LAW AND INTERPRETATION

Essays in Legal Philosophy

EDITED BY
ANDREI MARMOR

CLARENDON PRESS · OXFORD

This book has been printed digitally and produced in a standard specification in order to ensure its continuing availability

OXFORD
UNIVERSITY PRESS

Great Clarendon Street, Oxford OX2 6DP

Oxford University Press is a department of the University of Oxford.
It furthers the University's objective of excellence in research, scholarship,
and education by publishing worldwide in

Oxford New York

Auckland Cape Town Dar es Salaam Hong Kong Karachi
Kuala Lumpur Madrid Melbourne Mexico City Nairobi
New Delhi Shanghai Taipei Toronto
With offices in
Argentina Austria Brazil Chile Czech Republic France Greece
Guatemala Hungary Italy Japan South Korea Poland Portugal
Singapore Switzerland Thailand Turkey Ukraine Vietnam

Published in the United States
by Oxford University Press Inc., New York

Reprinted 2006

ISBN 0-19-826487-9

Preface

Interpretation has become one of the main intellectual paradigms of legal scholarship in the last fifteen years. Like the interest in rules during the 1960s and in legal principles during the 1970s, much of legal theorizing in the last decade has been built around the concept of interpretation. In one important respect, however, interpretation is a more ambitious paradigm: it is not only a subject-matter legal philosophers are interested in, but according to some influential philosophers, interpretation is also a general method, a meta-theory of legal theory. Ronald Dworkin, for instance, presents the interpretative method as a rival to the traditional analytical approach to jurisprudence. It has been a central presumption of the latter that there is a clear distinction between the philosophical question: 'What is law?' and the lawyer's question: 'What is *the* law on this or that matter?', and between these two and the moral question, 'What should the law be . . . ?'

Dworkin's recent interpretative theory of law challenges these conceptual distinctions. Accounting for the concept of law, he claims, is inevitably tied up with considerations about what the law is there to settle. Law, he claims, is not only an interpretative enterprise, but must also be accounted for by the very same methods employed by the participants; both theorists and practitioners are engaged in one and the same kind of reasoning, namely, in an attempt to impose the best interpretation on the practice they encounter. Thus, the concept of law and the justification of its particular requirements can no longer be seen as two separate issues.

Whether this methodological development is a turn for the better or worse is one of the main themes in dispute among the contributors to this volume. Dworkin's interpretative theory of law seems to support an anti-positivist stance in legal theory. Interestingly, however, some of those who are most sympathetic to his conclusions forcefully reject his interpretative method, and vice versa. Thus, some of those who would subscribe to many of H. L. A. Hart's conclusions about the relations between law and morality see considerable advantages in Dworkin's interpretative methodological turn. Both camps, however, acknowledge the centrality of interpretation to the understanding of law. After all, legal practice is pervasively interpretative, and unless we have an adequate grasp of what interpretation consists of, we cannot have a clear picture of the practice we purport to understand.

Interpretation is not uniquely, or even typically, a legal concept. In the realm of arts and art criticism it also plays a central role, and this suggests that there are interesting analogies between these two disciplines. Once again, the extent and usefulness of the analogy is subject to controversy, some of which is manifest in this collection. Few doubt, however, that theories about law and literature share a common interest in the concept of interpretation. Thus, for example, issues such as the role of intentions in the interpretation of texts, the question whether interpretation can ever be objectively true (or false), or whether texts determine, or significantly constrain, interpretations of them, are of obvious interest to both disciplines, and seem to call for a general theory of interpretation.

Most contributors to this collection seem to agree that there is a very close link between the concept of interpretation and the concept of meaning. Interpretation is basically an explanation of the meaning of its object. This shared starting-point, however, only opens the door for considerable controversy about the kind of meaning in question, its point, and its limits. That is, a general theory of interpretation should be expected to provide answers to at least three kinds of question: about the possible objects of interpretation; about its point, its normative basis; and the epistemological question, what is the possibility of knowledge in this field—for example, are there correct and incorrect interpretations? Is interpretation objective in any sense?

These and other general questions about interpretation have considerable implications for legal theory, particularly for a theory of adjudication. Judges, as we all know, are expected to interpret certain texts. But what are these texts? How, and what precisely do we identify as the object of interpretation here? Assuming that we have identified the texts, can we presume that these texts substantially constrain their possible interpretations? Have those interpretations any objective status? What would it mean for such an interpretation to be objectively true (or false)? These general questions about interpretation have important moral and political bearings on the legitimacy of adjudication. If, for example, texts do not constrain the interpretation in any significant way, what is the basis of the legitimacy of such interpretations? How can judges justify their interpretations of statutory law? Does interpretation differ at all from invention, and if not, is it warranted that judges invent the law?

Such moral and political concerns have always formed part of jurisprudence. Viewing them from the vantage-point of a general theory of interpretation, however, has been a fairly recent development. Thus, the analogies between law and literature, controversial and problematic as they may be, enable legal philosophers to have a fresh viewpoint on these traditional issues.

Not all the topics concerning law and interpretation are new; the role of legislative intent in the interpretation of statutes is one of those age-old jurisprudential issues that re-emerge one generation after another. Some of the contributors to this volume follow this tradition of debate, reaching, needless to say, different conclusions. They are more or less united in their belief, however, that the role of legislative intent in statutory interpretation is closely tied to an adequate theory about the authority of law. According to this line of thought, the justification of deference to legislative intent must be derived from considerations pertaining to the legitimacy of legal authorities. Once again, a close but controversial link emerges here between the concept of interpretation and the concept of law. Thus, by drawing on recent work on the analysis of authority, combined with contemporary research in the realm of interpretation, contributors to this volume have been able to offer new and refreshing insights into this age-old controversy.

The essays in this collection are like Janus' face; they are both backward and forward looking. In one sense, the collection offers something like a retrospect of one of the main themes in the last fifteen years of legal theorizing. Yet at the same time, the contributions to this volume raise new and challenging issues; some of them tentative, others more complete and comprehensive, and all call for more thinking and research.

All the contributions to this volume have been written especially for it, and are published here for the first time. The collection originated in a conference some of the contributors attended at Tel Aviv University in May 1993, and we would wish to express our gratitude to all the conference participants for their comments and the stimulating debate. Most of the essays, however, were specially commissioned for the book, and I am truly indebted to the contributors for their enthusiasm and wonderful co-operation.

A. M.

Contents

List of Contributors

Larry Alexander is Professor of Law, University of San Diego School of Law.

Brian Bix is Associate Professor of Law, Quinnipiac College School of Law.

Jules L. Coleman is John A. Graver Professor of Jurisprudence and Philosophy, Yale University.

Meir Dan-Cohen is Professor of Law, University of California, Berkeley.

Heidi M. Hurd is Professor of Law and Philosophy, University of Pennsylvania.

Kenneth Kress is Professor of Law, University of Iowa College of Law.

Brian Leiter is Joe A. Worsham Centennial Professor of Law and Philosophy, the University of Texas at Austin.

Andrei Marmor is Associate Professor of Jurisprudence, Faculty of Law, University of Tel Aviv.

Michael S. Moore is Leon Meltzer Professor of Law and Professor of Philosophy, University of Pennsylvania.

Stephen R. Perry is Associate Professor, Faculty of Law, McGill University.

Joseph Raz is Professor of the Philosophy of Law, Oxford University, and Fellow of Balliol College, Oxford.

Martin Stone is Professor of Law and Associate Professor of Philosophy, Duke University.

Jeremy Waldron is Professor of Law and Philosophy, Jurisprudence and Social Policy Program, School of Law (Boalt Hall), University of California, Berkeley.

1

Interpreting Interpretation

MICHAEL S. MOORE

INTRODUCTION

There is a simple life-cycle for metaphors. They are born of fresh insight about an unnoticed similarity, wither with over-use, and die by becoming so familiar that they are treated as established senses of words. Intellectual fashions are like metaphors in this respect. Although they may begin life fresh and full of promise, they eventually become the tired counters in a patter that prevents insight rather than conveys it.

This has happened to the current intellectual fashion built around interpretation. Like the 'form of life' patter of the 1950s, and the 'paradigm' patter of the 1960s, some mention of 'interpretation' has become *de rigueur* in articles on just about any subject. Like the 'form of life' and 'paradigm' patters that Wittgenstein and Kuhn visited upon earlier decades, our 'interpretive' patter does very little work in either discovering or justifying any conclusion; such patter is most often merely the ornamental dressing put on to generally sceptical conclusions about law, literary criticism, psychology, physics, or just about anything. 'It is only your interpretation' has descended to the level of cocktail party conversation as our preferred way of expressing metaphysical or epistemological scepticism about anything, but it rarely does any work in justifying such scepticism.

All this is distressing to those of us who were interested in interpretation before it became so fashionable. This is not just the unhappiness one feels when having the symbols of one's personality appropriated by the masses—as when hippies made blue jeans a uniform, or when yuppies made BMWs a high-status automobile. Rather, it is the dislike of seeing a useful concept turned into a piece of empty rhetoric. It is rather like the distress a surgeon

This paper originated from my Lectures on Interpretive Theory, given in 1986 to the Eighth Annual Session of the International Institute for Semiotic and Structural Studies, held at the English Department of Northwestern University, Evanston. It also benefited from the term-length research fellowship on interpretive theory held at the Humanities Research Institute, University of California, Irvine, Spring Quarter, 1989. The paper was written specifically for the Conference on Interpretation and Legal Theory, Tel Aviv University, 1993. My thanks go to participants (and particularly to my commentator at the latter, Gilead Bar-Elli) for their helpful comments.

might feel when, having honed his skills and his instruments to prepare for a delicate operation, he finds that others have thrown mud all over his scalpels.[1]

The mud in this case is what I have elsewhere called 'very ambitious interpretivism'.[2] What is so ambitious is the claim that all knowledge is interpretive, physics as much as psychology, astronomy as much as literary criticism. This is sometimes put into slogans, such as that 'all the world is a text', or that 'nothing exists outside the text', or that 'all understanding requires the prejudices of interpretation'.[3] These Derridan, Barthian, and Gadamerian slogans create a great deal of sympathy in me for reactions like that of Michael Devitt: 'when someone starts talking about "interpretation", reach for your gun.'[4] Still, even with bath-water this dirty, there may be a baby worth saving. What I wish to examine is the concept of interpretation that should be saved when the bloated interpretivism of current postmodernist fashion has run its course and died.

GENUINE INTERPRETATION

A good first stab at defining a useful notion of interpretation is that it is the activity we engage in when we are trying to find the meaning of something.[5] To elucidate this definition, we should pursue three questions: first, what sorts of things have meaning? Secondly, does the validity of an interpretation

[1] I owe the metaphor to David A. J. Richards, who at a conference many years ago when some very woolly comments were being directed to me leaned over to whisper, 'they're throwing mud on your scalpels'.

[2] Michael S. Moore, 'The Interpretive Turn in Modern Theory: A Turn for the Worse?', *Stanford Law Rev.*, 41 (1989), 871–957, at 891. For a recent expression of one form of such very ambitious interpretivism in law, see Stephen Feldman, 'The New Metaphysics: The Interpretive Turn in Metaphysics', *Iowa Law Rev.*, 76 (1991), 661–99 (commentary on Moore's rejection of Heidegger and Gadamer).

[3] Some of these slogans are explored in Joseph Margolis, 'Reinterpreting Interpretation', *Journal of Aesthetics*, 48 (1990), 1–15, at 7. Recognizing that very ambitious interpretivism is 'notably, even pecularily, fashionable in our own time' (ibid., at 1), Joe Margolis seeks to salvage what he can out of it.

[4] The realist metaphysician, Michael Devitt, is so quoted in W. Lycan, *Judgement and Justification* (Cambridge: Cambridge University Press, 1988), 195 n. 7.

[5] Cf. Sigmund Freud, *The Complete Introductory Lectures on Psychoanalysis*, James Strachey, trans. (New York: W. W. Norton, 1966), at 87: 'Interpreting means finding a hidden sense in something.' Note that Freud, like many others (e.g. Annette Barnes, *On Interpretation* (Oxford: Basil Blackwell, 1988), chs. 2–3; Andrei Marmor, *Interpretation and Legal Theory* (Oxford: Oxford University Press, 1992), 21), adds something to this most general notion of interpretation that I leave out, namely, that interpretation is the finding of something that is hidden or not obvious. In this sense, statutes with a plain meaning can be said to need no interpretation. This unhelpfully narrows interpretation, as I argue in Moore, 'A Natural Law Theory of Interpretation', *South. Calif. Law Rev.*, 58 (1985), 277–398, at 284–5. In Marmor's case, this restriction seems part of his general affirmation of the communicative model of interpretation, so that what is governed by semantics (and is thus obvious) is not part of interpretation.

consist in the discovery of such meanings, or can such validity exist even if we *create* such meanings by our interpretations? Thirdly, why should anyone ever engage in this activity, that is, what value is served by finding or creating a meaning for something? The first I shall call the basic question about interpretation; the second, the question of validity; and the third, the question of justification. Although these are analytically separable questions, the interrelations of any plausible answers to them prevent me from organizing this discussion around them. Rather, I shall ask all three of them simultaneously for each model of interpretation that I explore.

A place to start is by pursuing the basic question: what sorts of things have meanings? Let us sharpen this question before we try to answer it. The late Paul Grice once distinguished non-natural from natural meanings.[6] 'Clouds mean rain' was an example of the latter usage of 'meaning', while 'he means to hurt you' was an example of the former usage. With Grice, I take the natural meaning usage not to be of interest in this context, for 'natural meanings' are just animistic metaphors for causal connections between literally meaningless events. Causes and effects are natural signs for one another, but that just means that each is evidence for the other given the connection between the two. Clouds are a sign of rain, and if it rains, the raining is a sign that there were clouds from which the rain fell. In this uselessly broad sense of 'meaning', everything that is not causally inert (which is everything we know about) 'has meaning'.

Better for our purposes is non-natural meaning, what Grice called 'meaning'$_{nn}$. If we leave clouds for *talk* about clouds, for example, such talk seems to have a meaning that is not simply the causal connections between the clouds and other phenomena. Such talk may be an explicit utterance in ordinary, everyday conversation; it may be a legal utterance, such as a statute; it may appear in a novel or play; it may be part of an utterance of God; or it may form part of the manifest content of a dream. In all such cases, we are presented with phenomena that seem to possess meaning and seem to call for interpretation in order to be understood.

If we isolate what it is about ordinary conversational utterances, laws, novels, divine commands, and dreams that seems to give them meaning$_{nn}$, we come upon something that should be called a *text*. To say of each of these productions that they have meaning, is to say that each of them consists of a text. This of course is not to say much until we say what a text is (in some way that is freer of question-begging than, 'possessor of meaning').

A first impulse might be to think that there are texts in nature. Geologists often say, for example, that the various layers of rock form a textual history of the earth, and that to learn geology is to learn how to read this text. Such a reading of 'text', however, returns us to natural meaning. Layers of rocks

[6] H. P. Grice, 'Meaning', *Philosophical Review*, 66 (1957), 377–88.

are signs of past events—and thus, are texts 'about' those past events—only in the anaemic sense that such rocks are the effects of (and thus constitute evidence of) those earlier events.

The alternative that perhaps most readily suggests itself is to think that something can be a text only if a person or persons intentionally create it as a text. More specifically, one might think that *the* creative act of relevance here is that whereby persons create symbols that allow them to communicate what they mean to one another. On this view, texts are the medium (of representation devices) that author and audience share when one human agent is attempting to communicate to another. This, as I shall call it, is the communicative model of interpretation. The model has a powerful grip on our image of interpretation. Before showing how the model misleads, we need to understand the grip that it has on us.

The power of the communicative model of interpretation lies in its tidiness in answering the three questions I distinguished earlier. To the basic question of what has meaning, the model answers, only those representational systems (texts) that are created by human agents in order to communicate with one another. A system of signs becomes a representational system, on this view, when agents use the signs to form the object of intentions which they wish to communicate, and when the signs so used by authors are also used by audiences as the objects of the beliefs formed in response. Ultimately, thus, what is a text on this model is a function of the symbol system used in those propositional attitudes that are the intentions of communicators and the beliefs of their audiences. Since the propositional attitudes are what they are by virtue of their Intentionality, that makes texts too a function of the Intentionality of those agents who use them in this way.[7]

The second question—about validity—also has a very tidy answer on the communicative model of interpretation. An interpretation of an utterance—be it in a novel, dream, statute, or holy text—is valid on this model if and only if the interpretation corresponds to the intention with which the utterance was produced. There is no question here about *creating* something by interpretation, the validity of which then becomes mysterious. Rather, an interpretation is valid only if one discovers the true explanation of why the text was produced. Such an explanation does not create anything; it reproduces the object of the intention that caused the utterance to exist.

Similarly, the third question of justification has a ready answer on the communicative model of interpretation. For interpretation becomes a species of explanation (namely, explanations of communicative utterances).

[7] By Intentionality, I mean the directedness upon-an-object that Franz Brentano reintroduced to modern discussions. This rather technical notion is to be distinguished from the more ordinary, idiomatic 'intentional'. For an introduction, see Daniel Dennett, *Content and Consciousness* (London: Routledge, 1969), ch. 2.

We thus need have no special sort of activity, distinct from the normal descriptive or explanatory activities of science, that requires justification. Scientific curiosity about why some dream was produced, some novel written, some holy pronouncement made, or some statute passed, may suffice to justify interpreting these texts on this model of interpretation.[8]

The communicative model thus causes no ripples in the smooth waters of science. Moreover, the model no doubt accurately captures perhaps the most ordinary, most familiar usage of 'interpretation'. When we seek to 'find the meaning of something'—that is, when we engage in an activity properly called 'interpretation'—perhaps most often we are the audience of a communicative utterance by another. In which case our reasons and our methods are the standard reasons and methods of scientific description or explanation, with the only difference being that what we describe (a text) and explain it with (authorial intention) are both Intentional phenomena.

This is all so happily unproblematic that some may wish to stop here. Yet to do so ignores the insight that I take to have motivated late nineteenth-century theology to coin the English word 'hermeneutics' from the Greek. That insight is that there is something especially interpretive about disciplines like theology, literary criticism, law, and psychoanalysis. More precisely, the insight is that certain dominant *activities* within such disciplines cannot be forced to conform to the methods of ordinary scientific description or explanation, nor are such activities justified by the normal scientific goals of prediction, explanation, and understanding.

If we examine how such activities within such disciplines are in fact carried on, this sense that interpretation is richer than the communicative model can allow is reinforced. A problem with the communicative model lies in the strait-jacket it would force on to us about what we might properly conceive to be activities of literary, statutory, theological, or dream interpretation. For the model requires us to say that, only when literary critics are seeking to recapture the intended meaning of the author of some novel are they *interpreting* that novel; only when lawyers are seeking to recapture the intended meaning of the legislature that created some statute are they *interpreting* that statute; only when theologians are seeking to recapture what God meant in causing the Bible to be written are they *interpreting* the Bible; and only when psychoanalysts are seeking to recapture the wish that caused the dream to have the content that it did are they seeking to *interpret* that dream. There are, of course, well-known versions of literary criticism,

[8] On this view, interpretation is an activity in which one is justified in engaging on the normal scientific grounds: 'The basic reason for studying the cognitive processes has become as clear as the reason for studying anything else: because they are there.' U. Neisser, *Cognitive Psychology* (New York: Appleton-Century-Crofts, 1967), 12. On my view of interpretation developed below, interpretation is more like mountain-climbing than scientific explanation, in that both mountain-climbing and interpretation require more than George Mallory's famous 'because it is there' answer to justify the doing of them.

legal theory, theology, and psychoanalysis that promote just these intentionalist interpretive strategies. But there are other, competing interpretive strategies in each of these disciplines that do not seek to recapture authorial intention. Not only are these equally well regarded strategies; not only, indeed, are these *better* interpretive strategies, as I have argued in detail about some of these disciplines;[9] but it seems a woefully parochial and narrow-minded view of interpretation to dismiss these non-intentionalist strategies out of hand because they cannot—logically cannot—be *interpretive* in character.[10] Even if one ends up being an E. D. Hirsch about literary criticism, a Robert Bork about statutory and constitutional interpretation, an intentionalist about theological interpretation, or a Freud about dream interpretation, it should not be for lack of any truly *interpretive* alternatives. Even those literacy critics, lawyers, psychoanalysts, and theologians who end up being intentionalists need a broader notion of interpretation than that allowed by the communicative model in order to have substantive (as opposed to conceptual) arguments against their opponents.

I thus propose that we regard 'interpretation' as ambiguous. One sense is that involved in communication, where 'interpretation' names the description and explanation of communicative utterances. Such a social-scientific task is one sense of 'finding the meaning of something'. The distinct, non-communicative sense of 'interpretation' we have not yet described. Perhaps the most common analysis of this second sense is that bequeathed to us by Dilthey and the other original 'hermeneuts'. I refer to the dualistic tradition that divides the world between natural, meaningless phenomena, and social, meaningful phenomena, that divides the sciences between the *Naturwissenschaften* and the *Geisteswissenschaften*, that divides cognition between knowledge and *verstehen*, or understanding, and that divides the manner of doing science between explanation and interpretation.[11] These dualistic divisions are then used by such theorists to create a ghostly realm in which they may mimic the communicative model of interpretation. To the basic question of what is a text, they say that meaningful texts simply exist as a distinct kind of thing in the world, even though such texts need not be created by an author communicating to an audience. To the question of what makes an interpretation valid, they answer that an interpretation is valid if it corresponds to that meaning which is an essential feature of meaningful phenomena—even though that meaning is not to be equated with the datable state of authorial intention. To the question of why we

[9] Moore, *supra*, n. 5.

[10] As argued, for example, by Walter Benn Michaels, 'Response to Perry and Simon', *South. Calif. Law Rev.*, 58 (1985), 673–81.

[11] For description of this tradition and citations, see Moore, *supra*, n. 2, at 917–23. For an update, compare the differing views on dualistic interpretation in D. Hiley, J. Bohman, and R. Shusterman (eds.), *The Interpretive Turn* (Ithaca, NY: Cornell University Press, 1991).

should engage in interpretation, they answer that there need be no value justifying interpretation other than the value that motivates all science, namely to understand (in a special sense) the truth (in a special sense). What is mimicked is the communication model's subsumption of interpretation into ordinary scientific understanding, with the enormous caveat being added to the effect that this is a special sort of scientific understanding and a special sort of truth, to go along with this special sort of phenomena.

This dualistic model provides an unnecessarily mysterious and extravagant answer to our question of whether there is some non-communicative sense of 'interpretation'. Special notions of truth and understanding are notoriously the first refuge of those intellectual scoundrels who seek to escape their obligation to relate whatever it is that puzzles them (such as interpretation) with the rest of the world as they understand it.[12] Surely we can do better than this.

The dualist hermeneuts were right to seek to free another model of interpretation from the grip on the concept by the communication model, but the dualist tradition's 'special science' is no way to do this. Perhaps we can creep up on a better model, alternative to the communicative model, if we return to the basic question. What else might be a text besides a system of representations used by someone with the intention of communicating some intended meaning to others? To keep the communicative intentions of authors out of it, let us focus for the moment on examples where there are no authors. Imagine a formation of clouds in rare but suggestive shapes (we might call them 'Rorschach clouds'). Suppose further a set of individuals who purport to see their deepest secrets revealed in such clouds. Should we say that the clouds are a text, that they have meaning, so that those who see themselves revealed by the clouds can properly be said to *interpret* them?

The tug of the communicative model may be strong here. As we have seen, the general insight behind the communicative model is right: meaning$_{nn}$ is a function of the Intentionality of some human agents.[13] And if no human agent invested the clouds with meaning, how can they *have* meaning? Besides an author, there is of course the audience whose propositional attitudes of belief are eligible investors of meanings. A move tempting to some, such as

[12] See Moore, *supra* n. 2, at 919, for an example in psychoanalysis, where psychoanalytic theorists attempt to insulate their theory from scientific criticism by taking refuge in the tradition of dualist hermeneutics.

[13] Which is not to buy into John Searle's notion that persons possess an original, primitive, or irreducible Intentionality that a Turing machine (such as the human brain) cannot possess. I assume that human brains are ultimately syntactic engines whose complexity none the less produces states with semantic (i.e. Intentional) properties. Moore, 'Mind, Brain, and the Unconscious', in P. Clark and C. Wright (eds.), *Mind, Psychoanalysis, and Science* (Oxford: Basil Blackwell, 1988). One can accept this reductionist view about minds while accepting, as I do in the text, that persons are truly possessed of Intentional states and that it is the Intentionality of persons' propositional attitudes that invests other objects in the world with meaning.

the early Stanley Fish,[14] is to take the brute social fact that certain audiences ('interpretive communities') do regard certain phenomena as meaningful—do purport to form objects of beliefs by paying some kind of attention to such phenomena—as enough to constitute such phenomena as a text. Yet this sociological kind of answer brings with it all the dissatisfactions aroused whenever social facts are substituted for analysis. We all recognize that others sometimes regard a certain phenomenon as meaningful, but if what we want to know is in what sense such a phenomenon *is* meaningful, it is no help to be told that 'many so regard it'.

My own answer is in a sense 'audience-centred', but it focuses, not on the actual propositional attitudes or actions people might have in response to a phenomenon, but rather, on the attitudes and actions they have *reason* to have or to do. A person or group of persons staring at Rorschach clouds can give them meaning by finding some value (such as self-knowledge) in treating the clouds as a text. To treat them as a text is to treat the clouds as potentially giving us either reasons for belief or reasons for action, if we can just figure out what they mean. If there are such reasons to treat the clouds as a text, the clouds *are* a text.

This sounds circular, but it is not. There is a text, and thus interpretation in the desired sense, whenever: (1) people have some good reason, (2) to treat some phenomenon they do not yet know the meaning of, as being meaningful, (3) in the sense that such meanings give them either reasons for belief or reasons for action. Let us unpack this one step at a time.

Let us start with the second element, treating some phenomenon as meaningful. People do this whenever they impose a syntax–semantics distinction on to the phenomenon, that is, whenever they find the phenomenon to be meaningful even without knowing what it means. I call this the imposition of a syntax–semantics distinction because in order to do this they must have some criteria for isolating a meaningful phenomenon that does not depend on knowing the meaning of the phenomenon. If we call the meaning of the phenomenon its semantics, we should call the criteria for text individuation its syntax, for 'syntax' is the name we give in linguistics to those rules that determine which strings of symbols are well-formed formulas and thus eligible to be the bearers of meaning.

Two examples: in theology there is an old debate about whether the consummate goodness of God consists in the fact that whatever God commands is good (because she commands it), or whether that goodness consists in the fact that God, being omniscient, makes no mistakes about what is good in her commandings.[15] Suppose a believer seeks to do what God

[14] Stanley Fish, *Is There a Text in this Class?* (Cambridge, Mass.: Harvard University Press, 1980).

[15] Notice how Aquinas splits the difference here: 'the divine law commands certain things because they are good . . . while others are good because they are prescribed.' *The Political Ideas of St. Thomas Aquinas*, ed. Dino Bigongiani (New York: Hafner, 1953), 100.

commands. Under the first variation the believer is plainly interpreting God's commands, because he has a criterion of text individuation (God said it) independent of yet knowing what the text means. Under the second variation the situation is less clear. Eventually the believer may come to interpret God's commands because eventually he will grant God the (theoretical) authority he also grants to a good weatherman: both God and the weatherman get it right often enough that they should be listened to when it comes to morality or picnics. When the believer under the second variation grants such authority to God, he then has a criterion of text-individuation (God said it) independent of yet knowing what the text means. But initially, when the correspondence between the good and what God commands is in doubt, the believer will have to understand what the commands mean, check them against his own understanding of the good, and follow them only if they check out. This is not interpretation, because there is no criterion of text-individuation that is independent of knowing what the text means.

The second example is from law. While there is a debate in legal theory (about whether statutes possess practical or merely theoretical authority) that parallels exactly the above debate in theology,[16] another debate in legal theory reveals different aspects of this second criterion for the existence of a text. I refer to the debate about whether there is, can be, or should be a 'rule of recognition' that tests the validity of laws within any legal system. The late Herbert Hart's famous answer was that there is such a legal syntax, a set of rules that give the criteria for text-individuation independent of knowing the meaning of the text.[17] Critics of Hart have disagreed, arguing that one cannot know the text of the law without knowing (and judging to be good) what the law means. Somewhat ironically (given the rather different self-labellings of some of the critics), only the first of these positions about law reveals legal practice clearly to be interpretive. It takes some delicate footwork on the second of these views to make legal practice interpretive—one must talk about 'pre-interpretive data', 'obvious law (to be interpreted by non-obvious law)', 'rules (to be interpreted by non-rule-like principles)', 'concepts (to be interpreted by conceptions)', and the like to reintroduce the crucial notion of legal syntax in order for there to be something like a text to law.[18]

Why cannot one merge syntax and semantics so that whether there is a text, and what is the text, is a function of what such a text might mean?[19] The answer lies in the fact that with such merger one loses what is essential about interpretation, which is the guidance texts (and their correct

[16] See e.g. Heidi Hurd, 'Challenging Authority', *Yale LJ*, 100 (1991), 1611–77.

[17] H. L. A. Hart, *The Concept of Law* (Oxford: Clarendon Press, 1961).

[18] See e.g. Ronald Dworkin, *Law's Empire* (Cambridge, Mass.: Harvard University Press, 1986).

[19] Ronald Dworkin's kind of query. See ibid.

interpretations) are to give us in what we believe and what we do. Interpretive reasoning is distinct from ordinary moral or scientific reasoning in that it essentially involves a two-step dance: ask first whether there is a text and what it is; ask second what that text means in the sense of how it applies to the situation at hand. One can allow for a kind of reflective equilibrium to be reached between text-individuation ('syntax') and text-interpretation ('semantics'), so that whether a text produces good interpretations bears on the questions of whether it is a text at all, and if so, what the text is; but even so, when the epistemic equilibrium is reached, the reasoning must be a two-step dance to be an interpretive dance at all.

This brings us to the third aspect of my three-part answer to the basic question about texts. This third aspect is the distinctive reason-giving nature of texts and their interpretations. What makes interpretive reasoning so distinct a method of reasoning about what to think or what to do is the unique sort of reasons (for belief or action) such reasoning seeks to discover. Because these text-based reasons are themselves different depending on whether they are reasons for belief or reasons for action, let us consider each separately.

There is some debate about how texts can give reasons for action to those subject to the authority of such texts. Joseph Raz has developed in elegant detail the idea that texts can give those subject to them what he calls 'protected reasons' for action.[20] Such protected reasons are dual in nature: they are first-order reasons to do the act described in the text, a reason that did not exist prior to the creation of the text; and they are second-order reasons excluding all other reasons that might bear on the action from having any influence on the actor's decision. Texts, on this view, give conclusive reasons to act in the way described by the texts, for the text itself is a new reason for acting in conformity with it and that new reason is protected from any competition.

If there were a God, and if we had the text of her commands, this is undoubtedly how we should conceive of her text's influence on our practical reasoning. For less divine texts, however, such as those we find in the law, this is surely too strong. Democratically enacted statutes in reasonably just regimes, for example, give at least some legal actors new first-order reasons for action in conformity with them, but these reasons are unprotected from competition with the other reasons that may argue against doing the action. Or so I have argued in some detail.[21]

Whether one adopts Raz's view or my own does not here matter. On

[20] Joseph Raz, *Practical Reason and Norms* (Oxford: Oxford University Press, 1975); *The Authority of Law* (Oxford: Oxford University Press, 1979); *The Morality of Freedom* (Oxford: Oxford University Press, 1986), chs. 2–4.

[21] Michael S. Moore, 'Law, Authority, and Razian Reasons', *South. Calif. Law Rev.*, 62 (1989), 827–96.

either view, what is distinctive about texts is that they give actors reasons for action that did not exist before the text was created. When a friend requests an action, we promise to do an action, God commands an action, or a statute requires an action, we often have a reason to do the action requested, promised, commanded or required just because such a text was created.

Reasons for belief are different. When a text creates a new reason for belief, it is because we grant the text a kind of expertise over its subject-matter to which we are willing to defer. Weather reports are a good example. Because the weatherman has a better ability than do I to predict the weather, the texts he issues create for me new reasons for belief about the weather. The weatherman has no practical authority over me, so that his texts give me no reasons to act one way over another. Still, since my actions depend on what I believe, the weather-report texts can indirectly influence my actions by directly influencing my beliefs.[22]

Again, we can distinguish protected reasons for belief from unprotected but new first-order reasons for belief. And again, if there were a God, and if she were omniscient, God's texts would undoubtedly give us protected reasons for belief. For less divine texts, however, unprotected reasons for belief are more likely all we can expect. The important point again, however, is that such texts do give us reasons to believe that did not exist prior to the existence of such texts.

This notion of texts giving new reasons for action or belief must be sharpened if we are to use it in explicating text-hood and interpretation. For lots of things give us reasons for action or belief that are not texts. My decision in the past to allow my eldest child to attend a rock concert at the age of 14 created a reason, based in equality, to act now so as to allow my youngest daughter on her fourteenth birthday to attend her first rock concert; yet my past action is not a text. Similarly, the fact that a blade of grass is bent gives me reason to believe that some animal has passed by recently; but the bent blade of grass is not a text. To be sure, the existence of such events and states give me reasons for action or belief only because there are true generalizations of morality and science that include both them and the future act or event I have reason to do or believe. Yet these moral and scientific generalizations are also not texts, at least on any non-relativistic view of ethics and science.

The Intentionality of some intervening human agency is needed if we are to have the kinds of reasons for action or belief that are created by text. If

[22] Reasons for belief can have a more immediate implication for action than that mentioned in the text. One very important kind of theoretical authority is practical wisdom, that is, moral expertise about reasons for action. The utterances of such a theoretical authority do give us reasons for belief, not of action, yet *what* we have reason to believe because of such utterances is what reasons for action we have.

my youngest daughter requests that she go to the rock concert, or if I promise her that she may go, the acts of requesting and promising are texts; they not only give me a reason to do the act requested or promised, but they do so as Intentional states. That is, to have a reason to do the act requested or promised because the act was requested or promised means I have to figure out what my daughter requested, or what I promised to do. This is to enquire into the propositional attitudes expressed in the actions of requesting and promising.

Likewise for reasons for belief. The bent blade of grass has no Intentionality, and thus the reason for belief that it creates is not of the relevant sort. Contrast such ordinary evidence with the distinctive sort of evidence of relevance here: someone is holding the blade of grass and tells me that it will be bent because he intends to bend it; alternatively, an expert on the watering habits of animals at the water-hole around which the grass sits tells me that the blade of grass is bent because, at this time of the day, all of the grass is bent by animals watering. In both of these last cases, the expression of intention or of belief is a text because it gives me a reason for belief as the Intentional state of a person. That is, to know what it is this kind of evidence evidences, I will have to enquire into the propositional attitudes expressed by the relevant actors.[23]

It might seem that this reason-giving capacity of texts returns us to an intentionalist mode of interpretation.[24] For many examples of texts that give us new reasons for belief or for action do so only because the *authors* of those texts are either theoretical or practical authorities. And if the authority of the text wholly depends on the authority of the author of that text, one would usually interpret the text in a manner that seeks to elicit what the author *meant*.[25] One would, in other words, return to an intentionalist method of interpretation even while proceeding from a non-communicative model.

Are there then (syntactically individuated) texts that give us new reasons for belief or for action that do *not* depend on the authority of their author? This moves us to the first aspect of my three-part explication of what is a text—that is, to the question of value. We easily understand why we have reason to interpret requests, promises, and expert advice. Each of these give us reasons for action or belief, if we can only figure out what was meant by the requester, promisor, or expert; we thus in these instances have reason enough to engage in intentionalist interpretation. But our present

[23] I am indebted in this discussion to the notion of 'content-independent' reasons developed by Joseph Raz and Herbert Hart. See e.g. Raz, *The Morality of Freedom, supra*, n. 20, at 35–7. I have avoided their vocabulary because the label is a quite misleading one when used to refer to essentially Intentionality-dependent reasons.

[24] See e.g. Marmor, *supra*, n. 5, at ch. 8.

[25] But not always. Jeremy Waldron, in 'Legislators' Intentions and Unintentional Legislation (in this, volume, *infra* Ch. 9) nicely explores a variety of reasons for thinking that statutes may possess theoretical authority without any individual legislator possessing such authority.

enquiry is into what reason there might be to treat some text as creating new reasons for us when we do not care what the author meant. What values might be served by ceding authority to such texts when either they have no author, or the author they have lacks any theoretical or practical authority?

Suppose it were the case that clouds, like dreams, were in fact excellent devices for generating self-knowledge. Since self-knowledge is a good for persons, clouds and dreams should be treated as texts in the sense explicated, that is, they are treated as meaningful phenomena even before we know their meaning, and when we know their meaning we know the reasons for belief that they impart to us. The value of self-knowledge in such a case makes clouds and dreams a text even though there need be no author of them.

As another example, consider that used by Ronald Dworkin, the social practice of courtesy.[26] Social practices of courteous behaviour have no single author, and no intentional creation by anyone. They grow up gradually and unwittingly. None the less, we have reason to treat such practices as a text in the sense explicated: we have a syntactic mode of their individuation (past practice), and we treat the interpreted practice as giving us a reason to act in conformity with it. The value served by doing this is the value of respect. It is a good to treat others respectfully, and since others are so treated only when they realize that respect is being manifested, we each have reason to follow the practices of respect-giving (courtesy) by treating those practices as a text.

There is an important subtlety here that requires emphasis since it is so easily missed.[27] It is not that a social practice like courtesy becomes a text just because the practice is a valuable one. Our practices of kindness and justice are valuable practices, but those practices are not themselves texts that we must interpret in order to be either kind or just. Rather, there must be a value justifying why we should treat a practice as a text in the sense I have explicated. The value must show us why it is good to regard the practice as meaningful before we know its meaning, and why it is good to treat the interpreted practice as giving us reasons to behave in one way rather than another. Because courtesy must be understood by its recipients as courtesy in order for the good of respect to be achieved, we have reason to treat our practices of courtesy as a text. Because kindness and justice do not require their beneficiaries to understand that they are being treated kindly or justly for the goods of kindness and justice to be realized, we have no reason to treat our practices of kindness or justice as texts.

For a legal example, consider the American Constitution. This is a text with an author, or at least a set of them. It has thus tempted American

[26] See Dworkin, *supra*, n. 18, at 46–9.

[27] For criticism of Dworkin on this ground, see Moore, *supra* n. 2, at 946.

constitutional lawyers for decades to think that the authority of the text is due to the authority of its authors. This then leads to an intentionalist method of interpretation being applied to the document. Yet there is no good argument for why the framers of the Constitution had either theoretical or practical authority.[28] They were neither divinely inspired, nor notably more astute politically than are the educational élites of our own generation. They were not selected by us to lay down our fundamental law, nor have we in any meaningful sense consented, explicitly or tacitly, to their authority. I think it obvious that the framers had no authority over those of us who live 200 years later, so that we have no reason to care what they may have meant by what they said.

None the less, there is some value served by the present generation of Americans treating the written Constitution as a text. Like authorless clouds, dreams, and courtesy, that value has nothing to do with some supposed need to find out what the author of the document believed, wanted, or intended. Rather, that value has to do with the legitimation potential that the document has within American society. It is trite but true that the Constitution is America's civil religion. The result is that peaceful resolutions of fundamental disputes become easier if those disputes are framed as disputes about the meaning of Constitutional phrases like 'free expression', 'cruel and unusual punishment', and the like. Peaceful resolution of such disputes is a real good, giving each of us reason to grant the document the status of text even while we refuse to grant any authority to its authors.

These last examples, while freeing us from the inevitability of always seeking to discover an author's intention when we interpret, may seem to have flouted my earlier-stated requirement that the reasons given by a text be Intentionality-dependent. With social practices like courtesy, the American Constitution, and perhaps even with dreams (on a Freudian account), this flouting may not be so obvious, for at least these items were in some sense produced intentionally by someone or some group. But clouds, even Rorschach clouds, are intentionally produced by no one. In what sense can clouds give us 'Intentionality-dependent' reasons?

This worry leads many theorists about interpretation, such as Joseph Raz[29] and Andrei Marmor,[30] to disclaim such cases as instances of interpretation at all. Only items that are at least intentionally produced by their creators, and perhaps even intended to be a text by those creators, are eligible candidates for text-hood. This would include the American Constitution, and perhaps dreams and courtesy, but would certainly exclude clouds.

Yet notice how arbitrary is the line this view would draw. Once it is

[28] See Michael S. Moore, 'Do We Have an Unwritten Constitution?', *Southern California Law Review*, 63 (1989), 107–39, at 120–1.

[29] Joseph Raz, 'Interpretation Without Intention', this volume, *infra*, Ch. 5.

[30] Marmor, *supra*, n. 5, at ch. 6.

admitted that the meaning of texts such as dreams, courtesy, and the American Constitution is not to be sought in the propositional attitudes of their authors,[31] of what relevance is it whether a given phenomenon was intentionally produced, or intentionally produced as a text? Such a requirement seems an idle stipulation. If we have reason to treat dreams, for example, as a text, and if that reason justifies us in seeking a meaning to dreams *not* to be equated to any intention or wish that produced them, then surely it is irrelevant to their text-hood whether dreams are intentional productions or not.

One can, of course, seek to bolster this 'intentionally produced' criterion of text-hood by saying that we always do seek authorial intention when we interpret. Then the criterion is not idle. Yet one can only plausibly say this about dreams, courtesy, and the American Constitution if one fictionalizes the authorial intention a good interpretation recaptures.

Ronald Dworkin, for example, urges that when we interpret the American Constitution we seek the framer's intention—with the enormous *caveat* that such intention is not a psychological state.[32] Andrei Marmor likewise pays lip-service to intentionalist interpretation when he proclaims that 'interpretation is essentially a matter of attributing intentions', but then allows the attribution of purely fictional intentions of fictional authors to fit the bill so that he can account for what he (rightly) regards as undeniably interpretive practices of artistic criticism.[33] Similarly unhelpful are the evasions common to American legal practice with statutes, whereby one pretends that the value a statute serves (and that is therefore maximized by correct interpretations) is the 'intention in the statute'.[34] Equally unhelpful is the wilful trading on the ambiguity of 'purpose', so that one actually interprets so as to serve the purpose (in the sense of function, or value) of the statute, while pretending to be interpreting so as to serve the purpose (in the sense of further intended consequence) of the authors of the statute.[35] Similarly

[31] See e.g. ibid. Marmor distinguishes the use of intention to individuate the text from the use of authorial intention to find the text's meaning. According to Marmor, the latter use is occasional even while the former use is universal to all activities of interpretation.

[32] Ronald Dworkin, *A Matter of Principle* (Cambridge, Mass.: Harvard University Press, 1985), 34–57. See also *Law's Empire*, *supra*, n. 18, at 53–65.

[33] Marmor, *supra*, n. 5, at 30–1. For yet another example, see Stanley Fish, 'Play of Surfaces: Theory and Law', in Gregory Leyh (ed.), *Legal Hermeneutics: History, Theory, and Practice* (Berkeley: University of California Press, 1992), at 300–1.

[34] The 'intention in the words alone' obfuscation may be found in *United States* v. *Goldenberg*, 168 U.S. 95, 102–103 (1911). ('The primary and general rule of statutory construction is that the intent of the lawmaker is to be found in the language that he has used'); Donald Gustafson, 'On Unconscious Intentions', *Philosophy*, 48 (1973), 178–82 ('Exegetical and critical work makes use of the notion of *intention in* when it tries to bring out the intention in a piece of art without reference to the intention with which the artist produced it'). See generally Moore, 'The Semantics of Judging', *South. Calif. Law Rev.*, 54 (1981), 151–294, at 258–62; Moore, *supra*, n. 5, at 347.

[35] For this ambiguity, and its use, see Moore, *supra*, n. 34, at 263–5.

misleading is Plowden's old ploy of pretending that one's value-laden interpretations are really the recapturing of the hypothetical intention the author would have had had he directed his attention to the problem.[36]

If one is willing to fictionalize the authorial intention a good interpretation seeks in these ways, why would one not also fictionalize the intentional production of a text? Why not say of clouds, for example, that we regard them as a text because God intended them to be so treated, qualifying the latter by disavowing any belief in God or his intent? Alternatively, and preferably, we should dispense with both fictions. It neither matters to the existence of a text, nor to its proper interpretation, that someone intentionally created the phenomena as a text or that someone meant something by it. Justice Holmes's forthright disavowal of intention is preferable to the fictionalized evasions we have noted; with regard to legislative intent, Holmes noted, 'in fact intention is a residuary clause intended to gather up whatever other aids there may be to interpretation besides the particular words and the dictionary'.[37]

One might legitimately wonder at this point whether my own account does not fictionalize Intentionality in its requirement that texts give Intentionality-dependent reasons. In a sense this is true, for when I disavow the need for both authorial intention and audience belief I disavow the two obvious sources of Intentionality for texts. My notion of Intentionality-dependent reasons thus involves some fiction, but the fictionalization is not mine; rather, it is built into the relevant reasons themselves. Since this last sentence is hardly self-interpreting, let me explain.

Take the American Constitution. If I am right about it having authority while its authors have none, then one way to state the Intentionality-dependent reason the document gives us is to say that we have reason to treat the document as having more meaning than in fact it has. The reason itself is no fiction, because a real good is served by our treating the document as a text, interpretations of which legitimately resolve our political disputes. Yet the content of the reason contains a fiction, for what we have reason to do is to treat the document as if there existed a meaning sufficiently authoritative and sufficiently determinate to resolve our controversies.

Consider clouds again. On my earlier suppositions, we have reason to treat clouds as texts and that reason is no fiction, mental health being a real good. Yet the content of the reason contains a kind of fiction, for what we

[36] Plowdon's famous recommendation to look to the legislator's hypothetical intent are to be found in his reporter's remarks after *Eyston* v. *Studd*, 2 Plowdon 459, 75 Eng. Rep. 688 (1574). See also *Heydon's Case*, 76 Eng. Rep. 637 (Exch. 1584). For modern expressions, see Warren Lehmann, 'How to Interpret a Difficult Statute', *Wisconsin Law Rev.* [1979], 489–507; Richard Posner, 'Statutory Interpretation—in the Classroom and in the Courtroom', *University of Chicago Law Review*, 50 (1983), 800–22.

[37] Letter by Holmes, quoted in Felix Frankfurter, 'Some Reflections on the Reading of Statutes', *Columbia Law Rev.*, 47 (1947), 527–46, at 538.

have reason to do is to treat the phenomenon as if it were a description of our character, moods, and emotions, when of course the clouds are not a description by anyone.

This completes my general account of the basic question about interpretation, namely, what sorts of things have meaning. My answer, in terms of syntactically individuated texts whose interpretations give us new Intentionality-dependent reasons for belief or for action, also begins the answer to my third question, the question of justification. To that question (of what value is served by finding the meaning of something) the answer can be quite diverse: values of social peace, of treating people with respect, of knowing oneself, can justify treating different phenomena as texts requiring interpretation. Indeed, almost *any* value might give rise to treating *some* phenomenon as a text whose interpretations give us new reasons. The important point is that there must be some value justifying treating such a phenomenon as a text, else it is not a text nor is reasoning under it interpretation.

We have not yet answered the second of my three questions, that about validity. On the notion of interpretation here described, in what sense are interpreters discovering meaning (as opposed to creating it) and in what sense can their interpretations be true or valid? As we have seen, the communicative model of interpretation has an easy answer to these questions: interpreters discover meanings, not create them, and their interpretations are valid when, but only when, they discover what the author meant. But once we move to authorless texts, what are the analogous answers?

My own view about validity is this: an interpretation of some phenomenon is valid when, but only when, it maximally serves the value(s) that justifies the treating of the phenomenon as a text to begin with. In the case of clouds, the correct or valid interpretation—'what the clouds mean'—is that interpretation which maximally enhances our self-knowledge. In the case of a social practice like courtesy, the correct interpretation of our courteous practices is the one that maximally conveys respect to those to whom one is being courteous. In the case of the American Constitution, the matter is a bit more complicated. Prima facie, the correct interpretation of the Constitution is the one that maximally furthers the peaceful resolution of fundamental political disputes. I say 'prima facie', because the authority of the written Constitution only partly depends on the value of social peace. If the document made too many moral mistakes in what it required of us, we would not owe that text any allegiance; quite the contrary, amendment, civil war, or revolution would be our obligation. A more complete account of that document's authority thus includes some element of theoretical authority. This means that a correct interpretation of the Constitution is one that maximizes social peace while also seeking to eliminate moral mistakes.

In other cases the values that justify us in treating certain phenomena as texts justify us in interpreting those phenomena by reference either to what their author meant or to what their actual audience took them to mean. Two examples. In interpreting the request of a friend, we maximize the good of acceding to a friend's request—which is the reason that justifies us in treating it as a text at all—by seeking to discover what our friend meant by his request. In interpreting the defamatory utterance of another, courts maximize the good of corrective justice—which is (arguably) the reason that justifies courts in treating the utterance as a text at all—by seeking to discover, not what the speaker meant, but what any sizeable and respectable audience understood it to mean. In neither of these examples should one see a return to the communicative model of interpretation or to Fish's 'interpretive communities'. Rather, these author- or audience-centred interpretive strategies are instances of the more general, value-laden schema for interpretation that we have been examining. The same criteria for a valid interpretation hold even if those criteria sometimes yield intentionalist or belief-centred interpretive strategies.

The openly instrumental nature of this criterion of validity may give one pause. For how constraining can a text be if interpretations of it are valid simply because such interpretations maximally promote the value(s) justifying the treating of a text as a text? We should separate two strands to this worry. The first is nicely stated by Joseph Raz in his criticism of Ronald Dworkin's equally value-laden criterion of validity:

> If you regard the Constitution as an uninterpreted jumble of ink scratchings and regard legal theory [interpretation] as designed to give it meaning in accordance with the best moral theory there is, then there is no gap between ideal law and interpretation of existing law. Under these conditions one can interpret the Constitution to mean anything at all. It can be read to mean the same as Shakespeare's Hamlet.[38]

Raz worries that such instrumental interpretive reasoning ceases to be interpretive reasoning at all because the text in no way constrains doing what we would do if there were no text.

The answer to this worry lies again in the content of the Intentionality-dependent reasons essential to there being a text. When we have reason to treat some phenomenon as a text, it is not just that we have reason to treat it as *any* kind of text. The legitimization potential of the American Constitution, for example, not only gives us reason to consider that document as *some* kind of text; in addition, the kind of text it gives American citizens reason to interpret is one that respects the legitimizing potential of the document, which means that the ordinary English meanings of the words

[38] Joseph Raz, 'Dworkin: A New Link in the Chain', *Calif. Law Rev.*, 74 (1986), 1103–19, at 1103. I am indebted to both Joe Raz and to my commentator at the Tel Aviv Conference, Gilead Bar Elli, for stressing this point in the discussion on my paper at the Conference.

the document employs must be respected. Similarly, with the example of social practices like courtesy, the value of expressing respect gives us reason to take seriously the accepted parameters of courteous behaviours prevalent in a society, else the good of courteous behaviour expressing respect could not be realized.

At the level of generality of our concept of interpretation there is little to be said about these more particular constraints on interpretation. For these are local constraints, differing in their nature by the kind of text (and the kind of value justifying treating that text as a text). About the kinds of texts that appear in law, some generalization about these local constraints is certainly possible: because laws are framed in natural languages, and because one of the essential functions of all law is to realize the good of liberty (notice and opportunity to avoid legal sanctions) and substantive fairness (no retroactive surprises), the ordinary meaning of the words used in legal texts must always be given respect.[39] Yet even this generalization is better conceived as being part of a theory of interpretation, not part of the syntactic criteria of text individuation.[40] The local constraints (such as that of 'plain meaning' in law), in other words, are better thought of as markers of good versus bad interpretations, not of what is interpretation at all.

The second strand to this indeterminacy worry stems from the lack of there being any bright line blocking the slide down the slippery slope to fully instrumental reasoning, ignoring the text entirely. That is, granting the point just made—that local constraints such as plain meaning do constrain good interpretations—the distinct, second worry is that such constraints evaporate in the face of the pressure exerted by the values also guiding a good interpretation. This is the familiar worry about any form of what lawyers call 'purposive interpretation':[41] that the end or purpose (in the sense of value, not in the sense of authorial intention) will so dominate the reasoning that the means chosen (the text) will be ignored entirely. 'And' can be interpreted to mean 'or',[42] for example, or 'black' can be interpreted

[39] Which is not to say that such meanings may not be disregarded entirely in favour of a technical legal meaning; only, that such ordinary meanings carry great weight. See Moore, *supra*, n. 5; see also Brian Bix, *Law, Language, and Legal Determinacy* (Oxford: Clarendon Press, 1993), for another account of the local constraints put on legal interpretation by the semantics of natural languages.

[40] Argued for in Moore, *supra*, n. 28.

[41] See Moore, *supra*, n. 34, at 277–81. Some theorists seem to have imbibed so deeply of this fear that they refuse to conceptualize purposive interpretation of a rule to be following (or applying) the rule at all; according to Andrei Marmor, for example, when judges amend the ordinary meaning of the words appearing in a rule so as to make the rule better serve its purpose, they are 'disregarding', not 'following', the rule. Marmor, *supra*, n. 5, at 136–7. There are good reasons not to adopt this structural criterion of rules and rule-following and to adopt my functional criterion, namely, that doing the latter allows us to identify judicial obligation with following the (rules of the) law.

[42] *People* v. *Skinner*, 39 Cal. 3d. 765, 217 Cal. Rptr. 685, 704 P. 2d 752 (1985) (In the insanity defence, 'and' held to mean 'or' for purposes of conforming California initiative to the M'Naughten test).

to mean 'white';[43] 'death penalty' can be interpreted to mean 'life sentence',[44] once the validity of interpretation is made to turn exclusively on the ends served by the texts in which such words or phrases appear.

Yet this is a non-worry. Remember *what* it is that the value that guides interpretation first must justify: that the text be treated as a text by those who would interpret it. Even though, for example, a seeker of self-knowledge justifies his treatment of clouds or dreams as texts by the good of self-knowledge, and even though his interpretation of those phenomena is thus to be guided so as to maximize the self-knowledge attained, he must none the less pursue such self-knowledge indirectly. He must, in other words, focus on what the clouds mean, not on his own mental health, in order to serve the good of his own mental health. Similarly, the person who would be courteous must pursue respect for others indirectly. It does not maximize respect for others to ignore the forms of courtesy—say, by gushing constantly, 'I respect you'. Rather, one maximizes respect by behaviours that are recognizable interpretations of the forms of courtesy prevalent in that society. Similarly, the judge who would further the good of peaceful resolution of fundamental political disputes must pursue that good indirectly in his constitutional interpretations. It will not maximally serve that good to say that the Constitution means whatever a majority of Americans want it to mean; rather, he maximizes political peace by seeking an objective meaning to the document.

There is, to be sure, no bright line to be drawn as to when some value is sufficiently disserved (by giving the words of some legal text their ordinary meaning) that ordinary meaning should be overruled. Yet this is no more of a worry here than are slippery slopes generally. The inability to describe in general terms the right place to draw any line hardly betokens that in individual cases correct judgments of whether the line is crossed are not possible. It is not the case that everything (or nothing) is a heap, even if no clear general rule can be stated about how many stones make a heap.

APPLYING MODEST INTERPRETIVISM

Where are we? Having put aside the uselessly general very ambitious interpretivist model so popular today, I then distinguished four other models of

[43] This was one of Jonathan Swift's worries about the casuistry (purposive interpretation gone awry) of lawyers: 'There was a society of men among us, bred up from their youth in the art of proving by words multiplied for the purpose, that white is black, and black is white, according as they are paid.' *Travels by Lemuel Gulliver*, vol. 4, ch. v, repr. in C. V. Doren (ed.), *The Portable Swift* (Harmondsworth: Penguin, 1984), 472.

[44] As I took the Chief Justice of the California Supreme Court to be doing in her vote to reverse fifty-nine consecutive death sentences on allegedly procedural grounds. See Michael S. Moore, 'Politics is Not the Basis for Judging Judges', 'Justices' Personal Values Must at Times Give Way', 'Rose Bird Should Go', *Los Angeles Times*, 29, 30, 31, July 1985, repr. *USC Law* (Fall-Winter, 1986), 24–7.

interpretation: the communicative model, where necessarily one seeks authorial intention if one is interpreting anything; the metaphysical dualist model according to which objectively true interpretations are just there to be discovered in the special class of phenomena we call meaningful; the conventionalist or sociological model, according to which interpretation occurs whenever interpretive communities arise, developing concepts and practices of interpretation; and my own model, what I call the modest interpretivist model.[45] On this last model interpretation is an activity people do when they have some good reason to treat some phenomenon as a syntactically individuated text, valid interpretations of which will give them new, Intentionality-dependent reasons for belief or for action. We now should apply this model of interpretation to a variety of interpretive, or allegedly interpretive, activities.

Consider first the ordinary, communicative use of language in everyday conversations. When we as listeners seek to divine what the speaker meant by some utterance, are we engaged in an interpretive activity (on my 'modest interpretation' model)? The answer, perhaps surprisingly, is that it depends on what reason we have for listening. In ordinary, everyday conversations often there is no value that justifies us as listeners treating interpretations of the utterance as giving us either reasons to believe the proposition uttered, or reasons to act in accordance with the utterance. Conversational use of language looks interpretive in my sense (and is interpretive in the communicative sense I put aside at the beginning) because we often do have reason to seek to find out what the speaker meant by some utterance, and the conventional meaning of the sentence uttered is good evidence of that speaker's intent. It is part of the art of conversation to discover what the other meant so that one can respond appropriately, and we may plausibly suppose such pleasure of conversation to be something intrinsically good. Yet to serve this good does not require us to regard our interpretations as reasons for belief or action for us. Only when speakers are either theoretical authorities on the subject in question, or practical authorities (such as are friends with their requests), do we have reason to treat their utterances as giving us new reasons for belief or for action.

Ordinary, conversational use of language involves listeners in a standard, social-scientific task of description or explanation, not interpretation in the sense I have been attempting to isolate. Our curiosity about what such a conversational speaker meant is no different than our curiosity about what that speaker may have intended to achieve by saying what he did or, indeed, from what he may have intended with any action, speech-act or not. In all such cases, we wish to know the mental states of intention that moved him to action. This is a standard descriptive–explanatory question of social

[45] See Moore, *supra*, n. 2, at 934–41.

science even though it involves Intentional states, not the kind of non-descriptive, non-explanatory interpretive question that interests me.

It might be objected that the discovery of what someone intended on a given occasion is itself a matter of interpretation,[46] and thus that the social-scientific, communicative model of interpretation should be subsumed under my or some other more general model of interpretation. Yet this too would be a mistake. Describing what someone intended does, of course, involve one in describing the object or content of their intention. This is true for all Intentional states, not just for intentions. Yet describing a propositional attitude by describing its Intentional object is still to describe something, even if the thing described is itself a linguistic phenomenon. If you intend to go downtown, my description of what you intend is accurate if it corresponds to that object of your intention. That is, my description, 'he intends to go downtown' is true if and only if the description in his head—the object of his intention—is also that he go downtown.[47]

It is true that we often refer to both utterances and propositional attitudes in the language of indirect discourse. Instead of direct quotation, as in 'Mary said, "John is a louse"', we may paraphrase to, 'Mary said that John is a louse'. Likewise, instead of direct attribution, as in 'Mary intended "Mary go downtown"', we may paraphrase to, 'Mary intended that she should go downtown'. This indirect manner of referring to both utterances and propositional attitudes misleads many into thinking that therefore there is no fact of the matter about what Mary said or intended, and that we listeners therefore must fill in with our own interpretive efforts. Yet this is to take far too seriously our use of indirect discourse. One of Paul Grice's pragmatic injunctions was to convey no more information than your listener needs. We use indirect discourse because usually a listener does not need the precise wording of an utterance or an Intentional object—usually 'the gist' is sufficient.[48] That we have this intentionally vague way of referring to

[46] I discuss this possibility at somewhat greater length in *Law and Psychiatry: Rethinking the Relationship* (Cambridge: Cambridge University Press, 1984), ch. 1; and in *Act and Crime: The Implications of the Philosophy of Action for the Criminal Law* (Oxford: Clarendon Press, 1993), 63–5. The best working out of this possibility in the contemporary philosophy of mind is Dan Dennett's pragmatism about Intentional states. See Dennett, 'The Intentional Stance', in *Brainstorms* (Cambridge, Mass.: MIT Press, 1978) and *The Intentional Stance* (Cambridge, Mass.: MIT Press, 1987). This pragmatic or interpretive construal of intentions is assumed without argument by Ronald Dworkin (*supra*, n. 18) and by Dworkin's former student, Nicolas Stavropoulos ('Objectivity in Legal Interpretation', D.Phil. thesis, Oxford University, 1992). For a similar scepticism about the intentions of individuals, see Bix, *supra*, n. 39, at 188.

[47] This view of Intentional objects is, of course, not that of current eliminative materialists like Dan Dennett, Steven Stich, or Paul and Patricia Churchland. Rather, my own bets here are with those defenders of the folk psychology who believe that there is a language of thought in the brain that will allow realism about the propositional attitudes and their objects. See e.g. Jerry Fodor, *The Language of Thought* (Cambridge, Mass.: MIT Press, 1975). Compare the divergent views collected in John Greenwood (ed.), *The Future of Folk Psychology* (Cambridge: Cambridge University Press, 1991).

[48] Alternatively, we often do not know exactly what was either said or intended, so we use indirect discourse so as not to mislead as to the precision of our own knowledge.

utterances and propositional attitudes should not deflect us for a moment from the truth about both: there is a fact of the matter about both to which a description must correspond to be accurate.

If neither conversational use of language nor propositional attitude ascription are interpretive activities, what is? Quite a lot. Literary criticism, for example. There is (at least arguably—some literary critics make me doubt this) a point or value to treating novels, plays, poems, and so on as texts to be interpreted. If one has a moralistic view of literary criticism, such as that held by Matthew Arnold or John Gardner, then literature serves an educative function.[49] To the extent that the author is morally wiser than we the audience, we have reason to treat her productions as a text, interpretations of which give us new reasons to believe certain moral propositions to be true. This quickly leads to intentionalist literary interpretation. Alternatively, one might take certain literary productions to give us new reasons for moral belief (when those productions are correctly interpreted), even if the author of those productions is morally no wiser than are we. She may simply have hit upon a tale of compelling emotional power, allowing us to experience vicariously what life's lottery has not allowed us to experience directly in our own lives. For such novels, literary critics have reason to treat the novel as a text, interpreting it so as to further its experiential potential (and thus its capacity to give its audience new reasons for moral belief).

One might think literary criticism to have some quite different value justifying its interpretive attempts. One might think that literature can serve a therapeutic good, like clouds and dreams in my earlier examples. In which case it is the good of self-knowledge that justifies treating certain productions as texts, interpretations of which give us new reasons for believing truths about ourselves. Or the point of literary criticism might be beauty for its own sake (although this is more plausible for art than for literature), in which case it is the good of beauty (or appreciation of beauty, as G. E. Moore thought) that justifies literary critics interpreting the text so as to make it more beautiful (and thus to give its readers more reason to appreciate beauty).

Theology and psychoanalysis also contain activities properly thought of as interpretive by my modest conception of interpretation.[50] I probably, however, ought to say more about law (given that the text I am to interpret, the title of the symposium at which this paper was originally delivered, was 'Interpretation and Legal Theory').

Consider first statutory legal reasoning. This is plainly interpretive on the modest model of interpretation. There is a value served by judges regarding statutes as syntactically individuated texts, interpretations of which give them reasons for belief or for action. On one view of the matter, legislatures

[49] This view of literature is explored by Ron Garet, 'Comparative Normative Hermeneutics', *South. Calif. Law Rev.*, 58 (1985), 35–134.

[50] See Moore, *supra*, n. 2.

are theoretical authorities whose utterances, therefore, are the fit subjects for interpretation.[51] Such utterances, when properly interpreted,[52] give judges reasons for believing certain decisions to be more desirable than others. On my own view of the matter, legislatures are practical authorities because of their democratic composition; in addition, certain rule of law values justify judges in treating statutes as texts.[53] Such texts, when properly interpreted, give judges reasons for deciding one way rather than another. (Neither democracy nor the rule of law justifies judges in using intentionalist interpretive methods, but that is a detailed argument I have undertaken elsewhere).[54]

With common law (or precedential) reasoning, the situation is different. It is not difficult to imagine what an interpretive common law would look like. Indeed, with what is commonly called 'vertical precedent'—the deference lower courts give to prior opinions by courts higher in the appellate hierarchy—American courts regularly regard the prior opinions of higher courts as texts that they (the lower courts) have reason to interpret. Yet ordinary (or 'horizontal') precedent is not like this. Our courts do not treat prior opinions as texts. They broaden, narrow, reformulate, or throw out entirely the rule or the reasons stated by a prior court in its opinion, even while they 'follow' the decision of the prior court in deciding the later case.[55]

Our practice of horizontal precedent is correct in not regarding prior court opinions as texts. Those who have urged the contrary have often done so for the kind of reason given by Lord Mansfield, that earlier judges have 'worked the common law pure', so that their opinions possess a kind of theoretical authority for subsequent judges; alternatively, such proponents of an interpretive common law might think that being a judge in a legal system with a sitting legislature requires as little judicial lawmaking as possible and that therefore one's predecessors' opinions have some practical authority over one until changed by the legislature.[56] But neither of these views is very plausible. The value served by today's judges following precedent decisions is mainly the value of equality, but equality does not demand that cases that are alike *in the respects described in prior opinions* be treated alike; rather, equality demands that cases that are alike *in all morally relevant respects* be treated alike. Equality, thus, does not give a

[51] The view of Heidi Hurd and Donald Regan, among others. See Hurd, *supra*, n. 16; Regan, 'Law's Halo', in Jules Coleman and Ellen Frankel-Paul (eds.), *Philosophy and Law* (Oxford: Basil Blackwell, 1987).

[52] Either by finding what the legislature meant, or by some non-intentionalist interpretive strategy. Compare Marmor, *supra*, n. 5, ch. 8, with Waldron, *supra*, n. 25.

[53] See Moore, *supra*, n. 21; Moore *supra*, n. 5 at 313–18.

[54] Moore, *supra*, n. 5.

[55] Explored in Michael S. Moore, 'Precedent, Induction, and Ethical Generalization', in Laurence Goldstein (ed.), *Precedent in Law* (Oxford: Oxford University Press, 1987).

[56] The apparent view, for example, of Justice Heher in *Reimann* v. *Monmouth Consolidated Water Co.*, 9 N.J. 134 (1952).

judge any reason to treat the opinions of his predecessors as texts he must interpret.[57]

Why are not the particular decisions of earlier judges themselves a kind of text? For equality does give present judges reason to treat present litigants no differently than similarly situated, earlier litigants were treated by earlier judges. Why cannot we consider what was done to earlier litigants to be a kind of text? The reason we cannot do so lies in the Intentionality-dependent reasons that must exist for there to be a text. Although we might be able to formulate a syntactical rule (a rule of recognition) for what sort of judicial actions are to form the text for today's judges,[58] what the rule recognizes as authoritative—past judicial actions—will not give new, Intentionality-dependent reasons for belief or for action to subsequent judges. When judges generalize their decisions into common law *rules* in their opinions, such rules subsequently could be regarded as a text, if there were some value justifying subsequent judges in so treating them (as I have argued there is not). But the decisions themselves are simply meaningless events in the world, not Intentionality-dependent, reason-giving texts.

Common law reasoning is simply flat-out moral reasoning when the latter is done in the non-ideal case that past history must be respected so as not to violate the demands of equality. Moral reasoning in the ideal case (that is, ignoring the history of past treatments) is not interpretive reasoning for anyone whose meta-ethics is not relativist. Moral reasoning in the actual world, where equality demands that we respect our history, is similarly non-interpretive. Like common law reasoning, non-ideal moral reasoning itself generalizes past treatments, but those treatments, as we have seen, do not give Intentionality-dependent reasons for belief or for action.

American Constitutional reasoning has long been thought to hover—or oscillate—between being like statutory reasoning and being like common law reasoning. We are in a position to understand this uncertainty, for recall that the authority of the document lies both in its ability to resolve peacefully fundamental disputes and in the fact that the content of the document makes sufficiently few moral mistakes that the costs of revolution–radical amendment outweigh the gains. Only the first of these values justifies why judges should treat the document as a text even before they know what it means. The second requires judges to figure out what it means and only then decide whether it is good enough for government work. American Constitutional reasoning is thus an uncomfortable blend of genuinely

[57] Argued in Moore, *supra*, n. 55.

[58] Brian Simpson questions whether precedent as it is practised in Anglo-American legal systems in fact operates with such a rule of recognition. A. W. B. Simpson, 'The Common Law and Legal Theory', in id. (ed.), *Oxford Essays in Jurisprudence*, second series (Oxford: Oxford University Press, 1973).

interpretive reasoning and the kind of non-interpretive reasoning we find in common law adjudication.

Now let us consider, not legal practice, but legal theory. Since the work of Herbert Hart,[59] it has become common to distinguish two perspectives on law: one is the internal perspective on the law of a given legal system, taken by those who (actually or vicariously) participate as legal actors in the system; the other is the external perspective on law in general, taken by those who do not participate as a legal actor under that law. Theoreticians about law can work from either perspective. One can write, for example, judge-centred jurisprudence, advising judges in the American legal system what they should accept as American law and how they should go about interpreting (or otherwise applying) it. Or one can disengage from such vicarious judicial role-playing, writing one's legal theory about the (conceptual or real) essence of law as such.

Is the practice of either form of legal theory (usually labelled, respectively, particular or general jurisprudence) interpretive in character? It is easy to blurt out an unthinking 'yes' here, on the ground that because some of law practice is interpretive, so too must a study of that law practice be interpretive. This is a crude mistake, however. It is like the mistake of thinking that to study metaphors, one must do so metaphorically, or that to describe vagueness, one must do so vaguely. One can describe, explain, and fully understand an interpretive practice without necessarily being engaged in an interpretive practice.[60] So there is no necessity that legal theory of either kind be interpretive just because some of the legal reasoning studied by legal theory is itself interpretive.

Indeed, legal theory done from a perspective external to any particular legal system is quite plainly not interpretive in character. For there is no text of which theoreticians must seek the meaning in order to theorize about law in general. Such theorists are not judges, nor are they advising judges in some particular legal system, so that statutory or constitutional law does not bind them as it binds judges in those legal systems. Other legal theorist's writings are sometimes good heuristics, although more often good foils, but in any case, not *texts* for legal theorists.

It is true that a descriptive, general jurisprudence aims to describe law by giving a theory as to the nature of law, and that like any description, such a description of law must correspond to that which it describes, namely, law. Yet that does not make the kind, law, into a text legal theorists must

[59] Hart, *supra*, n. 17.

[60] Compare the often-criticized view of Peter Winch, whose Wittgensteinian fascinations lead him to assert that to understand a social practice one must join the natives in practising that practice: *The Idea of a Social Science* (London, Routledge, 1958). See also Dworkin, *supra*, n. 18, at 55 ('a social scientist must participate in a social practice if he hopes to understand it').

interpret—any more than similar truths about chemistry and descriptions of gold make chemists interpretivists about the periodic table. Describing something that has a nature hardly becomes interpretation just because the description must describe that nature in order to be accurate.[61]

All of this remains true for those general jurisprudes who seek to describe, not the thing, law, but a shared concept of law. When Herbert Hart and Joseph Raz wrote their justly celebrated books on this topic,[62] they were not interpreting anything. Rather they, like essentialists about law such as Aquinas, were seeking to describe something with a nature. In their case, that something was that set of shared propositional attitudes we call a concept, that is, common beliefs about law's nature. As we have seen, such propositional attitude ascriptions are not interpretations, irrespective of whether the propositional attitudes being described are about law or about anything else.

Does the case for legal theory being interpretive become stronger when that legal theory is done from the internal perspective? Since the legal theorist is giving advice to legal actors such as judges, presumably if the advice is to be taken seriously it well be because real judges ought to heed it. Since real judges are often engaged in interpretive reasoning, must the theorist who would advise them on how to reason also be engaging in interpretation? Since real judges have reason to treat statutes as texts, do not theorists who would advise judges how to judge not also have to treat statutes as texts?

Despite the appearances, these are not rhetorical questions. Indeed, the answer to them is 'no'. We must distinguish between advocates before judges—lawyers—from theorists advising judges how to judge. Lawyers arguing to judges must surely engage in the interpretive reasoning that they would have the judge himself go through in order to reach a result favourable to their client. But advising judges how to judge is not this sort of advocacy. For notice that, when I or other legal theorists advise judges how to interpret statutes—as I do regularly in my 'jurisprudence for judges' seminars in America—we are not interpreting statutes. Rather, we are trying to describe the best way to interpret statutes. Ours is a 'meta-' question. If there is any text for our meta-question, it would be the interpretive practices of judges, not the statutes being interpreted. And why should I, or the judges I advise, be bound (in how they do their interpretations) by how

[61] Such descriptions of law's nature remain just that, descriptions and not interpretations, even if the essential nature of law is given by the unique values ('functions') law serves and not by any structural features (like coercive sanctions). Functionalist description of law is not interpretive jurisprudence. For the difference, see Michael S. Moore, 'Law as a Functional Kind', in Robert George (ed.), *Natural Law Theories* (Oxford: Oxford University Press, 1992), 239 n. 79.

[62] Hart, *supra*, n. 17; Joseph Raz, *The Concept of a Legal System* (Oxford: Oxford University Press, 1970).

other judges have done their interpretations? Why should I or the judges I advise care a fig that American judicial practice is to interpret statutes by paying at least lip-service to legislative intent? Surely I as a theorist, like the judges I advise, are free of any obligation to treat other judges' interpretive practice as having any authority to constrain my recommendations about how to interpret statutes.[63]

I conclude that no legal theorist should wish to think of his theoretical activity as an interpretive activity. Only when legal theorists become advocates for particular interpretations—only when we act like lawyers who themselves act like judges, in other words—do we engage in interpretive reasoning.[64]

CONCLUSION

From what was just said, it should be clear that my title is misleading. I have not been interpreting interpretation—for such an activity would presuppose that I had some reason to treat our practices of interpretation as a kind of text, interpretations of which would give us reasons to believe certain facts about interpretation. And I can't think of any such reason that is at all plausible. Not being a very modest fellow, I am unwilling to grant any theoretical authority to the theories or practices of interpretation of others. Nor do I see any practical authority to such practices or to their practitioners. What I have been up to in this essay, thus, is *describing* a kind of activity. Even though that kind of activity is an interpretive one, that does not mean I have been doing anything other than describing the nature of this kind of activity. Such description becomes interpretation only on the very ambitious view that holds *all* descriptions or explanations to be interpretations, or on the communicative sense of 'interpretation' that identifies all descriptions of Intentional states as interpretation. But that is to abandon the useful, distinct notion of interpretation that I have sought to analyse in this essay.

In closing, let me taxonomize the various models of interpretation around their views on the relation between description and explanation, on the one hand, and interpretation on the other. The very ambitious interpretivist sees

[63] I can imagine that in a judicial world different from the one with which I am familiar—namely, a world in which there was some convergence of judicial interpretive practices—there could be a good of co-ordination giving each judge a reason to co-ordinate his interpretive practices with those of other judges. Presumably equality, enhanced predictability, and efficiency would be the goods served by such co-ordination. See Gerald Postema, 'Co-ordination and Convention at the Foundation of Law', *Journal of Legal Studies*, 11 (1982), 165–203, for suggestions in this direction.

[64] The conclusion that jurisprudence is not interpretive has been defended before, both by me and by Andrei Marmor, specifically against Dworkin's claims to the contrary, in Moore, *supra*, n. 2, at 948; Marmor, *supra*, n. 5, at ch. 3.

no difference between the two, because everything is interpretation. With a nice symmetry, the communicative model also sees no difference, but in this case, because interpretation just is a description of a natural phenomenon (an intention) and the explanation of another natural phenomenon (production of a text) as the causal product of it. Both of these reductionist views are wrong. Interpretation is an activity that is distinct from the descriptive and explanatory activities characteristic of science. But one must be modest about this difference. It will not do to elevate this difference into a metaphysical divide between two kinds of being, each with their own brand of science. That is the mistake of the metaphysically dualist model of interpretation. Interpretation is just another activity—like sleeping, eating, teaching, or writing—that people sometimes have reason to do. Such activities do not need the justification of science to make them worthwhile, and none of them can have that justification—the generation of understanding—since they are not descriptions or explanations. Interpretation as an activity makes perfectly good sense in the restricted domains that I have mentioned, without any more ambitious trappings.

2

Focusing the Law: What Legal Interpretation is Not

MARTIN STONE

Part I: Theory

This essay is about legal judgment—the judgment that focuses, applies, or elaborates the law—but it also touches on a cluster of related issues: the indeterminacy of rules, the 'politics of interpretation', and the misuse of Wittgenstein in recent legal theory.

My starting-point is a tension that is discernible in many contemporary theoretical discussions of law and legal judgment. Simply put, a great deal of contemporary legal theory finds itself in resistance to the commonplace. It tries to re-describe the law by means of a rhetoric borrowed from other disciplines but foreign to the materials closest to the lawyer's experience. Its aim is to go behind the law's own conception of itself. In American jurisprudence, with its legacy of 'legal realism', legal judgment has been a main target of such 'demystification', as emerges, for example, in the following remark from Edward Levi's *An Introduction to Legal Reasoning*:

> This [book] is an attempt to describe generally the process of legal reasoning in the field of case law and in the interpretation of statutes and of the constitution. It is important that the mechanism of legal reasoning should not be concealed by its pretense. The pretense is that the law is a system of known rules applied by a judge; the pretense has long been under attack. In an important sense legal rules are never clear . . . It cannot be said that the legal process is the application of known rules to diverse facts . . . The rules change as the rules are applied. (1949: 1, 3, 4)

The elements of this passage are familiar. (The passage comprises what many legal theorists in recent years take to be platitudes; part of my aim is to show how much philosophy there is in these apparent platitudes.) Levi speaks of a 'mechanism' of legal reasoning, a 'process' that occurs when cases are decided. The process is to be given a theoretical account, but the

This paper is indebted to conversations with Hilary Putnam and Ernest Weinrib, to the instructive writings on Wittgenstein by Stanley Cavell, Cora Diamond, and John McDowell, and to Katherine Bartlett, James Boyle, George Christie, Stanley Fish, Martin Golding, Toril Moi, Robert Post, Lisa Van Alstyne, and especially James Conant for their comments on an earlier draft.

law is not the source of the concepts that will figure in this account. On the contrary, it is necessary, from the beginning, to discard a 'pretence', one that belongs to legal reasoning as such ('*its* pretence'), that is to say, to the way the law represents—or rather 'conceals'—itself. The pretence has 'long been under attack', but it apparently continues to hold sway, for Levi suggests several lines of continued attack: The rules applied in the legal process are not known (they are continuously recreated as they are applied); the rules are never *simply* applied; the rules are never clear.

If the view Levi opposes is called by its traditional name of 'formalism', it appears to be a feature of formalism that it is historically enduring, for today the attack on it recurs in the guise of the claim that legal rules are *indeterminate* and that they are in need of *interpretation* in light of other normative considerations, say, political goals or social ideals. These claims go together: The claim that interpretation is needed to determine what a legal rule requires rests on the claim that legal rules are, in themselves, indeterminate—that there is a sort of gap between a legal rule and its application in the particular case.[1] Talk of indeterminacy is nowadays taken to represent the inheritance of a kind of 'realism' about law, but in the pages that follow I want to press the question: how *realistic* (the opposite, say, of obsessive or superstitious) is this most recent kind of realism?[2] Three observations will help to identify my concerns.

(1) The first point concerns a development whose intellectual mainsprings lie largely outside the law (in fields like anthropology and literary theory), but which in recent years has attracted many legal scholars who see in it the key to making sense of their own discipline and to providing it with an intellectual sophistication it would otherwise lack. Specifically, there is widespread interest today in using the notion of interpretation to conceptualize the humanities and social sciences—interpretation is supposed to be what distinguishes these fields from others. My concern is with this *foundational* interest in interpretation: the sort of interest that comes out in remarks to the effect that every reading, indeed every identification of a text, is an interpretation—you can't, so to speak, get free of interpretation. Clearly interpretation plays some role in legal adjudication, but the problems I have in mind grow out of attempts to see interpretation as a condition of *any* legal judgment.[3] It is the generality of this thesis about interpretation ('in an important sense legal rules are *never* clear') which makes it sound heady—and, to my ears, suspect as well.

(2) The pervasive indeterminacy of legal rules has struck many recent

[1] This alignment of these claims is helpfully noted by Marmor (1992: 146–7).

[2] I owe a debt, in the formulation of this question, to Diamond, 'Realism and the Realistic Spirit', in Diamond (1991*a*). See also n. 22.

[3] For examples of such attempts, see Fish (1989: 125, 121); Cornell (1992: 101). I discuss these examples below.

theorists as rendering it impossible to think of law as an autonomous discipline (a study with its own content). For if the legal rules do not determine the outcomes of adjudication, something else must. Admittedly, few theorists would go so far as to celebrate an image of law as an empty vessel waiting to be filled by whatever content is poured into it through judicial legislation (cf. Lyons 1993: 53). None the less, today a defence of the autonomy of law is often seen to be tied not only to a practical naïvety about the matter-of-fact entanglement of law with politics, but also to a theoretical naïvety concerning the nature of legal rules—a naïve misconception of their power to determine the particular case.

(3) These two theses of contemporary legal theory—the indeterminacy of legal rules and the heteronomy of law—combine to form a seductive revisionary conception of legal judgment. On the traditional view, legal systems articulate a distinction between legal and other substantive grounds of decision, and in this sense they consist in rules. To say that adjudication is governed by rules is to say that the grounds of a properly legal decision are fixed in a way that excludes other considerations that might otherwise be brought to bear in deciding the case. But if saying what the legal rules prescribe in the particular case requires an interpretation of the rules, then, according to the revisionist, the outcome of the case depends upon a judgment that is not uniquely fixed by the rules. The contrast between the legal and the political seems to hold up, on this view, only as long as adjudication is credulously understood to involve more or less mechanical or automatic reasoning from the general to the particular. But to speak of an interpretation is to imply that some other interpretation is possible; it is to evoke an activity that is not mechanical but in some sense creative. So the requirement that legal rules be interpreted means, the revisionist concludes, that there is a measure of pretence or self-deception present when a judge seems to resolve a case by means of the legal rules alone. In easy cases, the 'politics of interpretation' may be innocuous, importing into legal decision only considerations that are, at least for the moment, uncontested (and perhaps, therefore, hidden from view). But even such considerations, the revisionist enjoins us to think, are not *uncontestable*. To pretend that they are—or worse, that difficult cases can be resolved by direct application of the legal rules themselves—is, according to him, to repress potential conflict by means of a fictitious formalism (cf. Unger 1986: 1–2, 8). And in judicial practice, this is to present political judgments as purely legal conclusions.[4]

[4] I should emphasize that my concern in this essay is with the question of the inescapability of 'legal politics' and not with its political desirability. I suspect that any inference from a thesis about the heteronomy of law (e.g. its relation to the political) to a specific political orientation is a *non sequitur*. For the legal realists, legal politics tended to come under the sign of progressivism, but the opposite possibility is suggested by the example of Carl Schmitt, who wrote in 1934 that '[e]very interpretation must be an interpretation according to National Socialism' (cited in Muller 1991: 70). It should be mysterious, in light of Schmitt's sentence, why

Before introducing the preceding three observations, I posed the question: how *realistic* is (what legal theorists call) 'realism'. Law professors know that this 'realistic' revisionary account of legal judgment has had a long-standing play in our legal culture. As one commentator recently put it, 'a lesson that needs to be relearned in each generation is that the law can appear to be an objective, neutral, and determinate body of rules, but really is situated in social context, exposed to political bias, and indeterminate to a significant extent' (Burton 1992: 6–7). One might sense that there is something odd, however, about a lesson that cannot be done with, that needs to be continuously relearned. Might this be a sign that we are here in the tormented region of philosophy (and not dealing with straightforward lessons at all)? I have allowed myself to describe the argument that recently has accompanied this lesson in rather schematic terms.[5] For I do not want to criticize this or that theory of legal interpretation, so much as to raise a doubt about the tendency to theorize legal judgment as interpretation *tout court*. My aim is to identify the temptations that sometimes lead us to give interpretation a foundational role in law, if only to see in the end why our yielding to these temptations really yields little satisfaction.

THE LIMITS OF INTERPRETATION

> 'When you come tomorrow, bring my football boots. Also, if humanly possible, Irish water spaniel. Urgent. Regards. Tuppy.'
>
> 'What do you make of that, Jeeves?'
>
> 'As I interpret the document, sir, Mr. Glossop wishes you, when you come tomorrow, to bring his football boots. Also, if humanly possible, an Irish water spaniel. He hints that the matter is urgent, and sends his regards.'
>
> 'Yes, that's how I read it, too . . .'.
>
> (P. G. Wodehouse)[6]

> Let us ask ourselves: why do we feel a grammatical joke to be *deep*? (And that is what the depth of philosophy is.)
>
> (Wittgenstein, *Philosophical Investigations* § 111)

the contemporary reduction of law to politics is counted on by some theorists to underwrite progressive politics.

[5] A careful delineation of the details of various positions is not to my present purpose. For example, a theorist might hold fast to the idea that the outcome of each case is determined by the legal grounds of decision, but then take the necessity of interpretation to require a conception of these grounds that incorporates open-ended political considerations. There are important differences for legal theory in these variations, but I do not think they matter for my present concerns.

[6] Quoted in Schauer (1991: 207). Despite the joke's reliance on our recognition of situations in which a call for interpretation seems superfluous, Schauer maintains that '*every* application of a rule is also an interpretation'.

In our everyday affairs we encounter a more discriminating use of the notion of interpretation. If, in response to the waiter's inquiry, you nod and he takes your plate away, no one would count it a mark of your theoretical sophistication if you were to remark: 'See, he *interprets* my gesture as I intended it.' Does he understand your gesture without interpreting it? Here it seems best to say that talk of interpretation is not well motivated without the presence of some kind of doubt, something that makes it plausible to understand your gesture otherwise. Of course, you could cleverly insist that a vertical motion of the head might mean many things and might not even be a deliberate act at all; so he must (*implicitly* you will now say) be making an interpretation. But you ought to be clearer, in saying there was an interpretation, about whether you mean to imply that there were real and not just possible or imaginable doubts. Interpretations ordinarily function within a space of reasonable contrasting interpretations. Hence the maxims, *clara non sunt interpretanda, interpretatio cessat in claris*: interpretations come to an end when matters are clear.

But the question may be pressed: when is a legal rule clear? It would lead to a well-marked page of philosophy to say there comes a point when it is impossible to doubt, given the 'clearness and distinctness' of an idea, or when a sentence adheres to the thought it represents and brooks no other understanding.[7] Yet from contemporary discussions one is left with the impression that the legal formalist, in order to defend his position, must presuppose some such (apparently suspect) epistemology. According to Stanley Fish, for example, 'a formalist believes that words have clear meanings', and in order to believe this, 'he must also believe (1) that minds see those clear meanings clearly; (2) that clarity is a condition that persists through changes of context; (3) that nothing in the self interferes with the perception of clarity', and so on (1989: 6). Fish is certainly not alone among theorists today in taking the sense of phrases such as 'words have clear meanings' or 'the application of a legal rule is clear' to depend on a confused philosophical picture of meaning and interpretation. And while it is not part of my aim to deny the confusion in traditional—call them Cartesian—attempts to provide a philosophical story which underwrites such phrases, I do wish to call attention to a particular philosophical recoil: from the failure of such a story, to the inclination to see any impulse to respect such phrases as epistemologically suspect. Fish concludes—evidently from the failure of a certain philosophical picture—that the appeal to the clear meaning of a legal rule is itself already a symptom of philosophical confusion.

[7] Various historical connections obtain between the Latin maxims cited in the previous paragraph and the Cartesian epistemology of clear and distinct ideas. See Dascal and Wroblewski (1988). But my view is that the maxims are not circumscribed by that epistemology: they can be understood as expressing a notion of 'clarity' that is at home in legal activity and that is unproblematic once purged of that philosophical framework.

But why delineate the relevant notion of clarity in terms of such a picture? Isn't there a sense of 'clarity' that is at home in law and that remains useful once the requirements Fish attaches to that notion ('he must also believe . . .') fall away? It is a feature of law that its interpretation ends in positive decision, in its being followed in determinate judgments. The law may not always be followed, but if there is to be law it must be possible to follow it in the particular case. So it seems natural to say that a legal rule is clear or determinate when it serves in practice to guide legal judgment in a range of ordinary cases, and correlatively that it is indeterminate if there is significant disagreement in the practice of applying it—that is, actual disagreement, not the merest notional *possibility* that disagreement might arise. Any linguistic expression could be said to be subject, a priori, to such a possibility: no explanation of it can satisfy the demand to settle every possible doubt about how it is to be applied. But if this makes it appropriate to represent an expression as 'indeterminate' (cf. Fish 1989: 516), it is only because there is no such thing—in such a way of representing the matter—as its being determinate.

I shall argue in what follows that the thought that 'every application of a rule involves an interpretation of it' arises from the illusion that we have understood this demand for determinacy (as the *impossibility* of doubt): the disappointment of this demand then makes us feel that the law is defective—it cannot live up to this ideal. This recoil is what H. L. A. Hart had in mind when he remarked that 'the rule-skeptic is sometimes a disappointed absolutist' (1961: 135). The astuteness of Hart's remark can be seen in the way many of the slogans associated with legal realism—think of Holmes's '[g]eneral propositions do not decide concrete cases'[8] or 'the life of the law has not been logic' (1963: 1)—seem to be trying to deny something that, upon reflection, we will find we understand very poorly in the first place. (Is there such a thing as 'concrete cases being decided by general propositions'? What is it we imagine, when we repeat this slogan, that general propositions fail to do?) But the contemporary recourse to interpretation is more subtle and obscure than the often-repeated slogans of the realists. Indeed, the need for interpretation has been motivated in recent legal theory in a way that would regard the limitation of interpretation to a case of real doubt or uncertainty as largely misleading. The everyday notion of interpretation—where the sense of a call for interpretation depends upon the possibility of a significant contrast with clear cases in which there is no call for interpretation—thus comes to seem irrelevant to the task of understanding legal judgment. And this is where the real difficulty begins.

[8] *Lochner* v. *New York*, 198 US 45, 76 (1905).

INTERPRETATION UNBOUND

It is interpretation that gives us the rule, not the other way around.
(D. Cornell, 1992: 101)

What notion of interpretation *is* relevant to understanding legal judgment, if it is not the everyday one with its limited conditions of application?

The contemporary theories I have in mind sometimes represent the judicial decision that would occur *if* the law were determinate as the conclusion of a syllogism—a syllogism in which the major premiss gives the applicable rule of law and the minor premiss describes the transaction between the parties to the case. Since in even the easiest case the agreed upon or established description of the facts typically contains no legal language and certainly not the ultimate legal conclusion (for example, that the defendant acted negligently), it seems that there is always room for a question of the following sort: in virtue of what is *this* act and not *that* one an act of negligence? Or more generally: in virtue of what does this case, with its particular facts, fall within the class of cases designated, in principle, by the legal rule?[9] The answer is: in virtue of an *interpretation* of the legal rule. This answer is developed at length in a recent law-school textbook, Steven Burton's *An Introduction to Legal Reasoning* (1985). Burton believes that we go wrong if we think that legal rules can mark out their own application, and that this mistake should be corrected by acknowledging the need for interpretation.

Burton's discussion of legal judgment is notable, from my perspective, for the fact that it presents 'the necessity of an interpretive method' under a dual aspect or motivation. On the one hand, the concept of interpretation is introduced as part of an attempt to correct a confusion about legal reasoning, a confusion engendered by the widespread practice of presenting legal arguments in deductive or syllogistic form: 'The result commonly continues to be expressed in the form of a legal syllogism . . . But it is constructed by judging the importance of the facts in light of a judicial interpretation of the authoritative rule—an interpretation that itself is not a product of deduction . . .' (1985: 50). This is the moment of demystification, the legacy of legal realism. But although intending to demystify the law—to 'pierce through the forms of legal reasoning to its interpretive method' (153; cf. 36, 43)—Burton also presents the requirement that legal judgment pass through 'interpretation' as itself a kind of commonplace:[10] as the beginning of *any* sensible view of legal reasoning, an uncontroversial textbook point, suitable for catechizing beginning law-students who are learning, in

[9] For a similar formulation, see Burton (1985: 21, 42, 85–8).

[10] Burton states the point in various ways. For example: 'The forms [of legal reasoning] must be filled in through an interpretive method' (1985: 162).

the time-worn words of the Preface, to 'think like a lawyer' (p. xiii). 'One cannot reasonably deny the necessity', Burton tells the students, 'of an interpretive method' (83). So, oddly enough: although the need for interpretation cannot be reasonably denied, it does need to be continually reasserted against the misleading form of the law itself—a formula for obsession. And to learn to 'think like a lawyer' is to learn to see behind the forms in which legal arguments 'commonly continue to be expressed'.[11]

What is happening here? Is the word 'interpretation' simply doing notational duty for the idea of the 'application' of a rule? Or is something more than a mere gesture of renaming at stake, something in the order of an insight into the necessary conditions of any legal judgment?

If we think of a clear case as one which falls squarely within the extension of a legal rule, Burton's question of how the law applies to the particular case seems to demand an explanation of what makes a 'clear case' clear. What makes it possible for a legal judgment to be in accord with the rule it applies? Consider, in this regard, another remark of H. L. A. Hart's, one that appears to have influenced the direction of Burton's thinking (cf. Burton 1985: 88):

> [I]t is a matter of some difficulty to give any exhaustive account of what makes a 'clear case' clear or makes a general rule obviously and uniquely applicable to a particular case. Rules cannot claim their own instances, and fact situations do not await the judge neatly labeled with the rule applicable to them. Rules cannot provide for their own application, and even in the clearest case a human being must apply them.[12]

Hart doesn't doubt that we can reliably distinguish between hard and easy cases, but his remark presents an air of puzzlement that might lead his reader to think that an account of the basis of such a distinction is still pending.[13] Someone who understands a legal rule no doubt recognizes some cases as presenting standard instances of the relevant classification;

[11] Burton's textbook itself stages these tensions by re-creating within its form a certain dialectic of legal theory. Part One (the formalist moment) presents the analogical and deductive 'forms of legal reasoning' only to conclude by telling the student that in some respects legal reasoning 'is neither' (1985: 82). For in order to solve a crucial problem, the forms of legal reasoning must be supplemented by 'a workable method of legal interpretation' (82–3). Part Two (the realist moment) is then devoted to getting the student to see through the deceptive aspects of Part One: 'Though the forms of legal reasoning seem to presuppose a method like the romanticized popular conception of scientific reasoning, a workable method of legal interpretation must be different' (91). '[T]he promise of certainty implicit in the forms of legal reasoning is an illusory promise' (95).

[12] Hart, 'Problems in the Philosophy of Law', in Hart (1983: 106). See also Hart (1961: 123).

[13] The present essay may be taken in defence of a distinction (of the kind originally drawn by Hart 1961: ch. 6) between easy and hard cases. It should be clear from what follows that I cite this passage not to criticize the distinction, but because I think it invites a kind of confusion which has led some theorists to feel that they are not entitled—at least not without further theoretical work—to draw such a distinction.

and for practising lawyers who routinely draw analogies to clear cases, that might be enough to say about the matter. But in speaking of an 'exhaustive account of what makes a "clear case" clear', Hart seems to invite the theorist of law to push beyond this. And when Hart goes on to say that 'rules *cannot* claim their own instances' or that 'rules *cannot* provide for their own application', it may sound to a theorist like Burton as if there were *something* that rules were unable to do—as if (like Holmes's general propositions) rules were, in themselves, mere dead letters. Then, continuing this thought, since a rule does seem to make a normative demand on someone who endeavours to follow it, it will be natural to wonder how it gets animated—how (if not by the rule itself) its instances are claimed and its application provided for.

The demand for theory which Hart's remark seems to nurture can be brought out more clearly by noticing that his point about clear cases would have a different sense if it were taken to be specific to specific areas of adjudication. Suppose, for example, that a lawyer specializing in the law of nuisance informed us that 'it is difficult to give an exhaustive account of what makes a "clear case" clear'. He would most likely mean that while some occurrences are plainly (to any competent judge of the matter) actionable nuisances, the various factors that help determine this are such that it is inadequate to explain the concept of nuisance by giving (non-trivial) necessary and sufficient conditions for its application. This is how it is with nuisance: it can't be reduced to a rule of the form 'Occurrence O is a nuisance if and only if a, b, c . . .'. But to tell this lawyer that this difficulty about what makes a 'clear case' clear derives from the fact that 'rules cannot claim their own instances' would be to misunderstand him. His remark was meant to point to the absence of a certain kind of legal rule (a rule of the form 'O is a nuisance if and only if . . .'), and he would withdraw the remark if, say, the legislature laid down such a rule. That rule would, in effect, answer the question, in regard to nuisance, what makes a 'clear case' clear. The lawyer's conception of what makes it hard to say 'what makes a "clear case" clear', in short, derives its sense against the background of the possibility of a kind of account that would count as exhaustive for him and a kind of case that would count as clear for him. In contrast, Hart's remark that 'rules cannot claim their own instances' suggests some difficulty in accounting for clear cases under *any* rule, no matter how specific. That remark invites the supposition that the problem about legally clear cases is an instance of a perfectly general problem of explaining the possibility of judgment in accordance with a rule.

If one is inclined to accept such an invitation to undertake a general explanation of the possibility of judgment in accordance with a rule, then it can become enticing to appeal to interpretation to close the gap between a rule and the instances to which it applies. But before exploring the merits of this way of attempting to close the gap, it is worth pausing to reflect for a moment on what sort of gap is at issue here. I remarked, in introducing Burton, that it seems there is always room for a question of the following sort: in virtue of what is this and not that an act of *x* (putting a classificatory term of a legal rule in place of *x*)? An answer to this question would constitute an instruction about how to apply the legal rule. But a potential pitfall here is brought out in a brief remark of Kant's: 'judgment', Kant writes, 'is a peculiar talent which can be practised only, and cannot be taught' (1787: A133/B172). To give instructions about judgment (about how to subsume cases under rules) would be to supply the learner with further concepts or rules. This might be helpful or even indispensable on a particular occasion (as, for example, when a jury is instructed that 'reasonable care' is the care which persons of ordinary prudence use under similar circumstances). But the learner's ability to make use of the instruction he is given will itself require an exercise of judgment, so it can't *in general* be the case—on pain of a bad regress— that the connection between a rule and the particular cases that fall under it depends on some further, theoretically representable piece of understanding.[14] The question, 'in virtue of what is *this* and not *that*. . .' depicts a gap between a rule and its application in so far as it invites us to say what mediates our judgment in cases where we correctly apply a rule. But Kant's point is that the domain of this question is necessarily a limited one: at some point, instructions must give out and then judgment 'can only be practised'. Now, the logic of the point seems clear enough, but it can be very hard to see what moral one should draw from it. In particular, it may be tempting to take the threatened regress as showing that there is no general remedy for the inertness of rules—hence, that not every application of a rule can be, so to speak, 'rule-governed'.[15] And this is bound to make the possibility of determinate applications of rules seem paradoxical or at least difficult to fathom: the demand for an explanation of the connection between a rule and its applications will now be thought to be defeated, but in such a way that the demand remains in place—so one continues to look for something else (perhaps a theory of 'practice'?) to forge the connection.

As I hope to make clear in a moment, we are not compelled to take the regress in this way. We are not so compelled because we need not accede to the supposition that our entitlement to the notion of a legally 'clear case' needs to be shored up by any general (that is, not legally specific) account of what makes it clear. But to appreciate the options here it will be useful first to say something more about how, in contemporary discussions of law, these problems take hold. Those theorists who celebrate the thought that

[14] My explanation of Kant's remark follows Kant's own discussion.

[15] This is, for example, how Dallmayr (1992: 3) takes the regress. See note 45 below.

the application of the law requires the work of interpretation generally motivate this thesis, as I remarked, through an opposition to 'formalism'. Formalism, in this sense, is taken to be the thesis Hart's remark apparently means to deny: that legal rules *can* claim their own instances, *can* provide for their own application. So despite the regress that ensues if the subsumption of cases under a rule is made to depend on some intermediate kind of understanding, it continues to look as if we have a genuine controversy here—two conflicting opinions someone might hold about the nature of legal decision. On one opinion, to adjudicate—to say what the legal rules require in new cases—is to interpret the rules; on the other opinion, the legal rules themselves demand a certain result. I will urge a way of viewing the regress which does not take sides in this controversy—one which points in the direction of wondering whether these theses thrive on 'taking in each other's washing'[16] What is doubtful about each of these theses is to be discovered through an exploration of the character of the antithesis (between rules as requiring interpretation and rules as claiming their own instances).

To make this clearer, I think it would repay the effort to listen closely to how the turn to interpretation is motivated in a remark by another contemporary legal theorist. In a recent study of how the work of certain 'postmodern' theorists bears upon 'a concept of legal interpretation' (1992: 12), Drucilla Cornell approvingly reports the following:

> [Members of the Critical Legal Studies Movement] have not only shown that rules of procedure cannot escape an appeal to a substantive ethical justification, they have also shown us that the very idea of a rule as a force that pulls us down the track through each new fact situation, determining the outcome of a particular case, is false. Therefore, no line of precedent can fully determine a particular outcome in a particular case because the rule itself is always in the process of reinterpretation as it is applied. It is interpretation that gives us the rule, not the other way around. This insight is what has come to be known as the 'indeterminacy thesis'. . . [L]aw cannot be reduced to a set of technical rules, a self-sufficient mechanism that pulls us down the track through each new fact situation. (1992: 101–2)

What we are likely to notice in this passage (at least if we are attentive to how the turn to interpretation arises) is its reliance on a piece of mechanical imagery to express what legal decision is *not*: the rule is not a rail that pulls us down the track through each new case. The use of such imagery is, I think, philosophically significant, especially since it presents not merely a vivid illustration but also the primary characterization of the thesis Cornell seeks to oppose.[17] (I will return to this in a moment.) Imagery aside, Cornell

[16] The phrase is J. L. Austin's (1962: 4).

[17] Indeed, Cornell gives the imagery priority by presenting it as an explanation of the indeterminacy thesis (rather than the other way around). Thus, in an attempt to clarify the indeterminacy thesis in the face of a misunderstanding, Cornell maintains that the thesis

provides a catalogue of various things that *cannot* occur—'rules cannot escape . . .'; 'no line of precedent can . . .'; 'law cannot be reduced . . .'—without saying in what sense these things are impossible. In so far as Cornell offers an explanation, it invokes the inevitability of interpretation ('because the rule itself is always in the process of reinterpretation'), and she assumes we will know what this means. She goes on to say that 'an appeal to the beyond' is 'inherent in legal interpretation' (102). I take this to mean that interpretation makes legal decision political. Legal decision requires open-ended assessment of the merits of the case because the result is never 'fully determined' by the legal rule. Cornell calls this 'the indeterminacy thesis', and she calls this thesis an insight—that is, a piece of positive knowledge—opposing it to the false idea of a rule as that which compels us in a quasi-mechanical fashion.

Cornell speaks about the necessity of 'interpretation' as if it were something of a recent philosophical revelation, whereas for Burton it is what every undeceived lawyer already knows. But despite this difference in tone, their line of thought is the same. Two points may serve to characterize for us this line of thought.

First, the concept of interpretation is made to bear an explanatory burden. It appears to stand quite generally for whatever it is that mediates between the identification of the appropriate legal rule and its application to the particular case. Interpretation is the 'process' (Cornell 1992: 101) or 'method' (Burton 1985: 83) by which an otherwise indeterminate rule is attached to *these* cases and thus endowed with a concrete meaning.

Secondly, whereas the ordinary or everyday sense of interpretation connects the need for interpretation to hard cases, the present line of thought evidently seeks to revise our understanding of what occurs in every case. The difference between hard and easy cases will be poorly described, if we follow this line, as a difference between rules that require interpretation and rules that are clear enough to be directly or immediately applied (cf. Burton 1985: 129, 142, 191). For the appearance of clarity is, on this view, the effect of an interpretation—one that must be implicit or hidden from view, one that did not, at least on *this* particular occasion, come into question. 'Interpretation', as Cornell says, 'gives us the rule, not the other way around.' This suggests that the 'indeterminacy thesis' will be impervious to any contrary evidence based on easy cases because it will regard the apparent easiness of those cases as dependent on conditions that it seeks to unmask

'should . . . be understood to be that law cannot be reduced to a set of technical rules, a self-sufficient mechanism that pulls us down the track' (1992: 102). Cornell's prose here follows a tradition of thought opposing legal formalism. Starting with the legal realists, legal theorists have appealed to such mechanical imagery to represent what someone might mistakenly believe about legal judgment. See e.g. Frank (1963: 125–58); Kennedy (1973: 358–9); Burton (1985: 95, 97, 163); Lyons (1993: 41–57).

as interpretive. According to this thesis, the presence of plain meaning testifies to the hegemony, so to speak, of a particular interpretation, not to the absence or superfluousness of interpretation as such.

It would be wrong to think that this thesis is specific to the Critical Legal Studies Movement or to those who today try to pursue a political programme through an analysis of the nature of legal adjudication. It is upheld by others, not out of an attachment to its presumed political consequences, but simply as the right account of the nature of legal judgment. Here again is Stanley Fish: 'While there will always be paradigmatically plain cases—Hart is absolutely right to put them at the center of the adjudicative process—far from providing a stay against the force of interpretation, they will be precisely the result of interpretation's force; for they will have been written and rewritten by interpretive efforts.'[18] Since interpretive assumptions underlie the possibility of easy cases, it follows, for Fish, that the distinction between easy and hard cases is too innocently won and should be re-described as a distinction between cases in which the interpretive assumptions conditioning the judgment are uncontroversial and those in which they are not. Fish's notion of 'interpretation's force' is an instance of what I referred to earlier as a 'foundational' notion of interpretation. Interpretation does not come into play here only remedially, on specific occasions of unclarity; and correlatively, the sort of clarity that would obviate the need for interpretation (*Clara non sunt interpretanda*) is a clarity that 'cannot' be achieved.[19] In this sense, the omnipresence of interpretive force reveals not any ordinary inability on our part to be clear, but rather a *metaphysical* impotence. (Indeed, the notion of 'interpretive force' functions here as a metaphysical notion in the proper sense: it attempts to describe the conditions of intelligibility of the whole world, of everything.)[20] It now seems that any act of understanding or judgment requires the mediation of interpretation. So interpretation has become like a pair of glasses that colours everything we see. To take these glasses off would be to make the world disappear or at least to leave our normative practices without shape. And because we have come to think that such banal thoughts as 'there are easy cases and plain meanings' or 'determination by a rule is fundamental to law' are philosophically suspect, we come to imagine that the sophisticated thoughts—*plain cases are the result of interpretation's force, it is interpretation that gives us the rule*—are somehow clearer, less mysterious or less uncanny than these naïve commonplaces.

[18] Fish (1989: 153; see also 9). Fish (1980: 284) makes the same point about the interpretation of literature.

[19] It might be better to say that we are unable *to be able* to achieve it (but by the same token, unable *to be unable* to achieve it) since, given the priority of 'interpretive force', there is nothing that would constitute the achievement of such clarity.

[20] Fish declares that the implications of the thesis that no meaning 'is prior to interpretation' are 'almost boundless, for they extend to the very underpinnings of the universe' (1989: 4).

THE RULE AS A RAIL

The law is not a machine.

(Frank 1963: 129)

I think that something goes wrong when we embrace these sophisticated thoughts—thoughts that pervade a great deal of contemporary theory. The theorist begins by taking up what might be called the posture of realism: she does not want to be deceived, she wants to see through the mist of unnecessary pretences and fictions. The *legal* realist wants to attain a clear view of the notion of applying a legal rule. She thinks there is a tendency among lawyers to pretend that rules are mechanisms that spin out results in particular cases—'a self-sufficient mechanism that pulls us down the track'. Yet the attempt to be realistic often leads to a new kind of philosophical requirement, a new kind of fiction—one that is made in the philosophical mirror-image of the 'self-sufficient mechanism'. Today the impulse of realism can be heard not just in the claim that all legal meaning must be interpreted, but also in such claims as that it is all 'historical' (cf. Grey 1989: 787, 801–5) or all 'political',[21] and so on. When such requirements are conceived as part of a move towards a less metaphysical, more realistic view of the world, it is easy to miss how the words 'there are no plain facts, only the force of (historically and politically conditioned) interpretations' echo the words of the philosopher in the cave who says, 'there are only shadows here'. They are the words of someone who has looked hard into the sun. Repeatedly, our attempts to be realists fail in this way. Either we need more realism about realism—a more realistic conception of what realism amounts to—or we need to acknowledge that realism (or call it the demythological, the unsuperstitious, the secular) is still too hard for us.[22]

Cornell's remark concerning 'the very idea of a rule that pulls us down the track' affords an opportunity to explore how our attempts to be realists go awry. In its rejection of a mechanical image of rules, that remark refers directly to Wittgenstein's *Philosophical Investigations* (1958*a*).[23] It refers to a moment of Wittgenstein's writing that does indeed take aim at the conception of rules that Cornell also wishes to set her face against. But this moment in Wittgenstein occurs within the context of a discussion that attempts to reveal that a picture of rules as guided by rails and a picture of

[21] See e.g. Unger (1987: 10). I explore what motivates this claim in Stone (1991).

[22] I am indebted to Diamond, 'Realism and the Realistic Spirit' (*supra*, n. 2) for my sense, expressed in this paragraph, of how 'realism' in its ordinary, non-philosophical sense can give us the terms with which to describe both the motivation of certain kinds of philosophical theories, as well the ways in which they often betray their motivation and hence frustrate their own aspiration.

[23] Cornell cites *Philosophical Investigations* (henceforth *PI*) in two footnotes to the passage quoted.

rules as governed by interpretation are two sides of the same philosophical coin.

Wittgenstein writes: 'Whence comes the idea that the beginning of a series is a visible section of rails invisibly laid to infinity? Well, we might imagine rails instead of a rule. And infinitely long rails correspond to the unlimited application of a rule' (*PI* § 218). In the next section he continues:

> 'All the steps are really already taken' means: I no longer have any choice. The rule, once stamped with a particular meaning, traces the lines along which it is to be followed through the whole of space.—But if something of this sort really were the case, how would it help?
>
> No; my description only made sense if it was to be understood symbolically. (*PI* § 219)

'How would it help?': the question presents a doubt about whether the mechanical image of a rule does any real work at all in the context of a problem about the relation between understanding and judgment. We sometimes grasp the meaning of a rule instantaneously—'in a flash' (*PI* § 138, 139, 191). But since this is so, we may become tempted to wonder how a rule which we grasp instantaneously can determine what we are to do in innumerable future cases. How can a grasped meaning constrain the particular judgments we are to make when we endeavour to judge in accordance with it? Wittgenstein raises these questions in regard to the case of extending a series of numbers in a way determined by one's understanding of the rule governing it. If someone grasps the meaning of 'add 2', then in carrying out a series he must, if he is to remain faithful to what he grasps, write '1002' after he reaches '996, 998, 1000'; no other number he might write would accord with the rule. The image of a mechanism arises in the course of an attempt to give ourselves an explanation of how this could be—of what it is that *compels* this continuation. The meaning of the rule is pictured as an infinite rail and to grasp that meaning is mentally to hitch oneself to this rail so that, as long as one stays hitched to it, the rule will drive one to the correct applicative judgment in innumerable particular cases.

Cornell is certainly right to think that this imagery doesn't give us what we need if we have begun to lose our grip on the notion of a rule as something with which our judgments can keep faith (or not). But her reliance on interpretation as what will restore the threatened notion of a rule ('it is interpretation that gives us the rule') shows that she has a fixated conception of what is wrong with the imagery. Part of Wittgenstein's aim is to get us to see that what is wrong with it is not cured but rather exemplified or brought out by the notion that the normative demand of a rule is activated only through an interpretation of it. But to see this is to confront a number of fundamental issues about the way Cornell has framed her discussion.

Notice, to begin with, one way in which the idea of the mechanical rail is evidently not so much 'false' (Cornell 1992: 101) as confused. It assimilates the notions of normative determination (the red light means I *should* stop now) and causal determination (the red light may generally lead me to put on the brake, but if I fail to react this way that hardly makes the light *mean* something else). Clearly, it is the normative relation between a grasped meaning and the behaviour it constrains that puzzles us when we turn for help to the image of the rail. But the kind of constraint involved in a normative relation can be disentangled from the idea of a mechanism if we remind ourselves that any actual mechanism would be subject to breakdown: its parts might bend, break off, melt, or otherwise fail to function. The mechanism we appeal to in picturing the application of a rule is one assumed to be functioning *properly*. But to assume this is to move in a short circle: to think of a machine as functioning properly (that is, as it should, or in an ideally rigid way) is to think of it as conforming to a rule. The use of a mechanism to picture rule-guided behaviour seems to occur to us, in short, through the crossing of two different pictures of determination (causal and normative).[24] And this suggests one way in which, if we are seeking to explain the relation that obtains between a grasped meaning and the actions it determines, it is doubtful that the appeal to an infinite rail would help: an ordinary rail (a causal mechanism) is beside the point; yet the idea of an *ideally rigid* rail does not stand behind an account of the possibility of following a rule but presupposes it. If the rail is given that kind of normative characterization, then to describe the normative determination of our actions as our engagement with such a rail is just to re-describe the very relation that puzzles us.

The spurious explanation of meaning in terms of a rail reaching ahead of our actual performances (and on which they will have to lie if they are going to be judged correct) is often thought of, in contemporary philosophical discussion, as giving voice to 'Platonism'. Cornell, like many other theorists today, doesn't want to be a naïve Platonist,[25] and up to a point, she would be right to look for an ally in Wittgenstein. But that point comes for Wittgenstein at the beginning rather than the end of the story. For Wittgenstein's relationship to so-called 'Platonism' is not a relationship to a philosophical account of meaning which he takes—as Cornell takes it—to be *false*. (He is not, this is to say, an *anti*-Platonist—as if the problem were to decide which of a number of answers to a philosophical question about the possibility of determination by a rule is the right one.) Thus, just after the previous passage on the rail we find this: 'My symbolical expression was

[24] Cf. Wittgenstein's discussion of the 'Machine-as-Symbol' at *PI* § 193 (we tend to use the image of a mechanism as a symbol of its own (normatively characterized) action).

[25] Cf. D'Amato (1990: 151–4, 174–5) (the 'legal Formalist' could be helped by Wittgenstein to 'overcome . . . the Platonic view that words have determinate meanings').

really a mythological description of the use of a rule' (*PI* § 221). *A mythological description*—what sort of term of criticism is this?

Two points stand out in this difficult sentence. First, the appeal to mechanism involves a 'symbolical expression': the mechanism, as we remarked, is functioning not as an ordinary mechanism in the causal order of things, but as a symbol of its own normatively characterized action (see *PI* § 193). Secondly, this crossing of (causal and normative) pictures yields a 'mythological description of the use of a rule'. Here we are evidently meant to ask: what would an ordinary, a run-of-the-mill 'description of the use of a rule' be? Well, it is a commonplace feature of rules that they are used in a certain way: (1) they provide a standard of correct judgment; and (2) they can be applied in a temporally extended series of future cases. Putting these together, one might venture to say: the meaning of the rule reaches ahead of our applicative performances and claims its own instances in advance. Colourful as this way of putting the matter might be, part of Wittgenstein's aim is to show us that it is not in itself philosophically problematic—such pictures, properly understood, are perfectly all right (are, indeed, to be respected):[26]

> 'But I don't mean that what I do now (in grasping a sense) determines the future use causally and as a matter of experience, but that in a *queer* way, the use itself is in some sense present.'—But of course it is, 'in *some* sense'! Really the only thing wrong with what you say is the expression 'in a queer way'. The rest is all right; and the sentence only seems queer when one imagines a different language-game for it from the one in which we actually use it. (*PI* § 195)

Taking a cue from this passage, we might say that a 'mythological description' of the use of a rule is one that, while depicting the run-of-the-mill aspects of rules, is motivated by, and helps sustain the sense that there is something *queer* about them. In crossing the language of causal and normative determination (here we 'imagine a different language-game' both for the idea of 'mechanism' and for the commonplaces about rules), the idea of the rail offers the illusion that the commonplaces about rules are being not only re-described, but (at least in an incipient way) explained. In referring the application of a rule to a mechanism, the philosopher may think he is speaking at a level of greater depth; perhaps he will someday know more about this mechanism. Wittgenstein wants to take issue with this appearance of depth (see e.g. 1978: VI-31) and this invitation to further philosophical work, while allowing the idea that rules provide for their own future applications to remain what it is—something that is internal to our notion

[26] Cf. Wittgenstein (1980: 83): 'It is true that we can compare a picture that is firmly rooted in us to a superstition; but it is equally true that we *always* eventually have to reach some firm ground, either a picture or something else, so that a picture which is at the root of all our thinking is to be respected and not treated as a superstition.'

of a rule's extension, a notion whose sense is exhibited in our everyday talk of following a rule.[27]

What the Platonist wants to say—that the use of a rule is already present in the rule itself—is unproblematic; the problem lies in his thinking that in saying this he is describing a metaphysically queer or astounding fact. Wittgenstein's characterization of the rail imagery as a 'mythological description of the use of a rule' is thus consonant with the instruction he gives concerning his philosophical method: 'What we do is to bring words back from their metaphysical to their everyday use' (*PI* § 116). It is important, if this bringing back of words is to be possible, that the description not be fixed as a *false* one, an incorrect account of how it is when our judgment is determined by a rule. (If the sense of the words were so fixed, they could hardly be redeemed.) So Wittgenstein doesn't say: 'We think that the rule lays down a rail, but in fact there is no rail.' Rather, in speaking of a 'mythological description', he means us to see that the image of the rail might also be understood innocuously. The trouble comes only when we try to put such imagery to work in an explanation of rule-following. We realize that we don't mean to be speaking of ordinary causal determination, so we begin a search for the hidden mechanism of our normative capacities. Or, alternatively, we come to regard the picture as *false* (we replace it with a picture of the-*absence*-of-a-rail) and are then led to conclude that every application of a rule requires a new decision about the meaning of the rule.[28] Or again, we are led by the picture of the-absence-of-a-rail to think there must be something else besides the rule (something that now becomes the object of theoretical conjecture) that affixes a rule to its instances. In this way (that is, in being denied), the picture, which would otherwise only re-describe the commonplace, becomes captivating and intense. In the grip of this picture, we feel that there must be something like this rail (since the use of the rule is in some sense already present), yet we do not see how, in grasping the rule, its applications could be anticipated in this way (cf. *PI* §§ 188, 197). The picture, in short, becomes a proto-theory, and this opens and delimits for us the space of available philosophical positions.[29]

[27] On Wittgenstein's relation to Platonism I have benefited especially from McDowell (1992: 48–9). McDowell is particularly lucid about how, for Wittgenstein, the problem lies not in what the Platonist says (about a rule containing its future applications) but in a particular way of taking what he says ('in a queer way'). Thus, if one restricts oneself in reading Wittgenstein to the options of allowing him either to agree or to disagree with what the Platonist *says* (independently of the philosophical use to which one wants to put those words) one is bound to misunderstand Wittgenstein.

[28] Cf. Wright (1989: 240); *PI* § 186.

[29] For the notion that, for Wittgenstein, philosophy arises from and demands an intense (as opposed to an everyday) view of an everyday matter, and for the suggestion that the *Investigations* may be read as an exploration of the tension between these views, I am indebted to Cavell, 'Notes and Afterthoughts on Wittgenstein's "Investigations"', in Cavell (1994*b*), and to Goldfarb (1983).

We can see this happening—this origination of theory—in the quoted remark of Cornell's. Recoiling from the image of the rail, Cornell imagines that she is dealing not with a potentially misleading way of picturing the use of rules, but with an objectionable account of determination by a rule, one that is intelligible enough for her to reject it as 'false'. The rejection of this picture partakes of the same philosophical difficulties, the same unclarity, however, as the original picture; for what makes the picture potentially misleading is not that it suggests the wrong account of the facts but that it is liable to being taken as a representation of facts, hence as a substantive opinion (an answer to a clear question) calling for support or repudiation.[30] Thus, for Cornell, the true answer to the question about the determining power of rules appears to require the negation of a false answer (the rule as a rail). But to reject that answer as merely false is to endorse the question, thus continuing to saddle oneself with an explanatory gap. Cornell seeks to fill that gap by appealing to the notion of interpretation. And since it belongs to the idea of an interpretation that there are other possible interpretations—another interpretation may be adopted when the rule is next applied—it becomes natural for Cornell to contrast 'the rule as a rail' with the thesis that rules are continuously *re*-interpreted as they are applied: the indeterminacy thesis.

THE ABSENCE OF IDOLS

> All that philosophy can do is to destroy idols. And that means not making any new ones—say out of 'the absence of idols'.
>
> (Wittgenstein 1993: § 88)

Cornell goes wrong in attributing the indeterminacy thesis to Wittgenstein. For Wittgenstein's aim is to show that the question Cornell thinks she must answer (by recourse to interpretation) seems compulsory only on a peculiar picture of rules—call it the picture of rules as mere dead letter. 'Every sign by itself', Wittgenstein remarks, in characterizing this picture, 'seems dead.' And he indicates the question that is bound to follow on the heels of this thought: 'What gives it life?' (*PI* § 432).

The dead-letter picture arises when we try to account for the notion of a rule's normative reach from a standpoint outside our everyday practical activities, hence, when we try to view the rule *by itself*—independently of the use that we make of it. In the context of our everyday *legal* activities, the vitality of rules can be seen in the fact that the question, 'what makes a "clear case" clear?', derives its sense against the background of cases that

[30] See the instructive remarks on philosophical pictures in Diamond (1989).

are simply taken to be clear. But from the external standpoint that gives rise to the dead-letter picture, we are apt to suppose that our right to the notion of a clear case depends not simply on our practical ability to recognize clear cases, but on our being able to establish that there is something that, independently of our practical responses, 'makes it' clear (hence something against which our responses might—if only from a God's-eye perspective—be checked). The dead-letter picture is a tempting starting-point for thinking about rules when we attempt to view our practices, in an apt phrase of John McDowell's, 'from sideways on'.[31] To view our practice of following a particular rule from sideways on is to ask what the rule requires while removing it from the context in which it has its use; it is to ask how an item called 'a rule' determines our judgment while prescinding from the practical setting that is the life of—or better, our life with—rules. An answer to this question (what makes a judgment accord with the rule?) seeks to establish the connection in question from a vantage-point independent of our ordinary concourse with the rule—independent of the circumstances in which we ordinarily apply the rule, and independent of the responses that come naturally to us in those circumstances (for example, '1000, 1002, 1004' in carrying out the instruction 'add two').[32]

Wittgenstein wants us to see the dead-letter picture as a suspiciously abstract one. Once we attempt to consider rules apart from the practical activities of human beings, we are left to see them as simply possible mental or linguistic items; the rule, as Wittgenstein puts it in another characterization of this picture, 'stands there like a sign-post' (*PI* § 85; cf. § 431). Obviously a signpost, considered independently of the use we make of it (considered, say, as simply an inscribed block of wood), makes no demands on which way we are to go: 'But where is it said which way I am to follow it; whether in the direction of its finger or (e.g.) in the opposite one?' (*PI* § 85). We are apt to say that it can be interpreted like this or like that, and it looks like there needs to be *some* interpretation to make the sign come alive in a way that would give application to the notion of acting in accord with it. But if this is so—if, in Cornell's words, 'it is interpretation that gives us the rule'—the notion of accord will quickly come into trouble due to the kind of regress first pointed out by Kant.

In Wittgenstein's version of the regress, we have as much reason to wonder how an item called the 'interpretation' of the rule can bring about the

[31] McDowell (1981: 150). My sketch in this section of the relation of the rail imagery to the problem of the regress of interpretation generally follows McDowell (1992).

[32] This paragraph suggests one kind of motivation for the dead-letter picture: the desire for an external touchstone that could be seen as underlying our practical responses. There may, of course, be other (related) motivations, such as the thought that only such an external touchstone could secure the appropriate notion of objectivity in our dealings with the world—i.e. the notion that things are as they are independently of our judgment. McDowell (1984) provides a helpful discussion of these issues.

possibility of acting in accord with it, as we have to wonder how the rule itself can do this. If we have worked our way into thinking that rules must be activated by an interpretation, we are bound to realize that whatever we take as an interpretation of the rule ('"add two" means . . .'; 'the signpost means . . .')—and whatever form such an interpretation might take (an explicit directive, a mental image, a series of examples, a pointing finger)—can itself be understood in such a way as to make any action accord with the rule. 'But where is it said', we can now ask, 'which way I am to follow the *interpretation*? It looks like there needs to be some interpretation of *it*, if there is to be any application for the notion of acting in accord with it'; and so on. So instead of transforming the sign into something which expresses a genuine normative demand, the requirement of interpretation seems only to reproduce the problem of its impotence:

> [A]ny interpretation still hangs in the air along with what it interprets, and cannot give it any support. Interpretations by themselves do not determine meaning. (*PI* § 198)

> This was our paradox: no course of action could be determined by a rule, because every course of action can be made out to accord with the rule. The answer was: if everything can be made out to accord with the rule, then it can also be made out to conflict with it. And so there would be neither accord nor conflict here. (*PI* § 201)

Given the assumption that to follow a rule is to interpret it, the paradox of *PI* § 201 (in which the very notion of a rule as something capable of determining a course of action is on the brink of disappearing) follows from the conclusion of *PI* § 198—'any interpretation still hangs in the air along with what it interprets'. So unless we are willing to abandon this assumption, it can now look as if something like the Platonistic idea of meaning (as something capable of reaching ahead of our applications of a rule and determining the steps in advance), however mysterious or 'queer' this idea may seem, is our only alternative if we want to avoid this paradox. The dialectical relationship between the requirement of interpretation and Platonism so conceived can be schematized as follows:

1) A rule, considered *by itself* (apart from the use we make of it) is a lifeless sign. It can be applied like *this* or like *that*.

2) An 'interpretation' is needed to forge the connection between such a sign and a particular course of action. What a rule requires in the particular case is determined by its interpretation.

3) But if the interpretation of a sign requires its *own* interpretation, an infinite regress threatens, and the notion of a rule as something with which our actions might be brought into accord disappears into an abyss of interpretations.

4) So the connection between an otherwise dead sign and a particular course of action must depend on the possibility of endowing the sign

with a meaning not susceptible to further interpretation. It must depend on a special kind of interpretation, one that blocks the possibility of regress because it somehow contains all the future applications of the sign.

5) The idea that the meaning given to a sign can reach ahead and determine its correct applications in advance (in a way that the sign itself could not) seems mysterious or queer; but we are compelled to conclude that something like this must be the case if we are to make sense of the notion of accord (or conflict) with the meaning of the sign.

If we enter this dialectic, by embracing (1), we might reasonably end up trying to shore up the notion of accord with a rule (against the threat of a regress of interpretation) by depicting the 'meaning' of the rule as somehow (because it arises from the 'last' interpretation?) immune to further interpretation.[33] But the result looks 'queer' even to the committed Platonist: he has no notion of how meanings manage to exercise the powers of normative reach that mere signs fail to have; he simply concludes that there must be items with such powers. And it is at this point that the imagery of rails can appear to supply us with the sort of picture we feel we need to articulate this conclusion: 'The rule, once stamped with a particular meaning, traces the lines along which it is to be followed through the whole of space' (*PI* § 219). This does indeed offer a picture of the normative power of rules, one that answers the requirement of preventing the interpretive regress from taking off. But so motivated, the rail-image is not the innocuous, if somewhat colourful, expression of a familiar platitude about the use of rules (see section 3). Rather, it is meant to answer a demand for something to fill the explanatory gap between a rule and its application, a demand made all the more acute by the regress of interpretation. Here we may notice a difference between Wittgenstein's interlocutor and Cornell: where Cornell turns to the notion of interpretation to repudiate the idea of the rule-as-rail, on Wittgenstein's portrayal of the dialectic, the image of the rail emerges on the rebound from the regress of interpretation. But from a larger perspective—one that takes in the entire structure of the dialectic—we can begin to see each of these conceptions of rule-following as a mirror image of the other:

[33] Cf. Wittgenstein (1958*b*: 34): 'What one wishes to say is: "Every sign is capable of interpretation; but the *meaning* mustn't be capable of interpretation. It is the last interpretation."' McDowell (1992) helpfully suggests that we should trace the origins of the rail imagery (as a form of Platonism) to the thought which is expressed in this passage. Such imagery then looks like part of an attempt to hang on to the idea that accord with a rule is possible only through interpretation while at the same time blocking the meaning-destroying regress that comes in the wake of this idea (see McDowell 1992: 47–9). Cf. *PI* § 431 (quoting the thought that an 'act of understanding' is needed to bridge the gulf between an order and its execution: such an act would presumably fix what behaviour counts as executing an order without itself requiring a further act of understanding to connect *it* to the required behaviour; it would function as a regress-stopper).

both share a common presupposition, namely (1) in the schema above.[34] Both arise, that is, from trying to get rules satisfactorily into view after starting out with a picture that detaches them from the practical contexts in which we make use of them. Once we try to look at rules in this way, the problem of how acceptably to animate them becomes urgent, and the requirement of interpretation (with its intolerable regress), on the one hand, and the postulation of a rail-like 'meaning' (that somehow blocks the regress), on the other, emerge as two horns of a single dilemma.

It bears emphasizing that to take the rail image as the expression of a platitude about the use of a rule would *not* be to choose the Platonistic horn of this dilemma. It would simply indicate that one no longer feels compelled to reconstruct an adequate notion of accord with a rule out of whatever materials still remain in view after focusing our attention on signs considered *by themselves*—apart from the use that we make of them. It would be, in effect, to embrace the idea of the rail *before* (1) (before the dialectic so much as gets off the ground), rather than *after* (1–3), where, having divorced 'mere signs' from our activities with them, their reinvestment with a meaning that reaches ahead to their future applications (and hence which, in a sense, underlies our activities with them) seems to demand a kind of occultism about meaning.[35] Taking as an example the question from *PI* § 85 about how the signpost manages to show one the direction in which to go, we can illustrate the nature of the relevant platitude by giving the following response: there is an innocuous sense in which the signpost itself determines the action that accords with it—in which we can *see* what the signpost requires—without the need for interpretation. For, when we come upon the sign, we don't encounter mere marks on a block of wood. Rather, in the context of our mode of life (a life in which such things as directions, roads, paths, travellings, pointings, locations, destinations, distance, turnings, and so on, play a prominent part), the signpost gives a definite instruction. Peel off this context and the sign seems dead; a gap appears between the sign itself and its application, and the question arises: how does this gap come to be bridged? But the question only seems compulsory because we forget that the sign is alive in the practical affairs of human beings.[36]

[34] As often with philosophical problems (on Wittgenstein's view of them), 'the first step is the one that altogether escapes notice' (*PI* § 308).

[35] Here it is worth emphasizing the point that is implicit in this paragraph: What makes someone a Platonist (in the philosophically contentious sense) is not whether he endorses a certain formula (e.g. 'the use itself is in some sense present') but how he conceives of the formula: 'But of course it is, "in *some* sense"! Really the only thing wrong with what you say is the expression "in a queer way"' (*PI* § 195). What the Platonist says is all right; his mistake, according to this passage, lies in his taking himself to be remarking on a metaphysically puzzling fact.

[36] I owe a debt here to David Finkelstein's unpublished paper 'Constitutionism', which persuasively argues that Wittgenstein does not seek to take sides in the contemporary debate

The traditional Platonist (whose thought finds expression in the image of rules laying down invisible rails) is, in short, someone who starts by supposing that there is a gap between a rule and its applications, and then turns to 'meanings' in an attempt to close the gap. Keeping this motivation of the rail imagery in view, it becomes possible to understand why Cornell mistakenly imagines that she finds in Wittgenstein philosophical authority for the indeterminacy thesis. For Wittgenstein does indeed criticize the imagery of rails as a depiction of the relation between a rule and its application: he does not think that such imagery can help to restore a notion of accord with a rule, once that notion comes under threat in the dialectic that begins with (1). So, if one loses sight of how the dialectic begins—if one thinks that Platonistic rails and the requirement of interpretation are the only available options—it can look as if Wittgenstein's attack on the rail imagery gives support to the requirement of interpretation and fuels the resulting paradox about accord with a rule. But, as indicated above, Wittgenstein's aim is to question the assumption common to *both* horns of the dilemma. In his view, the right response—to the threat of interpretive regress, on the one hand, and the explanatory emptiness of the Platonic rail, on the other—is to realize that the felt need for a certain sort of explanation of a rule's normative reach arises only once we view rules in complete abstraction from the practical context in which we apply them. 'Following according to the rule', he remarks, 'is FUNDAMENTAL to our language game' (1978: VI-28)—as if what we need from philosophy is not the construction of a groundwork that would secure the notion of a rule's normative reach, but help in acknowledging the ground that lies before us.[37] The engagement

about Platonism, but seeks rather to recover an innocent or truistic sense in which the words the Platonist wants to say are to be taken. Finkelstein's use of a cooking recipe to elaborate Wittgenstein's point (about what is involved in applying a rule) suggested to me the 'response' imagined in this paragraph.

[37] See Wittgenstein (1978: VI-31). I borrow the word 'acknowledging' from Cavell's work on Wittgenstein (see e.g. Cavell 1979: 329–496), where it carries the point that, for Wittgenstein, the sceptical difficulties we get into in philosophy can be seen as a kind of alienation or turning away from the world, and hence that their resolution involves not (at least not in the way the sceptic understands this) establishing our claim to knowledge, but something like a change of attitude, attention, or attunement. Cf. Wittgenstein (1993: § 86) and (1979: § 378). To explore meaningfully Wittgenstein's engagement with scepticism would require another essay (at least), but with respect to the issue that concerns me here let me say this much: Wittgenstein's aim is not a theory connecting a rule to its instances, but 'complete clarity' (*PI* § 133)—i.e. the disappearance (at least on *this* occasion) of the philosophical problem. In the course of the discussion, Wittgenstein reminds us that we ordinarily take another person's correct application of a rule as a criterion that he understands it, and he then considers the difficulties with various attempts to bridge the supposed gap between understanding and application. A formula or picture fails to do the required work because it can itself be applied or projected in different ways (*PI* § 139, 141); and a 'mental state'—if it is not to be vacuous as an explanation—requires a criterion of identification other than the correct application of the rule (*PI* § 149). In each case, although the mediating item *may* occur, the criterion of its occurrence is different from that of grasping the rule—so it may also be regarded as unessential. The

with this therapeutic task informs Wittgenstein's own response to the regress of interpretation in the continuation of *PI* § 201:

> It can be seen that there is a misunderstanding here from the mere fact that in the course of our argument we give one interpretation after another; as if each one contented us at least for a moment, until we thought of yet another standing behind it. What this shews is that there is a way of grasping a rule that is *not* an *interpretation* which is exhibited in what we call 'obeying the rule' and 'going against it' in actual cases.
>
> Hence there is an inclination to say: every action according to the rule is an interpretation. But we ought to restrict the term 'interpretation' to the substitution of one expression of the rule for another. (*PI* § 201)
>
> And hence also 'obeying a rule' is a practice. (*PI* § 202)

The paradoxical regress of interpretation is to be avoided, on Wittgenstein's view, by dropping the assumption that causes all the trouble: namely, that one could not follow a rule unless one first attaches some interpretation to it. (We see here that, for Wittgenstein, Cornell's 'insight'—about the necessary mediation of interpretation in applying rules—is to be regarded as a 'misunderstanding'.) Wittgenstein is not denying that we are free to use the *word* 'interpretation' in any way we like, and we may still want to go on calling every application of a rule an interpretation of it. Wittgenstein, however, proposes that, for the sake of clarity, we restrict the word 'interpretation' to the substitution of one linguistic expression for another: if we follow this proposal we can allow that it is sometimes helpful, but not always necessary to interpret a rule in order to follow it. What is at stake here is not merely a terminological point. In Wittgenstein's invitation to think of 'a way of grasping a rule which is not an interpretation', the word 'interpretation' admits the broad sense of any *mediation* between grasping a rule and following it in the particular case. His point is that such mediation is no more necessary (or sufficient) for grasping a rule than mere linguistic substitution; and the proposed restriction of the word 'interpretation' serves its purpose in so far as it makes this perspicuous. Following the lead of *PI* § 202, we might say: in grasping a rule what is essential is not that one interpret it but that one become adept in a practice of applying it.[38]

It should be noted, however, that putting the matter this way (in terms

tendency of these remarks is to suggest that any explanation of how accord with a rule is possible is bound to be idle: even if it were true, it wouldn't help us to feel less puzzled. But then we may be left to see that it belongs to the very nature of our puzzlement that no explanation of the kind we thought we needed will resolve it.

[38] I might of course also show my grasp of a rule by giving a non-applicative explanation of it, but this only postpones the issue. What is it to grasp any explanation, any standard of correctness? Wittgenstein's point is not that interpretations do not manifest understanding, but that they do not do so 'by themselves' (*PI* § 198*a*), that is, independently of applicative behaviour.

of the necessary conditions of grasping a rule) can itself give rise to a further misunderstanding: 'isn't Wittgenstein himself trying to explain the normative reach of rules—only now by appealing not to interpretation or to rails but to human activity or practice?' It is important to observe, in this regard, that Wittgenstein does *not* say that obeying a rule is made possible or conditioned by a practice (much less that only appropriately conforming social behaviour would entitle us to say that a particular action accords with a rule) but rather: '"obeying a rule" *is* a practice' [*ist . . . eine Praxis*] (emphasis mine). But what is the point of saying that? From an exegetical point of view, the difficulty concerns the relationship between the negative thought that 'there is a way of grasping a rule that is not an interpretation' (which is 'exhibited' in our performances in actual cases), and the more positive-sounding thought about practice: '"obeying a rule" is a practice.' How is the second thought related to the first? The recourse to interpretation was an attempt to explain how accord with a rule is possible—an unhappy attempt since it led to an intolerable regress. But if one grasps the failure of this attempt in a way that leaves the demand for an explanation in place, one will be likely to take the reference to 'practice' as the beginning of an alternative constructive answer to the same seemingly genuine question (what does grasping a rule consist in? How is accord with a rule possible?). And if one takes the reference to practice in this way, one may be tempted to cash out (what one imagines to be) Wittgenstein's constructive solution to the problem in terms of an appeal to social interactions described in something other than normative terms. (For an explanatory appeal to 'practice' would be idle if the relevant notion of practice could only be made out in essentially normative terms—terms that presuppose such notions as 'accord with a rule'.) We go badly wrong, however, if we see Wittgenstein as continuing the philosophical attempt to dig beneath the normative in this way.[39]

If we are to be faithful to Wittgenstein's intentions, I think we must take this reference to practice to indicate the *place* in which we should look for rules if we are to begin to make sense of the idea that 'there is a way of grasping a rule which is not an interpretation'. In thrall to the 'dead-letter' picture, we look for rules in the wrong place—apart from their practical surroundings.[40] The remark about practice is thus an attempt, not to answer a question about the possibility of accord with a rule, but to re-direct our

[39] Such a reading of Wittgenstein would leave little room for such remarks as 'Following according to the rule is fundamental . . .'.

[40] I have borrowed the formulation—'looking in the wrong place'—from Diamond, 'Rules: Looking in the Right Place' (1989). The formulation is a vivid way of bringing out the way in which Wittgenstein's use, in this context, of such terms as 'practice' and 'use' (see e.g. *PI* § 432) does not stand in the same path of thought that leads to talk of interpretation and rails (i.e. the path that begins with (1) in the schema above), but rather calls for a change of direction, one that amounts to not entering the path at all (after seeing it as a philosophical dead-end).

attention: we cannot properly bring into view the phenomenon we wish to explain, Wittgenstein is saying, by leaving out of the picture the activities in which rules play a part. As long as we continue to consider rules apart from the use we make of them (apart from what Wittgenstein, in a related context, calls 'the weave of our life' (*PI*: II. i)), the question, 'how is it possible to follow a rule' will seem both urgent and—since it will seem that only an interpretation could give the rule life—perplexing. Wittgenstein's remarks here (including his remark about practice) are in the service of rejecting the assumption that informs these questions: that the possibility of determination by a rule rests on something that lies beneath whatever is already visible in our everyday use of rules—our obeying and going against them 'in actual cases'.[41] Putting the point positively, one might venture to say: it is our practical activity (in which the use of rules is routine and commonplace) and the kind of attention we exercise within this activity (and not a piece of theory in which we try to grasp this activity from the outside) that will bring into view—or 'exhibit' (*PI* § 201)—the normative demand of a rule we endeavour to follow.[42]

THE ABSENCE OF RAILS

> What I want to teach you isn't opinions but a method. In fact the method is to treat as irrelevant every question of opinions . . . I don't try to make you believe something you don't believe but to make you do something you won't do.
>
> (Wittgenstein, quoted in Rhees 1970: 42–3)

From the foregoing sketch, I think we can see that Wittgenstein is concerned with a philosophical anxiety that recurs in contemporary legal culture. On my reading, Wittgenstein is not denying that a rule can 'step forward to claim its own instances' (Hart 1961: 123), but only trying to call attention to our captivation by a notion of a 'rule by itself', according to which this 'stepping forward' seems queer in light of an otherwise unbridgeable gap. Here it is instructive to mark the contrast between Cornell's rejection of the

[41] Cf. *PI* § 435: 'If it is asked: "How do sentences manage to represent?"—the answer might be: "Don't you know? You certainly see it when you use them." For nothing is concealed.' The discussion in Diamond (1989) is helpful in bringing out how in the remarks on rules (as elsewhere), Wittgenstein wants to show that it belongs to the nature of philosophical difficulties that we resist the significance of what lies before our eyes, thinking that what we are able to see requires supports which are hidden from view and which it becomes the business of 'theory' to reveal. Cf. *PI* § 129.

[42] Although Wittgenstein will occasionally put the point in this positive manner, he will also caution that we should take this not as a thesis or doctrine about rule-following, but only as (what he calls) a 'reminder' (*PI* § 127) about where to look for rules, a reminder that may help to loosen the grip of a certain way of thinking that gets us into philosophical trouble.

rail image and Wittgenstein's own discussion of it. Cornell's remark contains three related moments:

First, *Cornell takes herself to oppose a false thesis.* She describes the suspect thought that a rule 'pulls us down the track through each new fact situation' as a demonstrated falsity. Leaving aside the question of how such a demonstration is to have been provided, to talk of falsity means that Cornell takes herself to grasp the objectionable content of this thought. She understands what it would be for rules to 'pull us down the track', or at least she understands it well enough to know that they don't. Cornell takes these words to assert a perfectly intelligible (rather than an empty) thesis which aims to shore up the notion of a rule's normative reach; and she declares that members of the Critical Legal Studies Movement have shown this thesis to be false. She thereby forecloses the possibility (which Wittgenstein labours to keep open) of taking the rail imagery as the expression of an innocuous platitude about the use of rules.

Secondly, *Cornell affirms the truth of the negation of the thesis she opposes.* By taking a mechanical account of rules to be straightforwardly false, Cornell commits herself to celebrating the truth of the negation of such an account, namely to thinking that rules are, in some significant sense, inert. In effect, by treating the rail image not as what Wittgenstein calls a 'picture' but as an objectionable thesis, something about which it is possible to have different philosophical opinions, Cornell replaces one piece of mythology (the rule as laying down a rail) with another piece (the-absence-of-a-rail). Indeed, the 'deconstructive' discourse of absence and defect which Cornell deploys would seem to depend on construing such philosophical pictures of meaning in this flat-footed way—as straightforward but false.[43] If, in contrast to this, we think of the rail imagery as simply a potentially confusing depiction of the way a class of cases is present through a rule, then it is not difficult to see that the denial of this image of presence gives at best a confused picture of absence; that the *denial* of an illusory notion of determinacy of meaning produces in the end not a correct account of indeterminacy but only the *illusion* that something has been denied.

Thirdly, *through her denial of the (mechanical) thesis, Cornell inherits the explanatory burden which that thesis sought to shoulder.* She thus feels the need to supplement her denial (of the existence of rails) with something (interpretation) which can now fill the role of mediating between a rule and its applications. It is interpretation which affixes the rule to the 'fact situation' it would otherwise be unable to reach, and hence which finally 'gives us the rule' in its normatively animated form. But why 'interpretation'? If a rule needs to cross a gap to determine the particular case, why not just speak of judgment in accord with the rule? The answer is that Cornell thinks

[43] See 'Appendix: A Note on Deconstruction', below.

that the notion of accord with a rule finds application only through our having recourse to something else: 'It is interpretation that gives us the rule, not the other way around.' Whatever interpretation is, it contrasts here with rule-governed judgment and is not just another name for it. Hence, it also seems to figure among Cornell's motivations for appealing to interpretation that following a rule by way of interpretation is something more creative than following a rule *simpliciter*. Interpretation involves an 'appeal to the beyond'; it shatters the illusion that law is distinct from politics.

Cornell reaches this dramatic conclusion not through anything she finds in the practice of law but through the theoretical requirements she brings to her view of it. If Wittgenstein's discussion of rules can help us here, it is by helping to free us from those requirements—and *not* by underwriting an alternative conclusion or by furnishing some other set of requirements with which to square our understanding of law. Regrettably, the recent tendency has been to introduce Wittgenstein's name into legal theory as if his thought provides an alternative (say, a social-pragmatic) conception of law,[44] or as if it supports the claim that 'law is an interpretive enterprise' (Patterson 1990: 940). More regrettable still, the regress argument is taken as showing that our ordinary idea of following a rule is naïve or confused, rather than as showing that the philosophical temptation to think that 'to follow a rule is to interpret it' is one which is disastrous for an understanding of what is involved in (the ordinary idea of) following a rule.[45] To the extent that such

[44] See e.g. Radin (1989). Radin also suggests that a Wittgensteinian or 'social practice conception of rules' would be 'incompatible with the traditional ideal of the Rule of Law' (810), and she presents several revisionary consequences of this conception: '[I]f we fail to follow a rule we undermine its existence as a rule.' Or again: 'Because a rule depends upon the existence of a social practice, it seems that an essential part of rule-application in a legal context is predicting the behavior of the community of judges and other legal actors including (it seems) one's own behavior if one is a legal actor' (807–8). Leaving aside the implausibility of these contentions (isn't legislative enactment often a sufficient condition of a rule's existence? In attempting to obey the red light does Radin attempt to predict whether she (or any one else) will in fact stop?), it seems that Radin has taken Wittgenstein's use of such terms as 'practice' and 'forms of life' as the beginning of a reductionist conception of rules rather than as part of a reminder that notions like 'following a rule' are commonplaces of our everyday world and of the shape it has for us. Here again Wittgenstein's remarks on rules seem easily subject to misunderstanding if they are read apart from his understanding of philosophical method.

[45] See e.g. D'Amato (1990: 174) and Tushnet (1988: 211). Consider also the following remark by Dallmayr, which both summarizes and approves what it takes to be the standard view: 'Ever since Wittgenstein's observations on "rule-following", it has been widely acknowledged that the application of rules cannot in turn be strictly rule-governed without conjuring up an infinite regress of stipulated rules (for their own application)' (1992: 3). If we take Wittgenstein's legacy to consist in a genuine question about whether the application of rules can be 'strictly rule governed' along with a regress argument in support of the opinion that they 'cannot', we are only too easily going to be made to feel the need for a constructive account of what *does* govern the application of rules. But we might notice, instead, how unclear the difference Dallmayr intimates between 'rule-governed' and 'strictly rule-governed' is bound to be. (What could that difference amount to? The thesis Dallmayr attributes to Wittgenstein is quite incredible if it is taken to mean that the application of a rule is never governed by another rule—

a conclusion is seen as the upshot of Wittgenstein's reflections on rules (rather than merely as one stage of the dialectic Wittgenstein seeks to depict), it may be said that Wittgenstein's availability in legal theory (but not only there)[46] has been conditioned by a misunderstanding.

LEGAL REASONING REVISITED

> [T]he rules and cases do not single out the important facts in a problem case mechanically.
>
> (S. Burton 1985: 97)

I want now to give this somewhat abstract discussion a more concrete cast by returning to the legal textbook by Burton mentioned earlier. To illustrate the need for an interpretive method, Burton asks us to consider the common law rule of negligence liability, according to which the defendant must compensate the plaintiff if the defendant was (1) under a duty to use reasonable care, (2) breached that duty, and in doing so was the (3) factual and (4) proximate cause of (5) injury to the plaintiff. 'The deductive form of reasoning', Burton comments, 'uses major premises that *appear* to state the necessary and sufficient factual conditions for any case to fall within the class of cases designated by the rule' (1985: 87). Burton wants to demystify this *appearance*. He acknowledges that the rule composed of these five conditions is the rule governing compensation in tort, but he none the less objects to the thought that 'compensation is required in any case in which these five facts are present and not when one or more of these five facts are not present—that all cases of negligence [liability] have in common the presence of these five facts' (ibid.). At first glance, this objection can seem

what could be more familiar in law?) The apparent point of Dallmayr's remark turns Wittgenstein's point inside-out. It converts Wittgenstein's reminder that it makes no sense to demand in general that the application of a rule be governed by another rule into the picture of a metaphysical lack: the application of a rule cannot be 'strictly' rule-governed. Against this, it might be of assistance to put the upshot of the regress like this: there no such thing as the application of a rule being *in general* rule-governed (there is nothing we actually want when, in the grip of the dead-letter picture, we seem to want this); so, by the same token, there is no such thing as the application of a rule *not* being in general rule-governed.

[46] Admittedly, the misunderstandings of Wittgenstein that have been imported into legal theory are ones to which Wittgenstein's thought has been widely subject, especially when it is seen through the lens of Kripke's interpretation (1982). It should be clear that I am at odds with Kripkean readings of Wittgenstein in both a general and a specific way. Generally, I give a central place to Wittgenstein's view that he is not advancing substantive claims or *theses* (cf. *PI* § 128). More specifically, I take the remarks on rule-following to offer a diagnosis of the difficulties we face in retaining our grasp on notions like 'meaning' and 'accord with a rule': the aim is to relieve our sense of a need for an explanation of such notions—*either* in terms of Platonist rails *or* in terms of practice or community. With respect to both the general and specific points I am indebted to a number of works: Cavell (1979; 1990: ch. 2); Conant (1993); Diamond (1989; 1991); Goldfarb (1983); McDowell (1984; 1992); Putnam (1991).

baffling. Doesn't the strangely complex and redoubling phrase Burton employs to characterize the major premiss—stating the necessary and sufficient factual conditions for any case to fall within *a class of cases* designated by the rule—describe just what it means to speak of there being a liability rule?

Burton, however, finds it queer to think that the rule itself determines the class of cases that fall under it. It would make sense to think so, he protests, only if '(1) all cases that are alike in the important respects, or members of the same legal class, have a fact or facts in common, and (2) the fact or facts in common among those cases correspond to the words of legal rules so that, by their presence, they signal the proper legal classification of the cases' (88). Burton tells us, in language that echoes the passage from Hart (about rules being unable to claim their own instances), that these conditions do not hold: 'It is highly doubtful . . . that facts in law cases so organize themselves, and therefore that the language of legal rules could be complete and determinate' (ibid.). Burton's argument to this heady conclusion about the indeterminacy of legal rules has the form of a *reductio ad absurdum*.

Now it is certainly unappealing to think that the world comes with labels instructing us how to apply words to it. So Burton is on safe ground in being suspicious of the idea that any facts—*by their very presence*—signal the proper legal classification of a case. But once one leaves behind this philosophically loaded picture of facts signalling to us (cf. 98), what should one say about the possibility of facts corresponding to the words of legal rules? Consider a simple legal rule, like the one requiring motorists to stop at a red light on penalty of being fined, and represent this, from the point of view of the judge charged with applying it, in the form of a conditional: 'If x is a motorist and x fails to stop at a red light, then x must pay a fine.' It seems innocuous to say that the rule states the conditions 'for any case to fall within the class of cases designated by the rule'. Nor would there seem to be anything especially odd in maintaining that (1) all cases in this class 'have a fact or facts in common' (namely, that some motorist fails to stop at a red light), or that (2) 'the facts in common correspond to the words of legal rules'. One could even add that any case that did not share these common facts would not fall under *this* rule,[47] and that any *other* facts—say that x's car is a Jaguar—whether common or not, are irrelevant to the classification of the cases under *this* rule. The point is a trivial one: the rule makes contact with the facts of the cases that fall under it precisely in (and in nowhere else than) the language of the rule itself: *this* is what is called 'going through a red light'. Is anything more needed to bring them together?

[47] For convenience, I am using 'fall under the rule' to mean 'fall within the classificatory term of the rule', as opposed to indicating simply a case to which the rule might be applied.

Of course, to speak of a rule making 'contact' with facts through language *can* sound philosophically fraught (as if we were saying that what particular facts there are depended on how we decided to label them). But the point only amounts to saying that what a rule requires a person to do is the same thing that a person might (or might fail to) do. If this does not seem enough to bring world and language together (for purposes of applying a legal rule), what could?

My analysis here is notably formal: there is nothing about it that is specific to the red-light rule and that could not be restated in the case of the more complex rule of negligence liability. It is that rule itself that determines the conditions—unreasonable conduct, causation, damage, and so on—comprising the class of cases that fall under it. Yet this seems so unexceptional that one might wonder whether one has not somehow missed Burton's point entirely. But can that point be stated? This is to ask: is there a genuine problem about how legal rules make contact with the particulars that fall under them (a problem that requires recourse to the notion of interpretation), or is there only the illusion of a problem—so that one's wording of the problem, if one reflects upon what the words mean, fails to correspond to one's sense of there being a problem that one is trying to word?

In the face of the platitudes I have offered, I imagine that there might be a tendency to feel that I have indeed missed Burton's point. In particular, it might seem that Burton's idea of a gap between the classificatory terms of legal rules and the facts of cases is, after all, only responsive to, or even descriptive of, a familiar feature of legal experience: the occurrence—in the face of the relevant legal rules and the agreed-upon facts—of intelligible disagreements in judgment. At the risk of putting words in Burton's mouth, the point might be put like this: 'While it is the legal rule that alone determines the class of cases to which it applies, the application of the rule to any particular instance (the identification of that instance as belonging to the class) requires an act of judgment.[48] And clearly the judgments that resolve cases in law often amount to describing the case with its singular facts in a controversial way.' This way of construing Burton's point comes out more clearly if we take note of an apparent asymmetry between easy and hard cases, between cases like those falling under the red-light rule and those falling under the rule of negligence liability. '*This* is what is called going through the red light' is uncontroversial in most instances, and it might even serve to explain to someone exactly what it is, according to the red-light rule, that one must not do. So it is unlikely to trouble us, with respect to *this* rule, that there may be nothing else other than their being so describable that all cases of 'going through the red light' have in common—

[48] Of course, this is still only a truism: One might have occasion to say it, for example, if one were trying to explain the word 'judgment' to someone who didn't know what it meant.

no other fact *in virtue of which* they can be so described. But with the negligence liability rule, the thought that there may be no independent way of picking out the class of cases falling under the rule can seem genuinely unsettling. For in a case of disagreement, it can look as if such an independent way—a rail, as it were, laid out prior to our judgments—is just what is acutely needed if we are to be able to take such a disagreement at its face value: as a disagreement about what *the rule requires* in the particular case. In the face of such disagreement, one would like to be able (or at least this is the fantasy) to point in a non-trivial way to the facts which make *this* (and not *that*) an instance of the rule; and short of being able to do this, one may feel unable to sustain the thought that the rule is making a specific normative demand, that it requires one thing rather than another.

Indeed, I think that this comes very near to the considerations that lead Burton to insist on an 'interpretive method'. In protesting that the facts of cases do not correspond to the words of legal rules in a way that *signals* the proper classification of the case, Burton seems to mean that there may be no facts that make it recognizable, independently of our judgments applying the terms of the rule, that a certain judgment or classification is the right one. And this is surely correct. But Burton then confronts us with a choice: either (1) defend the doubtful idea of such non-trivial or signalling facts; or (2) drop the pretence, sustained by the prevalent forms of legal reasoning, that legal judgments are nothing more than applications *simpliciter* (as opposed to applications-*cum*-interpretations) of the relevant rule. Burton's point in insisting on interpretation thus at bottom converges with Cornell's: he wants to tell us that the first choice is not a live option—there is no independent rail that stands surety for our judgment. Now confined to these choices, it is unlikely to deter someone from appealing to interpretation to point out that, by parity of reasoning, the application of rules in clear cases must also require interpretation (since the first choice is obviously no more attractive in such cases). Burton, for one, seems ready to embrace this consequence (see 1985: 126–9, 142). But consideration of clear cases should, in fact, lead us to find intolerable the choices that Burton presents. Is the only alternative to thinking that there are facts that enable us independently to pick out the class of cases falling under the red-light rule (that is, to do so without applying the terms of the rule itself) really to think that the rule can never be applied *simpliciter*? Rather than trying to embrace this consequence, it seems far more palatable to take a point here from Wittgenstein and extend it to the hard cases that seem to unsettle our sense of judging according to a rule. Simply put, there *need not* in general be anything independent of our judgments in applying the rule—for example, an independent 'rail'—that *makes* it correct to apply the rule in the way we do or that makes it recognizable ('signals') that a certain application of the rule is correct. In the case of disagreement, explanations may give out and we may be left simply with an appeal to the other's capacity to recognize an instance of the rule: 'But don't you see . . .'. But the fact that there is nothing against which such an appeal to good judgment can be checked (hence that an appeal to good judgment is an appeal to *nothing other* than good judgment) does not mean—this would be one way of characterizing Wittgenstein's point about the mythology (as opposed to what we may be tempted to regard as the absence) of the independent rail—that such judgments are any less instances of the rule they endeavour to apply.[49]

Burton, in short, is right to be suspicious of the idea that there are always facts that signal (except in a trivial sense) the proper legal classification of a case. But I am suggesting that we regard hard cases as standing on the same footing, with respect to this suspicion, as easy ones. What is sound in this suspicion lends no credibility to the thought that what makes a case an instance of a rule is an interpretation conferred upon the rule through the act of judgment.

In the first section of this paper I began by raising doubts, prompted by a bit of common sense, about the applicability of talk of interpretation in all cases. I can now summarize the three main conclusions of the preceding discussion—one which has uncovered nothing, at least in the work of several sophisticated theorists, which should lead us to give up this bit of sense.

(1) If in doing jurisprudence we keep one ear attuned to what we ordinarily say (and when we say it), we will respond to recent talk about interpretation in the following way: of course there are cases where it is useful or even necessary to make an interpretation. But is this so in *every* case? Must I interpret the traffic signal every time I stop or go? You can say this if you like, but that only shows that you are determined to represent the matter in a particular way: to call every application of a rule an interpretation of it. Yet given the far-reaching claims today made in the name of 'interpretation' (interpretation involves 'an appeal to the beyond'), it would be less confusing to keep the word moored, for the time being, in its original home—the useful substitution of one expression for another. Interpretation in this homely sense does play a significant role in adjudication. There are important interpretations of the equal protection clause of the Fourteenth Amendment or of the Sherman Act's prohibition of 'contracts, combinations, and conspiracies in restraint of trade', because such rules have been felt to require the intermediate formulations (familiar to every law student) that help guide judgment in particular cases.[50]

[49] My extension to legally hard cases of the point that Wittgenstein develops with respect to mathematically easy cases has benefited from the remarks on hard cases by McDowell (1981: 151–4).

[50] That this limitation of the notion of interpretation remains faithful to the practice of lawyers should not be too hastily counted against it. Typically, lawyers speak of interpretation

(2) The reasons for keeping our moorings in our ordinary ways of speaking in fact lie deeper than this. For the notion of interpretation was put forward by the theorists I cited in an attempt to *explain* the possibility of determination by a rule. And those theorists who offer this explanation do not think they are merely making a terminological point about the word 'interpretation', but that they are mounting a significant challenge to our naïve notion of clear cases under a rule. But an appeal to interpretation, even if it were found or presumed to occur in every case, wouldn't really be an explanation at all. Once we picture rules as unable to 'claim their own instances', the administration of interpretive aid only leads into the abyss where every interpretation hangs in the air along with what it interprets. Must we therefore conclude that the application of rules involves an unguided hunch, that it can never be 'strictly rule governed'?[51] That insistence on a kind of metaphysical absence seems attractive only against the background of a no-less metaphysical demand for a kind of presence: the rail that runs through our judgments and stands surety for them. If, however, we want to be truly realistic about law we will stop oscillating between these pictures and look closely at the law itself. Then we will be able to allow what the forms of legal reasoning themselves appear to suggest: that the judge sometimes follows the rules without interpreting them. (Or at least that, when this isn't so it is on account of considerations that belong to a specific body of law and do not implicate, as the theorists I have considered tend to suggest, legal rules *as such*.) What passes for realism in legal theory—namely, a demand to penetrate beyond the misleading appearance of the forms of legal reasoning—is to be seen as a failure of realism (in the non-theoretical sense of being realistic) about law.

(3) Am I trying to buttress a formalism that has long been under attack? It would be better to say that the worry about formalism in one distinct sense—the determining power of legal rules[52]—only arises from a certain picture of the law. In this picture we see a gap between legal rules and the results of particular cases, and then we think that there must be some theorizable thing in virtue of which this gap is bridged in practice—either the rails laid down by the legal rules themselves or an interpretation or a political theory or the goals of policy or the consensus of a community or the socialized hunches of the judge. This is the very matter of twentieth-century jurisprudence of legal judgment. We demand a theory that fills the

in relation to specific kinds of uncertainty or doubt: e.g. the ambiguity or vagueness of a word or clause, or a reason to think that the intention of parties to a contract does not conform with their expressed formulation, or the extreme generality of a rule (which may be intended as a rule of 'jurisdiction', conferring on subordinate agencies the power to develop intermediate standards), and so on.

[51] See note 45.

[52] The qualification is appropriate because the term 'formalism' has in fact meant a variety of things to different critics of it. See Schauer (1988); Radin (1989).

gap. But instead of trying to satisfy this demand, we might question the picture that gives rise to it.

Part II: Application

These problems about interpretation and indeterminacy come bundled together, as I noted early on, with the claim that legal judgment is inescapably 'political'. Or more precisely, the claim is that the indeterminacy of case results means that the traditional distinction between the legal and the political—a distinction appealing to the idea of a rule previously laid down—comes under threat. The best way to understand the motivation of this claim and to assess its merit, I think, is to consider some examples that present the problem of legal judgment in a concrete setting, and to this I want now to turn. But since the aim of my argument so far has been to cast doubt on the attempt to derive a thesis about the indeterminacy of legal rules from considerations about the nature of rule-following in general, the claim that indeterminacy opens legal decision to politics requires (if it is to be properly examined at all) a more plausible version of the indeterminacy thesis—one with a different pedigree.

Consider, in this regard, the following response to the argument presented so far. 'The law abounds in "hard cases", cases in which it is possible to apply the legal rules in different ways. *Possible*, not because clever doubts can be introduced that would never arise in the real world, but because there simply often are real doubts about what the law requires. Applying the law is not like nodding to the waiter or stopping at a red light. Perhaps not in every case, but certainly in the cases we care most about, interpretations are made and the doubts which make them necessary make them politically controversial as well. Common sense itself tells us that people would not generally take on the expense of litigation except in cases where divergent results are plausible under the existing rules. So cases tend, by self-selection, to be ones in which the legal rules require interpretation, and judgment in those cases tends to be, consequently, mainly an affair of politics at the penumbra—and not simply judgment at the undisputed core—of those rules.'

There is much that is right in this. In linking 'indeterminacy' specifically to adjudication, this response implicitly allows for a sense in which the law is *determinately* present in our everyday transactions—in the property we enjoy, the contracts we make, the risks we avoid, the regulations we obey, and so on. (After all, most legal questions are not—unless we simply stipulate them to be—officially adjudicated questions. If part of the legacy of legal realism has been to put the *results* of adjudicated cases at the center of contemporary legal theory, we may wonder whether this has not tended to blind us to the law's most ubiquitous aspects and occasions.)[53] Moreover, if a plausible version of the indeterminacy thesis is one thus rooted in 'hard cases', we should not expect to support it with considerations about the nature of legal, much less social, rules *as such*. This response accordingly affords a healthy invitation not merely to theorize about legal rules in the abstract but to *look and see* how the law behaves. Yet when we do this looking, I think we will see that the above appeal to the political (even with its limitation of indeterminacy to hard cases) really distorts the relations that obtain between the issues of interpretation, indeterminacy, and the political.

To begin with, however, a brief clarification is in order, for if we link the presence of interpretation to a 'hard case', it may be useful to distinguish two ways in which a case, in a legal system such as ours, might be said to be hard. (1) A case is 'hard' because there are doubts about what the relevant legal rules require in the particular circumstances. (2) A case is 'hard' because there are doubts about what, all things considered (including our sense of what would be a desirable result), ought to be done in the particular circumstances.[54] A hard case described by (1) may (but need not always) present an occasion of interpretation. Similarly, in (2) the rules may be perfectly clear, the question being whether to follow them or not—and that question calls for considerations that are significantly unlike the considerations present on occasions of interpretation.

To make this distinction more concrete, consider the hypothetical case of the driver who goes through a red light in order to obtain emergency medical treatment for her passenger. One can imagine a lawyer trying to argue in defence that her act furthers a worthy end, indeed, the very end that might be said to be the purpose, or the justification, of the red-light rule in the first place—the protection of life. It would be odd to say, however, that there is an *interpretive* question in this case, a question about the *meaning* of the red-light rule. What that rule requires in this case is clear—as clear, at any rate, as is our notion that (a) 'Stop at red lights' and (b) 'Stop at red lights except when . . .' are different possible legal rules. Of course, this is not to say that the distinction between interpretive questions and questions about what result in a case is generally desirable is *always* a clear one. The point of such jurisprudential chestnuts as Fuller's memorial statue (1958: 666), Pufendorf's surgeon, or the heir who murders his grandfather

[53] The fixation on results of adjudication that is a feature of the work of the legal realists comes out in the following statement by Jerome Frank: 'Until a court has passed on these facts, no law on that subject is yet in existence' (1963: 50). Since in deciding the case the court attempts to say what the legal norms require in particular circumstances, one is left to surmise that Frank has confused the truism that a conclusion is declared in legal judgment that is not given in the law with the absurdity that legal norms are created only when courts draw such conclusions. For contemporary versions of the demand that law be present not just as a ground of decision but as the particularity of results, see Hutchinson (1989: 7); Kairys (1984: 244).

[54] Schauer (1991) helpfully develops such a distinction.

to make the statute of wills operative,[55] may be expressed by saying that there are cases which are naturally described in either of two different ways: (a) as cases in which there are good reasons to set aside the result required by the relevant legal rule, and (b) as cases in which the relevant legal rule is indeterminate and needs to be interpreted in light of the normative considerations which are supposed to justify it.[56] None the less, it must in general be possible to know what a rule means (and what result it would require) without asking how the case would be decided on the basis of considerations that (independently of the rule) would provide a substantive justification of the result. If this were not the case, why have legal rules at all when one might as easily achieve the same result by analysing the merits of each case in the open-ended terms of what it is best to do—full stop?

Perhaps another way to grasp this point is to ask what an easy case would have to be if we were unable to draw such a distinction between two kinds of hard case. Not only would an easy case have to present no doubts about what result the relevant rules required, but that result would also have to be the desirable result, all things considered. It is plain that in this description of an easy case the idea of a legal rule drops out entirely. For if a judge's 'following a legal rule' means anything at all, it means that she has a reason for acting in a way that is at least potentially different from the way that would otherwise seem most desirable.[57] A legal system might be imagined in which judges thought of 'easy cases' without such a distinction, and they might express their jurisprudence like this: 'in every case, it is necessary not simply to identify the relevant rules but also to "interpret" the law-as-a-whole, in order to decide how (or whether) the rules are to be applied to the particular case—in order to decide what *the law* "means" in each case.' But such a system would contain rules only in the weak sense of 'rules of thumb'—ready to be discarded or emended when they give the 'wrong' result as judged on other grounds. Or rather, the one 'determinate' rule this system would acknowledge is a power-conferring rule, the one granting jurisdiction to some true statesman to do what is best.[58]

Rather than elaborate this distinction further here, I will turn to my examples, which pertain to hard cases in the first of these two senses—cases that

[55] *Riggs* v. *Palmer*, 22 N.E. 188 (N.Y. 1889). Pufendorf's surgeon is mentioned in this case as well.

[56] Dworkin's view that *Riggs* (the murdering heir) is about the proper interpretation of the statute of wills—about 'what the law actually was' (1986: 16), what it 'really said' (20)—is certainly plausible, but the description seems forced when it is used to support a general theoretical claim about law. It seems no less plausible to see *Riggs* as about whether the clear requirement of the statute controls the decision given that the result would conflict with common law equitable principles. See Silver (1987) for a discussion of the latter view.

[57] Here I follow Schauer (1991).

[58] I mean this statement to be reminiscent of the discussion of legal rules in Plato's *Statesman* (1984: 292*a*–302*b*).

involve doubts about what a legal rule requires, rather than about what to do in a more general sense.[59] But I will comment briefly at the end of my discussion on the contemporary tendency to elide this distinction and hence to describe all hard cases as cases in which the law needs to be interpreted.

FIRST EXAMPLE: THE NEGLIGENCE INSTRUCTIONS

In the civil-law jury instructions, the jury is asked to apply a very general formula: did the defendant act as a reasonable person would act under the circumstances. It is *not* asked to interpret it. In asking the jury to decide, the law knows that the legal rules alone do not specify a unique result of the case, but it apparently cares nothing for further interpretation of those rules. As one early commentator put it: 'The law recites its ritual and stops' (Green 1928: 1043): It does not attempt to translate the negligence formula into other terms. Indeed, contrary to Holmes's prediction that the accumulated findings of juries should eventually crystallize into increasingly precise rules of law, the historical development of negligence doctrine represents a movement towards less interpretive specificity, not more: a movement toward jury decision under one extremely general formula.[60] Thus, the judicial response to the defendant in *Vaughan* v. *Menlove*, who proposed an interpretation of the negligence standard designed to cure its imprecision, would seem as pertinent today as in 1837: 'The care taken by a prudent man has always been the rule laid down; and as to the supposed difficulty of applying it a jury has always been able to say, whether, taking that rule as their guide, there has been negligence on the occasion in question.'[61] Such a blank endorsement of the 'featureless generality' of the jury verdict (as Holmes anxiously called it)—this refusal to question, except for special reasons, the integrity of judgment under a very general standard—is worth thinking about. It is rich in implications that go beyond the specific institution of the jury and that bear on the nature of legal decision in general.

Every tort case that goes to the jury on negligence instructions is a 'hard case' with respect to the application of those instructions to the particular facts, for it involves conduct that falls between two limiting extremes at

[59] My examples all involve the common law of torts, and it may be that the conclusions I draw from them should be correspondingly restricted. But even so, those conclusions would hold true for a considerable domain of law.

[60] See Holmes (1963: 98–9). Holmes's view that whenever a judge sends a case to the jury he admits that he is unable to state the law governing the case before him (89) provides an illustration of the realist's tendency to identify the law with the results of the particular case. See *supra*, note 53. In contrast to Holmes's prediction of increasing precision, consider the erosion of the 19th-century status distinctions governing the duties owed to entrants on land, or the disappearance of special 'no duty' and 'limited duty' rules in cases involving claims of emotional harm and purely economic loss.

[61] *Vaughan* v. *Menlove*, 3 Bing. (N.C.) 468, 474 (1837).

which the legal disposition of the case would have been straightforward: at one extreme, conduct that, despite its causal relation to the plaintiff's injury, was clearly reasonable or prudent; at the other extreme, conduct that, in light of the available precautions, clearly involved an excessive risk of injury to the plaintiff. One of the court's familiar functions in a negligence case is to determine these extremes—typically by ruling on procedural motions for judgment by the lawyers. Such motions present, in essence, a question of 'reasonableness' at a higher level of abstraction: given the alleged facts or the evidence, could a jury 'reasonably conclude' that the defendant's conduct was somewhere within these extremes? Notice what is happening here. There is an area of difficulty in the application of a legal concept, that of an 'unreasonable risk'. While one response might be to see this as a defective vagueness in the law and then to interpret the concept,[62] this is not the law's response. The law only undertakes to determine the *intelligible* use of this concept—the limits, so to speak, of what can be said ('Can a jury reasonably conclude . . . ?'). That is its self-declared domain: if it is reasonable to say either of two opposing things about the defendant's conduct, the law doesn't take sides; it concerns itself with the reasonableness of conduct only in so far as there are some things about this which it would be unreasonable to say. To put it another way, the law does not appear to be concerned with the question *the parties* themselves may care most about (the question of liability, the 'result' of the case) but only with the point that it is *this* concept (the reasonableness of risk) and not some other concept which must be applied to determine that result.

If this is correct, then we should take seriously what is said in some of the model jury instructions, just after the legal standard is stated: 'The law does not say how a reasonably careful person would act under [the] circumstances. That is for you to decide.'[63] This is to be read in the following way: the law doesn't have an *indeterminate* view of the status of the defendant's conduct—as if the law were defective or subject to a general lack, or as if by using a general formula it were condemned to fall short of its own mark. It aspires to have *no* view—if the question can be reasonably entertained, if the matter is really *questionable*—about how to classify the defendant's conduct. By saying so—by declaring, in this way, its own limits—the law draws a distinction between its own determinations, which are conceptual or formal, and the positive decision which is needed to resolve the case. And just as the law declares itself distinct from positive decision, so too, the jury's decision, garnished by no explanation, traditionally creates no law and has no force as precedent; it is simply a judgment, without further currency, in the particular case. (The factors which might actually weigh

[62] Cf. Cooter and Ulen (1988: 347).

[63] *Illinois Pattern Jury Instructions Civil* § 10.01 (3rd edn. 1990). Similar instructions are recommended in other states.

with a particular agent of decision have no importance in a statement of the law.) Moreover, at the same time that the law has *no view* of the defendant's liability, it does apparently have a fully determinate view about the proper concept that must be applied for purposes of resolving his liability: 'The care taken by a prudent man has always been the rule laid down . . .'. The law brooks no further interpretations of this concept but only requires its application in an act of judgment.

If all this is in one way familiar to any student of tort law, here it is described in a manner that, given the legacy of legal realism, must appear peculiar—one that adheres not to the interested party's point of view, but, so to speak, to the law's own view of itself. For it is from the point of view of a party to the litigation that one might plausibly suppose that what matters most is the judgment entered in the case, the *result* (regardless of the grounds on which it is reached). Legal realism decisively took over that point of view. But I think we are bound to ask: isn't the possibility of a point of view which is not the point of view of this or that party (but is, one might even say, indifferent to the parties) the possibility of law itself? On this view, it is a constitutive feature of the law, a limitation which is nothing less than a condition of its possibility, that it does not offer opinions where different opinions are possible. On this view, the law is not lacking in anything, but it speaks with all the determinacy that it makes sense—short of its taking particular sides—for it to have: it is exactly this and not some other concept that must be applied if the case is to be resolved on *legal*, as opposed to some other political or administrative grounds.

Is the significance of this example limited to the institution of the jury? It would seem not, for the need for particular judgments that are distinct from 'the law' in a more primary sense would have to be a feature of any legal order that undertakes to apply general standards rather than to issue a series of specific decrees. Such a distinction between law and particular judgments can be seen not just in the fact of hard cases; more fundamentally, the very existence of official procedures for relating general legal norms to contingent circumstances expresses the law's recognition of potential uncertainty about what the prescribed norms require in those circumstances. Thus, the example of the jury instructions, taken in a more general way, can help us to see what is odd or unduly forced in the inference of some theorists today from the law's indeterminacy to its politicality. The loss of the distinction between the legal and the political would appear plausible, on the basis of an indeterminacy of result, only if one supposed that it must additionally be true that (1) the application of the law to the particular case must be mediated by an extra-legal ground (political, economic, moral, and so on) of judgment; and (2) achieving a result on such a ground still amounts (in something more than an attenuated sense) to legal judgment.

To illustrate the breadth of the problem, I turn now to a pair of cases that concern matters generally considered to be legal questions appropriate for resolution by the judge.

SECOND EXAMPLE: THE SCOPE OF THE DEFENDANT'S DUTY AND PROXIMATE CAUSE

Spartan Steel

Consider first a few sentences from *Spartan Steel*, a well-known decision by Lord Denning:

> The more I think about these cases, the more difficult I find it to put each into its proper pigeon-hole. Sometimes I say: 'There was no duty.' In others I say: 'The damage was too remote.' So much so that I think the time has come to discard those tests which have proved so elusive. It seems to me better to consider the particular relationship in hand, and see whether or not, as a matter of policy, economic loss should be recoverable or not.[64]

The question here was whether the plaintiff, in addition to recovering for physical damage, could recover for the economic loss that followed negligent damage by a contractor to an electrical cable owned by the power company that supplied power to the plaintiff. Since neither the contractor's negligence nor his causal relationship to the plaintiff's economic loss was in doubt, it was natural for the parties to argue the case in the common law terms of the scope of the defendant's 'duty' with respect to this kind of loss, and in terms of whether the loss was, given its manner of occurrence, sufficiently direct—not too remote. Denning, however, in a move that obviously signals his aspiration to a kind of realism, says that he will discard these elusive tests and decide the case on the basis of a number of considerations of policy. And that is what he does, basing his decision on such considerations as that the risk of economic loss 'should be suffered by the whole community' and not placed 'on the one pair of shoulders' (1 Q.B. at 39)—a far cry, certainly, from the traditional legal question posed in terms of 'duty' and 'remoteness'.

But this is not all. Denning wants to discard the old rhetoric, but he does not want to have simply changed the subject. Thus, he suggests that he is only doing what all judges *must* do when they are confronted with a case of uncertainty: 'Whenever the courts draw a line to mark out the bounds of *duty*, they do it as a matter of policy . . . Whenever the courts set bounds to the *damages* recoverable—saying that they are, or are not, too remote—

[64] *Spartan Steel & Alloys Ltd.* v. *Martin & Co.*, 1 Q.B. 27, 37 (1973). The case has become familiar to legal theorists through the extensive discussion by Dworkin (1977).

they do it as a matter of policy . . .' (1 Q.B. at 36). It looks as if we are meant to take what other judges in fact *say* as comparatively lacking in candour, just as we are invited to take the policy considerations that Denning invokes as an acknowledgment of the necessity of interpretation (of the otherwise elusive concepts of duty and remoteness)—for *some* interpretation, according to the thought of this passage, is inescapable if those concepts are to be seen as determining a particular result. On this brazenly self-conscious account, the difference between Denning and other judges is that he openly acknowledges what he is doing, whereas they artfully use the legal rhetoric of duty and remoteness to disguise the policies that actually govern their results.

But, for all of its loudly declared realism and transparency, there is a way in which Denning's procedure remains obscure. If loss-spreading is a desirable goal to pursue through a judicially administered regime of civil liability, why not bring it to bear in every case—not just in hard cases under the traditional rules but in easy ones as well? Indeed, the question goes further than this: if considerations of loss-spreading justify the result in this case, *must not* they be given the same normative reach in every other case? To give them such a reach, however, would be tantamount to applying a new legal rule that made the likelihood of a certain distributional effect— that is, a more inclusive sharing of the loss—a condition of fixing liability on one of the parties. Such a rule, we can surmise, is not really what Denning has in mind, for it is plain that there is no difference with respect to distributional effect between the imposition of liability on the contractor for physical harm (which Denning unhesitatingly allows) and the imposition of liability on the contractor for economic harm (which Denning, on the basis of the desirability of spreading the loss, doesn't allow). *Both* types of harm present a judicial opportunity for spreading loss by allowing it to remain where it falls; and conversely, a rule imposing liability on a negligent contractor for *either* type of harm will result (given the range of persons potentially effected by a break in electrical power) in a risk of loss being placed 'on one pair of shoulders'.

What happens, then, is that Denning introduces a new ground of justification (as a gloss on the traditional but elusive concepts of duty and remoteness), but then also implicitly limits the scope of its power to justify: it doesn't apply to the action to recover for physical damages. Is there any basis for this limitation? We may readily think that there is: is it not based on a judgment that the physical damage is sufficiently *direct* whereas the economic harm is not? Is it not based, then, paradoxically, on the traditional tort concepts which the recourse to 'policy' was supposed to have supplanted? In this light, Denning's reasoning appears not so much transparent as truncated. It invokes a policy justification that is supposed to replace the more abstract tort concepts (they are to be discarded); but it then limits the reach of the policy justification (capable on its own of refashioning the rule of tort liability)—and it limits it, by some unstated means, to fit the accepted contours of traditional tort liability.

The source of the trouble here appears to be nothing other than a contemporary dogma of legal realism according to which determinate judgment in the application of general legal concepts *must* involve some reference, however disguised, to political goals. Substantially similar trouble shows up in judicial decisions that self-consciously endeavour to understand the problem of legal judgment in terms of such a requirement. Consider my second example.

Kinsman Transit

In *Kinsman Transit* (now a standard part of the American curriculum on proximate cause), two ships careened into a municipally operated lift-bridge on the Buffalo River, and the entire wreckage of ships and bridge formed a dam that caused ice and water to back up causing property damage upstream. Three parties had been negligent: the ship-owner (Kinsman), because of an inadequate response to the danger of ice-jams that were moving downstream; the dock operator (Continental), because of failure to inspect a device at the dock; and the City of Buffalo, because it failed to raise the bridge. Addressing the question of liability for the property damage upstream, Judge Friendly writes:

> [T]he careless actor will [not] always be held for all damages for which the forces that he risked were a cause in fact. Somewhere a point will be reached when courts will agree that the link has become too tenuous—that what is claimed to be consequence is only fortuity. Thus, if the destruction of the Michigan Avenue Bridge had delayed the arrival of a doctor, with consequent loss of a patient's life, few judges would impose liability on any of the parties here . . .[65]

Up to this point Friendly is simply articulating the commonplace requirement of proximate cause. As with duty, it may be said that the point of that requirement is to link the injury suffered by the plaintiff to the negligent action of the defendant. A judgment is called for that makes the plaintiff's injury out as a consequence of the defendant's wrongdoing rather than, as Friendly says, a mere fortuity. In determining the City's liability, for example, it would be necessary to ask whether the flooding upstream is a consequence of the city's negligent failure to lift the bridge rather than the result of some other wrong or misfortune. Although there may be room for disagreement about this, the conceptual distinction between consequence and fortuity is one that has (as Friendly himself points out) clear instances

[65] *Petitions of the Kinsman Transit Co.*, 338 F.2d 708, 725 (2d Cir. 1964).

concerning which there is general agreement in judgment.[66] Friendly begins his argument by referring to such an instance, an easy case of a mere fortuity: if the destruction of the bridge 'had delayed the arrival of a doctor, with consequent loss of a patient's life, few judges would impose liability on any of the parties here'. But then what are we to make of Friendly's subsequent resolution of the case at hand?—

> It would be pleasant if greater certainty were possible . . . but the many efforts that have been made at defining the *locus* of the 'uncertain and wavering line' [quoting Andrews in *Palsgraf*] are not very promising; what courts do in such cases makes better sense than what they, or others, say. Where the line will be drawn will vary from age to age; as society has come to rely increasingly on insurance and other methods of loss-sharing, the point may lie further off than a century ago. Here it is surely more equitable that the losses from the operators' negligent failure to raise the Michigan Avenue Bridge should be ratably borne by Buffalo's taxpayers than left with the innocent victims of the flooding. (383 F.2d at 725–6)

Like Denning, Friendly takes the indeterminacy of the legal concepts to mean that the judicial exercise of judgment in accordance with them must be a political one. He apparenty moves from the realization that a line must be drawn, to the conclusion that the law authorizes him to draw that line on whatever grounds seem best to him. Thus, he uses his decision to create, in effect, a compensation scheme to be funded out of the City's tax revenues; what determines the city's liability is finally not whether the harm that occurred upstream is a consequence or a fortuity of its negligent failure to lift the bridge, but the purported fact that it is, given its taxing power, in a better position than the flood victims to spread the loss that has occurred.

Now it is plain that the goal of loss-spreading, whatever might be said for or against it, is essentially exogenous to a classification of the causal interaction between the parties. 'Loss-spreading' is intelligible independently of that interaction and it can be realized by various legislative means—taxation, insurance, accident compensation schemes, and so on. If private liability actions are to be a means of spreading accident losses, there is no reason, at least so far as concerns the realization of *this* goal, for there to be *any* causal relationship between the parties. (Quite possibly, a party not—even remotely—connected to the accident, say, the State of New York or a

[66] Here we may remind ourselves that, since the causal conditions of an injury extend back, as it were, to the beginning of time, no regime of personal liability for injury is possible without *some* distinction between actions that are merely necessary conditions of the injury and actions that are causes (in a sense implying responsibility). By the same token (looking forward from an action rather than backward from injury), the claim that a person has been wrongfully injured would be unintelligible without some distinction between the merely fortuitous results and the proper consequences of an action. The common law expresses this distinction in various idioms (foreseeable/unforeseeable, direct/indirect, proximate/remote), but all are essentially means of elaborating the proper 'consequences' of action. Such elaboration, in particular cases, would be part of the work of any positive body of tort law.

manufacturer with a large sales-base, would be an even more effective loss-spreader if *it* were made liable.) So there is a sense in which Friendly's opinion chafes against what is most commonplace in the lawsuit before him. These parties have been singled out and brought together in the bipolar form of plaintiff and defendant. As such they present an instance of causation, of the relationship between an action and its effects. But Friendly offers a justification for fixing liability on one of them which makes this central fact incidental and dispensable, but which none the less—precisely because it is given in the course of the judicial decision of a lawsuit—continues to be limited by it.[67]

To see the difficulty here it suffices to consider the very case that Friendly takes to be a clear one—the 'delayed arrival of a doctor with consequent loss of a patient's life'. If the possibility of spreading accident losses justifies the judicial imposition of liability, then the judicial consensus around the 'no-liability' result in that hypothetical case must be mistaken, for that case presents no less of an opportunity than the upstream property damage in *Kinsman* to compensate an innocent victim and to use the City of Buffalo's tax system to distribute the loss. In deciding the case of the patient's intestate, one could well repeat Friendly's appeal to these goals: 'here it is surely more equitable that the losses from the operators' negligent failure to raise the Michigan Avenue Bridge should be ratably borne by Buffalo's taxpayers than left with the innocent victims.' (One might even wonder whether it is not *inequitable* to use municipal taxes to compensate some victims of the accident while leaving others, identical in point of their innocence and their need for compensation, to bear their own losses.) But if, against this, one continues to tell the patient's intestate that the legal requirement of proximate cause operates as a limitation on judicial compensation and the shifting of losses (that is, if one refuses, on the grounds of causal remoteness, to regard the patient as a legally wronged victim), this implies that the defendants in *Kinsman* are entitled to a determination of whether *their* negligence was the proximate cause of the property damage upstream—a determination that is prior to and independent of the consideration that they might be good conduits for loss-spreading or that the plaintiff desires compensation. As a dissenting opinion in *Kinsman* tersely puts the point: 'before financial liability is imposed there should be some showing of legal liability' (338 F.2d at 728).

The trouble here evidently stems from the fact that in Friendly's decision two kinds of justification are merely yoked together. The result is (paradoxically) a double indeterminacy—an indeterminacy not only with respect to

[67] The importance of the form of the lawsuit for understanding the nature of private law liability is emphasized by Fuller (1978), and the idea is developed extensively by Weinrib (1995).

the result of the case but now also with respect to the considerations on which it is based. For, although we can follow Friendly's line of inference from an ensemble of considerations to the result in *this* case, we have no rule for extending these considerations to other cases. Without an explanation of how 'compensation' and 'loss-spreading' on the one hand, and 'proximate causation' on the other, fit together and limit each other, there is no basis for extrapolating how the pursuit of these goals will serve to fix liability in other cases, or alternatively, how the requirement of proximate causation (and more generally the bipolar, causal structure of the lawsuit) will interrupt and defeat the pursuit of these goals. To the original difficulty of determining the causal scope of liability, in short, is now added the difficulty of determining how that determination will limit the goals of compensation and loss-spreading, or in turn be limited by them.[68] To a certain degree these tensions are rhetorically camouflaged in Friendly's decision, which announces the pursuit of loss-spreading as if it were part of an interpretation of the legal requirement of proximate cause—part of an attempt to fix an 'uncertain and wavering line' between consequence and fortuity: 'Where the line will be drawn will vary from age to age; as society has come to rely increasingly on insurance and other methods of loss-sharing, the point may lie further off than a century ago.'[69] But what exactly is the relationship supposed to be between the goal of loss-spreading and the question of how to delimit the causal bounds of liability? It is apparent enough that there is no internal or predeterminable relationship at all. Whether the judicial pursuit of loss-spreading requires an *expansion* of the legal consequences of action (so that the point at which liability ceases lies 'farther off'), or whether it requires a *contraction* of them (so that the point lies closer in) depends on a wealth of contingent factors (for example, the structure of the insurance and other commodity markets surrounding the plaintiff's and the defendant's enterprise). Such contingences would have to be considered in any serious attempt to work out the distributional consequences of various legal rulings; but whether drawing the line of proximate cause at one point rather than another would tend to select the best party for spreading the loss could hardly be said in advance.

[68] Note, for example, that in *Kinsman II*, where plaintiff's grain shipments were delayed, the resultant economic losses were deemed too remote ('only fortuity') and considerations of loss-spreading were simply ignored. See *Petition of Kinsman Transit Co.*, 388 F.2d 821, 825 (1968). (In fact, the difficulties are even worse than I have described them, because the goals of compensation and loss-spreading must themselves sometimes pull the judicial decision in different directions. In *Spartan Steel*, for example, the goal of loss-spreading is thought to be furthered by denying the plaintiff compensation for his economic loss.)

[69] 338 F.2d at 725–6. Were it not so candid, this moment of Friendly's opinion could be seen as an example of Calabresi's approach in which concepts like proximate cause are viewed as judicial rhetoric disguising an analysis conducted in other terms. See Calabresi (1975).

DENNING'S AND FRIENDLY'S DISAPPOINTMENT

Although more could be said about the internal tensions in these decisions by Denning and Friendly, my main concern here is to see how they arise. In each decision we find a moment of severe or hyperbolic disappointment with the law. Denning's disappointment is conditioned by his demand that the concepts of duty and remoteness should function as what he calls tests ('I think the time has come to discard those tests which have proved so elusive'). Taking the legal concepts to be tests, Denning has discovered that they do not work, so they are to be discarded. Friendly, in a similar vein notes the failure of 'many efforts . . . at defining the *locus* of the "uncertain and wavering line" '—as if the law were defective because the requirement of proximate cause could not be made more precise through definition, but only through judgment in particular cases (and through run-of-the-mill judicial means: the analogic comparison of new cases to prior cases within a particular jurisdiction). The demands and disappointments expressed by these judges are certainly real in our legal culture, but they are not—in the sense of the word that represents not a compromise but an ideal—realistic.

It is surely a commonplace of tort law that the requirement of proximate cause—whether articulated in terms of foreseeability or directness—does not function as a test of the scope of liability (cf. Morris 1952: 198). Consider 'foreseeability': if the accident suffered by the plaintiff is described generally enough—say (to take the limiting case) as *some type* of harm occurring to *someone* by *some means* or other—then the plaintiff's injury must always be a foreseeable consequence of the defendant's misconduct. By the same token, if the accident is characterized with sufficient detail—in the limiting case as a uniquely particular event—it could never be 'foreseeable'. Thus, it may be said that when the law speaks of 'a foreseeable consequence', what is at stake is the proper description of the risk taken by the defendant along these three dimensions of generality: risk to *whom*, of *what*, and occurring in *what manner*. The classical idea in tort law is that the unreasonable risk taken by the defendant, described at the proper level of generality, must refer to the injury suffered by the plaintiff—otherwise the plaintiff is merely the victim of some other wrong or misfortune.[70] Strategically, this means that it will be in the interest of the plaintiff to describe the events of the case with less detail and in the interest of the defendant to describe them with more detail, emphasizing the unusual nature of what

[70] This is the point of Cardozo's relational analysis of negligence in *Palsgraf* v. *Long Island Ry. Co.*, 162 N.E. 99 (1928): the wrongdoing of the platform attendant does not properly refer to Mrs Palsgraf's injury. It would refer to her injury if it were described more generally—e.g. as involving a risk of some injury occurring in some manner, etc.—but then one looses one's purchase on its *wrongfulness*: so described the risk becomes indistinguishable from the normal, background risks present in all action.

has occurred.[71] But the idea of a legal judgment in this situation would be the idea of a judgment that privileges neither the point of view of the plaintiff nor that of the defendant: the judgment of a court implies that there is a way of describing the accident that is neither too general nor too specific, but rather neutral with respect to the two parties. One might say that such a description aspires to honour the equality of the parties.[72] This does not mean that there is some independent measure of the justness of the result; ultimately, the disappointment of these judges seems to be rooted in the demand for such a measure, for a law that moves behind history, as it were. But a judgment on the scope of causation that is sincerely made remains just that—a legal judgment, one that has no need to determine or support itself on other political grounds.[73]

Contrast the decisions by Denning and Friendly. Because the legal concepts give no 'test', but only a ground for decision, both Denning and Friendly feel justified in discarding them and judging the case on other grounds. Their decisions admittedly remain connected to the law in the sense that the law authorizes *them*, the judges, to decide. (They treat the law of tort as if it contained only power-conferring rules, granting them jurisdiction to decide.) At the same time, the traditional legal concepts continue to be present within each decision as more or less explicit limitations on the scope of the goal-based justifications that are proffered in support of the decision. But in so far as these traditional concepts are thereby acknowledged to have something more than mere jurisdictional significance (and in so far as the concept of causation is thereby treated as something more than a label to be attached to a decision reached by other means), these decisions must appear, from this *internal* point of view, to be an abandonment of legal judgment in favour of something else. The unhappy reasoning of these decisions resembles that of someone who, realizing that the concept of 'an appropriate reward' doesn't itself determine how much to pay someone, decides to abandon the concept and never offer a reward at all.

My first example concerning the jury instructions serves to illustrate the distinction between the law (in its primary or conceptual sense) and its

[71] For examples, see Morris (1952).

[72] This thesis is explored in detail by Weinrib (1995).

[73] An understanding of legal judgment along these lines is reflected in Judge Moore's dissent in *Kinsman*. Moore does not attempt to minimize the difficulty of the case, the possibility of reasonable disagreement in judgment. Indeed, he acknowledges that there is an element of the personal in his judgment: 'In final analysis the answers to the questions when the link is "too tenuous" and when "consequence is only fortuity" are dependent solely on the particular point of view of the particular judge . . . [T]o me the fortuitous circumstance of the vessels so arranging themselves as to create a dam is much "too tenuous"' 388 F.2d at 728. Moore recognizes that he must judge by his own lights. But for him, this means only that he must make a candid, good faith effort to apply the legal concepts; he does not take it as a reason for converting the judicial exercise into a political one.

application to a particular case (which calls for the reasonable exercise of judgment). My second pair of examples serves to illustrate what happens when a disappointment with the law's generality with respect to the particular case is experienced as a defect in the legal standard. Whatever their legal pertinence, it is clear that one source of the appeal of the policy considerations that Denning and Friendly invoke is that they seem to offer the promise of making assignments of liability a matter of calculation, and hence to domesticate the difficulty of judgment in hard cases. But the result is a framework of legal justification in which distinct, mutually limiting kinds of reason for decision coexist but fail to cohere. And this means that the judge is in the position of continuing to deploy the concepts the law prescribes (and upon which, it might be thought, his authority rests) while no longer being able to make sense of them. Thus, a disappointment over a legal rule's inability to 'claim its own instances' (in Denning's words, to provide a test for legal results), leads not only to perplexity in academic theory, but also to failures of justification in the court-room.

Part III: Conclusion

My examples in Part II are meant to suggest that legal judgment, even in hard cases, does not always require interpretation; nor do such cases in and of themselves pose a threat to the distinction between law and politics.

We have seen that some theorists (and not only theorists) are apt to feel disappointed with the law in so far as it does not concern itself with the legal *result* of a case but only with the concepts by which a *legal* result—hopefully with good judgment—is to be achieved. This disappointment was noted by Hegel well before he was taken by Holmes at the inception of legal realism to be the epitome of a way of thinking about law that ignored the positivity—indeed for Holmes, the violence—of judgment in the particular case. Consider a remark of Hegel's such as the following:

> It is in this focusing of the universal not just on the particular but on an individual case—i.e. in its immediate application—that the purely positive aspect of the law chiefly lies . . . There is essentially one aspect of law . . . which is subject to contingency, and this derives from the fact that the law is a universal determination which has to be applied to the individual case. If one were to object to this contingency, the objection would be merely abstract . . . [for] this contingency is itself necessary. (1821: § 214, 214A)

In identifying the resolution of the individual case with contingency and with the 'positive aspect' of law,[74] Hegel wishes to indicate the *limits* of

[74] Hegel speaks in § 214 of the '*purely* positive' (*das rein Positive*)—referring apparently not to the whole of legal judgment but to a more limited domain of judgment in which a decision

what he calls 'philosophical right'—that is, right in so far as it can be determined by thought or reason. But he is far from regarding this limitation as a defect or a ground for disappointment; contingency is necessary, hence 'it is reason itself which recognizes' such a limitation (1821: § 214). Surely something has gone awry in the jurisprudential story we tell ourselves if 'formalism' is supposed to have come to grief over indeterminacy, yet the archetypal formalist[75] maintains that indeterminacy is a necessary feature of the law, that the life of the law (in a phrase that could serve equally well as a paraphrase of either Hegel or Holmes) is not reason but contingent experience. But what (besides an evident failure to join issue) has happened here? This is to ask: what are the presuppositions about law under which a necessary condition of law—its generality with respect to the particular case—could have come to seem a shortcoming? I offer the following conjecture.[76]

Legal realism never succeeded in demystifying formalism because it never really encountered what is most significant in the previous tradition of philosophical thought about law, represented most notably by Kant and Hegel. Rather, it confined itself to the positive aspect of law (which it took to be the whole legal domain), and hence attacked, under the banner of opposing formalism, an account of law which was largely its own creation. Legal realism shared with the variety of formalism that it both invented and opposed a commitment to an account of law that was both positivist and instrumentalist. This variety of formalism was positivist in that the distinction between law and politics was never established in the first place except in the weak form of reference to the idea of a system of legal rules (so which considerations are legal or political at any given time is a matter of the rules that have been posited, 'the rules laid down'). And it was instrumentalist in that the generalizations entrenched in legal rules were thought to be justified (if at all) by their tendency to promote social goals which are identifiable independently of those rules (so strict adherence to legal rules might sometimes give an undesirable result from the point of view of the considerations thought to justify the rules in the first place). Given these assumptions, it was natural for legal theorists to ask: why should judges stick to following the rules at all? Why should they try to achieve substantively

needs to be made but there is no reason to decide one way or another (e.g. 'whether the just penalty . . . is . . . forty lashes or thirty-nine'). But elsewhere he speaks of legal judgment as 'positive' in a less restrictive sense: 'Right is in general *positive* . . . through the necessity whereby a system of legal right must contain the *application* of the universal concept' (§ 3; see also § 211). So evidently, the 'purely positive' is one example (and presumably the limiting case) of the more encompassing way in which right is 'positive'.

[75] At least that is who Hegel is for Holmes. See e.g. Howe's comments in Holmes (1963: pp. xv–xvii).

[76] I shouldn't call it more than a conjecture. It will serve its purpose if it suggests further lines of inquiry.

correct results by a formal procedure of rule-based decision? Why should they not decide each case directly on the basis of the goals that give normative point to the rules? Such questions were never far away for the realists.[77] The predominant answer—appealing to such administrative values as the cost of more open-ended decision-making, the limited capacities of decision-makers, or the need for certainty and predictability—made out a case for rule-based decision in law, but only at the cost of producing the 'hard case' as a moment of crisis. Given that the rules are only a means to a socially desirable outcome, in a hard case (*both* in cases in which the rules support different applicative judgments *and* in cases in which the straightforward application of the rules produces an undesirable result) the judge should be free to look beyond the rules to the substantive considerations which underlie them. Why not—unless one simply fetishizes rules and rule-based decision? Whence arose both: (1) the idea that in every hard case the judge must interpret 'the law' as such (that is, interpret the rules and decide whether to apply the rules); and (2) the idea that the judicial refusal to assume this freedom of interpretation is itself an interpretative decision about the law, an adherence to a particular and questionable model of 'formalism'.

Hegel's remark allows us to see the contours of this line of thinking more clearly because it stands apart from it in at least two ways. First, without denying the law's embodiment in a posited set of social rules, Hegel distinguishes case results in a particular jurisdiction from the conceptual aspect of the law. Secondly, Hegel understands this legal conceptuality as a ground of decision that is known by reason and that inheres in the very idea of the answerability of one person for the effects of his actions on another. Admittedly, a great deal more would need to be said to defend this conception of law. One would, however, not be defending it—but simply abandoning it—if one wished to render it invulnerable to a complaint concerning the indeterminacy of legal results. For Hegel counts indeterminacy not as a defect, but as a constitutive feature of the law, a condition of its possibility. What is essential to the rule of law, on this view, is not that the relevant legal concept should specify a unique result, but that it 'must always contain the basic principle, even for the particular instance' (Hegel 1821: § 101)—it must supply the *ground* of decision. The extent of the philosophical mis-encounter here can be seen in the fact that Hegel could well have said exactly what Holmes said—that general propositions do not decide concrete cases—but he would have understood this to mean not that the judge must willy-nilly engage in politics, but rather that the law, in its

[77] And they re-emerge in the contemporary attack on formalism. Cf. Kennedy (1973: 358–60).

philosophical aspect, aspires to be universal, not partisan.[78] The law does not take sides.

This classical idea of law was mentioned not long ago by Michel Foucault in a discussion with Maoists over the question of whether the people's courts (the revolutionary apparatus that carried out acts of substantive 'justice' in the name of the proletariat) should properly be thought of as courts in the judicial sense. Foucault said that he found this difficult to accept because:

> When we talk about courts we're talking about a place where the struggle between the contending forces is willy-nilly suspended; where in every case the decision arrived at is not the outcome of this struggle but of the intervention of an authority which necessarily stands above and is foreign to the contending forces, an authority which is in a position of neutrality between them and consequently can and must in every case decide which party to the dispute has justice on its side. The court implies, therefore, that there are categories which are common to the parties present . . . and that the parties to the dispute agree to submit to them. (1980: 27)

Foucault worried that to speak of courts in a context where judgment issues not from a disinterested third party ('an authority in a position of neutrality between them') but from a party which embodies the will of the aggrieved plaintiffs, would be to cast an ideological smoke-screen over acts which are really political decrees; it would be a camouflage of power. This point may also be turned in the other direction, however. For acknowledging the possibility of the distinction Foucault proposes (between a court and some other form of political administration) amounts to nothing less than acknowledging that our concept of adjudication stands for something more than a form of decree or legislation. As Michael Oakeshott once put it, 'to call a court political is to deny it the character of a court of law'.[79] Of course, to speak of legal neutrality is not yet to say anything which will assuage someone whose severe starting-point is that any reference to neutrality must represent the invidious camouflage of one party's triumphant will. And, maybe in the end, all we can say about this understanding of law is something like—what Foucault, in a characteristic turn of his thought, goes on to say—that 'it is all this that the bourgeoisie wants to have believed in relation to justice, to its justice' (1980: 27). But the case for such cynicism remains to be made, and made, moreover—in the only way it could be

[78] Holmes and Hegel appear to agree in so far as they both affirm the same words ('General concepts do not decide concrete cases'). But the difference between them lies in the kind of insight that they take these words to express. For Holmes, they express a substantive description of the character of the law as he happens to find it—one which, for him, points to a defect (albeit one he takes to be irremediable). For Hegel, they express a logical or constitutive (what Wittgenstein would call a 'grammatical') feature of law.

[79] Oakeshott (1975: 412); quoted in Weinrib (1995: ch. 8).

made—through what would amount to a philosophical critique of the possibility of law. The contemporary debate about the indeterminacy of rules is unfruitful because it fails so much as to encounter the classical idea of law; and so long as this debate continues to hold sway, the question becomes ever more urgent whether that idea, in the current jurisprudence of the legal academy, is in danger of being lost.

APPENDIX: A NOTE ON DECONSTRUCTION

1. The fact that Cornell's *Philosophy of the Limit* (1992) relies heavily on the thought of Jacques Derrida raises issues which deserve to be more carefully explored than the present context permits. Admittedly, Derrida's attitude toward traditional philosophical theses is more nuanced than my formulation, 'straightforward but false' (p. 58 above) suggests. (A significant difference between Derrida and his epigones often seems to lie in his willingness to affirm that a traditional philosophical thesis is not simply to be *opposed*—and thereby discarded.) None the less, the question remains whether Wittgenstein's and Derrida's thought can be harmoniously aligned in the manner Cornell, in the passage I quote, seems to suggest (Cornell 1992: 101–2). A reader who is appreciative of the intricacy of Derrida's thought may well feel that my criticism of this passage depends on my neglecting to take account of Cornell's philosophical motivations. Have I failed to appreciate Derrida's philosophical procedures? Perhaps so. But the purpose of this appendix is merely to provide such a reader with a brief sketch of how the questions I have raised about Cornell are questions that may be directed to deconstruction as well.

Consider the following statements:

> Deconstruction does not consist in moving from one concept to another, but in reversing and displacing a conceptual order . . . (Derrida 1988: 21).
>
> As I do philosophy, its entire task consists in expressing myself in such a way that certain troubles . . . disappear (Wittgenstein 1993: 181).

Both Wittgenstein and Derrida disavow philosophy's traditional constructive task and both seek to overcome certain ways of thinking that make this task seem imperative. Put another way, both continue on from Kant's sense of human reason facing an apparently compulsory but impossible task (Kant 1787: A vii). Cornell is right to find a likeness here. The likeness is what gives point to my question: what's the difference?

2. Part of Derrida's 'Signature Event Context' (1988) concerns a work that bears at least obvious affinities to Wittgenstein's thought: J. L. Austin's *How to Do Things with Words*.[80] Throughout this essay, Derrida is preoccupied with such questions as

[80] For this reason, 'Signature Event Context' is a salient starting-point for the questions I want to raise in this Appendix. It was the subject of an exchange between John Searle and Derrida

whether there is a concept of communication that is 'unique, univocal, rigorously controllable' (1988: 1), whether a context is ever 'absolutely determinable' (1988: 2; see also 14–15), and whether 'conscious intention' is 'totally present and immediately transparent to itself and to others' (1988: 18; see also 15). A negative answer to these questions is taken to problematize the notion of signature (and even to motivate the question 'Are there signatures?') since it follows from the considerations that support this answer that a sign must be 'detachable' from the intention and context of its origin. Austin had spoken of a signature as serving to 'tether' a written utterance to its origin (1975: 60–1). Since Derrida hears in this the assertion of an impossibly strong connection, he wishes to point out that 'in order for the tethering to the source to occur, what must be retained is the absolute singularity of a signature-event and a signature-form' (1988: 20). What must be retained doesn't make the right kind of room for the generality of a 'signifying form' and is therefore something doubtful.[81]

'Signature' here is only an example. The problem that concerns Derrida, more generally, is the relation between an utterance (an act of intending or meaning something) and its effects. One effect, when all goes well, is to communicate what is intended or meant. But a familiar philosophical question might be asked: what makes it the case that what is intended or meant is *this* and not *that*? On what basis can we distinguish effects that are internal to an utterance and mark its success from those that are mere consequences (and sometimes misfortunes). If I say 'Let's play a game of chess' and you start moving the pieces like checkers, I will say you misunderstand me—but by what right? Derrida thinks that Austin, in describing the conditions for the success of a (performative) utterance, relies on a suspect philosophical account of such matters, one that appeals to 'the conscious presence of the intention of the speaking subject . . . absolutely meaningful speech master of itself' (1988: 14, 15). The need for signatures to tether written utterances to their source, taken together with the doubtfulness of this tethering, illustrates for Derrida how it is generally with all utterances: their meaning cannot be secured by such a suspect notion of intention at their source.

An important question I cannot pursue here is whether Austin is asserting (e.g. in speaking of tethering) the metaphysically suspect thought of rigid connection that

over a decade ago. See Searle (1977). More recently, Stanley Cavell (1994: 53–127) has cast a complex light on the ways Derrida fails to reach Austin, while allowing that the differences between Derrida and Austin may well be—in the current state of philosophy's division—unsettleable (see 1994: 63). I owe a general debt to Cavell's discussion. It has helped me to see, much more clearly than I otherwise could have, how Derrida is involved in my topic. Other specific debts to Cavell are indicated in the following notes.

81 Derrida's idea about suspect 'singularity' seems to be that a 'signifying form' is the kind of thing whose recurrences can be recognized as 'the same' or as of the same 'type' (i.e. to identify a word as a particular object is not sufficient to identify it as a word). But it might be wondered: how are we so much as to imagine a 'tethering' of *utterances* that does not make room for this? But since this is also in a way Derrida's question, I am accepting such 'tethering', for present purposes, as representing a fantasy to which philosophy is prone. Derrida's analysis of the essential 'iterability' of the sign refers back to his early work on Husserl. Perhaps Condillac's—and originally Locke's—notion of words standing for ideas in the mind of the person using them would supply, in the terrain of early modern philosophy, a version of the relevant fantasy.

Derrida wishes to deny. Might not Austin mean something innocuous: that an utterance can be 'tethered' in the sense that ordinarily no doubt will arise about whose it is? Whatever the answer might be, my present purpose is served by assuming that *someone* (who Derrida calls 'Austin') is putting forward the metaphysical claim about signing that Derrida wishes to deny. What I want to focus on is the form that Derrida's denial of this suspect claim assumes: an invitation to feel the grip of a paradox.

Derrida's invitation has two main elements: (1) a commonplace; (2) the denial of the suspect philosophical claim. Thus consider: (1) Signatures function to make an act of meaning or intending something (a statement, a promise, an order) *mine*, that is, to identify a person as their source. We sign letters, contracts, deeds, drafts, and so on, and no doubt ordinarily arises as to what the effect will be: we have attached ourselves to what they say. (2) But for a sign to function as a sign it must be detachable from its origin; it cannot be 'tethered' in the metaphysically hard sense. Further acts of signing (a flock of them at the end of Derrida's essay calls attention to this) will not avail to secure the requisite connection: as with interpretations for securing the normative reach of rules, we have an unstoppable regress.[82] Now putting (1) and (2) together, it might be said that what makes the effects of signing possible is also what makes them impossible. And that is what Derrida says: 'The effects of signature are the most ordinary thing in the world. The condition of possibility of these effects is simultaneously, once again, the condition of their impossibility, of the impossibility of their rigorous purity' (1988: 20). Or rather, that is what he *seems to say* before adding the hedge 'of their rigorous purity'. The hedge softens, if it doesn't cancel, the suggestion of paradox. For in the end what is said to be possible—the everyday effects of signatures—and what is said to be impossible—*rigorously pure* effects—are not the same thing. Then why suggest the paradox in the first place?

The structure of the paradox, or of Derrida's suggestion of one, appears to be this: (1) The commonplace reminds us that something is possible. (2) The denial of the suspect claim tells us that what is supposed to make this something possible, its supposed foundation, is in fact impossible. But that isn't yet a paradox. There needs to be an additional thought, namely. (3) 'There *must*, none the less, be *something* that makes such commonplace things possible.' The paradox is now created by representing this enabling *something* as the *denial* or negation of the suspect claim, that is, by taking the enabling *something* to be just what is represented by (2). (The suspect claim had after all rendered the commonplace thing unintelligible—so the claim ought to be denied.) Thus, what makes the commonplace thing (e.g. signature) possible is now asserted to *be*: the impossibility of its supposed foundation (e.g. tethering, rigorous purity). The crucial significance of (3) is that it invites one to convert the mere denial of a foundation into a positive assertion of a 'condition of possibility'.

[82] As in Part I of my paper, a question here is how we are to take the regress. Multiple signing is like telling someone that you really mean it when you say that you mean what you say. Derrida seems impressed with the impotence of this. But why not see it as an obsessive assurance that corresponds to the sceptic's no-less obsessive kind of doubt? Then the possibility of the regress tells us no less about the nature of philosophical assurances than about the nature of philosophical doubt.

But the paradox depends, then, on something we should not take lightly, namely (3): 'There *must* be *something* that makes such commonplace things possible.' Must there? Without this thought all we have is the failure of a suspect attempt to provide a philosophical foundation for a commonplace. So it needs to be explained why the right conclusion to draw from the resulting paradox isn't just that we can do well enough without the excess baggage of this additional thought. One would have supposed, in any case, that the additional thought—which looks like a blanket demand for metaphysical foundations—is what *Derrida* wishes to refuse. Then is the point of the paradox just to get us to overcome the additional thought: to overcome the thought that philosophy must secure or ground, as if from a transcendent perspective, the things of our everyday experience? Then the point of the paradox, it might be said, is for the paradox to be thrown away.

3. Consider that one could construct a paradox along Derrida's lines concerning legal interpretation: '(1) In order for there to be a rule of law it must be possible to follow it in the particular case. (2) But for a rule to function as a rule, it must be interpretable. Can we so much as understand the notion of a rule which was *immune* to the possibility of interpretation? A rule that in every possible situation *must* be followed in just one way? Nothing under the philosophical sun—neither a "meaning" nor "intention" attaching a rule to its application—could *absolutely guarantee* this.[83] Nor could further rules or interpretive guide-lines eliminate the need for interpretation: we have an unstoppable regress.[84] The thought of a rule's immunity to interpretation—as if a super-hard rail connected it to its applications—renders rule-following unintelligible. So we may say—taking the invitation of (3)—that the impossibility of such immunity *is* what makes rule-following possible. Interpretation, in other words, is not something that besets the law from the outside but an internal condition of its very possibility. The mistake of traditional legal theory is to have *excluded* interpretation, to have treated it as a mere impurity. Of course, the effects of legal rules (determining the particular case) are the most ordinary thing in the world; we rely on them every day. The condition of the possibility of these effects is simultaneously the condition of their impossibility, of the impossibility of their rigorous purity.'

One could indeed represent matters like this. What Wittgenstein would like us to see is that there is nothing under the philosophical sun—nothing in the overturning of suspect notions of meaning or intention—that compels us to do so. It is a mark of Wittgenstein's thought—and an indication of its differences from Derrida's—that such paradoxes are not offered as philosophical conclusions (about 'conditions of possibility') but as moments in a dialectic that do not satisfy him.[85] Wittgenstein is commenting on this in a passage like the following: 'The concept of a perspicuous representation is of fundamental significance for us. It earmarks the form of account we give, the way we look at things' (PI, § 122).

[83] Starting with 'absolutely guarantee', the present paragraph uses several phrases from Derrida (1988).

[84] This is insisted on, along with the other points in this paragraph, by Fish, '*Fish* v. *Fiss*' in Fish (1989).

[85] Notice that the paradox about rule-following at PI, § 201 could easily be made into one of Derrida's: 'What makes determination by a rule possible', one could say, 'is the impossibility of securing the normative connection between a rule and what it requires.'

A mark of the form of account Wittgenstein seeks would be that it makes the philosophical problem 'disappear' (PI, § 133).[86] That does not mean that we are to stop thinking or to repress the problem, but to try to satisfy—in a way that the constructive doctrine initially demanded precisely does not—the urgent thoughts and feelings that gave rise to it. A picture Wittgenstein offers of this is of freeing our thinking from its own compulsions (cf. PI, §§ 133, 115). Of course not everyone struck by philosophy will want such freedom from it. Nor is there an uncontentious way—a way that does not go through such contentions as that the metaphysician's words have strayed from (hence depend on) their everyday use (PI, § 116)—to say why Wittgenstein makes this form of account 'fundamental'. But here all I wish to claim is this: these difficulties, formidable as they are, are also difficulties for Derrida. For they are difficulties about what is accomplished or achieved when everyday things such as signing or following rules are represented paradoxically in terms of conditions of possibility and impossibility. Indeed, in so far as Derrida (and Cornell) share Wittgenstein's suspicion of metaphysical philosophy, these appear to be aspects of the same difficulty.

The paradox (of transcendental conditions) earmarks Derrida's form of account, *his* way of looking at things. According to Cornell: '[Deconstruction] exposes the quasi-transcendental conditions that establish any system, including a legal system as a system. This exposure . . . demonstrates how the very establishment of the system as a system implies a beyond to it, precisely by virtue of what it excludes' (Cornell 1992: 1). The difficulty I am suggesting about 'what is accomplished' might be brought out by asking: Do we understand what Cornell's 'quasi' is supposed to add or subtract? It seems to express ambivalence about whether a deconstructive exposition is a further instance of traditional philosophy or not. If her point is that deconstruction is ambivalent in just this way (or that deconstruction *is* this ambivalence, the modern ambivalence of philosophy about itself), then the point offers little to quarrel with. But if in calling this an 'exposure', Cornell means that it uncovers a previously hidden fact—that what is exposed, then, is something other than the deconstructive way of representing things—that is something it does not seem easy to accept.

Consider again the 'indeterminacy thesis' Cornell attributes to Wittgenstein. It emerges elsewhere in her discussion when she brings forward the 'paradox' (1992: 133, 134) that the judge must appeal to rules yet—Cornell is here quoting Derrida—'each decision is different and requires an absolutely unique interpretation, which no existing, coded rule can or ought to guarantee absolutely' (1992: 133). It would be to Wittgenstein's purpose to ask: What do we understand this to mean? Do unconditional lifetime warranties (for example) 'guarantee absolutely'? If backed by further warranties? If not, do these words have some other use for us? If not, is Derrida saying anything? Or have his words gone astray? Like 'rigorous purity' with

[86] But compare Wittgenstein (1994: 185–7): 'As long as there is a verb "to be" which seems to function like "to eat" and "to drink", as long as there are adjectives like "identical", "true", "false", "possible" . . . humans will continue to bump up against the same mysterious difficulties, and stare at something that no explanations seem able to remove.' The idea of the philosophical problem 'completely disappearing' (PI, § 133), as I read it, is of philosophy's being satisfactorily brought to an end not once and for all but for the enduring moment—until philosophical perplexity arises again.

respect to signatures, the 'fact'—if that it is what it is—that a rule cannot 'guarantee absolutely' would presumably not challenge the commonplace that there are everyday—say, good enough—guarantees. Do we need more?[87] Would Derrida reply that 'guarantee absolutely' is philosophically autonomous (resting, if not on the ground or in a heaven of concepts, on itself) and so not in need of being brought back to its everyday use ('what *we* do')?[88] But if metaphysics, as the exposure of limiting conditions of possibility, is autonomous in this way, then the only deconstruction that could be relevant to it would itself belong to it as (more) metaphysics. Derrida may be saying as much. For Wittgenstein, this would mean that deconstruction is a further instance of philosophy's constructive ambition and not suitable for overcoming it.

Take as another instance of Cornell's interest in representing things paradoxically her assertion (drawing on Derrida on Levinas) that 'the possibility of the ethical lies in its impossibility'. This 'paradoxical formulation', she says, is 'necessary' if the ethical is not to be 'reduced to the actual' (1992: 83). Again, I do not doubt that a certain (transcendental) sense of the ethical *can* be conveyed like this, nor that there is considerable philosophical intelligence in it. But in declaring this way of conceiving the ethical to be 'necessary'—one of philosophy's requirements—I wonder if Cornell isn't cultivating blindness to the nature of the philosophical possibilities.[89]

[87] Concerning his own apparent denial of such 'absolute guarantees' as the sceptic seems to demand, Wittgenstein asks: 'What gives the impression that we want to deny anything?' (PI, § 305). For what is destroyed when philosophy punctures metaphysical demands is 'nothing but castles in the air [Luftgebäude]' (PI, § 118): i.e. nothing that was inhabitable in the first place, nothing that (when recognized without displacement) will be missed. (Cavell calls this a picture of philosophy's destructiveness. See 1994: 75–7.) Wittgenstein's picture occurs in the Preface of Kant's *Metaphysics of Morals* (1991: 38). It also refigures—both in its suggestion that philosophy destroys only fantasies and in its accompanying question about philosophy's 'importance'—the following remark from Kant's second edition Preface of the *Critique of Pure Reason*: 'Notwithstanding this important change in the field of the sciences, and the loss of its fancied possessions which speculative reason must suffer, general human interests remain in the same privileged position as hitherto, and the advantages which the world has hitherto derived from the teachings of pure reason are in no way diminished. The loss affects only the *monopoly of the schools*, in no respect the *interests of humanity*' (1787: B xxxi–xxxii). Kant is referring here to what emerges at the end of the *First Critique* as two concepts of philosophy: a *Schulbegriff* and a *Weltbegriff* (1787: A 838/B 866–A 840/B 868). One way of characterizing Wittgenstein's sense of philosophy's destructiveness might thus be to say: philosophy makes apparent that philosophy (as *Schulbegriff*) doesn't exist. In fact, Kant says as much himself: 'It sounds arrogant . . . to assert that before the coming of the critical philosophy there was as yet no philosophy at all. In order to decide about this apparent presumption, it need but be asked *whether there could really be more than one philosophy*' (1991: 36; original emphasis). Wittgenstein and Derrida appear to have different 'presumptions' about philosophy's existence, or to have different senses of where the initial presumption should lie: for Derrida, metaphysics is to be deconstructed; for Wittgenstein it has yet to make a prima facie case for itself. But this deserves closer attention than I can give it here.

[88] This is specifically Cavell's suggestion about how to frame the issue between Derrida and Wittgenstein: '[t]he question is as to the autonomy of metaphysical philosophy, of the direction of the burden of proof of its existence' (1994: 119). It is the question I put later of whether Derrida's characteristic assertions that we *can't* have something (e.g. 'an absolute guarantee') are genuinely intelligible—as opposed to something we only imagine we understand.

[89] Cornell may mean only that this paradoxical formulation is 'necessary' from where Derrida stands. A point at which to study other possibilities would be Wittgenstein's remark in the *Tractatus* that 'it is impossible for there to be propositions of ethics' (1961: 6.42). That is a

She is, in any case, begging the question I wish to raise about Wittgenstein's and Derrida's respective forms of account, and declining to take such opportunities as Wittgenstein would afford to think about the motivations of the form of account Derrida has 'mirrored' for her (1992: p. x). Is there a reason why she *should* take those opportunities? Perhaps not. A careful reading of Wittgenstein's *Investigations* would have been an obstacle to her conclusions about legal rules; and her immersion in deconstruction was already sufficient for Wittgenstein's text to drop out of view, its content becoming something she had merely glimpsed through Derrida. The costs (or benefits) of this can only be measured in terms of Cornell's own aspirations. As I read her, she wants to speak not just to those who already feel at home with Derrida's practice of philosophy, but also to legal theorists in the tradition stemming from H. L. A. Hart's *The Concept of Law*. Wittgenstein was bound to come up for her because he is already present in this tradition.[90] That Cornell finds this tradition naïve (in need of her kind of exposure) concerning the 'indeterminacy' of legal rules shows, as I have argued, her failure to encounter it.

4. Wittgenstein's response to a philosophical demand for 'meaning' to secure (or 'guarantee') the normative reach of rules is central to Part I of my paper. The point is that we can come to see the demand for security as unsatisfiable—that is, as having nothing that would satisfy it—without threat to what is expressed in our everyday talk of accord with a rule. The possibility of normative 'accord' is not peculiar to rules, however. Intentions, expectations, wishes (and thoughts in general) are all things that 'reach' into the world: they are things with which certain objects, events, actions, or states of affairs may or may not be 'in accord'. Hence the sceptical problem of securing a 'connection' (generally speaking between thought and the world) comes up, for Wittgenstein, in a number of forms:

> What kind of super-strong connexion exists between the act of intending and the thing intended? (PI, § 97)
>
> A wish seems already to know what will or would satisfy it; a proposition, a thought, what makes it true—even when that thing is not there at all! Whence this *determining* of what is not yet there? This despotic demand? (PI, § 437)

What Derrida has in common with Wittgenstein is an attempt to refuse the suspect metaphysical picture of thought that makes these questions seem compelling. Because of this point in common, we can at least clearly see Cornell's Derridian picture of Wittgenstein as a mis-recognition of *Wittgenstein*.

Where then lies the difference? I will put things now in a more pointed way, one that shows the direction from which I approach this philosophical divide.

Derrida does not countenance the possibility that his paradoxes are to be thrown

remark that might be turned in Derrida's deconstructive direction: 'So the possibility of ethics (as intelligible propositions, maxims, laws, etc.) is its impossibility', etc. I take it that a proper understanding of how the remark is meant to function in the *Tractatus* turns on an appreciation of how the reader is to be brought to a point at which he is able to throw such a remark away. For a helpful account, see Diamond (1991*b*).

[90] On Hart's indebtedness to both Wittgenstein and J. L. Austin, see Hart (1993: 1–6, 274–7). For an elaboration of some ways Wittgenstein is present in Hart's text, see Marmor (1992: 124–54); Bix (1993: 7–76).

away (see sect. 2 above). Admittedly, he is more complicated than many of his followers who do not countenance this possibility either. (A definition of a follower of Derrida, a 'deconstructivist' so-called, might be: someone who does not countenance this possibility.[91]) To throw the paradoxes away would be to see them as exposing nothing but philosophy's own fantasies. Perhaps some 'deconstructivists' do see them that way. But if they don't, what do they think deconstruction 'exposes'?

As I see it, the paradox invites us to think that, in undermining a suspect metaphysical picture of thought, our rational entitlement to everyday notions which had seemed to depend on this picture come under threat. I am not saying that I imagine Derrida feeling the tug of philosophical scruples when he says such serviceable everyday things as 'I was hoping you would call' or 'No, I meant the other brand of tuna', and so on. None the less, I think his invitation is seriously meant, as if in opposition to what may sometimes seem genuinely threatening in our everyday world—its thoughtlessness or naïvety. (This is merely to touch, inadequately, on the question of what gives deconstruction its evident sense of importance and ethical seriousness.)[92]

No complacency toward our everyday space of reasons need be involved, however, for us to decline the invitation on the following specific grounds: *this* way of calling our everyday notions into question is only attractive if we think that the metaphysical picture being undermined is something which we can genuinely make intelligible to ourselves in the first place. Only then does it seem that to undermine the suspect picture is to *deny* something, or does it come to look as if there is *something* that must be denied (e.g. a foundation for notions like 'signing' or 'following a rule' that is beyond attainment). Consider again one of Derrida's characteristic assertions to the effect that an 'absolute' or 'pure' something-or-other isn't possible: '[A] context is never absolutely determinable . . . its determination can never be entirely certain or saturated' (1988: 3). We can stop here and ask: 'But how "never absolutely determinable"? Are we acquainted with things that are "absolutely determinable" only a context is not one of them?'[93] If we can indeed draw on such an acquaintance, Derrida's remark would be an agreeable (or disagreeable) statement about contexts akin to, say 'Mountains in Vermont are never larger than . . .' But if all such acquaintance fails us, the remark, though offered in denial of a metaphysical picture, is bound to look like a recoil into an equally suspect metaphysical picture (something about which there is no agreement—or disagreement). In short, whatever difficulties stand in the way, on Derrida's own account, of giving application to the idea of an 'absolutely determinable context', should lead us to

[91] It may be that followers of Derrida, like followers of Wittgenstein, face the problem of how a work that defines its success in terms of the autonomy of the reader's thought is to be followed. This aim led Wittgenstein to 'doubtful feelings' (PI, p. viii) about the success of his own work.

[92] The same question can and should be asked (also at more length) about Wittgenstein's thought. When Wittgenstein himself asks it, he speaks of a change in our sense of value or importance, for example, our coming to see how little is achieved when philosophical problems are solved. See e.g. Wittgenstein (1961: 3–5); PI, § 118. That is also a kind of exposure—of false need or importance.

[93] Cf. PI, § 339. On the problem of philosophical recoil—apparently compelling us to deny something we don't understand in the first place—see also §§ 251, 305, 308.

question whether we have any clear idea of what it is that 'can never be'. (Indeed, if the sceptic's 'can never be' (e.g. certain, known, guaranteed)—this irremedial absence—becomes acute enough, the result may naturally be more philosophical oscillation: a new constructive attempt to shore up the connection between thought and the world.)

It can look as if this way of declining the paradox involves the thought that 'absolute' something-or-others are simply beyond the limits of what we can talk about. So it bears emphasizing that there is nothing wrong with the *words* 'absolutely determinable' or 'guarantee absolutely' or 'rigorous purity'. The words might be put to perfectly good work. For example, I might explain that for an extra $100 you can upgrade the 'standard guarantee' to the 'absolute guarantee': this covers the product not just against negligent manufacturing defects but against all defects and against accidental breakage as well. Or I might say: 'To win a medal the Canadian skater's triple toe-loops are going to have to be "rigorously pure", meaning that the following points will have to observed . . .' Or I might say that in '$x + 1 = y$' y is 'absolutely determinable' for any value of x, whereas in '$x = y^2$' it is not. But where these expressions do not refer to such cases (i.e. in philosophy), we may simply come to see them as unsuitable for our purposes. We may come to see them as a means for remaining in a state of confusion (cf. PI, § 339). Of course our purposes may lie in confusion: in supposing ourselves to grasp Derrida's use of these words to mark the limits of possibility, we may have the illusion that we are peering, however dimly, precisely beyond those limits; and that may have its satisfactions. But the way out of such confusion, if we want it, is just to find a more suitable way of describing things: one that allows us to stop feeling that we must either secure or deny the metaphysical foundation. That amounts to seeing the purported foundation as an illusory one (i.e. there is nothing to be secured or denied).

Does Derrida disagree with this? It may be that this is his very point.[94] But if the point is acknowledged then nothing—except the lingering spell of metaphysical illusion—compels the move Derrida wishes to make from the thought that a signature must be, in principle, detachable from its source to the paradoxical-sounding conclusion that 'the condition of possibility of [a signature's] effects is . . . the condition of their impossibility, of the impossibility of their rigorous purity' (1988: 20). Rather than accepting this conclusion as it stands, the way is open to ask what has led Derrida to conflate 'the impossibility' of a signature's effects with 'the impossibility of their rigorous purity'. Does Derrida suppose that our purchase on our everyday talk of signatures depends on our being able to have recourse to the suspect metaphysical picture of 'rigorous purity' he rejects?[95] What but the persisting

[94] See esp. Derrida (1988: 115 ff.).

[95] Note that Wittgenstein's way of overcoming an idea of 'crystalline purity' (PI, § 108) reverses the relation: his image of 'bringing words back' (PI, § 116) is an image of metaphysics depending, for its apparent intelligibility, on the work our words do for us everyday. That signing (like any intentional act) is subject to various kinds of failure, is, from this point of view, a commonplace. In the law, for example, a notion of 'intention' is employed that no one imagines to be controlling of the effects or normative significance of action. (Thus, lawyers speak of responsibility for unintended consequences of action: the field of torts.) And even where intention does control the significance of action, as in much of criminal law, it does so alongside a doctrine of 'excuses' (the subject of a paper of Austin's, 'A Plea for Excuses') which would appear richly to conceptualize nothing if not the possibility that the normative effects

grip of this very metaphysical picture could lead Derrida to suggest that we have something less than everything we could intelligibly want unless a signature could be made out to be 'tethered' (i.e. by some extraordinary means) to its source, secured against the possibility of detachment? The same question may be asked, *mutatis mutandis*, about the deconstructive treatment of legal rules and its corresponding dissatisfaction with the idea that a rule can determine the particular case without the mediation of interpretation.

Naturally, these very questions could be restated as paradoxes. In a sense, they are precisely *the* paradoxes of metaphysical philosophy, as Wittgenstein represented it in his early philosophical work: '[i]n order to be able to set a limit to thought, we should have to find both sides of the limit thinkable (i.e. we should have to be able to think what cannot be thought)' (1961: 3). But for Wittgenstein this calls not for more paradoxes but for a (dare one say *deconstructive?*) diagnosis of how we come into these philosophical difficulties: how do we come to feel that our grasp of the notion of a signature's effects demands that we make sense of the requirements imposed by a suspect picture of 'tethering'? Or that our grasp of the notion of accord with a rule demands that we make sense of similar pictures of super-strong connection? That will also be how we come to feel so much as a slip in our grasp when these demands are disappointed. The temptation to lay down new philosophical requirements, on this view, lies deep within us. So there is no call here to assume that satisfaction is to be gained through something less than interminable analysis. To so much as get off the ground, a shift in focus is needed. But we will think philosophy's paradoxes are its required conclusions only if we fail to see that there is another direction in which we might turn.

REFERENCES

AUSTIN, J. L. (1962), *Sense and Sensibilia* (Oxford: Oxford University Press).

—— (1975), *How to Do Things with Words*, 2nd edn. (Cambridge, Mass.: Harvard University Press).

BIX, B. (1993), *Law, Language, and Legal Determinacy* (Oxford: Oxford University Press).

BURTON, S. J. (1985), *An Introduction to Law and Legal Reasoning* (Boston: Little Brown and Co.).

—— (1992), *Judging in Good Faith* (Cambridge: Cambridge University Press).

CALABRESI, G. (1975), 'Concerning Cause and the Law of Torts: An Essay for Harry Kalven, Jr.', 69 *University of Chicago Law Review*, 69–108.

CAVELL, S. (1979), *The Claim of Reason: Wittgenstein, Skepticism, Morality and Tragedy* (Oxford: Oxford University Press).

—— (1990), *Conditions Handsome and Unhandsome: The Constitution of Emersonian Perfectionism* (Chicago: University of Chicago Press).

of action may be 'impure'. Cavell (1994: 53–127) points out the absence of this paper from Derrida's discussion and brings it to bear—as it should—at several points.

—— (1994), *A Pitch of Philosophy* (Cambridge, Mass.: Harvard University Press).

—— (1995), *Philosophical Passages: Wittgenstein, Emerson, Austin, Derrida* (Oxford: Blackwell).

Conant, J. (1993), 'The Search for Logically Alien Thought: Descartes, Kant, Frege, and the *Tractatus*', 20 *Philosophical Topics*, 115–80.

Cooter, R. and Ulen, T. (1988), *Law and Economics* (Glenview, Ill.: Scott, Foresman).

Cornell, D. (1992), *The Philosophy of the Limit* (New York: Routledge & Kegan Paul).

D'Amato, A. (1990), 'Pragmatic Indeterminacy', 85 *Northwestern University Law Review*, 148–89.

Dallmayr, F. (1992), 'Hermeneutics and the Rule of Law', in G. Leyh (ed.), *Legal Hermeneutics: History, Theory and Practice* (Berkeley: University of California Press).

Dascal, M. and Wroblewski, J. (1988), 'Transparency and Doubt', 7 *Law and Philosophy*, 203–24.

Derrida, J. (1988), *Limited Inc.* (Evanston, Ill.: Northwestern University Press).

Diamond, C. (1989), 'Rules: Looking in the Right Place', in D. Z. Phillips and P. Winch (eds.), *Wittgenstein: Attention to Particulars* (Basingstoke: McMillan).

—— (1991*a*), *The Realistic Spirit: Wittgenstein, Philosophy and the Mind* (Cambridge, Mass.: MIT Press).

—— (1991*b*), 'Ethics, Imagination and the Method of Wittgenstein's *Tractatus*', in R. Heinrich and H. Vetter (eds.), *Bilder der Philosophie*, 5 *Wiener Reihe*, 55–90.

Dworkin, R. (1977), *Taking Rights Seriously* (London: Duckworth).

—— (1986), *Law's Empire* (London: Fontana Press).

Fish, S. (1980), *Is There a Text in This Class: The Authority of Interpretive Communities* (Cambridge, Mass.: Harvard University Press).

—— (1989), *Doing What Comes Naturally: Change, Rhetoric, and the Practice of Theory in Literary and Legal Studies* (Durham: Duke University Press).

Foucault, M. (1980), 'On Popular Justice: A Discussion with Maoists', in C. Gordon (ed.), *Power/Knowledge: Selected Interviews and Other Writings 1972–1977* (New York: Pantheon Books).

Frank, J. (1963), *Law and the Modern Mind*, 2nd edn. (Gloucester, Mass.: Peter Smith).

Fuller, L. (1958), 'Positivism and Fidelity to Law: A Reply to Professor Hart', 71 *Harvard Law Review*, 630–72.

—— (1978), 'Forms and Limits of Adjudication', 92 *Harvard Law Review*, 353–409.

Goldfarb, W. (1983), 'I Want You to Bring Me a Slab: Remarks on the Opening Sections of the *Philosophical Investigations*', 56 *Synthese*, 265–82.

Green, L. (1928), 'The Negligence Issue', 37 *Yale Law Journal*, 1029–47.

Grey, T. C. (1989), 'Holmes and Legal Pragmatism', 89 *Stanford Law Review*, 787–870.

Hart, H. L. A. (1961), *The Concept of Law* (Oxford: Clarendon Press).

—— (1983), *Essays in Jurisprudence and Philosophy* (Oxford: Oxford University Press).

Hegel, G. W. F. (1821), *Philosophy of Right*, trans. H. B. Nisbet, ed. A. W. Wood (Cambridge: Cambridge University Press, 1991).

HOLMES, O. W. (1963), *The Common Law*, ed. Mark DeWolfe Howe (Cambridge, Mass.: Harvard University Press).

HUTCHINSON, A. (ed.) (1989), *Critical Legal Studies* (New Jersey: Rowman and Littlefield).

KAIRYS, D. (1984), 'Law and Politics', 57 *George Washington Law Review*, 243–62.

KANT, I. (1787), *Critique of Pure Reason*, trans. Norman Kemp Smith (New York: St Martin's Press, 1965).

—— (1991), *The Metaphysics of Morals*, trans. Mary Gregor (Cambridge: Cambridge University Press).

KENNEDY, D. (1973), 'Legal Formality', 2 *Journal of Legal Studies*, 351–98.

KRIPKE, S. A. (1982), *Wittgenstein: On Rules and Private Language* (Oxford: Blackwell).

LEVI, E. H. (1949), *An Introduction to Legal Reasoning* (Chicago: University of Chicago Press).

LYONS, D. (1984), 'Justification and Judicial Responsibility', 72 *California Law Review*, 178–99.

—— (1993), 'Legal Formalism and Instrumentalism—A Pathological Study', in *Moral Aspects of Legal Theory: Essays on Law, Justice and Political Responsibility* (Cambridge: Cambridge University Press), 41–63.

McDOWELL, J. (1981), 'Non-Cognitivism and Rule-Following', in S. Holtzman and C. Leich (eds.), *Wittgenstein: To Follow a Rule* (London: Routledge & Kegan Paul), 141–62.

—— (1984), 'Wittgenstein on Following a Rule', 58 *Synthese*, 325–63.

—— (1992), 'Meaning and Intentionality in Wittgenstein's Later Philosophy', 17 *Midwest Studies in Philosophy*, 40–52.

MARMOR, A. (1992), *Interpretation and Legal Theory* (Oxford: Clarendon Press).

MORRIS, C. (1952), 'Duty, Negligence, and Causation', 101 *University of Pennsylvania Law Review*, 189–222.

MULLER, I. (1991), *Hitler's Justice: The Courts of the Third Reich*, trans. D. L. Schneider (Cambridge, Mass.: Harvard University Press).

OAKESHOTT, M. (1975), 'The Vocabulary of a Modern European State (Part II)', 23 *Political Studies*, 409–14.

PATTERSON, D. (1990), 'Law's Pragmatism: Law as Practice and Narrative', 76 *Virginia Law Review*, 937–96.

PLATO (1984), *Plato's Statesman: Part III of The Being of the Beautiful*, trans. S. Benardete (Chicago: University of Chicago Press).

PUTNAM, H. (1991), 'Does the Disquotational Theory Really Solve All Philosophical Problems?', 22 *Metaphilosophy*, 1–13.

RADIN, M. J. (1989), 'Reconsidering the Rule of Law', 69 *Boston University Law Review*, 781–819.

RHEES, R. (1970), *Discussions of Wittgenstein* (London: Routledge & Kegan Paul).

SCHAUER, F. (1988), 'Formalism', 97 *Yale Law Journal*, 509–48.

—— (1991), *Playing by the Rules: A Philosophical Examination of Rule-Based Decision-Making in Law and in Life* (Oxford: Oxford University Press).

SILVER, C. (1987), 'Elmer's Case: A Legal Positivist Replies to Dworkin', 6 *Law and Philosophy*, 381–99.

STONE, M. J. (1991), 'The Placement of Politics in Roberto Unger's *Politics*', in R. Post (ed.), *Law and the Order of Culture* (Berkeley: University of California Press), 78–108.

TUSHNET, M. V. (1988), 'Following the Rules Laid Down: A Critique of Interpretivism and Neutral Principles', in S. Levinson and S. Mailloux (eds.), *Interpreting Law and Literature: A Hermeneutic Reader* (Evanston, Ill.: Northwestern University Press), 193–214.

UNGER, R. M. (1986), *The Critical Legal Studies Movement* (Cambridge, Mass.: Harvard University Press).

—— (1987), *Social Theory: Its Situation and Its Task* (Cambridge: Cambridge University Press).

WEINRIB, E. J. (1995), *The Idea of Private Law* (Cambridge, Mass.: Harvard University Press).

WITTGENSTEIN, L. (1958*a*), *Philosophical Investigations*, trans. G. E. M. Anscombe (Oxford: Blackwell).

—— (1958*b*), *The Blue and the Brown Books* (New York: Harper & Row).

—— (1961), *Tractatus Logico-Philosophicus*, trans. D. F. Pears and B. F. McGuiness (London: Routledge & Kegan Paul).

—— (1978), *Remarks on the Foundations of Mathematics*, ed. G. H. von Wright, R. Rhees, and G. E. M. Anscombe, trans. G. E. M. Anscombe (Cambridge, Mass.: MIT Press).

—— (1979), *On Certainty*, ed. G. E. M. Anscombe and G. H. von Wright, trans. D. Paul and G. E. M. Anscombe (Oxford: Blackwell).

—— (1980), *Culture and Value*, ed. G. H. Von Wright, trans. P. Winch (Chicago: University of Chicago Press).

—— (1993), 'Big Typescript Sections 86–93', in J. Klagge and A. Nordmann (eds.), *Philosophical Occasions: 1912–1951* (Indianapolis: Hackett Publishing Company), 100–99.

WRIGHT, C. (1989), 'Wittgenstein's Rule-Following Considerations and the Central Project of Theoretical Linguistics', in A. George (ed.), *Reflections on Chomsky* (Oxford: Blackwell).

3
Interpretation and Methodology in Legal Theory

STEPHEN R. PERRY

INTRODUCTION

At some point almost every major work in jurisprudence discusses issues of methodology, and often these seem to be the most difficult and intractable questions in the subject. Why should this be? Does jurisprudence raise special methodological problems that other disciplines do not face? Because law is both a social and a normative phenomenon, there is good reason for thinking that it does. In stating that law is both social and normative, I mean to say that it is a social institution that also systematically gives rise (or at least is perceived to give rise) to reasons for action. Now it is, of course, possible to study the reason-giving aspects of social practices from a purely philosophical perspective. One task of political philosophy, for example, is to describe ideal political practices, and to determine whether and under what circumstances they would affect people's reasons for action (usually by creating obligations for them). Similarly, it is possible to study social institutions from a purely descriptive perspective, without reference to anyone's reasons for action (or at least this is possible according to one school of thought in the social sciences). Some branches of sociology attempt to study law in this way. Jurisprudence gives rise to special methodological problems because it has both philosophical and descriptive aspirations; it attempts both to analyse the reason-giving dimension of social practices and at the same time to give a descriptively accurate characterization of an existing type of social institution. As a discipline jurisprudence claims, in effect, to be both a branch of practical philosophy (by which I mean the philosophy of practical reason), and a social science of a certain kind. The special problems of methodology it faces arise from this juxtaposition.[1]

 I am indebted to Brian Leiter both for extensive discussion of the arguments in this essay and for very helpful comments on an earlier draft. I have also benefited from comments received at a faculty seminar at the University of San Diego Law School. Work on the essay was supported by a research grant from the Social Sciences and Humanities Research Council of Canada.

[1] Cf. Gerald J. Postema, 'The Normativity of Law', in Ruth Gavison (ed.), *Issues in Contemporary Legal Philosophy: The Influence of H. L. A. Hart* (Oxford: Clarendon Press, 1987), 81, at 81.

Considered as a branch of practical philosophy, jurisprudence must deal with the following fundamental question: what kind of reasons for action, if any, can social practices give rise to? In the background, however, are a host of other questions. What, in general, is a reason for action? Are there moral as well as prudential reasons for action? Can social practices give people moral reasons that they would not independently have? The relevance of these and related questions, which are essentially philosophical in nature, will depend on the substantive claims of particular jurisprudential theories.

Considered as a social science, jurisprudence must deal with the problems of methodology that arise in the social sciences generally, including the following two questions. First, should social science employ the same methodology as natural science, or does it require a methodology of its own? According to one school of thought, with roots in scientific positivism, social phenomena can be adequately studied and explained by means of the same kinds of causal inquiries that characterize the natural sciences. According to another school of thought, with roots in the hermeneutic tradition in philosophy, we can only adequately understand a social practice by seeing it from the participants' point of view, from the inside. This is, in the hermeneutic tradition, the notion of *verstehen*. The second question of methodology in the social sciences with which jurisprudence must come to grips is this. Are social theories purely descriptive and value-free in nature, or do they necessarily involve evaluative or normative elements? The *special* problems jurisprudence faces as a discipline arise from the fact that it must respond to these two methodological questions within the framework of a necessarily philosophical account of how, if at all, law can give rise to reasons for action.

One might well wonder whether a single discipline can do all that seems to be expected of jurisprudence. One of the reasons why H. L. A. Hart's book *The Concept of Law*[2] is so justly renowned is that Hart attempted, within the bounds of a single theory, both to resolve the methodological questions that jurisprudence has inherited from the social sciences, and at the same time to show how and why law is a normative phenomenon. The key to both the methodological and normative questions, according to Hart, is 'the internal point of view'.[3] This is an application of the notion of *verstehen* mentioned earlier. In later work Hart described the methodological role that the internal point of view is supposed to play in legal theory in the following

[2] H. L. A. Hart, *The Concept of Law* (Oxford: Clarendon Press, 1961).

[3] Ibid., at 55–6, 82–8. In formulating the idea of the internal point of view, Hart cites Peter Winch, *The Idea of a Social Science* (London: Routledge & Kegan Paul, 1958). Winch held a particularly strong version of the *verstehen* thesis, according to which the theorist's perspective has to be the same as that of the participants. As we shall see later, Hart rejects this view, which I call the strong internalist thesis.

way: 'For the understanding of [not only law but any other form of normative social structure] the methodology of the empirical sciences is useless; what is needed is a "hermeneutic" method which involves portraying rule-governed behaviour as it appears to its participants, who see it as conforming or failing to conform to certain shared standards.'[4] Hart further argued that when participants as a group see their behaviour as rule-governed in this way—when, in other words, their behaviour has the appropriate 'internal aspect'—then they actually come under obligations of a certain kind, albeit not moral obligations. This was Hart's solution to the problem of the normativity of law.

It should be emphasized that, although Hart held that the methods of the empirical sciences cannot be applied to 'normative social structures', he was not rejecting the possibility that such structures could be the subject of a descriptive theory. On the contrary, he treated accurate description of social practices as one of the objects of the exercise. The claim was that such description requires, in the case of certain kinds of practice, reference to the subjects' own point of view. Thus, in the Preface to *The Concept of Law* Hart maintained that the book could be regarded as 'an essay in decriptive sociology'.[5] In more recent work he has similarly written that, while an analysis of what it is for a community to have an effective customary rule must utilize the internal point of view, the analysis will none the less be descriptive and not normative or justificatory in character.[6] Hart thus answered the two methodological questions inherited from the social sciences as follows. First, jurisprudence does require a distinct methodology of its own, which is based on the idea of the internal point of view. Secondly, the resulting theories about the nature of law are purely descriptive in character.

The general idea of the internal point of view is that an adequate jurisprudential account of law must at some point take into consideration how the practice looks to at least some of the practice's participants, from the inside. The theorist must in that sense 'interpret' the practice, so that the resulting methodology can appropriately be called 'interpretivist'. This term is also a natural one in light of the hermeneutic roots of Hart's methodological approach. Let me label the claim that an adequate jurisprudential account of at least certain kinds of social practice must refer to the point of view of some or all of the practice's participants as the 'internalist' thesis. Notice that the internalist thesis is not equivalent to the claim that the theorist's point of view must be the *same* as that of the participants. This latter claim, which I shall call the 'strong internalist' thesis, has been defended by Ronald

[4] H. L. A. Hart, *Essays in Jurisprudence and Philosophy* (Oxford: Clarendon Press, 1983), Introduction, at 13.

[5] Hart, *supra*, n. 2, at vii.

[6] H. L. A. Hart, 'Comment', in Gavison (ed.), *supra*, n. 1, 35, at 39. Such an analysis of customary rules lies, of course, at the heart of *The Concept of Law*.

Dworkin in *Law's Empire*.[7] Hart, as we shall see, explicitly rejects the stronger thesis.

The most appropriate understanding of the internalist thesis, I shall argue, holds that a theorist studying law and similar social practices must be able to understand how the practice could be regarded by its participants as creating *reasons for action* for them. This is the essential first step in reconciling the social and normative aspects of jurisprudence. If the internalist thesis is understood in this way, then there is a very good case to be made for treating the internal point of view as the methodological key to jurisprudence. But some interesting and perhaps surprising conclusions follow from this construal of the internalist thesis. One is that Hart himself misuses the notion of the internal point of view in his critique of the theories of law advanced by Austin and Holmes. Holmes's 'bad man' conception of law is as much concerned with reasons for action created by law as is Hart's version of positivism, and it too makes use of an 'internal point of view'. Holmes may have been wrong about the nature of law, but not because he observed it from a purely external perspective. The true basis of Hart's claim that his theory of law is superior to a theory like Holmes's turns out to be his unobtrusive and almost unnoticed invocation of a notion of the 'function' of law.

In fact, most minimally plausible theories of law invoke a similar notion of the value, point, or function of law. Hart's theory attributes a function to law from the point of view of the theorist, rather than from the point of view of the participants within the practice. While there is room in jurisprudence for such a methodology, it is in a number of respects unsatisfactory. The most important problem is that it effectively abandons the ambition of jurisprudence to explain the normativity of law. As we shall see, Hart's own solution to the problem of normativity fails, and his limited interpretivist methodology does not possess sufficient resources to permit the formulation of alternative accounts. The difficulty, I shall suggest, is that Hart's version of the internalist thesis is too weak. In order to offer an adequate explanation of the normativity of law, the theorist must ascribe a point or function to law from the *participants'* point of view. But to take this tack amounts to steering jurisprudential methodology much closer to Dworkin's version of interpretivism, and, in particular, towards a form of the strong internalist thesis. In this essay I only sketch the further consequences for jurisprudence, rather than develop them in detail. But one such consequence that deserves mention is that the most satisfactory jurisprudential theories turn out not to be purely descriptive and value-free, as Hart claimed.

[7] Ronald Dworkin, *Law's Empire* (Cambridge, Mass.: Harvard University Press, 1986), at 14: 'This book takes up the internal, participants' point of view; it tries to grasp the argumentative character of our legal practice by joining that practice and struggling with the issues of soundness and truth participants face.'

My main object in the essay is not, however, to demonstrate in detail how to turn Hart into Dworkin. It is simply to make the point that, despite the many disagreements between the two theorists, not least at the methodological level, the seeds of Dworkin's strong version of interpretivism were sown by Hart himself.

I shall begin by discussing Hart's own formulation and defence of the internal point of view. Before doing so, however, it is necessary to deal with a preliminary objection to the very possibility of an interpretivist methodology in jurisprudence. Michael Moore has argued that the only defensible form of interpretivism is based on the idea that it is sometimes rationally justifiable to treat an utterance, practice, or some other kind of entity as an authoritative 'text'. This is less mysterious than it sounds. Moore, who labels this understanding of interpretivism 'modest', describes the notion as follows: 'Modestly interpretive activities presuppose some theory that justifies why particular decisions are warranted by some preexisting text.'[8] R. L. Schwartz makes a related point when he states that authoritative texts provide 'sources of norms and standards of action'.[9] In other words, to treat something as an 'authoritative text' is to treat it as a source of reasons for action. Such treatment is justified when, *inter alia*, there is in fact good reason for regarding the text as giving rise to reasons for action. Candidates for texthood range from sacred writings in religion to dreams in the field of psychoanalysis, and to constitutions and statutes in law. Modest interpretivism is a non-explanatory rather than a descriptive enterprise, because it involves a type of *activity* in which one can engage when there is some point or value to doing so. There will be such a point when one has a justification for treating the potential text as authoritiative in the sense explained.

Moore argues that while *law* may in some respects be a modestly interpretive activity, the same cannot be said of *jurisprudence*. This is because the legal theorist has no justification for treating either particular laws or some more general aspect of legal practice, such as the activities of judges, as an authoritative text: these would-be texts cannot serve the legal theorist as sources of reasons for action, or at least they cannot do so with respect to her project of doing legal theory.[10] For similar reasons Dworkin's strong version of the internalist thesis must also be rejected: 'As legal theorists, we need not be committed to some internal point of view such as that of a judge: Texts like statutes that are authoritative for judges, lawyers and citizens need not be authoritative for us *qua* legal theorists.'[11] Since there is no other acceptable understanding of interpretation, the upshot, according to

[8] Michael S. Moore, 'The Interpretive Turn in Modern Theory: A Turn for the Worse?', *Stanford Law Rev*., 41 (1989), 871, at 936.

[9] R. L. Schwartz, 'Internal and External Method in the Study of Law', in *Law and Philosophy*, 11 (1992), 179, at 188.

[10] Moore, *supra*, n. 8, at 948.

[11] Ibid., at 955.

Moore, is that jurisprudence is best viewed as a non-interpretive, explanatory or descriptive activity that is essentially no different from any other scientific endeavour.

Moore's conclusion that modest interpretivism cannot ground an interpretivist methodology for jurisprudence is clearly justified. But his further conclusion that jurisprudence must be regarded as non-interpretive is too hasty, since he simply does not consider the possibility of an interpretivism based on the internalist thesis. Hart's methodological proposals for jurisprudence obviously do not incorporate anything like modest interpretivism. He does not think that legal practices are texts that legal theorists should treat as authoritative, and he clearly accepts that at least one of the objects of jurisprudence is, as for Moore, descriptive accuracy. But Hart none the less concludes that, because there is something special about the subject-matter of jurisprudence, this object cannot be attained by means of the usual methods of the natural sciences. In the case of law and other normative structures, descriptive accuracy requires a methodological precept peculiar to this area of inquiry, namely, the internalist thesis. For reasons already explained, the resulting approach to methodology is appropriately labelled 'interpretivist'. There are, in effect, more twists to the interpretive turn than Moore acknowledges.[12]

HART ON THE INTERNAL AND EXTERNAL POINTS OF VIEW

In *The Concept of Law* Hart introduces the internal point of view in the course of explaining the difference between social rules and mere habits.[13] Both habits and social rules are characterized as aspects of group behaviour. In each case the pattern of behaviour in question has to be general and generally convergent. But rules differ from habits in that divergence from the pattern typically leads to criticism, and the fact of divergence is regarded as a good reason for making the criticism. Moreover a rule, unlike a habit, is marked by an *internal aspect*, which consists of 'a reflective critical attitude' to the relevant pattern of behaviour. Criticism of deviations from the pattern, and demands for conformity with it, are regarded as legitimate by both the criticizer and, typically, the criticizee. Both the criticism of deviations and the acknowledgement of that criticism tend to be marked

[12] 'Interpretation' has, of course, other meanings besides those associated with modest interpretivism and the internalist thesis, but these are not at issue in the methodological debate. The most important of these other meanings is given by what is usually referred to as the communication or conversational model of interpretation. The essential idea is that interpretation aims, at least in its central instances, to grasp the meaning that some person or body intended to convey by means of an utterance or text. See Dworkin, *supra*, n. 7, at 50; Andrei Marmor, *Interpretation and Legal Theory* (Oxford: Clarendon Press, 1992), at 28–34.

[13] Hart, *supra*, n. 2, at 54–5.

by the use of such normative terms as 'ought', 'must', 'right', and 'wrong'. In some cases the normative terms 'obligation' and 'duty' are used. Rules are regarded as imposing *obligations* 'when the general demand for conformity is insistent and the social pressure brought to bear upon those who deviate or threaten to deviate is great'.[14] Obligations are marked, in effect, by a particularly strong manifestation of the internal aspect of rules. One of the distinctive themes of *The Concept of Law* is that not only are social rules of this kind *regarded* as giving rise to obligations by (a majority of) members of the group, they *do in fact* create obligations, albeit not moral obligations. As Hart puts it, the existence of law 'means that certain kinds of human conduct are no longer optional, but in *some* sense obligatory'.[15] These obligations extend even to those members of the group who do not accept that they are bound by the rules.[16]

The internal aspect of rules is contrasted with the external aspect, which Hart variously describes as 'the regular uniform behaviour which an observer could record', 'externally observable physical behaviour', and 'regularities of physical behaviour'.[17] Later Hart introduces the idea of the internal and external *points of view*. The internal point of view is just the point of view of a person who accepts the rule in question. That there must be such a point of view follows more or less automatically from the definition of a rule, since one of the defining marks of a rule is that it has an internal aspect. The external point of view is more complicated, however. For one thing, Hart says that statements made from the external point of view may be of different kinds. For example, 'the observer may, without accepting the rules himself, assert that the group accepts the rules, and thus may from outside refer to the way in which *they* are concerned with them from the internal point of view'.[18] Although Hart is not explicit about this, it is clearly just this kind of statement that jurisprudence requires in order accurately to describe normative practices and, in particular, law. This type of statement takes account of the internal point of view, but it is not made *from* that point of view; since the internal point of view is only referred to, not utilized, such external statements (and the theories of which they are a part) can be characterized as descriptive rather than normative in character. Let me call external statements of this type 'engaged' external statements.

Engaged statements are obviously very important, but they are not the only kind of external statement Hart recognizes. It is also possible for an observer simply to describe 'the regularities of physical behaviour' that comprise the external aspect of rules, without mentioning either the rules

[14] Ibid., at 84.

[15] Ibid., at 6 (emphasis in original). Cf. ibid., at 96: 'Reference to . . . the internal point of view is required for the analysis of the basic concepts of obligation and duty.'

[16] Ibid., at 80–1, 85–6. [17] Ibid., at 55, 56, 87.

[18] Ibid., at 86–7 (emphasis in original). Cf. ibid., at 99.

themselves or their internal aspect. An observer who 'keeps austerely to this extreme external point of view' will describe what he sees in terms such as these:

> His view will be like the view of one who, having observed the working of a traffic signal in a busy street for some time, limits himself to saying that when the light turns red there is a high probability that the traffic will stop. He treats the light merely as a natural *sign that* people will behave in certain ways, as clouds are a *sign that* rain will come.[19]

Let me call statements of this type 'disengaged', or 'extreme' external statements.

Hart is clearly of the opinion that a satisfactory jurisprudential theory requires engaged external statements, and thus requires reference to the internal point of view. But why is this, exactly? What would be wrong with a theory that simply employed disengaged external statements? From the perspective of the methodological debate in the social sciences one would expect the answer to this question to turn on the formulation and application of epistemological criteria of some kind: which type of theory, engaged or disengaged, provides a more unified account of apparently disparate phenomena, or which type of theory has greater predictive power?[20] Hart has nothing to say about such matters, however, and so far as one can tell he does not regard them as relevant. One of the few clues as to why he thinks engaged theories are preferable to disengaged theories (or, perhaps, why they are necessary in addition to disengaged theories), is to be found in the continuation of the passage just quoted:

> [The observer who takes the extreme external point of view] will miss out a whole dimension of the social life of those whom he is watching, since for them the red light is not merely a sign that others will stop: they look upon it as a *signal for* them to stop, and so as a reason for stopping in conformity to rules which make stopping when the light is red a standard of behaviour and an obligation. To mention this is to bring into the account the way in which the group regards its own behaviour. It is to refer to the internal aspect of rules seen from their internal point of view.[21]

This suggests that Hart is concerned, at least in part, with pure description for pure description's sake.[22] Even if disengaged theories that attempt to give causal/explanatory accounts of law are useful for some purposes—and at no point does Hart say that they are not—still, there is room and need

[19] Ibid., at 87 (emphasis in original).

[20] I am grateful to Brian Leiter for clarification on this point.

[21] Ibid., at 87–8 (emphasis in original).

[22] Cf. Hart, *supra*, n. 6, at 36: '[T]here is a standing need for a form of legal theory or jurisprudence that is descriptive and general in scope, the perspective of which is not that of a judge deciding "what the law is", that is, what the law requires in particular cases (such as those examined by Dworkin in the first section of his paper) but is that of an external observer of a form of social institution with a normative aspect, which in its recurrence in different societies and periods exhibits many common features of form, structure, and content.'

for a type of theory that does not simply treat the internal point of view as epiphenomenal. An accurate description of 'the way in which the group regards its own behaviour' is important in order to give us a complete picture of the social practice under study.

But there is clearly more to Hart's insistence on the need for an engaged theory than a preference for accurate description. The key here is that the rule, in connection with facts about the world made pertinent by the rule (such as the light being red), is regarded by those who accept the rule as giving rise to a *reason for action*. As Hart says at another point, for those who take the internal point of view, rules serve as 'guides to the conduct of social life'.[23] Law is a practical phenomenon that systematically creates, or at least affects, persons' reasons for action. Hart clearly takes seriously the aspiration of jurisprudence not only to describe law accurately, but also to explain its normative dimension. As mentioned earlier, Hart regards social rules of the kind he analyses as giving rise not just to a *belief* among a majority of persons within the group that they are obligated, but to actual (non-moral) obligations. He thus explains the normativity of social rules and, ultimately, of law, in terms of what we might call *social* obligations. Such obligations apply only within the group, and they might or might not coincide with more general obligations that derive from what Hart calls 'critical' morality.

The internalist thesis, as characterized earlier, holds that an adequate jurisprudential account of law and, perhaps, of other, related social practices must refer to the point of view of some or all of the practice's participants. We can now see that, for Hart, the content of the internalist thesis is more specific: the theorist must be able to grasp how law is believed by at least some of its participants to give them reasons for action. In fact his formulation of the thesis is more specific still: the theorist must understand and take account of the viewpoint of those who accept social rules, because such acceptance *in fact* gives them reasons for action. The justification for construing the internalist thesis in this way takes us back to the dual ambitions of jurisprudence. The jurisprudential theorist is trying not just to describe law, but to understand its normative character. The fact that some persons accept social rules is significant from a purely descriptive perspective, but beyond that it also explains, according to Hart, why a normative practice is normative. On Hart's philosophical analysis of social rules, the fact that the members of a group adopt the internal point of view towards their own behaviour is enough to give them reasons for action, in the form of social obligations. Thus, even though Hart borrowed the notion of the internal point of view from the methodological debate in the social sciences, he was not primarily concerned with the epistemological issues that

[23] Hart, *supra*, n. 2, at 88.

that debate addresses. He was, to be sure, interested in accurate description, but beyond that he thought that the internal point of view also solved the *philosophical* problem of how law could be truly normative.

It is important to emphasize that, on Hart's account, social obligations are not moral obligations. If this were not so, he could not claim to be a legal positivist. Thus, it has been a constant theme of Hart's work that there is a form of normativity distinct from that of (critical) morality. An associated theme is that normative language bears a different meaning in legal and moral contexts. Since social obligations pertain only to the group under study, all that is required of the theorist is that she understand how the members of the group regard their own behaviour. She does not have to *share* their point of view, nor does she have to regard herself as similarly obligated. As Hart has subsequently made clear, this would be so even if an explanation of the internal point of view required reference to moral beliefs. Assuming, for the sake of argument, that a satisfactory account of what it is for a community to have a customary rule will show that conformity to the rule must be motivated by a belief that the rule is morally valuable, he continues:

> [A]n analysis referring in this way to moral beliefs will only be intelligible to those who can understand what it is to be motivated by such beliefs and to regard moral considerations as justifying conduct. *In that sense* the theorist must 'put himself in the place' of those whose practice he is attempting to elucidate in order to portray their conduct as it appears to them. But he need not share or endorse their beliefs or regard his descriptive account as also claiming that their conduct is justified.[24]

Hart does not, as we shall see, accept that the correct analysis of a community (or social) rule shows that conformity must be motivated by moral beliefs. Either way, however, the legal theorist still needs to be able to grasp how the practice's participants think that the practice gives them reasons for action. To that extent she must be able to see the practice from their point of view, and in that limited sense must adopt what can properly be labelled an interpretive or hermeneutic methodology. But the theorist need not share the participants' belief that the practice is morally justified (although, in order to explain the normativity of law, she must presumably still accept that it gives *them*, even if not her, *social* obligations). It is for this reason that Hart rejects the strong internalist thesis.

The methodological position I have just attributed to Hart bears some resemblance to Moore's modest interpretivism, since both are concerned with the manner in which social practices give rise to reasons for action. But the two notions are not equivalent. Modest interpretivism considers two problems of practical reason: first, determining whether an individual is

[24] Hart, *supra*, n. 6, at 39 (emphasis in original), commenting on Dworkin's summary of the argument of *Law's Empire* in Gavison, (ed.), *supra*, n. 1.

justified in treating something or other as an authoritative text and second, assuming an appropriate justification exists, determining what reasons for action the text creates for that individual. It is true that this 'something'—the would-be text—might be an existing social practice, and one reason for deciding that the practice gives someone a reason for action might be, in appropriate circumstances, that other people already regard it as giving *them* a reason for action. Even so, modest interpretivism is concerned not with social practices as such, but rather with issues of individual practical reason. By contrast, Hart's internalist methodology is concerned with the study of social practices. It is true that the internalist thesis takes hold when the members of the group in question regard the practice as reason-creating. It is also true that the theorist must be able, in the sense previously explained, to put herself in the position of (some of) the group's members. It may even be the case that she herself is a member of the group. The fact remains that her project is an exercise in theoretical, not practical, reason.

It is worth emphasizing that Hart's internalist methodology appears to be quite compatible with non-jurisprudential theories of law, also intended to be descriptive, that take up a disengaged, external point of view. It is compatible, for example, with functional/causal accounts that attempt to explain, by reference to certain social functions and without taking account of anyone's reasons for action, why law exists, or continues to exist, or takes the form that it does.[25] Thus one might make the causal claim that law takes the form that it does because it serves the function of, say, promoting the interests of the dominant economic class. There is in the philosophy of the social sciences a continuing debate, the resolution of which is not of present concern, over whether functions of this kind can really be causes.[26] My point here is simply that, in principle, law can simultaneously be the subject of both internal and external theories, just as human beings can simultaneously be the subject of both biological and psychological theories. Hart's methodological claim thus should not be that *any* theory which takes law as its subject-matter must be sensitive to the internal point of view. Rather it should be that reason-givingness is a distinctive aspect of law and certain other social practices, and that we would be missing something important about those practices if our social theories at no point studied this feature of them. There is thus both room and need for theories that make the reason-givingness of these practices the main object of scrutiny, and which are therefore sensitive to the internal point of view. Jurisprudence, as a discipline, defines one class of such theories.

Now that we have a better idea of what part the internal point of view

[25] Leslie Green, 'The Political Content of Legal Theory', *Philosophy of the Social Sciences*, 17 (1987), 1, at 4–5, 11.

[26] See e.g. Richard W. Miller, *Fact and Method: Explanation, Confirmation and Reality in the Natural and Social Sciences* (Princeton NJ: Princeton University Press, 1987), at 118–26.

plays in Hart's jurisprudential methodology, I want briefly to consider how he employs the notion in developing his own positivist theory of law. I am not interested in the substantive issues for their own sake, but only in so far as they help us to make sense of the methodological issues. As is well known, Hart maintains that the officials of a legal system, and in particular its judges, accept a fundamental duty-imposing social rule that he calls the rule of recognition. This rule is to be understood in terms of Hart's general analysis of social rules that was summarized earlier. The rule of recognition provides criteria for determining the validity of other rules in the legal system, and imposes upon judges a duty to enforce those rules. Judges take the internal point of view towards the rule of recognition, which means that they regard it as 'a public, common standard of correct judicial decision'.[27] In accordance with Hart's view of the normativity of law, judges thus come under a social obligation to enforce the valid rules of the system. Existence of a legal system also requires a minimal level of compliance with the valid rules by citizens generally, and while citizens might share the internal point of view, they need not; it is enough that for the most part they obey the rules, and it does not matter whether they do so out of fear, inertia, or for some other reason. Thus Hart says that

> [a]t any given moment the life of a society which lives by rules, legal or not, is likely to consist in a tension between those who, on the one hand, accept and voluntarily co-operate in maintaining the rules . . . and those who, on the other hand, reject the rules and attend to them only from the external point of view as a sign of possible punishment.[28]

Hart states that an adequate legal theory must take account of both the internal and external points of view, and hence must be careful not to define one or the other out of existence. Yet there is an asymmetry here, since a Hartian legal system could exist if everyone took the internal point of view, but not if everyone took the external point of view. Hart may not define the external point of view out of existence, but he clearly assigns the internal point of view a more central role in his theory. The reason for this might seem to follow fairly straightforwardly from our earlier discussion of methodology: law is a reason-creating social insititution, and this could only be so if at least some of its participants took the internal point of view. But this answer begs some important questions. To see why, we must examine more carefully what Hart has to say about the external point of view.

As previously noted, Hart distinguishes two types of external statement, both of which are made from the perspective of an observer. Engaged statements are not at present at issue, since they take account of the internal point of view. Rather, our concern is with disengaged external statements.

[27] Hart, *supra*, n. 2, at 112. [28] Ibid., at 88.

These simply describe, from an observer's perspective, 'the regularities of physical behaviour'. Hart says that an observer who takes up what he calls the extreme external viewpoint—in my terminology, the disengaged viewpoint—will miss out on a whole dimension of the social life of those whom he is watching. What he will miss, presumably, is that they are acting for *reasons*, and that those reasons are systematically related to the practice he is supposedly studying. In fact, it is not clear why someone who took the extreme external point of view would even be led to describe what he saw in terms of *actions*. Hart himself comes close to conceding as much when he says of his traffic-signal example that the external observer will treat the red light 'merely as a natural *sign that* people will behave in certain ways, as clouds are a *sign that* rain will come'.[29] In the context of the cloud and rain analogy, the word 'behave' seems to suggest bodily motions more than it does purposive actions. In any event, whatever the background theoretical framework for extreme external statements is supposed to be,[30] it is clear that such statements abstract from the reasons for action of the persons observed. An observer who takes the extreme external viewpoint may become aware of empirical regularities that permit him to make predictions about what people will do, but he will not be aware of their processes of practical reasoning, and may not even be aware that they are agents.

Consider now Hart's claim that some members of any given society can be expected to reject the rules 'and attend to them only from the external point of view . . .'.[31] In what sense can it be said that persons who reject the rules—let's call them alienated participants—are taking up the external viewpoint? Hart says of such persons that they 'are only concerned with [the rules] when and because they judge that unpleasant consequences are likely to follow violation'. In other words they pay attention to the rules, but with the sole aim of avoiding criticism or punishment. This prudential perspective, as I shall call it, is clearly very different from Hart's earlier characterization of the external point of view. That characterization referred to an observer who takes note of the regularities of conduct among a group of persons. Such an observer is engaged in a process of *theoretical* reasoning, the aim of which is not action but description. Moreover, in formulating her descriptions she is not aware of (or at least omits to mention) the reasons for action of the persons she is watching. The contrast with the prudential perspective could hardly be greater, since persons who take up this perspective are engaged in a process of *practical* reasoning. Their reasoning is quite different, it is true, from the practical reasoning of persons who have adopted the internal viewpoint (socialized participants, we might call them).

[29] Ibid., at 87 (emphasis in original).

[30] The concern here is with Quine's point that it is impossible to specify a neutral, non-theory-laden language of observation.

[31] Ibid., at 88.

For alienated participants, it is not the rules as such, understood as group norms, that serve as reasons for action; their concern, rather, is with the criticism or punishment that might follow a deviation from the pattern of behaviour the rule demands. They are attending, in other words, to *prudential* reasons for action. But the important point for present purposes is that for both alienated and socialized participants the social practice in question is a source of reasons for action.

It is thus clear that, even apart from the possibility of engaged external statements, Hart's notion of the external point of view is systematically ambiguous. The official understanding concerns a form of theoretical reasoning about regularities of group conduct. But this official understanding is tacitly merged with a second, unofficial understanding, the focus of which is a certain kind of *practical* reasoning that some members of a group might engage in. Given that the rationale for taking account of the internal point of view in theorizing about social practices like law is precisely to elucidate the reason-giving character of those practices, one would have thought that the prudential perspective should, rather than being conflated with the extreme external point of view, be treated as a second kind of *internal* point of view. But it is only by excluding the prudential perspective from the magic circle of internal viewpoints that Hart is able to make his most important argument for the centrality of social rules within the concept of law. That argument can be paraphrased as follows. An appropriate methodology for studying law requires the internal point of view. The internal point of view must be understood by reference to social rules. Therefore, a satisfactory analysis of law must place social rules at its centre. This is a bad argument, however, because the second step begs an important question; the internal point of view should be characterized in terms of the reason-giving character of the practice generally, and not just in terms of social rules.

To put the point another way, the internalist thesis should leave open the (partly philosophical) question of which types of reasons a social practice creates for its participants (as well as the empirical question of which reasons or perceived reasons *move* them to act), rather than *defining* the internal point of view by reference to a single such type. (There is thus a sense, after all, in which Hart defines away the external point of view, or at least one branch of a systematically ambiguous characterization of the external point of view.) When we understand the internalist thesis in this more open way, we can see that the question of whether the internal or external point of view should have pride of place in Hart's theory of law is simply misplaced. We have already accepted that there is room for a type of theory that focuses on the reason-giving character of social practices. The more appropriate question then becomes: *which* internal point of view should be treated as more significant for a given social practice, and in particular for law? In other words, which type of reason for action, social obligations or prudential reasons, should be conceived as quintessentially *legal* reasons for action? I shall suggest in the following section that these questions can only be answered by reference to a moral argument of a certain kind. First, however, I want to ask how Hart might have been led to conflate the extreme external point of view with the prudential perspective. The answer, I shall argue, has to do with two different ways that the notion of prediction might be thought to figure in a theory of law.

Hart summarizes his various criticisms of the predictive theory of obligation, versions of which were held by Austin, Bentham, and Holmes, by saying that it defines the internal aspect of obligatory rules out of existence.[32] The predictive theory holds that obligations should be analysed in terms of the predictability of punishment. Theories of law that adopt this analysis are not always very clear, however, about the precise role prediction is supposed to play. Consider, for example, Holmes's discussion in 'The Path of the Law'. Holmes states at the outset that '[t]he object of our study . . . is prediction, the prediction of the incidence of the public force through the instrumentality of the courts'.[33] But Holmes does not tell us here who is supposed to be doing the predicting. Later he gives the following characterization of law: 'The prophecies of what the courts will do in fact, and nothing more pretentious, are what I mean by the law.'[34] Similarly, a legal duty is defined as 'nothing but a prediction that if a man does or omits certain things he will be made to suffer in this or that way by judgment of the court'.[35] These two passages suggest a disengaged external theory of law and legal obligation: the person doing the predicting is an external observer who takes note of regularities in the behaviour of courts; he need not, it would seem, be concerned with anyone's reasons for action, either those of the judges themselves or those of citizens generally.[36]

But this apparently external cast to Holmes's thinking about law is misleading. A more accurate clue to the type of theory he really had in mind is to be found in the following famous passage from his essay: 'If you want to know the law and nothing else, you must look at it as a bad man, who cares only for the material consequences which such knowledge enables him to predict, not as a good one, who finds his reasons for conduct, whether inside the law or outside of it, in the vaguer sanctions of conscience.'[37] Here the notion of prediction clearly does not serve to demarcate the disengaged, external point of view of an observer. It serves, rather, to

[32] Ibid.

[33] Oliver Wendell Holmes, 'The Path of the Law', in *Collected Legal Papers* (New York: Harcourt, Brace, 1920), 167.

[34] Ibid., at 173. [35] Ibid., at 169.

[36] Dworkin accepts that Holmes's theory is 'external' in character, by which he means that it lacks the 'participant's understanding'. Dworkin, *supra*, n. 7, at 14.

[37] Holmes, *supra*, n. 33, at 171.

characterize prudential reasons for action that the law creates for ordinary citizens. A citizen's prudential reasons depend on the probability of being punished, which in a less precise terminology is just the predictability of punishment. Holmes is thus building his account of law on a particular *internal* point of view, in the broader sense of that notion sketched earlier. Later I shall say something more about the substance of that account. My present point is just that Holmes uses the notion of prediction in two different but not very clearly differentiated ways. One of these is most plausibly associated with an external view of law, while the other is most plausibly associated with an internal view. Given this failure on the part of at least one proponent of the predictive theory to distinguish clearly between two quite different uses of the notion of prediction, it is perhaps not surprising that Hart would be led to subsume both under the single rubric of the external point of view.

THE POINT OF LAW

We saw in the preceding section that the internalist thesis, properly understood, is not sufficient by itself to rule out a theory of law like Holmes's. Contrary to Hart's assertion, the predictive theory does not define the internal point of view out of existence. We are thus left with two competing theories of law, each of which takes as its point of departure a different understanding of the internal point of view. Each of these understandings represents the perspective of a different group of participants within the social practice of law, and each is associated with a different mode of practical reasoning (that is, a different type of reason for action that law is claimed to create). There are, of course, many more possible theories of law besides these two, each of which has its own understanding of which reasons for action are fundamentally legal in character. For the moment, however, it will be helpful to continue to focus on the theories of Hart and Holmes. As we have seen, Hart holds social rules and the perspective of judges to be central to the proper understanding of law. Holmes, by contrast, has a different starting-point, which he calls the point of view of the bad man. Holmes argues, in effect, that the quintessentially *legal* reasons for action are those prudential reasons created by legal institutions to which a bad man, that is, a person concerned only for his own self-interest, would systematically attend. Given that both these accounts of law begin with an internal point of view, the obvious question is: how do we choose between them?

It might seem that one could make this choice on the basis of conceptual argument, that is, on the basis of which theory offers the best analysis of various concepts that figure in the social practice being studied. Thus Hart argues, for example, that his theory offers a better analysis of what we mean by the notions of legal obligation and legal authority than does the predictive theory of obligation or the related Austinian view of law as orders backed by threats. Now it is certainly true, as we shall see below, that conceptual argument is part of the story. But it is not the whole story, at least not if we regard conceptual argument as completely distinct from normative argument. There is no doubt that the predictive theory of obligation does not offer a very accurate analysis of what we ordinarily mean by a legal obligation, or indeed any kind of obligation. But it still seems open to a defender of the Holmesian theory to say that the various conceptual elements we associate with law are complex and not necessarily in complete harmony with one another. He is not so much concerned to analyse the concept of obligation as to argue that that concept, as ordinarily understood, is not theoretically fundamental. The theoretically fundamental concept, he will continue, is that of sanctions, because it is sanctions, not Hartian obligations, that create the reasons for action which are truly central to an accurate understanding of law. The conceptual 'reduction' of obligations to prudential reasons is really just meant to emphasize this fact. Hart, for his part, emphasizes the concept of obligation, as analysed by his account of social rules, and down-plays the role of sanctions.[38]

There is in fact a deeper point here. For it is necessary to ask: from whose point of view is the conceptual analysis to be carried out? The answer for Hart, as we shall see shortly, is the theorist's point of view. But the theorist's conceptualization of the social practice in question need not correspond to that of the participants. To the charge that his analysis of obligations does not respect 'our' concept, where 'our' presumably refers to participants in the social practice of law, the Holmesian can respond: 'It is not meant to respect your concept, and moreover, it does not have to; my conceptualization of obligations is theoretically preferable to yours, and since Hart's own methodology makes the theorist's point of view determinative on such matters, mine is the one I should use.' The justification for dealing with such matters from the theorist's point of view, together with the basis for determining that a particular conceptualization is superior, will be considered below.

The conceptual manœuvre thus seems to leave us no further ahead. We are still faced with the question: how do we choose between the Hartian and Holmesian theories of law? As it happens, Hart has an answer to this question that does not appeal to conceptual analysis (or at least not to pure conceptual analysis, untainted by normative considerations). After referring

[38] Hart, *supra*, n. 2, at 34: 'In the case of the rules of the criminal law, it is logically possible and might be desirable that there should be such rules even though no punishment or other evil were threatened . . . We can, in a sense, subtract the sanction and still leave an intelligible standard of behaviour which it was designed to maintain.'

to Holmes's claim that the law should be understood in terms of what the 'bad man' would want to know, he continues:

> Why should not law be equally if not more concerned with the 'puzzled man' or 'ignorant man' who is willing to do what is required, if only he can be told what it is? Or with 'the man who wishes to arrange his affairs' if only he can be told how to do it? . . . The principal functions of the law as a means of social control are not to be seen in private litigation or prosecutions, which represent vital but still ancillary provisions for the failures of the system. It is to be seen in the diverse ways in which the law is used to control, to guide, and to plan life out of court.[39]

The key word here is 'function'. Hart is clearly not using the term to refer to social functions of the kind discussed earlier, which might figure in a causal explanation of some kind. Nor could he simply mean that guidance of conduct is one of the *effects* of law, since the law's influence on bad men is also one of its functions in this sense; there is nothing in these purely factual statements to determine which is the *principal* function. In any event, to understand 'function' as meaning 'effect' is inconsistent with Hart's expressing his point in terms of what the law *should* be concerned with. Rather, the term is most plausibly interpreted as referring to the *moral value*, or *point*, of the institution of law.[40] Hart appears to be saying that when law is understood in accordance with his analysis, then it has moral value, or at least potential moral value, because it is capable of guiding conduct in a way that is socially beneficial. This idea is to some extent fleshed out by Hart's thesis of the minimum content of natural law.[41] Of course, if this is to be an argument against Holmes's 'bad man' theory, Hart cannot suppose that most ordinary citizens take the prudential perspective, as his own theory seems in fact to allow. Interestingly, Hart thus seems to be attributing a value to law that emphasizes the role of the internal point of view (as he understands it) not just for judges, but for ordinary citizens as well. This, as we shall see below, is an idea that has been taken up and developed with great sophistication by Joseph Raz. My present point, however, is simply this. Although Hart's original theoretical ambitions were apparently limited to pure social description on the one hand and explanation of normativity on the other, one of the principal arguments he makes in favour of his own theory of law over a rival theory seems to be *moral* in character: it is grounded in a certain understanding of the moral point or value of the institution of law.

Although he does not do so himself, one could envisage someone defending Holmes's determination of which elements of law are theoretically significant by ascribing to the institution a different moral point or value.

[39] Ibid., at 39.
[40] Cf. John Finnis, *Natural Law and Natural Rights* (Oxford: Clarendon Press, 1980), at 6–7.
[41] Hart, *supra*, n. 2, at 189–95.

The obvious line of argument would begin with a Hobbesian conception of the person and then maintain, in light of the primary goals and motivations of such persons, that the point of law is to preserve social peace and order through coercion. In these circumstances the coercion would be regarded as justified. Normative accounts of law that take roughly this form have, of course, been put forward,[42] but I shall not discuss them here. My concern is not with the substance of the moral debate that might ensue between Holmes and Hart (or their successors) about what the point or value of law should be taken to be. My concern, rather, is with the methodological status of such a debate. How, if at all, does the claim Hart makes about the moral value of law fit into his more general conception of legal theory? Does it implicitly change that conception in some way? In order to answer these questions it will be helpful first to address the following question: from what point of view does Hart make the claim that the 'primary functions' of law are its uses in controlling, guiding, and planning life out of court?

One possibility is that this claim is meant to represent the perspective of those who take the internal point of view (in Hart's sense of those who accept the rule of recognition). It would thus be, in essence, the point of view of judges. At one point Hart does say that social rules giving rise to obligations 'are thought to be important because they are believed to be necessary to the maintenance of social life or some highly prized feature of it'.[43] Elsewhere in *The Concept of Law*, however, Hart suggests that to ask questions about the moral worth of the rule of recognition or the legal system to which it belongs is to move to an external point of view.[44] Consistent with this idea is the explication of his views that Hart has offered in his later work. In *Essays on Bentham* he argues that persons who accept social rules may have very diverse reasons for doing so: some may, it is true, adopt the internal attitude on the basis of a moral belief—a belief, it should be added, that might or might not be true—but others will do so as part of a traditional way of life, or out of fear, or because they wish to please someone, or to conform with what others do, or for any of a number of other possible reasons.[45] In the case of law in particular, Hart says that acceptance by judges of the rule of recognition gives rise for them to a specific kind of reason, which he calls an 'authoritative legal reason'.[46] This reason is institutionalized in the sense that 'a duty to conform to [legal] standards is attached to the office of judge and assumed by individual judges when they take up that office'; they are 'committed as judges' to maintain

[42] See e.g. Robert Ladenson, 'In Defence of a Hobbesian Conception of Law', *Philosophy and Public Affairs*, 9 (1980), 134.

[43] Hart, *supra*, n. 2, at 85. [44] Ibid., at 104–5.

[45] H. L. A. Hart, *Essays on Bentham: Studies in Jurisprudence and Political Theory* (Oxford: Clarendon Press, 1982), at 256–7.

[46] Ibid., at 160.

the instititution, and speak of the subject's legal duty 'in a technically confined way'.[47] It is only in this sense that a judge can be said to be committed to following the rules: his view of the moral merits is, Hart says, irrelevant.[48]

Hart's discussion of the nature of judicial duty makes it quite clear that he regards social rules, and the rule of recognition in particular, as giving rise to a non-moral obligation of the kind I earlier called a social obligation. This, it will be recalled, is how he explains the normativity of law. In the case of judges, Hart calls this non-moral obligation an authoritative legal reason. The thesis that the notion of judicial duty is to be explained in terms of such a reason goes hand in hand with a semantic thesis to the effect that normative terms like 'duty' and 'obligation' have a different meaning in legal and moral contexts. It would be beyond the scope of this essay to discuss the substance of either of these theses, both of which have met with powerful criticism from other quarters.[49] My concern, rather, is with the fact that Hart treats the acceptance of a social rule as a kind of brute social fact, the nature of which will not, at least so far as legal theory is concerned, repay further investigation. Hart states in *The Concept of Law* that the internal point of view is marked by a 'reflective critical attitude to [the appropriate] pattern of behaviour'.[50] But this apparently just means that the participants regard that pattern as a standard of conduct, deviation from which legitimately invites criticism. It does not mean that that they reflect upon the justification, moral or otherwise, of the rule or the practice in which it is embedded. Acceptance of a social rule is, in this sense, an essentially unreflective phenomenon. Hart does not assume that judges and other persons who adopt the internal point of view within law have any views at all on the moral value of law as an institution, let alone a shared, canonical view of some kind. Reflection about the point or value of law is thus not, according to Hart, itself an aspect of the social practice.

Presumably the same thing is true of Holmes's view of law. As Holmes envisages the bad man, not only does he appear to be a creature who is motivated purely by self-interest, but he does not engage in second-order reflections about either his own practical reasoning or about the legal institutions that are the source of his prudential reasons for action. Holmes also

[47] Ibid., at 258, 266.

[48] Ibid., at 159. Hart's views on the nature of judicial acceptance of the rule of recognition are underpinned by what he calls a non-cognitive theory of duty. According to this theory, 'committed statements asserting that others have a duty do not refer to actions which they have a categorical duty to do but . . . to actions which are due from or owed by the subjects having the duty, in the sense that they may be properly demanded or exacted from them'. Ibid., at 160. This seems to bring Hart perilously close to a Holmesian or Hobbesian theory of law, the central feature of which would be, not a duty to comply with legitimate authority, but rather justified coercion.

[49] Cf. Joseph Raz, 'Hart on Moral Rights and Legal Duties', *Oxford Jo. of Legal Stud.*, 4 (1984), 123, at 129–31; Postema, *supra*, n. 1.

[50] Hart, *supra*, n. 2, at 55.

seems to regard judges as essentially unreflective beings who are moved primarily by tradition rather than by 'weighing considerations of social advantage', which is what he thinks they should be doing.[51] At any rate let us assume, in order to facilitate comparison with Hart's theory, that Holmesian judges and bad men are unreflective in the ways described. The moral point that one would be led to attribute to law on a more fully developed Holmesian theory would not then be taken to represent the viewpoint either of participants generally within the practice, or of any particular group of participants, such as judges. Notice, though, that this is not a necessary corollary of a theory of law of this general type. It is reasonable to think that Hobbesian persons who had agreed to be subject to coercion by the sovereign (and/or the sovereign's courts) would be capable of appreciating the argument that such coercion was morally justified. But this is not how Holmes conceived of the law, or so I shall assume.

Thus, a debate between a Hartian and a Holmesian about the moral point of law as a social practice would not be a debate conducted from the point of view of participants within that practice. It would be a moral argument carried on by the theorists themselves, from their own individual standpoints (or, more accurately, from the standpoint of the background moral framework that at some level of generality they presumably shared). This might seem to entail that their respective theories must be normative rather than descriptive in nature, but this is not necessarily so. Of course it is *possible* that their theories are best regarded as normative, in which case their debate would simply be about the best kinds of social institution to have; they would be doing pure political philosophy rather than jurisprudence. There is, however, another possibility. Our two theorists might be having a *methodological* disagreement, about the appropriate concepts to use in investigating a roughly delineated and provisionally agreed-upon range of social phenomena. This is an important issue, because we require concepts to individuate social practices in a more precise and theoretically satisfactory way. It seems plausible to think, as Weber suggested, that the question of which concepts would be the most interesting or fruitful to employ in a given branch of social theory will raise evaluative and even moral considerations. The moral debate between Hart and Holmes would, on the view under consideration, take place at this level; it would be a debate about concept formation. But once each theorist had formulated his concepts, the resulting characterizations of actual social practices could presumably be, again in Weberian fashion, purely descriptive and value-free.

In recent work Hart has explicitly acknowledged that he accepts an approach to concept formation that is very much along the Weberian lines just sketched:

[51] Holmes, *supra*, n. 33, at 184.

[A]n analysis which allots a place to moral claims and beliefs as constituents of a social phenomenon must itself be guided, in focusing on those features rather than others, by some criteria of importance of which the chief will be the explanatory power of what his analysis picks out. So his analysis will be guided by judgements, often controversial, of what is important and will therefore reflect such meta-theoretic values and not be neutral between all values. But again there is nothing to show that this analysis is not descriptive but normative or justificatory.[52]

Hart clearly applies such a methodology in *The Concept of Law* when he limits law to normative systems with a rule of recognition, thereby excluding social practices that consist of primary social rules alone. A social regime of the latter kind will, Hart says, be *defective* in certain ways: the manner in which it provides guidance for conduct will be uncertain, static, and inefficient. Moving to a system of the kind Hart calls law, which contains a rule of recognition and other so-called secondary rules, will *remedy* these defects.[53] Hart is thus delimiting the concept of law by appealing to the values of certainty, flexibility, and efficiency. (It is worth remarking that this appeal presupposes a yet more fundamental feature of law, namely, that its primary function is to guide conduct. This is, of course, the function Hart attributes to law in his direct response to Holmes.) Once the concept has been formulated, however, it can be used to describe existing social practices in a purely descriptive, value-free way. Notice that the resulting concept is the creation of the theorist; it may or may not coincide with any conceptualization of social practices that the subjects under study might happen to possess.

The Weberian exercise in concept formation just described distinguishes among *different* social practices that would be found in different societies. It does not involve distinguishing between different conceptual analyses of the *same* practice, within the same society. The postulated Hart–Holmes debate about the concept of law would, however, be an exercise of the latter kind. Two related points should be noted about the nature of this debate under the proposed 'methodological' interpretation. The first is that if the two theorists formulate their preferred concepts in different ways, then both are likely to diverge from their original, tentative, and presumably shared characterization of the relevant social phenomena. (The most plausible scenario is that they start out by focusing on just one or two specific social practices, for example, the American and English legal systems.) Their newly formulated concepts will individuate social practices, and hence cut up reality, in different ways. This point is illustrated by Hart's exercise in Weberian analysis that was just described: Hart's concept of law excludes systems of primary rules, but another theorist who was less concerned with

[52] Hart, *supra*, n. 6, at 39. Cf. Green, *supra*, n. 25, at 14–16.
[53] Hart, *supra*, n. 2, at 89–96.

certainty, flexibility, and efficiency, and more concerned about other values, might be led to formulate *her* concept of law so as to include such systems.

Let us consider how this point might apply to the postulated Hart–Holmes debate. The extension of the Holmesian concept of law is coercive institutions of a specified type. Hart's concept, on the other hand, applies to social practices in which, among other defining conditions, a group of persons identified as judges accept a certain kind of master social rule. There could easily be extensive overlap between these two concepts, and in particular both might apply to the specific practices the theorists began by examining (the American and English legal systems, in our example). This would be the case so long as both concepts provided accurate descriptions of those practices, which is of course perfectly feasible. Such convergence could all the more easily occur given that the respective descriptions do not have to respect the *participants'* conceptualization of their practices. Let us assume, for the sake of argument, that the Hartian and the Holmesian concepts both accurately describe modern legal systems. This is not in fact implausible, given that such systems give rise both to prudential reasons for action based on sanctions and to social norms that have a Hartian internal aspect.

The second point to be noted about the postulated Hart–Holmes debate is really a corollary of the first. It is that, strictly speaking, our two theorists cannot be debating the moral value of 'law' at all, since they have no shared concept of law. Indeed, at the stage of methodological disagreement they do not even have precise *individual* concepts of law: the whole point of the exercise is, after all, concept formation. But the debate can none the less proceed by reference to the perceived moral merits of particular social practices within the provisionally agreed-upon range of social phenomena, on the one hand, and to arguments within pure political theory about the moral merits of ideal types of legal and political institutions, on the other. If they ultimately formulate their individual concepts in different ways, they cannot then conceive of their disagreement as being about the moral merits of the same general type of social practice. If they did, they would be victims of a version of Dworkin's semantic sting.[54]

[54] Dworkin, *supra*, n. 7, at 31–46. Dworkin argues that positivist theories like Hart's are 'semantic' theories. Semantic theories suppose that lawyers and others agree, at least implicitly, on the 'grounds' of law. (The grounds of law can be very roughly equated, for present purposes, with the criteria for determining which reasons are legal reasons.) But then, according to Dworkin, semantic theories have a great deal of trouble accounting for apparently 'theoretical' disagreement about what the grounds of law really are. As the discussion in the text should make clear, however, Hart's theory is not a semantic theory in this sense. The aim of the theory is, to be sure, to formulate a concept of law, but that is an enterprise carried out by the theorist. At no point does Hart assume that all lawyers agree about the grounds of law. Moreover, two theorists can have a perfectly sensible discussion, at the theoretical level of concept formation, about how the grounds of law—the criteria for determining legal reasons—should be understood. They would only be subject to the semantic sting if they stupidly happened to conceive of their disagreement in the manner described in the text. What they cannot suppose, however,

Rather oddly, despite criticizing Holmes's 'bad man' theory of law on the basis of an ultimately moral claim about the function of law, Hart seems to assume throughout his work on jurisprudence that there is really only one possible conceptual analysis of modern legal systems, namely, his own. Thus, of his attempt in *The Concept of Law* to answer such questions as, what are rules, how do rules form a system, and so on, Hart has written the following: 'I found and still find a need for a clarifying, descriptive enterprise which would answer such questions as I have mentioned and would have some claim to universality.'[55] Hart envisages this enterprise, the core of which is his analysis of social rules and the internal point of view, as having explanatory priority over what he takes to be the preoccupation of Dworkinian interpretivism with 'the articulation of controversial claims concerning the fitness of legal practices to justify the use of legal coercion'.[56] Thus Hart sees his own analysis of law as the *foundation* of Dworkinian interpretations, rather than as a *competitor* among them. This, however, is a mistake. Dworkinian interpretations of law do require some agreed-upon set of raw (or pre-interpretive) social data,[57] but that data is not to be found at the level of Hart's social rules. This is because Hart's conceptualization of the data is, like that of Dworkinian interpretations, relative to a view of the point or function of law. It is true that this attribution of a point to law is carried out from a theorist's perspective that is assumed by Hart, unlike Dworkin, to be distinct from the participants' perspective. But for present purposes this does not matter: Hart's theory is, so far as the present issue is concerned, on the same footing as theories within Dworkin's interpretive methodology. Because it ultimately depends on a moral argument, Hart's analysis of law lacks the neutrality it would require to be capable of providing a foundational set of social data.

is that they are having a disagreement *within* the social practice of law. That is because their point of view is an external, theoretical perspective that is not to be equated with the point of view of participants. In brief, Dworkin does not properly formulate his methodological objection to Hart's theory. The real point of his critique is that the theorist *should* adopt the participants' point of view, since that permits the theorist to explain, among other things, how theoretical disagreement can take place *within* law.

[55] Hart, *supra*, n. 6, at 38.

[56] Hart, *supra*, n. 6, at 38. Dworkin describes and defends his interpretivist methodology for legal theory in *Law's Empire*, *supra*, n. 7. See particularly chs. 2 and 3.

[57] At points Dworkin suggests that pre-interpretive data consist of 'rules and standards', or even 'social rules'. Dworkin, *supra*, n. 7, at 65–6. This misleads critics such as Steven Burton into thinking that Dworkinian interpretivism presupposes something like Hart's model of rules. See Steven J. Burton, 'Ronald Dworkin and Legal Positivism', *Iowa Law Rev.*, 73 (1987), 109, at 117–21. In fact, the better view is that the pre-interpretive data are, for Dworkin, roughly identified *institutions* such as legislatures, courts, and administrative agencies, which 'count as legal practices in our own culture'. Dworkin, *supra*, n. 7, at 91. This is not to deny that the notion of pre-interpretive data gives rise to some very tricky issues. See further Gerald J. Postema, '"Protestant" Interpretation and Social Practices', *Law and Philosophy*, 6 (1987), 283, at 302–8.

Why does Hart overlook the fact that his theory of law depends in part on the attribution of a function to law, thereby leading him to claim foundational status for the theory? The reason goes back, I believe, to the systematic ambiguity in the external point of view and to the privileged status that is consequently accorded to Hart's preferred understanding of the internal point of view. Hart is correct that there is room and need for a type of theory that utilizes the internalist thesis, but he construes that thesis in a narrow and question-begging way. He claims foundational status for his conceptual analysis of law because, in effect, he defines away the competition. He is led to do this because he wrongly believes that the internal point of view can only be understood by reference to the analysis he gives of social rules (or some similar analysis).[58] Given this mistaken belief, Hart would presumably regard his argument based on the function of law as a peripheral or even superfluous feature of his overall theory. In fact, it is absolutely central.

THE PARTICIPANTS' POINT OF VIEW

Hart's theory of law and, in the reconstructed version I have sketched, Holmes's as well, can be regarded as weakly interpretive theories, in the sense that both take account of the internal point of view of some designated group of participants within the practice. In each case the internal point of view has to do, as we have seen, with reasons for action to which the practice is claimed by the theorist give rise. This is, however, the extent of their interpretiveness, so to speak. It is true that each also attributes a moral point or function to law, and this is obviously reminiscent of Dworkin's interpretive methodology in *Law's Empire*. But the comparison with Dworkin's approach cannot be taken too far, since Hart's theory and (as I have construed it) the Holmesian theory do not attribute a point to law *from the participant's perspective*. The attribution of a moral point to law is a step in the process of concept formation at the theoretical level, rather than an aspect of the description of the actual practices studied. In each case the resulting concept of law is the theorist's concept, not the participants'. The reason for this limitation is, presumably, that Hart does not think that there *is* a coherent participants' viewpoint. Acceptance of a social rule is just a brute social fact that is not necessarily or even typically accompanied by a

[58] Other theorists follow Hart in this regard. Thus Andrei Marmor suggests that the interpretive attitude that Dworkin says is a mark of law and certain other social practices 'characterizes social practices which are constituted by norms'. Marmor, *supra*, n. 12, at 41. Marmor goes on to make the Hartian point that '[t]he distinction here is between normative rules which constitute a social practice, and rules which merely reflect social regularities'. As I argue later in the text, the question of whether legal reasons are best conceived in terms of Hartian (or Razzian) rules, or in some other way, is an interpretive question in Dworkin's sense.

belief in the moral justifiability of the rule. The social practice of law does not, according to Hart, extend to reflection about the nature and justification of law.

Hart's theory of law does not, in the end, accomplish what it sets out to do. We should take note in this regard of three points in particular. First, Hart's explanation of the normativity of law does not hold up. His account of the normativity of social rules, in terms of what I earlier called social obligations, has been very persuasively criticized by Dworkin and Raz.[59] While the details of their objections cannot be discussed here, the essential point is easy to state: a binding obligation does not necessarily come into being merely because (a majority of) a group of persons adopt the internal attitude, in Hart's sense, towards a rule. Put even more simply, believing does not make it so. Thus, the internal point of view is not a factor in explaining how and whether law really gives people reasons for action; its role could only be to help us understand how they *perceive* law to create reasons for action.[60]

Secondly, the internal point of view does not figure in the theory in a way that would permit it to fulfil the role just described. Thus, the theory does not have the resources to formulate an alternative philosophical account of the normativity of law, the starting-point for which would be the participants' *perception* that law gives them reasons for action. This is because in both the Hartian and Holmesian theories the choice between internal points of view is determined by a completely external factor, namely, the theorist's own attribution of a moral point to law. Moreover, the perceived reasons for action that each theory picks out as quintessentially legal reasons are not, because of the assumption that law is an essentially unreflective phenomenon, directly related to the moral point ascribed to law; it is not because they have grasped that point that citizens think that law gives them reasons for action. For both theories the ultimate function for law is, as Hart says in his response to Holmes, 'social control'. This is obtained in the one case by coercion, in the other by unreflective socialization. In neither case is the connection between the point of law and the reasons for action law creates assumed to be transparent to participants within the practice. The fact that participants act for reasons enters the theory in only a secondary and instrumental fashion, as part of an explanation of how the institution is able to serve the value it is supposed to serve. The attribution of a point to law cannot assist in explaining why the *participants* think that law gives

[59] Joseph Raz, *Practical Reason and Norms* (London: Hutchinson, 1975), at 50–8; Ronald Dworkin, *Taking Rights Seriously*, 2nd edn. (London: Duckworth, 1978), at 48–58.

[60] This is true not only of Hart's social rules, but also of Holmes's prudential reasons; the existence and character of a prudential reason depend on the objective probability of both the occurrence of a sanction and of its severity, and people might radically mis-estimate these probabilities.

them reasons for action, and the theory offers no other avenue for understanding the normativity of law. Of course one could turn to psychology for the desired explanation of why law is perceived to give rise to reasons for action, but then the philosophical aspirations of jurisprudence would have been effectively abandoned.

Thirdly, Hart's aim of pure description for pure description's sake cannot be attained, at least within a *jurisprudential* theory. This point was illustrated by our discussion of the imagined Hart–Holmes debate. The elements of the particular, usually local, social practices that we identify at a pre-theoretical stage as law are extremely complex and often difficult to reconcile with one another; without a conceptual framework of some kind, we would simply have an unsystematic welter of discrete observations. Perhaps a head-count of how many people are moved by prudential reasons and how many by socializing Hartian rules would be interesting for some purposes, but it would not be a jurisprudential theory; this would be, again, to abandon the philosophical ambitions of jurisprudence. Jurisprudence requires a conceptual framework. The difficulty is that the data can plausibly be conceptualized in more than one way, and choosing among conceptualizations seems to requires the attribution to law of a point or function. This in turn involves not just evaluative considerations, but moral argument. It is true that the concepts themselves, once formulated, can be applied in a value-free way, and that the moral argument in question takes place at the level of concept formation. But, as became clear in our discussion of Hart's claim to provide a purely descriptive foundation for Dworkinian interpretations of normative social practices, Hart's ascription of a moral point to law, even at the level of concept formation, ensures that his analysis cannot constitute a neutral set of social data that all other theorists could agree upon as a starting-point for further theorizing.

None of this is meant to show that a limited interpretive methodology like Hart's can serve no purpose. It is at least conceivable that law is unreflective in the way he supposes, and in any event we should not rule out that possibility on methodological grounds. Moreover, even if law is not an unreflective practice, no doubt there are other normative social practices that are, and we need some suitable method for studying them. (These are the practices Dworkin refers to as 'runic orders'.)[61] Finally, there may be some point to applying a limited interpretive methodology like Hart's to social practices whether we regard them as unreflective or not. Rather ironically, Hart's methodology can easily be viewed in natural-law terms. It offers a method for picking out a category of social institution every instance of which has moral value of a certain kind, or at least possesses properties (such as being able to guide conduct in a certain way) that are

[61] Dworkin, *supra*, n. 7, at 47.

required if the institution is to be capable of having moral value of some contemplated kind. It is thus not surprising that Michael Moore employs a variation on Hart's methodology in developing his 'functionalist' approach to natural law.[62] The natural-law concept that results from applying this methodology may not be *our* concept of law, of course; more generally, it may not coincide with the concept of the persons whose practices are being studied. Because the concept yielded by this methodology is constructed by the theorist, there is an ever-present danger that the accompanying natural-law conclusion, to the effect that law 'necessarily' possesses moral value of such and such a kind, will simply be a tautology: it will be true because the theorist has defined the concept so as to ensure its truth. Whether a natural-law theory developed in accordance with a Hartian methodology can avoid this danger is not, however, a question that can be considered here.[63]

[62] See Michael S. Moore, 'Law as a Functional Kind', in Robert P. George (ed.), *Natural Law Theory: Contemporary Essays* (Oxford: Clarendon Press, 1992). Moore seeks a description of social practices that will show law to be a 'functional kind', that is, a type of institution that uniquely serves some good. This good—let me use the term 'value', to maintain terminological consistency—will then be the necessary goal of law; it will be law's essence. The theorist, by a process of reflective equilibrium, provisionally assigns some value to law, understood in terms of some provisional structural description, and then tinkers with both the attribution of value and the structural description until the hoped-for description of a functional kind emerges. Moore concedes the process might not produce a goal that law can uniquely serve, in which case law is not a functional kind. But what if the process is capable of producing many descriptions of social practices, with different but overlapping extensions, where each description correctly and uniquely assigns a different goal to the set of practices it covers? The imagined Hart–Holmes debate suggests that this is far from a remote possibility. Which description, if any, represents the functional kind? Moore tries to get around such difficulties by claiming that functional kinds are similar to Saul Kripke's natural kinds, such as gold and water, that exist in the world *as* a kind and hence possess necessary properties; they are not just the creatures of someone's concept. But Moore's main argument to this effect is that the investigation of natural kinds will proceed, as in the case of functional kinds, by means of a similar, 'circular' process of reflective equilibrium. Ibid., at 219–21. This is no doubt true. It seems very unlikely, however, that in a scientific investigation of natural phenomena we could *end up with* accurate but overlapping descriptions, each of which had an equally good claim to refer to a natural kind. Moreover, in science we have independent reasons for thinking that there are such things as natural kinds, such as the role they play in general scientific laws, but we have no such reason for thinking there are functional kinds. Cf. Hilary Putnam, *Realism and Reason* (Cambridge: Cambridge University Press, 1983), at 74–5. Thus, although Moore claims not to be engaged in Hartian concept-formation (Moore, *supra*, at 204–6), that is exactly what he appears to be doing. Even if his functionalist methodology produced only *one* description of a type of institution that uniquely served some value, we would still have no grounds for thinking that it referred to a kind of thing that existed independently of the concept, and hence could be said to have necessary properties.

[63] But see the discussion of difficulties with Michael Moore's 'functionalist' methodology in the previous note. John Finnis, in developing his version of natural law, might at first glance also appear to be relying on a methodology similar to Hart's. After invoking Weber, Finnis continues: '[T]he evaluations of the theorist himself are an indispensable and decisive component in the selection or formation of any concepts for use in description of such aspects of human affairs as law and legal order.' Finnis, *supra*, n. 40, at 16. But Finnis clearly does not regard law as an unreflective practice in the way that Hart does, and he takes the participant's reflective point of view into account in developing what he calls the central case of the legal viewpoint: 'If there is a point of view in which legal obligation is treated as at least presumptively a moral

While there may thus be a place for a limited interpretive methodology like Hart's, it would be an unsatisfactory state of affairs if legal theory were to employ this approach alone. There are two main points to note in this regard.

First, law is not, after all, very plausibly understood as an unreflective practice. It is best viewed as self-reflective in the sense that, first, reflection on the practice's character and point is widespread and properly regarded as a part of the practice, and secondly, different views about the point of law influence how the practice is conceptualized by its participants. This is essentially what Dworkin means when he says that law is a social practice marked by the *interpretive attitude*.[64] And while it may sometimes be appropriate to study self-reflective practices using Hart's approach, to do so exclusively will leave something out of account. The concern here is with juriprudence's descriptive ambitions. Consider Joseph Raz's observation that, 'unlike concepts like "mass" or "electron", "the law" is a concept used by people to understand themselves. We are not free to pick any fruitful concepts. It is a major task of legal theory to advance our understanding of society by helping us to understand how people understand themselves.'[65] We have seen that jurisprudential descriptions cannot, as Hart hoped, be completely neutral. A conceptual framework is required, and the usual method for constructing that framework involves the attribution to law of a point or function. Raz suggests, in effect, that in the case of practices in which people use the associated concepts for purposes of self-understanding—these being practices that will inevitably possess at least the first characteristic of self-reflectiveness noted above—it will be particularly fruitful and illuminating to engage in description from the participants' own point of view. Raz himself takes up this task by attributing to law the function of guiding conduct by means of general, publicly ascertainable rules.[66] This is the first step in an illuminating analysis that is intended to clarify, from the participants' own point of view, the concept of legal authority.[67]

obligation . . . then such a viewpoint will constitute the central case of the legal viewpoint.' Ibid., at 14–15. The legal viewpoint is, clearly, an *internal* viewpoint. Finnis also makes it clear that the theorist is to some extent bound, although in no way completely bound, by the concepts that the societies he is studying use in their own self-interpretation. Ibid., at 15–16.

[64] Dworkin, *supra*, n. 7, at 47, 87. The interpretive attitude has two aspects. The first is an assumption that the practice not only exists but has a value or point that can be stated independently of the 'rules' that make up the practice. The second is the further assumption that the requirements of the practice are taken to be sensitive to its point, 'so that the strict rules must be understood or applied or extended or modified or qualified or limited by that point'. Ibid., at 47.

[65] Joseph Raz, 'Authority, Law and Morality', *The Monist*, 68 (1985), 295, at 322. Cf. Gerald J. Postema, *Bentham and the Common Law Tradition* (Oxford: Clarendon Press, 1986), at 333. Postema's approach to methodology in jurisprudence is in a number of respects quite similar to the approach I sketch in this essay. See ibid., at 328–36.

[66] Joseph Raz, *The Authority of Law* (Oxford: Clarendon Press, 1979), at 50–1.

[67] See particularly Raz, *supra*, n. 65.

The second point is that Hart's methodological approach does not, as we have seen, assist us in understanding the normativity of law. Hart was correct to point out that the internal point of view, understood in terms of (perceived) reasons for action, plays a crucial role in explaining the normativity of law. But the only way of taking advantage of this insight, as Hart himself did not, is to broaden the role that the internal point of view plays in legal theory. Full understanding of the normativity of a self-reflective practice is only possible if the theorist inquires into how and why the practice is perceived by its participants as giving rise to reasons for action, and in order to do this she must ask about the (possible) point or value of the practice *from their point of view.* Once again Raz's views are illuminating.

Consider, to begin with, Raz's account of the normativity of law.[68] Unlike Hart, Raz accepts that normative language has the same meaning in both moral and legal contexts. Thus, legal statements, when used in a fully committed way, make claims about one's moral duties, rights, and so on. But it is possible to make normative statements, and hence legal statements, that are non-committed, or *detached.* A detached normative statement does not carry its full normative force, and so does not commit the speaker to the normative view expressed. But a detached statement is still made from the same normative point of view as a fully committed statement. An example would be the non-vegetarian who advises her vegetarian friend that she should not eat a particular dish, because it contains meat. Raz thus explains the normativity of law not by supposing, like Hart, that law gives rise to a special kind of social obligation, but by pointing to the fact that many people *believe* that law gives rise to *moral* reasons for action. In other words, he explains the normativity of law in terms of the reasons it is *perceived* to create. The more general use of normative language is then explained by the possibility of parasitic, detached statements. But Raz's theory of law offers a fuller understanding of the normativity of law than the mere observation that the law is perceived to give rise to reasons for action. The theory's point of departure, it will be recalled, is the attribution to law of a certain point or function, namely, the guidance of conduct by means of general, publicly ascertainable, rules. But one of the conceptual constraints that the theory must take into account is the fact that the law claims moral authority for itself. From the perspective of a theorist who is looking at the practice with a participant's eyes, this claim is a conceptual feature of the practice that must be treated as a given.

Raz formulates and defends the *service conception* of authority, which regards authorities as '*mediating* between people and the right reasons which apply to them, so that the authority judges and pronounces what they ought to do according to right reason'.[69] Raz says that, in advancing the

[68] See particularly Raz, *supra*, n. 66, at 153–9.
[69] Raz, *supra*, n. 65, at 299 (emphasis in original).

service conception, he is not simply reporting what people believe. Nor is he saying that the law's claim to authority is, in fact, justified. What the service conception does is to offer a philosophical argument showing that the law's claim to moral authority *could* be justified under certain conditions. Summarized in a very crude and incomplete form, the argument holds that the law's claim to authority will be justified (or partially justified) when some or all persons would do better, with reference to the reasons (including moral reasons) that are actually applicable to them, to follow the law's publicly ascertainable, source-based rules rather than trying to decide what to do on the basis of their own judgment; for someone for whom that condition holds, the rules will serve as *new* (moral) reasons for action that that person actually has. The service conception thus establishes a connection between, on the one hand, a function that, given the law's internal conceptual structure, it makes sense to attribute to law—that function being, to repeat, the provision of publicly ascertainable guides to conduct—and, on the other hand, the perception many people have that law is for them reason-creating. The connection consists in the fact that authoritative legal rules could indeed, under certain conditions, give rise to actual reasons that people ought to follow. In this way Raz's theory leads to a deeper understanding of the normativity of law. It does so by taking up the participants' point of view and offering to participants a form of *self*-understanding.[70]

Raz's theory attributes to law a similar function to the one posited by Hart's theory, and indeed Raz's theory explicitly builds on Hart's positivist premisses. But Raz is much more successful in achieving the twin ambitions of jurisprudence, namely, the social scientific ambition of describing law and the philosophical ambition of explaining law's normativity. He achieves this success by, unlike Hart, taking up a participant's perspective. Among other things, this permits Raz to respond, in a way that would not be available to Hart, to a Hobbesian theory of law advanced by Robert Ladenson that in several respects is reminiscent of the reconstructed Holmesian theory discussed earlier.[71] Ladenson in essence takes the point of law to be the maintenance of peace and social stability: a *de facto* authority is thus presumptively legitimate simply because its subjects acquiesce to its exercise of governmental power. Raz's argument in reply is, in brief, that Ladenson's construal of authority is not faithful to the main features of the notion of

[70] Cf. ibid., at 321: 'The concept of law is part of our culture and our cultural traditions. It plays a role in the way in which ordinary people as well as the legal profession understand their own and other people's actions. It is part of the way they "conceptualize" social reality. But the culture and tradition of which the concept is a part provide it with neither sharply defined contours nor a clearly identifiable focus. Various, sometimes conflicting, ideas are displayed in them. It falls to legal theory to pick on those which are central and significant to the way the concept plays its role in people's understanding of society, to elaborate and explain them.'

[71] Ladenson, *supra*, n. 42.

political authority prevalent in our culture; in particular, it ignores the fact that authorities claim to impose duties and create rights.[72] Raz would presumably wish to add that even Holmesian bad men conceptualize the law in this way, despite the fact that they do not accept, or at least are not moved by, its (possible) moral authority.

In taking up a participants' viewpoint in this way Raz appears to come very close to the strong internalist thesis, which, as defined at the beginning of this essay, is just the idea that the theorist's point of view must be the *same* as that of the participants. This does not quite capture Raz's position, however. These are not matters that can be properly considered in the present essay, but the main point to note is that there is more than one way to take up a participants' point of view, and, indeed, there is more than one such point of view. (The discussion of Holmes illustrated the latter point.) The Razzian theorist appears to look at law from the perspective of a participant who identifies himself with the institution (although possibly in some fairly loose sense), who uses the normative language and conceptual apparatus of the law, but who does not *necessarily* endorse the moral authority of the law, either in full or in part. His use of normative legal language may thus be detached rather than fully committed.[73] He will, however, be inclined to reflect on the empirical and conceptual nature of law, and to inquire into the justifiability of the assumption made by many of his fellow participants that law does in fact have a moral point or value. But he may personally have witheld judgment on whether that assumption is true.[74] Let me call the point of view of such a participant the *reflective* point of view. The claim that the legal theorist should adopt the reflective point of view we may call the moderate internalist thesis. We can now redefine the strong internalist thesis in a more precise fashion as the claim that the theorist should take up the point of view of the fully committed participant, that is, the participant who unreservedly endorses the moral value and authority of law.

It seems preferable that a theorist who is studying a social practice should not have to be fully committed, simply as a *methodological* matter, to the moral justifiability of the practice in question. For that reason moderate internalism has more appeal, as a methodological stance for jurisprudence, than strong internalism. At times Ronald Dworkin appears in *Law's Empire*

[72] Joseph Raz, *The Morality of Freedom* (Oxford: Clarendon Press, 1986), at 24–8.

[73] For reasons not entirely clear to me, the possibility of such a detached perspective is denied in H. Hamner Hill, 'H. L. A. Hart's Hermeneutic Positivism: On Some Methodological Difficulties in *The Concept of Law*', *Canadian Jo. of Law and Jurisprudence*, 3 (1990), 113. Hill seems to think, putting the point in my terminology, that if a theorist takes up any version of the internalist thesis it must be the strong version.

[74] It is thus possible that his ultimate conclusion will be that any entrenched belief in the moral justifiability of law is a form of collective self-delusion, or false consciousness. Cf. Green, *supra*, n. 25, at 14.

to endorse the strong internalist thesis, although the matter is by no means crystal clear.[75] We should not, however, allow this fact to obscure the otherwise strong resemblance that exists between moderate internalism, even as reflected in Raz's own work, and Dworkin's interpretivist approach to jurisprudence.[76] It will not be possible to discuss Dworkin's interpretivism in detail in this essay. I would, however, like to offer preliminary arguments in support of two of the more important points that must be established if the claimed resemblance between moderate internalism and Dworkinian interpretivism is to seem credible.

The first point is that different theories of law constitute plausible competing *interpretations* of law, in the sense that they offer, from the reflective point of view, differing conceptualizations of the practice that are sensitive to the point or value ascribed to the practice by the relevant theory.[77] Raz himself seems to assume that the concepts embedded in legal practice are sufficiently determinate that they can be spelled out and clarified in one way only, namely, his. (In Dworkinian terms, this amounts to the assumption that only one interpretation fits the practice.) But this is a dubious assumption. Consider, by way of example, Dworkin's early work on jurisprudence. Dworkin explicitly rejected the positivist thesis that the point of law is to guide conduct by means of general, publicly ascertainable rules, suggesting instead that law's most basic function is principled adjudication.[78] It was for this reason that he treated law not as a closed set of source-based rules but

[75] The following passage suggests strong internalism: '[F]or us, legal argument takes place on a plateau of rough consensus that if law exists it provides a justification of the use of collective power against individual citizens or groups.' Dworkin, *supra*, n. 7, at 109. But the distinction that Dworkin immediately goes on to draw between the grounds and the force of law is more compatible with moderate internalism. The fact that Dworkin allows global internal scepticism as one possible interpretation of law also suggests that his theorist adopts a reflective rather than a fully committed attitude to law. Ibid., at 79.

[76] Cf. Stephen R. Perry, 'Second-Order Reasons, Uncertainty and Legal Theory', *South. Calif. Law Rev.*, 62 (1989), 913, at 946–9.

[77] That this must be shown follows from Dworkin's characterization of law as a social practice exhibiting the interpretive attitude. See *supra*, n. 64. Gerald Postema points out that the second assumption of the interpretive attitude, which holds that the requirements of the practice are sensitive to its point, should not be understood, as Dworkin suggests in his discussion of the 'post-interpretive' stage of interpretation, as a matter of *reforming* the practice. Dworkin, *supra*, n. 7, at 66. Rather, differing views on the point or value of law 'must, on Dworkin's view, be regarded not as proposals for changes in the practice, but as conflicting views about what the practice as presently constituted really is and what, as a result, it really requires of participants. In this respect, theory drives practice, for the practice is what the (best) general interpretive/justificatory theory says it is . . .'. Postema, *supra*, n. 57, at 293. Of course if different theories—i.e. different interpretations—are not simply to be talking past one another, there must be *some* agreement, at some level, about the nature of the social data to be interpreted. This give rise to the very difficult problem, which cannot be considered here, of how the 'pre-interpretive data' are to be characterized. The only point I would emphasize for present purposes is that, despite some misleading terminology on Dworkin's part, pre-interpretive data are not best understood in terms of a positivist theory of social rules. See *supra*, n. 57.

[78] Dworkin, *supra*, n. 59, at 338, 347–8.

rather as an open-ended set of principles that are, in part, a function of background morality: on this view, quintessentially *legal* reasons are principles binding upon judges rather than rules directed to the population at large.[79] This may not be a plausible function to attribute to law as a whole, but I have argued elsewhere that it makes a great deal of sense in the case of private common law. The result, however, is a very different conceptualization of the common law from the one offered by Raz's theory. On the view I defend, the common law gives rise to reasons for action that for both judges and citizens cannot be understood in terms of Raz's general characterization of legal reasons as source-based and exclusionary.[80] This permits us, among other things, to make sense of such locutions as that common law principles possess a variable weight or authority, and to reject the idea, accepted by Raz, that the common law consists of rules that are valid in an all-or-nothing sense.

By way of further example, consider the disagreement that exists even among positivists concerning the proper characterization of legal reasons, usually because they understand the point or value of law in somewhat different ways. Jules Coleman, for example, denies that legal reasons must have solely social sources, as Raz maintains, because Coleman implicitly accepts that the point of law extends beyond the provision of source-based guidance to include principled adjudication.[81] By contrast, Bentham, as

[79] See further Stephen R. Perry, 'Judicial Obligation, Precedent and the Common Law', *Oxford Jo. of Legal Stud.*, 7 (1987), 215, at 223–6, 254–5. Dworkin clearly regarded a rule as just a summary of the all-in result that is determined by a balance of principles, so that the notion of a rule is logically subordinate to that of a principle. Dworkin, *supra*, n. 59, at 37–8. Dworkin's conception of a rule is thus, at this stage in his work, very different from the 'exclusionary' conception defended by Raz. (On Raz's exclusionary conception, see *infra*, n. 80.) Note that in his later work, from 'Hard Cases' on, Dworkin essentially reversed the logical priority of rules and principles. The rules determined by previously settled law now constitute a fixed starting-point for judges rather than the provisional upshot of a balance of principles. This conception of rules is clearly much closer to Raz's notion of exclusionary rules than it is to Dworkin's own earlier conception. Principles, on the other hand, now play a subordinate role: a principle is said to be a legal principle, not because it is morally applicable to the case at hand, but because it figures in the soundest justification of the settled law.

[80] A source-based reason is one the existence and content of which can be established on the basis of social facts alone, without resort to moral argument. See Raz, *supra*, n. 66, at 39–40. An exclusionary reason is a (second-order) reason to refrain from acting on one or more (first-order) reasons. See ibid., at 17. Raz's claim that legal reasons are both source-based and exclusionary plays an integral role in the service conception of authority and its associated understanding of the point or function of law. See *infra*, n. 81. Raz maintains that the common law doctrine of precedent yields reasons for action that have the same theoretical character as legislated rules, i.e. general, exclusionary, source-based norms that citizens must follow and judges must apply. I argue, by contrast, that the common law gives citizens first-order, non-exclusionary reasons for action, and judges 'weighted', non-source-based, second-order reasons. (I define a second-order reason as a reason to treat a first-order reason as having greater or lesser weight than it in fact possesses.) See Perry, *supra*, n. 79 and *supra*, n. 76, at 957–94.

[81] Jules Coleman, 'Negative and Positive Positivism', in *Jo. of Legal Stud.*, 11 (1982), 139. Raz says of the sources thesis, which holds that legal reasons must be identifiable on the basis of social facts alone, that it serves a systematizing or tidying-up role because it 'reflects and

interpreted by Gerald Postema, views the point of law as giving citizens guidance by *adding to* their reasons rather than, as Raz argues, by exclusionarily *replacing* reasons.[82] Thus, Coleman's and Bentham's respective versions of positivism conceptualize legal reasons in ways quite different from Raz's version. Taken together the observations in this and the preceding paragraph suggest that Raz's theory is one possible interpretation, plausible in many respects but by no means inevitable, that can be offered of the social practice of law in general and of the nature of legal reasons in particular; it is no more foundational in character than Hart's theory turned out to be.[83] These observations further suggest that many other jurisprudential theories should also be understood as intepretations of legal practice (contrary, it should be added, to Dworkin's claim in *Law's Empire* that most are really semantic in character).[84]

The second point that has to be established in order to demonstrate that moderate internalism is a close cousin to Dworkin's interpretivism is that the *content* of different interpretations of law involves moral argument.[85]

explicates our conception of the law'. Raz, *supra*, n. 66, at 48. But this very much understates the strength of the controversy about the status of the sources thesis that exists within legal theory, and that would presumably exist among judges and ordinary lawyers if they were asked. Raz's better argument for the sources thesis is the *moral* argument that he makes in the course of defending the service conception of authority, to the effect that the subjects of an authority can only benefit from its directives if they can establish the existence and content of those directives by means that are independent of the reasons the directive is supposed to be based upon and then replace. See Raz, *supra*, n. 65, at 304. (There is, of course, nothing contradictory about giving a moral argument for the conclusion that moral argument should not be used in a certain context.) The sources thesis is part of a controversial, morally based *interpretation* of legal practice and its associated concepts, and not just a straightforward *clarification*.

82 See Postema, *supra*, n. 65, at 323–7.

83 In my view Raz's theory offers the best interpretation of the legislative aspects of legal practice, whereas a theory more akin to Dworkin's offers the best interpretation of the common law. See Perry, *supra*, n. 79, at 217–18, 255–7, and *supra*, n. 76, at 957–63, 994. This illustrates, it should be remarked in passing, that we are not limited to theories that assign a single point or value to law; pluralism regarding the value of law is not only possible but plausible. It is also worth noting that Dworkin's reconstructed version of positivism, which he calls conventionalism, bears little resemblance either to Raz's version of positivism or to any other plausible version. See ibid., at 950 n. 108.

84 See *supra*, n. 54.

85 Dworkin holds that the interpretation of a social practice has two dimensions, namely, the dimension of fit and the dimension of value. Fit concerns the extent to which a particular interpretation must account for 'the standing features of the practice'. Dworkin, *supra*, n. 7, at 67. Value, which is our present concern, is a matter of showing the practice 'in its best light'. Ibid., at 52–3, 67, 90. Dworkin clearly conceives of the dimension of value as involving moral (or political) argument. Ibid., at 98, 430 n. 3. Andrei Marmor has criticized the 'best light' aspect of Dworkin's theory on the grounds that an interpretation of a work of art need not show the work in its best light. Marmor, *supra*, n. 12, at 52–3. This is clearly correct, but that shows only that Dworkin should not have begun with a comprehensive notion of 'creative' interpretation; he should have first developed a methodology for studying social practices, and only afterwards asked if it bore any relation to other forms of interpretation. So far as the study of social practices is concerned, a theorist who takes up the reflective point of view is inquiring into the

The idea here is that when a theory attributes a moral point or value to law from the participants' perspective rather than the theorist's, the accompanying moral argument becomes part of the theory rather than a preliminary step in concept formation. From the point of view of the participant, which differs in this respect from the point of view of the Hartian theorist, conceptual and normative argument are inextricably entangled. This general point is illustrated by Raz's own theory. The content of that theory is, Raz's claim to the contrary notwithstanding,[86] thoroughly moral in character. It involves far more than making evaluative judgments, in the course of a Weberian process of concept selection, about what is important or significant. We can see this by recognizing that if the service conception offers a correct rendering of the concept of authority, then the anarchist thesis that it is always irrational to act on the basis of someone else's judgment rather than one's own is, as a position in political morality, simply wrong. The service conception redeems the belief held by many participants that the law embodies a moral ideal. As such, it clearly incorporates moral argument. And while it may not make a moral judgment in the strict sense, it does makes a *conditional* moral judgment: if certain conditions are met, then the law's claim to moral authority is wholly or partially justified. That Raz's theory has moral content is not accidental. It is the consequence of adopting a methodology that calls on the theorist not just to report people's beliefs about the law's conceptual apparatus, but also to clarify those beliefs. For clarification of beliefs about reasons for action will almost inevitably involve moral, or at least normative, argument.

There are two final observations I would like to make about moderate internalism. The first is that it envisages jurisprudence as an exercise in theoretical rather than practical reason. In other words, the theorist who adopts a methodology based on the moderate internalist thesis does so because she wishes to understand the institution of law rather than to decide what she or anyone else should do. Thus, she does not treat the institution as authoritative in the sense of Moore's modest interpretivism; she does not treat it as giving her, in her capacity of legal theorist, any reasons for action. This is true even though her characterization of the institution may include moral argument, since moral argument can play a role in theoretical as well as in practical reason. It remains true despite the fact that she has taken up the point of view of a participant, since she is simply attempting, from that point of view, to gain a better understanding

moral justifiability of the practice; it is hard to see what this could mean, other than putting the practice in its morally best light.

[86] See Raz, *supra*, n. 65, at 321: 'All that is claimed is the centrality to our social experience of institutions which express what they claim to be the collective and binding judgment of their society as to how people should behave . . . [W]hile this is an evaluative judgment, it is not a judgment of the moral merit of anything.'

of the practice; she is not trying to determine what she or anyone else ought to do. In fact nothing turns in this regard on whether or not she personally endorses the law's claim to possess moral force. Even if she believes that the institution of law has the full moral authority it claims, she is not, *qua* legal theorist, trying to determine what reasons for action that it gives her. Rather she is attempting, first, to give an accurate internal description of law, and secondly, to ascertain whether her belief in the moral authority of law is justified. Thus, a methodology that takes up the participants' point of view, whether understood as embodying a full-blooded normative commitment or only a detached, reflective attitude, is not equivalent to modest interpretivism.[87]

Dworkin perhaps encourages the idea that an intepretivist methodology must regard theories of law as exercises in practical rather than theoretical reason when he states that 'no firm line divides jurisprudence from adjudication or any other aspect of legal practice'.[88] This might be taken to suggest that legal theorists are engaged in exactly the same sort of activity as judges, which is, of course, a form of practical reasoning. But the better interpretation of this passage is not that theorists must do what judges do, but rather that judges must do what theorists do. In other words, the practical reasoning of judges must presuppose some account of the point or value of law, and hence must presuppose an interpretive theory of the kind called for by Dworkin's jurisprudential methodology. As Dworkin goes on to say, '[j]urisprudence is the general part of adjudication, silent prologue to any decision at law'.[89] But it does not follow that, considered on its own, jurisprudence involves adjudication or any other form of practical reasoning.

My final observation on moderate internalism is that while the central task of jurisprudence is taken to be, on this understanding of the subject, the explication of the concept of law within a particular culture—in practice, our own culture—that does not deny the possibility of what is often referred to as general jurisprudence. It just means that we will look at the practices of other cultures using our own concepts. Raz puts the point well:

There is nothing wrong in interpreting the institutions of other societies in terms of our typologies. This is an inevitable part of any intelligent attempt to understand

[87] This is also part of the answer to Marmor's argument that for a theorist, unlike a participant, Dworkin's requirement that a practice be put in its best light does not necessarily mean morally best light. Marmor, *supra*, n. 12, at 56–7. That 'best' would mean 'morally best' makes sense for participants, according to Marmor, because they must regard law as giving them reasons for action. If, however, the purpose of jurisprudence is 'to reveal those features of law which are common to all legal systems', then 'best' will mean something like '[the best] understanding of our concepts, and of the conceptual scheme which constitutes our intellectual world'. I have argued at length that to obtain the best understanding of our concepts, we must take up the (possibly detached) participants' point of view, and then engage in moral argument. The point I am now making is that this exercise is none the less a matter of theoretical, rather than practical, reason.

[88] Dworkin, *supra*, n. 7, at 90. [89] Ibid.

other cultures. It does not imply that in interpreting alien institutions you disregard the intentions, beliefs or value-schemes of their participants. It only means that at some stage you classify their activities, thus interpreted, in terms of a scheme for analyzing social institutions of which the participants themselves may have been ignorant.[90]

It has been claimed that Dworkin views jurisprudence as a debate that is 'consciously situated within and responsible to our culture's practice', whereas Hart and Raz are engaged in a different activity called general jurisprudence, 'the philosophical effort to *understand* law and legal systems as abstract concepts transcending any one contingent, culturally situated, practice'.[91] As the quote displayed above should make clear, this characterization does not very accurately reflect the way that Raz, at least, views general jurisprudence. Dworkin and Raz are in fact not very far apart on this question (and indeed on many other questions, as should be starting to become clear). It is true that Dworkin says that '[i]nterpretive theories are by their nature addressed to a particular legal culture, generally the culture to which their authors belong'.[92] But there is no reason why the theorist who espoused such a theory could not employ its concepts to engage in general jurisprudence, as Raz describes it above.[93]

CONCLUSION

H. L. A. Hart argued that a satisfactory jurisprudential theory must take account of the internal point of view. As we have seen, this is best understood to mean that the theorist must, by means of external but engaged statements, take account of how the law is believed by at least some participants to give them reasons for action. But theories of law based on this weak form of interpretivism are unlikely to prove satisfactory from the perspective of the twin ambitions of jurisprudence, namely, accurate description and explanation of normativity. Particularly troublesome is the explanation of normativity. The solution is to adopt a more robust version of the internalist thesis, as Joseph Raz implicitly does, thereby calling on the theorist to take up a participant's point of view. The resulting methodology, which I have called moderate internalism, has much to recommend it. But even though moderate internalism does not commit the theorist to morally

[90] Raz, *supra*, n. 66, at 50.

[91] Burton, *supra*, n. 57, at 110–11 (emphasis in original).

[92] Dworkin, *supra*, n. 7, at 102.

[93] It is true that Dworkin says (ibid., at 102–3) that 'there is no reason to expect even a very abstract conception [of law] to fit foreign legal systems developed in and reflecting political ideologies of a sharply different character'. But he then makes it clear that even though one's interpretive theory did not 'fit', say, the Nazi regime, one could still employ the theory to help elucidate the nature of the regime. This is quite close to Raz's understanding of general jurisprudence.

endorsing law, it appears to be very close to the methodological interpretivism of Ronald Dworkin. Dworkin's interpretivism regards theories of law as competing interpretations of the social data, in which the correct description of the social practice is in part a function of moral argument. This is a conclusion that Raz resists. Perhaps, however, the moral of the story is this. If you dance with the interpretivist devil, it's not easy to keep your distance.[94]

[94] Since this article went to press, I have had the opportunity to read Hart's Postscript to the second edition of *The Concept of Law* (Oxford: Clarendon Press, 1994). His discussion there of methodological issues, and of Dworkin's interpretive methodology in particular, generally follows the approach he has taken in other recent writings that I consider in the article. But Hart does take up a new point in the following passage at 248–9: 'Like other forms of positivism my theory makes no claim to identify the point or purpose of law and legal practices as such; so there is nothing in my theory to support Dworkin's view, which I certainly do not share, that the purpose of law is to justify the use of coercion. In fact I think it is quite vain to seek any more specific purpose which law serves beyond providing guides to human conduct and standards of criticism of such conduct.' But Hart's assertion that his theory does not attempt to identify the point or purpose of law as such seems odd in light of the fact that he immediately goes on to single out the guidance of conduct as that very purpose. (This is, of course, the view I attribute to him in this article). And while Hart implicitly suggests that his understanding of the purpose of law is sufficiently broad and general as to be uncontroversial, I have tried to show that this is not the case: see *supra*, at 129–31. (As that discussion also shows, positivists disagree strenuously among themselves, in ways that have theoretical significance, about how the general purpose of guiding conduct is to be more specifically formulated.) It bears mention in this regard that Dworkin has explicitly rejected the view that the purpose of law is to provide guidance for conduct (Dworkin, *supra*, note 59, at 347–48). Moreover Dworkin's talk of justifying coercion is really just a roundabout way of making his standard point that the primary function of law is principled adjudication (Dworkin, *supra*, note 7, at 400–1). Since this cannot be characterized as an obviously implausible view, there is a real debate here. Hart's theory, rather than setting out the neutral presuppositions of that debate, takes up one position within it.

4
Questions in Legal Interpretation

BRIAN BIX

INTRODUCTION

Philosophers in a variety of fields have recently put forward theories in which practice has a significant role within the analysis. Most of these theories, to a greater or lesser extent, are inspired by Wittgenstein's later writings. The turn to practice-based theories has occurred, if unevenly, in jurisprudence as well.

The first part of this paper considers some of H. L. A. Hart's early work, aspects of which may be better understood if seen as an early attempt at a practice-based approach to law.[1] In passing, possible connections and parallels between that work and Wittgenstein's writings will be considered. The second part of the paper analyses questions about legislative intention and Ronald Dworkin's interpretative theory from the point of view of a practice-based approach.

While the paper to some extent works as an advocate for practice-based analyses, I hope the discussions also indicate that there are a variety of ways 'practice' can be used within a theory, and that each has difficulties as well as advantages.

HART AND WITTGENSTEIN

Wittgenstein (1960: 1) warned us against 'one of the great sources of philosophical bewilderment: a substantive makes us look for a thing that corresponds to it.' Many of the more difficult questions in philosophy occur when a particular way of thinking leads us from everyday life to difficult-sounding metaphysical investigations and to the positing of strange abstract entities as a way of resolving the problems we think we have discovered.

This is a revised version of a paper given at the Law and Interpretation Conference at the University of Tel Aviv in May 1993. I am grateful for the comments and suggestions made by Andrei Marmor, and by the other participants at the Conference.

[1] Joseph Raz (1990: 49–58) has analysed (and criticized) aspects of Hart's later writings on rules as part of a critique of 'the practice theory of norms'.

The proper response then, Wittgenstein would say, is not to try to find a better answer to the problems which lead us to metaphysical speculations, but to understand why we thought there were problems in the first place. Once we understand the cause of this urge to metaphysics, we will understand that our real concerns can be met by a clearer overview of our situation, with no necessity for positing or arguing about various non-natural entities. Our belief that the way we use language requires explanation in metaphysical terms is incorrect; no explanation is needed beyond that which can be given by a simple restatement of what we actually do.

Similar themes can be found in H. L. A. Hart's writings on law and legal theory, particularly, though not exclusively, in his earliest work (e.g. 1954, 1955). There are obvious parallels between Hart's approach and that of Wittgenstein: in their discussions of philosophy as a type of therapy,[2] their attempts to avoid metaphysical questions and explanations,[3] and their emphasis on defeasibility as an important, if not central, aspect of concepts.[4] As a historical matter, however, Hart's approach probably derives from J. L. Austin and the advocates of 'ordinary language philosophy' at Oxford (Hart 1983: 2–6; Baker 1977: 28–33). The similarities between Hart's work and Wittgenstein's ideas may be explained by the influence of Friedrich Waismann on Hart (as well as by a convergence of ideas between Austin and Wittgenstein). Waismann was Hart's colleague at Oxford and many of Waismann's ideas derived directly from Wittgenstein. The most obvious example of this influence via Waismann was Hart's well-known discussion (1961: 119–26) of 'open texture', which derived from Waismann's idea of the same name.[5]

The theme of Hart's work in his early writings was that the more difficult questions in legal theory, those that centred on trying to determine the meaning of a legal term or concept (like 'corporation' or 'right'), could be resolved by avoiding the old path of trying to discover what thing in the world the term named. Instead, the focus should be on how the term is used within legal discourse, within legal practice. (In philosophical

[2] Cf. Wittgenstein (1968: §§ 133, 255) with Hart (1955: 241). In the latter text, Hart wrote of inquiries which are 'designed not to teach [the use of legal concepts within a legal system] but to dissipate a certain kind of perplexity about it'.

[3] Both writers thought that such false metaphysical speculations were caused by surface similarities between concepts and aspects of language that in fact had quite different uses. (Hart 1955: 241; Wittgenstein 1968: §§ 90, 109).

[4] While Wittgenstein seemed to believe that defeasibility was a general aspect of thought and language, Hart saw the importance of defeasibility as something that distinguished legal concepts from ordinary concepts. The emphasis on defeasibility was particularly strong in one of Hart's earliest publications (1948–9); for a discussion of defeasibility, criteria, and certainty in Wittgenstein's work, see Hacker (1986: 307–18).

[5] I discuss elsewhere (1993: 7–17) the similarities and differences between Waismann's and Hart's notions of 'open texture'.

parlance, it would probably be accurate to say that Hart was advocating an approach focused on 'warranted assertability'.)[6]

In 'Definition and Theory in Jurisprudence' (1954), Hart urged us to avoid the temptation to find a thing, or even a set of facts (whether future facts, complex facts, or psychological facts), that corresponds to legal terms like 'right' and 'corporation' (45–6). Instead, when asked about some legal term or legal concept, we should only offer descriptions of how, and under what conditions, propositions using the term ('X has a right' or 'Smith & Co. Ltd. owes me five dollars') are used (47–8, 50). Such a response, Hart suggested (50–1), would answer all that had puzzled the interlocutor, and there would be no further temptation to ask metaphysically sounding questions like, 'but what *is* a right (or a corporation)?'

The problem is the extent to which we should ask questions of ontology about concepts within legal discourse, the 'what is the essence of X?' or 'what is the real nature of X?' type of question. In practice, Hart's prescription may seem to have its fullest importance against those who favour metaphysical realism, and thus argue that the enquiry about an object or a concept should never end with an assessment of other people's beliefs about it (community consensus) or statements about it (for example, legislative definitions). However, I think the claim is broader, and applies equally to those who might prefer a non-realist approach to ontology.

The argument is that in the practice of law (and in theories about the practice of law), it is usually not helpful, and it is often misleading, to venture into ontological inquiries. Here again, Hart's writings about law can be compared with Wittgenstein's writings about language and philosophy. It is very difficult to determine what Wittgenstein's position actually was on matters of ontology; most of the time when his real (in lectures) or imaginary (in his writings) interlocutors press him on ontological questions, his response is merely to point out that these sorts of questions are unhelpful, unnecessary, and tend to mislead.

An objection to Hart's position might run as follows: stating the conditions under which we use a term does not explain why we apply those conditions rather than others. There are at least two kinds of situations where a mere description would not seem to be adequate. First, if there appeared to be an inconsistency in the practice; and secondly, if a new case arose where previous practice and the criteria we might derive from it did not offer conclusive guidance as to how the new case should be treated. In both types of situations, we would want an explanation of (or in Ronald Dworkin's terminology, an interpretation of) the past practice which would give us broad principles we could use both for criticism and for guidance.

[6] e.g. at one point (1954: 60), Hart wrote: 'legal words can only be elucidated by considering the conditions under which statements in which they have their characteristic use are true.'

Some aspects of this objection were considered in Hart's work. In his discussion (1954: 49–59) of corporations and attempts to define or theorize about them, Hart briefly mentioned the then-novel question of whether certain crimes could be attributed to corporations, and the question, not then resolved, of whether corporations could be held responsible for *ultra vires* torts. Surely it is for novel cases like these that we need some explanation regarding why the legal system has treated corporations the way it has, and we would expect the explanation to be in terms of corporations 'actually' being real entities, legal fictions, or whatever. However, this was not the approach Hart suggested had been taken, or should have been taken; again, Hart's focus was solely on the past practices.

Hart's belief that a practice-based approach is sufficient even for apparently inconsistent past decisions and for novel questions appeared to be based on a faith that traditional legal analysis is adequate for resolving such problems. In particular, Hart appeared to believe that judges resolve these difficult legal issues through consideration of how far various analogies with other doctrines can and should be used (1954: 57).

It was not part of Hart's concern to consider to what extent traditional legal reasoning or analogical reasoning is in fact neutral, objective, or non-political, though these are obviously questions that would arise in the current jurisprudential climate if similar assertions were made. What is important for present purposes is Hart's contention (1954: 56–60) that judges *should*—and almost always do—confine themselves to traditional forms of analysis that do not require recourse to ontological claims. There is no reason to go beyond what we are familiar with from daily practice into the airless realm of metaphysical speculation. As Hart pointed out (1954: 40), as often as not, the ontological claims are equally consistent with—and equally indifferent to—the possible resolutions of the legal question at hand.

The answer to the question of whether Hart's approach in his earlier works is sufficient in embryo, just requiring further elaboration, is not clear to me.[7] In particular, I do not know how to evaluate the faith Hart appeared to have that legal analysis, simply understood, was sufficient for deciding most legal issues. On one hand, it may just be a naïve position, reflecting the absence of sharp Critical Legal Studies or metaphysical realist challenges in the legal literature of that time.[8] On the other hand, it may be an undeveloped (or underdeveloped) version of a full practice theory, that is, claiming

[7] Also not immediately clear is whether or how the theory would need to be modified to meet the challenge of the modern metaphysical-realist legal theories, of which Michael Moore's work (1985, 1992) is the most prominent example.

[8] There are other topics where Hart's discussion seems to ignore or overlook some of the questions which seem in the context of current debates immediate and crucial—elsewhere (Bix 1993: 23–4), I analyse one such example, involving Hart's discussion of 'open texture' and judicial discretion. Again, the explanation may be simply that writers at different times are responding to different concerns and different challenges.

that no reference to abstract entities or political power is necessary to explain or participate in our legal practices (a position not far from some modern practice-based theorists, for example, Patterson (1993) and Bobbitt (1991)). I must leave this exegetical question for another person or another time.

APPLICATIONS—LEGAL INTERPRETATION

As Wittgenstein (1968: §§ 133, 255) described philosophy in general, one could argue that legal philosophy should see its primary purpose as a kind of therapy: a way of overcoming the temptation to see questions within the law and about the law as ones which require answers in abstract or metaphysical terms (for example, the 'nature' or 'essence' of 'law' or of 'rights').

The Hart–Wittgenstein approach, as characterized, is about seeking to answer questions about law and legal theory from within the practice of law: that is, focusing on the practice and emphasizing the extent to which most, if not all, problems in legal theory can be answered by nothing more than a better description of our practices.[9]

Within discussions of law and legal theory, the topic of interpretation receives attention primarily in connection with prescriptions for judges: how they should apply constitutional provisions, statutes, and past judicial decisions (and to what extent the reasoning or the interpretation of texts should differ over these three categories). The first topic of this section will be taken from matters of this kind: it involves the problem of legislative intention.

An additional set of questions about the role of interpretation in law has been raised by Ronald Dworkin's important recent works (1986, 1987),

[9] Other theorists have recently put forward approaches to law which are similar. In particular I have in mind the Wittgensteinian approaches of Dennis Patterson (1993) and Philip Bobbitt (1991), though there are aspects of those approaches with which I would disagree.

In Hart's later work, he can still be seen to be arguing that finding the right answers to the problems of legal theory is based to a large extent on making sure that one is asking the right questions. For example, at the beginning of *The Concept of Law* (1961: 1–6), he considered the standard question of legal theory, 'What is Law?' Past theorists had given various answers to this question, from the mundane but unsatisfactory to the bizarre. Hart proposed (13) that the question 'What is Law?' is usually best seen as an attempt to consider one of three issues: 'How does law differ from and how is it related to orders backed by threats? How does legal obligation differ from, and how is it related to moral obligation? [and] What are rules and to what extent is law an affair of rules?'

Whether one agrees with his proposal or not, one can see how Hart has succeeded in diverting attention from definitional obsessions to more mundane and manageable questions, and to questions and answers rooted in our practices. Hart's response to the question, 'What is Law?' was basically to counter, 'Why do you ask?' This is the Wittgensteinian response I summarized earlier: it is an attempt to simplify, or dissolve, a seemingly difficult question, which tempts some to answers in terms of ontology and essences, by trying to convert it or reduce it to questions relating to the proper description of our practices.

where he has argued that all attempts to determine what the law requires, to understand a particular legal system, or to understand law in general, are basically acts of interpretation. The second topic of this section is the consideration of certain aspects of Dworkin's recent work, in particular, the connection between his analysis and our practices.

Legislative Intent

Discussions of 'legislative intention' have often been less clear than they might be, and it seems likely that this confusion is caused by a number of factors. For my purposes, I want to focus on three of those factors: (1) the temptation to define legal terms in the same way that non-legal terms are defined (discussed earlier, in connection with Hart's earlier writings); (2) the assumption that the term 'intention' must have roughly the same meaning and use in a legislative context (and with other collective entities) as it does in the context of individuals; and (3) the assumption that since the same term (legislative intent) is used within (or in discussions about) a number of legal systems, the term must name the same thing in each system.

Regarding the first point, debates about 'legislative intent' sometimes use the term as if it named some thing, and the debate is then about how one can best discover that thing, or whether its existence is indeed only a figment of our imagination.[10] Hart pointed out that we are likely to create misunderstandings and confusion if we try to understand legal concepts in terms of standard definitions ('genus and differentia'—Hart 1954: 46). Hart's proposal, as discussed earlier, was that instead of using a form of analysis that (expressly or implicitly) tries to match a legal concept with some thing in the world, it is better to analyse the concept in terms of the circumstances in which sentences using the concept would be true.

This analysis works particularly well for 'legislative intent'. The standard discussion regarding that term is that it must name some collective mental state, and the question then becomes how one discovers such an entity, or whether it makes sense to talk about collective mental states at all. A Hart-like analysis would place the focus on the way the term 'legislative intent' is actually used by lawyers and judges. To the extent that there are consistent and coherent rules guiding when reference to legislative intent is appropriate and when inappropriate, and such rules can be (at least roughly) articulated, there seems no need to become involved in questions of ontology and epistemology.[11] Meaning is use; one understands a term, even a

[10] e.g. compare Marmor (1992: 155–84) with Dworkin (1986: 313–27); the question was also raised in a number of papers at the Tel Aviv conference.

[11] A similar analysis seems to be assumed by Raz (1993: 14), when he writes: 'How can institutions have intentions? The answer is that if they can act intentionally, after much deliberation (e.g. "after discussing the matter for 7 hours the House of Commons approved the Bill

legal term, when one understands when it is appropriate and when inappropriate to use it, and one can explain those rules to another person.

There can, of course, be difficulties even for this method of analysis. One is that within a single context there may be a number of different concepts, each with separate rules for warranted assertion, which coexist under that the same label. For example, in recent American legal literature, the references to legislative intention are often ambiguous between a technical concept specific to American constitutional theory and a more general concept derived from analytical jurisprudence.

A recent discussion by Joseph Raz is quite helpful in distinguishing one of the uses of legislative intention from the others. Raz proposes (1993: 18) a basic or minimal aspect of legislative intention: noting that 'whenever one legislates one intends, under some description, to make the law one is enacting'. This basic or minimal aspect of intention is important to recognize, as against those who might believe that intention plays no role in understanding legislation, or who might doubt the connection between legislation, authority, and legitimacy in the law. However, Raz's basic (and universal) point about legislation does not purport to determine how legislation should be interpreted in particular legal systems,[12] which I believe is the focus of most uses of the term 'legislative intent', as I will discuss below.

The aspect of legislative intention in which I am interested could be understood as being the next step in the analysis: the conventions of interpretation that are needed beyond the minimal intention. When courts in England or America discuss legislative intention, it is usually in the context of supporting or refuting a particular reading of a statute or series of statutes, clarifying ambiguities in a legislative text, or justifying the conclusion that the text should be interpreted in a way contrary to its (apparently) unambiguous meaning.

In most cases, the reference to legislative intention will involve using the statements of legislators (usually statements within institutional bounds during the legislative process) to ground a particular reading. However, in at least one group of cases the reference to legislative intention in the context of statutory interpretation had no connection with the comments or the mental states of legislators.

In England, it was the case until recently that the record of legislative debates could not be consulted to determine the meaning of a statute. The

as amended in committee") they can have intentions. We find no problem in attributing intentions to corporations, groups and institutions in ordinary life, and the law assumes that corporations and some other legal subjects who are not human beings can act intentionally.'

[12] Though Raz (1993: 21) does argue that this aspect of legislative intention does impose a significant constraint on interpretation, in that one must understand legislation according to what the 'words [enacted] mean, given the circumstances of the promulgation of the legislation, and the conventions of interpretation prevailing at the time'.

focus instead was (and still is) on the 'literal' or 'plain' meaning of the statute. Lord Reid explained: 'We are seeking the meaning of the words which Parliament used. We are seeking not what Parliament meant but the true meaning of what they said.'[13] Yet judges and commentators continued to refer to 'Parliamentary intent'. If one tried to determine the meaning within the English legal system of 'the intention(s) of Parliament' (and similar phrasings) from the way such terms were used, one would conclude—and I think correctly—that the term was merely a place-holder for all the (text-centred) rules of interpreting legislation, and nothing more than that.

As regards the second topic, the comparison of 'legislative intentions' and individual 'intentions', various theorists have pointed out that one cannot speak of a legislature having intentions regarding a statute in the same way that one speaks of an individual intending a certain meaning when stating something during a conversation (e.g. Dworkin 1986: 313–27). This is surely correct, and to the extent that anyone was under a contrary impression, it is certainly a point worth making. However, it is not necessarily the case (in fact, I would argue that it is rarely the case) that when judges or commentators in a particular legal system refer to 'legislative intent' in interpreting statutes, they are using the phrase no differently from the way they use 'intentions' in an individual or conversational context.

That two terms—here '(individual, conversational) intent' and 'legislative intent'—are similar does not necessarily mean that they have identical uses (and this can even be true for the same term used in two different contexts). An analogous situation is described by Wittgenstein (1980: 77): 'On railway stations there are dials with two hands; they show when the next train leaves. They look like clocks though they aren't; but they have a use of their own.' Just as the special railway station clock has a use and significance different from normal clocks, so we should consider the concept of legislative intent with the possibility that its use and significance is different from that of the concept of individual, conversational intent.

If legislative intent cannot be understood in terms of individual intention, that does not mean that the concept is incoherent, only that it is a distinctly different concept. The obvious differences in the two types of situations, with legislatures being collective bodies and legislative texts being applicable to unforeseen circumstances, and so on, are usually taken into account in the way the phrase 'legislative intent' is defined and used.

Thirdly, one must consider to what extent one can speak generally about legislative intent. The argument against a general view is that it is potentially misleading to use any legal term in a way which implies that it (necessarily) has the same meaning in all legal systems. If a legal term is best defined by

[13] *Black-Clauson International, Ltd.* v. *Papierwerke Waldhof-Aschaffenburg A.G.* [1975] 1 All ER 810, at 814. As the law is currently, only the speech of the proposer of the act can be referred to, and even then only in limited circumstances.

the circumstances in which its use is warranted, then a general definition will usually be inappropriate, for the rules of warranted assertion can (and generally will) vary from one legal system to another (although the common history and interaction among systems often serve to limit the divergence).

The position I am arguing against is one which sees legislative intent as having a single meaning, a single referent, for which the different approaches in different legal systems can be seen as nothing other than different evidentiary rules for trying to determine the same matter. References to '*the* meaning' of legislation can be misleading, in that one might conclude that there is but one correct way to interpret legislation, or to interpret a particular piece of legislation, independent of or transcending any particular legal system, instead of seeing the understanding of legislation, like the understanding of language, as dependent on (a vast and intricate) context. There is no one method for 'extracting' meaning or determining meaning which will work for all legal systems, and to the extent that legislative intent is a shorthand for all or part of that process, the term will have significantly different meanings in different legal systems.

In England, the convention in interpreting statutes is still (despite the inroad made by *Pepper* v. *Hart*, discussed below) to place a great deal of emphasis on the literal meaning of the words that Parliament enacted. In America, the convention is to place a great deal of emphasis on committee reports and the exchanges in legislative floor debates.[14] These and similar definitions are not different, perhaps inefficient, attempts to capture some entity called 'legislative intent'; that is to get things the wrong way around. There is no Platonic idea of 'legislative intent' that we must discover and try to describe. These various definitions in the various legal systems define what legislative intent *is* for the purposes of those legal systems.

In favour of the possibility of a general theory or a general discussion of legislative intent, one can offer two suggestions. First, there can be a general study of a legal term, if one were to choose to define the concept in a more or less arbitrary manner, selecting an aspect of our legal system and then looking to see if other legal systems have characteristics that are roughly analogous.[15]

[14] One could argue that the American courts' approach to 'legislative intent' indicates that they are giving the term the same meaning that it has in individual, conversational contexts. If that is the case, it would of course be worth stating that such an attempt is untenable. I do not have sufficient time here to consider fully the argument (or assumption) that this reading of the American practice is the only one available. If another reading is possible, then we should certainly prefer that reading to one which leaves the practice incoherent or untenable. Dworkin's approach in *Law's Empire* (1986: 313–54) is similar, though his alternative reading is to see legislative intent as part of an interpretative approach to statutory interpretation. My alternative is in some ways more straightforward: that 'legislative intent' is a tenable and coherent concept—simply one different from individual, conversational intent.

[15] I offered some brief comments in another place (1993: 190–5) on the analogous topic of the possibility and limitations of a general theory of law.

Secondly, a general study of legislative intent may be warranted by what is common to its uses in different legal systems. As indicated, the term might best be seen not as naming a thing, but as a shorthand for the process (and the result) of interpretation. Legislative intent in England and America at least (I cannot speak for the extent to which this is a general phenomena) appears to stand for whatever aspect of legislative texts or the legislative record is used to clarify or settle the meaning and application of legislation, and the way in which such material might be so used.

Finally, I should note as an aside that there is a sense in which one could say that legislative intent within the English legal system has recently undergone a change of meaning, through the important decision of *Pepper* v. *Hart*.[16] In that decision, the House of Lords decided, contrary to 250 years of precedent, that judges may refer to the record of legislative debates (Hansard), in at least some circumstances, to help elucidate the meaning of legislation. The 'meaning' of the term has changed in the Hartian sense that the conditions under which sentences using the term would be true has changed. The House of Lords, when acting in its legislative capacity, changes the conditions under which expressions which indicate conclusions of law are warranted. Thus, there is a sense in which the House of Lords can change—and has changed—the meaning of terms like 'contract', 'recklessness', and 'consideration' for the purposes of English law.[17]

Ronald Dworkin's Interpretative Approach

For Ronald Dworkin (1986, 1987), interpretation is not a mere facet of legal practice about which we might ask questions; it is the primary and incessant answer to almost any question one might want to ask about law or about legal theory. An interpretative approach is appropriate for describing what goes on in legal theory and what judges do, and it is also the proper description for determining what the law requires on any single issue.

Dworkin's theory is tied to practices in two different ways. First, the theory argues that legal theories should be interpretations of particular legal systems, interpretations of the actions and attitudes of the participants and officials of the system as well as the relevant statutes and judicial decisions. Secondly, Dworkin on a number of occasions has argued for particular controversial views about the nature of law by stating that his theory better reflects our practices than alternative approaches do.

[16] *Pepper* v. *Hart* [1993] AC 593. The reaction to this case has at times been extreme. One commentator (Styles 1994: 154) described the result in *Pepper* v. *Hart* as 'a change which clearly violates the rule of law, making a fundamental change in the British Constitution'.

[17] For an interesting contrasting view see Moore (1985: 328–38; 1989: 881–90), who holds that all such legal terms are best understood in a Platonic (metaphysically realist) way.

Dworkin's work has elicited two types of general questioning, discussed below, which have some claim to being in the Hart–Wittgenstein tradition.

Debunking Questions

The first type of question is to wonder what 'the real reason' for or 'the real motivation' behind Dworkin's analysis is. Debunking is sometimes characterized as a practice-based approach, in that it claims that theorists' descriptions of what occurs within law are false or misleading relative to what our practices actually are (what is '*really* going on'); debunking theories will sometimes go so far as to claim that the (self-) characterizations and descriptions used by officials within the system are similarly false and misleading.

This type of challenge has its roots in American Legal Realism (e.g. Cohen 1935) and its most enthusiastic recent proponents are in the Critical Legal Studies movement (e.g. Kelman 1984; Freeman 1981). The connection with the Hart/Wittgenstein approach is in the belief that terms used by practitioners or theorists are labels without content, which only serve to mislead. If we look at the actual practice, the argument goes, we would find only an attempt to rationalize particular results. Additionally (as conclusion if not as premiss), these arguments usually hold that it is all but nonsensical to say that one theory is better than another at explaining law. All that is going on in descriptive legal theory, this approach states, is an attempt to legitimate particular judicial decisions or methods.

This is an interesting game, often entertaining, and not terribly difficult to play. For example: the early American theorists, like Christopher Columbus Langdell, who tried to portray legal reasoning and the judicial process as scientific, were trying to defend unpopular conservative judicial decisions as 'objective', as required by deductive reasoning that the judges could not legitimately side-step. The American Legal Realists who debunked this formalistic approach could themselves be debunked: their positive programme legitimized legal reform and justified the use of policy arguments in the courts (Horwitz 1992: 185–212).

Similarly, H. L. A. Hart, with his arguments based on the 'open texture' of language, could be seen as justifying limited judicial legislation in difficult cases. Ronald Dworkin's response, in terms first of the 'right answer thesis' and later with the 'interpretive approach', could be seen as offering a way of legitimizing the apparently political nature of the Warren Court's jurisprudence in the United States when the decisions of that court were attacked as 'anti-democratic' (Gabel 1977).

One might argue that theories of interpretation merely decorate and legitimate the choices made by judges, while hiding the real reasons (motivations) for the decisions, and that few decisions are actually determined (or precluded) by the theoretical prescriptions (for example, 'neutral principles'—Wechsler 1959; 'the Grand Style of Judging'—Llewellyn 1960; or 'the judicial virtues'—Hart 1961: 200) judges are told to follow.

Dworkin has responded (1986: 271–4; 1991*b*: 369–70) to attempted debunkings of this type by claiming that they are irrelevant to his project. Why does it matter, he asks, that there might be historical, psychological, or sociological explanations for why a particular theory was put forward or was well received? Even if it can be proved that a theory serves the interests of a certain class or group at the expense of others, or that the theory expresses the *Zeitgeist* of its era of origin, why should this matter? In the end, the question is whether the theory is right, or whether it is at least better than alternative theories. Historical, psychological, and sociological explanations are marginal to investigations into a theory's correctness.

Debunking explanations may not be completely irrelevant, in that we can rightly be suspicious of philosophical positions—whether these be ethical, social, or legal theories—that match the theorist's self-interest or that theorist's particular prejudices regarding how the world should be. However, suspicion is not proof, and as long as argument about the merits of a theory can be conducted on neutral grounds (according to criteria accepted by the participants in the field regarding what makes for stronger and weaker arguments and for better and worse theories),[18] then the debunking arguments can work only to justify beginning a debate about the theory in question; the eventual judgment about its merits will be based on other grounds.

Questions of Clarification

The second kind of question about Dworkin's work is more directly connected with the Hart–Wittgenstein approach, in that it asks for clarification of the meaning of some of the more abstract concepts and ideas that appear in his writings.

For example, it is important to Dworkin's interpretative approach that we are able to distinguish a meaning which is an *interpretation of* a comment, novel, or statute from 'an invention', a meaning *imposed on* the text.[19] In discussing this distinction in seminars, Dworkin said that a particular reading of *Hamlet*, for example, is legitimate if that meaning or theme were *already present* in the play. An illegitimate reading of the play is one that claims a meaning that was not *in* the play to begin with.[20]

[18] The sceptic might argue that there are no 'neutral grounds': all criteria already express the interests or the preconceptions of certain groups. I do not have time to consider this argument here.

[19] See Dworkin (1986: 67): 'He also needs convictions about how far the justification he proposes at the interpretive stage must fit the standing features of the practice to count as an interpretation of it rather than the invention of something new.' (See also ibid., referring to an interpretation that is 'too ill-fitting a justification to count as an interpretation at all'.)

[20] As an interesting comparison, Dworkin once commented that he thought that a particular interpretation or meaning of a play is 'already in' the text of a play in a way that a particular interpretation of a Rorschach Test pattern is not 'already in' that pattern.

Dworkin is elsewhere (1983, 1991*b*) conscious of avoiding metaphysical-sounding references, for example, to the 'objectivity' of legal or moral right answers, based on answers being 'out there' as part of the 'furniture of the universe'. Therefore, he would not be happy with my focusing too much on meanings being 'in the text' as contrasted with 'imposed on the text', and so on. However, such metaphors aside, the success, indeed the workability, of Dworkin's interpretative approach obviously depends on (among other things) our being able to distinguish tenable interpretations from untenable ones (and our ability, at least most of the time, to be able to persuade other participants that a proffered interpretation fits in one category rather than the other).

To what extent is Dworkin's analysis based purely on subjective impressions, or on the participants' intuitive reactions? (And if the analysis is grounded in intuitions, on what are those intuitions based?) If I offer an interpretation of a book, a play, a practice, or a string of past judicial decisions, offering textual citations, analogies, and moral arguments to support my argument, and you are not persuaded—in fact, you find my proffered reading bizarre or 'off the wall'—on what grounds can I persuade you (or a neutral third party) that my reading is correct, or at least that it deserves serious consideration, other than by simply repeating my argument? In the end, there seems to be only the practice in which I participate, and the fact that I, a competent practitioner, fully trained in this practice, find this set of arguments persuasive.

Does this mean that the success of an interpretation is merely a function of its acceptance, that the only question that we can ask is whether a majority of competent practitioners would in fact see the interpretation as tenable?[21] This cannot be. After all, the people making the evaluation must themselves have some basis for judging the interpretation right, wrong, or 'clearly wrong', and presumably that basis is not simply a prediction that other people will judge similarly.

In Wittgenstein's discussions of rule-following (1968: §§ 198–242), he connected meaning with individual judgments, but there are two matters worth noting in comparing this connection with any possible comparable connection within legal analyses. First, for Wittgenstein the rule-following connection was indirect: it was the agreement in judgments (regarding 'how we go on') which made the practice *possible*. Without consensus, language

[21] Where we draw the line between the interesting and creative on one side, and the bizarre and untenable on the other may be relative to an era, a society, or an intellectual community. Here, John Bell's (1986) analysis about the 'acceptability' of arguments might be helpful. How close must the analogy be before the example will seem to be on point? Bell's analysis was that there was no a priori way to distinguish good or acceptable analogical arguments from bad ones in legal discourse. His argument was that the line between acceptable and unacceptable arguments is set by a consensus of the legal community, and that newcomers to the legal profession learn the community's standards through training.

and communication as we know them would not be possible. However, consensus is not part of the grammar of 'correct' and 'incorrect': we do not usually refer to majority opinion as part of our justification for evaluating usage as correct or incorrect. (Wittgenstein 1967: § 431) Secondly, the judgments in the context of the rule-following considerations were immediate, unreflective reactions. This would hardly be the case with legal questions, where we do not give priority to people's first intuitive responses to difficult legal questions, and where we think detailed and reasoned arguments for a conclusion are appropriate and often required.[22]

Again, if the reference to practice is challenged regarding the standard topics of Wittgenstein's rule-following considerations (simple descriptive terms and simple mathematical series), the response is, 'there is nothing more that *could* be offered as justification; we have reached bedrock' (Wittgenstein 1968: § 217). If someone were to ask me, 'how do I know that following the instruction "add 2" the next number in the series "1004, 1006, 1008" is 1010?' or 'how do I know that this tomato is red?', all I could say in reply is that this is simply *what we call* 'adding 2' or 'the colour red'. (Baker and Hacker 1984: 85) These practices are in no further need of justification, nor is it clear what a further justification of such basic practices would look like.

Does Dworkin's interpretative approach have a similar connection of practices and judgment? The answer appears to be both yes and no. As mentioned above, when Dworkin is challenged regarding the meaning of the metaphors within his interpretative approach—an interpretation 'fitting' a text or set of texts, or the contrast between 'finding the meaning of' a text rather than 'imposing a meaning on' it—he resists the natural move of seeing his theory in terms of metaphysical questions and ontological answers.[23] All attempts to find a deeper reality beneath the images in the end evoke only the response: this matches the way we actually act and think. (e.g. Dworkin 1985: 144–5) Thus, in a sense, Dworkin follows the advice of theorists like Hart and Wittgenstein: in the end, all there is, all we can strive for, is a better description of, a better overview of, our actual practices.

However, there is another sense in which Dworkin's characterization and interpretation of legal practice appear to be significantly different from Wittgenstein's rule-following considerations. While the descriptive terms and simple mathematical series Wittgenstein discussed resist further analysis and justification, the surface grammar of Dworkin's concepts seems to invite it.

[22] Compare Blackburn (1981: 170) on the importance for Wittgenstein's analysis of the 'automatic and compelling nature of rule-following' in easy cases.

[23] A more precise picture of the role of 'fit' within Dworkin's theory is given by Andrei Marmor's helpful analysis (1992: 72–3) that fit has two functions: in the interpretative stage, it sets a threshold that determines whether something is indeed an interpretation of that text or practice; while in the post-interpretative stage it is one of the criteria to be applied to determine which of the tenable interpretations of the text or practice is the correct (or best) one.

When Dworkin writes of there having to be a sufficient fit with the material for a meaning to be 'found in' a text or a practice rather then 'imposed upon it', of 'balancing fit and moral value' to determine which of two interpretations of past legal materials is correct, or of determining as a moral matter what weight is to be given to fit in a particular area (Dworkin 1986: 249–50), all such comments seem to indicate that further elaboration and justification are possible.

However, what would such further analysis look like? There are obvious difficulties with trying to quantify the fit or textual support of the interpretations we put forward. Consider what might happen if someone were to offer such an analysis. Imagine someone individuating the parts of a text and then, after studying past interpretations and their critical reception, coming to the following conclusion: 'an interpretation is justified if and only if it is consistent with at least 75 per cent of the text's individual units.' Even if that description were consistent with every judgment we made in the past, we would not accept it as the rule to follow in evaluating texts, because it is not the way we actually reach decisions. More to the point, if there were a case where this quantitative analysis said that an interpretation should be rejected, but our own conclusions (reached in the traditional, non-quantitative way) were to the contrary, our inclination would be to reject the theory, not to change our conclusions. This is just a roundabout way of saying that our practices here resist being put on a scientific basis or placed under any rubric that might allow demonstrability or consensus.[24]

In a recent article, Dworkin (1991*b*: 377–80) emphasized that the distinction between interpretation and invention is not based on anything else (and certainly not on any sort of 'furniture of the universe'-type claim). Rather, all one can say—and all one need say—is that it is a distinction that we (participants in the practice) use, and that we understand the distinction when others use it.

There is a parallel between aspects of Dworkin's work and Hart's early writing, discussed at the beginning of this article. In both cases there are claims made at two levels: first, that the description offered matches the practice (including characterization of the practice by participants) better than alternative theories do; and secondly, that the practice can be explained without complex references to meta-theory or ontology.

[24] Some of the problems discussed in this section (and in this article generally) might be clarified by a better understanding of the (differing?) metaphysical positions underlying Dworkin's theory and the Wittgensteinian approaches (e.g. the extent to which they presuppose a realist or conventionalist ontology). However, even as to Dworkin the task is difficult, as is shown by the way even the better writers on the subject disagree sharply on the extent to which Dworkin should be read as a metaphysical realist or a conventionalist (compare, e.g. Marmor (1992: 61–84); Patterson (1993: 281–6); and Moore (1987: 457–75); see also Dworkin (1991*a*), where he discusses some aspects of the 'ontology' of his ideas). A fuller consideration of these questions must wait for another time.

The argument (Dworkin 1991*b*: 376–81) that the distinction between interpretation and invention needs no further grounding other than the acceptability and use of that distinction in our daily legal practices, assumes certain facts about the practice. More to the point, it assumes that these facts are true at a variety of levels. It is one thing to say that legal practitioners understand arguments regarding whether a reading of legal precedent is a tenable interpretation rather than an invention (and that there is sufficient overlap in our judgments about such things for the practice to be workable); it is another to say that the distinction is similarly grounded in our general and theoretical reflections about the law.[25]

That is, the analysis might work at the level of lawyers and judges arguing about the proper reading of a certain line of precedent, but it does not follow that it works in a similar way for characterizations of the nature of a particular legal system. (For example, it must first be established that theorists analysing legal systems are (always) engaged in an interpretative task, a notion many theorists strongly resist, e.g. Hart 1987: 36–40.) However, for Dworkin the analysis must work at all levels, both within the practice of law and within the practice of legal theory, because his interpretative approach is meant to be the required analysis for all aspects of legal analysis (1987: 13–15).

At least two further responses to Dworkin's approach also remain open. First, it is of course open to a critic to argue that Dworkin does not in fact capture our practice, the way we act and talk within the law and think about it. For example, one might argue that Dworkin's analysis gives insufficient emphasis to the importance of consensus or authority within law (see e.g. Marmor 1992: 35–84; Bix 1993: 106–32). Secondly, even within Dworkin's theory, practices are not seen as absolutely beyond question. If the practitioners' perceptions are incoherent or indefensible in some way, then they have to be re-characterized (-interpreted) charitably, restating them in a way which makes them more defensible without requiring a rejection of too much of the practice. Thus, while Dworkin did not deny that reference to legislative intent is an important part of American legal practice, he believed the concept (as generally understood) to be incoherent (or at least unworkable); he offered (1986: 313–54) an interpretation of the practice which understands the references to legislative intent in a significantly different way. As J. W. Harris has pointed out (1992: 693–4), a similar re-characterization or reinterpretation could be applied to Dworkin's own ideas about fit, and the points raised earlier may (or may not) help to justify such a re-characterization.

[25] Marmor (1992: 39–44, 56–7) offers a similar analysis of Dworkin's interpretative approach: the fact that participants within the practice take a constructive-interpretative approach to the questions within the practice does not entail that theorists of the practice should take a similar approach.

CONCLUSION

An emphasis on actual practices can have a healthy effect on theory, in that it discourages unnecessary metaphysical speculation. It is far too easy to be 'ensnared by language': to assume that there must be an object of some type which corresponds to every label, to become misled by the images and metaphors we use so that they confuse more often than they clarify, and so on. Periodically returning to what it is we actually do—what it is that our theories are trying to explain—may help to avoid some of these snares. This paper has discussed examples of practice-based approaches, ranging from H. L. A. Hart to Ronald Dworkin, and from statutory interpretation to criminal law. While I think that the examples show some of the strengths of the approach, I would stop short of the position, advocated by some, that a focus on practices will by itself cure all that puzzles us within law and legal theory. Some of those problems go beyond the snares of language, and reflect genuine—and genuinely difficult—moral and political dilemmas.

REFERENCES

Baker, Gordon (1977), 'Defeasibility and Meaning', in P. M. S. Hacker and J. Raz (eds.), *Law, Morality and Society* (Oxford: Clarendon Press), 26–57.

—— and Hacker, Peter (1984), *Scepticism, Rules and Language* (Oxford: Basil Blackwell).

Bell, John (1986), 'The Acceptability of Legal Arguments', in N. MacCormick and P. Birks, (eds.), *The Legal Mind* (Oxford: Clarendon Press), 45–65.

Bix, Brian (1993), *Law, Language, and Legal Determinacy* (Oxford: Clarendon Press).

Blackburn, Simon (1981), 'Rule-Following and Moral Realism', in S. Holtzman and C. Leich (eds.), *Wittgenstein: To Follow a Rule* (London: Routledge & Kegan Paul), 163–87.

Bobbitt, Philip (1991), *Constitutional Interpretation* (Oxford: Basil Blackwell).

Cohen, Felix (1935), 'Transcendental Nonsense and the Functional Response', 35 *Columbia Law Review*, 809.

Dworkin, Ronald (1983), 'My Reply to Stanley Fish (and Walter Benn Michaels): Please Don't Talk About Objectivity Any More', in W. J. T. Mitchell (ed.), *The Politics of Interpretation* (London: University of Chicago Press), 287–313.

—— (1985), *A Matter of Principle* (Cambridge, Mass.: Harvard University Press).

—— (1986), *Law's Empire* (Cambridge, Mass.: Harvard University Press).

—— (1987), 'Legal Theory and the Problem of Sense', in R. Gavison (ed.), *Issues in Contemporary Legal Philosophy* (Oxford: Clarendon Press), 9–20.

—— (1991*a*), 'On Gaps in the Law', in P. Amselek and N. MacCormick, (eds.), *Controversies about Law's Ontology* (Edinburgh: Edinburgh University Press), 84–90.

—— (1991*b*), 'Pragmatism, Right Answers, and True Banality', in M. Brint and W.

Weaver (eds.), *Pragmatism in Law and Society* (Boulder, Colo.: Westview Press), 359–88.

FREEMAN, ALAN (1981), 'Truth and Mystification in Legal Scholarship', 90 *Yale Law Journal*, 1229.

GABEL, PETER (1977), Book Review, 91 *Harvard Law Review*, 302.

GRIFFITH, JOHN (1985), *The Politics of the Judiciary* (London: Fontana).

HACKER, PETER (1986), *Insight and Illusion*, revised edn. (Oxford: Clarendon Press).

HARRIS, J. W. (1992), Book Review, 109 *Law Quarterly Review*, 693.

HART, H. L. A. (1948–9), 'The Ascription of Responsibility and Rights', 49 *Proceedings of the Aristotelian Society*, 171.

—— (1954), 'Definition and Theory in Jurisprudence', 70 *Law Quarterly Review*, 37–60, repr. in (1983), *Essays in Jurisprudence and Philosophy* (Oxford: Clarendon Press), 21–48.

—— (1955), 'Theory and Definition in Jurisprudence', 29 *Proceedings of the Aristotelian Society* (supp. vol.), 239.

—— (1961), *The Concept of Law* (Oxford: Clarendon Press).

—— (1983), 'Introduction', in *Essays in Jurisprudence and Philosophy* (Oxford: Clarendon Press), 1–18.

—— (1987), 'Comment [on Dworkin]', in R. Gavison (ed.), *Issues in Contemporary Legal Philosophy* (Oxford: Clarendon Press), 35–42.

HORWITZ, MORTON (1992), *The Transformation of American Law 1870–1960: The Crisis of Legal Orthodoxy* (Oxford: Oxford University Press).

KELMAN, MARK (1984), 'Trashing', 36 *Stanford Law Review*, 293.

LLEWELLYN, KARL (1960), *The Common Law Tradition: Deciding Appeals* (Boston: Little, Brown & Co.).

MARMOR, ANDREI (1992), *Interpretation and Legal Theory* (Oxford: Clarendon Press).

MOORE, MICHAEL (1985), 'A Natural Law Theory of Interpretation', 58 *Southern California Law Review*, 277.

—— (1987), 'Metaphysics, Epistemology and Legal Theory', 60 *Southern California Law Review*, 453.

—— (1989), 'The Interpretive Turn in Legal Theory: A Turn for the Worse?', 41 *Stanford Law Review*, 871.

—— (1992), 'Moral Reality Revisited', 90 *Michigan Law Review*, 2424.

PATTERSON, DENNIS (1993), 'Conscience and the Constitution' (Book Review), 93 *Columbia Law Review*, 270.

RAZ, JOSEPH (1990), *Practical Reason and Norms* (Princeton, NJ: Princeton University Press).

—— (1993), 'Intention in Interpretation' (unpublished MS).

STYLES, SCOTT (1994), 'The Rule of Parliament: Statutory Interpretation after *Pepper* v. *Hart*', 14 *Oxford Journal of Legal Studies*, 151.

WECHSLER, HERBERT (1959), 'Toward Neutral Principles in Constitutional Law', 73 *Harvard Law Review*, 15.

WITTGENSTEIN, LUDWIG (1960), *The Blue and Brown Books* (New York: Harper Torchbooks).

—— (1967), *Zettel* (Berkeley: University of California Press).

—— (1968), *Philosophical Investigations*, 3rd edn. (New York: Macmillan).

—— (1980), *Culture and Value* (Chicago: University of Chicago Press).

5

Interpretation Without Retrieval

JOSEPH RAZ

When interpreting we explain, show, or display the meaning of the object of interpretation ('the original', as I will refer to it). Interpretation is therefore often thought to be retrieval, a process of retrieving and elucidating the meaning the original has. After all, if interpretation is a display or an explanation of the meaning of an original, that original must have meaning to be capable of being interpreted, and interpretation is the retrieval of that meaning, making it plain to those who might be unaware of it. The role of an author's, or, more generally, a creator's intention in interpretation is closely connected with the retrieval picture. If interpretation is retrieval it is often tempting to think that the only thing there to retrieve is the intention of the creator.

The purpose of this essay is to show that the ideas associated with the retrieval picture are mistaken or misleading. I have chosen to concentrate on interpretation of works of art, music, and literature for two reasons. First, such works are among the paradigmatic objects of interpretation. Secondly, we are all familiar with good interpretations of such works which are innovative, and therefore appear to be at odds with the view of interpretation as retrieval.

I will offer an abstract account of the interpretation of works of art, music, and literature[1] which can, I hope, be modified to apply to other standard objects of interpretation (for example, the law, historical events, rituals, and social customs). That account allows for a more balanced view of the different ways in which authors' intentions can play a role in interpretation.

LEVELS OF MEANING

It is convenient to distinguish broadly between three types or levels of question about the meanings of works of art and literature. At one end there is the question of the significance of the fact that a work of a certain kind was created, or became popular at a certain time, as well as other questions

[1] I will often use 'art' in its broad sense to include music and literature.

about its reception and influence. These questions shade into historical issues, which may not be about meaning and interpretation at all, or which may concern the interpretation of a culture or its mood at a particular time. Those of them which deal with the interpretation of the work of art call for conserving interpretations, that is, they deal with interpreting how other people interpreted the work: 'What did the Romantics see in the Don Giovanni story?', 'How did attitudes to McCarthyism influence the reception of Miller's *The Crucible* at the time of its first performance?', and so on. This level of meaning has little to contribute to our enquiry.

For the purposes of this essay I will distinguish two levels of meaning which I will call 'deep' and 'basic' meaning, though one should not make anything of the choice of these terms. The basic meaning of a work concerns the question of the subject of the work ('a portrait of Alexander VI') or its literal content ('Is this Salomé holding the head of John on a platter?', 'What do the words of a poem mean?', and so on). The identification of a work's subject and literal meaning does give rise to interpretive issues and there is an understandable feeling that if nowhere else surely here the author's intention reigns supreme. Take portraiture: is it not the case that if Giacometti makes a sculpture which he declares to be the portrait of Annette then a portrait of Annette it is? It is made so by being baptized by him as such, and nothing else counts. I will return to this argument later. To begin with I will focus on the deep level of meaning. It is captured by observations such as: 'the painting portrays the compassion of the Christian victors towards the vanquished Muslims', 'the play contrasts the new sophisticated metropolitan culture with the crudity of the traditional mores of the provinces', 'the music is an expression of the passion of love, followed by the depths of despair when it is not requited', and so on. This distinction between the levels of meaning and interpretation is not a sharp one, but it can render useful service for many purposes, including ours. The deep, more than literal meaning is the subject of most discussions of the meaning of works of art. 'Why did Hamlet turn against Ophelia?'; 'Did Hamlet's delay in revenging his father expose an ambivalence in his attitude to his father?', etc. These questions are the standard stuff of critical discussions in art and literature. Are such questions illuminated by the picture of interpretation as retrieval? Are they to be settled by reference to the author's intention?[2]

FROM INTENTION TO EXPRESSION

If interpretation explains or displays the meaning of the work being interpreted, what meaning can a work of art have other than that given it by its

[2] Whether or not every work of art has meaning at one or both of these levels is a question which will not be taken up here.

creator? One answer which springs to mind is both right and inadequate. Meaning, we may say (indeed people have said), just like beauty, is in the eye of the beholder. The performer or spectator, in interpreting the work, is displaying or explaining a meaning which he sees in it.[3] This is correct as far as it goes, and the implication that the meaning he sees in it may not have been put there by the author, or anybody else, may be correct as well. But it is false to conclude that the interpreter can find any meaning whatsoever in the work. Interpreting a work of art differs from reacting to it as to a Rorschach test, or from being inspired or moved by it to have or express certain thoughts, emotions, or attitudes. A sculptor may be inspired by the grain of a block of marble in carving a piece of sculpture out of it. But that would not make the sculpture into an interpretation of the block of marble.

Part of what is missing is an intention to interpret.[4] But what is that intention if not the intention to display, state, or explain the meaning of the work, that is, the meaning it in some sense already has? So we are back to square one. If interpretation requires an intention to bring out the meaning the work has is it not a process of retrieval, and what can there be to retrieve other than what was put into the work by the intention of its author?

The first step towards liberation from the power of the intention paradigm is to note that even interpretations which take the creator's attitudes as the key to success are not confined to viewing interpretation as a retrieval of the author's intention. We need to distinguish the meaning of a work to its author, the meaning he intends it to have, and the views, emotions, attitudes, and so on that he expresses in it.

The meaning of a work to its author can differ from the meaning he intended to express in it in several ways. It may mean something to him because of his memories of events in his life associated with the time of its creation, or publication, and so on, or because of its success with the public, or because of his ultimately unsuccessful struggle to express his vision of this or that in it. It may come to be for him a record of his failure or success. Typically the work may also mean something to the author because of what it and the process of its making reveal to him about himself. Just as the work can mean something to its author, so it can mean various things to other people, who saw the work for the first time on their honeymoon, whose life was transformed by an experience in which it played a role, or in many other ways.

[3] To guard against the mistaken assumption that the interpreter must believe that the work has one correct or best interpretation I refrain from saying that he explains or displays the meaning he sees in it.

[4] In 'Morality as Interpretation: on Walzer's *Interpretation and Social Criticism*', *Ethics*, 101 (1991), 392, I have argued that one interprets only if one intends to do so (under this or some other description).

The question is whether what the work means to its author is special in fixing (at least in part) the meaning of the work. But in all cases what the work means to its author, just like what it means to anyone else, is distinct from, and external to, the meaning the work has. When someone says 'this work means a lot to me', or 'it has a special meaning for me', and we ask 'what does it mean to you?', the answer is not, nor can it be 'it means to me that Hamlet felt frustrated at having lost his mother a second time, first to his father and now to his uncle'. That may be (part of) what *Hamlet* means, and our interlocutor may be aware of that, but it cannot be what it means to him, nor what it meant to Shakespeare or to anyone else. It is rather the meaning he, or they, see in it.[5]

So the meaning of the work is different from what it means to its creator. Is it what he intended it to mean? Why should it be that? Presumably because that is what works of art and literature are. They are vehicles for people to express their views, attitudes, emotions, feelings about beauty, and so on. Whatever else art is, the argument goes, it is a framework, a language for self-expression and for communicating one's thoughts, feelings, and the like by expressing them. But if this is so then the author's intention does not always prevail in interpretation, for what authors of works of art and literature express in their work is not always what they intend to express. They may be surprised by what they learn about themselves from reading, watching, or listening to the works they created. A work can express guilt about one's attitude to one's parents which the author never suspected that he felt. (Is *Don Giovanni* a case in point?)

If the underlying thought is that art is a vehicle for self-expression then authors' intentions are important, but they by no means dominate interpretation. Should we then opt for the view that the work means that which the author expressed in it? If we do we should not do so for lack of rival ways of understanding the meaning of works of art. Clearly some interpretations can proceed without reference to what an author expressed, if only because we can interpret customs, rituals, ceremonies, and such things which do not have authors. Such ceremonies, rituals and their like can be conveniently called 'cultural objects' to mark the fact that—in some sense yet to be explained—they possess their meaning within cultures. Flying or waving a flag expresses pride in or loyalty to one's nation only within a culture or against the background of a culture in which such acts bear this meaning.

[5] Possibly this exaggerates the degree to which 'what does the work mean to X?' can only be answered by reference to X's personal experience of it and personal associations with it. This and kindred expressions range from a usage which excludes what X takes the work to mean, to a usage in which they refer primarily to the meaning which X believes the work to have (as in 'what did *The Sorrows of Werther* mean to the Romantics?'), and on many occasions they refer both to the meaning X believes the work to have, and to the personal associations connected with it.

One mistake to avoid is to regard the interpretation of cultural objects as a conserving interpretation. First, it is useful to remember that the fact that cultural objects have the meaning they have only against the background of certain practices does not mean that their meaning is the meaning they have in the eyes of any particular person, or of the majority of people in the society in which the practices obtain. The meaning of cultural objects is not to be reduced to a statistical fact. It is related to the meaning people believe cultural objects to have, but it does not follow that all aspects of their meanings are understood or known to everyone or to many. Secondly, while we can always look for conserving interpretations such as 'What did a work mean to the Victorians?', conserving interpretations are always secondary or parasitic on non-conserving ones. It is always possible that the two questions: 'What is the meaning of the work?' and 'What is or was the meaning of the work to this public or that, or at this period or that?' have the same answer.[6] But they are always two different questions. Ours is the first of the two.

Works of art, I will argue in the next section, are cultural objects and as such their interpretation is, in principle, independent of the intention of their creator. Later sections will qualify this conclusion. But before we embark on the main argument a brief clarification of its relation to the view of art as a vehicle for self-expression is in place. First, the strong view I have put forward above, that is, that it is the essence of art to provide vehicles for self-expression, is at best misleading, and possibly wrong. It is wrong if it suggests that necessarily artists create art-works in order to express themselves. They can do so to fulfil a commission, aiming to meet detailed specifications and bringing only their skills to the task. They can make randomly produced works, or use 'ready-mades' in order to make theoretical points about the nature of art. And there are other ways in which the self-expression view understood in that way can fail. More importantly, whatever truth there is in it has to accommodate the following distinctions:

The attitudes, emotions, or views which the work expresses need not be those that its creator expressed in it, and what its creator expressed in it differs from those attitudes, emotions, and views for whose existence in the author it contains evidence. To start from the end, a psychologist, or just anyone who knows the artist or author, can find the work revealing in the way in which slips of the tongue or malapropisms are. In our actions, and in the products of our actions we betray our thoughts and feelings in a variety of ways, and not only through expressing them. Furthermore, an artist can create a work or write a poem expressing passionate love or

[6] It may even be a necessary truth that any statement of the form 'this is the meaning (or one meaning or part of the meaning) of the work' is true only if there is a public or a period for which it is its meaning. We will return to this question later.

anything else without feeling such emotions or having such thoughts. As I have just remarked, it may simply be his commission to do so. It is then true that he has created a work which expresses these feelings and thoughts, and in a sense, that he has found a way, or invented a way, of expressing such thoughts or feelings. But it is not the case that he has expressed himself or his feelings or thoughts in the work. He expressed himself or his feelings and thoughts only if he felt or thought what the work expresses. So we need to understand what the work expresses, what it means, independently of what its creator expressed in it.

WORKS OF ART AS CULTURAL OBJECTS

Works of art not only may become, they are meant to become cultural objects. It is the nature of works of art and literature that they are cultural objects, in the sense that they are judged by their success as cultural objects. Let me explain. One aspect of the concept of art is that works of art are meant to be of interest to people who are not merely interested in their creator. They are meant to be of a wider interest, in the sense that their success is judged by the degree and the way in which they do deserve such wider interest. A very bad work of art may still be of great interest to the friends or relations of its creator, for it may be every bit as revealing of his life or personality as a good work. No one else need pay it any attention, if—as we are assuming—it is a bad work of art in all relevant respects. Nor is the general significance of works of art, that is, their interest beyond any interest in the author, to be confused with their significance as historical evidence of the mores of the time, of the language of their day, evidence of the eating habits, and so on, of one period or another. Their general significance, which makes them into cultural objects, is in what they express or represent, in their meaning when that is understood to exclude what they express about the author.

The fact that works of art are cultural objects with cultural meaning does not entail, but goes well with, a further feature of art, namely that they are meant to be understood in a relatively context-independent way. I should heavily underline the word 'relatively' in this sentence. Much of the meaning of a work of art may be missed by someone who is unaware of the fact that it was created under severe censorship, or shortly after widespread race-riots, or in a literary tradition which valued allusions to Greek myths and literature, and so on and so forth. Context is highly relevant to the appreciation of the meaning of art-works. But the context which is relevant is the public context. The reader–listener–spectator is not expected to know that the work's creator has moved house, that his cousin has recently been divorced, or that his first child has reached school age. Such events may have greatly influenced the work he produced (and his biographers may dwell on them), but while the work may have special appeal to people who have experienced or are interested in changing places, divorce, separation, loss of love, joy in children, and the like, the meaning of the work must be available to those who have no knowledge of the circumstances of its creator. I will refer to this point by saying that the meaning of a work of art depends on its public context, but not on its private context. This means that its success is to be judged by reference to what it expresses as it can be understood without reference to the circumstances of the author's life.[7]

The convention that the meaning of the work is to be available to people without reference to the private context[8] is consistent with the fact that art-works are necessarily works deliberately created by their authors. This may suggest an analogy with the general argument for the intention thesis regarding legislation.[9] Artists, like legislators know (when they do)[10] that the meaning of their work is that which can be gauged without regard to the private context, and therefore they will create works which have the meaning they intend when so understood. But the analogy, while valid, disguises a basic difference between art-works and legislation. This fundamental feature of art, that art-works are meant to carry meaning to people who have no interest in their creator, makes the intentions of the artists relatively unimportant. What counts is the work of art. If an artist attracts our admiration it is because he or she produces great art. We often suspect that some admire certain art-works for no reason other than that they were made by a famous or fashionable artist. But it is commonly agreed that this is a perversion of the proper appreciation of art. Even those who are guilty of it know as much, and disguise their true reasons, sometimes even from themselves.

An enactment, on the other hand, is binding not because its content is exceptional, but because it was promulgated by this person or body, which is endowed with authority to legislate. Legislation is to be interpreted in accordance with convention because this is the way of establishing the intention of the lawmaker. Art is to be understood independently of the private context of its creation because what counts is its public meaning. If

[7] Can there be a convention to the contrary, i.e. a convention that the work is to be understood as, say, a lament on lost love—and judged by the degree to which it is good as such, only if the author suffered such loss before writing the work? Not really.

[8] Though there is no denying that it may reveal itself more readily to those aware of the private context of its creation.

[9] I am here relying on my article 'Intention in Interpretation', in R. George (ed.), *The Autonomy of Law* (Oxford: Oxford University Press, 1995).

[10] Which need not be the case. Many art-works were made in civilizations which did not have the concept of art, and did not conceive of them as art. Many works were created in civilizations which did have the concept, by so-called primitive artists who did not think of their work as art.

this meaning is the one intended by the artist, so be it. But if the work brings out something in the artist which even he is unaware of, and the expression of which is publicly perceived, and becomes crucial to the interpretation, that is, to the common understanding of the work, this belittles neither this understanding of the work nor the work's merit.

This dual independence of art from the artist (its meaning is meant to be relevant to people who are uninterested in the artist, and is determined independently of the private context of its creation) is crucial to an explanation of the role of interpretation in determining the meaning of works of art. But it has to be supplemented by another feature. In the main the aspects of the context which determine the meaning of works of art can be divided into two: first, the state of the art in question; and secondly, other reflections on or representations of the meaning of human life, man's place in the world, and aspects of human experience. The relevance of the first type of contextual feature, which includes technical developments such as use of pigments, musical instruments, methods of projection such as perspective, or techniques of amplification, iconographic conventions, narrative techniques, and their like, is inescapable given that the arts are identified, classified, and therefore understood by their techniques and by the skills that they display. The relevance of the second type of feature derives in part from the public nature of art, that is, from its dual independence of the artist. This makes it natural to expect its meaning to be in the portrayal and expression of matters of relevance to human beings in general.

This consideration, however, does not fully account for the involvement of art with the 'higher' meanings of human life. It is an aspect of art which can only be explained historically, by reference to the way the concept of art developed. In the West the arts of the modern era, and the concept of art, grew out of the traditions of Christian art. In Medieval Europe what we recognize as art was, as life generally was meant to be, created for the glory of God. It re-enacted, and where appropriate celebrated, in icons the stories which embodied the meaning of human existence, and of divine existence and intervention. When in early modern Europe some of the crafts of the Middle Ages were separated in status and in the understanding of their meaning from the rest and elevated to the status of 'Art', they kept their significance as expressing and speaking about the meaning of human life, of the world, its tribulations and triumphs, social and metaphysical. The further they appeared to stray from this self-conception towards a view of art for art's sake only, the closer they approached it. For the art-for-art's-sake movement is associated, and not by accident, with the most extravagant claims ever made for art and artistic beauty as being the quintessentially human value, supreme in its ability to endow human life with meaning.

A resulting standing temptation is the 'high' view of art. It holds that the difference between 'art' and the crafts which lie outside its boundary is that it expresses and represents views on and attitudes to nature and to human life. But while much art does so, this feature cannot be used as part of its definition. The distinction between art and the merely decorative (allegedly the only aesthetic property of wallpaper, and all other 'mere' artefacts) does not apply to music and to some other areas in the arts. This having been said, it has also to be pointed out that art is biased towards the 'higher' meaning in a specific way: it is always legitimate to see any work of art as expressing an attitude to life or experience, to nature or God, if its content when seen against the context of its creation will bear this meaning. It is judged as merely decorative only if no such understanding of it is possible.

In this section I have argued that works of art are cultural objects, and that therefore their interpretation is relatively independent of the intentions of their creators. Being cultural objects in this context means that they can legitimately be seen as bearers of meaning for their culture, that is, be judged as good or bad depending—in part—on their meaning (bad works of art, or insignificant ones, may have 'no meaning'). Having a meaning for a culture means being a suitable object of certain attitudes, responses, and uses. Meaning and interpretation are reciprocal notions. Interpretation is the elucidation of a meaning, and what has meaning which is not trivially obvious can be interpreted. It follows that an essential feature of the arts is that works of art can be interpreted. The arts come with interpretive traditions, the meaning of works of art can be perceived only by those who, through familiarity with these traditions, can interpret, that is, come to understand, their meanings.

The connection between art and its interpretation is neither trivial nor accidental. It is no accident that one cannot interpret a kitchen-sink in the kitchen, but that a kitchen-sink in an art gallery, or otherwise presented or used as art, calls for interpretation. There is much more to art than interpretation, but there is no art without interpretation, and there is no art without a practice of the interpretation of works of art. The sense in which this is so has to be carefully stated. Clearly many works of art were created at times and in cultures in which there was nothing resembling our traditions of art interpretation. Many were created in cultures which did not recognize the notion of art itself. The good sense in the remark that there is no art without interpretation is that our understanding of art makes all works of art suitable objects of interpretation of a certain kind, art interpretation. Therefore, in recognizing works as works of art we recognize them as objects of interpretation of that kind, whether or not they were so regarded by their creators or by their early public. As a result, we can focus on these works in our attempts to understand the meaning of the cultures in which they were born and of life in those cultures.

BASIC MEANING IN ART AND LITERATURE

Granting the argument of the previous section, is it not the case that meaning and interpretation there discussed presuppose a more basic meaning, meaning in the sense used when we say that the ermine in Leonardo's portrait of Cecilia Gallerani (in Cracow) symbolizes the sitter,[11] or that blue in Italian Renaissance Madonna paintings symbolizes her virginity, or that 'vanished power of the usual reign' in T. S. Eliot's 'Ash Wednesday' refers to the speaker's declining powers at the end of his life. I will refer to meaning in this sense as the 'basic meaning' of elements of the work, and contrast it with the 'deeper' meaning of the work as a whole or of parts or aspects of it as discussed in the previous section.

The case for the sovereignty of author's intention seems stronger with regard to the interpretation of basic meaning. Two points militate in that direction. First, works of art and literature are intentional creations. In the normal case only what is made to be a novel or a poem or a painting, and so on is a novel, poem, or painting, and so on. As Duchamp's urinal reminds us, sometimes what makes a work of art is no more than that an object has been christened by its author (that is, its author as a work of art, who need not have made the physical object itself) *as* a work of art. It has been noted in the previous section that this point is not without exception. We are used to co-opting into art works produced in cultures or subcultures where the notion of art did not exist, or where the authors did not think of their creations as art. But this co-option can be understood only as an exceptional extension of the application of the notion of a work of art.

Secondly, the boundaries of the work are determined by its creator. Whether or not a piece of dialogue is part of *Henry V* depends on whether Shakespeare intended it to be part of that play. Given that Anselm Kiefer wanted the frame to be part of his painting, it is part of the painting. Admittedly, the answer can be far from straightforward. Did Aristophanes intend his later revisions of *The Clouds* to be part of the play? He may have intended them to be part of a version of the play to be read, but not to be part of a performing version.[12] But that does not mean that the boundaries

[11] According to Kenneth Clark it is doubly symbolical of her identity: first, because the ermine was frequently used as Ludovico's emblem, and secondly, because the Greek for ermine: has a punning reference to her name. Kenneth Clark, *Leonardo Da Vinci* (Harmondsworth, Penguin Books, 1939), p. 54. To understand this reference one had to know Greek and to know that Gallerani was Ludovico's mistress at the time of the painting. This shows the elasticity of the contrast between the public and the private context I have been relying on. Given that the portrait was painted for her, and was to be seen by her family and friends, what was common knowledge to them was the public context against which the portrait was to be interpreted.

[12] Aristophanes *Clouds*, ed. K. J. Dover (Oxford: Oxford University Press, 1958) p. xcviii. I am grateful to Dr Bulloch for having drawn my attention to this example.

of the work are not determined by its creator. It merely shows that sometimes there is no simple answer to the question 'what are the boundaries of this work?'

Given that works of art are meant to be intentionally created, and that their boundaries are created by their authors, can we make sense of the basic meaning of any work except by reference to its author's intention? The problem with this argument is that it runs counter to the basic feature of art highlighted in the previous section, that works of art belong to the domain of cultural objects, to be understood independently of the private context of their creation. This aspect of art applies to its basic meaning as much as to its deeper meaning.

In Italian Renaissance paintings of the Madonna the blue of her dress symbolizes her virginity. We know this because we know the public meaning of the iconography of those paintings. We need know nothing about the intentions of the painter. Admittedly, the assumption is that the painter knew that and used blue to refer to the virginity of the Madonna, but he may have been a hack painter who knew of the meaning of the colour but cared little. He may even not have known—though in fact this is unlikely. He may have painted her dress blue because that is how it is done, and his patron will complain if he does not follow convention. He may not have cared about what it signified, and may have had no intention of signifying anything. Regardless of that, the Madonna's blue dress in the painting does symbolize her virginity. The patron could not have complained that he was offered a painting of the Madonna lacking a reference to her virginity. He could not have complained that, though the dress was blue, it did not refer to her virginity for the painter did not intend it to do so.

We see in this the difference between art and the law. In the law, prima facie, the fact that the text is interpreted contrary to the lawmaker's intentions denies it legitimacy. Its legitimacy derives from the authority of the lawmaker to make the law it judged right to make. The application of this argument is both limited and indirect.[13] But it is always there in the background of any interpretation of enacted law. Not so interpretation in the arts. The autonomy of works of art means that the author's intention can be said to be irrelevant to the interpretation of his work, except where there are special considerations to take it into account.

Can this conclusion be reconciled with the fact that works of art are intentional creations, whose boundaries are determined by their author? It can, for it leaves untouched the basic understanding of art and literature as fields of human self-expression, which is at the core of the fact that it is of the essence of art that works of art are normally products of intentional

[13] See, on the case for the role of intention in legal interpretation, 'Intention in Interpretation', *supra*, n. 9.

creation. Art bears a dual relation to self-expression. Being cultural objects makes works of art both works through which their creators can express themselves, and works which provide a focus for reflection, emotion, and even identification for their public. Members of the public express themselves through their relations to the works.

This statement should be cautiously interpreted. First, it does not subscribe to an expressionist view of art. It refers to expressing beliefs about the glory of god, the order of the angels, the piety of a donor, as well as to the despair of frustrated ambition or love, or of the futility of human life, or of the overpowering joy of conquest, and other more conventional subjects of expressionism in the arts. Secondly, it is not meant to deny that much art is created by craftsmen or even hacks who work to a formula and express nothing. Nor does it deny that many works never see the light of day, as they remain confined to drawers or cellars, and many others are stillborn, never becoming an object of contemplation or identification to anyone. Yet I am saying more than that sometimes they do serve as vehicles of self-expression to their author and public. That much is true about almost everything. Art-works are meant to be vehicles of self-expression. They are evaluated in part by the degree to which they are good vehicles for self-expression.

This both assures the connection between works of art and their creator's intention, and secures their distance from it. It is open to people to make works which will express what they intend to express. That possibility is assured by the fact that they intentionally create the work and determine its boundaries. Since it is what they make it, they can—in principle—make it mean what they want it to mean. But to do that they have to take note of what makes works of art mean one thing or another, and in the light of that make the work so that it will have the meaning they want it to have. They cannot make it mean something just by intending it to mean that. Nor can they deny it a meaning simply by not having it in mind.

INTERPRETATION AS DISCOVERY

The argument so far has undermined the case for author's intention as the foundation of interpretation. It has done little either to challenge the broader conception of interpretation as retrieval, or to explain the nature of interpretation of works of art. To do both we should concentrate on the test case of innovative interpretation. How is it possible? If interpretation is retrieval, how can it be new? If it is not, what is the difference between a novel interpretation of a work and reacting to it as to a Rorschach test?

The retrieval picture offers an answer through a threefold distinction: there are two ways in which an interpretation can be new, and one in which it cannot. It can be a new statement of a familiar meaning, a new way of articulating it. An illuminating simile, a striking phrase, a bold statement of a familiar meaning strikes home precisely because it articulates a familiar point in such a strikingly new way. This kind of novelty, novelty in articulation, is possible and often attractive. It is different from an innovative interpretation which assigns a new meaning to the work. Such interpretations are inconsistent with the retrieval picture. Interpretation is a retrieval of the meaning the work has. It cannot reveal in it a meaning it did not have before.

It is, however, the third way of being innovative which is the most interesting. An interpretation may do no more than retrieve the meaning that was always there, and yet its novelty may not be just in re-describing a familiar meaning in a fresh way. It may rather be a matter of revealing a meaning which was so far hidden. When *Hamlet* was first given a psychoanalytic interpretation that did not give it a new meaning. Rather, it claimed to display the meaning of the play by explaining Hamlet's motivation as it has always been—what else can it be? After all, the play has not changed with the advent of psychoanalysis. So the motivation of its characters and the meaning of its action cannot change either. An interpretation can only retrieve and disclose what is there already. It is innovative when that meaning was hidden from sight. There are innovative interpretations, but there are no new meanings. On the retrieval model, innovative interpretation is a discovery of a hitherto unknown meaning.

The case of the psychoanalytic interpretation of *Hamlet* illustrates this idea. It is an example of how innovative interpretation is arrived at (at least some of the time). The 'discovery' of psychoanalysis makes possible novel interpretations of many works of art. We can now reinterpret *Hamlet* as the working out of an Oedipal complex, or something like that. It is fairly clear how innovative interpretations are possible in such cases: the discovery of the truth of some general theory, or just of a general truth about people, reveals that certain facts about the interpreted work which were not seen as significant before are significant. Interpretation consists in pointing to connections and analogies. The test of a good interpretation is that those connections and interrelations are significant in terms of, or by reference to, some general theory or general truths about people, society, or whatever. An interpretation is innovative if the significance of the aspect of the work highlighted by it has not been appreciated before, and this is most commonly due to the fact that the general truths were not known before.

Sometimes new interpretations are not prompted by new discoveries of general truths, but by a novel realization of how some known truths bear on the events of a story or the features of some other works. We come to recognize that the work instantiates known general propositions in ways not hitherto realized. Sometimes authors deliberately disguise clues to the significance of their work, and only with time does their work yield its secrets.[14]

There is some truth in this picture of innovative interpretation as discovery. No doubt many new interpretations are new in the way described. Yet this cannot be the full story. It regards innovative interpretations as discoveries of hidden meaning. This was the meaning of *Hamlet* all along, although no one knew it until Freud. But the idea of hidden meaning, meaning hidden not from some but from all, is puzzling. How can this be the meaning of *Hamlet* if *Hamlet* did not have that meaning for anyone? Can there be an expression in English that has a meaning which is hidden and unknown, awaiting discovery? Why should things be different with works of art? The idea of hidden meaning seems odd there as well.

The discovery view of interpretation makes it too much like a scientific explanation or interpretation. The discovery of special relativity explains the deviation of Mercury from the course predicted by Newtonian physics. Here interpretation means just that: explanation of an event as an instance of a general law. But that is not an explanation of the meaning of the event. It is just an explanation of the event. The interpretations we are after are explanations of meaning. But if innovative interpretations can be arrived at simply by realizing how general truths are instantiated in the interpreted work, what is wrong with the discovery view of interpretation? What does it leave out?

We can be helped here by examining some of the ways in which interpretations can be criticized. Some criticism is fairly straightforward: our belief that a psychoanalytic interpretation of *Hamlet* is not a very good one may be due to doubts about psychoanalysis, or to a feeling that that interpretation leaves too much of the play outside its ambit, thus making it incomplete, or that the story of Hamlet does not fit analytic theory and does not warrant the construction put on it.

There is, however, an additional and far less obvious way of criticizing an interpretation. Imagine someone offering the absurdity of a physics-based interpretation of *Hamlet*. His interpretation consists in showing that all the events described in the play are consistent with physics and that all of them are instances of the laws of motion (speaking being interpreted as mouth and lung movement for this purpose, and so on). All our interpreter says—let us assume—is true. We are still entitled to say that his is no interpretation of the play at all. Why not? Because it altogether misses the meaning of the play. If this is right then a psychoanalytic interpretation cannot be a good interpretation just because it is true that the actions depicted in the play instantiate truths revealed by psychoanalysis. To put the point in other

[14] I am glossing over many complications; e.g., does the significance of the Ghost in *Hamlet* depend on whether there are ghosts? Or is it the same whether or not there are ghosts, since it depends only on whether Shakespeare believed in ghosts, or perhaps whether he expected his audience to believe in them?

words: a psychoanalytic interpretation can be rejected as bad, or even as no interpretation at all (that is, as very bad) even though it is a true explanation of the motivations of the personae in the play, just as a physics-based interpretation can be rejected as no interpretation at all even though it is a true explanation of the physical events in the play. I am not saying that the two interpretations deserve the same verdict. I am saying that if they do not, then the difference between them is to be accounted for by factors which still elude our grasp. And while they do we are still ignorant of what innovative interpretation, and therefore what interpretation in general, is.

INNOVATIVE INTERPRETATION

It is tempting to say that we have all the pieces of the jigsaw puzzle in place. Our only problem is that we do not—at least I do not—understand the most important among them. My ruminations so far suggest that an interpretation is an explanation of the work interpreted which points to connections and interrelations among its parts, and between them and other aspects of the world, so that it (a) covers adequately the significant aspects of the work interpreted (that is, does not relate just to one part of a novel, or just to one of its themes, and so on), and is not inconsistent with any aspect of the work; (b) it shows the elements of the work to be instances of some general truths; and (c) in doing the above it elucidates the meaning of the work. The more successful it is in meeting these criteria the better the interpretation.

At least in one respect this way of elucidating the nature of interpretation is on the right lines: it proceeds by setting criteria for excellence as an interpretation, rather than by setting necessary and sufficient conditions for anything being an interpretation. There are no such necessary and sufficient conditions. At the limit the boundary between a very bad interpretation and one which is not an interpretation at all is usually pointless to draw or argue about.[15]

Yet this characterization includes both too much and too little. It includes too little because it overlooks how the way an interpretation affects the value of the work interpreted contributes to the evaluation of the interpretation itself.[16] The evaluation of works of art depends only to a limited

[15] Though sometimes it is clear that something is no interpretation, and is not a bad interpretation. For example, if it is not intended to be an interpretation. Though the fact that an interpretation must be intended as such is the closest we get to a necessary condition, it is not strictly speaking one. If someone says 'this is a splendid interpretation of Hamlet', meaning 'this would make a splendid interpretation of Hamlet were it presented as such', he is not to be charged with abuse of language. Language has a way of stretching itself.

[16] The recognition that that is so is the core of Dworkin's view of interpretation. His mistake is not in emphasizing the importance of this factor, but in ignoring others, as well as in assuming that there is normally only one correct interpretation.

degree on their interpretation. A large component in the evaluation of works of art is the degree to which they are skilfully executed, the degree to which they meet internal criteria of excellence for that genre of art. (When it comes to randomly produced art the two aspects of this test come apart: the generic criteria for the success of the product are no longer criteria for skill in its execution.) But to a degree the evaluation depends on the importance of the subject-matter of the work. If a work is merely a display of a minor aspect of human relations then it is less valuable than, or not as excellent a work of art as, one which deals with the fundamental dilemma of human life, if there is such a dilemma.[17] At the same time an interpretation which shows the work's meaning as dealing with what is more important is, *pro tanto*, a better interpretation than one which shows it as dealing only with what is less important.[18] Disagreement about what is important and what is not is a constant source of disagreement about which interpretation is better.

Where the characterization of interpretation I offered goes too far is in insisting that showing that aspects of the work are instances of general truths is the only way of showing or explaining its meaning. This is hardly consistent with performances being interpretations, and generally there are other ways of bringing out the meaning of a work than by showing it to be an instance of some general truths. Not all explanations refer to or presuppose exceptionless general truths, at least not in any significant way. Explanations of human action by reference to people's reasons and motives notoriously defy such generalizations. An interpretation of an art-work will include an explanation of the work. But any pattern of explanation will do.

All this is helpful and relevant. But we are still short of a general characterization of what counts as showing or explaining *the meaning* of the work. But is there really a problem here? All we need—you may say—is an explanation of what it is for a work of art to have a certain meaning. Once we understand that, there will not be any problem about interpretation left. An interpretation is whatever makes one understand that meaning. That is true as well. Right at the outset I insisted on the close connection between interpretation and meaning. If we understand either of these concepts we understand both. But it follows that to explain one is to explain both: we cannot be deemed to have explained interpretation without explaining meaning, at least to a degree.

There is a simple, though perhaps not altogether perspicacious, way of elucidating the missing element in our account. An interpretation is an

[17] Notice that the beauty of a work of art is not the most fundamental category for its evaluation. The importance of its subject does not affect the beauty of an art-work, but it does affect its excellence.

[18] These points further elaborate the presumption noted in the third section of this paper, that any work of art is fair game for 'profound' interpretations.

explanation of the work interpreted which explains why it is important, to the extent that it is. This shows what was right in the idea that a novel interpretation can arise out of a discovery of some general truths. Since any interpretation is an explanation of the work it can become available as new discoveries are made. Yet, as we have seen, and as this augmented account allows, not every explanation, however successful as an explanation, is an interpretation. It is an interpretation only if in explaining the work it also elucidates, makes plain, why it is important, to the extent that it is. The physics-based explanation of *Hamlet* I dreamt up earlier fails that test.

The following is an attempt to integrate all the points made so far: an interpretation is an explanation of the work interpreted which highlights some of its elements and points to connections and interrelations among its parts, and between them and other aspects of the world, so that (a) it covers adequately the significant aspects of the work interpreted (that is, it does not relate just to one part of a novel, or just to one of its themes, and so on), and is not inconsistent with any aspect of the work; (b) it explains the aspects of the work it focuses on; and (c) in doing the above it elucidates what is important in the work, and accounts—to the extent that this is possible—for whatever reasons there are for paying attention to the work as a work of art of its kind. The more successful it is in meeting these criteria, and the more important the meaning it justifiably attributes to the work, the better the interpretation.

In brief:

AN INTERPRETATION IS AN EXPLANATION OF ASPECTS OF THE WORK, WHICH ACCOUNTS FOR REASONS TO PAY IT ATTENTION AS A WORK OF ART OF ITS KIND.

My reference to 'reasons to pay it attention as a work of art' is meant to exclude primarily whatever reasons there are to pay attention to the work as evidence about the character or life of its author, or of other people, or of the practices of a period which it portrays, and so on. It assumes a concept of art defining what counts as an appropriate attitude to it, what kind of reasons could be reasons for attending to works of art. This stops the definition from being too subjectivist. Different people have different reasons, and the definition allows for that. But only certain reasons are proper reasons for attending to art as art, and that puts a limit to the degree to which variations in the reasons different people have lead to different interpretations. Even so this way of understanding interpretation offers the beginning of an explanation of why several incompatible interpretations may attract each person. Developing this explanation requires further discussion of the subjectivity of interpretation—a topic which cannot be undertaken here.

Instead, let me note that this account implies that some of the variety of good, though possibly incompatible, explanations, while appealing to some people quite properly and legitimately, leave others cold. An interpretation is a good one if the explanation it produces displays valid reasons for (some) people to pay attention to the work of art. But people differ, and while all have to concede that the interpretation is good, for it displays reasons why some people (say children) may do well to pay attention to the work, these are not reasons for them (not being children themselves), and therefore they have no interest in the interpretation.

A spirit of intolerance often makes people deny the validity of interpretations they have no interest in. But clear-sighted people know better. They know that a good interpretation may be so because of the way it displays reasons which some people have to attend to the work, and they know that there is no need—indeed that it would be foolish—to deny an interpretation's value just because it holds no interest for them.

THE INSTABILITY OF INTERPRETATION

The characterization of interpretation offered above is very abstract. It requires careful fleshing out to illustrate its application to various forms of art, and careful adaptation to be applicable to the interpretation of objects other than works of art. One respect in which the account is both specific to the interpretation of works of art, and at the same time seriously incomplete, is in its reliance on the existence of genre-defining standards, and ways of identifying which genre the work belongs to. I believe, though the matter cannot be investigated here, that the interpretation of works of art essentially presupposes that works belong to kinds with their own defining standards of excellence.[19] Only by reference to the work's genre can the reason to pay attention to it be identified. If it is a psychological novel then a psychoanalytic interpretation may be acceptable, while if it is a religious allegory such an interpretation would be like one showing that everything in the novel can be explained by reference to physics: a true statement which is no interpretation at all or, at any rate, a bad interpretation which misses the point of the work. Interpretations bring out reasons to pay attention to the work, to the extent that there are any. But—to repeat—not every reason will lead to an interpretation. The evidence the work provides for the culinary habits of its time is not relevant. The relevant reasons differ from the irrelevant ones in being reasons to attend to the work as a work of art of its kind. Hence an understanding of art and its genres is presupposed.

Naturally, works may belong to more than one genre, which is another source for the possibility of a multiplicity of good and incompatible

[19] Thus giving rise to the theoretical and—more painfully—the practical problems of understanding and appreciating genre-breaking works.

interpretations. The account I have offered makes it plain that the interpretations and meanings of works of art are not only potentially many, but that they can and do change. They change when the reasons for attending to the work change. The reasons people have change because their circumstances change. The reasons people in modern post-industrial societies have for being interested in the works of classical Athens are not those of the Renaissance, nor those of Athenians of the Periclean period. For those Athenians the art of their day did not reveal—as it did to the people of the Renaissance—a culture lost for many generations, nor did it disclose to them—as it does to us—the source of so much western art of the last two millennia. As one work influences another, or influences people's lives or perceptions in certain ways, it acquires new meanings, that is, as prefiguring later development. These are but some of the innumerable ways in which the reasons for attending to a work of art may change.

The process of change is not a process of accretion. Some reasons lose their force. A period piece is a piece which portrays and illuminates, sometimes brilliantly, matters which preoccupied a certain period, and which may be of no interest any more. Most works of art have their 'period aspect', that is, a meaning for their generation which they do not have for later generations. Works of art acquire new meanings, and shed some of their old meanings.

Does this make interpretation and meaning subjective? No. It makes them—in a sense—relative. To have meaning is to have meaning for someone. I say that this makes them relative in a sense, for we commonly use the terms 'meaning' and 'interpretation' in a non-relativized sense. This is the sense in which I am using the terms, and which enables me to say that the meaning of works of art changes. In a relativized sense the meaning does not change. The meaning of Periclean art to the Athenians at the time of Pericles remains the same, as does its meaning to the Renaissance, or to the nineteenth century. If we understand 'interpretation' and 'meaning' in a relativized sense, new meanings emerge but none die. So are 'meaning' and 'interpretation' relative or not? They are both, or rather we follow both a relativized and a non-relativized use of the terms.

Apart from the fact that the reasons people have vary with their circumstances, the reasons which count as relevant for the interpretation of art change with changes in the notion of art. The names of some 'schools' in the arts suggest such changes: Expressionism brings with it a new understanding of what art is about and how it is to be understood; the use of *objets trouvés*, or collages of ready-made items, and so on, effects a transformation in our understanding of the meaning of art, as does the emergence of op-art, the use of strobes, and so on.

Do these reflections on the instability of interpretation, on the fact that interpretations, as well as coexisting with their rivals, come and go, presuppose that interpretations are imposed on the work rather than discovered in it? And does it follow from this that judgment of how good an interpretation is has to be subjective, expressive of one's own feeling, rather than objective? Not in the least. Judgment of the value of interpretations is no more subjective than is judgment of the value of cars, even though in both cases the reasons why it is good to attend to the work or to have the car are, in an obvious sense, not in the work but in the circumstances of one's life, for example, in one's daily need to travel long distances.

THE REJECTION OF RETRIEVAL

The normative character of interpretation, its dependence on reasons, by explaining the possibility of change refutes the picture of interpretation as retrieval. Too many writers have triumphantly exclaimed that the meaning of a text is not 'in the text itself', on the ground that marks on paper, and so on, are meaningless except in the context of a linguistic practice, which requires the existence, at one time or another, of a population sharing an understanding of the same linguistic practices. This trivial point, never disputed by anyone, has nothing to do with the sense in which the interpretation of a work of art can be new in that it shows the work to have a meaning which it did not always have. If all there was to say was that works of art also have meaning only if there is a society whose practices establish artistic genres and the standards which apply to them, then the retrieval picture would be accurate, and there would be no truth in the thought that meaning is in the eye of the beholder.

What defeats the retrieval picture is the normativity of interpretation, its dependence on reasons, and the fact that those reasons may vary, and change. Two difficulties with this suggestion should be mentioned. First, how can the meaning of a work change without the work itself changing? Secondly, the problem raised above: how can an interpretation be new? Must not the meaning of anything be on the surface, that is, known to those who know the relevant 'language'?

Our concepts are complex and flexible. We should not be captives of some features of our concepts to the exclusion of others. To be sure, Hamlet's motivation cannot change, except as Hamlet himself changes in the course of the play. That is why some new interpretations, for example, a psychoanalytic interpretation, are discoveries about Hamlet's motivation. But these, like all interpretations, are relative to a certain perspective on the work, a certain set of reasons for seeing it as interesting. The perspectives can change as our reasons for taking an interest in the work change. We can understand Hamlet as representing the loss of orientation of a person who, under the influence of a new culture (that of the Renaissance in this case), loses the secure bearing that the culture he was brought up in gave him, and suffers a collapse of self-confidence, a collapse which is made manifest by the murder of his father and the hasty remarriage of his mother.

This interpretation comes from a different perspective than the psychoanalytic one. Here the interest is not in individual psychology, but in the interaction of culture and sense of self. From this perspective interpretive points are made which are, if true at all, true of Hamlet in a timeless way—which have always been true of him. The play has not changed, and what is true of it was, so seen, always true of it. But the perspective itself is new. This interest in the play is new, and therefore the interpretations offered from this perspective are new. With the emergence of this perspective the play has acquired a new meaning. Since meaning is relative to a normative perspective, it can change as that perspective changes. Our concepts are rich enough to accommodate both ways of thinking of meaning: as timeless, from one and the same perspective, and as changing, with the change in perspective.

Perspectives emerge with changes in culture and in the conditions of life. Being normative, they emerge as new reasons for new interests emerge. Revolutionary interpretations capitalize on that. They are offered by those whose view of the work is infused by the new perspective before it reaches others, or before it finds articulation in the hands of others. They capture the significance of the work from this newly emerging perspective. Their interpretations may themselves hasten that emergence, and affect the direction and content of the new perspective. Less revolutionary, but still novel, interpretations bring a perspective which by now is well established in the culture to a work which has not yet been seen in that light. There is here a wide range of different cases for the study of cultures to explore. They all display the varied and subtle combinations of the familiar and the novel, the range of ways in which meaning is there, and the interpretation merely articulates it, and the ways in which the articulation can itself be seen as contributing to the meaning, as in part investing the work with a new meaning—the sense in which the interpretation of works of art is part and parcel of the creative artistic enterprise.

The interpretation of works of art may be thought to be unique in this respect. Surely, the interpretation of history does not invest history with a meaning; history is not made through its interpretation, but by the people whose history it is. Art is special in that it is part of its nature—captured by the presumption in favour of interpretations which show the interpreted work to bear on important issues—to be a mirror to our lives and world. History and law are not mirrors; they are there, made by those who forged them, and are merely to be understood by those who interpret them. Or are they? The account offered here applies directly to the interpretation of works of art only. It requires careful modification to apply to other objects of interpretation. But, I believe, the similarities between different domains of interpretation are at least as striking as the differences.

6
Three Concepts of Objectivity

ANDREI MARMOR

This essay is about the concept of objectivity and its possible roles in the interpretation of works of art. 'Objectivity', however, is one of those notions philosophy students are well advised to avoid in their essays. There is very little agreement on what it means, and there is a great deal of confusion about its different and often conflicting uses. This may sound puzzling, and perhaps it is; however, unlike philosophical concepts such as 'realism' and 'cognitivism', which have received extensive philosophical attention in the last two or three decades, the concept(s) of objectivity has been left pretty much in the lurch. Consequently, any discussion of the objectivity or subjectivity of a certain realm must begin with a clarification of what one means by these terms. I shall begin with an outline of the distinction between three different concepts of objectivity which, I will suggest, are philosophically useful. Once the boundaries between these different uses of objectivity are clearly drawn, we shall be able to see that there are several aspects of interpretation which can be characterized as 'objective' or 'subjective' in a rather non-controversial manner; that is, depending on the kind of 'objectivity' ascribed. Other aspects of the objectivity of interpretation, however, remain genuinely controversial, and I will try to add a few drops of my own to this ocean of philosophical literature. I will have nothing directly to say, however, about legal interpretation; my main concern will be with interpretation in the realm of the arts.

Part I: Some Basic Distinctions

The objective–subjective dichotomy is a philosophical invention (and one, in fact, with a rather peculiar history).[1] There is very little to gain, then, from

I am indebted to Meir Dan-Cohen, Chaim Gans, Ruth Gavison, Alon Harel, David Heyd, Dori Kimel, Brian Leiter, Ariel Porat, Joseph Raz, Timothy Williamson, Jeremy Waldron, and Zahava Zevit, for their invaluable comments on earlier drafts of this essay.

[1] The philosophical discourse about the objective–subjective dichotomy probably stems from 17th-century Rationalism. Interestingly, however, the Cartesian use of these notions was almost the opposite of their current one; for Descartes, the idea of objectivity carried sceptical connotations with it, whereas the subjective realm was associated with truth and certainty. See his *Meditations on First Philosophy* (1641), trans. L. J. Laflens (Bobbs Merril, 1960).

an ordinary-language analysis of these concepts. The definitions of the objective–subjective dichotomy must be based on theoretical considerations, and their usefulness must be tested against theoretical objectives. This much, at least, I will take for granted.

I will also assume that the objectivity–subjectivity pair, like that of realism and anti-realism, is a distinction usefully applied to *classes* of statement. It is only about certain kinds of statement, as a kind, that we normally want to know whether they are objective or subjective. Those who assert, for example, the objectivity of statements about mid-sized physical objects, make a claim about the objective standing of each and every statement in this particular class only as an instance of its belonging to the class of statements about mid-sized physical objects. It is the objectivity (or subjectivity) of the class of statements as such that is normally the subject of philosophical controversy, not the standing of a particular statement as such.

There are (at least) three different and, as I shall argue, basically independent concepts of objectivity. First, there is objectivity or subjectivity in what I shall call the *semantic* sense. In this sense, statements (or, perhaps more precisely, speech-acts) are either semantically objective or subjective, regardless of their validity or truth. In the second sense, the objective–subjective dichotomy is a matter of *metaphysical truth*. The question of objectivity in this metaphysical sense is a question about the world, and not about the meaning of the statements. Finally, there is what I shall call *logical objectivity*: a certain class of statements is objective in this sense if it makes sense to ascribe truth values to statements of that class.

Before we proceed to the elaboration of these three concepts of objectivity, however, a clarification is called for: it should not be assumed that these three concepts are meant to be taken as exhausting all the prevalent uses of objectivity in ordinary language. For instance, 'objectivity' is often used as a synonym or a quasi-synonym for 'impartiality'. It is often in this sense that judges and arbitrators are required to be objective, or that we seek the objectivity of scientists, namely, as a quest for impartiality in the rendering of judgments. This, and perhaps some other prevalent uses of objectivity, will not be part of the analysis offered below.[2]

[2] It may be questioned whether the three different uses of objectivity described in the following discussion are three different *concepts* of objectivity, or only different *conceptions* of one concept. As it is not altogether clear why the distinction would matter in the present context, I have allowed myself to suspend judgment on it, and I beg the reader to do the same. If one assumes, however, that the conceptions of a given concept must be competing conceptions, then, of course, the notions of objectivity described below cannot be conceptions of one and the same concept, simply because they are not mutually exclusive. I am indebted to Joseph Raz for bringing this to my attention.

SEMANTIC OBJECTIVITY

The semantic sense of the objectivity–subjectivity dichotomy is basically a characterization of a given type of discourse. Roughly, a statement is semantically objective if and only if it is a statement *about an object*; and it is a subjective statement if and only if it is about an aspect of one's self, that is, about some mental state of the subject making the statement. Thus, a statement is subjective in this semantic sense if it is (or if it is equivalent in meaning to) the expression of the speaker's tastes, desires, perceptions, and so on.[3] And a statement is objective if it has as its grammatical subject an object in the world, other than the speaker's state of mind, as it were.[4] This, I take it, is the most simple (but not useless) sense of the objective–subjective dichotomy. The most important feature of this sense of objectivity is that it is purely a matter of the meaning of the speech act in question, independent of the statement's truth or falsehood. More precisely, a given class of statements can be objective in the semantic sense, even if there is no truth of the matter about the objects described by those statements (for example, because they do not exist at all). And vice versa, a class of statements can be subjective in the semantic sense, even if there is a truth of the matter about the meaning of those statements. As an example of the former, consider the discourse about God; people can talk about Him (or Her, as the case may be) even if there is no such an entity. And vice versa: many kinds of subjective statement can easily be conceived as determinedly true or false. For instance, 'I love Sarah' is a semantically subjective statement, but of course, it can be true (or false) in a fairly standard manner.

Is it the case, then, that all statements are either semantically objective or subjective? Not necessarily: first, there may be types of mixed statement, which involve subjective and objective elements inextricably.[5] Secondly, there may be statements which are neither objective or subjective in the semantic sense, simply because such statements do not appear in what might be called, a propositional discourse, or context (for example, like a move in a game, or as part of a greeting, and so on). Be this as it may, the important point is that there is a sense of objectivity and subjectivity which

[3] In a more formal way, perhaps we can say that a statement like 'x is P', as uttered by S, is semantically subjective if it means that x induces in S a certain reaction or sentiment, etc., which is publicly recognized or expressed as 'P'. See e.g. Wiggins (1991*b*: 185).

[4] For those who deny that there is a metaphysically plausible concept of one's self, anything like semantic subjectivity would have to be analysed in terms of an error theory: semantically subjective discourse would turn out to be a widespread error.

[5] One such case occurs when the statement is basically about the subject asserting it, but it involves certain objective presuppositions rendering the statement intelligible. Other examples could be statements expressing a relation between the subject and an external object like, for example, the statement 'I am Sarah's best friend'. I am indebted to Chaim Gans for bringing this to my attention.

only pertains to the characterization of the given discourse, independently of its objectivity or subjectivity in any other sense.

One might wonder why this semantic distinction between objective and subjective statements would be of any philosophical interest, particularly, as it is alleged that the objectivity of a statement in this sense is no indication of its truth. The answer lies in the distinction between the superficial and the deeper layers of grammar. It is quite common for philosophers to claim in various contexts that the superficial appearance of grammar is misleading; sentences that appear semantically objective can turn out to be semantically subjective (or vice versa) on closer scrutiny. To take one familiar example, consider the meta-ethical theory Richard Hare (1981: 76) dubbed 'old-fashioned subjectivism'. This view suggests that moral judgments—despite appearances to the contrary—are actually equivalent in meaning to reports of the subject about his or her psychological state (for example, of disapproval of the act being judged). Thus, the judgment 'act *x* is cruel', which appears to be semantically objective, namely, a statement about the properties of an act *x*, becomes according to the analysis of 'old-fashioned subjectivism' semantically subjective: it is a statement about a certain kind of reaction experienced and reported by the subject asserting it. Whether this is a plausible meta-ethical stance (or indeed, whether any philosopher has ever held such a view)[6] does not matter for our purposes. What does matter, however, is the philosophical relevance of this semantic sense of the objectivity–subjectivity dichotomy. 'Old-fashioned subjectivism' as a semantically subjectivist stance on the appropriate analysis of the meaning of ethical judgments is anything but trivial. If true (and again, I certainly don't claim that it is), it would render our understanding of ethical discourse radically different from what we normally take it to be. Indeed, so radically different as to render it highly implausible; as Hare (1981: 77) rightly points out, 'old-fashioned subjectivism' cannot make any sense of ethical disputes and arguments. (More on this later, however.)

Furthermore, although I wish to reiterate that semantic objectivity is never an indication of the truth of a statement, it does have, nevertheless, a bearing on the *kind* of truth-conditions appropriate for the statement in question. According to 'old-fashioned subjectivism', for example, the truth conditions of an ethical judgment must always refer to the mental state of the subject asserting it. If, on the other hand, ethical judgments are semantically objective (as they appear to be according to their superficial grammar), the mental

[6] It is important to emphasize that the so called 'old-fashioned subjectivism' should not be confused with Emotivism. The latter is perhaps a subjectivist account of the ethical discourse, but not along the lines suggested by this 'old-fashioned' version. (Hare 1981: 77) The latter is sometimes associated with David Hume's subjectivism about ethical discourse, but it is far from certain that this association does Hume adequate justice (see e.g. Wiggins 1991*b*).

state of the subject asserting the statement in question would not be a constituent of the statement's truth conditions.

Semantic objectivity then, is basically a matter of grammar, but not necessarily of the superficial grammar. Statements that look like objective ones, can turn out to be subjective, and vice versa.[7] The importance of this sense of objectivity, however, lies mainly in what it does not imply: namely, truth or validity. There is no contradiction involved in asserting that a given class of statements is objective in the semantic sense, while maintaining that there are no objects of the kind purportedly described by the class of statements in question.

Furthermore, people often tend to talk in semantically objective terms even if they are perfectly aware of the fact that the discourse is not objective in any other sense. Certain elements of aesthetic discourse may be precisely of this kind. Many people talk about beauty, for example, *as if* it were a property of objects in the world, despite the fact that they do not really believe this to be the case. Aesthetic discourse, in other words, is for many people a bit like the atheist's discourse about God. Now, this 'as if' kind of discourse, namely, one which is cast in objective terms despite the common assumption that there are no objects in the world of the kind purportedly described by it, is not so bewildering as it may seem on first impression. Many types of discourse have a social or a psychological rationale, and serve social and cultural functions, in ways which have very little to do with truth or falsehood. A certain kind of discourse may serve such functions as enhancing social cohesion or institutional identification, and the like, regardless of truth or validity. In other words, we don't always expect people to believe in the truths of their statements even if those statements are cast in semantically objective terms.[8]

METAPHYSICAL OBJECTIVITY

Objectivity in the metaphysical sense does imply truth, and in a rather special manner. Roughly, it implies that there is a truth of the matter consisting in the fact that there is an object with properties corresponding to its description by the statement in question. It would be safe to assume that most philosophers (and laymen) interested in the objectivity or subjectivity of a certain type of statements have the metaphysical sense of objectivity in

[7] As an example of statements which look like subjective statements but are in fact semantically objective, consider statements such as 'I have to visit Jones'; this is not a statement about the subject making it, but about a reason which is claimed to apply to the subject. Statements about reasons, are, most plausibly, semantically objective.

[8] See e.g. Dan-Cohen (1989).

mind. Two kinds of confusion regarding metaphysical objectivity are prevalent, however. Objectivity in this sense is all too often conflated with realism (and subjectivism with anti-realism).[9] Although there is a close link between these two pairs of philosophical concepts, they are not identical. Secondly, metaphysical objectivity is often confused with the third, logical, sense of objectivity and this confusion, I will argue, is the source of many superfluous controversies.

The metaphysical objectivity–subjectivity dichotomy must be defined in terms of the relations between types of statement and the existence of the appropriate categories of objects. A given type of statements is objective in the metaphysical sense if, and only if, there exist objects of the kind purportedly described by that type of statements; and a class of statements is subjective if no such objects exist in the world. Thus, a given statement is *objectively true* in the metaphysical sense if, and only if, there exists an object in the world with the properties attributed to it by the statement in question; and it is *objectively false* if the object it purports to describe does not have the properties attributed to it by the statement. A statement cannot be objectively either true or false, however, if there are no objects of the kind purportedly described by the type of statements in question. Thus, the typical subjectivist or sceptical stance on the objectivity of a given type of statements consists in the contention that those statements which are semantically objective turn out to be subjective in the metaphysical sense. (Note that the objective-subjective pair is not always symmetrical; subjectivity in the metaphysical sense is simply the denial of objectivity, and hence, it is merely a negative view. In the semantic sense, however, subjectivity is a kind of opposite to objectivity, and not its denial.)

The definition of metaphysical objectivity seems to imply two presuppositions: first, that the kind of statements which can be metaphysically objective are only of the *descriptive* kind. They must be statements which purport to describe objects in the world, and they are objective if and only if there are objects of the kind referred to by the description. Secondly, as indicated by the latter sentence, metaphysical objectivity seems to assume the *correspondence theory of truth* (at least with respect to the kind of statements about which one is objectivist). Both assumptions are indispensable. Beginning with the latter, it is easy to see that metaphysical objectivity assumes that a statement is objectively true if and only if there is an accurate correspondence between the statement and the world. For example, the proposition 'this chair is black' would be objectively true in this metaphysical sense if and only if there is an object, namely, the chair referred to, and it is black. Does this imply that the truth of the statement consists in this

[9] Brink (1989: 5–10, 14–22), for example, uses the terms 'objectivity' and 'realism' in metaethics almost interchangeably. See also Coleman and Leiter's contribution to this volume, *infra*, Ch. 7.

relation of 'correspondence'? Basically, yes. Whatever the flaws of the correspondence theory of truth, something like it must be assumed for sentences to be metaphysically objective. Even if we take the notion of 'truth' as simple or primitive, not analysable in terms of other notions like 'correspondence', it must be assumed, at some intuitive level, that a statement is rendered objectively true or false by the constitution of reality. If it does not make sense to say that truth somehow consists in the relation between sentences and the world, metaphysical objectivity would not make sense either.

Metaphysical objectivity is most easily grasped with respect to propositions ascribing a predicate to a subject.[10] Hence the rendering of evaluative judgments can be subjected to the analysis required by metaphysical objectivity only if the evaluative judgments in question *purport to describe* some aspects of reality. Not surprisingly, then, objectivism in ethics, to take a prominent example, is commonly associated with descriptivism.[11] This is correct, as far as it goes. It is a mistake, however, to assume that metaphysical objectivism (as defined here) is the only kind of objectivity of interest in ethics. More on this later, however.

There is a considerable overlap between metaphysical objectivism and realism. Realism, like objectivism, is seen as a position on a metaphysical issue, a view on the way our thoughts and language relate to the world. Since much of the current debate on realism has been initiated by Michael Dummett, it may be useful to base the discussion on his formulation of realism, which runs as follows: 'The primary tenet of realism, as applied to some given class of statements, is that each statement in that class is determined as true or not true, independently of our knowledge, by some objective reality whose existence and constitution is, again, independent of our knowledge' (1981: 434).

One is tempted to say that the difference between realism and objectivism is that realism is even 'more metaphysical' than metaphysical objectivism, if I may use this terrible expression. This is so, as realism presumes the existence of an objective reality which is ontologically *independent* of our knowledge. On the other hand, one can be an objectivist about kinds of object that do not meet this independence condition. Objectivism, in other words, does not entail, as realism does, the possibility of verification-transcendent truths within the realm about which one is objectivist.[12] For example, the

[10] By this I do not mean to take sides in the age-old (and rather obscure) controversy over the question whether 'existence' is a genuine predicate or not. I do mean, however, to include in the definition of metaphysical objectivity those statements which affirm or deny the existence of an object in the world. Namely, statements of the kind $(\exists x)$ Ax or $\sim(\exists x)$ Ax.

[11] Cf. Mackie (1977: 24); Hare (1981: 85).

[12] Cf. Wright (1993: 9–10). Notably, Putnam's modified version of realism—which he dubs 'internal realism' (1983: p. xvii)—is based on an epistemic notion of truth, and hence it would not entail the possibility of verification-transcendent truths either. In fact, there may be some

existence and constitution of many types of object is a matter of social or cultural production. There is no reason to deny the possibility of objectivism about such cultural objects. There is, in fact, a whole range of concepts and classes of statement about which it would make perfect sense to hold an anti-realist and objectivist stance. Consider, for example, statements describing: the annual rate of inflation in the UK; the rules of chess; the legal speed-limit for driving in California; the ordinary perceptions of colours; the ordinary meanings of words in a natural language (?!?); and, say, the basic plot of *Pride and Prejudice*. It would be utterly obscure to deny, I believe, the applicability of metaphysical objectivism to all these, and doubtless many other, kinds of statement. Yet it seems equally clear that (Dummettian) realism does not apply here. The reference of concepts like inflation, chess, or the legal speed-limit, and so on, cannot be conceived as ontologically independent of our knowledge and culture. Moreover, at least with respect to some of these examples, one cannot separate the meaning of the concept from its verification conditions. Our concept of inflation, for instance, is closely tied to the way in which economists think that one can verify the existence and constitution of its reference.

Objectivism about a given class of statements, then, does not necessarily entail realism about that class. On the other hand, it would be safe to presume that realism does entail objectivism. If one is a realist about a given class of statements, one is, *ipso facto*, a metaphysical objectivist about that class of statements.

Finally, the question arises whether one can be an objectivist even with respect to non-existent entities? Would metaphysical objectivism make any sense with respect to, for example, statements about fictional characters, or mythological ones? On first impression, it might all seem to depend on the appropriate definition of the idea of 'objects existing in the world' one is willing to allow. Once we allow objectivism (as opposed to realism) about cultural objects, this argument would run, there is no reason to deny its application to non-existent objects as well. (Perhaps the example of fictional characters is potentially misleading. I do not intend to deny that they can be objects, of course, *qua* fictional characters. The oddity concerns the actual reference of such characters, which, I gather, do not exist in any sensible way.) Now, if this were true without further qualifications, it would show that metaphysical objectivism almost collapses into semantic objectivism: if there is no limitation on the kinds of object about which one can be an ojectivist, that is, in the metaphysical sense, then potentially each and every statement which is grammatically about an object could also be objective in the metaphysical sense. Which is to say that the semantic and the

affinities between what I describe here as metaphysical objectivism and Putnam's modified version of realism, but I cannot point out the affinities and differences here. See also Coleman and Leiter's contribution to this volume, *infra*, Ch. 7.

metaphysical senses of objectivism can turn out to be almost equivalent in extension. But this, I think, would be a serious distortion. The distinctions between the various senses of objectivity are basically a matter of theoretical convenience; I do not believe that there can be an independent truth of the matter about these philosophical classifications. From a theoretical vantage-point, however, there is a very good reason for holding on to the distinction between the semantic and the metaphysical senses of objectivity. Generally speaking, the former is a stance on the characterization of the discourse whereas the latter is a characterization of the world. In other words, it must be possible to describe various forms of discourse in the semantically objective sense, even if the discourse is such that the pertinent kind of objects does not really exist, and hence, there can be no truth of the matter about the properties of those objects.

All this is just another way of saying that metaphysical objectivism must always be accompanied by a well-defined notion of the kinds of object one is willing to allow and their existence conditions. There is no logical constraint on the kinds of object to which metaphysical objectivism is applicable, as long as the objectivist can make it clear what would distinguish objects of the kind about which he or she is objectivist, and which exist, and those which do not exist. To be sure, the existence of objects need not be, necessarily, spatio-temporal existence; but it must be distinguishable from non-existence. Otherwise, metaphysical objectivism would make very little difference indeed.[13]

LOGICAL OBJECTIVITY

Metaphysical objectivism about a given class of statements, as we have seen, is only applicable to statements of the descriptive kind. A statement can be objectively true (or false) in this sense, only if it is, or can be reduced to, a description of an object in the world.[14] Some philosophers believe that

[13] I have been told by some of those who have read a draft of this essay that I should specify what I mean by 'objects' here, and what I take to be their existence conditions. I have not been convinced, however, that I should try to carry out this daunting task, and for two main reasons. First, it is not part of my project to argue for the plausibility of metaphysical objectivism in any particular field, and I am not trying to say that it can be done; only that this is what many philosophers have been trying to do, and many others have been trying to refute. More importantly, however, I don't think that it is possible to say anything sufficiently general about the kind of objects one is willing to allow, and their existence conditions, that is, in abstraction of particular domains. Those who argue, for example, about the objectivity of values, and those who argue for the objectivity of mathematical entities, need not base their arguments on the same grounds, even though both try to substantiate a sort of metaphysical objectivism in their respective domains. This, I think, is one modest lesson we could learn from the failure of Platonism.

[14] That may include, as we have noted, the subject's own mental state.

only descriptive propositions can be true or false. According to this view, nothing but metaphysical objectivism about a given class of statements admits of truth values for the statements in that class. This need not be the case, however. Equally respectable is the philosophical stance that allows for the validity or truth of statements which are not descriptive (or reducible to descriptive) statements. Kant's (but perhaps not the contemporary 'Kantian') constructivism in ethics is one prominent example.[15] R. M. Hare's prescriptivism may be another. According to these, and doubtless many other views, statements which do not purport to describe anything can still be true or false, valid or invalid. This indicates that there is at least a logical space for a third kind of objectivism, one which would not necessarily require descriptivism. Logical objectivism, as I will call this view, holds that a given class of statements is objective if and only if each and every statement in that class has a determinate truth value.[16] Consequently, logical subjectivism is the denial of the above, and hence amounts to one of the most common forms of scepticism about the class of statements in question. The logical subjectivist denies the possibility of ascribing truth values to the statements of the kind about which he or she is subjectivist.

Logical objectivism has very close affinities to cognitivism (particularly in meta-ethics), and so before we proceed perhaps I should clarify some of the differences (others will become clear, I hope, as we go along). Cognitivism is a complex doctrine, and it normally involves a two-stage position. First and foremost, it is a view about the possibility of attaining knowledge in the realm about which one is cognitivist. If one is a cognitivist about morality, for example, one holds that moral judgments purport to represent moral knowledge, and that this aspiration is at least sometimes attainable and warranted. (Wiggins 1991*a*: 62). The second stage involves the notion of truth. The cognitivist is expected to maintain that one can come to know that p, because p is true (or, more precisely, perhaps, one can come to know that *p* if and only if one can come to believe that *p* because *p* is true). Now, it is in this second stage that cognitivism and logical objectivism more or less converge, that is, as long as the cognitivist's explanation for the possibility of attaining knowledge is based on the availability of truth (which is not necessarily the case).[17] In other words, logical

[15] On the differences between Kant's and contemporary Kantian constructivism, see O'Neill (1989: ch. 11).

[16] A very difficult question arises here, whether the concept of logical objectivity must assume the law of excluded middle and the bivalence principle. I tend to think that objectivism, as opposed to realism, does not necessarily require a commitment to bivalence, but this is a complicated matter which I cannot discuss here.

[17] Intuitionism in mathematics may well be one such exception; but it is difficult to generalize here, since intuitionism can be understood as espousing a constructive notion of 'truth' which, according to certain interpretations, may well be compatible with logical objectivism. See e.g. Putnam (1983: 20); Dummett (1981: 66).

objectivism is a standard (but again, not necessary) component of cognitivism.[18]

It need not be assumed that the logical objectivity–subjectivity dichotomy is only applicable to non-descriptive statements (as some of the examples mentioned above may be thought to suggest). This will become apparent once we take a closer look at the relations between the logical and the metaphysical senses of objectivity. These relations are somewhat complex. Basically, metaphysical objectivism about a given class of statements entails logical objectivism about that class, but not vice versa. The relation of entailment is pretty clear. One who maintains that a given class of statements can be objectively true or false in the metaphysical sense, *ipso facto* must also maintain that statements in that class can be assigned determinate truth values. Note that a parallel relation of entailment holds between logical subjectivism and metaphysical subjectivism: if one denies the possibility of logical objectivism about a given class of statements, one must also deny the possibility of metaphysical objectivism about that class, and for the same reason. Now the important point is that the reverse does not hold—logical objectivism does not entail metaphysical objectivism—even with respect to statements of the descriptive kind. In other words, there are classes of statement about which it is possible to subscribe to the following three theses:

1. Statements of class A are semantically descriptive: they purport to describe objects of type *x*.
2. Objects of type *x* do not exist in the world.
3. Each and every (well-formed) statement in class A has a determinate truth value.

How is it possible, then, to maintain these three theses about a given type of statements? What kind of discourse could fit such a characterization? Admittedly, it would be very difficult to think of non-controversial examples. There is one, trivial and perhaps, as such, not very interesting example: it is always possible simply to *construct* an artificial language game, or as a matter of fact, just a game, that will fit the conditions mentioned above. But again, such examples would not show a great deal.[19] Thus, consider the

[18] Is it possible to conclude, then, that logical objectivism entails cognitivism? The relation of entailment would seem to follow straightforwardly, since the possibility of truth about a given realm would naturally allow the possibility of knowledge as well. It does not follow, however, if one is both a realist (in the Dummettian sense) about a given realm, and a verificationist about knowledge. Realism, needless to say, entails logical objectivism. But it also entails, as we have seen above, the possibility of verification-transcendent truths, and hence, oddly enough, realism might actually undermine the possibility of cognitivism in certain areas.

[19] Another easy, but perhaps not very interesting, example would be the example of a coherence theory of truth. For those who maintain that the concept of truth consists in the relation of coherence, all statements can be objective only in the logical, but not the metaphysical, sense. The question whether a coherence theory of knowledge admits of objectivity

analysis of our discourse describing mental events according to those who believe in something like central-state materialism. According to such a reductionist conception of the mental to the physical, mental events as such, namely, as forming a separate ontological category, do not really exist. When we describe a mental event or a mental process, our description is of objects (that is, of the mental kind) that do not really exist. Nevertheless, central-state materialism need not deny the possibility of ascribing truth values to statements describing mental events and processes. On the contrary: as each and every statement about the mental sphere is assumed to be reducible to statements about the physical, if one is a logical objectivist about the physical, one must also admit logical objectivism about the reduced class, that is, about the mental sphere. This, in fact, is precisely what is meant by the possibility of complete reduction. Thus, far from denying the logical objectivity of mental statements, central-state materialism reinforces it, despite its outright denial of the metaphysical objectivity of the mental sphere.[20]

To take another example, consider the traditional empiricist analysis of concepts such as causation. Hume, for example, presumably did not intend to deny the possibility of truth and falsehood about causal relations; what he meant to deny, is the metaphysical objectivity of such relations. Thus, at least according to a fairly standard interpretation of Hume, we can say that he advocated metaphysical subjectivism—without denying the possibility of logical objectivism—about the concept of causation. On this interpretation, then, Hume would subscribe to all three conditions mentioned above: (1) statements about causal relations are semantically descriptive; (2) such statements describe objects of a certain type that do not exist, as such, in the world; and (3) statements about casual relations can be assigned determinate truth values.

To be sure, nothing should be understood here as commending a particular theory about the mental or about the Humean analysis of causation. These examples are meant to illustrate a fairly limited point, namely, that there is a philosophically useful notion of logical objectivity which does not necessarily entail metaphysical objectivity. If I am right about this, it will enable us to see that there are two distinct forms of scepticism one can hold about the objectivity of a given kind of discourse. All too often, moreover, these two forms of scepticism are not properly distinguished by their advocates and foes alike. They consist in the denial of metaphysical and logical objectivism, respectively. What usually goes unnoticed is the fact that the denial of the former does not entail the repudiation of the latter as well. In

in the metaphysical sense is a very difficult one, and it involves intricate issues which I cannot discuss here. See Davidson 1986.

[20] Cf. Dummett's discussion of the distinction between naïve and sophisticated realism (1981: 448). See also Marmor (1992: 88–9).

the realm of interpretation this confusion is of considerable importance. Before we get to interpretation, however, it might be useful to demonstrate this by a well-known example of scepticism about objectivity in ethics.

THE ERROR IN MACKIE'S ERROR THEORY

In his celebrated book *Ethics, Inventing Right and Wrong* (1977) John Mackie sets out to establish moral subjectivism. His argument in chapter 1, called 'The Error Theory of Meta-Ethics', runs basically as follows: ethical discourse, Mackie admits, is by and large semantically objective. The ordinary language of morals includes, in a very pervasive manner, a claim to objectivity: the assumption 'that there are objective values' (35), that is, in the metaphysically objective sense. But this claim to objectivity, Mackie argues, is based on a factual/metaphysical mistake. Simply put, there are no objects in the universe of the kind purportedly described by ethical discourse. Hence, he concludes, regardless of the superficial grammar of ethical discourse (or more precisely, despite it), one must adopt outright scepticism about its objective status.

Mackie advances two well-known arguments in favour of his crucial claim that ethical discourse is based on a metaphysical mistake: the argument from relativity and the argument from queerness. The first is utterly inconclusive even on Mackie's own account. It is based on the (basically correct) contention that moral objectivism would make it necessary to attribute a very considerable amount of moral mistake to whole cultures and communities (1977: 36). This is so, as the moral codes of different cultures vary extensively, and widespread moral views are at odds with each other. The only problem for Mackie, though, is that his own meta-ethical conclusions also make it necessary to attribute a very considerable amount of mistake to most of us. Namely, a meta-ethical mistake. The claim to objectivity, inherent in moral discourse, turns out to be, on Mackie's own account, a mistake. Thus, either morality is objective, in which case whole cultures and communities are liable to ethical mistakes; or else, morality is not objective, in which case whole cultures are liable to a widespread meta-ethical mistake. Why we should prefer the attribution of one type of mistake to another remains unexplained.[21]

[21] There is no particular reason to suppose that we are generally more willing to accept the possibility of widespread mistakes which are meta-theoretical compared with substantive errors. In the realm of science, for example, the opposite is true: we feel much more certain about our conceptions of 'how to go about' doing science, than about the substantive scientific theories we now hold true. None of this proves, of course, that Mackie's argument is completely misguided, but only that it is utterly incomplete. What is needed, above all, is a careful and detailed account of various types of moral disagreement and an account of the possibility of moral change (across time and cultures). Only once we posses such an account, can we begin to asses the force of Mackie's argument from relativity. (See e.g. Wiggins 1991*a*: 75–8.)

Be this as it may, the argument from queerness is much more instructive for our purposes. It contends that 'if there were objective values, then they would be entities or qualities or relations of a very strange sort, utterly different from anything else in the universe' (1977: 38). This queerness of moral entities or qualities, Mackie maintains, is enough to cast a serious doubt on the plausibility of objectivism in ethics. Undoubtedly, this argument is far from complete and, as Mackie readily admits (39), there is a great deal more to be shown here before one can draw the sceptical conclusions he wishes to draw (for example, why the same argument from queerness cannot be applied to a great many other concepts, such as numbers, identity, solidity, and so on). Nevertheless, one important point seems to have eluded Mackie with respect to the possible scope of his argument: the argument from queerness can show, at most, the implausibility of *metaphysical* objectivism. It cuts no ice with those who subscribe to logical objectivism in ethics. In other words, the argument from queerness has a bite only against those who conceive of the objectivity in ethics consisting in an objective moral reality 'out there in the universe', so to speak. Logical objectivism remains intact. Hence Mackie could have established only one of the two possible forms of scepticism about morality, namely, about metaphysical objectivism; scepticism about the possibility of ascribing truth values to moral statements (that is, about logical objectivism) simply cannot follow from his argument.

The conclusion that Mackie's argument establishes, at best, only metaphysical subjectivism, is of considerable importance to the assessment of the error theory in meta-ethics. This is so, mainly because the more respectable forms of objectivism in ethics have long eschewed the metaphysical kind.[22] As we have seen earlier, metaphysical objectivism is only applicable to ethical discourse if one can make sense of it in terms of descriptive statements. Yet descriptivism in ethics is extremely problematic, to say the least. Nothing in Mackie's error theory can shake the belief of the non-descriptivist in ethics about the objectivity of moral discourse, as the latter must be presumed to be of the logical kind anyway.[23]

Needless to say, I have not tried to establish the plausibility of logical objectivism in ethics, or in any other field, for that matter. Whether one can

[22] The current revival of metaphysical realism in ethics (e.g. Brink 1989) might cast a serious doubt on the accuracy of this statement, as it would be natural to suppose that Realism presupposes descriptivism. If this is true (and I am not claiming here that it is), then perhaps one should see it as yet another reason to side with the anti-realists in ethics, particularly if one accepts Wiggins's position (as I do), that anti-realism is compatible with moral cognitivism. See Wiggins (1991*a*: 64).

[23] There are clear indications that Mackie has meant his arguments to have a greater significance than they actually have. For instance, he thought to have repudiated the kind of objectivity assumed by Kant as well (1977: 29), yet Kantian ethics can hardly be taken to be a species of descriptivism.

make sense of moral discourse as logically objective must remain an open question, one which I shall not try to resolve here. My purpose has been much more limited; I have attempted to illustrate the importance of the distinction between these three kinds of objectivism. In the next part of this essay I will try to resolve some of the puzzles concerning objectivity in interpretation drawing on these distinctions.

Part II: Objectivity in Interpretation

Objectivity in the realm of the interpretation of works of art is almost universally discredited. In its popular manifestation, the subjectivism associated with interpretation is often expressed by people saying 'it is only your interpretation', or something like that, as if the label 'interpretation' is equivalent to subjectivism. This popular scepticism is largely echoed in the philosophical literature as well. The philosophical origins of this scepticism are not difficult to trace. Most of them are based on sound observations, but the conclusions drawn from them are not always carefully stated. Generally speaking, I will try to show that the interpretation of works of art is typically objective in the semantic sense; rarely, and only in a subordinate manner, objective in the metaphysical sense; and under certain conditions, it is often objective in the logical sense.

It may be useful, then, to take a closer look at some of the main sources of subjectivism in interpretation, following the three concepts of objectivity distinguished in Part I.

INTERPRETATION AND SEMANTIC SUBJECTIVISM

The idea that interpretations of works of art are typically subjective in the semantic sense is widely shared, though, admittedly, more so by laymen than by philosophers and art critics. The first point to notice here is that people are led to the conclusion that interpretative statements are typically subjective in the semantic sense, not because of, but despite the superficial grammar of such statements. Most interpretations of works of art are not presented by the interpreter as a report of his or her state of mind; rarely, if at all, would an interpreter present the interpretation only as a subjective reaction to the object interpreted. Subjective preferences of, and reactions to, aspects of works of art make perfect sense as expressions of personal taste, and are indeed quite common as such. Interpretations, however, are rarely presented as expressions of personal taste. Why the common assumption to the contrary, then? Why is it so tempting to suggest that superficial grammar is misleading here?

The puzzle is increased when we recall that the subjectivist account of the interpretative discourse involves a very high price: it renders the phenomenon of a dispute or an argument about the interpretation of a work of art quite irrational. After all, if interpretative statements are semantically subjective, namely, reports of personal impressions, there is no point whatsoever in arguing about them. More precisely, if interpretative discourse is semantically subjective, two people with different views on the appropriate interpretation of a work of art could never be in a real disagreement with each other; each would be simply stating that he or she had a certain attitude, feeling, or whatever, and these statements would always be mutually consistent.[24]

Undoubtedly, the failure to separate between the semantic and the metaphysical senses of objectivity can explain at least part of the tendency to describe interpretative discourse in subjectivist terms. Since most commentators are inclined to deny the possibility of objectivity in the metaphysical sense (and rightly so, I shall argue), they assume that despite the superficial grammar, interpretative statements are equivalent in meaning to statements about the subject's state of mind. But this move is quite unnecessary, as the previous sections have argued at length.

There is, perhaps, another source for this confusion, one which is based on a sounder point. It is often assumed, and rightly so, I believe, that interpretation involves a rather special notion of epistemic tolerance. One important aspect of this tolerance is captured by the idea that whenever there is one interpretation of a work of art, there must also be others that do not necessarily coincide with it. As Joseph Raz puts it, 'the very idea of interpretation imports the possibility of more than one interpretation, of several good or acceptable interpretations'.[25] This is a crucially important observation, and we shall have to explain it in some detail. Any account of interpretation must explain this paradoxical feature of it, namely, that interpretations admit, on the one hand, of plurality and inconsistency, and on the other hand, of ascriptions of good or bad, right and wrong, and the like. I will try to offer at least a partial explanation for this in the last section. For the time being, however, suffice it to say that nothing in this epistemic tolerance requires the characterization of interpretative discourse in semantically subjectivist terms. On the contrary: interpretative statements could not be good or bad, acceptable or unacceptable *at all*, if the semantic subjectivism attributed to them were true. Interpretations can be commensurable,

[24] Cf. Hare 1981: 77. Wiggins (1991*b*: 185 ff.) has made an interesting attempt to overcome this, and related difficulties, by articulating a much more sophisticated version of subjectivism, one which affirms both relativism and cognitivism. An assessment of Wiggins's views, however, exceeds the scope of this essay.

[25] See Raz's contribution to this volume, *supra*, Ch. 5.

and subject to appraisals and intelligible controversies, only if they are by and large objective (at least) in the semantic sense.

Finally, there is an important distinction between an interpretation of a work of art and its description that might account for the tendency to describe the former in semantically subjectivist terms. Once again, the subjectivist conclusion is unwarranted, but the confusion stems from a sound point. Grammatically, by and large, interpretative statements are descriptive; they purport to describe certain aspects of the work interpreted. But in this case we must be very careful not to be misled by the superficial appearance of grammar. A statement describing an aspect of a work of art is never, by itself, an interpretation of the work in question. The latter always involves, explicitly or implicitly, evaluative judgments of various kinds which give the descriptive part of the interpretation its particular significance. When this evaluative significance is absent, or perhaps when it eludes us, the description is not grasped as an interpretation of the work of art. Saying, for example, that 'the *American Gothic* is a picture of a man and his daughter' is part of an interpretation of the picture, only if it is somehow significant, or important, to know this piece of information. When this significance is absent, like when someone informs us that the length of a novel is 500 pages, the description in question is not grasped as interpretative.[26] Needless to say, often the very same piece of information can be significant within one interpretative framework and insignificant within another. There is no hard and fast line to draw here between descriptions which are part of interpretations, and those which are not. The important point is, however, that descriptive statements about a work of art are always subordinate to a larger framework of the interpretative explanation, and this framework must include evaluative judgments about the significance of the descriptions offered.[27]

We have not equipped the subjectivist, however, with the weapon she needs. Semantic subjectivism would follow from the considerations mentioned above if, but only if, it could also be shown that the kind of evaluative judgments pertinent to the interpretation of works of art is, by and large, semantically subjective. But this, of course, does not follow. Those evaluative judgments which provide the significance and relevance of the descriptive parts of a given interpretation, need not be semantically subjective. On the contrary, as we have already noted, interpretative discourse would not make much sense if it were based on semantically subjectivist terms. People can only have a genuine and intelligent argument or disagreement

[26] It is possible, of course, that the length of a novel would be relevant and significant.

[27] Cf. Dworkin (1986: 59–61) and Marmor (1992: 38). Needless to say, evaluations without any descriptive element whatsoever are not normally considered interpretations either. Saying something like 'this is a wonderful novel' does not amount to an interpretation of the novel.

if their judgments are not meant to reflect only preferences of taste, as it were; it is not enough that they are talking about one and the same object if the former condition is not met. If I say, for example, that I like this picture and you say that you don't, there is not much left to argue about, as both statements are mutually consistent. We may, of course, attempt to influence each other's personal tastes, but this is not normally achieved effectively by an interpretative argument. Sometimes a change in another's personal taste or preference is an additional (and perhaps welcome) achievement of a good interpretation; but this is hardly the main point of interpretations generally.

As a final remark about semantic subjectivism, it should be kept in mind that we are talking about generalizations that do not always hold. My contention is that, by and large, interpretative discourse cannot be presumed to be based on semantically subjectivist terms. This does not rule out the possibility that sometimes it is. Impressionistic interpretations, so to speak, make perfect sense, as such.[28] But again, the point is that they cannot be characteristic of the discourse; they do not present the paradigm of an interpretation of a work of art.

INTERPRETATION AND METAPHYSICAL SUBJECTIVISM

There are several lines of thought purporting to repudiate the possibility of metaphysical objectivism in the realm of artistic interpretation. Most of them, I shall argue, are basically sound. Let me begin, however, with one prevalent type of argument which is misconceived, as it confuses subjectivism with anti-realism. The argument under consideration would basically run as follows.

The interpretation of works of art is paradigmatically the interpretation of cultural products. Works of art, as objects existing in the world, exist only as such cultural entities. No interpreter is interested in, for example, Michelangelo's *David* as a piece of marble *qua* physical object; the object of interpretation is the statue. There is a clear sense, however, in which it is possible to deny the reality of this statue, namely, as an object whose properties are independent of our perceptions, conventions, culture, and so on. As an object which is totally independent of our knowledge and culture, Michelangelo's *David* exists only as a piece of marble. Now this much can be conceded without much difficulty. The simple point about its significance, however, is that it only shows, at best, the repudiation of realism as applied to the construal of interpretation of works of art. That is, one can

[28] By 'impressionistic interpretations' I mean those which basically amount to an articulation of personal tastes, impressions, and the like.

hardly be a realist about the interpretation of works of art, as such interpretative statements cannot be assumed to be rendered either true or false by some objective reality whose existence and constitution are independent of our knowledge. But, as we have observed earlier, the denial of realism about a given class of statements does not necessarily amount to the denial of objectivism, even in its metaphysical sense, about that class of statements. Objectivism without realism, as we have seen, makes perfect sense.

This distinction between metaphysical objectivism and realism, however, does not rescue the former; there are other considerations which support metaphysical subjectivism as applied to the interpretation of works of art. Something like Mackie's argument from queerness might be one of them. Note that there is a distinction between a Mackie-like argument concerning the queerness of the existence of objects purportedly described by interpretations of works of art, and the anti-realist argument criticized above. The latter relies on the cultural nature of the objects of art. This, as we have just seen, is not enought to cast a doubt on the possible objectivity of interpretation. The argument from queerness, however, aims to show that the entities, or qualities or characters, and so on, purportedly described by typical interpretations of works of art do not exist at all; they are queer entities, so to speak. In other words, the argument from queerness would deny that features of works of art meet any reasonable conditions of existence. Whether this is a plausible line of thought is rather doubtful, but in any case I shall not try to develop it further. I will offer a different line of thought instead, drawing on the idea that metaphysical objectivism presupposes descriptivism. In other words, I will try to show that metaphysical objectivity about interpretations of works of art is rendered implausible because a descriptivist account of interpretation is misguided.

There are two prevalent accounts of interpretation of works of art which are basically descriptive and hence potentially support the objectivist stance. The more familiar one is the authorial intent doctrine.[29] Roughly, it maintains that an interpretation of a work of art should strive to retrieve the author's intentions with respect to the work he or she has created, and the interpretation is successful—and objective—if and only if it succeeds in doing so. Note that one need not hold this intentionalist doctrine *tout court* for the purposes of our discussion: in order to show the *possibility* of metaphysical objectivism in interpretation, it is sufficient to show that at least in certain (but not-insignificant number of) cases the intentionalist doctrine holds. After all, no one has to claim that interpretations of works of art are always objective. The second type of interpretation which seems descriptive in the requisite sense is the historic interpretation. An interpretation of a

[29] Notably, Hirsch's famous essay (1967) advocating intentionalism has been explicitly motivated by the point of securing the objectivity of interpretation.

work of art sometimes tells us a story about the way in which the work has been conceived, appreciated, and so on, by the culture in which it has been created, or by later cultures in which it played a certain part. In other words, historic interpretations are descriptions of the cultural significance of the work in question, and hence they are basically descriptive.

Neither of these two accounts, however, suffices to show the possibility of metaphysical objectivism as a significant aspect of the interpretation of works of art. The fallacy of intentionalism is more readily apparent. It is, of course, quite correct to maintain that if an interpretation of a work of art consists in the description of its author's intentions, such an interpretation is objective in the metaphysical sense (that is, of course, as long as it makes sense to hold an objectivist position about the relevant kind of mental states); it will be objectively true if the description fits the intentions the author had, and objectively false if it doesn't. But the point is that an interpretation can never be thoroughly descriptive in this sense, even if it focuses on the author's intentions, and even if it makes perfect sense to do so. In other words, a description of the author's intention does not constitute by itself an interpretation of the work he or she has created. There is always the implicit assumption that the author's intentions are relevant, important, or significant for our understanding of the work in question. Even the most devout intentionalists do not assume that just about any fact about the author's state of mind bears on the interpretation of his or her work. The fact that the author has had a terrible headache, or that she has been bothered by domestic problems, may or may not have such a bearing on the meaning of her work, depending on numerous, *inter alia* evaluative, considerations. Similarly, the fact that the author has intended her readers to understand the motives of one of the characters in her novel, say, in a sinister manner, may or may not shed light on the meaning of her work. Whether it does or does not, however, cannot be determined by a closer scrutiny of her intentions. Not, primarily, because there simply may not be anything to discover there (which is very often the case), but mainly because it would be absurd to assume that authors are infallible interpreters of their own works of art. I shall not dwell on this point further, as it is well known and rarely disputed. Its significance, however, needs to be stated. The point is that even if there are certain aspects of an interpretation of a work of art that admit of metaphysical objectivity (for example, the description of the author's state of mind), such aspects are always *subordinate* to other, more evaluative aspects of the interpretation in question. Hence it is simply misleading to say that *the* interpretation is (metaphysically) objective; only an aspect of it, and one whose significance is always to be determined on non-descriptive grounds, can be objective in the requisite sense.

To be sure, I have not been assuming that evaluative judgments, as such, cannot be objective in the metaphysical sense. The argument offered here is limited to showing that the reference to authors' intentions, even where plausible, does not render *by itself* the interpretation objective. The objectivist must also show that the evaluative judgments grounding the significance of the authors' intentions are metaphysically objective.[30] But this, I imagine, is a rather daunting task.

Now, similar, but not identical, considerations apply to historic interpretations. Such interpretations vary a great deal; some are closer to straightforward descriptions, while others are better described as critical interpretations set against an historic background. The plausibility of metaphysical objectivity here depends on its plausibility in the realm of historical explanations generally. The latter involves intricate issues that cannot be discussed here. Suffice it to emphasize one point, namely, that the more an interpretation is descriptive, the less of an interpretation it is, as it were. The cultural history of art is what it purports to be, namely, history; and the more it is so, the less it can count as a piece of interpretation of a work of art. The fact that there is no hard and fast line to be drawn between the history of art and its interpretation should not obscure the functional and conceptual differences between the two. There is a clear conceptual distinction between an historic interpretation, which basically attempts to describe how a given work of art has been understood *by others*, and a critical interpretation which purports to suggest how the work should be understood. It should be readily admitted that, as far as one can be objectivist about the construal of others' understanding of a work of art, objectivity is applicable to historic interpretations. Nothing follows from this about the objective standing of critical interpretations.

Once again, it may not be pointless to emphasize the limited scope of the arguments presented in this section. I have not tried to deny any possible role for metaphysically objective statements in the realm of interpretation of works of art. As we have seen, certain aspects of interpretation can be objective in this sense. What remains very doubtful, however, is the assumption that metaphysical objectivism can be regarded as a paradigm, or as a significant aspect, of interpretation of works of art.

INTERPRETATION AND LOGICAL SUBJECTIVISM

Perhaps I should not complain if the reader has gained the impression that I am over-simplifying the controversies over the objectivity of interpretation in the realm of art. This impression is premature, however. Most of the genuine controversies over the possibility of objectivism in this field should

[30] Cf. Barnes (1988: ch. 4).

be seen as concerning the possibility of objectivism in the logical sense. And here I think that we must face a very intriguing puzzle indeed, concerning what I have called the epistemic tolerance of interpretations of works of art. To reiterate, the puzzle is this: on the one hand, we must account for the fact that interpretations admit of plurality—the very idea of an interpretation of a work of art imports the possibility of other interpretations of the same work which are potentially inconsistent with it. On the other hand, we must also account for the fact that interpretations of works of art can be good or bad, interesting or silly, right or wrong, and so on. Of course, if one espouses logical subjectivism about appraisals of interpretations in terms of right or wrong, good or bad, there is not much of a puzzle left. Such a sceptical approach to interpretations of works of art would simply reinforce their plurality. If anything goes in interpretation, as it were, no wonder that we should be 'tolerant' with respect to conflicting interpretations of the same work. As a matter of fact, for most sceptics it is precisely this plurality of interpretations which leads them to their subjectivist conclusions. But this move, I shall argue, is unwarranted. In other words, I will try to show that we can account for the epistemic tolerance of interpretations of works of art without eschewing the possibility of them being objective in the logical sense. Notably, this is a modest claim; it would not prove the correctness of logical objectivism as applied to interpretations of works of art, as there might be other reasons for denying it, besides this one (that is, the argument from plurality). But at least it could show that one prevalent source of subjectivism is unsound.

Consider this question: can it be the case that logical objectivism is consistent with relativism? If the answer is basically yes, as I shall now argue, then we have the key to the solution of our puzzle. In brief, the idea is this: interpretations admit of plurality, of epistemic tolerance, mainly because they are based on different frameworks of reference, as it were; they are always relative to a certain scheme (or 'myth', as Margolis (1980: ch. 7) has called it), and these different schemes of reference need not be consistent with each other. If it can be shown, however, that this relativism inherent in the interpretation of works of art is consistent with logical objectivism, the puzzle about the epistemic tolerance would be solved. Let us now take it step by step.

Interpretations of works of art normally work from a certain scheme, whether it is explicit or only implicit. Authorial intent, historical context, Freudian psychology, Catholic religion, Marxist political theory, and feminist critique are but a few, familiar examples of such perspectives or schemes guiding interpretations of works of art. Moreover, as we have seen above, the fact that there is such a perspective underlying the interpretation is essential for distinguishing an interpretation of a work of art from mere description on the one hand, and from expressions of personal tastes and impressions on the other. Now, the plurality of interpretations in the relativist sense is secured not merely by this plurality of possible schemes, but mainly by the fact that none of them can be accorded a privileged status. Or at least, this is what the subjectivist assumes, and we need not argue with this assumption. Furthermore, the acceptability of an interpretation of a work of art is rarely affected by the truth or falsehood of the scheme upon which it is based. An interpretation of Dante's *Commedia*, for example, could hardly be affected by the truth or falsehood of Catholicism.[31] Now these three points, namely, that interpretations are typically guided by a certain scheme, that none of these schemes can be accorded a privileged status, and that the truth or falsehood of these schemes does not normally affect the acceptability of the interpretations based on them, establish a fairly strong relativist position.

The only question we need to ask, however, is whether this relativism characteristic of interpretations of works of art is compatible with logical objectivity. The answer would seem to be as follows: as long as one can hold an objectivist stance about the scheme of reference, one must also allow objectivity about the interpretations based on it. Thus, for example, as long as one may assume that certain kinds of statement about, for example, Catholicism are objective in the logical sense, one would have to admit that the same is true about interpretative statements concerning Dante's *Commedia* which are based on the Catholic scheme. For instance, if there is a truth of the matter about the meaning of a certain symbol according to Catholicism, there can also be a truth of the matter about the meaning of that symbol in Dante's work, if it is interpreted from the perspective of the Catholic scheme. There may not be a truth of the matter about the choice of the appropriate scheme, but that does not undermine the logical, as opposed to the metaphysical, objectivity of the particular interpretation offered. From the Catholic perspective, one can easily be mistaken about the meaning of a certain symbol in Dante's work, and there is no reason to deny that this would be a mistake, objectively speaking, even if it is not a mistake to strive to interpret Dante's *Commedia* according to a totally different scheme.

It should be conceded, however, that interpretations admit of plurality and inconsistency even from within one and the same scheme. For example, from the perspective of psychoanalysis it may be controversial whether Hamlet's character is best described in terms of an Oedipus complex, or not. But this internal plurality of interpretations is explicable on the following grounds: very often, interpretations of works of art which stem from a certain scheme are concomitantly interpretations of both the work in question

[31] Note that there are possible exceptions: psychoanalytic, and perhaps even Marxist, interpretations are not totally unaffected by the scientific truths of these theories.

and certain aspects of the scheme itself. A psychoanalytic interpretation of *Hamlet* may be both an interpretation of the play and of certain aspects of psychoanalytic theory. Whether the interpretation of the scheme admits of logical or metaphysical objectivity would obviously depend of the nature of the particular scheme in question, and the nature of the particular controversy.

Generally speaking, then, logical objectivity is not necessarily at odds with relativism. Yet there is one important proviso that must be taken into account here: we must draw a distinction between modest and comprehensive interpretative claims. An interpretative claim is *modest* if it does not claim truth (that is, in terms of exclusivity, or some other form of privileged status) for the choice of its underlying scheme, but only for the truth of the interpretation from the perspective of the scheme chosen; and an interpretative claim is *comprehensive* if it does claim truth for the choice of the scheme as well. Obviously, then, relativism would not be compatible with logical objectivity if the interpretations of works of art are typically of the comprehensive kind. I do not believe that they are, however. Epistemic tolerance is so widely acknowledged in this field, precisely because it is characteristic of interpretations of works of art that they are not comprehensive. After all, art is basically a cultural product, and it is reasonable to suppose that there are as many ways of interpreting works of art as there are imaginative schemes embodied in our cultures.[32] In other words, interpreters and art critics normally assume that there is no truth of the matter about the choice of the appropriate scheme for the interpretation of a work of art. Note that it is the claim for the *truth* of the choice of the underlying scheme which is being denied here; not its relevance or relative importance from a cultural (or some other theoretical) point of view. We can easily understand, for example, why the Catholic scheme is more appropriate for Dante's work than for Shakespeare's. But this appropriateness, so to speak, is a matter of cultural significance, not of truth and falsehood.

The fact that interpretations of works of art are typically of the modest kind may serve well to illustrate a fairly obvious point, namely, that objectivity is only one aspect of the appraisal of interpretations of works of art, and probably not the most important one. In other realms of interpretation the case may be quite different, of course. Interpretation in law, for example, may well be intelligible only if it claims to be comprehensive. Whether legal interpretation can be objective in the metaphysical or in the logical sense is a difficult question, calling for an essay of its own.

[32] Dworkin's constructive model of interpretation presupposes, I think, that interpretations are typically comprehensive. Otherwise, it would be very difficult to understand his insistence on the general availability of 'the best' interpretation. See Dworkin (1986), mainly ch. 2, and cf. Marmor (1992: 51–7).

REFERENCES

BARNES, A. (1988), *On Interpretation* (Oxford: Blackwell).

BRINK, D. (1989), *Moral Realism and the Foundations of Ethics* (Cambridge: Cambridge University Press).

DAN-COHEN, M. (1989), 'Law, Community, and Communication', *Duke Law Journal*, 1654–76.

DAVIDSON, D. (1986), 'A Coherence Theory of Truth and Knowledge', in Le Pore (ed.), *Truth and Interpretation: Perspectives on the Philosophy of Donald Davidson* (Oxford: Blackwell).

DUMMETT, M. (1981), *The Interpretation of Frege's Philosophy* (London: Duckworth).

DWORKIN, R. (1986), *Law's Empire* (London: Fontana Press).

HARE, R. M. (1981), *Moral Thinking* (Oxford: Clarendon Press).

HIRSCH, E. D. H. (1967), *Validity in Interpretation* (New Haven, Conn.: Yale University Press).

MACKIE, J. L. (1977), *Ethics, Inventing Right and Wrong* (New York: Penguin Books).

MARGOLIS, J. (1980), *Art and Philosophy* (Brighton: Harvester Press).

MARMOR, A. (1992), *Interpretation and Legal Theory* (Oxford: Clarendon Press).

O'NEILL, O. (1989), *Constructions of Reason* (Cambridge: Cambridge University Press).

PUTNAM, H. (1983), *Realism and Reason* (Cambridge: Cambridge University Press).

WIGGINS, D. (1991*a*), 'Moral Cognitivism, Moral Relativism and Motivating Moral Beliefs', *Proceedings of the Aristotelian Society* (Fall), 61–85.

—— (1991*b*), *Needs, Values, Truth*, 2nd edn. (Oxford: Blackwell).

WRIGHT, C. (1986, 1993), *Meaning, Realism, and Truth*, 2nd edn. (Oxford: Blackwell).

7

Determinacy, Objectivity, and Authority

JULES L. COLEMAN AND BRIAN LEITER

INTRODUCTION

Since the 1970s analytic jurisprudence has been under attack from what has come to be known as the Critical Legal Studies ('CLS') movement. CLS has been joined in this attack by proponents of Feminist Jurisprudence, and, most recently, by proponents of Critical Race Theory. When the battle lines are drawn in this way, the importance of the distinctions between the Natural Law and Positivist traditions are easily missed. Whatever distinguishes Hart from Dworkin, and both from Lon Fuller, matters very little from this point of view, as compared to what (theoretically at least) unites them, and that, according to its critics, is a commitment to the ideals of 'legal liberalism'.

If Joseph Singer's 'The Player and the Cards: Nihilism and Legal Theory'[1] is representative of the CLS critique, liberalism is committed to the law being determinate, objective, and neutral. According to CLS, the problem with liberalism is that none of these ideals obtain in legal practice. Law is neither determinate, objective, nor neutral.[2]

Earlier versions of this article were presented at the Tel Aviv Conference on Interpretation where it benefited from excellent comments by Andrei Marmor, Joseph Raz, Jeremy Waldron, and Michael Moore, and at Oxford University where it benefited from more comments by Raz and Waldron, a splendid commentary by Howard Chang, and thoughtful criticisms by Ruth Chang, Wil Woluchow, John Finnis, John Gardner, Carl Wellman, and Liam Murphy. The article also improved as a result of conversations with Peter Railton, Larry Alexander, Chris Kutz, Scott Shapiro, and Jack Balkin.

This article is part of a series of papers on objectivity in law by the authors. Some in the series will be co-authored, others will not. The reader is directed to Leiter, *infra*, nn. 20, 29, 60, 113, and to Jules Coleman's book-length MS, 'Reason, Objectivity and Authority' (in progress) (MS on file with author), for related discussions of the materials in this article. In the next, jointly authored piece, we plan to take up the question of whether legal facts are minimally or modestly objective. See Coleman and Leiter, *infra*, n. 154.

[1] Joseph W. Singer, 'The Player and the Cards: Nihilism and Legal Theory', 94 *Yale LJ* 1 (1984).

[2] Critical Race Theorists have been especially critical of law's claim to objectivity. See e.g. Derrick Bell and Preeta Bansal, 'The Republican Revival and Racial Politics', 97 *Yale LJ* 1609, 1611 (1988) (noting that many scholars have identified the 'objective' stance as distinctively white and male); John O. Calmore, 'Critical Race Theory, Archie Shepp, and Fire Music: Securing an Authentic Intellectual Life in a Multicultural World', 65 *S. Cal. L. Rev.* 2129, 2162 n. 107 (1992) ('[C]ritical race theory unmasks certain themes that dominate mainstream legal disclosure,

Although liberalism is sometimes associated with neutrality regarding alternative conceptions of the good,[3] and less frequently with forms of neutral dialogue,[4] the status of neutrality as a defining characteristic of liberalism is quite contestable—even among liberals.[5] Liberalism is a political philosophy built on the premiss that authorities often govern in the face of *a plurality* of conceptions of the good. Legitimate authority must respect and respond to pluralism, and while being neutral among divergent conceptions of the good is one way of doing so, it is neither the only way nor the uniquely liberal way. Let us, then, set aside the question of whether liberal legal institutions are neutral in a suitable way, and focus instead on the claim that legal authority presupposes or requires that the outcomes of legal disputes be determinate and the legal facts to which judicial opinions refer be objective.

We sympathize with many of the substantive concerns Crits, Feminists, and Critical Race Theorists have expressed about existing legal *practices*. We have two problems with the prevailing critique, however. First, and of most immediate concern, the arguments against determinacy and objectivity are unsound. Secondly, the prevailing critique often misunderstands the nature of philosophic argument and the manner in which philosophical theories bear on our understanding and evaluation of legal practice, and on legal practice itself. It appears to be essential to the critique that substantive

such as formal equality, individualized opportunity, neutrality, objectivity, color blindness, and meritocracy.'); Anthony E. Cook, 'Beyond Critical Legal Studies: The Reconstructive Theology of Dr. Martin Luther King, Jr.', 103 *Harv. L. Rev.* 985, 992 (1990) (noting 'disproven values of neutrality and objectivity'); Kimberle W. Crenshaw, 'Race, Reform, and Retrenchment: Transformation and Legitimation in Antidiscrimination Law', 101 *Harv. L. Rev.* 1331, 1341 (1988) (questioning Thomas Sowell's 'expectations that he will eventually identity some determinate, clearly discernible version of [the], law); Richard Delgado, 'The Inward Turn in Outsider Jurisprudence', 34 *Wm. & Mary L. Rev.* 741, 748 (1993) (reflecting on observation that 'feminism and Critical Race Theory are defined by a commitment to the interests of people of color and women, by rejection of abstraction and dispassionate "objectivity"'); id., 'Shadowboxing: An Essay on Power', 77 *Cornell L. Rev.* 813, 814 (1992), (arguing that powerful parties prefer 'objective' to 'subjective' standards); id., 'Storytelling for Oppositionists and Others: A Plea for Narrative', 87 *Mich. L. Rev.* 2411, 2441 (1989) ('Implying that objective, correct answers can be given to legal questions . . . obscures the moral and political value judgments that lie at the heart of any legal inquiry.'); Patricia J. Williams, 'Alchemical Notes: Reconstructing Ideals from Deconstructed Rights', 22 *Harv. CR-CL L. Rev.* 401, 404 (1987) (speculating that rights discourse may prove 'contradictory, indeterminate, reified and marginally decisive'). But see Mari J. Matsuda, 'Pragmatism Modified and the False Consciousness Problem', 63 *S. Cal. L. Rev.* 1763, 1769 (1990) (noting 'contradiction between the critique of objectivity and the critique of present injustice . . . well known to . . . critical race theorists'); Symposium, 'Minority Critiques of the Critical Legal Studies Movement', 22 *Harv. CR-CL L. Rev.* 297 (1987); Veronica Gentilli, Comment, 'A Double Challenge for Critical Race Scholars: The Moral Context', 65 *S. Cal. L. Rev.* 2361, 2366 (1992) (arguing that Critical Race Theory is committed ultimately to a form of moral realism).

[3] See e.g. Ronald Dworkin, *Taking Rights Seriously* (p. xiv 1977) London: Duckworth, John Rawls, *A Theory of Justice* (Oxford: Oxford University Press, 1972), 136–42.

[4] See Bruce A. Ackerman, *Social Justice in the Liberal State* (New Harven, Conn.: Yale University Press, 1980), 357–9.

[5] See Joseph Raz, *The Morality of Freedom* (Oxford: Clarendon Press, 1986), 113–14.

problems with liberal legal regimes are either problems in the 'philosophy of liberalism', or are otherwise connected with 'liberal philosophy' because liberal practice and philosophy are somehow inseparable.[6] Thus, some critics have suggested that the problem with liberalism (and why it is an enemy of women, for example) is its commitment to abstraction and the correspondence theory of truth.[7] Others have claimed that the problem is essentialism.[8] The most prevalent confusion is the identification of liberal theory with epistemological foundationalism.[9] Then, citing Rorty, Kuhn, and Wittgenstein as if they were citing a holding in an unanimous Supreme Court decision, critics are satisfied to reject foundationalism, the possibility of objective epistemology, and liberalism all in one fell swoop.

Foundationalism, however, is only one of many possible epistemologies of justified belief, and not one currently favoured.[10] The correspondence

[6] Ironically, the same views we are concerned with rejecting here enjoyed a certain currency in Germany in the later stages of the first wave of Hegelianism in the 1830s and 1840s. Indeed, such views were lampooned by Marx and Engels in 1845–6. See Karl Marx and Frederick Engels, 'The German Ideology: Part I', in *The Marx–Engels Reader,* ed. Robert C. Tucker, 2nd edn. (New York: W. W. Nortan, 1978), 146. It is a curious feature of the intellectual history of CLS that it should have revived—apparently unselfconsciously—the very neo-Hegelian critical themes that had been ridiculed by Marx and Engels more than a century ago. For a further discussion, see *infra,* n. 12.

[7] See e.g. Ann C. Scales, 'The Emergence of Feminist Jurisprudence: An Essay', 95 *Yale LJ* 1373, 1377 (1986) ('The philosophical basis of [the liberal] approach is "abstract universality" . . . Underlying this approach is the correspondence theory of truth . . .').

[8] See e.g. Marie Ashe, 'Inventing Choreographies: Feminism and Deconstruction', 90 *Colum. L. Rev.* 1123, 1132 (1990) (reviewing Zillah Eisenstein, *The Female Body and the Law* (Berkeley: University of California Press, 1988), which criticizes MacKinnon's 'essentialist error'); Drucilla Cornell, 'Sexual Difference, the Feminine, and Equivalency: A Critique of MacKinnon's Toward a Feminist Theory of the State', 100 *Yale LJ* 2247, 2264 (1991), (claiming that MacKinnon 'remains a specific kind of essentialist'); Angela P. Harris, 'Race and Essentialism in Feminist Legal Theory', 42 *Stan. L. Rev.* 581, 591 (1990) (contending that '[d]espite its power, MacKinnon's dominance theory is flawed by its essentialism'); Allan C. Hutchinson, 'Inessentially Speaking (Is There Politics After Postmodernism?)', 89 *Mich. L. Rev.* 1549, 1560 (1991) (reviewing Martha Minow, *Making All the Difference* (Ithaca, NY: Cornell University Press, 1990), and observing, 'essentialist leanings' of MacKinnon's 'standpoint epistemology'); Catherine A. MacKinnon, 'From Practice to Theory, or What is a White Woman Anyway?', 4 *Yale JL & Feminism* 13, 18–22 (1991) (responding to gender essentialism critiques); Jeanne L. Schroeder, 'Abduction From the Seraglio: Feminist Methodologies and the Logic of Imagination', 70 *Tex. L. Rev.* 109, 193 (1991) (charging MacKinnon with 'external essentialist understanding of woman's nature'); Jeanne L. Schroeder, 'Feminism Historicized: Medieval Misogynist Stereotypes in Contemporary Feminist Jurisprudence', 75 *Iowa L. Rev.* 1135, 1149 n. 33 (1990) (agreeing with Robin West that 'there seems to be an underlying unadmitted strain of essentialism running through MacKinnon's work').

[9] See Steven L. Winter, 'Bull Durham and the Uses of Theory', 42 *Stan. L. Rev.* 639 (1990) (criticizing anti-foundationalist denials of a concept of theory); id., 'Transcendental Nonsense, Metaphoric Reasoning, and the Cognitive Stakes for Law', 137 *U. Pa. L. Rev.* 1105 (1989).

[10] There have been at least two different foundationalist traditions in epistemology: Cartesian foundationalism and logical empiricism. Foundationalism (roughly) is the view that beliefs are ultimately justified only if they rest on beliefs that themselves are not justified by appeal to yet other beliefs. Understood narrowly, foundationalism is associated with the view that those beliefs that are not justified by yet other beliefs are themselves indubitable or otherwise certain. In the Cartesian tradition the foundation is the belief that 'I think, therefore I am'. In the logical empiricist tradition, ultimate beliefs are normally associated with reports of sensory

theory of truth is simply one of many alternative accounts of the nature of truth, and a fairly controversial one at that.[11] Truth itself can hardly be the enemy. Remarks like these seriously misunderstand philosophy and its relationships to both legal theory and practice. Worse, to think that anything of substance hangs on a semantic, metaphysical, epistemological, or other philosophical thesis may well be counter-productive to the desirable goals of righting substantive wrongs and improving people's lives.[12]

Phrases like 'legal liberalism' have found their way into modern jurisprudence, but do little to clarify the underlying issues. There is no such thing as a 'liberal philosophy', that is, an all-encompassing philosophy that includes, among other things, a distinct metaphysics, epistemology, philosophy of language, and meta- and normative ethics. Some liberals are metaphysical realists, others are anti-realists. Some are epistemic coherentists, others are externalists. Some are ethical deontologists, others are consequentialists. And so on.

The same can be said about liberal jurisprudence. No analytic jurisprudent —not Dworkin, not Hart, not Fuller, not Raz, nor anyone else—has ever referred to his or her *jurisprudence* as 'liberal'. This is so in spite of the fact that Dworkin, Hart, and Raz are arguably among the most important figures in political liberalism of the last half of this century.

We will do two things in this essay. First, we will consider and reject certain arguments about determinacy and objectivity. Secondly, we will get the debate back on the right track by eradicating several confusing conflations

experience, e.g. 'I am now being appeared to greenly'. Neither of the narrower forms of foundationalism have been favoured in philosophy at least since the publication in the 1950s of W. V. O. Quine's 'Two Dogmas of Empiricism' (in *From A Logical Point of View*, 3rd edn. (Cambridge, Mass.: Harvard University Press, 1980), 20; see also Wilfred Sellars, 'Empiricism and the Philosophy of the Mind', in *Science, Perception and Reality* (London: Routledge & Kegan Paul, 1963),127–56. Richard Rorty popularized these Quinean and Sellarsian themes in *Philosophy and the Mirror of Nature* (Princeton University Press, 1980), 170–209.

[11] See e.g. Donald Davidson, 'A Coherence Theory of Truth and Knowledge', in *Truth and Interpretation: Perspectives on the Philosophy of Donald Davidson*, ed. Ernest LePore (Oxford: Basil Blackwell, 1986), 307, 307–10 (favouring coherence theory of truth over correspondence theory of truth); id., 'The Structure and Content of Truth', 87 *J. Phil.* 279, 301–5 (1990) (same).

[12] This point was put well enough some 150 years ago by two writers whose credentials on the political left are, we imagine, still unimpeachable: 'Since [here, the Crits] consider conceptions, thoughts, ideas, in fact all the products of consciousness . . . as the real chains of men . . . it is evident that [the Crits] have to fight only against these illusions of the consciousness. Since, according to their fantasy, the relationships of men, all their doings, their chains and their limitations are products of their consciousness, [the Crits] logically put to men the moral postulate of exchanging their present consciousness for human, critical or egoistic consciousness, and thus of removing their limitations. This demand to change consciousness amounts to a demand to interpret reality in another way, i.e., to recognize it by means of another interpretation . . . They forget, however, that to these phrases [constituting the old interpretation] they themselves are only opposing other phrases, and that they are in no way combating the real existing world when they are merely combating the phrases of this world.' Marx and Engels, *supra*, n. 6, at 149. There are obvious emendations to the text above. We do not mean to suggest that this passage is applicable to all the writings associated with CLS. Still, it is strikingly apt with respect to some of the best-known CLS work.

of ideas and concepts. It would be a mistake, however, to read us as being concerned primarily with responding to liberalism's critics. Therefore, rather than arguing that liberalism's critics have failed to show that liberal political philosophy is committed to legal determinacy, we will ask whether any of the deep commitments of liberalism require that the outcomes of legal disputes be determinate. In doing so, we hope to say something fresh about what determinacy consists of, as well as about its connection to predictability, stability, and the possibility of democratic rule. Similarly, rather than arguing that its critics have failed to establish liberalism's commitment to objectivity, we will argue that liberalism is committed to objectivity, and that our ordinary understanding of judicial practice presupposes a form of metaphysical objectivity with respect to legal facts. In making good on those claims, we distinguish among a number of senses of objectivity, introduce a new conception of it, and argue for its coherence and its plausibility as an account of the kind of objectivity presupposed by our legal practices.

Understood in this way, the criticisms of liberalism presented by Crits, Critical Race Theorists, and Feminists (among others) will be employed largely as a springboard to a wider discussion of determinacy and objectivity in their relationship to liberal political theory and the legitimacy of legal authority.

We begin by drawing some simple but important distinctions. Initially, there are political and legal institutions on the one hand, and there are philosophical, analytic, and normative theories about these institutions on the other. With respect to philosophical theories, we can distinguish the analytic from the normative. Analytic theories offer accounts of human practices, particularly their theoretical and conceptual commitments.[13] The claim that philosophical theories are accounts of human practices might suggest that they are largely *descriptive*, that philosophy is really a branch of sociology, that metaphysics or philosophy of science is really something like a sociology of science, that epistemology is really sociology of knowledge, and so on.

Philosophical accounts are not mere descriptions, however. They are contestable conceptions or characterizations of practices and the concepts central to them. They provide *analyses*, not reports.[14] They are pictures of

[13] Problems in a philosophical theory do not provide a reason for rejecting the practice it is designed to illuminate. By the same token, the moral undesirability of a practice is not a reason for rejecting the best philosophical account of it.

[14] A report presupposes a well-defined or understood object. This is not true of all philosophical accounts, especially metaphysical ones, which are themselves accounts of the objects of understanding. A philosophical account, moreover, illuminates a practice from a point of view, in the light of certain interests or goals. Furthermore, arguments on behalf of one kind of philosophical account, say, a metaphysical theory, may point out how well that account fits with philosophical accounts of other practices, say, with more settled accounts of our linguistic and epistemic practices. Many of the considerations that support a philosophical account have little to do with the accuracy of the account, which would not be the case were philosophical theories primarily reports.

our practices, windows through which we view the practices of making and defending moral judgments, carrying on scientific inquiry, making and sustaining claims to knowledge, and so on.

Not all philosophical theories seek to explain or provide an understanding of the theoretical and conceptual commitments of human practices. Some are *normative*. Instead of illuminating the conceptual or theoretical commitments of our practices, normative theories set out the conditions under which certain practices and institutions could be *justified* or defended. Though analytic and normative theories differ in their purposes, they are not always unconnected. As the following example illustrates, certain analytic theories have normative dimensions.

A philosophy of language provides an account of the conceptual and theoretical commitments of our linguistic practices, the central aspect of which is the ascription of meaning. As part of the practice of ascribing meaning to words and sentences, we intend that the meaning of the word or sentence serve to *constrain* the uses to which the word or sentence can be put. Linguistic constraint is a normative concept; thus, analysis of meaning will be partially normative, setting out the conditions of *justifiable* use of words or sentences. Accordingly, an account of meaning that focused entirely on the history of the use of a term would fail because it could not explain the sense in which the meaning was intended, not merely to describe customary practice, but to constrain future use.[15]

So we can distinguish between legal and political practices on the one hand and philosophical theories of those practices on the other. Similarly, we can distinguish between analytic and normative theories of those practices. The former illuminate the practice, especially its theoretical and conceptual presuppositions and commitments, by providing analyses of the concepts implicated or presupposed by them. The latter set out justification conditions, that is, criteria that must be satisfied if a political practice or

[15] For a further discussion of the normative aspects of meaning, see *infra*, Pt. II.A.2, discussing Kripkenstein's and Wright's rejection of realist semantics. There are normative dimensions to jurisprudential theories as well. In this regard, consider Ronald Dworkin's account of adjudication. His view is that in interpreting legal texts judges are committed to seeing the law in its best light; that means that they are committed to seeing it as normatively defensible in a certain way. Thus, his view is that there is a normative or aspirational dimension of adjudication. See Dworkin, *supra*, n. 3, at pp. vii–viii ('A general theory of law must be normative as well as conceptual . . . It must have a theory . . . of adjudication . . . [that views] normative questions of law from the standpoint[ ] of . . . a judge'). Sometimes his critics charge Dworkin with confusing normative with descriptive jurisprudence, but they misunderstand his project. Like positivism, Dworkin's is not a normative jurisprudence; it is an *analytic* jurisprudence that claims that part of the practice being illuminated by the theory is normative. Judges share a commitment to seeing the law as prima facie defensible, as justifiably enforceable by the use of coercive means. The important point for our purposes is that the aspirational component is an element of the practice, not a statement of the conditions under which adjudication could be justified.

institution is to be defensible, worthy of our allegiance, or otherwise morally acceptable.[16]

Where does the term 'liberalism' fit into these categories? Liberalism can refer both to a set of institutions and political and legal practices *and* to a *normative* philosophical theory of the conditions that must be satisfied in order that certain aspects of our practices, for example, adjudication or coercion, can be justified.

To which of these categories does jurisprudence apply? It is plainly not a political or legal practice or institution. For the most part, jurisprudence is an *analytic* theory about certain legal practices. A distinction exists as well between particular and general analytic jurisprudence. Particular jurisprudence provides an account of the legal practice of a particular community; general jurisprudence provides an account of what, if anything, is true of the concept of law, of legal practice everywhere. Typically, analytic jurisprudence has an important normative component: It aims to set out the conditions that must be satisfied in order for something to count as law. It

[16] The distinction between analytic and normative theories may seem artificial in another way as well. We say that analytic theories offer accounts of our practices, whereas normative theories set out justification conditions. But, of course, that just means that there is a practice of justification—indeed, there are many practices of justification. If philosophical theories provide accounts of our practices, we would expect there to be accounts of our justificatory practices. Different theories will apply to different justificatory practices. A theory about the nature of political justification may not coincide with a theory about the nature of justification in legal argument.

Is it part of the practice of political justification that the norms that set forth the conditions under which authority is to be justified must themselves transcend the practices of the community, or might they be embedded in some ways within the practices of the community? Some have thought that it is part of our practice of political justification that the norms of justification be universal and practice transcendent. Recently, however, liberal political theory has focused on the possibility of understanding our practices of justification differently; that, for example, justification begins with certain norms and practices that at a certain level of abstraction can be seen to be embedded in a particular community; that, moreover, justification is particular to communities of a particular type and need not be universal. According to John Rawls, '[Political liberalism] does not criticize . . . any particular theory of the truth of moral judgments . . . [I]t simply supposes that judgments . . . are made from the point of view of some comprehensive moral doctrine . . . Which moral judgments are true, all things considered, is not a matter for political liberalism, as it approaches all questions from within its own limited point of view.' John Rawls, *Political Liberalism* (New York: Columbia University Press, 1993), pp. xix–xx. As one important consequence, this trend in political philosophy undermines the very standard, oft-heard objection that because we are always situated in a particular time and place, we cannot have a view of the matter that transcends our 'positionality'. Because we cannot transcend our position, the objection continues, we connot provide justifications that are objective. All our justifications merely reflect our positions (our contingency) and do so while hiding behind a mask of objectivity. In the first place, it may be no part of our practice of justification that justification proceed from an Archimedean point. Secondly, there are a variety of senses of objectivity—as we explore below—that do not presuppose a position outside human practices altogether. Justification can rely on norms that are constitutive of practices, not external to them. And the mere fact that such practices or norms have a causal history or explanation does not entail that they lack justificatory force. To assume otherwise is to assume, in effect, that justification requires a view from nowhere.

is normative with regard to the conditions for applying the concept; it is not normative in the sense of setting out the conditions that must be satisfied in order that legal practice be justified.[17]

When critics claim that the problem with liberalism is that it is committed (among other things) to determinacy and objectivity, what precisely is the target? Is indeterminacy an objection to *liberal judicial practice*, in the sense that if such institutions are indeterminate that would in principle render them less (or in-) defensible? Or is it instead a problem in 'liberalism' as an 'analytic' account of our practices, in the sense that the best available 'liberal' account of our practices coheres only because it treats adjudication as determinate? In establishing that law is indeterminate, then, have we lost hope of finding a way to see our practices as liberal? Or is the determinacy of adjudication part of normative liberalism in the sense that the only kind of adjudicatory process that could be defended on liberal grounds is one in which outcomes were determinate? In that case, establishing law's indeterminacy would show that our adjudicatory processes did not measure up to liberal ideals, and could not be defended on those grounds.

Similar remarks are in order regarding objectivity. Is the problem that important legal practices, like adjudication, are not objective in the relevant sense, and so less (or in-) defensible in principle? Or is it that the best available 'liberal' jurisprudence of that practice is coherent just because it sees adjudication as objective when in fact it is not? The failure of objectivity, then, would leave us without a way of understanding our practices as liberal. Or is the problem that whereas liberalism as a normative political theory is committed to objectivity, our adjudicatory practices do not exemplify objectivity of the relevant sort, and so cannot be defended on liberal grounds?

As we shall understand them, the criticisms of liberalism as indeterminate and not objective have the same basic structure. The argument proceeds as follows:

(1) liberal political theory (liberalism as a normative theory) is committed to determinacy (objectivity);

(2) legal practice (adjudication) is indeterminate (not objective);

(3) therefore, existing liberal practices cannot be defended on (because they are inconsistent with) liberal principles.

[17] One can run these two ideas together, of course, by advancing a normative jurisprudence according to which the term law could only be correctly applied to a practice if the practice itself were normatively defensible. Such an account could not be shown to be false by pointing out that we use the term 'law' to refer to many practices that do not satisfy this condition, because as a normative account it makes no descriptive claim. It merely recommends or prescribes. Instead, one would have to argue against the attractiveness of the recommended use, and one obvious thing to say is that such a proposal makes it difficult, if not impossible, to criticize legal regimes as unjust. Rather than treating them as unjust, we are left treating them as not being law at all; and it is hard to see that anything would be gained by such a strategy.

In making this argument, the critic often does not argue for premiss (1). Typically, citations to various philosophers, such as Rawls, are treated as if they suffice to establish its truth.[18] Premiss (2) is supported in a variety of ways, sometimes by appeal to contestable interpretations of our existing practice, often, however, by appeal to philosophical theories, typically about the nature of reasons generally, or legal reasons in particular.[19] Proposition (3) is then said to follow from the premisses, thus assuring the argument's validity. Given its validity, the truth of the premisses assure its soundness.

We do not deny the *validity* of the argument with respect to its claims about either determinacy or objectivity; we do deny its *soundness* in both cases, however. Consequently, this essay falls into two distinct parts. In the first part we evaluate the above argument with respect to its claims about indeterminacy. In that section our first goal is to clarify the so-called 'indeterminacy thesis'. Then we argue that law can be and often is indeterminate in the way critics take it to be. Though we accept the truth of the second premiss with regard to determinacy, we argue that many of the claims made on behalf of that premiss are based on philosophical confusions, and are often (on other grounds) unpersuasive. In contrast to liberalism's critics, however, we reject the first premiss. Instead, we argue that liberalism as a normative political theory is not committed to determinacy, though it has several other commitments with which determinacy might be easily confused.

In the second part of the essay we reject the argument with respect to its claims about objectivity. With respect to objectivity, we accept the first premiss, but reject the second. In our view, legal practice is objective in a suitable sense, and thus the argument against liberalism fails.

Our thought is that, as a first approximation, those who worry about law's objectivity are concerned about whether the decisions judges reach are *objectively* correct or whether instead they are correct just because the judge so regards them. Let us characterize this as a worry about the metaphysical objectivity of 'legal facts'. Any time a judge renders a decision, she asserts the existence of what we are calling a legal fact; for example, 'Coleman's failure to inspect constitutes negligence', or 'Leiter's failure to deliver constitutes a breach of contract'. The question about metaphysical objectivity, then, is the question about the *status* of these facts, that is, about whether they hold independently of what a particular judge happens to

[18] See Singer, *supra*, n. 1, at 25 n. 74 (citing Rawls's statement that the principles of justice are objective).

[19] Ibid., at 6 (stating that 'legal reasoning is indeterminate and contradictory [and] cannot resolve legal questions in an "objective" manner'); see also James Boyle, 'The Politics of Reason: Critical Legal Theory and Local Social Thought', 133 *U. Pa. L. Rev.* 685, 695 n. 29 (1985) (agreeing with Legal Realists that 'dogma of objectivity . . . in legal reasoning serves to obscure the fact that judicial opinions arise from a matrix of social and political forces'); Gary Peller, 'The Metaphysics of American Law', 73 *Cal. L. Rev.* 1151, 1152 (1985) (noting that 'legal analysis cannot be neutral and determinate').

think, or perhaps independently of what all lawyers and judges would think.

We distinguish among three conceptions of metaphysical objectivity: minimal, strong, and modest. Minimal and strong objectivity are, under different names, more or less familiar to philosophers of law; modest objectivity is not. The remainder of this essay is devoted to explaining and defending the plausibility of modest objectivity as the kind of metaphysical objectivity presupposed by our legal practice of adjudication.

Part I: Determinacy

A. VARIETIES OF LEGAL INDETERMINACY

1. Reasons and Causes

We begin by drawing a distinction between *(in) determinacy of reasons* and *(in) determinacy of causes*.[20] Often we want to know whether a particular legal outcome or result is *justified*. Justification is provided by reasons. The thesis that law suffers from indeterminacy of reasons is a claim about the relationship between the set of available legal reasons and the justification of legal outcomes. On other occasions, we seek an *explanation* of the outcome a judge (or panel of judges) has reached in a particular case. On the theory that explanations are primarily causal, an explanation of an outcome is provided by identifying its causes. The thesis that law suffers from indeterminacy of causes is a claim about the inadequacy of the set of legal reasons as causes of judicial opinions. In short, indeterminacy theses make claims about the relationship between legal reasons and the outcomes of cases: the indeterminacy of reasons thesis claims that the relationship of the former to the latter is *justificatorily* inadequate; the indeterminacy of causes thesis claims that the relationship of the former to the latter is *explanatorily* inadequate.

Our immediate concern is with indeterminacy of reasons. Given that, our next task is to distinguish between two forms of indeterminacy. In one sense, a rule is indeterminate if there is more than one way of fulfilling its demands. In the other, to say that a rule is indeterminate is to make a claim about the lack of uniqueness with respect to what the rule is. Indeterminacy of the first type is not only unavoidable; it is both necessary and desirable. The duty to be charitable, for example, imposes constraints on behaviour even if no way of understanding it eliminates entirely one's latitude in discharging the duty it imposes. What is not legitimate is failing to discharge

[20] This distinction is drawn and explored in Brian Leiter, 'Legal Realism and Varieties of Legal Indeterminacy' (27 Sept. 1993) (unpublished MS, on file with authors).

the duty in some plausible way. An agent who acts according to such principles is not subject to criticism simply because she took one rather than another justified course of conduct. One might even argue that the absence of latitude in satisfying the demands of moral rules would be a failing in a moral theory: a failing, because it would be based on an inappropriate conception of the person, of human cognitive and psychological capacities, and of the nature of practical reason. Because indeterminacy of this sort is both unavoidable and desirable in any system of norms, it cannot be the kind of indeterminacy that troubles liberalism's critics. Therefore, we take it that the kind of indeterminacy that is thought to create a problem for liberalism is indeterminacy about what the rule is—not about how the rule can be satisfied.

Indeterminacy of reasons is a thesis about the inadequacy of legal reasons as (full) justifications of the outcomes they are offered to support. The set of legal reasons is a function of two elements: (i) the set of valid or binding legal sources; and (ii) the set of *interpretive* operations that can be legitimately performed on those sources (to generate rules and principles of law) and the set of *rational* operations that can be performed on law and facts (to generate outcomes). Valid sources will invariably include *at least* statutes and precedents; typical (interpretive and rational) operations will include canons of interpretation (for example, for constructing the 'rule of a prior decision') as well as forms of legal reasoning, including deduction and analogy.

Every theory of law (or jurisprudence) provides an account of the conditions of membership in the class of legal reasons. The indeterminacy thesis is the claim that the set of legal reasons, regardless of its actual content, will be indeterminate with respect to its justificatory relationship to the outcomes judges reach. At its core, the indeterminacy thesis is a claim about the ability of reasons—legal reasons in particular, but perhaps also reasons in general—to justify fully the outcomes in favour of which they are adduced. And this is one way in which the indeterminacy argument might be said to draw, at least in part, on traditional philosophical theories about meaning and metaphysics—in this case, the meaning and essence of reasons. Before we explore the extent to which such efforts are warranted, we need to provide a more precise formulation of the indeterminacy thesis. In what sense is the class of legal reasons invariably indeterminate? What form of justificatory inadequacy is marked by indeterminacy?

One formulation of the indeterminacy of reasons thesis is the claim that:

(1) The set of legal reasons is never adequate to warrant any result.

Understood in this way, law is indeterminate only if no legal outcome can be justified in the light of the class of available legal reasons. If that is so, then the possibility of legitimate legal authority is thrown into doubt, since, at the very least, authority presupposes that some of the outcomes that are enforced by law are warranted by law. This formulation is too strong, however. Even indeterminists who believe that proposition (1) is true are not likely to believe that it must be true in order for indeterminacy to pose a serious obstacle to the possibility of legitimate governance by law.

The claim can be weakened so that:

(2) The set of legal reasons is sufficient to warrant any result.

Instead of claiming that no outcomes are warranted, this version of the thesis holds that, theoretically at least, all outcomes are warranted by the set of legal reasons. If all outcomes can be warranted by the set of available legal reasons, then a judge would be justified in reaching any decision whatsoever. That too would pose a problem for legal authority, since part of our ordinary understanding of authority is that judges are not generally free to pick any possible outcome and enforce it through the coercive power of the state. Again, even indeterminists who believe that proposition (2) is true are not likely to believe that it must be true in order for indeterminacy to pose a threat to the possibility of legitimate governance by law.

Instead of claiming either that all outcomes are justified by legal sources or that none are, the indeterminist could be understood as claiming that:

(3) The set of legal reasons never uniquely warrants (or justifies) one and only one result in a particular case.

This indeterminist does not claim that the available legal resources justify all outcomes or no outcomes, nor does she deny that the set of legal reasons constrains or limits available outcomes. Instead, she claims that the set of legal reasons is inadequate to warrant unique outcomes. If proposition (3) poses a problem for the possibility of legitimate governance by law, it can only be because legitimacy requires that outcomes be uniquely warranted by the set of legal reasons. The indeterminist who accepts (3) clearly believes that legal liberalism adheres to what we might call 'the unique outcome' requirement. Whether analytic jurisprudence is committed to any such claim is not clear.[21] For a very long time the leading analytic jurisprudent, Ronald Dworkin, appears to have defended the claim that adjudication was about finding the right answer to legal disputes,[22] although he no longer claims that there are right answers to all cases.[23]

[21] See e.g. Steven J. Burton, *Judging in Good Faith* (Cambridge: Cambridge University Press, 1992).

[22] See Dworkin, *supra*, n. 3, at 81–130; id., 'No Right Answer?', 53 *NYU L. Rev.* 1 (1978).

[23] One reason for the change is the following. In his earlier work, including *Taking Rights Seriously*, Dworkin had a 'right-based' political theory, according to which the point of adjudication was primarily to determine which of the litigants had the pre-existing right. See Dworkin, *supra*, n. 3, at 184–205. If there was a pre-existing right in each case, then there was a right answer in each case: namely, that which answered the question: 'which litigant has the right?' In his more recent work, especially *Law's Empire*, adjudication is a practice within a

Whereas the typical indeterminist may well believe that either proposition (1) or (2) is true, she does not have to defend either in order to make indeterminacy a potentially interesting thesis; proposition (3) may be interesting enough. On the other hand, even (3) may be stronger than necessary. Instead of claiming that the set of legal reasons never warrants a unique outcome, the indeterminist might claim that even if legal reasons sometimes warrant unique outcomes, they do not do so in important or controversial cases—precisely the sorts of cases that make it to the stage of appellate review.[24] In this view, indeterminacy of reasons asserts:

(4) The set of legal reasons never uniquely warrants (or justifies) one and only one outcome in important or hard cases.

Interestingly, if Dworkin is right about positivism, proposition (4) represents the classic positivist account of judicial discretion. In that account there is a distinction between 'easy' cases in which there are unique, determinate outcomes, and 'hard' cases in which judges must exercise discretion precisely because the set of legal reasons is inadequate to determine or warrant one unique outcome.

If we accept proposition (4) as a plausible formulation of the indeterminacy of reasons thesis, we can draw some interesting connections between the indeterminists, the positivists, and Dworkin. In the first place, both the indeterminists and Dworkin accept the claim that, if true, proposition (4) poses a serious problem for legal authority. They differ in that the indeterminists believe that proposition (4) is in fact true, while Dworkin believes it is almost always false. In the second place, both the indeterminists and the positivists believe that proposition (4) is true. They differ in that the indeterminists believe that the truth of (4) spells trouble for a liberal conception of legal authority, whereas the positivists do not believe that the truth of (4) is incompatible with liberal legal authority (neither, arguably, does the Legal Realist).

differently conceived political morality—one that emphasizes the bonds of liberal community. See Ronald Dworkin, *Law's Empire* (London: Fontana, 1986), 95–6. In such an account there is no need that adjudication settle on uniquely correct answers to all disputes, and thus Dworkin relaxes the constraint. That does not mean that he no longer believes that there are correct answers almost all the time. His continued use of the Hercules construct as a way of fixing right answers to legal disputes indicates that he is still committed to much more in the way of determinacy than most positivists. But, as we suggest below, the importance of judges aspiring to act like Hercules changes in the most recent work; there is a different political theory that motivates Hercules, and it is not one based on right answers. Consequently, the determinacy claim is no longer at the heart of Dworkin's jurisprudence. (The reader should note that we are offering an interpretation of the development of Dworkin's thinking; there are few, if any, explicit acknowledgements in Dworkin indicating that this is the way he sees his work developing.)

[24] Indeterminists should not dispute the existence of easy cases, but point out that the legitimacy of adjudication turns only on the cases that are *really* adjudicated—namely, the hard cases, in which indeterminacy seems indisputably to be a real threat.

We now have a working formulation of the indeterminacy thesis. Next, we need to distinguish among the various arguments for the existence of indeterminacy. In doing so, we will put ourselves in a position to assess the truth of the claim that law is indeterminate. If the law is indeterminate, then the issue will be whether, and to what extent, indeterminacy poses a problem for the possibility of legitimate governance by law. We begin with a summary of the possible sources of legal indeterminacy, keeping in mind that different kinds or sources of indeterminacy may pose different challenges to the possibility of legitimate governance by law.

2. Sources of Indeterminacy

We begin by distinguishing between two levels of indeterminacy: *specific* and *general*.[25] Specific indeterminacy of reasons makes a claim about law. It makes no claim about any other domains of discourse. In contrast, general indeterminacy of reasons is a thesis about all domains of reason-giving discourse. We might distinguish, then, between those arguments for law's indeterminacy that follow from more general concerns about language or reason-giving discourse and those that derive from features peculiar to legal discourse. Let us begin with the former.

A range of arguments for legal indeterminacy draw support from considerations that bear on language generally. All natural languages contain *vague predicates* and *family-resemblance concepts*, and legal discourse is no exception. It may be impossible to determine whether, in some cases, a person without much hair is bald, a scribbling art, compensation just, or process due.

In law, these concerns have been addressed in H. L. A. Hart's discussion of the distinction between the 'core' and 'penumbra' of general terms.[26] Judges follow law when the rules apply to core instances of general terms, but must exercise discretion when the question is whether the rule applies to a case involving the penumbra of a general term. When faced with a case involving the penumbra of legal meaning, a judge has no option but to help fix the meaning through the exercise of a discretionary authority. In his earlier essays, Dworkin took issue with this argument for judicial discretion.[27] By allowing that moral principles as well as social policies are binding legal sources in terms of which other legal directives are to be understood, Dworkin argued that the extent to which judges must exercise a discretionary authority would be significantly reduced.[28] Understood in this way, the

[25] See Leiter, *supra*, n. 20, at 6–7.

[26] See H. L. A. Hart, 'Positivism and the Separation of Law and Morals', 71 *Harv. L. Rev.* 593, 607–15 (1958).

[27] See Ronald Dworkin, 'Judicial Discretion', 60 *J. Phil.* 624 *passim* (1963) (hereinafter Dworkin, 'Judicial Discretion'); id., 'The Model of Rules', 35 *U. Chi. L. Rev.* 14, 3240 (1967) (hereinafter Dworkin, 'Model of Rules').

[28] For an application of this Dworkinian line of reasoning to various indeterminacy arguments, see Ken Kress, 'Legal Indeterminacy', 77 *Cal. L. Rev.* 283, 295 (1989).

penumbra argument for judicial discretion appears to depend in part on the poverty of legal sources and is thought to be mitigated by a richer domain of legally binding standards.

This line of argument, however, cannot resolve a worry about vague predicates; the moral principles that are supposed to enrich the domain of legal sources will, themselves, contain vague predicates—namely, moral ones (for example, 'just', 'fair', 'equal'). Some writers—notably Dworkin and Michael Moore—think this does not in principle create a problem for legal determinacy; assessing their views, however, would also require a meaning the plausibility of their views about the determinacy of moral reasoning and the truth of moral realism. Instead, we propose to leave these tasks for another occasion.[29] We want to concentrate on a different and more far-reaching concern about language—the nature of meaning in general.

There are a variety of considerations normally associated with Wittgenstein's private language argument[30] that we can capture under the rubric of *semantic scepticism*. The semantic sceptic denies that there are objective facts of a suitable sort that constitute or determine a word's or a sentence's meaning. Because there is no fact that is the meaning of a sentence, the meaning of a sentence, directive, command, or request invariably will be indeterminate. In other words, what a sentence means cannot be adduced by pointing to some fact that is its meaning. Thus, the meaning of a sentence is indeterminate because there are no objective facts that would render it determinate. If this is true of language generally, then it is true of law *a fortiori*.

Semantic scepticism supports a form of *general* indeterminacy of reasons, which applies to law as well as to any other semantic domain. We want to begin, however, by examining forms of indeterminacy that are *specific* to law. We will be concerned with two. First, one worry about the determinacy of law is that at some appropriate level of abstraction, legal sources are *inconsistent* or fundamentally *contradictory* (or that the legitimate operations performed on them lead to inconsistent rules or principles). If legal sources are contradictory in the formal sense, then any outcome can be derived from them; any proposition, true or false, can be derived from a contradiction.[31] If all possible legal outcomes follow from inconsistent

[29] For some doubts, see Brian Leiter, 'Introduction: The Varieties of Objectivity,' in *Objectivity in Law and Morals*, ed. Brian Leiter (New York: Cambridge University Press, forthcoming).

[30] See Ludwig Wittgenstein, *Philosophical Investigations* G. E. M. Anscombe, trans. (Oxford: Basil Blackwell, 1953) § 203.

[31] Sentences of the form 'if p then q' are conditionals, written in logic as '$p \rightarrow q$'. Such sentences are materially equivalent to sentences of the form 'not p or q' written in logic as '$\bar{p} \vee q$'. These two sentences have the same truth value which means that whenever one is true (or false), so too is the other. '$\bar{p} \vee q$' is true whenever either '$\bar{p}$' is true or 'q' is true. '$\bar{p}$' is true whenever 'p' is false. Therefore '$\bar{p} \vee q$' is true whenever 'p' is false. A contradiction always has the truth value 'false'. So whenever 'p' is a contradiction, 'p' is false: '$\bar{p} \vee q$' is true. Whenever '$\bar{p} \vee q$' is true, so too is '$p \rightarrow q$'. Thus, the claim is that anything follows from a contradiction. Whatever 'q' is, '$p \rightarrow q$' is true, provided 'p' is a contradiction.

premisses, then the law is indeterminate in the senses expressed by propositions (4), (3), and (2) above.

A second source of the indeterminacy thesis specific to law is the claim that the set of legal reasons is either too impoverished or too rich. This has the air of paradox about it and so needs clarification. There is a natural way of thinking about legal sources and the operations that can be performed on them that suggests both sources of indeterminacy. On the one hand, it is natural to suppose that a legal system that had few sources, few canons of interpretation, and few restrictive forms of reasoning from those sources would find itself with insufficient resources to resolve legal disputes authoritatively. Judges would often find themselves unavoidably having to resort to non-legal sources and forms of argument in order to resolve disputes. This way of thinking suggests that the richer the stock of legal sources and operations on them, the less likely judges will be to appeal to extra-legal norms to resolve disputes before them. The natural inference is that the degree of indeterminacy in a legal regime is a function of the richness of the set of legal reasons. The richer the set, the more complete it is; the more complete, the fewer the 'gaps'; the fewer the gaps, the less indeterminate.

This argument suggests that indeterminacy is a by-product of a poverty of available or authoritative sources and operations on them. It is natural to understand this argument as grounded in the idea that an impoverished set of authoritative standards and interpretive resources will yield numerous 'gaps'. Law is necessarily indeterminate simply because no matter how rich the set of authoritative standards and operations are, there will always be cases that fall under no binding standard; there will always be gaps. To be sure, the extent of the problem of indeterminacy that results from gaps will be diminished by ever enriching the set of authoritative standards and sources; still, it cannot be eliminated altogether. There will always be gaps in the law.

Enriching the class of legal reasons will reduce indeterminacy owing to gaps, but it creates its own set of problems and sources of indeterminacy. As a legal system enriches the set of available binding legal sources, judges will always have more than one norm or rule that is arguably applicable or controlling. If that is so, then there may be no one rule or norm that uniquely controls a case. There may, then, be too many standards available for adjudicating a case to claim that there is only one uniquely warranted outcome.

Arguments for indeterminacy, then, can be grounded on considerations of law's internal and unavoidable inconsistency, the relative poverty or richness of legal reasons, and general semantic scepticism. In the next few sections we explore these sources of indeterminacy. In doing so, we will try to assess the general merits of the arguments in favor of indeterminacy. Whereas we believe that the arguments for indeterminacy, as usually presented, are often unconvincing and typically overstate its scope, we do not deny that there are important ways in which the set of legal reasons will be indeterminate. Nor do we intend to deny that certain forms of indeterminacy can pose a problem for the possibility of legitimate governance by law. Nevertheless, the problems posed by indeterminacy are in no way fatal to the possibility of legitimate authority—or so we argue. In considering the sources of indeterminacy, we begin by considering one type of general indeterminacy of reasons, what we have been calling semantic scepticism.

3. Semantic Scepticism

The core of semantic scepticism is the claim that there are no facts that constitute or determine a sentence's meaning, so that language is indeterminate at the most basic level: there are no *objective* facts that make it the case that language means one thing rather than another. Thus, there is no point to claiming that a legal rule can be satisfied by some actions but not others since the meaning of the rule is always 'up for grabs'.

This line of argument is motivated largely by Saul Kripke's sceptical reading of Wittgenstein's private language argument.[32] Let us briefly set out Kripke's interpretation of Wittgenstein's argument.[33] In philosophy, it is customary to draw a distinction between discourses that are *cognitivist* (or fact-stating) and those that are *non-cognitivist.* A cognitivist discourse is one in which the sentences state facts, and in which the meaning of those sentences is given by the conditions in the world under which the sentences would be true (that is, the meaning is given by the truth-conditions).[34] We typically identify cognitivist discourses by their *syntactic* form; thus, for example, sentences which are *assertoric* or *declarative* we generally view as cognitive. So the sentence, 'Guido is in the room', asserts a particular fact—that Guido is in the room—and the meaning of the sentence is given by the circumstances under which it would be true (that is, Guido is, in fact, in the room).

It has been an important lesson of twentieth-century philosophy that *syntactic* form can be misleading as to *semantics* (or meaning). *Non-cognitivism* is the view that a particular discourse is not primarily descriptive or fact-stating, and thus that the meaning of its sentences is not given by truth-conditions (that is, by the obtaining of the facts asserted in the

[32] See Saul A. Kripke, *Wittgenstein on Rules and Private Language* (Oxford: Basil Blackwell, 1982), 55–113. Kripke's reading was prefigured by others, notably, Robert J. Fogelin, *Wittgenstein* (London: Routledge & Kegun Paul, 1976) and Crispin Wright, *Wittgenstein on the Foundations of Mathematics* (Cambridge, Mass.: Harvard University Press, 1980).

[33] We follow in broad outline the illuminating account in Alexander Miller, 'Kripke's Wittgenstein' (2 Sept. 1990) (unpublished MS, on file with authors), 2–13.

[34] See Donald Davidson, 'Truth and Meaning', in *Inquiries into Truth and Interpretation* (Oxford: Blackwell, 1984), 17, 17–36; Alfred Tarski, 'The Semantic Conception of Truth', 4 *Phil. and Phenomenological Res.* 341, 341–76 (1944).

sentences). Thus, non-cognitivists about ethics, from A. J. Ayer to Allan Gibbard,[35] hold that, notwithstanding the surface syntax of moral discourse ('Guido is a just man'[36]), such discourse states no facts, but instead gives *expression* to certain attitudes: its meaning, then, comes not from its truth-conditions (there are none), but rather from its expressive role.

Kripke's Wittgenstein—or Kripkenstein—can be read as arguing that sentences that ascribe meaning are, despite their syntactic appearance, also *non-cognitive*: they state no facts, in the sense that there are no facts by virtue of which the sentence would be made true. When we say, 'this rule *means X*', there are no facts we can identify that would constitute the rule's *meaning X*. While Hume had argued that sentences about morality or causation are essentially non-cognitive—such sentences state no facts in the sense that there are no facts that constitute something *causing* something else—Kripkenstein advances the startling position that sentences about meaning itself are non-cognitive: there are no facts constituting or determining an expression *meaning* one thing rather than another.

In order to establish this thesis, Kripkenstein allows that there might be two domains in which we might search for the relevant objective facts: the speaker's previous verbal and non-verbal behaviour and the speaker's mental states. Kripkenstein then allows that we have full information about these domains. His argument is designed to show that there can be no facts that constitute meaning, since even with full access to these domains we can find no property or fact that constitutes the meaning of the sentence, that is, no fact which establishes that the sentence *means* one thing rather than another.

Kripke offers the following (now) famous example to illustrate the argument. Take the sentence, '57 + 65 = 5', and compare it with the sentence '57 + 65 = 122'. Suppose we wanted to know what the '+' expression *means*. The sceptical argument is that there is no fact about a person's past behaviour with respect to '+' that would fix its meaning such that one, but not the other, of the above uses is correct. To see this, suppose that I have performed simple arithmetic sums in the past only involving numbers below 57. Then that past behaviour is perfectly compatible with '+' meaning either 'the sum of the integers' (addition) or 'the sum of the integers except when adding numbers above 56 in which case always give the answer 5' (quaddition).

[35] See A. J. Ayer, *Language, Truth and Logic* (1936, repr. New York: Doner, 1952), 20–2, 107–8, 110–12 ; Allan Gibbard, *Wise Choices, Apt Feelings* (Cambridge, Mass.: Harvard University Press, 1990), 105–25.

[36] Compare this with the syntax of 'Guido is a large man', which we are inclined to understand in cognitivist terms: i.e. it states a fact (about Guido's size), and its meaning is equivalent to the conditions under which the statement is true (i.e. Guido is, in fact, large in size).

Note what the argument here is *not*. The argument is not that we do not know that 57 + 65 = 5 is wrong while 57 + 65 = 122 is correct. We do know that the former is incorrect and that the latter is correct. Rather, the argument is that we can identify no objective fact that justifies our correctness judgments: that is, no fact about our usage of the '+' sign such that it is compatible with only one of the two sums. If we are still able to make correctness judgments about meaning—and we are—it is *not* because there are objective facts that constitute meaning: such correctness must have some other source. This source is identified in what Kripke calls the 'sceptical solution'.

In short, the Kripkensteinian solution[37] is to accept the conclusion of the sceptical argument—there are no facts determinative or constitutive of meaning—but to suggest that we look for the criterion of correctness with respect to meaning elsewhere: not in some fact that makes it the case that X means Y, but rather in the circumstances and conditions under which our community will let us assert particular sentences. Meaning, then, is not a matter of truth-conditions, but rather of *assertibility-conditions* (that is, the conditions under which a community of language users permits assertion of a particular sentence). The sentence '57 + 65 = 122' is correct not because there is some fact that constitutes the meaning of the '+' sign, but rather because in our community we are only permitted to use the '+' sign consistent with addition rather than quaddition.

Critics of liberalism might read Kripkenstein as showing that the law must be radically indeterminate. For if meanings are indeterminate—in the sense that there are no objective facts about meaning, only what the community will and will not allow us to assert—then the law, which depends on meaning (for example, on rules meaning one thing rather than another), must also be indeterminate. If language itself is indeterminate, then legal language is indeterminate *a fortiori*.

There are three possible responses to this line of argument. The first is to deny the soundness of Kripke's construal of Wittgenstein, for Kripke's reading is, in fact, quite controversial.[38] This line of response, however, is really beside the point since it is not the accuracy of Kripke's reading of Wittgenstein

[37] Arguably, this solution is not Wittgenstein's because his original problem is not a sceptical one. See John McDowell, 'Wittgenstein on Following a Rule', 58 *Synthese* 325, 331 (1984) ('The right response to the paradox, Wittgenstein in effect tells us, is not to accept it but to correct the misunderstanding on which it depends: that is, to realize that there is a way of grasping a rule which *is not* an *interpretation*; Crispin Wright, 'Kripke's Account of The Argument Against Private Language', 81 *J. Phil.* 759, 778 (1984) ('Wittgenstein's conclusion, however, is emphatically *not* that there is no such thing as the fulfilment of a prior intention—the conclusion, in effect, of Kripke's skeptic').

[38] See McDowell, *supra*, n. 37, at 330–2 (emphasizing the distinction between Kripke's endorsement of the 'misunderstanding' and Wittgenstein's attempt to correct it).

that is at issue. Kripke can be all wrong about Wittgenstein, but right about meaning. Instead of attacking the accuracy of the attribution of the argument to Wittgenstein, a good response will have to attack the argument itself, or its alleged consequences. In this vein, a second response might be this: even if Kripkenstein is right in his sceptical argument, it does not follow that meaning is indeterminate in any problematic sense. All that follows is that there are no facts about meaning that are completely independent of how we are disposed to construe meanings. Meaning is not radically indeterminate; instead, meaning is public—fixed by public behaviour, beliefs, and understandings. There is no reason to assume that such conventions cannot fix the meaning of terms determinately. Indeed, such a response would be fully acceptable to Kripkenstein himself: the sceptical solution shows precisely how there can be 'communal' facts—but not *objective* facts—about meaning. Moreover, even if communal conventions are themselves indeterminate in important ways, it will not be for the kinds of reasons we are considering in this section, namely, that the meaning of sentences cannot be fixed by strongly objective facts about the speaker's previous verbal and non-verbal behaviour or her mental states.[39]

This response is closely related to a third response to the Kripkensteinian argument for legal indeterminacy. As we noted in the Introduction,[40] philosophical arguments are often offered primarily for the purposes of giving an explanation or a justification of our existing practices. Criticisms of philosophical theses are not normally intended to call into doubt the underlying practice; rather, they are offered to raise doubts about a certain picture or way of understanding the practice. This is an important point, but easy to miss.

Quine's indeterminacy of translation thesis, for example, is not designed to prevent us from buying or reading texts in translation, but to raise doubts about the picture of meaning that emphasizes intentionality.[41] The very same point can be made about Wittgenstein. Wittgenstein's goal—as opposed to Kripkenstein's—is to call into question a certain Platonic picture of the foundation of semantics that some might have thought explains or justifies important features of our linguistic practices. If the argument completely succeeds, it does not, for example, raise doubts about our ability to know the determinate meaning of a rule, but only about the source of that knowledge. If Kripkenstein's sceptical solution is right, then that source is

[39] Other questions have been raised about the coherence and viability of the sceptical solution. For example, some writers have worried that scepticism about meaning facts will also warrant scepticism about other facts, like facts about communal dispositions of use. For some discussion, see Warren Goldfarb, 'Kripke on Wittgenstein on Rules', 82 *J. Phil.* 471, 485 (1985); Wright, *supra*, n. 37, at 761–6. We do not pursue these difficult issues here.

[40] See *supra*, text accompanying nn. 6–12.

[41] See W. V. O. Quine, *Word and Object* (Cambridge, Mass.: MIT Press, 1960), 26–79. We are grateful to Yale law student Chris Kutz for suggesting this illustration of our general point.

not some semantic fact in Platonic heaven, but rather the conventions of use that comprise our linguistic community. The practice of rule-following —by judges or anyone else—remains intact, but our philosophical picture of its possibility changes.

4. Legal Contradiction

Whereas semantic scepticism argues that legal discourse is fundamentally indeterminate, the claim that law is indeterminate because it is fundamentally and internally inconsistent or contradictory depends on legal rules having determinate meanings, or meanings sufficiently determinate to allow that they might contradict one another. At some level, it is obviously an empirical question whether the available set of legal sources is inconsistent. Suppose, however, that the set of binding legal standards has a formal contradiction embedded within it. Since every outcome is implied by a formal contradiction, all outcomes are entailed by the set of legal reasons, and therefore all outcomes are warranted. No unique outcome is warranted, and the law is indeterminate.[42]

It would be impossible to deny that law is indeterminate under these conditions. It is also true, however, that legal standards are rarely formally contradictory. If they were, the problem with legal authority would not be that outcomes would be indeterminate; rather, it would be that the law would be formally contradictory. Indeterminacy is just one of the many undesirable consequences of law's inconsistency—and hardly the most troubling either. If the indeterminacy thesis is really the claim that law is formally contradictory, then apart from noting that law is rarely formally contradictory in the way the argument envisions, there is no denying that under those conditions the law would be indeterminate.[43]

The indeterminacy theorist may object that we are underestimating the extent to which legal regimes are contradictory. One idea, associated with CLS, is that liberalism suffers from a 'fundamental contradiction'.[44] The fundamental contradiction refers to the purportedly inescapable tension between our need for others and our fear of them, which has as one of its more significant political analogues our need for centralized powers to

[42] See *supra*, n. 31 and accompanying text.

[43] In the next section we discuss a different—and genuine—source of legal indeterminacy under the rubric 'conflicting norms'. see *infra*, Pt. I.A.5. This rubric is often described as involving 'contradictions'. We eschew that loose usage in order to distinguish that case from the cases discussed in the present section.

[44] See e.g. Roberto Unger, *Passion* (New York: Free Press, 1984), 20 ('We present to one another both an unlimited need and unlimited danger, and the very resources by which we attempt to satisfy the former aggravate the latter.'); Duncan Kennedy, 'The Structure of Blackstone's Commentaries', 28 *Buff. L. Rev.* 209, 213 (1979) ('The fundamental contradiction—that relations with others are both necessary to and incompatible with our freedom—is not only intense. It is also pervasive.').

protect our autonomy and our fear that these same powers will usurp that autonomy.[45]

As many writers have already observed, this is not, of course, a contradiction.[46] Indeed, it is a complex matter how one mediates between the need for coercive political powers to protect autonomy and the threat those same powers pose to autonomy; and it has been a central theme of liberal political theory to explore the boundaries of legitimate coercion. But complexity is not contradiction, and simply calling it otherwise does not make it so. To be sure, there have been some powerful philosophical challenges to this liberal programme—for example, from Robert Paul Wolff[47]—which have met equally powerful replies.[48] But in the absence of some demonstration of the impossibility of liberal political theory—that is, the impossibility of providing a theory of the terms of legitimate mediation between coercion and autonomy—there is little more that can be said at this juncture.[49]

[45] The analogy is this: we *need* others to constitute our individual identity (through friendship, love, etc.), yet at the same time there is the risk that they will destroy our individual autonomy (through rejecting us, betraying us, objectifying us, etc.).

[46] See e.g. Phillip E. Johnson, 'Do You Sincerely Want to Be Radical?', 36 *Stan. L. Rev.* 247, 257 (1984) ('[W]hat Kennedy calls a "contradiction" is not a logical contradiction at all but merely a reflection of the complexity of human relationship.').

[47] See Robert P. Wolff, *The Poverty of Liberalism* (Boston: Bercon Press, 1968), 3–50 (arguing that in so far as our enterprises are inherently social, the central problem of government cannot be, as liberalism presupposes, the regulation of each person's infringement on the sphere of other persons' actions, but rather the co-ordination of actions and the choice of collective goals).

[48] See e.g. Raz, *supra*, n. 5, at 18 ('While not denying that governments can and often do pose a threat to individual liberty, there is another conception which regards them also as a possible source of liberty. [Governments] can create conditions which enable their subjects to enjoy greater liberty than they otherwise would.').

[49] Talk of the 'fundamental contradiction' in the CLS literature has echoes of anti-Kantian and anti-liberal arguments in Hegel. Hegel's arguments, however, *can* be reconstructed in ways that demonstrate his opponents' involvement in genuine *logical* contradictions once one grants Hegel certain strong metaphysical theses. Thus, in the famous master-and-slave section of *The Phenomenology of the Spirit*, Hegel shows that the putatively Kantian ideal of an independent self-consciousness is contradictory because: (i) to be *independent* is not to be *dependent* on anything or anyone; but (ii) to be *self-conscious* is to depend upon the recognition of other persons. See G. W. F. Hegel, *The Phenomenology of the Spirit*, A. V. Miller, trans. (Oxford: Oxford University Press, 1977), 111–19. Granted (ii), it follows that an independent self-consciousness is a contradiction in terms. Similar Hegelian arguments can be constructed against the liberal ideal of freedom as involving a separate and protected sphere of autonomy, into which the community cannot intrude. Ibid., at 211–17. But since freedom, for Hegel, involves rational action, and *rational action is* only possible for the person whose actions are harmonious with the purposes of a *rational* community, it is a contradiction to think of freedom in terms of separation from, rather than immersion in, the (perhaps coercive) purposes of the community. These are hasty summaries of difficult arguments, but they should remind us that there is a genuine set of anti-liberal arguments based on contradictions in liberal theory. While the Crits, through their superficial engagement with Hegel and Lukács, have picked up similar-sounding themes, they have actually abandoned all the philosophical content of genuine anti-liberal positions.

5. Gaps and Conflicting Norms

Indeterminacy that is thought to arise because of either the relative poverty or richness of legal sources and interpretive operations represents two very different, indeed contrary, ideas. One is that law is indeterminate whenever the set of legal reasons is impoverished; the other is that law is indeterminate whenever the set of legal reasons is too rich. The poverty claim draws on the notion of 'gaps' in the law. The idea is simple enough. In a primitive or immature legal system, legally binding sources for resolving disputes will be in relatively short supply. Therefore, there are bound to be cases in which no controlling legal source exists. While enriching the set of sources will reduce the extent of indeterminacy, it can never eradicate indeterminacy altogether; it will always be possible to imagine a case in which no binding legal standard applies. Thus, because there will always be gaps in the law, there will always be some degree of indeterminacy.

Without denying the possibility that a legal system bereft of binding legal sources will be indeterminate in important ways, it is worth noting that the argument for indeterminacy from the existence of gaps can be more misleading than illuminating, for three separate reasons. In the first place, if there are gaps in the law, their existence is not likely to depend on features of the legal practice that are peculiarly liberal; gaps do not appear to discriminate between liberal and other legal regimes. Secondly, the existence of gaps is insufficient to establish the indeterminacy thesis, namely proposition (4) above.[50] All that the possibility of gaps in the law establishes is the possibility of novel cases not governed by existing standards and interpretive resources; it does not establish that important or controversial cases (for example, abortion, the death-penalty) lack determinate answers. Nor does the existence of gaps in the law establish, without the benefit of further argument, that indeterminacy is widespread or problematic.

Most importantly, the claim that there are genuine gaps in mature legal systems (which liberal regimes presumably are) is misleading at best. Given the set of standards and accepted tools for thinking about the relationship between binding standards and various fact patterns available in a reasonably mature legal system, it is unlikely that genuine gaps exist. For almost any dispute that we could imagine arising, there exists some legal norm or rule that bears on its resolution. It may well be that the relationship between the rules from which judges could legitimately draw and the issue before them is so weak that no decision could be said to be warranted by the rules, but that is very different from saying that no rule applies, that, in other words, there is a genuine gap in the law.

There is an important distinction between the claim that no binding

[50] See *supra*, Pt. I.A.1.

source—principle or rule—is available as a legitimate resource to enable a judge to think fruitfully about a dispute before her (a genuine gap), and the claim that in most legal systems there will always be norms that bear on every dispute, but that, in some cases, the relationship between the norms and any outcome a judge might reach is too weak to warrant or justify the decision. In such cases, we might say that no outcome is warranted by the set of legal standards, and that the outcomes judges reach in those cases are indeterminate in the requisite sense. Thus, even in mature legal systems law can be indeterminate without its indeterminacy arising from the existence of gaps in the law. Talk of gaps is, at best, simply a misleading way of referring to indeterminacy that arises when the justificatory relationship between existing legal reasons and outcomes is too weak to support the claim that any of the available outcomes a judge could reach is justified or adequately warranted by the class of legal reasons. While we are not comfortable with the term 'gaps-in-the-law', we do not deny that the kind of indeterminacy intended to be signalled by that phrase exists in all legal systems. Still, as we note above, that form of indeterminacy does not discriminate between liberal and non-liberal legal regimes, nor does its existence establish the truth of the indeterminacy thesis.

If we focus instead on legal regimes rich in authoritative legal resources, we can identify at least two possible sources of indeterminacy. The first we have considered above:[51] indeterminacy that arises because those reasons do not sufficiently support any outcome in particular, even though the set of legal sources provides resources with which a judge might reason fruitfully about cases. In contrast, we can focus on the case in which differing legal resources warrant conflicting outcomes. The idea is that in any legal regime richly endowed with argumentative resources, binding legal sources, while not strictly contradictory, will nevertheless support conflicting outcomes or decisions. Thus, instead of no legal reason sufficing to warrant an outcome, the problem more often will be that different legal reasons to which we are otherwise committed warrant conflicting outcomes or decisions.[52]

One obvious response to this line of argument maintains that even

[51] See *supra*, text following n. 31.

[52] Sometimes critics of liberalism who talk about the 'contradictions' in law can be understood in a way that makes such 'contradictions' equivalent to the source of indeterminacy we are now considering. In this sense, two or more valid legal sources each fully warrant conflicting outcomes. Thus, we might loosely say that the sources contradict each other. In some views, this type of contradiction is thought to arise because of the existence of the more fundamental, or global contradiction of liberalism, discussed *supra*, Pt. I.A.4. It is important to note, however, that this putative form of contradiction in virtue of conflicting norms or outcomes is no contradiction at all. It is just another way of saying that different norms that apply to us, that are part of the system of principles and policies which govern our actions, draw us in different directions. There is nothing contradictory in this fact alone, and it is hardly so much a misfortune of liberal political or legal theory as it is a consequence or feature of an enlightened sense of the complexity of human motivation.

conflicting norms can be ordered in their appropriateness or importance, or their relative weights accounted for in some way that resolves the apparent conflict. Against this response, note that it is possible that no common scale along which the conflicting values are to be compared, measured, evaluated, and in virtue of which be ordered, exists. Norms and the underlying values they express may be incommensurable in important ways.[53]

We need to distinguish between two conclusions a critic might draw from the incommensurability of values and the legal standards expressing them. The first is that legal outcomes will be indeterminate. The second is that legal argument cannot be rational. If the argument is sound, it that legal outcomes will be indeterminate—in the sense that no unique outcome is warranted. On the other hand, it does not follow that legal discourse cannot be largely rational. Rational disagreement about law (or morals) is perfectly compatible with the lack of unique determination, and so it does not follow from the fact that outcomes are indeterminate over some domain or range of cases that all choices are equally defensible or that no exercise of rational judgment can be defended.

In our account, indeterminacy is a failure of *warrant*, of the justificatory relationship between reasons provided by legal sources and the outcomes they are presumed to support. Therefore, to the extent that rational judgment can be defended in the face of disagreement caused by the fact that different norms support conflicting conclusions, it will not follow that indeterminacy understood as a failure of justification or warrant exists, or, to the extent that it exists, that its existence is problematic. Indeterminacy is a problem when it suggests that the exercise of rational judgment cannot be defended as against a different exercise of judgment. If the existence of conflicting norms entailed the impossibility of defending the choice of one over another, *that* would be a problem.

Having said that, we have no reason to deny that sometimes the conflicts among norms will be sufficiently great and the arguments on all sides strong enough to justify the claim that no unique outcome can be defended to the exclusion of others. In that case, we do not intend to deny that in mature legal systems conflicting norms can present genuine cases of indeterminacy. Nor do we intend to deny that sometimes even when only coherent and non-conflicting norms apply to a case, the justificatory relationship between

[53] See Raz, *supra*, n. 5, at 321–66 (defining the concept of incommensurability and explaining why values are incommensurable); see also Elizabeth Anderson, *Value in Ethics and Economics* (Cambridge, Mass.: Harvard University Press, 1993), 56 ('The more a given scale of value encompasses very different, categorically unranked ways of meeting it, the more scope there is for incommensurability.'); Charles Taylor, 'The Diversity of Goods', in 2 *Philosophy and the Human Sciences: Philosophical Papers* 230, 230–47 (Charles Taylor (ed.), Cambridge: Cambridge University Press, 1985) (arguing against those ethical and political theories which, informed by utilitarianism, ignore the fact that certain goals such as integrity, charity, and liberation merit a special kind of pursuit and are incommensurable with our other goals).

the norms and any outcome a judge might reach is too weak to claim that the norms warrant the outcome. Thus, we accept that indeterminacy is a feature of both mature and less well-stocked legal systems.

6. Summary

In sum: first, if employed to establish radical indeterminacy, arguments from general semantic considerations are unpersuasive. Secondly, the familiar argument for indeterminacy based on the fundamental liberal contradiction has the misfortune of being based on a false premiss, namely, that liberalism is deeply and fundamentally contradictory. Thirdly, there are nevertheless good reasons for thinking that law will be indeterminate in a range of important cases. Legal norms may not sufficiently warrant any outcome in a case. Different but binding norms within the legal system may each warrant conflicting outcomes.

B. INDETERMINACY AND AUTHORITY

1. Why Indeterminacy Matters

It would be foolish to deny the possibility of indeterminacy, though reasonable disagreement about the extent of it in particular legal systems is obviously possible. Given the likelihood, if not the inevitability, of indeterminacy, it is reasonable to wonder why someone might think that its existence poses a problem for the possibility of legitimate governance by law, or for the possibility of liberal authority. Why does indeterminacy matter?

There are a variety of plausible answers one could give to this question, only some of which we can take up here. One idea is that indeterminacy causes us to rethink the lawyer's conception of legal practice. In this view, the existence of determinate or right answers to legal disputes is part of the working framework of legal practice into which lawyers are socialized. This conception is part of a larger network of beliefs or presuppositions that form the conceptual framework of liberal, legal culture. The existence of non-trivial indeterminacy in the law requires a reconceptualization of liberal legal culture.[54]

A second reason for thinking indeterminacy important is demonstrated by the following example. Suppose we discover a pattern of unjust decisions

[54] See Mark Tushnet, 'The Indeterminacy Thesis' (1993) (unpublished MS, on file with authors). Tushnet argues that the lawyer's conception of adjudication presupposes determinacy. Thus, finding out that law is in fact indeterminate forces the lawyer to rethink the *descriptive* account of it. The problem with this argument is that it probably mis-describes the practising lawyer's working conception of legal practice. Only ordinary citizens, some jurisprudents, and first-year law students have a working conception of law as determinate.

in some domain of law. We may feel it appropriate to criticize the law or judges for these decisions. To meet our objection, judges might respond that they too view the outcomes as unjust, but are incapable of doing otherwise; their hands are tied in that the decisions they have reached are determined uniquely by the law which binds them. The existence of legal indeterminacy might be thought to be important in so far as appeal to it would help undermine arguments of this sort. For if the law is indeterminate, it is not possible for a judge to say that he was compelled by law to reach and enforce an unjust decision.[55]

This argument, however, has only a superficial plausibility, and legal indeterminacy has nothing to do with it. If a judge reaches a series of obviously unjust decisions by applying the law, then there is something morally reprehensible about the law; and what is reprehensible about it has nothing to do with its being either determinate or indeterminate. Moreover, liberal theory does not allow a judge to escape moral disapprobation or sanction by claiming that the law was determinate. If the law is determinate and does require morally unjust outcomes—that could not otherwise be defended (even slightly)[56]—then liberal theory does not excuse the judge from doing what he ought morally to do, all things considered, and that is to reach some other, more just, solution.

There are at least three other motivations for attributing to liberalism (as a normative political theory) a commitment to determinacy as a *political ideal*. Two of these have to do with 'rule-of-law' considerations. First, legal outcomes must be determinate if individuals are to be put on notice as to their duties under the law and be provided with an opportunity to conform their behaviour accordingly. Secondly, legal outcomes are enforceable by force, and if those outcomes are not warranted by the set of legal reasons, then the exercise of coercion seems unjustified. The third concern of liberalism that bears on law's determinacy has to do with the very possibility of democratic rule. Democracy presupposes that a duly elected legislature can form a judgment, enact it through legislation, and have its will followed by the courts. This presupposition of democratic rule is incompatible with indeterminacy, or at least with more radical forms of it. In the remainder of this part of the essay we take up each of these arguments.

2. Indeterminacy and Predictability

Sometimes we want to know not whether a particular outcome in a case is justified, that is, whether there are reasons sufficient to warrant it, but whether an outcome can be *explained or predicted*. Reasons can figure in explanations

[55] This line of argument was brought to our attention by Professor Jack Balkin.
[56] By appeal, for example, to the settled expectations of the litigants.

and predictions provided they are causes.[57] The set of legal reasons is causally indeterminate just in case it is inadequate to explain or predict the outcomes judges reach. If we put the two indeterminacy theses together, we get the claim that the set of legal reasons is insufficient to justify a unique outcome, or to predict or explain it.

Leiter has observed that the primary legacy of Legal Realism has been the indeterminacy of reasons hypothesis, whereas the realists themselves were at least as concerned with causal indeterminacy.[58] The Legal Realists were as interested in understanding why judges reach the decisions they do as they were in determining whether those decisions could be justified.[59] This emphasis on explanation and prediction is of a piece with well-known realist slogans, including 'the law is what judges say it is', or that 'the law is the best prediction of what judges will do in a particular case', and so on.

Not surprisingly, according to the realist, the ideal lawyer is the one who is in the best position to counsel his clients about what to expect from litigation. That lawyer will need to know what leads judges to decide as they do, not what legal reasons, if any, would justify their decisions. Of course, most judges are educated in a way that would suggest that binding legal reasons will play a prominent role in their decision-making, but the indeterminacy (of causes) thesis holds that even where binding legal reasons have a causal role, they are insufficient to predict or explain judicial decisions. The best explanation of judicial decisions may include the set of binding legal reasons, but cannot be limited to them. Instead, explanations will point to psychological and sociological facts about judges as part, if not all, of the causal story.[60]

Legal Realists claim that the class of legal reasons is causally indeterminate. On the other hand, like the positivists, the realists do not seem to doubt the possibility of legitimate governance by law.[61] Why? We cannot be

[57] See Donald Davidson, 'Actions, Reasons and Causes', in *Essays on Actions and Events* (Oxford: Clarendon Press, 1980), 3, 3–19 (defending the position that 'rationalization is a species of causal explanation').

[58] See Leiter, *supra*, n. 20.

[59] See e.g. Jerome Frank, *Courts on Trial: Myth and Reality in American Justice* (Princeton, NJ: Princeton University Press, 1949, repr. 1973), 20–1, 146–64, 262–89, 316–25.

[60] For the complete picture of realism in this regard, see Leiter, *supra*, n. 20, at 145–67, and id., 'Legal Realism', in *A Companion to the Philosophy of Law and Legal Theory*, ed. Dennis Patterson (Oxford: Blackwell, forthcoming 1996).

[61] This is clearest in Karl N. Llewellyn, *The Common Law Tradition* (Boston: Little, Brown, 1960) (implicitly acknowledging that legitimate government by law is possible). We take Llewellyn as representative of the core of realism, though, admittedly, some who claimed the label took more extreme views. Of course, Llewellyn himself, by 1960, had perhaps retreated too far from some important realist themes. For a seminal discussion, see Charles E. Clark and David M. Trubek, 'The Creative Role of the Judge: Restraint and Freedom in the Common Law Tradition', 71 *Yale LJ* 255, 256 (1961) (criticizing Llewellyn's *The Common Law Tradition*, for 'recogniz[ing] judicial creativity as part of the common law tradition, but . . . reject[ing] the notion of judicial freedom').

sure, since the realists are relatively silent on questions like these. Still, one plausible reason for thinking that the realists do not view indeterminacy as incompatible with authority may have something to do with the relationship between determinacy and predictability.

How does the realists' emphasis on predictability relate to the claim that legal authority requires determinacy? To answer this question, we have to answer another question first, namely, what is the concern or problem for which determinacy is supposed to provide the only acceptable solution? Here is one possibility. Law is coercive. At a minimum, in order for the exercise of coercive power to be justified, it must be imposed on individuals who are capable of conforming their behaviour to its demands and who have the opportunity to do so. Thus, agents must be put on notice of what is expected of them. Indeterminate law is presumably a problem for the rule of law because if the law is indeterminate, then agents are left unaware of what the law requires of them and are unable to conform their behaviour accordingly.

Here is where the realists' emphasis on prediction and causation comes in. If the need for agents to have the opportunity to conform their behaviour to the law's demands is the concern that motivates the worry about indeterminacy, then all that is really required is predictability. If individuals can predict what the law will require of them, then, in principle, they are on notice and have the opportunity to conform their behaviour to the law's demands. Notice requires predictability, not determinacy. And the very point of the realist tradition is that rationally indeterminate outcomes can nevertheless be reliably predictable—even if the prediction cannot be made entirely on the basis of the class of legal reasons.

The second reason for thinking that liberals require determinacy relates to the role of autonomy in the liberal tradition. Liberal autonomy requires stable, predictable frameworks within which agents are free to pursue their projects, plans, and aspirations.[62] Only against this background in which much can be taken for granted, and is not otherwise 'up in the air', can individuals formulate meaningful long-term projects and goals and be confident in their investments in resources necessary to execute them. This is the kind of liberal political theory that Coleman has begun to outline in *Risks and Wrongs*.[63] In this kind of liberal framework, determinate outcomes might be thought to matter because of their relationship to an agent's ability to form reliable expectations and to the rationality of his investments in resources—including human capital—necessary to their execution. Once

[62] See e.g. Loren Lomasky, *Persons, Rights and the Moral Community* (New York: Oxford University Press, 1987) (developing a system of rights based on a view of human beings as individuals concerned with personal projects).

[63] See Jules Coleman, *Risks and Wrongs* (Cambridge: Cambridge University Press, 1992), 436.

again, if the concern is that determinacy is necessary for autonomy, then it is unfounded. Concerns about conformity and autonomy can be met by stability and predictability, not determinacy. An agent's ability to conform his behaviour to the law's commands *ex ante* depends on his capacity to predict what judges will do in applying the law to various fact patterns, and the sort of stability required for liberal autonomy also invites the underlying concern for predictable authoritative actions.

In short, indeterminacy will not pose the threat to liberalism one would otherwise expect, provided that indeterminate judicial decisions are nevertheless reliably predictable. Establishing that indeterminacy is compatible with predictability is part of the unintended Legal Realist legacy, and is in fact a presupposition of the jurisprudence of liberalism's harshest critics.[64] The realists emphasize that indeterminate outcomes can be predictable, but what reason do we have for supposing that they are right? After all, the realists themselves claim that the class of legal reasons is itself causally indeterminate. That means that predictions cannot be based entirely on legal reasons.[65] On what else might such predictions be based?

One suggestion is that reliable predictions about how judges decide cases requires the existence of a suitable social-scientific theory of judging. Several realists believed in the existence of such theories. Jerome Frank, for one, thought that Freudian psychoanalytic theory provided in principle, the right kind of social-scientific theory for accomplishing just that.[66] Underhill Moore sometimes favoured a form of Watsonian behaviourism.[67]

The particulars of various theories do not matter for our current purposes. All we need do is assume that some such theory is a reliable predictor of what judges will do in particular cases. If such a theory is available, all agents can in principle predict with a reasonable degree of confidence what the law will expect of them. If that is the case, then even though the set of legal sources may be indeterminate both as reasons and causes, the law itself is predictable and 'determinate' in the sense requisite for legitimate authority. The problem, then, is not indeterminacy *per se*. Rather, it is identifying and developing the right kind of reliable social-scientific theory of judicial behaviour. Ironically, in a rough and ready way that identification

[64] See e.g. Clare Dalton, 'An Essay in The Deconstruction of Contract Doctrine', 94 *Yale LJ* 997, 1009–10 (1985) (asserting that the idea of indeterminate judicial decision-making is not inconsistent with the predictability of judicial decisions); David Kairys, 'Legal Reasoning', in *The Politics of Law: A Progressive Critique*, ed. David Kairys (New York: Pantheon, 1982), 11, 14–15 (asserting that although judicial decisions are based on indeterminate judicial values and priorities, such decisions are not necessarily unpredictable).

[65] See e.g. Dalton, *supra*, n. 64, at 1009–10 (asserting that because judicial decisions are indeterminate yet predictable, predictability must be based on something other than legal doctrine).

[66] See generally Jerome Frank, *Law and the Modern Mind* (London: Stevens, 1930).

[67] See Leiter, *supra*, n. 20, at 81–90 (discussing Underhill Moore's theory of adjudication).

and development is precisely what the vast majority of liberalism's critics are really pursuing.

3. Folk Theories and Predictability

Legal Realists like Frank and Moore believed in certain social-scientific theories of judging, but there may be no reason to think that armchair psychoanalysis and Watsonian behaviourism are correct accounts of judicial behaviour. The problem does not lie solely in the possibility that Frank and Moore might be wrong; rather, it is that there may be no social-scientific theory of the appropriate sort. And if no theory of the appropriate sort exists, then prediction is not possible; and if prediction is not possible, then we are back where we started—with liberal concerns and worries that are not met by existing practice. That is only half the problem. Suppose such a theory did in fact exist. The relevant theory would be either insufficiently well known to allow ordinary citizens to avail themselves of it (in which case, judicial outcomes will not be predictable for them), or it may be sufficiently well known such that judges themselves will be aware of it (in which case, judges will respond to it in ways that will undermine its predictive power).[68] We now have two objections to respond to. The first is that prediction requires a full theory which may not be available. The second is that if such a theory is available, it will either be inaccessible, or, if accessible, self-defeating. Let us take these up in turn.

The existence of a full and satisfactory theory is less important than it at first appears: lawyers can and do predict, with a fairly high degree of accuracy, what outcomes judges will reach, and they do so without anything like Jerome Frank's armchair psychoanalysis or Underhill Moore's behaviourism. How do lawyers do it, then? Presumably they do it with some degree of informal psychological, political, and cultural knowledge constituting a 'folk' social-scientific theory of adjudication. The success of this folk theory, which is, after all, largely coextensive with the talents of lawyers (that is, their ability to advise clients what to do, when to go to trial, when to settle, and so on), may constitute success enough for the purposes of predictability and authority, regardless of the prospects of social-scientific theories. Even liberalism's harshest critics do not appear to deny the possibility of 'folk' theories of judicial behaviour.[69] Thus, Crits and Feminists correlate judicial decisions with wealth, gender, race, cultural mores, and

[68] We are indebted to Professor Andrei Marmor of the faculty of law at the University of Tel Aviv for this objection.

[69] See e.g. Kairys, *supra*, n. 64, at 15 (asserting that the 'shared backgrounds, socialization, and experience of our judges . . . yield definite patterns in the ways they categorize, approach, and resolve social and political conflict').

ideologies. Indeed, doing so is essential to part of their programme, which is to establish the ideological bases of adjudication.

If a correct social-scientific theory of judging did exist, most ordinary citizens would not be aware of it. Then again, they need not have such a theory in mind in order to steer clear of the law's wrath. Most people, most of the time, can arrange their affairs to avoid coming into conflict with the law; like lawyers, ordinary people can avail themselves of informal psychological, political, and cultural knowledge in anticipating what courts will do. In those few cases in which they have genuine doubt about what the law requires of them, they can (and often do) consult counsel who can deploy the relevant folk theory. Thus, a theory that is not well known across the population as a whole is compatible with legal authority as long as there is the relevant folk theory to fill in the gaps in their knowledge.

Suppose the predictive theory is well known, however. We can assume that judges are familiar with it. Another possible objection suggests that judges will not passively participate in a fraud while the rest of the world knows the true grounds of their decisions. Surely, judges will respond by making decisions on other grounds, thus undermining the predictive power of the relevant theory.

The plausibility of this objection depends on the type of predictive theory at issue. Suppose someone has the following predictive 'theory': 'Coleman and Leiter eat when hungry.' Suppose this hypothesis is widely known and becomes known to Coleman and Leiter. It hardly follows that either Coleman or Leiter will stop eating when each is hungry or start eating when either is not hungry. In fact, it may appeal to both Coleman and Leiter to learn why they eat when they do. Such a theory may give them an understanding of their behaviour that they would not otherwise have, and so on.

This type of predictive or explanatory theory *vindicates* the behaviour or decisions in question. But some of the predictive theories associated with Legal Realism do not seem to have this character. For example, if Jerome Frank is right, then judges make decisions because of various neurotic unconscious desires;[70] bringing these causes of decision to light surely would change judicial behaviour! Of course, Frank's armchair psychoanalysis never delivered a powerful predictive theory; and it is surely not the folk theory of which most lawyers avail themselves. More promising is the sort of theory envisioned by realists like Karl Llewellyn and Underhill Moore, according to which judges decide commercial law cases based on their sense of what would be fair or appropriate in the particular commercial context, rather than on the basis of legal rules or prior court decisions.[71] This type

[70] See Frank, *supra*, n. 59, at 146–64.

[71] See Underhill Moore and Theodore S. Hope, Jr., 'An Institutional Approach to the Law of Commercial Banking', 38 *Yale LJ* 703, 719 (1929); Underhill Moore and Gilbert Sussman, 'Legal and Institutional Methods Applied to the Debiting of Direct Discounts—Institutional Method',

of predicative theory, should judges become more aware of it, would presumably vindicate their decisions rather than cause them to act otherwise.

In short, prediction does not require a full theory of judicial behaviour. It requires only an informal 'folk' theory of judicial behaviour, or precisely the sort that most lawyers and many citizens already seem to have. Moreover, no perverse consequences would follow from judicial knowledge of this theory.

We close this section by considering one final concern about causation and adjudication. The argument we have offered accepts that legal reasons may be causally inadequate to explain or predict judicial behaviour. However, it is based on the idea that such behaviour is causally explicable. Thus, whereas our argument appears to accept the Legal Realist view of legal reasons as causally indeterminate, it is not sceptical about the causal efficacy of reasons generally. Is this a problem? Is it inconsistent? It is neither. In accepting the indeterminacy of causes thesis, we accept that legal reasons might not themselves fully cause judicial decisions. We are not rejecting the possibility that reasons can be causes. To accept the notion that judicial behaviour is not fully caused by the legal reasons to which judges might be expected to appeal hardly entails that judicial behaviour is itself mysterious or otherwise not subject to ordinary causal explanation.

4. Determinacy and Warrant by Reason

To this point, we have focused on concerns about determinacy that can be met by rationally indeterminate but predictable outcomes. These worries arise by virtue of liberalism's commitment to the rule of law and from a certain kind of liberal political theory that emphasizes the centrality of personal autonomy. At first blush, these considerations suggest that the indeterminacy of the law is inconsistent with liberal normative theory because rule-of-law and autonomy considerations essential to the theory require determinacy. If our analysis is correct, however, closer examination reveals that these concerns require only that the law be reliably predictable, not that it be determinate.[72] So indeterminate, but predictable, law satisfies these rule-of-law and autonomy considerations, and does not, on these grounds at least, fall short of the liberal normative ideal.

There is no doubt that predictability and stability are important elements

40 *Yale LJ* 555, 560 (1931); see also Llewellyn, *supra*, n. 61. In Llewellyn's later works, and in Moore's work, this theory took on considerably more theoretical baggage, but its core is eminently simple and plausible, and a central component of any commercial lawyer's folk theory. It was common wisdom among the commercial litigators with whom Leiter practised in New York City that judges want to 'do what's fair'; the lawyer's job was, first, to present the facts in such a way that fairness seemed to demand a decision for her client and, secondly, to provide the judge with some law on which the judge could 'hang his hat'.

[72] See *supra*, Pt. I.B.3.

of liberal normative theory. There are, however, other aspects of liberal normative theory that have considerably less to do with predictability and stability; aspects of liberalism that one might think entail a commitment to determinacy. Conceptually at least, determinacy and predictability are mutually exclusive. Recall that an outcome is determinate,[73] provided it is uniquely *warranted* by the set of legal reasons.[74] Outcomes may be uniquely warranted without being predictable. The right decision in a case may not have been predictable *ex ante*, even if it comes to be viewed as the natural solution *ex post*. The determinacy thesis makes a claim about *justification*: the set of legal reasons justifies a unique outcome. The focus on predictability has nothing to do with justification, whereas determinacy has everything to do with justification.

In the previous sections we have explored the ways in which certain constraints of liberal political theory draw our attention to the predictability and stability of judicial decisions.[75] What commitments, if any, draw our attention to the justificatory relationship between legal reasons and judicial decisions?

Once again, the obvious candidate is the fact that legal outcomes are coercively enforceable.[76] Because the decisions judges reach are coercively enforceable, it is not enough that those decisions be predictable. For coercion to be justified, individuals must be able to conform their conduct to the law's demands and have the opportunity to do so. This condition is not sufficient, however. Predictable, but nevertheless unwarranted (or unjustified) outcomes may not be justifiably enforceable by coercion. In order for the coercive power of the state to be legitimately employed, judges' decisions must be justified by something more.

In order to be justified, judicial decisions must be warranted by the available set of legal reasons. Depending on one's theory of justification (and of law), being warranted by legal reasons may also be insufficient to justify coercive enforcement, since even legally required outcomes may sometimes prove morally indefensible. At the very least, though, compelling compliance with judicial decisions can be justified only if those outcomes are warranted by the class of legal reasons. Thus, predictability may allay some of the concerns liberals have about coercion, but it cannot allay all of them. The missing component is determinacy.

This argument correctly points out that concerns about justification are not reducible entirely to considerations of predictability. In order to be justified, coercion must, at least, enforce outcomes warranted by the set of legal reasons. That seems right. But it does not follow that such outcomes must be determinate, that is, warranted uniquely by the class of legal reasons.

[73] Determinate in the sense associated with indeterminacy of reasons.

[74] See *supra*, Pt. I.A.1. [75] See *supra*, Pts. I.B.1–3. [76] See *supra*, Pt. I.B.1.

Political coercion is unjustified when it is employed to enforce an *unjustifiable* decision, not when it is used to enforce a justifiable (if not uniquely so) decision. The problem with coercion is its use to enforce outcomes that are not justified; it is not that coercion is being employed to enforce justified outcomes that happen not to be uniquely warranted. Coercion requires warrant, not uniqueness. Uniqueness, we shall argue, is not a requirement of legitimate authority.

Is it enough to say that the coercion argument requires only warrant by dint of legal reasons and not uniqueness (determinacy)? Consider the situation of the losing litigant, say, the plaintiff in a suit. Is it enough that a decision for the defendant is warranted by the class of legal reasons even in the case in which a decision in favour of the losing litigant could have also been warranted by the class of legal reasons? Surely, the plaintiff will feel that the power of the state has been unjustly imposed against him.

Of course, two outcomes could be warranted by the class of legal reasons, but one could be more warranted than the other. Warrant has both a threshold and an ordinal dimension. It is not the case that outcomes are either warranted or not, and that those which are warranted are equally warranted, while those that are not warranted are equally unwarranted. Among those outcomes that are warranted will be some that are better supported by the class of relevant reasons than others. So the fact that the losing plaintiff 'has a case' (that is, a decision in his favour would be rationalizable under the class of legal reasons) hardly leads to the conclusion that he has a claim in justice when a decision against him is rendered.[77] In order to make this line of argument interesting, we have to restrict it to cases in which a decision either way would have been equally warranted by the class of legal reasons.

Before considering what to say about this kind of case, notice how this line of argument could lead a thoughtful theorist to wonder whether the best interpretation of the practice will reflect a commitment to legal determinacy. The plaintiff says, in effect, 'to justify a decision against me it is not enough that the defendant has as good a case; the case on his side has to be better than mine'. Coercion can be justified only to support the best case, not a case that is merely good enough. A plausible way of understanding the notion of a correct answer is in precisely this way: the correct answer is the better one. Thus, litigants may have a working conception of the practice that commits them to the view that there are correct answers

[77] The losing plaintiff may have a valid complaint, however, when a decision in his favour is better supported by the class of legal reasons than the decision reached in support of the defendant's claim—even if that outcome is warranted by the class of legal reasons. In that case, it is not sufficient that an outcome be warranted by reason in order justifiably to compel compliance with it. If both outcomes are warranted, then only the argument that is given greater support by the class of legal reasons is justifiably enforceable. The real dilemma occurs when both outcomes are equally warranted. We consider this problem next.

to legal disputes; otherwise, the exercise of coercion against them lacks justification. This is one kind of reason a theorist might have for trying to understand adjudication as being committed to determinate outcomes.[78]

Getting back to the issue before us: we are imagining a case in which decisions for either the plaintiff or the defendant are equally warranted by the set of legal reasons. What can we say to the losing plaintiff in such a case that could justify (to her) the use of coercion to force her compliance (if necessary)? Would it help matters if a decision against her was the *predictable* outcome? Predictability will not do all the work we need. Initially, the original defence of coercion based on the predictability of outcomes was not intended to apply to each and every case; instead, it was intended to justify the general use of force. All that was required was that outcomes be predictable enough to provide guidance and allow individuals to conform their behaviour to the law. The argument did not require that each outcome be predictable with certainty, and the decision in our example may not have been.

For the sake of argument, suppose that the plaintiff's loss was predictable by her. In that case, she would not have been justified in forming any expectations of winning the suit. If her claim is that the decision against her is unjust because it frustrates expectations she has about winning, the following response is appropriate: her expectations are not well grounded, and so frustrating them is not unjustified. This suggests that whether predictability of outcome is helpful to fend off the charge of injustice depends in part on the source of her claim of unjust treatment.

The plaintiff's claim, after all, may not be that her expectations were frustrated. Instead, her claim may simply be that she has just as solid a case as does the defendant. She wonders why the coercive power of the law is being used against her rather than for her?

There are several points to be made at this juncture. First, it does not follow that when the class of legal reasons is inadequate to distinguish the plaintiff's from the defendant's case that the judge's decision for the defendant is arbitrary in the sense of being *unreasoned* or *unreasonable*. The charge of injustice cannot be seen as the charge that the decision lacks a justifying reason. More likely, the objection is that the decision lacks a conclusory reason. But even this may not be the case. Recall the important distinction between the class of legal reasons and the class of reasons that the state has authority to implement or act upon.[79] Not every area in which a state has authority to act has its authority fully implemented in legislation or prior adjudication. The class of legal reasons may fall within the set of

[78] An argument very much like this is part of the pre-*Law's Empire* argument Dworkin has for the right-answer thesis. See Dworkin, *supra*, n. 22, at 28 (citing id., 'Hard Cases', 88 *Harv. L. Rev.* 1057 (1976), repr. in Dworkin, *supra*, n. 3, at 81).

[79] See *supra*, Pt. I.B.3.

reasons the state can implement, but it is not identical to that set. The scope of legal reasons will be set by 'a rule of recognition' or binding sources and conventions, whereas the scope of legitimating reasons for acting will be set by the relevant political theory of the state.

In the event that there is a tie as judged by the class of legal reasons, there may be other reasons a judge may be authorized to apply. While these are not strictly speaking legal reasons, they fall within the judge's *discretionary* authority to implement. Such reasons may ground a decision for one litigant rather than the other even when the class of legal reasons cannot. It may be part of our existing legal practice that when legal reasons are indeterminate a judge has authority to appeal to applicable extra-legal reasons to resolve a dispute. Our losing plaintiff would surely have grounds for complaint were the judge to appeal to reasons that were not applicable to the case, or that the judge was not authorized to consult, but she would have no complaint otherwise.[80]

Our losing plaintiff will not be satisfied, however, if in addition to the extra-legal reason adduced in favour of the defendant, there existed similar reasons to support her case. Her concerns will simply arise at a different level. Rather than claiming that the outcome is unjust because she has just as good a case under the law as the defendant has, she now claims that she also has just as good a case given whatever other legitimate sources or reasons for deciding a judge might have. What can we say when there is no substantive reason of law or of political morality that distinguishes the plaintiff's case from the defendant's?

There are at least two things we might say. In some cases there will exist cultural norms and practices that are shared by both plaintiffs and defendants. These norms and conventions may make one outcome more salient than another; in certain settings the community understands that the right decision is of a certain sort. To the extent that both litigants participate in the same culture, adopt the same practices, and follow the same norms, these informal considerations will reinforce the decision even if there is no

[80] Most commentators agree that something like this is what occurs in our practices, but disagree about how to describe it. Dworkin, for one, has argued that in appealing to such reasons, judges are actually appealing to *legal* standards, not to reasons beyond law (but nevertheless within their authority to consult). It is easy to see how this view of the class of legal reasons fits with Dworkin's earlier views about determinacy and right answers. Positivists, notably Raz and Coleman, argue that not every reason a judge may appeal to is, for that reason alone, a legal reason, that is, one, given the criteria of legality, they must consult. Part of the difference is that Dworkin constructs his theory of law—his account of what law is—from a theory of adjudication, whereas positivists like Hart, Raz, and Coleman claim that the theory of law and adjudication are distinct but related components of a jurisprudence. See Dworkin, *supra*, n. 3, at p. xii (identifying legal rights as an 'institutional right to the decision of a court in its adjudicative function'); Joseph Raz, *The Authority of Law: Essays on Law and Morality* (Oxford Clarendon Press, 1979), 180, 206–9; Jules L. Coleman, 'Negative and Positive Positivism', 11 *J. Legal Stud.* 139, 148–9 (1982).

binding or authorizing reason that requires it. This view reflects the realists' conception of the commercial realm.[81]

This kind of response has only a limited application, however. The more general argument is simply that in cases in which the reasons offered are equally strong on both sides, if the judge decided against the defendant, the defendant would have been in a position to make the same allegation. As long as we opt for a system of formal dispute resolution, someone has to win and someone has to lose. Provided that the operative political theory of the state is that decisions based on reasoned judgment are better than no decision at all, that it is better to have authorized decisions than no decision, the judgment against the plaintiff can be justified. In the end, a decision for either the plaintiff or the defendant will be arbitrary, but it does not necessarily follow that the decision will be utterly unreasoned or unreasonable. Thus, the objection that deciding against the plaintiff is unjust rings hollow.

5. Determinacy and Democracy

Liberal autonomy requires stable political, social, and economic institutions. (Stable does not mean 'fixed'.) At the same time, liberal constraints on coercion require predictability and warrant by dint of legal reasons. We have found no deep commitment of liberalism that requires determinacy. In addition, although liberalism requires that the decisions judges reach be warranted by the class of legal reasons, we have found no argument that requires that those same decisions be *caused* by the class of legal reasons. For all we have shown, a judge could decide cases on bases other than the class of legal reasons provided that her decision could be independently warranted by the class of legal reasons.[82] Is this a problem?

The answer is 'yes' and 'no'. The problem does not involve the determinacy of reasons, which is a claim about justification and warrant by reason. Indeterminacy of causes and indeterminacy of reasons occupy different places in liberal theory. Nevertheless, liberal political theory envisions judges acting responsibly, reaching decisions based on the reasons that apply to them. If it happens that judges typically decide cases on other grounds in which the class of legal reasons plays no causal role or only an insignificant one, then that may well mark a serious failing in the practice, not in the theory. The theory would neither endorse nor rationalize it. The determinacy objection draws our attention to the scope of judicial leeway or discretion, not to the causal mechanism by which decisions are reached.

Before closing this part of the article, let us pursue briefly one last argument for the claim that liberalism is committed to determinacy: the argument from

[81] See Moore and Hope, *supra*, n. 71, at 719; Moore and Sussman, *supra*, n. 71, at 560; See also Llewellyn, *supra*, n. 61.

[82] See *supra*, Pt. I.B.4.

democracy. The basic idea is that duly elected legislatures can only reflect the will of the populace if judges are in a suitable sense bound by democratically created legislation. Since liberalism is ordinarily committed to some form of democratic legislation, liberalism is committed to determinacy, as judges must decide cases on the basis of the reasons legislatures provide. To the extent those reasons fail to constrain judicial behaviour, the very possibility of democratic rule is in doubt.[83]

There are several things to note about the argument, not all of which, strictly speaking, bear on the problem of determinacy. First, the argument implies that judges must be constrained by the reasons provided in legislation, not just that their decisions be defensible by appeal to those reasons. If sound, the argument from democratic rule is that the outcomes judges reach must be in some significant way *caused* by the reasons legislation supplies. This is not a matter of determinacy, although critics of judicial behaviour would be justified in complaining that judges who did not so regard the class of legal reasons were acting in bad faith.

Secondly, even if democratic rule requires that the outcomes judges reach be constrained by legislation, it does not follow that judges are unconstrained when the reasons legislation provides do not warrant unique outcomes. To have leeway within boundaries, is, after all, to be constrained.

The argument of this part of the article can be summed up very briefly. Liberal political theory is committed to a variety of ideals that can be confused with a commitment to determinacy. In fact, however, liberalism is not committed to determinacy in the sense of uniquely warranted outcomes. The existence of indeterminacy in adjudication, therefore, poses no substantial threat to the possibility of legitimate governance by law.

Part II: Objectivity

A. THE IMPORTANCE OF OBJECTIVITY

1. Procedural Objectivity

Recall the argument about law's objectivity:

(1) liberal political theory is committed to objectivity;
(2) legal practice is not in fact objective in the relevant sense;
(3) therefore, existing practices cannot be defended on liberal grounds.

The burden of establishing premisses (1) and (2) would normally fall to the critic who would advance proposition (3). In fact, no critic has yet shouldered

[83] The argument applies primarily to statutory law and not to the common law, where no analogous problem about democratic rule would be thought to arise.

this burden for two different, but related reasons. First, there are too many political theories that claim to be liberal, so that as a practical matter it is simply too difficult to *establish* that 'political liberalism' is committed to the objectivity of adjudication. Secondly, the concept of objectivity is itself quite complex, cutting across a variety of philosophical disciplines, including epistemology, semantics, and metaphysics. No existing critical discussion has even tried to address problems of objectivity in all these areas of philosophy or examined the possible connection of each to a distinctly liberal conception of adjudication.

Since no one who argues that liberalism is committed to a kind of objectivity that legal practice fails to exhibit has ever presented anything like a satisfactory argument to this effect, perhaps we should simply suggest that until such an argument is offered there is no reason to suppose that liberalism is committed to objectivity, or, if it is, that the kind of objectivity to which it is committed is not in fact exemplified by legal practice. This is not the tack we have chosen. Our view is that liberalism may well be committed to objectivity, and, more importantly, that legal practice is objective in the relevant sense.[84] To put this in terms of the argument about objectivity sketched above, we accept premiss (1), but reject premiss (2).

Before moving to a discussion of premiss (2), we would like to outline some of the reasons for thinking that liberalism is committed to objectivity. Doing so will have the additional benefit of allowing us to introduce different senses of objectivity, while identifying different domains in which concerns about objectivity arise. We can distinguish between two different kinds of reasons for thinking that legal practice is objective in an important sense. The first of these has to do with concerns in *political philosophy*; the second has to do with concerns in *jurisprudence*. We consider both in turn.

With respect to objectivity and liberal political theory, the important distinction is between procedural (or epistemic) and metaphysical objectivity. A familiar view about the foundations of liberalism begins with the idea that, in order to endure, political associations must find a compromise among conflicting conceptions of value and the good, as well as among conflicting all-encompassing philosophical theories. In a liberal political community

[84] We argue below that there are good reasons for ascribing objectivity to liberalism, but the argument in this part of the article does not depend on this ascription being fully warranted. For even if liberalism is not, and need not be, committed to objectivity of any sort, important aspects of legal practice are in fact objective. The critic who claims that liberalism fails to justify existing legal practice because that practice is not objective will be mistaken in so far as legal practice is in fact objective. The central issue is not whether liberalism is committed to objectivity, but whether law is objective in the appropriate sense. Thus, much of this part of the article is devoted to specifying the relevant conception of objectivity.

law allows individuals with competing conceptions to coexist (more or less) peacefully.[85]

Legal decision-making procedures are designed to forge compromises among conflicting interests as well as to establish ground-rules on which individuals with conflicting all-encompassing theories or political and philosophical conceptions might agree. These procedures are defensible, not because they provide correct answers to legal and political disputes, but because they resolve such disputes in a fair and impartial, that is, objective manner. This is a rough and ready formulation of the classic conception of procedural or epistemic objectivity. The decisions judges come to, by applying such procedures, may or may not be correct in the sense of corresponding to some independent set of moral or political facts; indeed, some proponents of procedural objectivity are themselves sceptical about the existence of such facts (though scepticism is not a necessary condition for subscribing to procedural objectivity). Whether motivated by scepticism or not, procedural objectivists share the view that what justifies the outcomes of legal disputes is the fact that judges reach them by following objective procedures.

Though objectivity is all that matters to the procedural objectivist, it matters to different procedural objectivists for different reasons. We have already considered the case of the sceptic who is dubious about objectively correct answers to legal, moral, and political questions. For her, objective procedures are all that she could hope for. We can distinguish between at least two other kinds of procedural objectivists whose commitment does not depend on scepticism about the existence of correct answers to pressing

[85] 'Objectivity' in this procedural sense essentially involves the absence of *partiality*: a procedure for reaching decisions is objective by virtue of its relative freedom from partiality to one side or the other. We could also think of this type of objectivity as *epistemological*, i.e. pertaining to the cognitive procedures by which we form beliefs about which side is entitled to a decision in its favour. In general, we form our conceptions of what features should comprise an objective epistemic procedure by reference to some conception of what outcomes would be correct: an epistemologically objective procedure is a 'reality-tracker'. Thus, impartiality is a mark of epistemic objectivity in adjudication because pre-existing partiality to one side or the other is not relevant to what outcome the law deems correct; impartiality helps judicial decision-making track (legal) reality because legal reality is not partial. ('Legal reality' here means 'what the law requires' not 'what actually happens in court', which may be tainted with partiality, and so not objective.) As we observe in the text below, procedural or epistemological objectivity, though typically characterized by implicit reference to a conception of a reality-to-be-tracked, need not be defended by reference to what is really legally correct. It can instead be defended on the grounds that it is an impartial procedure for resolving disputes that is acceptable to individuals wedded to conflicting claims about what is right. Procedural objectivists need not deny that there are correct answers to political disputes, nor need they believe that objective decision-making procedures are unconnected to those answers. Their point is that the defence of those procedures is independent of the relationship between the procedures and the correctness (or incorrectness) of the answers secured by following the procedures.

legal, moral, and political questions. First there are the Hobbesians. Hobbesians see procedural objectivity as a *modus vivendi*—a strategically motivated compromise among self-interested parties.[86] Having decisions reached by objective procedures is the only way to forge compromise among individuals with conflicting interests and philosophical conceptions. Objective decision procedures can be defended on Hobbesian grounds even if there are correct answers to most pressing legal, moral, and political questions. All that is required to support agreement on objective procedures are (i) sufficient disagreement about what those answers are, and (ii) a collective interest in mutually advantageous co-operative endeavours.

We can now distinguish Rawlsians from Hobbesians. Like Hobbesians, Rawlsians need not be sceptics about the existence of correct answers to pressing moral, legal, and political questions. Unlike Hobbesians, however, Rawlsians believe that there are substantive grounds of political morality, not merely of self-interest or expediency, for agreeing to objective decision procedures; Rawlsians believe that liberalism requires that objective procedures be employed to settle disputes in a pluralistic setting.[87] In sum, procedural objectivity can be defended on sceptical grounds (as in the case of James Buchanan[88]), substantive grounds of political morality (as in the work of the later Rawls[89]), or strategic grounds (as in Hobbes[90]).

In contrast to procedural objectivity, we can distinguish *metaphysical* objectivity. According to metaphysical objectivity, there are correct answers to pressing legal, political, and moral questions: answers whose correctness is independent of people's beliefs about them and are, in a sense to be clarified below, objectively correct. The legitimacy of authority depends, not on judges following objective procedures, but rather on the accuracy of their decisions in reporting objective legal facts.[91] Recall that a 'legal fact' is simply any statement of what the law requires on some point: for example, 'it is a legal fact that Coleman's failure to inspect constitutes negligence' just in case it is true that as a matter of law Coleman's failure to inspect really does constitute negligence. Adjudication is objective in the metaphysical sense when the outcome of the adjudication coincides with the relevant legal fact. Some liberal political theories accept the view that the justification of coercion depends in part on the state's having an adjudicatory system whose outcomes track the objective legal facts; indeed, natural lawyers typically hold such a view.[92]

To see why political liberalism might be committed to objectivity in either

[86] See e.g. Thomas Hobbes, *Leviathan* (1650, repr. Dutton & Co. 1950), 228.

[87] See e.g. Rawls, *supra*, n. 16, at 38.

[88] See generally James M. Buchanan, *The Limits of Liberty: Between Anarchy and Leviathan* (Chicago: University of Chicago Press, 1975).

[89] See Rawls, *supra*, n. 16, at 137.

[90] See Hobbes, *supra*, n. 86, at 107–8.

[91] See *infra*, Pt. II.A.2.

[92] See e.g. Michael Moore, 'Moral Reality Revisited', 90 *Mich. L. Rev.* 2424, 2477 (1992).

the procedural or the metaphysical sense, notice what subjectivity would consist in. Adjudication is subjective in the procedural sense just in case judges reach decisions by relying on their feelings of bias and partiality toward one side or the other. Adjudication is subjective in the metaphysical sense when something is a legal fact by virtue of the individual judge believing it to be a legal fact. Were adjudication subjective in either sense, there would be little reason to suppose that a citizen would have a prima facie duty or moral reason to comply with the judgments of officials. Similarly, it would be hard to see how the use of coercion to enforce such decisions could be justified. The liberal conception of political obligation and the conditions under which coercion is justified both support the view that liberalism is committed to either epistemic or metaphysical objectivity.

The above arguments for objectivity are drawn from normative considerations. The view that legal practice has an important objectivist component need not rely entirely on normative considerations, however. For it is part of our ordinary conception of adjudication that judges seek to resolve disputes by determining what result the law requires. What the law requires, in turn, is thought to be independent of how judges regard the law in the sense that judges and lawyers can be wrong about what the law requires, and in the additional sense that adjudication is about discovering the law's requirements. This suggests that the ordinary conception of legal facts treats them as being objective in some sense. Our goal is to specify that sense of objectivity.

One consequence of defending objectivity on liberal normative grounds is that if liberalism's critics are correct in arguing that legal practice is not objective in either the procedural or the metaphysical sense, then current legal practice cannot be defended on liberal grounds. If our current practices are to be defended, we will have to look to other political conceptions. If, however, the claim about objectivity is motivated by considerations of analytic jurisprudence rather than substantive political theory, then the failure of legal facts to be metaphysically objective would imply something else: not that liberal legal practice is indefensible, but rather that our ordinary understanding of legal practice is deeply mistaken. If it were the case that the objects referred to in the domain of legal discourse were not objective, we would need to provide another explanation of our practice of referring to legal facts as if they were objective, when in fact they are not.

As our mission here is to uncover the relevant conception of objectivity, we do not assume adjudication will turn out to be objective in any sense. Some sort of metaphysical objectivity may be a theoretical or conceptual commitment of our discourse about law, but upon closer inspection it may well turn out that our discourse is misleading, and that our apparent commitment to objectivity is based on a mistake. John Mackie famously held a similar view about our ethical discourse.[93] That is, when we make moral judgments we talk as if moral facts were part of the fabric of the universe in the same way that tables and chairs are. Our ethical discourse is based on a commitment to this kind of objectivity of moral facts. Thus, because moral facts are not objective in this sense, Mackie argues that our ethical views are based on a mistake.[94]

The same may be true of our legal discourse. We talk as if some legal decisions are right whereas others are not, and not just because a judge so regards them. This suggests that judgments are not merely reports of a judge's preference, but that there is a sense in which legal facts that make such judgments right or wrong are, or can be, objective. It is perfectly possible that we are wrong, our discourse misleading. We cannot assume that our discourse has it right. That is what needs to be argued.

It is important, at this point, not to confuse objectivity with determinacy.[95] To say that the law is determinate is to say that there are correct answers to legal disputes. An answer is correct if it coincides with the relevant legal fact of the matter. Thus, the judge's ruling that Coleman's failure to inspect is negligent is correct if the legal fact of the matter is that Coleman's failure to inspect constitutes negligence. The determinacy thesis claims in effect that in all cases there are legal facts-of-the-matter: the point of adjudication is to reach decisions that coincide with what those facts are.

The worry about objectivity concerns the status of those legal facts—when there are such facts. Are they facts because a judge or most lawyers would regard them as such, or are they facts independent of whether judges or lawyers so regard them? In this section of the article we presume that, to the extent that the law is determinate (as it is, for example, in easy cases), the correct answers must be *objectively* correct; our concern, however, is with what sense of objectivity is at issue here. Of course, indeterminacy is still compatible with legitimate authority for the reasons given in the first half of this article.[96] But to the extent that the law is determinate, objectivity (of some sort still to be specified) is required.

[93] See J. L. Mackie, *Ethics: Inventing Right and Wrong* (Harmondsworth: Penguin, 1977), 40.

[94] More precisely, Mackie agrees with the realist that ethical discourse is essentially cognitive, i.e. it aims to describe and state facts. But for various reasons, Mackie argues there are no such facts. Thus, ethical discourse is systematically in error because it purports to describe and state facts where there are none. See ibid. at 35. In meta-ethics this doctrine is called 'error theory'. Most who agree with Mackie on the metaphysical point—that there are no moral facts—disagree with him on the semantic point—that ethical discourse is essentially cognitive. While it is hard to understand the point of a putatively fact-stating discourse that never succeeds in stating any facts, ethical discourse seems to play *some* important role in our lives. The non-cognitivist suggests that we look for that role not in any ability of ethical language to state facts, but rather in its ability to *express* certain sorts of important attitudes and feelings.

[95] The natural tendency to conflate objectivity and determinacy stems from the fact that we sometimes say that the law is objective just in case it is largely determinative of outcomes in individual cases. In spite of this tendency, and perhaps because of it, we need to distinguish the claims of determinacy from those of objectivity.

[96] See *supra*, Pt. I.B.

To accept indeterminacy, then, is to allow that sometimes there are no legal facts of the matter: for example, it is not a legal fact that Coleman's failure to inspect constitutes negligence and it is not a legal fact that Coleman's failure to inspect does not constitute negligence. To accept (metaphysical) subjectivity is to allow that where there are such facts what makes them so is that judges or lawyers so regard them.

While we are on the subject of exploring the relationships between determinacy and objectivity, it is worth noting that there is an important connection between *in*determinacy and subjectivity, a connection that raises a serious concern about the cogency of the critical attack on liberalism. Liberalism's critics reject both determinacy and objectivity, and therefore accept both indeterminacy and subjectivity. The problem is that one cannot coherently maintain both indeterminacy and subjectivity. Once one accepts subjectivity, one is committed to the view that legal facts are as judges regard them, because they regard them as such. Since correct answers are those that correspond to the facts and the facts are simply those that the judge regards as such, there must be determinate answers to all legal disputes. Thus, because subjectivity entails determinacy, no critic of liberalism can coherently maintain both subjectivity and indeterminacy. This means that when liberalism's critics claim that law is indeterminate, they must really have in mind an objectivist account of legal facts!

In what follows, we reject the procedural conception of objectivity in favor of the metaphysical one, at least as a first approximation. We are attempting to provide an analytic jurisprudence, that is, a philosophic account of our practices—including adjudication—and our pre-theoretic view is that legal discourse presupposes a form of metaphysical objectivity.[97]

With these preliminaries out of the way, let us now turn our attention to the second premiss.

2. Metaphysics and Semantics

Claims about the objectivity of law can be cast in either metaphysical or semantic terms. That is, they might be expressed as claims about legal discourse (semantics) or about the objects referred to by the discourse (metaphysics). While we focus on the metaphysical side of the divide, it will prove helpful to understand the relationship between objectivity in metaphysics and semantics. We begin with metaphysics. In its simplest and most

[97] As we noted before, it may well happen that there is no satisfactory conception of metaphysical objectivity that applies to law. If that turns out to be the case, legal facts would not be objective, but subjective. But it would not follow, and this is the important point, that adjudication would be subjective, for it might yet be procedurally or epistemically objective. That form of objectivity is compatible both with metaphysical subjectivity about legal facts and with our liberal tradition regarding the terms of legitimate coercion.

basic form, metaphysics is concerned with 'what there is'.[98] Metaphysical realism[99] is the view that what there is—the world—is independent of human minds in two senses. First, the existence and character of the world is not simply the extension of human mind (metaphysical or constitutive independence). Secondly, the existence and character of the world does not depend on the evidentiary tools available to us for gaining access to it (epistemic independence). For the time being we shall speak simply of the 'independence of the world from evidence and belief', and that because of its conception of the independence of the world, metaphysical realism is committed to the 'strong objectivity' of 'what there is'.

Metaphysical anti-realism denies that the world is independent in one or both senses, though the epistemic sense has been the most important in the twentieth century ('what there is' depends on what we take there to be). If realism entails strong objectivity, then it would be natural to assume that anti-realism entails subjectivity. But that would be a mistake, or so we will argue. The view that we want to press below is that one can reject metaphysical realism and yet embrace objectivity.

Note two further points. First, one can be a metaphysical realist about certain objects in certain domains (mid-size physical objects, for example, tables and chairs) and an anti-realist about the objects in other domains (for example, moral properties or the theoretical entities in scientific theories). Secondly, metaphysical realism typically involves more than a view about the objectivity of the world. Crispin Wright has helpfully characterized metaphysical realism as the conjunction of both a modest and a presumptuous thesis.[100] The modesty derives from its view of the world as independent of our experiences of it and our beliefs about it. The presumptuousness derives from its view that, in spite of this independence, individuals can come to know important truths about the world, including those concerning its deep structure. Thus, the metaphysical modesty of realism is typically conjoined with an epistemological presumptuousness: yes, the world is the way it is independent of our beliefs and evidence; nevertheless, we can come to know things about the way the world really is.

We need now another set of preliminary distinctions between realism and anti-realism in semantics. Semantic theories provide accounts of what meaning itself consists of—that is, what kind of property it is—as well as

[98] There are reasons and contexts in which it makes sense to distinguish metaphysics from ontology; in our usage here, metaphysics encompasses ontology.

[99] The reader should not confuse Legal Realism, which is the name of a jurisprudential school, with metaphysical or semantic realism, which are theses about the nature of what there is and meaning respectively. Metaphysical realists believe that there is a way the world is that is independent of human beliefs and minds, whereas Legal Realists sometimes seem to believe, among other things, that legal facts are what judges determine them to be. So one reason for insisting that the reader keep the distinction in mind is that, though the two views share the word 'realism', they stand for nearly opposite claims with respect to the status of (legal) facts.

[100] See Crispin Wright, *Realism, Meaning and Truth* (Oxford: Blackwell, 1987), 1–2 (stating that '[r]ealism is a mixture of modesty and presumption').

how sentences (or words) get their meaning. Semantic realists make two claims. The first is that the meaning of a sentence is given by its truth conditions; the second is that those truth conditions can themselves be evidence-transcendent. Thus, evidence-transcendence is a central element of both metaphysical and semantic realism.

Anti-realism in semantics is characterized by its denial of either or both of these claims. So a semantic anti-realist might deny that meaning is given by truth conditions, or she might deny that meaning is evidence-transcendent. An anti-realist can accept that the meaning of sentences is given by truth conditions and deny that truth-conditions can be evidence-transcendent.[101] Or an anti-realist can deny that meaning is given by truth conditions. Instead, for example, she could argue that the meaning of a sentence is given by its 'assertibility conditions' (that is, the conditions under which it can be asserted); this is the approach many semanticists who have been influenced by Wittgenstein have taken.[102] The fact remains, however, that most anti-realists deny both of the central tenets of semantic realism.

Before moving on, we have to say something about conventionalism in its relationship to both realism and anti-realism. There are many senses of conventionalism, but there is one usage of 'conventionalism' that is common to both realism and anti-realism. We take note of this usage because failing to distinguish it from other senses of conventionalism invites the confusing and mistaken view that all theories of meaning are ultimately conventional. Choosing a particular word to stand for something is conventional. We choose the word 'water' to refer to something when we could have just as easily made up another word to serve the same function, say, 'wetski'. Languages are always conventional in this sense, but this sort of conventionality is independent of the realist–anti-realist divide. For the realist, once we use the word 'water' to stand for something that has the chemical property of being H_2O, the meaning of water is fixed by the way the world is. The word 'water' cannot be correctly employed in some other way to refer to objects that do not have the appropriate chemical structure. In contrast, for the anti-realist, water is just whatever the community of language-users permits us to say it is, whether or not it has the property H_2O.[103]

[101] This is a recurring theme in Crispin Wright's form of anti-realism. See e.g. Crispin Wright, 'Realism, Antirealism, Irrealism, Quasi-Realism', in 12 *Midwest Stud. in Phil.* 25, 27 (ed. Peter A. French *et al.*, 1988) (stating that anti-realism 'is exactly the view that the notion of truth cannot intelligibly be evidentially unconstrained . . . [but that an antirealist has] no motive to forswear all use of the notion of truth').

[102] See e.g. Kripke, *supra*, n. 32, at 74.

[103] The confusion is similar to another confusion that applies to metaphysics. It is common to accept realism about tables and chairs, which means that tables and chairs exist independently of human beliefs about them. But we have heard many otherwise intelligent people deny the objectivity of tables and chairs on the grounds that people construct tables and chairs. Neither exists in nature as a natural kind. They are constructed by humans. But the metaphysical realist's claim is not that tables and chairs are *causally* independent of human behaviour, but rather that they are epistemically and constitutively independent of human minds.

Semantic realism presupposes metaphysical realism. The claim that meaning is fixed by the way the world is (semantic realism) presupposes that there is a way that the world is independent of human evidence and belief (metaphysical realism). Metaphysical realism, however, does not entail or presuppose semantic realism. One can believe that the character of the world is independent of our epistemic access to it, but that the nature of meaning itself is not. In such a case, semantic anti-realists would provide us with a picture of language that would be inadequate for depicting the world as the metaphysical realist conceives it; not surprisingly, then, it is common for metaphysical realists to be semantic realists.

Given our concerns regarding objectivity, realism is important because of its relationship to objectivity. If one wanted to establish the objectivity of legal discourse, then one might be inclined to defend a semantic realist's perspective of the legal domain. And if one wanted to defend the objectivity of the facts or the objects referred to in the legal domain, then one natural way of doing that would be to defend a metaphysical realist conception of legal facts. Among contemporary jurisprudents, Michael Moore defends realism about both legal facts and the semantics of legal discourse.[104]

There are, however, serious problems for all forms of semantic realism, whether in the legal domain or not, and there are specific problems with pursuing a metaphysical realist conception of legal facts. We take up some of the problems facing realism about legal facts below. For now we want to draw the reader's attention to familiar concerns about semantic realism in all domains of discourse. The key arguments here are associated with Kripkenstein, Michael Dummett, and Crispin Wright.[105]

One way of understanding the semantic scepticism associated with Kripkenstein is to view it as an attempt to undermine what we might call semantic Platonism: the view that meaning is given by facts that exist independently of the semantic practices and beliefs of humans.[106] Kripkenstein is not alone in this effort. Dummett's influential essays have raised doubts about the ability of semantic realism to explain 'meaning acquisition' and 'manifestation',[107] and Crispin Wright has formulated a novel and important objection to realist semantics that is based on the normativity of meaning

[104] See Moore, *supra*, n. 92, at 2469–70.

[105] Purely for reasons of philosophical currency, *not* cogency, we concentrate on Kripkenstein and Wright.

[106] See Wright, *supra*, n. 32, at 10.

[107] See generally Michael Dummett, *Truth and Other Enigmas* (Cambridge, Mass.: Harvard University Press, 1978) (discussing the philosophical interrelationship between meaning and understanding). McDowell, in criticizing Dummett, identifies a core of shared assumptions between Dummett and Platonists and proposes a new way to move beyond both. See John McDowell, 'Anti-Realism and the Epistemology of Understanding', in *Meaning and Understanding*, ed. Herman Parret and Jacques Bouveresse (Berlin: W. de Gruyter, 1981), 225, 242.

(of which Kripkenstein's argument may be just a special case).[108] Here is the basic idea behind Wright's objection.[109]

According to the realist, the meaning of a sentence is given by its truth conditions, the set of conditions that must obtain in order for it to be true. Sentences, for the realist, may be true even if we are unable to grasp their truth or to have access to it. On the other hand, it is central to our concept of meaning that it play a normative role by constraining the uses to which sentences can be legitimately put. For example, the *meaning* of 'the cat is on the mat' constrains the uses to which the sentence can be put; thus, it prevents us from 'correctly' using it to refer to a pig being on my bed.[110] But if the meaning of a sentence is given by its truth conditions in a world independent of our evidentiary capacities to access it, then how can the meaning constrain our use of it? How can we be constrained by something possibly beyond our access?[111]

In short, meaning constrains usage. But meaning that is given by facts that we may have no access to cannot constrain our use in the appropriate way. Semantic realism has the problem of explaining the way in which meaning can be normative, that is, how it can constrain usage. The anti-realist semantics of the Kripkensteinian communitarian, for example, does not face this problem. If the meaning is set by what the community of language-users will allow Leiter to assert, then the meaning of 'the cat is on the mat' may not prevent Leiter from using it to refer to a pig being on the bed, if that is an allowable assertion under the prevailing practice. So it is the practice of the community of language-users with which each language-user is adequately familiar that constrains usage.[112]

For the foregoing reasons, we reject the application of semantic realism to legal discourse. As we noted earlier, it is (logically) possible to accept metaphysical realism but reject semantic realism. However, we also noted

[108] See Wright, *supra*, n. 100, at 23–6.

[109] We do not mean to slight Dummett, though we think Wright's argument is particularly meaningful in the legal context. Dummett argued that the semantic realist will have trouble explaining both how we can acquire new meanings, and how we can manifest our understanding of a meaning, when meaning, for the realist, is given by possibly evidence-transcendent truth-conditions. See Dummett, *supra*, n. 107, at 420–30. That is, the dilemma facing the realist is that if it is possible that we could never detect the conditions that would constitute the meaning of a sentence, how then can we acquire this meaning (i.e. come to understand it) or manifest our grasp of the meaning (i.e. display our understanding of it)?

[110] That is, we cannot *correctly* use the sentence 'the cat is on the mat' to refer to a pig on my bed under normal circumstances, i.e. where I am trying to assert a true proposition.

[111] Or, as Nietzsche put the same point regarding Kant's attempt to give a metaphysical foundation to morality: '[H]ow could something unknown obligate us?' Friedreich Nietzsche, *Twilight of the Idols (1888)*, in *The Portable Nietzsche*, Walter Kaufmann, trans. (New York: Viking, 1954), 463, 485.

[112] A further question, beyond the scope of the present enquiry, is how conventions or practices constrain. How does the mere convergence of behaviour (as in a convention) impose normative constraints?

that if one took this tack, one would be committed to the odd view that the discourse in question could not describe the world as the metaphysical realist conceives it. Thus, semantic and metaphysical realism typically go hand in hand. The considerations that invite us to abandon semantic realism in a domain of discourse appear to suggest that we abandon metaphysical realism in that domain as well. And if we give up both semantic and metaphysical realism, does not that imply that we have abandoned all hope of providing an objective conception of the relevant discourse or of the objects referred to by the discourse as objective?

Realism entails objectivity, but objectivity does not entail realism. Anti-realism, in other words, does not entail subjectivity. We intend to defend a form of anti-realist objectivity. But how can a position that denies that the world is independent of the ways in which we happen to construe it be compatible with objectivity? Our task is to show how a discourse and the objects referred to in the discourse can be objective even if the domain of discourse does not invite a realist interpretation. That is the task to which we now turn.

3. Objectivity and Subjectivity

We begin by attending more carefully to what it means to talk about 'objectivity' and 'subjectivity'. Consider, in this regard, the distinction between what 'seems right' (with respect to the truth of some judgment) and what 'is right' (that is, what really is the case).[113] *Subjectivism* is the view that denies the distinction. To say that something *is* right under subjectivism is to say that it seems right to me, no more, no less. We might call this doctrine pure Protagoreanism,[114] since it literally suggests that *each* individual is the measure of all things.[115]

At the other end of the continuum from subjectivism is the doctrine we will call 'strong objectivism'. According to this view, what 'seems right' never determines what 'is right'. According to the strong *metaphysical* objectivist, what is the case about the world never depends on what humans take there to be (even under ideal epistemic conditions). According to the strong *semantic* objectivist, the meaning of a sentence never depends on what any speaker or community of speakers takes it to mean. We will call

[113] For a more complete development of these distinctions, see Brian Leiter, 'Objectivity and the Problems of Jurisprudence', 72 *Tex. L. Rev.* 187, 192–6 (1993). We also ignore here certain philosophical details and difficulties that are taken up in Leiter's article.

[114] This doctrine is an allusion to Plato's *Theaetetus* (152a, 166a–b).

[115] What, someone might wonder, is the meaning or content of the thought, 'It seems right to me that X means Y'? If subjectivism is true, then it must only be: 'It seems right to me that it seems right to me that X means Y.' But what, then, is the content of that thought? Clearly, an infinite regress is in the offing. This might be one reason—one among several, no doubt—for rejecting subjectivism about meaning.

strong objectivism the 'Platonic' position.[116] Thus, at one end of the subjectivism–objectivism divide we have Protagorean subjectivism; at the other end we have Platonic objectivism.

'Minimal objectivity'[117] occupies some of the space between these two extremes. According to minimal objectivity, what seems right to the majority of the community determines what is right. As regards the theory of meaning, this is simply a form of 'linguistic communitarianism': how most speakers are disposed to use a word fixes its meaning. Minimal objectivity preserves the essential anthropocentrism of the Protagorean doctrine in that neither the meaning of sentences in the discourse nor the metaphysical status of the objects referred to by those sentences are independent of human practices with regard to them. But it introduces an element of objectivity that consists in taking from the individual the measure of all things and placing that power in the community as a whole. According to minimal objectivity, individuals are not the measure of all things, but their collective or convergent practices are. Because it denies the epistemic transcendence of meaning and ontology, minimal objectivity is essentially anti-realist; because it denies that the world is just how any particular person takes it to be, it is essentially objectivist. Whether it is a powerful enough conception of objectivity to allay our fears about the subjectivity of adjudication remains to be seen.

We now have two conceptions of objectivity that may be applicable to the legal domain: strong and minimal objectivity. Both conceptions of objectivity play a role in various of our non-legal practices. Strong objectivity, for example, figures in our conception of scientific inquiry. We view scientists as trying to uncover the way the world really is; and the way the world is is independent of anyone's beliefs or theories about it, all of which could turn out to be false.[118]

On the other hand, there are several predicates that are naturally interpreted as being minimally objective. Being fashionable is an obvious example.[119] Something is (objectively) fashionable provided the majority of the community treats it as such, not otherwise. It is impossible to conceive of the property of being fashionable in any other way. It makes no sense, for example, to say that a style of dress is fashionable and mean by that nothing more than that I alone regard it as such. At the same time, it makes no sense to say that whether a style of dress is fashionable is altogether independent of how people regard it. So being fashionable is neither purely subjective nor strongly objective; it is minimally objective.

116 See Plato, *Phaedo* 74*a*–75*b*; *Republic* 475–80, 508d–e; *Symposium* 211a–b.

117 See Leiter, *supra*, n. 113, at 192–3.

118 This may even be the way in which scientists see their practice, but interestingly, it is not the only way philosophers of science see scientific practice and its metaphysical commitments. In this regard, see Larry Laudan, *Science and Relativism* (Chicago: University of Chicago Press, 1990), p. xii.

119 See Leiter, *supra*, n. 113, at 195.

Just to complete the picture, it is also obvious that some predicates naturally admit of a subjective interpretation. A good example is tastiness.[120] When we try to make sense of someone's claim that a certain ice cream flavour tastes good, it is natural to understand her to be claiming that it tastes good to her. It makes no sense to understand her to be asserting that it tastes good independently of how anyone regards it as tasting; and it makes only slightly more sense to understand her to be claiming that it tastes good because most people would so regard it.

These various conceptions of objectivity and subjectivity all play a role in our accounts and understandings of different features of our experience. It is simply false, and not merely unhelpful, to claim that 'everything is subjective'. If our theories are supposed to illuminate our practices, then it is worth noting that much of our discourse employs predicates that invite objectivist interpretations. The only meaningful or worthwhile endeavor is to try to determine which domains of discourse admit of objective and subjective accounts. Which conception of objectivity or subjectivity applies to a particular domain? Which applies to the legal domain?

As important as it is not to conflate concerns about objectivity with concerns about determinacy, it is equally important not to conflate theories of *metaphysical* objectivity with general semantic claims. The former are concerned with the degree of mind- and evidence-independence of facts of various kinds;[121] the latter give an account of meaning in some or all regions of discourse. For example, minimal objectivism about *moral facts* (the view that the community determines what is morally right and wrong) is a metaphysical view—a view about the status of moral facts. Though it may be a plausible metaphysical view, it is obviously not a very plausible account of the semantics of moral discourse. In moral discourse—in our discussions and debates about moral issues—we do not justify our judgments about the morality and immorality of various acts by averting to the fact that 'most people around here believe it to be so'. The surface of our moral discourse seems to aspire to higher forms of objectivity. What this means is that even if minimal objectivity provides the best interpretation of the way in which moral facts are regarded, it does not provide a particularly plausible semantics of moral discourse. Even if moral facts are fixed by community practices, the discourse of moral argument invites a somewhat different interpretation. It is no part of the practice of making and defending moral judgments that those who do so are satisfied to show that the bulk of the members of a community regard conduct as good, bad, right, wrong, and so on.

[120] Ibid., at 194.

[121] We can think of theories of semantic objectivity—theories about the objectivity of meaning—as a subset of theories of metaphysical objectivity. Instead of being concerned with mind- and evidence-independence of facts in general, theories of semantic objectivity are concerned with the degree of mind- and evidence-independence of semantic facts (or facts about meaning).

Consequently, a philosopher who thinks that moral facts are subjective or minimally objective (as a metaphysical matter)[122] still owes some account of the semantics of our moral discourse: what do we mean when we purport to defend moral claims without averting to what the speaker or the community of speakers takes to be true. Recent philosophical work has shown that there can be an account of the semantics of moral discourse and its purported claims to strong forms of objectivity ('what the Serbs are doing in Bosnia is really wrong, whether or not they know it') that is compatible with denying comparably strong forms of (metaphysical) objectivity.[123] There may be no moral facts, but we can still have an account of the meaning of ethical discourse which proceeds as though there were.

Unsurprisingly, there are cases where the same theory of objectivity will suffice for both the metaphysics and the semantics. What is fashionable is determined by what the bulk of the community regards as fashionable. Moreover, in discussions about what is fashionable, we can properly avert to majority opinion as a gauge for the correctness or incorrectness of particular judgments of fashionability. As we suggested above, however, even if moral facts are—metaphysically—subjective or minimally objective, it is not part of meaningful moral discourse to establish the immorality of torture by averting to the speaker's or the community's dislike of it.

As with moral discourse, there may be reasons to think that sceptical positions regarding the metaphysics of legal facts (for example, subjectivism or minimal objectivism) may have to be conjoined with different views of legal semantics. Judges, after all, do offer reasons for their decisions, and in the course of doing so seem to aspire to certain forms of objectivity that are stronger than subjectivism and minimal objectivism—a point exploited to good effect by Ronald Dworkin over the past twenty-five years.[124]

Averting to the semantics of legal discourse as a way of establishing metaphysical claims has been a large part of Dworkin's arsenal of weapons used against his enemy, the legal positivist. Here are two examples. First, in arguing that principles and policies other than legal rules are binding legal standards, Dworkin claims that judges do not appear to write or speak as if they treated such standards as extra-legal. Then, in defending the claim that there are right answers to legal disputes, Dworkin argues that judges argue as if there were right answers even if they do not agree about what

[122] Our locution here may not be standard: a philosopher who thought moral facts were metaphysically subjective in the sense defined above might prefer to say that there are no moral facts at all, suggesting that the very concept of a moral fact presupposes some form of objectivity

[123] See Allan Gibbard, *Wise Choices, Apt Feelings: A Theory of Normative Judgment* (Cambridge, Mass.: Harvard University Press, 1990), 153–250 (providing a seminal treatment of this issue).

[124] See e.g. Dworkin, 'Model of Rules', *supra*, n. 27, at 14, repr. in Dworkin, *supra*, n. 3, at 14.

those answers are. In both cases Dworkin employs features of the discourses as a way of suggesting or establishing claims about the status of the objects referred to in the discourse.[125]

The concepts of minimal and strong objectivity are far from unfamiliar in jurisprudence, even if they have not been discussed previously in these terms. Minimal objectivity is very close to conventionalism, and most contemporary legal positivists (Coleman is an exception) have favoured some or other version of it. Strong objectivity is associated with the natural law tradition and most recently with the works of Michael Moore and David Brink.[126] Both minimal and strong objectivity are subject to important criticisms, especially when construed as semantic theories. Some of these criticisms are quite general; others are more limited to one or the other as a conception of objectivity in law. In taking up these objections, we want not only to raise doubts about the applicability of either to law; we want as well to motivate consideration of yet another conception of objectivity that is largely unfamiliar to legal scholarship, modest objectivity.

B. SETTING THE STAGE FOR MODEST OBJECTIVITY

1. Problems with Strong Objectivity

Following Crispin Wright, we have characterized metaphysical realism as the conjunction of two premisses: one affirming the independence of facts from our epistemic access to them (their independence from human evidence and belief); the second affirming the possibility of securing knowledge of such facts.[127] The most pressing problem with metaphysical realism about legal facts has to do with the tension between these two claims. If the

[125] Coleman, for one, is a positivist who has never found this line of argument persuasive, since it rests on a philosophically dubious form of argument, employing features of the semantics of legal discourse to establish a metaphysical claim about the objects referred to by the discourse.

The analogy with the case of ethics is again apt and likely to be illuminating. Many writers who agree on the metaphysical question (about the status of moral facts) disagree on the semantics. Ayer, Gibbard, Mackie, and Stevenson are all metaphysical anti-objectivists about morality (i.e. ours is a world without moral facts), and they all disagree, in some cases dramatically, on the best account of the meaning of moral language and moral discourse. See A. J. Ayer, *Language, Truth and Logic* (New York: Dover 1952); Gibbard, *supra*, n. 123; Mackie, *supra*, n. 93; Charles Stevenson, *Ethics and Language* (New Haven, Conn.: Yale University Press, 1944). We think it more fruitful to begin with the metaphysical question—what there is—and deal with the semantics afterward. Semantics always has the option of revisionism (i.e. maybe the pretensions of language cannot be realized, and so must be revised), but revisionism in metaphysics, as a picture of what there is and its status, seems less promising.

[126] See generally David O. Brink, 'Legal Theory, Legal Interpretation, and Judicial Review', 17 *Phil. & Pub. Aff.* 105 (1988); Michael S. Moore, 'A Natural Law Theory of Interpretation', 58 S. *Cal. L. Rev.* 279 (1985).

[127] See Wright, *supra*, n. 100, at 1–2.

existence and nature of legal facts are independent of what all lawyers and judges believe (or might have reason to believe), then how do judges gain access to them? Put differently, what reason is there for thinking that conventional adjudicatory practices involve reliable mechanisms for identifying legal facts?

The realist about legal facts might simply deny that there is a problem here. She might offer two responses. First, she might say that it does not matter whether judges have access to the legal facts of the matter. Legitimate authority depends only on there being correct answers to legal disputes, not on any judge's ability to access them. But this ought to be unconvincing. The fact that there are right answers would count for very little if judges were invariably to come to the wrong conclusions about them. Why would anyone have a reason to comply with the law's demands if there were no reason to believe that the decisions judges arrive at were generally correct? In order for coercion to be justified it must be employed to enforce answers that are generally correct, not just ones judges happen to reach. So there is no escaping the problem of access.

Metaphysical realists about legal facts, like Michael Moore,[128] are well aware that this answer will not do. Instead, they offer a second kind of response: judges can have access to the correct answers to legal disputes in the same way that ordinary citizens can have access to ordinary facts of the matter. The problem is somewhat different in the case of judging, however. The evidence on which a judge bases his beliefs about what is the correct answer to a dispute is presented in a special way through an adjudicatory process. Our question, therefore, becomes what reason do we have for thinking that the adjudicatory practices we have developed will yield judgments or beliefs that accurately track what the law in fact (objectively) requires?

If we think of an adjudicatory process as the mechanism through which a judge forms *justified beliefs* about what the law requires, then the question becomes what conception of the adjudicatory process will ensure that those justified beliefs are also true, that they coincide with what the law actually requires. Philosophically, we would put the question this way: what *epistemology* of judging is appropriate to a metaphysical realist conception of legal facts?

The leading metaphysical realist about legal facts, Michael Moore, is a *coherentist* about justification. Justified beliefs about what the law requires of officials are those that cohere in an appropriate way with the set of beliefs about the law that the judge already has. Beliefs cohere to the extent that they are, for example, consistent and display a maximum of inferential

[128] Although we say, 'like Michael Moore', Moore and David Brink (as well as some natural lawyers) are probably the only adherents of the view that legal facts are strongly objective. See *supra*, n. 126 and accompanying text; cf. Leiter, *supra*, n. 113, at 201–2.

support for each other.[129] The adjudicatory process, then, is best seen as the vehicle through which judges try to provide an account of the law that makes the law's demands cohere in the relevant way. The outcome a judge should give in a particular case is the one that maximally coheres, and, provided the judge has gone about things in the right way, she is justified in believing that the outcome she reaches is what the law *really* requires. Coherence in our beliefs is supposed to track the strongly objective requirements of the law.[130]

The problem is that coherence as an account of justified belief (that is, as an epistemology of judging) is a poor match for metaphysical realism regarding the content of legal judgments and the status of legal facts. Why should the fact that a set of beliefs cohere for a judge (or for us) be a reason for thinking that those beliefs track the way the world really is? This is just the familiar philosophical worry that in the absence of a mechanism through which a coherent set of beliefs comes to be connected to facts about the world that are independent of those beliefs, there are no grounds for believing that justified beliefs, so conceived, track the way the world is. The problem is not eliminated even on the assumption that the world is itself coherent or consistent. For why should the kind of coherence among our beliefs (which is justificatory or inferential) correspond to the consistency or coherence of things in the world? Coherence among beliefs has nothing to do with the kind of coherence that objects in the world are thought to exhibit.[131]

Our objection here is not to strong objectivity about legal facts *per se.* Rather, it is an objection to mating strong objectivity with coherence theories of justified belief as a satisfactory account of how judges can have

[129] See Laurence Bonjour, *The Structure of Empirical Knowledge* (Cambridge, Mass.: Harvard University Press, 1985), 93–101.

[130] There are numerous formulations of the requirements of coherence, and the interested reader would do best by consulting the epistemology literature rather than the legal literature. But see Joseph Raz, 'The Relevance of Coherence', 72 *B. U. L. Rev.* 273 (1992) (providing an illuminating treatment of the topic). There are well-known problems with coherentist accounts of justified belief, but our concern here is with the narrower problem of mixing a coherentist account of justified belief with a metaphysical realist picture of legal facts.

[131] Suppose the required coherence *includes* coherence among our predictive beliefs (e.g. water will boil at 100°C) and our beliefs based on subsequent experience (e.g. water did in fact boil at 100°C). Will not this sort of coherence warrant the inference that our predictive beliefs described the world as it really is? Although this strategy might seem completely inapposite in the legal case, it may seem to harmonize coherentism and metaphysical realism in other domains. We do not take up this strategy of argument here, except to note that it is parasitic on what is known as the explanatory argument for realism. For powerful criticisms of this underlying explanatory argument, see Arthur Fine, 'The Natural Ontological Attitude', in *Scientific Realism*, ed. Jarrett Leplin (Berkeley: University of California Press, 1984), 83, 84–91 (discussing inherent flaws to various methodological defences of realism); Peter Railton, 'Explanation and Metaphysical Controversy', in *Scientific Explanation*, ed. Philip Kitcher and Wesley C. Salmon (Minneapolis: University of Minnesota Press, 1989), 220, 224–30; Bas C. Van Fraassen, *Laws and Symmetry* (Oxford: Clarendon Press, 1989), 142–9.

access to strongly objective legal facts (which, on the view under consideration, is a precondition for legal authority). In areas outside of law, the vast majority of contemporary metaphysical realists are 'externalists' in epistemology.[132] Externalism holds that beliefs are justified provided they result from a reliable causal mechanism; that is, if the fact of which one claims to have knowledge causes one to have the beliefs one has in a suitable way, then one's beliefs are justified. Coherence has nothing to do with the justification of beliefs on an externalist account; the right kind of causal relationship between fact and belief is all that is required for a belief to be justified. Externalism is not subject to the same criticisms we have levelled against coherence accounts because externalism requires a mechanism (causation) through which the way the world is—is connected to justified beliefs so that the set of those beliefs tracks this world. Justified beliefs are caused (in an appropriate and reliable way) by those facts.

If externalism solves the mechanism problem that haunts coherentism, why would a metaphysical realist about legal facts not simply abandon coherentist accounts of justified belief about legal facts in favour of some form of externalism? Fortunately, we can answer this question without getting into the details of various forms of externalism. In fact, pursuing the externalist approach may well prove fruitful in a variety of domains,[133] but there is good reason for being troubled by its application to legal knowledge. The problem is that externalism rejects the doxastic requirement of justified belief.[134] One's beliefs are justified externally, that is, independent of one's own experience or awareness of them as being justified. And such an account, even if plausible in other areas of knowledge, seems especially inappropriate to the adjudicatory process. A judge sees herself as being justified in defending a particular outcome as required by law by considering the grounds for her judgment. It is an entirely self-conscious activity. Externalism requires only a suitable causal mechanism, of which the agent need not be aware. And this seems terribly out of place in the context of adjudication in which the justification of belief has everything to do with the judge's self-conscious reasoning.

The realist is on to something in claiming that the ordinary conception of adjudication seems committed to the idea that judges try to determine what

[132] See e.g. Richard Boyd, 'How to Be a Moral Realist', in *Essays on Moral Realism* ed. G. Sayre-McCord (Ithaca, NY: Cornell University Press, 1988), 181, 181–228 (exploring how realist philosophy of science can be employed in the articulation and defence of moral realism); Peter Railton, 'Moral Realism', 95 *Phil. Rev.* 163, 166–71 (1986) (arguing that a naturalistic realist view of epistemology requires the adoption of external criteria). Perhaps the leading contemporary externalist is Alvin Goldman. For his original articulation of the view, see Alvin I. Goldman, 'A Causal Theory of Knowing', 64 *J. Phil.* 357 (1967).

[133] For some general doubts about externalism, however, see Bonjour, *supra*, n. 129, at 41–5.

[134] For a discussion of the doxastic requirement, see ibid. 101–6.

the law requires—that, in effect, judges find the law, rather than make it in the sense subjectivism claims they must. The problem is that if the law judges find is epistemically transcendent—if its existence and character are independent of how judges and others regard it—then how can judges come to hold true beliefs about its requirements? Coherence among a set of beliefs about what the law requires simply will not do the trick.

2. Problems with Minimal Objectivity

With this discussion in mind, it is easy to understand the attraction of minimal objectivity. According to minimal objectivity, legal facts are fixed by what the majority of judges take them to be. Thus, there is no problem of epistemic access. Indeed, the very concept of minimal objectivity is defined in epistemic terms, in terms of how the relevant community takes things to be. Though legal discourse may appear to implicate strongly objective legal facts, the objects of that discourse, legal facts, are only minimally objective.

Minimal objectivity is not unproblematic, however. There are at least three different kinds of objections that have been offered to minimal objectivity both as a semantic and metaphysical theory. The first concerns its difficulty in explaining the possibility of global or large-scale error; the second concerns its inability to explain rational disagreement that is not settled by convention; the third concerns what we will call the problem of the dominant ideology. We begin with the last, not because it is the most telling or troublesome, but because versions of it are so fashionable.

Recall that liberalism's critics mistakenly argue that Kripkenstein-like considerations establish a radical indeterminacy of meaning when in fact that meaning is fixed by conventional human practices.[135] The human practices that fix meaning, one might worry, are, like other human practices, reflections of the dominant hierarchies and power relationships within the community. And this invites the objection that ultimately the meaning of the various rules and principles that comprise the law will reflect the dominant culture in ways that threaten the law's legitimacy as an arbiter among conflicting interests and conceptions of the good. The law is really no more than an enforcer of the dominant ideology and culture hiding behind a mask of objectivity. This is the semantic version of the dominant-ideology objection.

The metaphysical version has an even greater initial force. If legal facts are fixed by the practices of judges, then legal facts will reflect how judges regard them. Judges are generally well-to-do white males. Thus, what we regard as objective legal facts turn out to be nothing more than expressions of the biases of wealthy white men.

[135] See *supra*, Pt. I.A.3. Meaning so determined can still be quite determinate.

These objections are of differing merit. The semantic version of the objection, to start with, is simply confused and implausible. That communal practices fix the meaning of *particular* words and sentences can hardly preclude those meaningful words and sentences from being employed in new ways to express new semantic content. The sentences 'workers are exploited under capitalism' and 'in patriarchal societies, men on average enjoy benefits and privileges not enjoyed on average by women' are perfectly intelligible, even if semantic conventionalism is true.[136] The writings of Marxists, Crits, or Feminists seem perfectly intelligible, Kripkenstein notwithstanding.

The objection to metaphysical conventionalism is slightly more worrisome. There are good grounds for expecting some correlations between race, gender, and class and ideology or system of belief.[137] But the correlation is neither obvious nor uniform; and in the legal case, it surely requires some detailed explication to demonstrate that there is a real determination relation between judicial race, gender, and class and the metaphysical universe of legal facts. Surely, too, it is worth remembering in this context the lesson of the 'sociological' wing of Legal Realism (the Karl Llewellyn/ Underhill Moore wing):[138] of the psycho-social facts about judges that explain and determine what they do, significant weight must be assigned to the fact that they are socialized as judges, rather than as journalists, pundits, revolutionaries, or psychotherapists. The sociological fact that judges are, quite strikingly, people possessed of a self-conscious sense of themselves as judges, as persons occupying roles with defined expectations and norms, means that any simple-minded correlation between race, gender, class, and legal decision may be the exception rather than the norm.

That being said, we think the worry about minimal objectivity as an account of the metaphysical status of legal facts is a genuine one. An 'on-average', but not uniform, correlation between race, gender, and class and legal decisions would be significant enough to raise doubts about whether minimal objectivity could suffice as the kind of objectivity of legal facts that would be consistent with legal authority. Indeed, this objection provides part of the impetus for exploring a conception of the law as *modestly* objective, a topic to which we turn shortly.

[136] See *infra*, text accompanying n. 139 (discussing a more serious worry about conventionalism as a theory of legal semantics).

[137] Of race, gender, and class, class affiliations seem the most powerful predictors and determinants of ideology, though race and gender have been more popular topics for bourgeois academics in American law schools and elsewhere. Greater subtlety in the application of these categories would be welcome in all cases. Most great radical theorists, after all, came from the bourgeois classes; and need we remark upon the pertinent racial differences between William Brennan, a jurist possessed of exceptional powers of empathy and imagination, and Clarence Thomas, a jurist of equally exceptional callousness and narrowness of vision?

[138] See Leiter, *supra*, n. 60.

Conventionalism (or minimal objectivity) as a semantic theory confronts another problem: if conventional practice fixes the meaning of a word, then participants in the practice cannot be wrong in using the word as they do. This problem leads to quite general philosophical problems, especially for concepts about which our knowledge grows. If everyone agrees, for example, about the meaning of 'gold' or 'death', then the conventional understanding fixes the reference of gold or death. Suppose, however, that as a result of developments in chemistry and biology, metal that was formerly referred to as gold and states of being that were formerly referred to as death are no longer plausibly viewed that way. Suppose that, as a consequence, the relevant linguistic practices change to reflect this change in the state of scientific knowledge. Conventionalism or minimal objectivity provides a rather odd characterization of what has transpired. Rather than saying that previous speakers of the language were wrong, it must say instead that the meaning of the terms have changed because the properties conventionally associated with the terms have changed.

A more plausible account, it seems, would claim that chemists and biologists have learned more about the way things really are. It makes more sense to say that scientific discovery warrants the conclusion that previous speakers of the language were simply wrong about the way things really are, not that things were one way once, but are no longer. It makes even less sense to say that things have changed just because the conventions adopted by language speakers have changed. And it has seemed to those who are persuaded by such objections that the only plausible alternative is to reject conventionalism (or, in the language used so far, the thesis that semantic facts are 'minimally objective') in favour of some form of semantic realism (that is, the view that meaning is fixed by reference, and not the other way around).[139]

There is one final problem for minimal objectivity: the problem of rational disagreement. Suppose there is a general practice among members of a community that has a certain reasonably well-defined boundary. Everyone, say, stops at red lights. Now suppose someone comes on to the scene, does not know the people very well, but wants to make the right kind of impression. She wants to do what everyone else does. Such a person might ask herself the following question: what must I do in order to conform my behaviour to what others do as a rule? This is just another way of asking the question: what rule are the others following?

The conventionalist or minimal objectivist holds the view that the normative dimension of the rule is fixed by convergent behaviour. If an agent wants to know what she must do in order to follow the rule, then she should do what others do, or what is conventionally understood to be what

[139] See Moore, *supra*, n. 126, at 323–8.

the rule requires. This means that to the extent to which there is disagreement about what the rule requires, there is no action the rule requires of her; and that is because what the rule requires is fixed by convergent behaviour. In a nutshell, the problem is this: according to minimal objectivity or conventionalism, the scope of the duty imposed by rules is set by convergent behaviour. In the absence of convergence, there is no duty. This means, in the case of the red light, that everybody has a duty to stop at the red light, but if people disagree about whether one should stop in an emergency, then there is no duty to stop.

This is just another way of raising a doubt about the ability of minimal objectivity to provide a plausible account of rational disagreement. One reason individuals may not converge on a practice with respect to emergencies is that they disagree about what the rule regarding stopping at red lights means. Their convergent behaviour under-determines which rule they are following.[140] They may disagree about what the rule requires, yet all believe that the rule actually requires something. In other words, none of them really believes that the rule requires nothing simply because they disagree about what it requires. This is a problem for minimal objectivity because it is understood as the claim that what a rule requires is fixed by convergent practice. Presumably, part of the commitment to objectivity in law is the idea that there are objective answers to legal disputes, answers that may be connected to judicial practices, but not absolutely fixed by them, answers that are correct in spite of even widespread disagreement about what they are.[141]

3. Modest Objectivity

We have now surveyed some of the more troubling and more or less familiar problems facing strong and minimal objectivity respectively. Minimal and strong objectivity are not, however, the only candidates for the kind of objectivity involved in adjudication; there is an additional conception of objectivity we want to develop which we call 'modest objectivity'. According to modest objectivity, what seems right under 'ideal epistemic conditions' determines what is right.[142] In pure Protagorean subjectivism the individual is the measure of all things in the very straightforward sense that

[140] X 'under-determines' Y when X does not justify only Y.

[141] We do not mean to suggest that conventionalists have nothing to say in response to these objections. Andrei Marmor, for one, persuasively responds to at least one version of the problem of mistakes. See Andrei Marmor, *Interpretation and Legal Theory* (Oxford: Clarendon Press, 1992), 124–54. Additionally, when Coleman was a committed conventionalist he did not find the Dworkinian line of argument compelling. See Coleman, *supra*, n. 80, at 139, 150.

[142] We develop the content of 'ideal epistemic conditions' *infra*, Pt. II.C.2, but for now let us say that such conditions are those that are the best for gaining reliable knowledge of something.

if something seems right to her, then it is right.[143] Minimal objectivity takes the judgment out of the hands of each person, so that it is possible that a person could be wrong in asserting that something is right on the grounds that it seems right to her. Minimal objectivity introduces the possibility of an agent's being wrong about whether something is right without her being wrong depending in any way on any form of realism.

Modest objectivity allows the possibility that everybody could be wrong about what a rule requires; what seems right even to everyone about what a rule requires may not be right. Only what seems right to individuals placed in an epistemically ideal position determines what is right. At the same time, modest objectivity provides a sense in which sentences can be objective that does not depend on their truth-conditions being fully independent of our epistemic resources and access to them. As a metaphysical theory, it makes the existence and character of facts of various kinds dependent on us, but not on our actual or existing beliefs and evidence.

4. Modest Objectivity, Access, and Error

We have not yet said much about the concept of modest objectivity other than to point out that it shares with minimal objectivity an anti-realist metaphysical stance, and that it shares with strong objectivity the idea that the world is not necessarily just how the majority regards it. Why prefer modest objectivity as an account of adjudication and law? It would not make much sense to try to develop the concept of modest objectivity with much care unless there was some reason to believe that it would improve our understanding of legal practice. One way to do that is to show how modest objectivity avoids some of the problems that beset strong and minimal objectivity.

Modest objectivity is not committed to a realist or strongly objective metaphysics. According to modest objectivity, legal facts are not evidence-transcendent. Legal facts are fixed by judgments under epistemically ideal conditions. Therefore, modest objectivity does not face the same problem that realism does in explaining how a judge could gain access to strongly objective facts.[144]

If meanings are minimally objective, then the extant convergent practice fixes the meaning. This is what generates the problem of mistakes, because where the practice changes (for example, because of new scientific discoveries about the chemical composition of gold), so does meaning. But this radical discontinuity—in which our understanding of gold does not *increase*, but rather the subject simply changes when we learn more about

[143] See *supra*, nn. 114–15 and accompanying text.

[144] It faces another problem, however, of showing how adjudication approximates or exemplifies ideal epistemic conditions. See *infra*, Pt. II.C.5.

it—is avoided if we think of meaning as being modestly objective. That is, what gold means depends on what speakers of the language would take it to mean under *epistemically ideal conditions*. For natural kind terms like 'gold' the ideal epistemic conditions must, of course, include relevant scientific knowledge about gold. Thus, the meaning of the term is fixed not by extant convergent practice, but by the convergence that would occur under conditions of maximum scientific information.

Roughly the same considerations apply in the case of determining the prescriptive dimension of (legal) rules. A judge intent on doing what the rule requires would not look to do what judges as a rule do; there may be no convergence of behaviour. Instead, a judge should try to uncover what a judge or panel of judges would do under ideal epistemic conditions. That is, according to modest objectivity, the scope of the duty under a rule is not fixed by existing convergent practices, nor is it settled by what the law is independent of anyone's beliefs about it; rather, the scope of duty is given by the sort of convergence that would occur under ideal conditions. Thus, a judge who wants to know what the scope of that (modestly objective) duty is wants to know what judges would do under the relevant conditions. Disputes about the requirements of a rule, then, are really best understood as disputes about what practice judges would converge upon under ideal conditions (conditions which presumably will include, for example, full information and maximum rational and legal capabilities).

In short, we have reason to pursue the concept of modest objectivity further. In doing so, we will have to say a good bit more about its central idea, 'ideal epistemic conditions', a concept that we have relied upon above, but that we have so far left perhaps maddeningly vague. We turn now to begin, but only begin, the difficult task of remedying this situation.

C. THE CONTENT OF MODEST OBJECTIVITY

1. Objectivity as the Absence of Subjectivity

Note, first, that someone defending modest objectivity does not have to defend it as a general metaphysics applicable to all domains. In other words, it is possible to think strong objectivity applicable to mid-size physical objects like tables and chairs, while thinking modest objectivity appropriate to our concepts of the moral, social, or legal domain.[145] Or one can defend modest objectivity with respect to mid-size physical objects and subjectivism or minimal objectivity about the moral and social domains.

Secondly, whatever account of ideal epistemic conditions we settle on

[145] See Leiter, *supra*, n. 113, at 194–5, 201–2.

may vary from one domain to another. What might constitute ideal conditions for fixing the existence of scientific facts (should these be modestly objective) may bear no relation to what counts as ideal conditions for fixing the existence of legal or moral facts.

Thirdly, there is at least one general theme that underlies our conception of things as modestly objective (and that also underlies, consequently, the specification of the relevant ideal conditions). All the conceptions of objectivity—strong, modest, minimal—involve severing the dependence of some entity or property from elements of our 'subjectivity', such as our beliefs, prejudices, ideologies, and personal characteristics. Where strong objectivity seems untenable (for whatever reason), we are drawn to modest objectivity where it still seems important to sever at least some of the ties between the existence and character of some object or property and our immediate subjectivity; our existing subjective condition is more likely to distort the object than to present it in its 'true' light. An attempt to specify idealized conditions so that what 'seems right' would determine what 'is right' is just the attempt to abstract away from some of these elements of our subjectivity.

Thus, modest objectivity is not objectivity in the sense of a world whose character is independent of our epistemic tools for gaining access to it; rather, it is objectivity that involves the substantial (but not total) absence of subjectivity. It is an attempt to abstract away from the kinds of subjectivity that might intercede between us and items in the world that we conceive of as possessing some measure of independence from our existing subjective propensities. It is not (as we shall see shortly) a kind of objectivity that requires abstraction from all aspects of subjective human experience, however.

2. Understanding Epistemically Ideal Conditions

Take the case of colour properties. Suppose, as seems likely, that we conceive of colours as modestly objective; something is red just in case it seems red to observers under ideal conditions. What are those conditions? Well, observations would have to be made in the light, not in darkness; the light would have to be reasonably bright; it would have to be white light (Day-Glo would not do); observers would require normal vision, and they would have to be able to distinguish between colours (everything cannot appear blue to them). But these *ideal* conditions are not necessarily our normal or presently existing conditions. We do not want to say that the colour of an object is determined by however we presently take it to be, regardless of our existing subjective condition. Hence, a need for idealization exists.

But how do we know what the ideal conditions are? We have no resource at this point other than our *existing concept* of the property at issue; we simply 'unpack' our concept of colour, of how colour properties figure in our practices. If the specification of the idealized conditions is accurate, then the claim must be that anyone who uses colour concepts otherwise (for example, someone who claims that something is red if it appears to be red under Day-Glo) would simply not understand our concept of colour.

Note, then, that a property can only be modestly objective when there exists a sufficiently clear concept to 'unpack'. Most of us are inclined to say, for example, that the tastiness of ice cream flavours is not objective, precisely because we have no conception of what the appropriate or ideal conditions are for rendering judgments about tastiness. If chocolate seems tasty to Coleman, and vanilla seems tasty to Leiter, there is really nothing more to be said; there is no objective fact about which flavour is really tasty (that is, no conditions we could specify for *fixing* the tastiness of ice cream flavours).

Moral judgments present a special, and more problematic case. If morality is modestly objective, then we might want to say that X is morally right only if judges under appropriate conditions would so judge it. But what are the appropriate conditions? Will they not be contestable in important ways that cannot be resolved other than by substantive moral argument, if they are resolvable at all? Yet surely everyone would agree, would they not, that moral judges should have accurate and complete factual information, should be impartial and free of bias, should weigh all affected interests equally, and so on? Are not these conditions part of the concept of morality that figures in our practices? Would not a person who was unwilling to count these as appropriate or ideal conditions of moral judgment be revealing herself to be someone who did not understand the concept of morality? Would she not be just like the person who thought that colour properties should be fixed by observation under Day-Glo?

It may be plausible to claim that these conditions of judgment are part of our concept of morality in the same way that the conditions of observation are part of our concept of colour. But it can only be plausible if we possess a sufficiently coherent and well-defined concept of morality (of what it means for something to be morally right), so that there is something in the concept to unpack. The question of whether morality is sufficiently coherent and well-defined is just one of the issues that separate moral realists from moral anti-realists. If the realist is right, then our concept of morality hangs together sufficiently well that we can specify the conditions under which persons would properly detect what it is we are talking about when we are talking about the morality of an act. When we say an act is morally incorrect we are, perhaps, just saying something like, 'it has a negative effect on aggregate well-being'. In that case, the appropriate conditions under which judgments will fix the morality of an act will include full information about effects upon well-being, the capacity to weigh affected interests, and impartiality as between the well-being of different parties.

The anti-realist denies all this. According to the anti-realist, sometimes when we say an act is 'morally incorrect' we mean what the utilitarian thinks it means; but other times, we mean that it 'fails to respect the dignity of persons' (or some other appropriate Kantian surrogate). At still other times, we use the language of morality to express other judgments in other circumstances. For the anti-realist, in short, our concept of morality does not cohere around a group of descriptive or empirical properties (like facts about well-being); talk about the morality of an act has an entirely different role—not to pick out some cluster of facts, but perhaps to express approval or to recommend or endorse an action.[146]

3. Objectivity in Law and Morals

Properties can be modestly objective only if they are sufficiently coherent to enable us to identify what would count as the conditions under which judgments about such properties would fix their existence and character. We have suggested that our concept of colour is sufficiently coherent to admit of an account of it as modestly objective. It is less clear whether the same could be said of moral properties. So, for example, is impartiality really a condition of adequate *moral* judgment? Can not a refined moral sensibility include *partiality* to family and close friends? Is morality really about aggregate well-being, the dignity and autonomy of persons, or something else altogether?

If law and morality are connected in the strong sense that the truth of legal propositions often depends on the truth of moral judgments, then this dispute between moral realists and anti-realists can be extremely relevant to certain forms of legal theory. Some legal theories, including all forms of substantive natural law theory, make the truth of some moral claims part of the truth-conditions of various legal claims. Michael Moore has dubbed this view 'relationalism'.[147] For such theories, the objectivity of morality is, then, a necessary condition of the objectivity of law. If the authority of law depends on its objectivity, then legal authority turns on the very possibility of the objectivity of morality. Morality must be objective in some sense if law is. Moore, himself, defends a form of moral realism.[148] For him, both law and morality are strongly objective.

The interesting case is Dworkin. Positivism can be understood as the claim that the truth conditions of legal sentences typically do not implicate the truth of moral judgments.[149] Positivists reject relationalism. As one of

[146] See Gibbard, *supra*, n. 123, at 6–22.

[147] See Moore, *supra*, n. 92, at 2425.

[148] Ibid., at 2491–533.

[149] This is not quite the conception of positivism Coleman defends. See generally Coleman, *supra*, n. 80.

positivism's earliest and most powerful critics, Dworkin accepts some version of the relational thesis.[150] On the other hand, unlike Moore, Dworkin (as we read him) rejects moral realism and the strong objectivity of legal facts. For him, legal facts are not part of the ' "fabric" of the universe'.[151] Both law and morality must be objective for Dworkin, but not strongly objective. We will argue momentarily that Dworkin is committed to the modest objectivity of both law and morality.[152]

The debate between moral realists and anti-realists has less of a bearing on the jurisprudential views that we hold. We are both positivists, which means that we reject a strong interpretation of the relational thesis, that is, the view that the truth of legal claims is invariably or often related to the truth of certain moral claims. The objectivity of law is, in our view, independent of the objectivity of morality in part because the truth conditions of legal propositions do not entail the truth of moral claims. We are free to adopt an anti-realist view about morality, which, in fact, both of us are inclined to do, while maintaining the view that legal facts can still be minimally (Leiter) or modestly (Coleman) objective.[153] Because we are positivists, there is no real need here to pursue the question of how morality, which seems so unlike colour, could be modestly objective; it is enough if law is.

[150] See Dworkin, *supra*, n. 3, at 2245.

[151] Dworkin, *supra*, n. 23, at 80. Dworkin's use of this kind of rhetoric seems to betray various confusions about the metaphysical issues. None the less, it seems correct to say that Dworkin holds a weaker view of the objectivity of morality than, say, Moore does.

[152] See *infra* Pt. II.C. 7.

[153] It may be worth emphasizing our differences with both Moore and Dworkin. Each of us are committed to the objectivity of law as a conceptual or normative matter. (Being a sceptic and a Legal Realist of sorts, Leiter is somewhat less certain about actual legal practice.) Unlike Dworkin and us, Moore is committed to law being strongly objective. Both Dworkin and Moore accept the relational thesis, namely, the claim that the truth conditions for legal propositions implicate the truth of moral claims. We reject this thesis. Moore adopts strong objectivity about both law and morals. Dworkin accepts the objectivity of law, and because he adopts the relational thesis, he is committed to the objectivity of morality. But he rejects the strong objectivity of both. In our view, he is committed to the modest objectivity of both.

Because we reject the relational thesis, our views about the objectivity of law and of morals are not linked in the way they are for both Moore and Dworkin. Coleman shares with Dworkin the conception of law as modestly, not strongly, objective. And we both disagree with Moore and Dworkin about morality. Moore is committed to morality being strongly objective; Dworkin is, we think, committed to law being modestly objective; we doubt that morality is objective in either sense.

We are committed to what might be called 'legal cognitivism'. We are committed to the claim that statements of the form, 'it is the law in our community that *P*' can be either true or false; statements about what the law requires are apt for truth predicates. We are not committed to the idea that there are right answers to all legal disputes. However, because we are committed to law's objectivity, we are committed to the objectivity of the claims that there are right answers to legal disputes.

4. Is Modest Objectivity Conventional?

We come now to a series of philosophically demanding and important points. The objectivity of a concept (for example, colour, morality, or law) presupposes a coherent practice regarding the use of that concept. Only such practices can admit of ideal conditions of observation or judgment. When properties can be modestly objective, their being so depends on the existence of epistemically ideal conditions for judgment. In the case of colour properties, it is fairly obvious what those conditions are. This will not always be the case. Suppose there is disagreement as to what is to count as epistemically ideal positions. How is that disagreement to be resolved? Is there a fact of the matter regarding what counts as suitable constraints on observation and judgment? If so, what is its source? The answer seems to be (as we hinted above) that what counts as appropriate constraints on observation is given by accepted practices within a domain of discourse. Scientists agree that observations made only under white light are appropriate to forming judgments about colour properties, and so on; common sense follows science in this regard. But if it is this kind of scientific and common-sense agreement that renders observation conditions legitimate or appropriate, why, then, does not modest objectivity merely collapse into conventionalism?

There is a difference, however, between saying that the nature of X is determined by what the community believes about X (conventionalism or minimal objectivity) and saying that the nature of X is determined by what people under *appropriate or ideal* conditions would believe about X. Even where what counts as an idealization depends on our 'conventional' practice (as in the case of colour concepts), the account of objectivity still obviously differs. All the objection shows is that modest objectivity still honours the Protagorean doctrine that 'man is the measure of all things', by relying, in this case, on our practices involving the concept to generate the idealization. But this hardly shows that there is no difference between minimal objectivity about colour and modest objectivity.

Two other points need to be emphasized. First, in cases like this we have no other way of proceeding than by trying to unpack the concepts that figure in our practices. The fact that these concepts figure in our practices does not make the task of unpacking them a version of conventionalism. The practices may be conventional, but conventional practices may be committed to practice-transcendent or non-conventional concepts.

Secondly, it is highly misleading to claim that in explicating concepts that are modestly objective, like colour properties, the epistemically ideal conditions are *set* or *fixed* by conventions. Those conditions are not set or fixed at all. Instead of pointing out that the conditions of observation appropriate to colour properties are set by convention, we should be read as trying to uncover the conditions of observation that are presupposed by the concept of colour properties. These are conditions that are part of the concept; they are not independently set or determined. The whole question of how epistemically ideal conditions are set or fixed misunderstands the inquiry. In every case of a property or fact that is potentially modestly objective, we are looking to see if we can identify the conditions of observation or judgment that the practices involving that concept presuppose. When we are unable to identify a set of such conditions, we do not fix a set arbitrarily. Rather, the failure to uncover a set of such conditions gives us reason to doubt that the concept in question is or can be modestly objective. So the thought that modest objectivity collapses into conventionalism because the conditions of judgment are fixed by convention simply misses the point.

5. The Content of Modest Objectivity and the Problem of Access

Legal facts are modestly objective when what is a legal fact is what judges under ideal epistemic conditions would take that fact to be. For example, Coleman is *in fact* liable for his negligence when judges under ideal epistemic conditions would find him liable for his negligence. In suggesting that this concept of objectivity is implicit in our legal practice we are claiming that, among other things, it may provide the best explanation for various features of that practice.[154] For example, we willingly allow the possibility that individual judges can be mistaken about legal facts, that an entire legal community during a particular historical period can be mistaken about what the law is (for example, the Court in the era of *Plessy* v. *Ferguson*[155]), but that what the law is does depend, at some level, upon the judgment of lawyers. An in-principle undetectable legal fact—of the sort whose existence is possible under strong objectivity—is, we suggest, not part of the conceptual apparatus of our legal practice.

But now let us try to be more precise and flesh out this notion of objectivity with some details. There is a legal fact about whether Coleman is liable for his negligence just in case judges under ideal conditions would find him liable. What are these conditions? Does the concept of 'law', or the 'legal', cohere sufficiently well to admit of characterization as modestly objective? Is law going to be more like the case of 'colour' (in which ideal conditions seem easy to specify) or 'morality' (in which it may be impossible to specify such conditions)?

We want to suggest that law is more like colour than morality in this respect.[156] At least some of the ideal conditions for rendering (objective)

[154] We tackle this very question at length in Jules Coleman and Brian Leiter, 'Legal Objectivity: Minimal or Modest?' (in progress; MS on file with authors).

[155] 163 US 537 (1896).

[156] Though it should go without saying, the ideal conditions for rendering colour judgments are nothing like the ideal conditions for rendering legal judgments.

legal—as opposed to moral—judgment seem easy to specify. The ideal judge must be:

(1) fully informed both about
  (a) all relevant factual information; and
  (b) all authoritative legal sources (statues, prior court decisions);
(2) fully rational, for example, observant of the rules of logic;
(3) free of personal bias for or against either party;
(4) maximally empathetic and imaginative, where cases require, for example, the weighing of affected interests; and
(5) conversant with and sensitive to informal cultural and social knowledge of the sort essential to analogical reasoning, in which differences and distinctions must be marked as 'relevant' or 'irrelevant'.

Our claim, then, is that a legal judgment rendered under conditions like these would fix what the law is on that point.[157] The idea that a legal judgment rendered under these conditions would not fix the law on that point is, if modest objectivity is correct as an account of the metaphysics of legal facts, foreign to our legal practice. Conversely, the idea that a legal judgment rendered under ordinary conditions (of incomplete information, bias, irrationality, and so on) fixes the legal fact in the case at hand is, if modest objectivity is correct, also foreign to legal practice. What judges believe matters, even though all judges can at present be wrong about the law. But judges under ideal conditions of the sort just specified cannot be wrong.

But now comes the 'natural' objection: surely, judges in the real world are not, in fact, rendering judgments under ideal conditions! So framed, however, this is no objection to the position just described because our claim here is only that the appropriate concept of objectivity in law is that of modest objectivity. The claim is not that actual adjudication is necessarily objective in the metaphysical sense of reliably reporting objective legal facts. Modest objectivity is a normative conception of objectivity in the sense that it provides a criterion for assessing whether adjudication is legitimate or justifiable. The critic of liberalism who faults adjudication for not being objective is precisely in need of an account of the concept of objectivity appropriate in law to which actual adjudication falls short. Modest objectivity provides criteria by which to *criticize* actual adjudicatory practice as falling short of objectivity, for example, for its lack of impartiality, complete information, imaginative empathy, logic, and so on.

Having said this, the natural objection just rehearsed points to a far more important philosophical difficulty with the theory of modest objectivity.

[157] We are definitely not claiming that judgment under these conditions would always identify one legal fact; since we accept that law can be indeterminate, legal judgment under ideal conditions will sometimes identify no legal fact of the matter.

Recall that modest objectivity was presented earlier as an objection to strong objectivity in that it rendered legal facts in-principle inaccessible to judges at the very same time accessibility was thought to be a condition of legal authority. And if real judges are not ideal judges, and if law is modestly objective in the sense just described, then will it not turn out that legal facts are equally inaccessible to actual judges rendering decisions for actual litigants?[158] If that is so, will not a conception of law as modestly objective fall foul of the very same objection we levelled against strong objectivity, and in so doing undermine the conditions for legal authority?

Once again, we have to be careful not to conflate two distinct notions; let us call them '*de jure* inaccessibility' and '*de facto* inaccessibility'. According to strong objectivity, legal facts are *de jure* inaccessible because, given the terms of the theory, it must be the case that what we are capable of determining does not determine what is the case.[159] By contrast, modestly objective legal facts will only be *de jure* inaccessible if the ideal conditions specified by the theory are themselves *de jure* (that is, in principle or by the terms of the theory) unattainable by humans. The ideal conditions for rendering legal judgment, however, do not seem to be beyond human reach; indeed, it seems that judges sometimes approximate them well enough to succeed in reporting legal facts (as in any standard 'easy case'). As framed, the objection shows only that legal facts are sometimes *de facto* inaccessible, that is, unknown (or undetected), because of the failure of judges to be objective in precisely the sense specified by the criteria for the ideal conditions. Modestly objective legal facts—unlike strongly objective ones—are *de jure*, or in-principle accessible, and thus can survive the earlier objection that the conditions of objectivity ultimately undermine rather than support the liberal conception of legal authority.

6. Modest Objectivity and Contemporary Jurisprudence

As it is normally conceived, the debate about objectivity in law is a debate between conventionalists and realists. We have tried to show that there is an alternative conception of objectivity, modest objectivity, that explains the possibility of general mistake and provides a sense of objective legal duty that extends beyond convergent behaviour, and does so without commitment to full-blown realism about legal facts. It is our view not only that this is a coherent conception of objectivity, but also that it is the conception of objectivity at work in much of the current jurisprudential debate. It is, we suggest, the conception of objectivity to which Dworkin is committed, and to which Critical Race Theorists (and also Feminists) ought to be committed.

[158] Cf. the 'Normativity Argument' in Leiter, *supra*, n. 113, at 207–8.

[159] This does not entail the view that *de jure* inaccessible legal facts are unknowable to humans, however, only that their being legal facts does not depend on their being knowable.

In the closing sections of this article, we seek to make good on these claims. Our remarks are tentative in part because Dworkin, and Critical Race Theorists, can be understood as explicitly rejecting the notion of objectivity in law.[160] But we cannot allow their explicit rejection of objectivity to divert us from showing that there is a viable form of objectivity in the legal domain to which they could and should be committed.

7. Dworkin and Modest Objectivity

It is plain that Dworkin means to reject conventionalism and plausible (if less plain) that he wants to resist the strong objectivity of realism. He wants to give an account of the way in which legal propositions can be true without their truth-conditions being set either by convention or by correspondence to facts that are part of 'the "fabric" of the universe'.[161] Although he does not explicitly embrace a legal metaphysics, we want to suggest that the metaphysics to which he is committed is what we have called modest objectivity, at least with regard to the status of 'right answers'.[162]

There is a difference between Dworkin's right-answer thesis as presented in his discussion of 'hard cases',[163] and the argument Dworkin settles on in *Law's Empire*.[164] In his earliest essays, for example, 'Judicial Discretion'[165] and 'Model of Rules',[166] Dworkin's target was legal positivism's commitment to judicial discretion in hard cases. At first it looked like Dworkin's main

[160] Anyone who believes that there are right answers to legal disputes is unavoidably committed to the idea of objectivity. Thus, despite his protestations to the contrary, Dworkin is certainly committed to metaphysically objective legal facts. Similar remarks apply to many of his most ardent critics. See *supra*, n. 2. Much writing by Feminists and Critical Race Theorists, on the other hand, seems to have fallen under the influence of a lot of bad philosophy, with the result that such writers often seem to believe that there are no objective facts about the world. Rather than providing new perspectives (female, minority) that enrich our understanding of an objective world or offering new discursive modes (e.g. narrative) for accessing heretofore ignored facts about this objective world, these critical writers often seem to view themselves as offering simple alternatives to the 'white male' perspective (if there is such a thing), alternatives that may have ethical and aesthetic merits, but certainly no epistemic merits (like being true). We urge that these writers should not be so quick to abandon claims to objectivity. It seems a distinct advantage to be able to reject sexist and racist views not simply because they are ethically or aesthetically unappealing to our 'perspective' but because they are objectively false, i.e. predicated on false claims about gender, race, social structure, and social causation. We suggest in the text an account of objectivity that is compatible with the spirit of such critical work.

[161] Dworkin, *supra*, n. 23, at 80.

[162] This may also be Kent Greenawalt's view. See Kent Greenawalt, *Law and Objectivity* (New York: Oxford University Press, 1992), 210; cf. Leiter, *supra*, n. 113, at 198–200.

[163] Dworkin, *supra*, n. 3, at 81–130.

[164] See Dworkin, *supra*, n. 23.

[165] See Dworkin, 'Judicial Discretion', *supra*, n. 27, at 624 (arguing that the view of discretion that is 'grounded on the realization that some of the reasons courts give for decisions do not operate like rules is inaccurate and misleading').

[166] Ibid., at 31 (critically assessing the positivist acceptance of judicial discretion in hard cases when other principles exist to guide and bind judges).

point was that positivism had too impoverished a conception of binding legal standards. Increase the set of binding legal standards, and the scope or extent of judicial discretion will diminish accordingly. By the time one reaches his chapter on 'hard cases', Dworkin should be read as developing a general theory of adjudication, applicable to all cases, and not just to hard ones. In the account developed there, right answers to legal disputes were defined as those to which Dworkin's idealized judge, Hercules, would come.[167] Hercules's judgment fixes what counts as a right answer to a legal dispute. Thus, the kind of objectivity involved in the right-answer thesis is not independent of epistemic access to legal facts. Indeed, Hercules is nothing other than a judge perched precisely in an ideal epistemic condition. He has the entirety of the law before him. He is fully rational and informed. He has maximum capacities for philosophical and moral reflection. The kind of objectivity exhibited by legal facts on this account is modest.

Under the theory of 'Hard Cases', judges have a duty to aspire to decide cases as would Hercules so that they might develop a practice that enables them to find the right answers to legal disputes.

By the time we get to *Law's Empire* Dworkin's argument has changed significantly, even if his basic philosophical (especially metaphysical) commitments have not. He is still committed to the existence of right answers that are, in our terms, modestly objective, and this is because answers are correct if they are the decisions reached by Hercules. The argument for judges aspiring to decide cases as would Hercules has altered significantly, however. The relevant components of the theory of adjudication are not defended because they are essential to fixing or finding correct answers to legal disputes. Rather, they are defended on different grounds of political morality. The relevant theory of adjudication is defended on the grounds that it embodies the political virtues of integrity, justice, and due process.[168] Hercules' decision-making process embodies these ideals, and judges should aspire to Herculean heights, not because doing so is necessary to secure right answers, but because doing so is required by these political ideals.[169] These political ideals are themselves defended in terms of a theory of political community, which is itself defended by its relationship to the value of fraternity.[170] Whereas the argument for the right-answer thesis of 'hard cases' derives ultimately from a liberal political theory that takes individual rights as fundamental, the argument of *Law's Empire* is grounded in the ideal of liberal community.

Whatever the differences may be between the underlying political morality of *Taking Rights Seriously* and *Law's Empire*, and they are substantial, Dworkin remains committed to a conception of right answers to legal

[167] See Dworkin, *supra*, n. 3, at 105–30 (outlining Hercules' decision-making process).
[168] See Dworkin, *supra*, n. 23, at 225. [169] Ibid., at 176–216.
[170] Ibid., at 187.

disputes: answers that can be right whatever the prevailing conventions among lawyers may be, answers that can be right without their correctness requiring strong objectivity, answers that are right and modestly objective.

8. Critical Race Theory and Modest Objectivity

We conclude with a few brief remarks about the relationship between Critical Race Theories and modest objectivity. We begin by revisiting a remark made earlier about the sense in which modest objectivity seeks to abstract from those aspects of subjective human experience that might infect judgment.

While it is true that objectivity suggests the rejection of subjectivity, it is not true that the epistemically preferred position will always abstract from aspects of subjective experience. Quite generally, in so far as there are objective facts about subjective experience, ideal conditions for rendering judgments about these facts will necessarily incorporate aspects of subjective experience. More particularly, in so far as the application of some legal categories requires the weighing of the affected interests of individuals, then the ideal conditions for rendering judgments about such matters will require information about subjective experience.

In this light, the familiar emphasis in Critical Race Theory on 'narrative' can be understood not as a rejection of objectivity—'it's narrative all the way down'—but rather as a specification of the conditions for detecting objective legal facts in certain types of cases.[171] Narratives, after all, are supposed to recount subjective experience, typically of oppression by law or by other means. They are best understood as providing access to real facts about oppression that would be inaccessible to ordinary discursive modes of legal reasoning. In cases, then, where minority interests are at stake (are to be 'weighed', 'balanced', and so on), the claim that the legal facts are modestly objective amounts to the claim that the ideal conditions for rendering judgment include access to narrative depictions of the affected parties.

It probably goes without saying, but it might bear repeating none the less, that subjectivism is not the friend of those who view themselves as alienated and disempowered. The claim that everything comes down to power cannot help those who view themselves as outside the corridors of power. The kind of account of legal facts that is compatible both with the possibility of their objectivity as well as the centrality of narrative is, we suggest modest objectivity.

[171] See *supra*, n. 2.

CONCLUSION

Philosophical theses are offered to help us understand and, on occasion, to defend our practices. Liberalism is offered as an account of a defensible political and legal practice. Its critics have raised a variety of objections to liberalism both as an account of our existing practices and as an ideal to which social and political arrangements ought to aspire. Our ambition has not been to defend liberalism against all of the criticisms levelled against it. Instead, we have focused on two different, but related, objections to liberalism as a family of jurisprudential theses: the claims that law is both indeterminate and subjective.

Our argument has been that liberalism is not in fact committed to legal determinacy. Instead, it is committed to a variety of political ideals, including the claims that political coercion must be justified, individuals must have an opportunity to conform their behaviour to the law's demands, institutions must enhance autonomy and well-being, and democratic rule must be possible. None of these entail a commitment to determinacy in the sense of uniquely warranted outcomes. Determinacy is not part of the liberal conception of law. Objectivity is.

For some, objectivity is not metaphysical, but procedural or (broadly speaking) epistemic; it is motivated by commitment to certain values that themselves do not depend on the truth of any metaphysical claims. For reasons similar to the ones Joseph Raz has raised against political liberalism without metaphysics,[172] we have chosen not to pursue this approach to the concept of objectivity implicated by law. Instead, we have pursued a metaphysical conception of objectivity. In so doing, we have distinguished among a variety of conceptions of objectivity and have tried to set out a new conception of objectivity for the field of jurisprudence, modest objectivity.[173]

In setting out the concept of modest objectivity, we have tried to put some flesh on its bones, establish its coherence, and explore its relationship to both minimal and strong objectivity. We have outlined some of the ways in which modest objectivity answers important objections raised against both minimal and strong objectivity. We have also argued that the notion of 'ideal epistemic conditions' is central to much of the current jurisprudential

[172] See Joseph Raz, 'Facing Diversity: The Case of Epistemic Abstinence', 19 *Phil. & Pub. Aff.* 3, 4 (1990) (challenging the cogency of the reasons offered by John Rawls and Thomas Nagel for epistemic abstinence).

[173] When we say 'new', we do not mean to say that this conception of objectivity is original to us—although we believe its application to the legal domain is lacking in philosophical pedigree. For a general metaphysical picture of modest objectivity, see Hilary Putnam, *Reason, Truth and History* (Cambridge: Cambridge University Press, 1981), 49–74. For an account of value as modestly objective, see Bruce Brower, 'Dispositional Ethical Realism', 103 *Ethics* 221, 222 (1993) and Mark Johnston, 'Dispositional Theories of Value', 63 *Proc. Aristotelian Soc'y.* 134, 145 (1989).

debate, figuring prominently in both Dworkin's and his strongest critics' most important arguments. To that extent, we have suggested that (implicitly at least) the thought that law is modestly objective is part of the working conception of legal practice among many different jurisprudential theses.

Much work remains. We have not completely fleshed out the idea of 'ideal epistemic conditions' as applied to law. We have not yet shown that our working conception of law is sufficiently coherent to admit of (metaphysical) objectivity of any sort. In short, it remains for us to show that modest objectivity figures not only in the various jurisprudential accounts of legal practice, but also in our legal practices themselves. That is a formidable task, one on which we differ, and which we hope to explore shortly. For now, we have to be satisfied with putting the concept of modest objectivity on the table.

8

Against Legal Principles

LARRY ALEXANDER AND KEN KRESS

I. INTRODUCTION

Conventional Anglo-American jurisprudential wisdom accords legal principles central and even honorific status in determining how legal reasoning does and ought to proceed, and how cases are and ought to be interpreted and adjudicated. Reference to legal principles permeates both philosophical commentary on and doctrinal discussion of law, interpretation, and adjudication. Indeed, reference to legal principles is a staple of the instruction of law students and of the arguments of practising lawyers. For many—including Ronald Dworkin—rules in effect drop out of the picture, leaving the field to principles.[1] Just as the nineteenth-century physicists invoked the ether to explain past observations and predict future ones, traditional legal reasoning and theories of interpretation invoke legal principles to explain the outcomes in past cases and to justify conclusions about how future cases should be decided. And like the invocation of the ether, the invocation of legal principles is misguided. Traditional theories of interpretation and legal reasoning, and the jurisprudential theories that build upon them, rest on a fundamental mistake. So, at least, we shall argue.

We shall establish the case against legal principles as follows. In Section II, drawing heavily on the work of Ronald Dworkin, we shall describe various types of norms and show where legal principles fit within the universe of norm-types. In Section III, we shall point out the ubiquity of references to legal principles in jurisprudential literature, legal scholarship, and case law. We shall conclude that section by returning to Dworkin's jurisprudential theory, which is the most powerful extant theory that builds upon legal principles, in no small part because it so faithfully tracks traditional legal methodology. Then, in Section IV, we shall set forth different but ultimately related arguments for why legal principles cannot exist except perhaps as theoretically possible but practically inert entities. More

The authors would like to thank Steven Burton, William Edmundson, Brian Leiter, Frederick Schauer, and Jeremy Waldron for their helpful comments on the ideas discussed herein.

[1] See Frederick Schauer, 'The Jurisprudence of Reason', 85 *Mich. L. Rev.* 847 (1987) (reviewing Ronald Dworkin, *Law's Empire* (1986)).

importantly, we shall show that Dworkin's argument for applying morally incorrect legal principles which manifest integrity fails. It is better to follow correct moral principles. Finally, in Section V, we shall set forth the implications for legal methodology that follow from the non-existence and normative emptiness of legal principles.

II. THE LEGAL PRINCIPLE AS A NORM-TYPE

Legal norms can be divided up in two ways. First, there is the familiar dichotomy of rules and standards. Rules are legal norms that are formal and mechanical. They are triggered by a few easily identified factual matters and are opaque in application to the values that they are designed to serve. Standards, on the other hand, are flexible, context-sensitive legal norms that require evaluative judgments in their application. A paradigmatic rule is 'drive at 55 m.p.h. or under'. A paradigmatic standard is 'drive safely'. Most legal norms are hybrids, in that they have both rule-like and standard-like elements.

The rule–standard dichotomy has been a favorite topic of the Critical Legal Studies camp of scholars ever since Duncan Kennedy, one of the camp's founding fathers, wrote an illuminating article on the subject of legal formality.[2] Frequently, but not always, rules are the scholars' whipping boy and standards their favoured norm-type.[3] On the other hand, rules and the methodological formalism with which they are associated have also had their champions in the literature, the most notable one being Fred Schauer.[4]

The second way that legal norms can be divided up is into rules and principles. It is this categorization of legal norms that is the focus of this article.

The rule–principle dichotomy should be clearly distinguished from the rule–standard dichotomy. This distinction should be observed because the term 'rule' appears in both but means something different in each, and because frequently the term 'principle' is used in place of the term 'standard' in discussions of the rule–standard dichotomy. For purposes of the rule–principle dichotomy, rules and principles are not distinguishable by how mechanical or flexible they are in form, nor by how factual or evaluative they are in content. Rather, they are distinguishable by whether they are posited in a canonical form by a specific institution at a particular time, and by whether they are determinative of the outcomes of whatever transactions come within their terms. For purposes of this dichotomy of legal

[2] See Duncan Kennedy, 'Legal Formality', 2 *J. Legal Stud.* 351 (1973).

[3] Kennedy appears to favour standards over rules. See Duncan Kennedy, 'Form and Substance in Private Law Adjudication', 89 *Harv. L. Rev.* 1685 (1976).

[4] See Frederick Schauer, 'Formalism', 97 *Yale LJ* 509 (1988).

norm-types, rules—which can include *both* rules *and* standards (the first dichotomy)—are identified by having been posited by a specific institution at a specific time and in a specific canonical form. Moreover, rules determine how transactions that fall within their terms are to be legally treated.[5] Conversely, principles are not posited and have no canonical form, though they supposedly reflect and can be changed by changes in posited, canonical legal norms (rules).[6] Moreover, principles do not determine legal outcomes in all cases in which they apply, though they can influence legal outcomes through adding normative *weight* to one outcome as opposed to another.[7] (Rules, which apply in an all-or-nothing way, are sometimes said to have no weight; but the more accurate way of characterizing rules is to say that, at least in the absence of conflict with other rules, because they are determinative when applicable, their weight is infinite.)[8]

[5] Are cases where two valid legal rules conflict counter-examples to our claim that rules are outcome determinative for all transactions that fall within their terms? We think not. Frequently, such cases are handled by higher-order rules that designate which of the conflicting rules is applicable (e.g. the rule later in time repeals inconsistent earlier rules, or the rule of a superior court repeals inconsistent rules of inferior courts). In those cases, the inapplicable rule is deemed amended or repealed and thus is not accurately formulated if the formulation results in a conflict. In the rare cases where no such higher-order rule resolves the conflict, the court must essentially enact a rule that operates as a higher-order rule for purposes of the conflict. In either case, the *ex post* formulation of the rules does not produce a conflict but rather resolves one by making one of the rules determinative of the outcome.

[6] This is not to deny that legislatures sometimes attempt to enact principles. See e.g. *California Civil Code Maxim of Jurisprudence*, § 3517: 'No one can take advantage of his own wrong.' But if such enactments are truly enactments of principles and not rules, then they are constrained in their effect in the following ways. First, if the enactments are referring to *legal* principles, then they have no effect, since legal principles cannot be directly enacted. Legal principles can only arise from—supervene upon—other posited legal materials (rules, decisions). Their very nature as principles, with the dimension of weight, means that legal principles cannot be enacted, since weight cannot be posited for all contexts. Indeed, given Dworkin's account of legal principles, there is no guarantee that the legislature or courts can even formulate or enact a legal principle: principles must arise from the legal materials, and even enacted principles would be authoritative only if they formed part of the morally best set of principles that meets or exceeds the threshold of fit—and not merely because they are enacted. See *infra*, n. 22–5.

Secondly, if the enactments are referring to moral principles, then their effect depends upon whether these principles (1) actually exist as moral principles and (2) are moral principles that are and can therefore be treated as independent of other moral principles and the moral theory of which they are all part. (Consider, for example, whether the 'principle' of freedom of speech is an independent principle. See Lawrence Alexander and Paul Horton, 'The Impossibility of a Free Speech Principle', 78 *Nw. U. L. Rev.* 1319, 1346–52 (1983).) Note, however, that even if these conditions are met—the principle referred to in an enactment or decision does exist as a moral principle and is independent of other moral principles—the only possible effect of its positive enactment is to convert it from a principle, which might be outweighed by non-enacted principles, either into a rule, which has an artificial weight of infinity, or into a norm with an indeterminate weight (because weight itself cannot be posited). Thus, as a principle, it cannot be enacted.

[7] Principles may determine outcomes only where they are absolute or where there are no opposing principles.

[8] In private correspondence, Jeremy Waldron has maintained that we have not dealt with the possibility of norms that have both canonical form and weight and norms that have no

The leading theoretical expositor of the rule–principle distinction is Ronald Dworkin. He introduced the distinction in chapter 2 of *Taking Rights Seriously*, where he distinguished posited, canonical, applicable, all-or-nothing rules from legal norms that 'operate . . . as principles, policies, and other sorts of standards'.[9] He gave as an example of a legal principle 'no man may profit from his own wrong', the principle that Dworkin claimed was decisive in the case of *Riggs* v. *Palmer*.[10] Another example was the principle of freedom of contract, a principle that was operative, but none the less outweighed, in the case of *Henningsen* v. *Bloomfield Motors, Inc.*[11] by the competing principles that 'the courts must examine purchase agreements closely to see if consumer and public interests are treated fairly'[12] and that 'courts will not permit themselves to be used as instruments of inequity and injustice' and 'generally refuse to lend themselves to the enforcement of [unfair] bargains'.[13]

For Dworkin, principles were distinguishable from policies in that principles expressed basic standards of justice and morality, while policies—such as reduction of auto accidents or protection of the environment—stated social goals to be achieved.[14] This difference between principles and policies, which was criticized by many commentators on Dworkin's work,[15] is less visible by the time of *Law's Empire*. Principles, which generate legal rights, have become paramount. In part this is because Dworkin's opponent has shifted from utilitarianism in *Taking Rights Seriously* to communitarianism in *Law's Empire*.

The crucial distinction for our purposes is the one Dworkin draws between legal principles and legal rules.

> The difference between legal principles and legal rules is a logical distinction. Both sets of standards point to particular decisions about legal obligation in particular circumstances, but they differ in the character of the direction they give. Rules are applicable in all-or-nothing fashion. If the facts a rule stipulates are given, then either the rule is valid, in which case the answer it supplies must be accepted, or it is not, in which case it contributes nothing to the decision.
>
> This all-or-nothing [character] is seen most plainly if we look at the way rules

canonical form but apply in an all-or-nothing manner. (Correspondence with Ken Kress, 27 Apr. 1994.) We do not believe that such types of norms are important for our purposes. The former type is impossible because weight, as opposed to lexical ranking, cannot be canonically specified; and weight is an integral part of any norm that has such a dimension. The latter type is just an absolute principle of less than universal scope, that is, one that outweighs all competing principles within a specific domain. See *supra*, n. 7.

[9] Ronald Dworkin, *Taking Rights Seriously* (rev. edn., 1978), 22.

[10] 115 NY 506, 22 N.E. 188 (1889).

[11] 32 NJ 358, 161 A.2d 69 (1960).

[12] Ibid., at 387, 161 A.2d at 85.

[13] Ibid., at 389, 161 A.2d at 86.

[14] Dworkin, *supra*, n. 9.

[15] See e.g. Lawrence Alexander and Michael Bayles, 'Hercules or Proteus? The Many Theses of Ronald Dworkin', 5 *Social Theory & Practice* 267, 286–93 (1980); Kent Greenawalt, 'Policy, Rights, and Judicial Decisions', 11 *Ga. L. Rev.* 991 (1977).

operate, not in law, but in . . . a game, for example. In baseball, a rule provides that if the batter has three strikes, he is out. An official cannot consistently acknowledge that this is an accurate statement of a baseball rule, and decide that a batter who has had three strikes is not out. Of course, a rule may have exceptions (the batter who has had three strikes is not out if the catcher drops the third strike). However, an accurate statement of the rule would take this exception into account, and any that did not would be incomplete.[16]

Principles, on the other hand, do not operate like rules. There are many instances in the legal system where people are allowed to profit from their wrongs (for example, adverse possession).[17] These are not repudiations of or exceptions to the principle that people should not profit from their wrongs. A principle is merely 'a reason that argues in one direction but does not necessitate a particular decision'.[18] It may compete with principles that argue in the opposite direction. 'Principles have a dimension that rules do not—the dimension of weight or importance.'[19]

Dworkin argues that principles are legal standards every bit as much as are legal rules, and that this refutes the legal positivist account of law. For the legal validity and weight of legal principles cannot be specified or explained by a master rule such as H. L. A. Hart's rule of recognition[20] or in any other way brought within a system of rules. Dworkin claims that positivism, with its pyramidical structure of valid rules, requires that the truth of all legal propositions be testable by reference to rules, and principles, because of their dimension of weight, cannot be restated as complex rules. Additionally, Dworkin argues that the determination of legal principles and their weight is often a matter of complex moral and theoretical argument and is thus a counter-example to the positivist claims that law and morality are logically separate and that law is public and certain.[21]

What is crucial about Dworkin's theory of legal principles does not become fully apparent until chapter 4 of *Taking Rights Seriously*. Up to this point one might take Dworkin to be asserting that there are *moral* principles as well as *legal* rules, and that judges in our legal system frequently

[16] Dworkin, *supra*, n. 9, at 24–5.

[17] See also *Simon & Schuster, Inc.* v. *New York Crime Victims Board*, 112 S. Ct. 501 (1991) (freedom of speech trumps state policy against having criminals profit from their accounts of their crimes).

[18] Dworkin, *supra*, n. 9, at 26.

[19] Ibid. Dworkin fails to notice that his substantive and logical definitions for policies and principles are inconsistent. Where a standard of justice or morality—a principle—outweighs all competing norms, it is absolute and functions like a rule, as a conclusive reason for action, not as a prima-facie reason for action to be weighed in the balance. See David Lyons, 'Principles, Positivism and Legal Theory', 87 *Yale LJ* 415 (1977) (reviewing *Taking Rights Seriously*).

[20] H. L. A. Hart, *The Concept of Law* (1961), 92–107.

[21] Dworkin, *supra*, n. 9, at 66–8. Some recent positivist writings have moved away from the claim that law be certain but not that law and morality are logically separate. See e.g. Joseph Raz, 'Authority, Law and Morality', 68 *The Monist* 295 (1985); Jules L. Coleman, 'Negative and Positive Positivism', 11 *J. Leg. Stud.* 139 (1982).

advert to those moral principles in deciding cases, even when a clear legal rule applies.

But in chapter 4 ('Hard Cases'), Dworkin makes clear that the principles he is concerned with are distinctly *legal* principles and not necessarily moral ones. In a mature, decent legal system, we should expect significant overlap between the classes of legal and moral principles, but neither identity between nor subsumption of one class under the other.

In chapter 4 of *Taking Rights Seriously* and throughout his later writings Dworkin distinguishes legal from (mere) moral principles in two ways. First, legal principles must have institutional support in the legal system. That is, their influence must be reflected in constitutional, statutory, administrative, and decisional law.[22]

If institutional support were all that distinguished legal from moral principles, then legal principles might be merely a subset of moral principles, that subset which has been manifested in positive law. But what if, as is surely the case, positive law is not completely consistent with moral principles, or any subset of moral principles? In other words, what if no subset of moral principles, with appropriate moral weights, would have produced the existing legal rules? Or, to put it still differently, what if the existing legal rules cannot be perfectly reconciled with, and thus do not properly reflect, either the entire set of correct moral principles or any set of correct moral principles less than the entire set? Do we then say that there are no 'principles' reflected in the legal system?

Dworkin's answer to this question is no, and it is his move to salvage *legal* principles in the face of the legal system's deviation from moral principles that is significant and the topic of this article. In essence, Dworkin's move is to divorce legal principles from moral principles to the following extent: legal principles are principles that would justify most of the extant positive law—that 'fit' the positive law beyond a (vague) threshold level—and they are the morally best principles (as gauged by correct moral principles) among all possible principles that meet or exceed the threshold of 'fit'. In other words, legal principles are principles some or all of which may not be morally correct but that score highest on the 'moral acceptability' axis while meeting the 'fit' requirement.[23] This possibility of moral incorrectness is the second sense in which legal principles differ from moral principles for Dworkin.

[22] See Dworkin, *supra*, n. 9, at 110–23, 340–1.

[23] See ibid., at 340–1, 360; Dworkin, *supra*, n. 1, at chs. 6, 7; Larry Alexander, 'Striking Back at the Empire: A Brief Survey of Problems in Dworkin's Theory of Law', 6 *Law & Philosophy* 419, 420–1 (1987); Alexander and Bayles, *supra*, n. 15, at 276–8 (1980); Kenneth J. Kress, 'Legal Reasoning and Coherence Theories: Dworkin's Rights Thesis, Retroactivity, and the Linear Order of Decisions', 72 *Cal. L. Rev.* 369, 378 n. 53 (1984).

Dworkin thus first, by means of the moral acceptability criterion, divorces legal principles from norms that fit the legal system perfectly,[24] and secondly, by means of the threshold of fit criterion, differentiates legal principles from principles of pure moral-political theory. In doing so, he sabotages the obvious motivations and justifications for following legal principles: authority and certainty for theories dominated by fit; justice for theories following moral-political theory.[25]

In what sense are legal principles 'legal'? We know they are not necessarily moral principles because moral principles may not meet the requirement of 'fit'. That is, there may be an insufficient number of legal rules that are consistent with what moral principles would dictate. Moral principles play the background role of assessing the relative moral attractiveness of all the possible principles that fit the legal rules. The principles that fit the legal rules and that are assessed for moral attractiveness are not themselves moral principles.

What makes the principles in question 'legal' is the requirement of fit. Although legal principles are unlike legal rules in that they are not posited—they are not laid down by particular institutions at a particular time—and lack a canonical formulation, they arise from the body of posited, canonical legal rules. They are theoretical entities, like the physicists' ether, in that they justify the bulk of the legal rules. And although in chapter 2 of *Taking Rights Seriously* ('The Model of Rules—I'), Dworkin could be read as requiring that legal principles be actually adverted to by judges in their opinions in order to 'exist', Dworkin is quite clear in his subsequent writings that legal principles are the (morally) best principles among those that fit the rules and decision whether or not they are mentioned or even consciously adverted to by any official.[26]

III. LEGAL PRINCIPLES IN JURISPRUDENTIAL THOUGHT

No one has explicated the distinction between legal rules and legal principles with as much care and attention as Dworkin. Nor has anyone given as precise an account of how legal principles are related to, but differ from, moral principles. None the less, Dworkin, in drawing these distinctions, is speaking not merely for himself, but is speaking from and for an entire

[24] Cf. Sartorius, who holds that law consists of what follows from the principles that entail the surface rules, decisions, and constitutional provisions. R. Sartorius, *Individual Conduct and Social Norms* (1975), 192.

[25] For a fuller examination, see the discussion of Alexander and Bayles, *supra*, n. 15; examined also *infra*, at nn. 69–76.

[26] See esp. Dworkin, *supra*, n. 9, at chs. 4 (pp. 118–19), 6, 7.

jurisprudential tradition, a tradition that has shaped not only academic thought on these matters but also how lawyers and judges think and operate.

In this section we shall survey some representative jurisprudential works for evidence of reliance on the distinctions between legal rules and legal principles and between legal principles and moral principles that are so central in Dworkin's work. We shall then return to Dworkin's explication of these distinctions, which we believe is the clearest and most powerful account. And we shall conclude by illustrating its power through demonstrating how pervasively it reflects deeply ingrained methodologies of legal scholars, legal advocates, and judges.

A. Legal Principles in other Jurisprudential Theories

Steven Burton, in his recent book *Judging in Good Faith*,[27] argues that in deciding cases judges must consult not only formal legal rules, but also legal reasons and their weights. For Burton, a legal reason (for action) consists in a fact plus a legal standard in concrete context.[28] Ignoring the factual aspect, legal reasons are those moral principles and social policies and other standards 'that form the background justification for the particular legal standard understood in its legal context'.[29] The weight of legal reasons varies from context to context,[30] and is a function of all the other relevant legal reasons.[31] Reasons that do not prevail at the legislative stage are excluded from consideration by the judge,[32] although they may be relevant in those parts of the law where they have prevailed.[33]

Although Burton disagrees with Dworkin on certain points,[34] like Dworkin, he believes that there are distinctly *legal* principles, which in particular cases he calls legal reasons.

Cass Sunstein, in his recent article 'On Analogical Reasoning',[35] describes the familiar process of legal reasoning in which mid-level principles are posited that cover the existing legal rules and decisions and in terms of which those rules and decisions are analogous or dis-analogous to adjudicatory decisions under consideration. These mid-level principles are not the morally correct principles that one might reach through the process of moral reasoning by which one reaches reflective equilibrium between specific moral judgments and general moral principles.[36] That is so because unlike specific moral judgments, which are revisable, many specific legal rules and decisions are unrevisable even if morally flawed.[37] Sunstein points

[27] (1992). [28] Ibid., at 39. [29] Ibid., at 48. [30] Ibid., at 61.

[31] Ibid., at 57, 88–9. [32] Ibid., at 48. [33] See ibid., at 59–60, 64.

[34] Ibid., at 188–9. For example, Burton believes that the authoritative nature of legal standards is grounded in legal conventions, not Dworkinian interpretation along the fit and moral acceptability axes.

[35] 106 *Harv. L. Rev.* 741 (1993). [36] Ibid., at 778. [37] Ibid., at 778, 782–3.

out the similarity between identifying principles by which contemplated decisions are analogous to those already reached by the legal system and Dworkin's method of adjudication, with its requirement that legal principles 'fit' the existing body of settled law.[38] Sunstein emphasizes more than Dworkin, however, the inference from the existing legal materials 'up' to the legal principles, and stresses less than Dworkin the moral-acceptability axis.

Kenneth Henley, in 'Abstract Principles, Mid-Level Principles, and the Rule of Law',[39] makes a case for mid-level principles in legal decision-making that is similar to Sunstein's. For Henley, mid-level principles, unlike rules, have the dimension of weight.[40] They 'justify' the existing body of rules and can be resorted to when the rules themselves do not resolve a legal dispute. In contrast to abstract moral principles, which theoretically could also be resorted to in cases not determined by legal rules, mid-level principles are much more constraining and provide a better check on unbridled official discretion.

Henley, however, never discloses how the weight of these mid-level principles is to be ascertained, except to posit that there will be 'some shared sense of weightings'.[41] Nor does he indicate whether these principles have some canonical formulation. If they do, through what process are they formulated and how does that process bear on their weight? If they do not, then how are they to be identified? Thus, it is not clear how he imagines the principles will actually constrain.

B. Dworkin's Account of Legal Principles and the Standard Methodologies of Legal Analysis

Let us return now to Dworkin's account of legal principles, which, as we have said, is the most careful jurisprudential treatment of them in the literature. On Dworkin's account, legal principles are distinguishable from legal rules in three respects: legal principles are not posited; they have no canonical formulation; and they have the characteristic of (finite) weight. They are connected to legal rules—those legal norms that are posited, do have canonical formulations, and have all-or-nothing application (infinite weight)—in that they are the morally best principles that would justify the promulgation of a high percentage of the extant legal rules. They are connected to moral principles in that moral principles determine which set of legal principles among those sets that 'fit' the legal rules is the morally best set of principles. In other words, legal rules govern the 'fit' axis,[42] moral principles govern the

[38] Ibid., at 784–7. [39] 12 *Law and Philosophy* 121 (1993).
[40] Ibid., at 122–3. [41] Ibid., at 127.
[42] In conjunction with other aspects of institutional fact: precedents, legislative history, administrative regulations, actual and proposed, repeals of statutes, and the like.

'acceptability' axis, and the fit and acceptability axes determine the set of weighted principles that are legal principles. These legal principles are the theoretical entities that justify the legal rules, determine how they should be extended and modified, and resolve conflicts among them. Legal principles —the (morally) best (morally) incorrect principles that 'fit'—ultimately determine all legal decisions, even those clearly covered by non-conflicting rules, since the decision to apply the rules rather than overrule or modify them is itself a product of the legal principles.[43]

Dworkin's account of legal principles is, of course, abstract and theoretical. But its force as an account comes from how well it tracks the standard methodologies of legal scholars, advocates, and judges. Anyone who has ever written legal briefs, legal opinions, or scholarly articles at the mid-level of doctrine will be familiar with the following procedure. You have a particular issue that you desire, as an academic or judge or advocate, to resolve. You first collect the cases in the particular area of law. You then cast about for an attractive principle or policy that, if consistently followed, would have generated most of the outcomes in those cases. In other words, you look for a normatively attractive covering theory of the cases. The theory need not be morally correct, since correct moral principles might produce too many outcomes at odds with the existing outcomes in the area. The theory just has to be as morally attractive an incorrect theory as it can be and still account for the outcomes.[44] Moreover, the theory need not account for all outcomes, though the more it accounts for, the better. Some outcomes may be deemed 'mistakes' if the covering theory is otherwise sufficiently morally attractive. The theory just needs to account for most of the outcomes. We will call this methodology the reconstructive theory.[45]

This method is so commonplace that it might be almost invisible to us. It is the dominant methodology in both the practice of law and in legal scholarship.[46] 'The (morally) best (morally) incorrect set of principles that "fit" the legal rules'—legal principles—appear to be the theoretical foundation of legal practice.[47]

[43] See Dworkin, *supra*, n. 9, at 37–8; Kress, *supra*, n. 23, at 394–5.

[44] Brian Leiter has suggested that instead of characterizing legal principles as 'incorrect' moral principles, we should instead characterize them as 'non-ideal' moral principles. (Correspondence with Larry Alexander, 19 Apr. 1993.) Presumably a moral principle is 'non-ideal' if following it is consistent with following ideal moral principles in some (many?) cases. Indeed, one author does characterize Dworkin's legal principles as 'non-ideal'. See David Lyons, *Moral Aspects of Legal Theory: Essays on Law, Justice, and Political Responsibility* (1993), 208.

[45] See Ken Kress, 'Legal Indeterminacy', 77 *Cal. L. Rev.* 283, 299–301 (1989).

[46] See *supra*, § III.A. and *infra* text at nn. 48–66.

[47] Another way of understanding Dworkin's account of legal principles is to view them as counter-factual moral principles. Thus, we might say that legal principles are principles that would be correct moral principles in a world in which most of the extant legal rules and decisions, including those that are morally incorrect, were morally correct. See n. 96 *infra* (penultimate paragraph). Such a counter-factual approach is in fact the best description of the dominant methodology for dealing with precedential constraint, what Alexander has called the

The Dworkinian judicial technique of surveying the past decisions in an area of law and distilling a legal principle from those decisions that is not (necessarily) the stated ground for any of them is so commonplace as to be the standard of orthodoxy. Indeed, a case that exemplifies this use of Dworkinian legal principles, *MacPherson* v. *Buick Motor Company*,[48] and the cases that it draws upon, are the cases selected by such expositors of common law methodology as Melvin Eisenberg, Edward Levi, and Henry Hart and Albert Sacks to illustrate common law legal reasoning.[49]

In *MacPherson*, the defendant had manufactured an automobile that it sold to a retail dealer, who in turn sold it to the plaintiff. The car collapsed while being driven by the plaintiff, injuring him. The cause of its collapse was a defective wheel, which the defendant had purchased from another manufacturer and apparently failed to inspect adequately.

The difficulty in allowing recovery for the plaintiff stemmed from the fact that there was no privity of contract between plaintiff and defendant. The leading case in which the absence of privity was held not to bar recovery, *Thomas* v. *Winchester*,[50] a case involving the sale and resale of a falsely labelled poison, had been taken by subsequent courts to stand for a distinction between items inherently dangerous (such as poison) and items dangerous only if defective, with privity considerations set aside only in cases involving the former. (The opinion in *Thomas* appears explicitly to reject liability in cases like *MacPherson*.)

None the less, Justice Cardozo, writing for the majority of the New York Court of Appeals, held that a manufacturer owes a duty to inspect its goods for defects to anyone who might foreseeably be injured because of such defects regardless of whether privity of contract exists between the manufacturer and the potential victims. Moreover, Cardozo purported to induce that principle from the prior case law, even though the prior cases had never announced so sweeping a principle. Cardozo admitted that some of the earlier cases following *Thomas* did not fit the principle he was announcing

result model of precedent. See Larry Alexander, 'Constrained by Precedent', 63 *S. Cal. L. Rev.* 1, 28–34, 38 (1989). According to the result model, an incorrectly decided precedent case binds the court in a subsequent case to the extent that, relative to the subsequent case, the precedent case is an *a fortiori* case in favor of a particular result, even if in the absence of the precedent neither case should be decided that way. And what makes a precedent case an *a fortiori* case is that, *in a world in which its incorrect decision were correct*, the analogous decision in the subsequent case would also be correct and even more strongly supported. The counter-factual test for employing the result model of precedential constraint is identical to Dworkin's account of legal principles, the principles that would be morally correct in a world in which certain morally incorrect decisions and rules were morally correct. Ibid., at 38–9.

48 217 NY 382, 111 N.E. 1050 (1916).

49 Melvin Aron Eisenberg, *The Nature of the Common Law* (1988), 58–61; Edward H. Levi, *An Introduction to Legal Reasoning* (1948), 7–18; Henry Hart and Albert Sacks, 'The Legal Process' (mimeographed materials published by the *Harvard Law Review*, 1958), 574–7.

50 6 NY 397 (1852).

and that he found implicit in *Thomas*: 'In the application of . . . [the principle of *Thomas* v. *Winchester*] there may, at times, have been uncertainty or even error.'[51] He went on to discuss some of these 'erroneous' decisions, which he pointed out had been criticized by scholars,[52] as well as English cases, such as *Winterbottom* v. *Wright*,[53] that also were inconsistent with the principle of negligence liability for all foreseeable injuries.[54]

Cardozo's method in *MacPherson*—the reconstructive method—fits perfectly Dworkin's account of how legal principles are derived. Cardozo purports to derive his principle from the extant law, not from morality. Moreover, he relies on what was decided in prior cases, not on the announced grounds of those decisions. (In other words, he does not just apply a previously posited canonical rule.) Finally, he is willing to settle for less than perfect fit with those past decisions. In other words, Cardozo's principle is a paradigmatic Dworkinian legal principle because, while Cardozo views it as morally more attractive than the stated grounds for earlier decisions, it is none the less derived from most (but not all) of these decisions and not directly from morality.

Levi asserts that Cardozo's method in *MacPherson* is paradigmatic of common law adjudication. We agree, and will provide one additional illustration. In *Hannah* v. *Peel*,[55] the plaintiff, a British soldier, was staying in the defendant's house, the house having been requisitioned for use by military personnel. While adjusting the black-out curtains, the plaintiff discovered a valuable brooch in the crevice of a window frame. The plaintiff turned the brooch over to the police, who eventually gave it to the defendant. The plaintiff sued for the brooch. The King's Bench held in favour of the plaintiff on the basis of a principle favouring finders of personalty over landowners.

In fashioning its opinion, the King's Bench had to confront a number of troublesome authorities, particularly *South Staffordshire Water Company* v. *Sharman*.[56] In that case, a workman, who had been employed to drain a pool, discovered two gold rings at the pool's bottom. The court held that the rings should go to the landowners notwithstanding their lack of knowledge of the rings. The court's expressed reason for so holding was that possession of land entails possession of what is attached to it. The King's Bench in *Hannah*, however, ignored the court's reason in *Sharman* and instead pointed out that the finder there, unlike plaintiff in *Hannah*, was in the landowner's employ.[57] (*Sharman* itself had 'reinterpreted' an earlier case, *Bridges* v. *Hawkesworth*,[58] in which someone who found banknotes on a shop floor prevailed against the shop's owner.)

Hannah, like *MacPherson*, induced a covering principle for the previous

[51] 217 NY at 385; 111 N.E. at 1051.
[52] 217 NY at 385–6; 111 N.E. at 1051–2.
[53] 10 Meeson and Welsby 109 (1842).
[54] 217 NY at 394; 111 N.E. at 1054.
[55] 1 KB 509 (King's Bench, 1945).
[56] 2 QB 44 (Court of Queen's Bench, 1896).
[57] 1 KB at 517–18.
[58] 21 L.J., N.S., 75 (Court of Queen's Bench, 1851).

cases that had not been announced in any of them and under which some previous cases were 'mistakes'. It thus supports our contention that Dworkin's account of legal principles reflects the dominant legal methodology.[59]

The doctrinal arguments of legal scholars lend further support for this contention. In article after article, treatise after treatise, legal scholars survey a doctrinal field and conclude that the legal materials in that field are best justified as expressions of this or that set of legal principles. Their arguments are not that such principles are moral principles, for they may not be morally ideal, and they owe their very existence to specific human decisions. Nor do their arguments depend upon these principles having been explicitly adopted by courts or legislatures, for frequently no court or legislature has done so. Rather, their arguments for these principles consist of showing that the principles are morally attractive even if not ideal, and that following these principles would have resulted in most of the legal decisions in the field, even if not their actual rationales. We will illustrate this scholarly methodology with two examples.

In 'The Right of Privacy',[60] Brandeis and Warren argue that decisions by courts in a variety of doctrinal areas indicate the emergence of a new legal principle that they label the 'right of privacy' or 'the right to be let alone'.[61] They regarded this principle as highly desirable, given the ever-greater intrusiveness into private life that modern technology had made possible. However, it was not the principle's desirability that led Brandeis and Warren to assert its existence. Rather, the principle existed because it was implicit in numerous judicial decisions.

What is important to note is that the cases that Brandeis and Warren relied upon to establish the general right of privacy did not themselves assert such a general principle. The cases included those protecting artistic and intellectual property, those enforcing contractual and fiduciary relations, and those protecting trade secrets. What Brandeis and Warren say about the first set of cases extends to all the cases they discuss:

> These considerations lead to the conclusion that the protection afforded to thoughts, sentiments, and emotions, expressed through the medium of writing or of the arts, so far as it consists in preventing publication, is merely an instance of the enforcement of the more general right to be left alone.[62]

Brandeis and Warren, like Dworkin's Hercules and the common law courts in *MacPherson* and *Hannah*, thus discovered a principle that, unlike moral principles, arose from decisions in legal cases, but unlike the rules authored

[59] Another case illustrating the reconstructive method is the treatment of *Christensen* v. *Thornby*, 255 N.W. 620 (1934) in *Sherlock* v. *Stillwater Clinic*, 260 N.W. 2d. 169 (1977). For an illuminating discussion of these cases, see Eisenberg, *supra*, n. 49, at 56–8.

[60] Samuel D. Warren and Louis D. Brandeis, 'The Right of Privacy', 4 *Harv. L. Rev.* 193 (1890).

[61] Ibid., at 195, 205. [62] Ibid., at 205.

in those cases, was not itself an intentionally created norm and could extend beyond and revise the rules that were its source.[63] The Brandeis and Warren methodology, which is the dominant model of doctrinal legal scholarship, reflects perfectly Dworkin's reconstructive account of legal principles.

Our final example is a representative passage from *The Law of Torts* by William Prosser and Page Keeton.[64] In discussing the doctrine of 'coming to a nuisance', Prosser and Keeton point out a decision by the Supreme Court of Wisconsin allowing a mink ranch to recover damages from the operation of a pre-existing village dump. The court in that case had stated that 'while coming to the nuisance may properly be entertained while weighing the equities in an abatement action, it is irrelevant in a damage suit'.[65] Prosser and Keeton respond: 'Such a general proposition would seem to be questionable. The result reached in the case can be justified because of other circumstances . . .'.[66]

What is notable about this response is that it invokes neither strictly moral considerations nor posited legal rules. A moral argument against the Supreme Court of Wisconsin's position would not have required 'justifying' the result reached in the case. And there can be no gainsaying the Wisconsin Supreme Court on the question of what legal rule governs Wisconsin with respect to coming to a nuisance in a damage action. To reject the Wisconsin court's rule but accept the materiality of its result requires recourse to a principle that arises from such results rather than from morality standing alone but that is not itself posited by any court or lawmaker. In other words, the kind of principle Prosser and Keeton rely upon fits the reconstructive theory of legal principles: legal principles need not be any legal decision-maker's intended grounds for decision and need not be moral principles; they are influenced by both but not necessarily identical to either.

IV. THE ARGUMENTS AGAINST LEGAL PRINCIPLES

Notwithstanding their dominance in legal practice, the case for the existence of legal principles fails miserably.[67] Our argument focuses on Dworkin's account of legal principles, which we believe to be the most careful account

[63] See Dworkin, *supra*, n. 9, at 119 (discussing Brandeis and Warren's analysis of privacy as an example of the Herculean method); Kress, *supra*, n. 45, at 304.

[64] W. Page Keeton, *et al.*, *Prosser and Keeton on the Law of Torts* (5th edn. 1984).

[65] *Kellogg* v. *Village of Viola*, 67 Wis. 2d 345, 349, 227 N.W. 2d 55, 58 (1975).

[66] *Prosser and Keeton*, *supra*, n. 64, at 635.

[67] See n. 96 *infra* for discussion of whether the case against employing legal principles is a case against their existence. We believe that it is, though we shall have accomplished our goal if we have established, not that legal principles do not exist, but that they should not be employed in legal decision-making.

in the literature. Most other accounts of legal principles share the crucial flaw of Dworkin's, for they are based on the mistaken assumption that there can be norms that are not correct moral norms, that are not posited in canonical form like legal rules, but that arise out of the posited legal rules.[68]

A. Past Arguments Against Dworkin's Legal Principles

1. *The Normative Unattractiveness of Legal Principles*

One of the earliest arguments against legal principles is found in Alexander and Bayles's criticism of *Taking Rights Seriously*.[69] Alexander and Bayles point out that moral principles are morally attractive because they *are* our moral ideals. They are the very standards of moral attractiveness. Moral principles are what ideally should govern our conduct in all instances, both within the legal system and without.[70]

Legal *rules* can be morally attractive because they can be formulated to give better guidance than the moral principles themselves.[71] How moral principles apply to particular cases will frequently be controversial. Having everyone individually determine how the moral principles apply may lead to moral errors, lack of co-ordination, and other ills. Thus, the resulting state of affairs is, in light of the moral principles themselves, morally inferior to the state of affairs emerging from clear, blunt, formal rules. This may be so even if the rules, because of their blunt, formal nature, produce morally incorrect results (in terms of the moral principles) in some particular cases.[72] Indeed, this may be so even if there are better rules available than those actually in place, for there may be higher order rules that authorize the (non-ideal) lower-order rules and which themselves are ideal (or as near ideal as can be agreed upon and morally preferable to anarchy).[73]

Moral principles have the virtue of moral correctness; legal rules have the virtues of being the creations of those with the authority to make law and of giving clear guidance. Legal principles, however, have none of these virtues. They are neither morally correct nor uncontroversial in application. Nor have they been promulgated by authorities whose power to create norms is rule-based, for they are not posited norms.[74] They represent the

[68] Joseph Raz's account avoids this flaw because he accepts as authoritative only posited principles. See Joseph Raz, 'Legal Principles and the Limits of Law', 81 *Yale LJ* 823, 848 (1972). Raz's account, however, runs into the problem regarding whether principles can be enacted. See *supra*, n. 6.

[69] See Alexander and Bayles, *supra*, n. 15, at 271–8.

[70] Ibid., at 277. [71] Ibid., at 272.

[72] See Alexander, *supra*, n. 47, at 48–51; id., *supra*, n. 23, at 432–3; Larry Alexander, 'Pursuing the Good—Indirectly', 95 *Ethics* 315, 317–30 (1985); Larry A. Alexander, 'Modern Equal Protection Theory: A Meta-theoretical Taxonomy and Critique', 42 *Ohio St. LJ* 3, 12–14 (1981).

[73] See Larry Alexander, 'The Constitution as Law', 6 *Const. Comment* 103, 107–9 (1989).

[74] See *supra*, n. 6. Again, legal principles are not just those correct moral principles explicitly recognized as legally controlling in cases, legislation, and constitutions. Such a description of

worst of all worlds.[75] Alexander and Bayles concluded that Dworkin had made out no case for legal principles as appropriate norms.[76]

2. *Legal Principles and the Spurious Claims of Equality and Integrity*

In *Law's Empire* Dworkin continues to press the case for legal principles derived from the axes of fit and moral acceptability, but he buttresses the case for such legal principles by arguments appealing to 'integrity'.[77] Integrity

legal principles as enacted moral principles fails to account for the role legal principles are supposed to play in justifying the bulk of the legal materials, much of which may be morally incorrect. The claim that legal principles are enacted moral principles requires an ontology of legal rules, legally enacted moral principles, and moral principles that have not been legally enacted. This ontology depends upon an unlikely severability of moral principles from each other (so that some but not others can be legally enacted). In most moral theories of which we are aware, however, moral principles are far too interrelated to lend themselves to legal severance.

[75] Alexander has pointed out that because of their 'worst of all worlds' nature, enacted norms that appear to be principles will be interpreted either as correct moral principles (to the extent that is possible—see *supra*, nn. 6 and 74) or as rules. See Alexander, 'Modern Equal Protection Theory', *supra*, n. 72, at 15–16.

Brian Leiter has objected to our 'worst of all worlds' characterization of legal principles as follows: 'Surely [legal principles] . . . have this virtue: they provide some guidance in cases where rules provide none, and they approximate moral correctness in so doing. Approximately morally correct partial guidance in cases where no guidance would be had otherwise strikes me as a virtue in adjudication.' (Correspondence, *supra*, n. 44.) Leiter overlooks a crucial point, however—namely, that in order to know the legal principles and their weights, we must already know the correct moral principles and their weights, or at least know what is morally more ideal than the legal principles (which are constrained by the fit requirement). Correct moral principles govern the axis of moral acceptability which, together with the axis of fit, determines the legal principles. We cannot be guided by legal principles unless we are also guided by moral principles. But why should we be guided by what Leiter calls 'approximately correct moral principles' when we can be guided by fully correct, or at least more nearly correct, moral principles?

The argument above in response to Leiter answers any claim that Dworkin's account of legal principles is compelling as a theory of proper adjudication even if it is not compelling as a theory of law. Each theory of adjudication that requires judges to resort to correct moral principles but not to follow them in deciding cases is at a distinct disadvantage compared to one that requires judges to follow correct moral principles (as an indirect strategy for getting judges to reach morally correct results more often than alternative strategies). See Alexander, *supra*, n. 23, at 434.

We should also point out that arguments for 'mid-level principles' as part of a theory of adjudication—arguments such as those given by Kenneth Henley, *supra*, n. 39, and Cass Sunstein, *supra*, n. 35—are most compelling as arguments for various levels (in terms of abstractness) of *rules*. In other words, they are most compelling as arguments for fairly abstract rules that are incompletely specified and potentially conflicting. When conflicts among these higher-order rules occur and compel refinement, it is not *their* weights (as mid-level *principles*) but the weights of the moral principles from which they are derived that should determine their specification.

[76] Alexander and Bayles, *supra*, n. 15, at 277–8.

[77] Dworkin, *supra*, n. 1, at chs. 6, 7. In *Taking Rights Seriously*, the case for principles was grounded in the duty of political officials to act on the basis of an articulated, consistent justification applying to past, present, and hypothetical governmental actions. Dworkin, *supra*, n. 9, at 162–3.

is Dworkin's name for a particular version of equality, namely, the equality that is manifested by acting in a 'principled' way and applying the same legal principles to X that one has applied to Y. When one determines what are the most morally attractive principles that 'fit' past legal decisions at the threshold level, and then applies those principles in the present, one is treating present litigants in a principled way and maintaining equality between them and past litigants. Dworkin also requires that the principles underlying various aspects of doctrine be consistently applied and fit coherently together into an overall scheme of principles expressing 'a single and comprehensive vision of justice'.[78]

Alexander, in commenting on *Law's Empire*, argues that Dworkin's supports of legal principles by reference to equality is confused.[79] If 'equality' is a value, it is not a free-standing one. Rather, it is theory-dependent. In other words, each moral theory—each set of moral principles—will generate its own conception of equality. And each moral theory will dictate the pursuit of equality through following the theory itself. Thus, there cannot be a coherent reason in terms of the true moral value of equality for ever departing from the requirements of the correct moral theory. The true moral value of equality is internal to the correct moral theory, not a reason to depart from it in favour of morally incorrect legal principles.[80]

3. *The Retroactivity of Legal Principles*

In *Taking Rights Seriously* and thereafter, Dworkin argues that adjudicating by reference to legal principles protects legal rights against retroactive upsets.[81] Legal positivists, who argue that legal rules exhaust the legal norms available in adjudication, must decide cases on grounds other than legal grounds whenever those cases are not covered by legal rules. That, argues

[78] Ken Kress, 'Coherence and Formalism', 16 *Harv. J. L. Pub. Pol'y* 639, 652–3 n. 46 (1993); Dworkin, *supra*, n. 9, at 134.

[79] Alexander, *supra*, n. 23, at 426–31.

[80] Although Dworkin is vague on this point, it appears that integrity serves both as a constraining principle on other moral principles and (ambiguously) as simply one moral principle among equals. In its capacity as just one principle among others, it would presumably be theory-dependent, just as are 'justice' and 'due process'. In its role as a constraining principle on others, it would serve as a test that the other principles must meet. Integrity cannot coherently play both roles.

To meet the criticism in the text of integrity as a theory-independent test of moral principles, Dworkin might concede that integrity is theory-dependent and argue that it is just one of our liberal-egalitarian principles. The problem with such a rejoinder is that it leads to intractable theoretical difficulties through self-reference. Integrity (I) is part of correct moral theory (CMT). I, when coupled with legal decisions that are inconsistent with CMT (morally incorrect legal decisions), requires us to adopt covering principles that are inconsistent with CMT. In other words, I requires us to change the covering moral principles of which it is itself a component. Thus I requires that it itself be changed. I requires ~I. Integrity, therefore, cannot be both theory-dependent *and* a test for selecting the principles that make up moral theories. For a fuller elaboration of Dworkin's conception of Integrity and its difficulties, see *infra*, § IV.E.

[81] See Dworkin, *supra*, n. 9, at 30, 44, 84.

Dworkin, leads to applying new legal rules—those formulated in cases without pre-existing legal rules—to transactions that arise before the legal rules are promulgated, which is akin to legislating retroactively. Legal principles, on the other hand, are already immanent in past decisions, define the legal rights to which those past decisions give rise, and can determine outcomes in cases not governed by legal rules.

Alexander and Bayles, along with others, argue that Dworkin's argument from retroactivity is both confused and question-begging.[82] It is confused because any moral arguments against retroactivity could be accommodated by judges through recourse to correct moral principles whenever the legal rules failed to resolve a case. (In other words, in deciding based on correct moral principles which party should prevail in a lawsuit, the parties' expectations, the extent of their reliance on those expectations, and the countervailing benefits of upsetting their expectations would be among the factors that correct moral principles would dictate be taken into account.)[83] It is question-begging because it assumes that legal rights exist and thus could be retroactively upset in cases not covered by legal rules, a proposition legal positivists would dispute.

Perhaps the most interesting criticism of the argument from retroactivity is a *tu quoque* response by Kress.[84] Kress demonstrates that Dworkin's own theory of adjudication grounded in legal principles results in retroactive application of legal rights.

Kress's argument builds upon the role of authoritative institutional acts, such as constitutions, statutes, and judicial decisions, within Dworkin's theory. Legally authoritative principles and the rights that they describe are, for Dworkin, a function of institutional history and moral-political theory. Outcomes in concrete cases at law are in turn a function of the application and elaboration of legal principles (and rights). Thus, by transitivity, correct outcomes are a function of institutional history (along with moral-political theory). This much is obvious. Differences in constitutional and statutory provisions, precedents, and administrative rulings result in varying legal rights and principles, that is, in different law.

Suppose that, as a consequence of a judicial decision, a change in legal

[82] See Alexander and Bayles, *supra*, n. 15, at 284–5.

[83] Reliance values, like equality, are theory-dependent, that is, internal to whatever moral theory is correct. No set of incorrect decisions, no matter how numerous, can ever give one reason to depart from applying correct moral principles. Incorrect decisions are, of course, part of the furniture of the world to which correct moral principles apply, and they can and certainly do affect how those principles apply (and whether the principles should be directly or indirectly applied). That is, incorrect decisions in the past can alter what are correct outcomes in the present. But incorrect decisions can never alter the principles by which correctness is gauged. See Alexander, *supra*, n. 23, at 430; Alexander and Bayles, *supra*, n. 15, at 272.

[84] See Kress, *supra*, n. 23. The arguments on the following pages are developed in greater detail in Ken Kress, 'Precedent, Coherence and Moral "Mathematics" in Adjudication' (MS in progress).

rights occurs after the facts giving rise to a lawsuit but before the case is adjudicated. With only rare exceptions,[85] the case will be adjudicated on the basis of the legal rights existing at the time of trial (and final adjudication) and not on the basis of the legal rights that existed at the time of the events giving rise to the lawsuit. If one of the legal rights that changes in consequence of the judicial decision is dispositive of the lawsuit, then the litigant who would have won (based upon the law existing at the time of the underlying events) will lose, and the litigant who would have lost will win. This is nothing less than retroactive application of law.

The same result can be established more elegantly by first noticing that, in Dworkin's theory, the legal principles—the morally best principles, T_1, that meet or exceed the threshold of fit—will always be precisely at the minimum threshold of fit. This can be demonstrated by *reductio ad absurdum*. Suppose the legal principles T_1 exceed the threshold of fit. T_1 could then be 'transformed' into a morally more attractive set of principles T_2 by replacing one or more morally unattractive principles p_1 of T_1 that fit the institutional history well with morally more attractive principles p_2 that fit less well, yet still leave T_2 over the threshold of fit. But then T_2 is a better set of principles than T_1 because it is morally better than T_1 yet exceeds the threshold of fit. This contradicts the assumption that T_1 was the morally best set of principles exceeding the threshold of fit. QED.

The same conclusion can be reached by a positive argument. If the alleged set of legal principles exceeds the threshold of fit, we can substitute principles, trading off fit for greater moral appeal until we reach the minimum threshold of fit and maximum moral appeal at that threshold. The set of principles reached at that point are the veridical legal principles.

Some may object that principles are not as abundant, nor as finely discriminable, as the proof requires. Dworkin is estopped from raising that objection. He argues that no Hartian master test for law could distinguish legal from non-legal principles based upon institutional support. *A fortiori*, he claims, no test of institutional support could 'fix [a principle's] weight at a particular order of magnitude'.[86] Besides the *ad hominem* against Dworkin, infinite differentiation of principles may be justified in several ways. Principles' weights may vary along a real-valued continuum. Natural, normative, or legal language may be rich enough to provide subtly differing articulations of principles and their weights. Normative considerations may require infinite discriminability. Mathematical construction may provide it. A metaphysical principle of sufficient reason may establish it. Even if principles were not infinitely divisible, but only finely so, this would only mean that

[85] The main exception is when courts apply law prospectively only, in any of a number of variations. See sources cited in Kress, *supra*, n. 23, at 386 n. 77; Linda Meyer, '"Nothing We Say Matters": *Teague* and New Rules', 61 *U. Chi. L. Rev.* 423 (1994).

[86] Dworkin, *supra*, n. 9, at 40.

the best set of principles may slightly exceed the threshold of fit but need not be precisely equal to it. Under this condition, the results to follow would still be true, although the proofs of them would be less elegant.

That Dworkinian legal principles are always at the threshold of fit entails that principles are continuously changing. Applying these new principles to events arising before the new principles become legally authoritative amounts to retroactive application of law. We shall elaborate upon these claims.

Suppose that the minimum threshold of fit in a given jurisdiction is 80 per cent of judicial decisions. (Ignore, for simplicity, enactments, regulations, judicial hierarchies, and so on. The argument is sound even with these added complications.) Suppose that there have been 100 decisions to date, and that there is only one judge.

We have just seen that Dworkinian legal principles will just meet the threshold. Since the threshold is 80 per cent, Dworkinian legal principles T_1 will fit 80 per cent of the cases. They will explain 80 and fail to explain 20 of the 100 cases.

Now suppose that 100 new decisions arise and the judge correctly applies Dworkinian legal principles T_1 in resolving the cases. T_1 fits 100 of the new cases, since it was followed in deciding them. There are now 200 decisions. T_1 fits 80 of the first 100, and 100 of the second 100. Thus, T_1 fits $180/200 = 90$ per cent of the total decisions. This exceeds the threshold of fit, 80 per cent, so T_1 can no longer be the Dworkinian legal principles by the result just proven since T_1 substantially exceeds the threshold of fit. We can construct a T_2 with 80 per cent fit and morally better principles, by trading off fit for moral appeal until we reach the threshold of fit.

For one or more principles, T_2 differs from T_1. This means that T_2 will decide some cases differently from how T_1 would. Litigants whose cause of action arises when T_1 is the set of legal principles, but whose cases are decided when T_2 is the set of legal principles, will be subject to retroactive application of law whenever the differences between T_1 and T_2 are relevant to their lawsuit. If a changed principle is dispositive, the litigant who would have won loses, and vice versa.

In fact, T_1 will cease to be at the threshold of fit before 100 decisions have been rendered, and the law will therefore change sooner. Principles continuously evolve in Dworkinian legal theory. (This may explain some of the woolly statements in chapter 11 of *Law's Empire* about a law beyond the law, and about the law working itself (morally?) pure.)

Susan Hurley rejects Kress's intervening case argument for retroactivity in Dworkin's theory.[87] Although her exposition is subtle and complicated, the essence of her objection can be conveyed simply.

[87] Susan Hurley, 'Coherence, Hypothetical Cases, and Precedent', 10 *Ox. J. Leg. Stud.* 221 (1990).

Hurley argues, following a suggestion of Dworkin's, that precedent changes the truth value of legal propositions only when judges make mistakes, and never when they make correct decisions.[88] The retroactivity resulting from mistaken judicial decisions is not of substantial, abstract, theoretical import —although it is significant to theories that take consequences into account and to theories that are concerned with human limitations. It is also of no great practical moment. If intervening case retroactivity could be confined to when judges make mistakes, the damage would be limited.

Hurley issues the following 'challenge': 'How, on coherentist assumptions, could the precedential force of a decision . . . change the law itself, as opposed to our *beliefs* about it, if that decision were *ex ante* correct?'[89]

It appears that Hurley has mistaken Kress's intervening-case argument. The intervening-case argument does not suppose that when a judge makes a correct decision, the truth of the proposition decided in that opinion has been changed by the judge. Rather, the position is that when the judge makes a correct decision, the judge may well increase the weight of the principles or propositions supporting that decision (not necessarily their truth value). As a ripple effect of the increase in the weight of those principles or propositions, the decision may change the truth value of some other (logically? theoretically? normatively?) related propositions, resulting in ripple-effect retroactivity for some litigant whose case depends upon those other propositions.

Thus, Hurley is mistaken when she writes: 'suppose the decision was *ex ante* correct and settled [and the judge decides it correctly]. In this case there is change neither in the law nor beliefs about it, so no retroactivity problem can arise.'[90] There may be no change respecting beliefs or the truth of the law respecting the decision, but principles (or policies) supporting the decision may gain weight or strength, thus leading to a change in the law respecting a related proposition.

Hurley, and by Hurley's reporting, Dworkin,[91] have fallen victim to the following fallacy. They have a myopic view of the possibilities for coherentist theories of legal reasoning. Their view of coherence theories of law is too crude, and misses the potential richness of coherentist methodology. They appear to presuppose or believe that within coherentist methodology, all that can be relevant to a proposition of law, either before or after a judge decides it, is its truth value. They forget, what each has noted elsewhere, that propositions of law, or at least the principles which support them, have a dimension of weight,[92] or they have forgotten the significance of this

[88] Ibid., at 228 n. 40. Dworkin made roughly the same suggestion to Kress in informal conversation on 7 Mar. 1985.

[89] Hurley, *supra*, n. 87, at 247.

[90] Ibid., at 249.

[91] Ibid., at 248 and n. 40. See also *supra*, n. 88 (Dworkin's conversation with Kress).

[92] Ibid., at 225, 240, 247; Dworkin, *supra*, n. 9, at 26–7.

dimension for judicial decision-making. When the judge correctly decides a case in which the dispositive issue is P, and the judge so holds, the truth value of P does not change, but its weight or the weight of the principles underlying it does. This increase in weight is what makes possible the change in weight and in truth value of other principles in subsequent cases, which gives rise to dispositive ripple effects and retroactivity.

Hurley's interpretation of precedent is undesirable on independent grounds. It cannot explain how law evolved from a clean slate to its current state. More importantly, what justification can be given for a doctrine of precedent which operates only when judges make mistaken decisions? According to Hurley, Dworkin's claim is that when a judge makes a correct decision, that decision does not change the truth value of the dispositive proposition (or of any other). However, when a judge makes a mistake and holds that P when prior to the decision in fact not-P was true, then the doctrine of precedent will sometimes operate to make P true thereafter. This may be so, for example, when the competition between P and not-P is relatively fierce, with not-P barely edging out P, so that the additional values behind following precedents suffice to give P the edge after the decision. So it appears that, according to Hurley and Dworkin, precedent makes a difference only when judges make mistakes. What could possibly be the underlying moral justification for a doctrine which operates to give people a right to the same incorrect decisions that have previously been made but is ineffective to make any difference when a judge makes a correct decision?[93]

Of course, there might be reasons of notice, efficiency, justified reliance, liberty, practical uncertainty, separation of powers, comparative justice, and the like, supporting a doctrine of precedent which will sometimes take a legally mistaken proposition, say P, and make it correct thereafter in consequence of a mistaken judicial decision supporting it. But such reasons will also have some effect in giving further support to a correct legal proposition P which is so decided by a judge.

We shall provide one further reason why the Hurley doctrine of precedent does not comport with legal practice. Suppose that Q is legally true, but has never been explicitly so decided. According to Hurley, when it is first explicitly decided, that adds no additional force or weight to the principles recommending Q. Nor, presumably, the second time Q is explicitly decided, nor the fifth, nor the hundredth. So let Q be explicitly decided in a hundred decisions. According to Hurley, the best theory of law will be

[93] If Dworkin truly takes this position, it shows that law as integrity diverges from pragmatism (pure natural law) further than readers of *Law's Empire* would have supposed. For an argument that pragmatism is normatively superior to law as integrity, see Ken Kress and Jeremy Waldron, 'Integrity is Our Vulcan' (MS in progress presented at ITT—Chicago Kent College of Law, 6 Apr. 1990); Alexander, *supra*, n. 23, at 432–4; *infra*, § IV.E.

precisely the same after a hundred decisions of Q as it was before Q was even once correctly or explicitly decided. But now let us suppose that three decisions or five or some moderate number come out explicitly rejecting Q. Where there are *one hundred* decisions embedding Q and three or one or a modest number rejecting Q, the best theory of law on a coherentist account will, all other things being equal, be more likely to include Q than it will when there are *no* decisions explicitly deciding Q and one or three or a moderate number proclaiming not-Q. The explicit decision that Q, particularly the repeated explicit decision that Q, has some force in withstanding a small number of incorrect decisions that not-Q. What better way is there to understand this phenomenon within a coherentist framework than that the explicit decisions of Q increase the weight of Q and its underlying principles, and the principles which those principles support and rely on for support? What better way to explain this phenomenon within a coherentist framework than to say that decisions have ripple effects throughout the seamless web? And if this is correct, then Kress's retroactivity argument against Dworkin's coherentist methodology stands.

B. New and Conclusive Arguments Against Legal Principles: The Arguments from Weight and Fit

1. *The Argument from Weight*

Legal principles, as we have said, are not the same as correct moral principles. They are, instead, incorrect moral principles, or just plain incorrect principles. But are there such things?

There are, of course, incorrect *rules*, norms posited by particular people at a particular time and with a particular canonical form and intentional structure that demarcates their extensions. Rules, correct or incorrect, are weightless. They either apply or don't apply, but they cannot be 'weighed'. (Actually, rules are not weightless; rather, they claim to have *infinite* weight where they apply.) Principles, however, are supposed to have (finite) weight. Indeed, weight is essential to their being principles, since they have neither canonical form nor dependence on particular persons' datable intentions to govern their application. Their application is a function of their weight.

An *incorrect* principle, in so far as it is a principle, must, therefore, have weight. How else could we determine in a particular case whether the incorrect principle outweighs competing principles? (If incorrect principles never outweigh competing principles, correct and incorrect, then they can never determine the outcome of any case, since competing principles are always available to govern the case. At a minimum, the entire set of morally correct principles is available.) But what weight will incorrect principles have, and how will such weight be determined? No set of past cases, no matter how large the set, can fix as a matter of logical entailment the weight in the context of a present case of any principle that would explain those past cases, as Quine's indeterminacy thesis demonstrates.

We can, of course, 'assign' a weight to an incorrect principle by deciding a case in accord with it or against it. In doing so we are declaring that the incorrect principle P_1 shall outweigh correct principle P_c in Case C. We are not *discovering* that it is the case, however, for there is nothing to discover. Our declaration that it is the case cannot be correct or incorrect. The weight of P_1 in case C does not determine the outcome in Case C; rather, the outcome in Case C determines the weight of P_1 in Case C.

Suppose one were to argue that we induce the weight in the same way we induce the incorrect principle, by looking at past cases. Assume, for example, that there have been N cases in which plaintiffs named Green have won even though correct principles P_c would have dictated that they lose. Suppose we induce the existence of incorrect principle P_G, 'plaintiffs named Green should be preferred'. Suppose we have a new case with a plaintiff named Green where P_c would dictate that Green lose. Does P_c outweigh P_G or does P_G outweigh P_c? All we know is that P_G outweighed P_c in past cases C_N. This does not tell us whether P_G outweighs P_C in the present case. What other arguments might determine P_G's weight in this case? Arguments about how this case ought (really) to come out? Those arguments will all be based on correct principles P_C. They will dictate that P_G be followed from now on only when it is consistent with P_C, which means P_G has no weight of its own, which means it does not exist. The argument for inducing the weight of incorrect principles mistakenly views the adjudicative enterprise as predictive, while in fact it is normative.

Suppose we do not induce the 'correct' incorrect principle and its weight from past cases. Assume, instead, that we rely on the incorrect principle's *promulgation*. Take freedom of speech, for example. Suppose that there is no independent moral principle of freedom of speech. Rather, the freedom of speech we should endorse is the product of moral principles regarding liberty and anti-paternalism.

Now suppose the constitutional framers declare that 'the principle of freedom of speech shall be recognized'. There is no problem treating this as a *rule* (with infinite weight within the scope of its application), as Justice Black tried (unsuccessfully) to treat the first amendment.[94] But suppose we try to take the framers at their word and treat free speech as a principle, albeit an incorrect one. What weight do we give it when it conflicts with P_c? Not its real weight (for, being incorrect, what would its *real* weight be?). Its promulgation cannot help us here, for unless the framers tell us how it is

[94] See e.g. *Kongisberg* v. *State Bar of California*, 366 U.S. 36, 60–71 (1961) (Black, J., dissenting).

to be applied in each possible case—in which case they have made it into a *rule*—all we know from its promulgation is its promulgation. We do not know *it*. Nor can we. What is *there* to know?[95]

Incorrect principles have a problematic metaphysical status.[96] Our argument

[95] See also *supra*, n. 6 for another version of the argument in this paragraph.

[96] We initially intended to claim that legal principles were strictly analogous to the ether because the case we make against legal principles, like the scientific case against the ether, showed that legal principles did not exist. We have resisted that inclination because it might be misunderstood. Some might think that the case against legal principles is strictly analogous to the scientific case against the ether, perhaps even to the point of claiming that just as the ether has turned out not to exist physically, so legal principles have no similar existence. This, however, is not the claim we intend, because of the normative character of legal principles.

The ether was thought to exist in the realm of fact. The best current explanation of the data regarding the realm of fact is inconsistent with the ether's existence. Legal principles are norms, and in just what sense norms exist, how that existence is established, and how the ontological realm of norms relates to the ontological realm of facts are hotly controverted metaphysical issues. Legal principles exist either in social, Platonic/realist, or Meinongian metaphysical space. They are, after all, believed in and invoked by legal practitioners and academics, and no doubt this belief in and invocation of them influences legal decisions. Indeed, it is because they are so influential in this way that we think it important to make our case against them. Therefore, if belief and invocation of legal principles can establish their metaphysical existence—even though, in the ontological realm of facts, beliefs in and references to the ether (or to unicorns) would not establish *their* metaphysical existence—legal principles exist. (Less problematically, legal actors can hold certain incorrect principles and can act as if these principles have a particular weight *vis-à-vis* other principles the actors hold. The legal principles we are attacking, however, do not exist in the realm of particular legal actors' beliefs; rather, they are supposed to exist independently of any legal actor's holding them and acting upon them.)

Our case against legal principles is primarily a normative case. Legal principles are either normatively unattractive or superfluous. If legal principles dictate outcomes different from what moral principles and legal rules dictate, they are normatively unattractive. If, on the other hand, they dictate the same outcomes that legal rules and moral principles dictate, they are normatively superfluous. If normative unattractiveness or superfluity counts against the metaphysical existence of a norm, then the case we make against legal principles is a case against their existence.

Some additional points should be made regarding the metaphysical status of legal principles. First, legal rules exist and belong to the ontological realm of fact. Their existence consists of their canonical formulation and the possibly complex, combined intentions of the rules' authors that their canonical formulation represents. The ontological status of moral principles is, of course, the stuff of metaphysical debate. We need not and do not here take any stand on the ontological status of moral principles, whether they supervene upon matters of fact, whether they are matters of construction or projection, etc.

Secondly, legal principles cannot unproblematically claim the same ontological status as legal rules. Though legal principles, like legal rules, are formulated by judges and legislators, the formulation and the legal principle are ontologically distinct. The formulation of a legal principle *refers* to it, whereas the formulation of a legal rule *is* the legal rule.

Thirdly, if legal principles exist, then, according to the conventional understanding, they must be potentially infinite in number. Each possible substantive variation in the development of legal rules will produce its own distinctive configuration of legal principles with their distinctive weights.

Fourthly, legal principles have the following metaphysical oddity. They arise not from the realm of fact, and not from the realm of value, but from the combination of fact and value. Unlike the straightforward supervenience on facts that many philosophers claim is the best ontological account of moral values, the supervenience of legal principles is on a combination of facts (legal rules) and moral values. Thus, if moral values are themselves supervenient on is that determining their weight may be like assigning a property to 'the ether'; it cannot be done correctly or incorrectly, since there is nothing in the world that is 'the ether with (or without) the property'.[97]

2. *The Argument from Fit*

If there are legal principles that are morally incorrect principles, then Dworkin's account of them is the best there is. Namely, the incorrect principles (P_1) that exist are those principles that 'fit' above some threshold with past government actions and that are the morally best such principles, 'best' being measured by normative distance to correct principles (P_C). But in fact, $P_1 = P_C$. Dworkin's case for legal principles is nothing more than a case for correct moral principles. Why?

facts, legal principles supervene on facts both directly and indirectly (through moral values). This is a very odd ontology: if moral norms are metaphysically 'queer' (see John Mackie, *Ethics: Inventing Right and Wrong* (1977), 38–42), legal principles are metaphysically superqueer. See Larry Alexander, 'Practical Reason and Statutory Interpretation', 12 *Law and Philosophy* 319, 322, 327 n. 15 (1993).

Finally, as we have explained, the best account of legal principles is that they are counter-factually correct moral principles; that is, they are principles that would be correct moral principles if the world were such that certain legal decisions and rules that are actually morally incorrect were morally correct. Thus, legal principles possess whatever metaphysical reality counter-factual moralities possess.

The discussion in this footnote was prompted by Brian Leiter's and Jeremy Waldron's comments and criticisms on an earlier draft. Correspondence with Ken Kress, *supra*, n. 8; correspondence with Larry Alexander, *supra*, n. 44.

[97] T. R. S. Allan shares our intuitions about incorrect principles. He, too, argues that principles cannot exist without weight, and that Dworkin's legal principles, being morally incorrect, are always outweighed by correct principles: 'It is important to see that the weight of a principle is a function of the relevant facts. It is the nature of a principle to argue in favour of a certain result, but not conclusively: it does not dictate a decision in the manner of a rule, which applies absolutely (subject only to stated or acknowledged exceptions). The weight of a principle can only be determined by the court seised of the particular case and acquainted with the proven facts . . . A rule may be applied, at least in the case of statutes, by a process of definition. Where a set of circumstances fall within the ambit of the rule, as determined by its enacted terms, no further deliberation is normally required: the rule dictates a particular result. It is precisely the function of rules to foreclose such deliberation in advance of particular cases arising for decision. By contrast, a principle makes an appeal directly to reason. It follows that Hercules can only apply a principle he understands and shares and therefore values. Since the weight of a principle inevitably depends on all the circumstances of the case, its application is always a matter of judgment—necessarily personal judgment.

It is hard to see how Hercules could determine the weight of a principle whose results he thought unfortunate, perhaps pernicious. If he applied the principle to the extent he thought truly appropriate—ascertaining its weight—he would inevitably reject it altogether. He could not, then, discriminate between particular cases, distinguishing or following precedents in all their complexity, on the basis of a popular conception of principle he himself rejected. It follows that it makes no sense to attempt to compare principles one accepts with those one rejects, even if the latter are popular. The comparison would by wholly theoretical: it could gain no purchase on the particular facts of concrete cases.' T. R. S. Allan, 'Justice and Fairness in *Law's Empire*', 52 *Cambridge LJ* 64, 69–71 (1993) (footnotes omitted). See also M. J. Detmold, *The Unity of Law and Morality* (1984), 83–93; Alexander, *supra*, n. 23, at 431–2 n. 20.

Suppose there are in the past N cases, C_N, that have not been decided in accord with correct principles P_C. Of all the incorrect principles P_1 that would 'fit' the past cases, there is one principle that 'fits' perfectly and is also morally best. That is the principle that is coextensive with P_C except for cases C_N (where it dictates the results reached in C_N). Let us call this principle $P_C - C_N$.

It is clear that no set of incorrect principles P_1 fits better than $P_C - C_N$, since the latter exhibits 100 per cent fit. Nor is any set morally better, since $P_C - C_N$ will dictate exactly the same results in all future cases and hypothetical cases as P_C. Therefore, Dworkin would have to urge that we decide based on incorrect principle $P_C - C_N$.

Is there anything wrong with this? Well, $P_C - C_N$ is not an *elegant* principle. But why should that disqualify it *normatively*, as opposed to aesthetically, given that it scores highest on both the fit and moral dimensions?

$P_C - C_N$ might be condemned as arbitrary and *ad hoc*. That is true. But if so, *all* incorrect principles are arbitrary and *ad hoc*, constructed to 'justify' mistaken decisions.[98]

Ronald Dworkin argues that a legal system that manifests *ad hoc* principles lacking integrity is unable to generate the associative bonds necessary for legal obligation and moral legitimacy. In Section E below we will address this claim.

$P_C - C_N$ might be condemned as failing to accord persons equal treatment in those future cases that are 'like' cases C_N but in which $P_C - C_N$ will have a 'different' outcome (one in accord with P_C, not C_N). This objection is confused. Equality is in one sense completely dependent on substantive principles;[99] therefore, $P_C - C_N$ generates its own conception of equality. On the other hand, if the point is that true equality, that mandated by P_C, differs from $P_C - C_N$, the point is correct but supports $P_C - C_N$. The litigants in C_N and in $P_C - C_N$ are being treated equally in the sense that our best view of what is just at the time is being applied to each of them. C_N is in the past and cannot be undone. $P_C - C_N$ will produce all the true equality (P_C equality) one can now achieve.[100]

[98] Dworkin sometimes treats his value of 'integrity', reflecting the ideals of community and fraternity, as on a par with other values, such as justice, due process, etc., and sometimes treats it as a value capable of trumping other values. In the latter sense, integrity as the queen of values might urge the rejection of principles that, while more just, are too complex to form the basis of a 'community of principle' relative to simpler though less just principles. We find such a view, resting as it does on the fragmentation of moral theory, to be objectionable. See *supra*, n. 80 and *infra*, § IV.E.

[99] See Peter Westen, 'The Empty Idea of Equality', 95 *Harv. L. Rev.* 537 (1982).

[100] We cannot do better in terms of morally significant equal treatment than to treat everyone in accordance with our current best view of justice. A past injustice creates no reason, not even a very weak one, to commit a present injustice. See Alexander, *supra*, n. 47, at 9–13; id., *supra*, n. 23, at 426–31; *infra*, § IV.E.

Thus, the objections based on inelegance, *ad hoc* principles, and equality all fail to dislodge $P_C - C_N$ as the preferred incorrect principle P_1.

Finally, since the past is past, and since $P_C - C_N$ dictates exactly the same results in the future as P_C does, there is no practical difference between $P_C - C_N$ and P_C. And since $P_C - C_N$ is the incorrect principle—P_1—that we are supposed to choose, $P_1 = P_C$. There are no incorrect principles of any practical (what other?) consequence.

C. A Misleading Analogy: Legal Principles and the Methodology of Reflective Equilibrium

Some might argue that the case for legal principles rests on the case for employing the methodology of reflective equilibrium. In the moral realm, reflective equilibrium is championed as the correct epistemological method for discovering (constructing?) correct moral principles.[101] One moves between one's considered moral judgments regarding particular cases and more general moral principles that would account for such judgments, adjusting the principles and reconsidering particular judgments until the principles and judgments reach an equilibrium state. Could we not say by analogy that legal principles are those principles that are in equilibrium with (most of) the cases?[102]

The answer is no. First, in moral reflective equilibrium, it is considered judgments that we have to bring into reflective equilibrium with our principles (and vice versa). In law, it is authoritative legal acts that must be brought into equilibrium with a theory of justice.

Secondly, and relatedly, in the moral methodology of reflective equilibrium we consider everything that can possibly bear on our judgments (what we know about psychology, sociology, economics, and so forth).[103] In constructing legal principles, however, we are limited to primary legal materials (decisions, statutes, and so forth) and, importantly, cannot consider more than a certain percentage of those materials to be mistaken (the threshold of 'fit'). There is no such limitation on moral reflective equilibrium.[104]

Finally, assume, as its proponents claim, that the method of reflective equilibrium does lead to correct moral principles. If so, the method would also lead to correct moral principles when applied to legal materials. For although those correct moral principles would not necessarily be consistent with any particular percentage of the primary legal materials—the method would presumably lead to dropping *all* morally misguided legal materials

[101] See John Rawls, 'Outline of a Decision Procedure for Ethics', 60 *Phil. Rev.* 177 (1951); John Rawls, *A Theory of Justice* (1971), 14–21 (esp. 19–21), 43–53, 578–82; Norman Daniels, 'Wide Reflective Equilibrium and Theory Acceptance', 76 *J. Phil.* 256 (1979).

[102] See Dworkin, *supra*, n. 9, at 159–66.

[103] See Daniels, *supra*, n. 101.

[104] See Sunstein, *supra*, n. 35, at 778, 781.

and supplanting them with morally correct notions that might have no legal pedigree—those moral principles *would* be consistent with our considered judgments *about* the primary legal materials.

Thus, reflective equilibrium does not support the use of morally incorrect legal principles.

The arguments from weight and fit are two sides of a single coin. For suppose one were to argue that all possible incorrect principles with all possible weights exist in some Platonic way. Then among those incorrect principles with Platonic existence would be an incorrect principle with a weight such that it would always be outweighed by correct moral principles except in those past cases that were decided inconsistently with correct moral principles. Indeed, that incorrect principle would be the morally best incorrect principle we could choose as well as one with total fit: it would be morally best because it is completely consistent with correct moral principles for all future cases, and it has total fit because it coheres with all past cases. But *that* 'incorrect' principle is really identical for all practical purposes to correct moral principles and so is not a counter-example to the claim that incorrect principles do not, for practical purposes, exist in any way that matters. Either legal principles are just (correct) moral principles, or they are nothing.

D. Legal Principles and Agreement Among Competent Practitioners

One final objection to our case against legal principles goes as follows: Legal principles, like legal rules, are established through the practices and conventions of competent professionals. In cases where legal rules do not determine the results, those practices and conventions establish the governing legal principles and their weights. Legal principles and their weights are whatever competent practitioners would agree they were.[105]

We have several responses to this objection. First, the objection implies that when competent practitioners disagree about legal principles and their weights, there are no legal principles about which to agree or disagree. If legal principles and their weights are completely determined by professionals' conventions, then the absence of convention means the absence of legal principle. Professionals could never meaningfully disagree about what the legal principles are.[106]

[105] Owen Fiss, 'Objectivity and Interpretation', 34 *Stan. L. Rev.* 739 (1982); Dworkin, *supra*, n. 1, ch. 3 (discussing conventionalism).

[106] Conventionalist theories not requiring agreement or near agreement have been advocated in recent years. See e.g. Steven J. Burton, *An Introduction to Law and Legal Reasoning* (1985) (law is the coherent reconstruction of the practices and dispositions of the legal community); Coleman, *supra*, n. 21. We have serious doubts that conventionalism can ever dispense with agreement. In any event, against these conventionalist theories, we would urge the

When professionals do agree, however, they could be agreeing about legal principles, as this argument we are constructing has it, or they could be agreeing about moral principles and establishing a higher-order legal rule to govern the case based on those moral principles. How would we tell whether, when professionals agree about a case not determined by legal rules, they are agreeing about legal principles or establishing a higher-order legal rule based on their moral principles? We submit that so long as agreement is what constitutes legal principles and their weights, we will never be able to distinguish legal principles from higher-order legal rules. The argument from convention does not support legal principles.[107]

The argument we have just made against agreement among competent practitioners as establishing legal principles assumes that what practitioners are agreeing about is how particular cases ought to be resolved. At that level, we have argued, legal principles cannot be distinguished from higher-order legal rules. Suppose, however, it is argued that the objects of these agreements are not particular outcomes but are legal principles themselves (and their weights). In other words, what establishes legal principles just *is* agreement among competent practitioners about what those legal principles are.

This position has two variants, neither of which is tenable. On one, the practitioners *posit* the legal principles through their agreement. As we have already noted, however, legal principles cannot be posited.[108]

The alternative is to argue that it is the practitioners' agreement about what the legal principles *are* that establishes them. This alternative, however, involves fatal self-reference. If the agreement establishes legal principles, how can the practitioners agree *about* legal principles?

E. Is There a Moral Argument for Extending Past Decisions Into the Future?[109]

To this point we have argued that Dworkinian legal principles, which correspond to the reconstructive method of common law reasoning, represent an unattractive response to past mistaken decisions.

normative superiority of following correct moral principles rather than conventional legal principles. We do not mean to imply that *moral* principles are not, at some deep level, matters of agreement. See Jurgen Habermas, *Legitimation Crisis* (1973); Rawls, *A Theory of Justice*, *supra*, n. 101, at 11–17. Legal principles that were matters of agreement at *that* level would be identical to (correct) moral principles. Therefore, if legal principles are distinct from correct moral principles, they must be so at a more superficial level; and at that level, disagreement undermines their existence.

107 Dworkin would agree with us on this point. See Dworkin, *supra*, n. 1, at 120–39.

108 See *supra*, n. 6.

109 The material included here in § IV.E. has been developed over years of discussion on these matters between Ken Kress and Professor and Associate Dean Jeremy Waldron, University of California, Berkeley, and in a MS they have in progress (*supra*, n. 93). We are grateful to Professor Waldron for permission to include material from this draft here.

(1) Legal principles produce results different from those which correct moral principles produce.

(2) Legal principles do not have the indirect consequentialist virtues of determinate rules, which, though capable of producing morally incorrect results in particular applications, may produce on balance more morally correct results overall.

(3) Legal principles are not required for treating present and past litigants 'equally'; the correct conception of equality is internal to correct moral theory and can never require departure from that theory.[110]

(4) Legal principles produce retroactivity in the law.[111]

(5) If legal principles differ from correct moral principles, the weight of legal principles will be indeterminate, which means the principles themselves will be indeterminate. Reconstructive methodology cannot yield determinate weight, nor can weight be posited or a matter of agreement.[112]

(6) The method by which legal principles are derived requires fit. Fit is neither sufficient by itself to yield legal principles (because an indefinite number of different principles can fit any set of legal materials, no matter how extensive), nor is fit capable of constraining its necessary complement of moral acceptability. The best incorrect principles that fit past mistakes are morally correct principles with exceptions corresponding precisely to those mistakes. Such incorrect principles will be the practical equivalents of correct principles. Legal principles correctly derived will thus always collapse into moral principles.[113]

(7) Legal methodology requires only posited legal materials and correct moral principles. In Dworkin's terms, it requires 'pragmatism',[114] though a pragmatism that shows a proper regard for the rule-of-law values of conventions.[115] Legal principles will be either otiose (if they behave no differently from correct moral principles) or morally pernicious.

One consequence of our argument is that there is no reason to extend past morally incorrect decisions into the future by departing from correct moral principles. That is not to say that past morally incorrect decisions leave no traces, such as rules, reliance, and so forth. It is rather to say that morally correct decisions in the present will take proper account of the traces of past incorrect decisions.

The case for legal principles requires, therefore, an argument for *abandoning* correct moral principles in the present when they conflict with legal principles, not merely an argument that correct moral principles heed the past and its traces. We shall assume, contrary to points (5) and (6) above, that legal principles can be derived that have determinate weight and yet do

[110] See *supra*, text at n. 99. [111] See *supra*, § IV.A.3. [112] See *supra*, § IV.B.1.
[113] See *supra*, § IV.B.2. [114] See Dworkin, *supra*, n. 1, at 147–53.
[115] See Alexander, *supra*, n. 23, at 432–4.

not collapse into correct moral principles. What is the argument *for* them, given the powerful arguments against them?

In this section we will explicate and respond to the most powerful argument of this kind we know of: Dworkin's claim in *Law's Empire* that we must follow the past in the sense that our current governmental acts must manifest integrity.

Before we describe and criticize in detail Dworkin's argument that integrity is necessary for the associational bonds required for obligation and legitimacy, we wish to remark briefly on some connotations and implications of the term 'integrity'.

Dworkin obtains a patina of legitimacy by calling his theory 'law as integrity', yet his opponents' 'pragmatism' and 'conventionalism'.[116] He also receives an unfair rhetorical advantage from illegitimately extending the analogy of integrity as a personal virtue to integrity as an institutional virtue. That is to say, integrity is a virtue in a person who acts consistently according to some set of principles.

Yet for Dworkin, integrity as an *institutional virtue* does not entail that the government act on the basis of consistent principles or motivations. Rather, integrity is a virtue of institutions in so far as the *interpreter* can imaginatively reconstruct or interpret the institutional history to reflect a set of principles, even if the governmental actors whose acts constitute the institutional practices acted from very different principles or motivations. Thus it may be that one governmental actor acted on the basis of right-wing motivations, another on the basis of moderate motivations, and a third from left-wing motivations. Nevertheless, all three acts can be said to display integrity if the interpreter can reinterpret those three acts as all flowing from a consistent set of principles which fit the acts reasonably well. This concern might be thought exaggerated, because one aspect of fit is fitting the justifications given by the governmental actors. But while that is one aspect of fit, it need not be the most important, and it appears that for Dworkin it is not a crucial or necessary aspect of fit.

In the personal realm, in contrast, an actor would not be said to be displaying integrity if his acts were motivated by very different sets of principles, even if they could be reconstructed so as to be seen to flow from a single set of principles. Thus, Dworkin obtains an unfair rhetorical advantage by the use of the term 'integrity' when he transfers it from the personal to the institutional realm.

More importantly, 'integrity' in its ordinary usage requires a natural law interpretation of pragmatism. We shall establish this claim in four stages.

First, integrity as a personal virtue surely requires—with a caveat to be discussed later—consistency in its underlying justifications. We would not

[116] See Dworkin, *supra*, n. 1, at 114–17.

call someone a person of integrity if some of her acts were based upon one set of principles and others were built upon inconsistent principles and still others were performed without justification at all (if that is possible). Moreover, the term 'integrity' can only be applied to actors whose justifications, rationales, or motivations are intelligible to us.[117] Thirdly, it appears that integrity requires not only consistent application of some set of principles but also that the set of principles is within some range of principles that are thought plausible. If the principles are thought silly, or worse yet incoherent, we would not call a person who follows them a person of integrity.

Finally, and most controversially, yet most importantly, a person who acts on the basis of one set of justifications while agreeing that a better justificatory scheme is available does not display integrity. Integrity demands not only action consistent with a set of principles, but also action based on the set of principles which one believes to be best. So, for example, an individual who has consistently followed principles of nepotism and becomes convinced that equal opportunity is preferable would lack integrity if he continued to follow nepotistic principles. Suppose he were to say: 'You have now convinced me that equal opportunity is morally preferable to nepotism. Yet, I am a person of integrity. In order to maintain my integrity, I will continue to act on nepotistic justifications, even though I now agree that equality of opportunity is superior as a matter of morality and justice.' Surely such a person lacks integrity. Integrity requires that one act on the basis of the principles which one believes to be best. Put differently, integrity entails natural law, that one act on correct moral principles.

We now return to the fine detail of Dworkin's argument. By integrity, Dworkin means at least:

> (a) the principles which underlie the official acts must be coherent individually, they must be intelligible, and they must have been consistently applied;
>
> (b) the principles as a whole must be consistently applied, with applicable principles applying similar weight to relevantly similar situations; and
>
> (c) the principles as a whole must fit together into a single and comprehensive vision of justice.[118]

Moreover, the reason for each of (a)–(c) is the same: 'Consistency in principle . . . requires that the various standards governing the state's use of coercion against its citizens be consistent in the sense that they express a single and comprehensive vision of justice.'[119]

[117] This notion of intelligibility is context sensitive.

[118] Dworkin, *supra*, n. 1, at 88, 116–17, 134, 166; Kress, *supra*, n. 78, at 653 and nn. 45, 46.

[119] Dworkin, *supra*, n. 1, at 134. Dworkin's phrase 'single and comprehensive vision of justice' is puzzling. If all government officials always acted on the *same single* vision of justice, there would be no need for the virtue of integrity.

What account does Dworkin give of the point of integrity? Why is integrity a political virtue, to be ranked alongside such other undoubted virtues as substantive justice, political fairness, and procedural due process?

Dworkin provides two or more (depending how you count) answers to this question, which we shall examine. First, though, we should look at what he says about the general *form* such an answer is likely to take.

In chapter 3 of *Law's Empire*, Dworkin suggests that many (though not all) jurists will agree on the following rather abstract account of the point or function of *law* in the political life of a community. The point concerns the legitimacy of governmental coercion:

> Governments have goals: they aim to make the nations they govern prosperous or powerful or religious or eminent; they also aim to remain in power. They use the collective force they monopolize to these and other ends. Our discussions about law by and large assume, we suggest, that the most abstract and fundamental point of legal practice is to constrain the power of government in the following way. Law insists that force not be used or withheld, no matter how useful that would be to ends in view, no matter how beneficial and noble those ends, except as licensed or required by individual rights and responsibilities flowing from past political decisions about when collective force is justified.[120]

That according to Dworkin is the *concept* of law or legality: 'The law of a community . . . is the scheme of rights and responsibilities that meet that complex standard: they license coercion because they flow from past decisions of the right sort. They are therefore "legal" rights and responsibilities.'[121]

But a particular theory or, as Dworkin terms it, a particular *conception* of law needs to be more detailed than this. It needs to say in detail what the point is of this constraint on the use of governmental coercion. It needs to clarify this metaphor of 'flowing from'. Exactly what relation is to hold between the governmental act whose legitimacy is in question and the set of 'past political decisions' to which we are looking back? And, of course, it needs to indicate, again in detail, which past acts in the history of the community are members of the set from which the act presently under consideration must be shown to flow.

It looks, then, as though we will find our defence or justification of the virtue of integrity in the first of these questions. What is the point of insisting that present political decisions must 'flow from' political decisions rendered in the past?

Notice several things about this question. First, it is a complex question. What is at stake is not the justifiability of coercion *simpliciter*; rather, what is at stake is the justifiability of placing a certain constraint on the justification of coercion. Some critics reading *Law's Empire* too quickly have taken Dworkin to suggest that the point of integrity is to justify governmental

[120] Ibid., at 93. [121] Ibid.

coercion. But on Dworkin's account (at least in this passage), the basic justification for any governmental act comes from the aims and goals to which it is oriented—for example, the aim of making the society more prosperous, more civilized, or more just. These aims are the sorts of reasons why governmental coercion is undertaken in the first place, and they have little or nothing to do with integrity. The idea of integrity operates to constrain the exercise of political power even when it is undertaken for the sake of these worthy ends. It says to the government official: 'We know you have a very good reason, of economic policy or social justice, for the action you are about to undertake. But the existence of that reason, by itself, is not enough to legitimate the use of power that you are contemplating. You must *also* show that the action you are contemplating flows from or coheres with other actions that have been taken in the name of the community in the past. Otherwise your use of force, for all its worthy motivation, must be condemned as illegitimate.' The point of integrity is the point of insisting on that. By contrast, the position Dworkin denominates 'pragmatism', and which we shall interpret here in a natural law version, would not constrain worthy acts simply because they do not cohere with the past.[122]

There is, however, an interesting ambiguity in Dworkin's formulation of the position. As we read it, it has the form of a necessary condition on the justifiability of coercion:

> (I) a coercive act, A, by government is justified *only if* A flows from the relevant set, S, of past political decisions.

This, as we argued earlier, is compatible with A's being justified substantively by some consideration of justice or policy, P, which is formulated in the first instance quite independently of S. All the necessary condition requires is that A must also flow from S. For example, if 'A flows from S' is read as 'the principle, P, justifying A is not inconsistent with the set of principles justifying the members of S', then A may be said to flow from S even though P is not a member of that set of principles.

We might, however, read 'flows from' in a more restrictive way. 'A flows from S' might mean that either A or the principle adduced to justify A must be *entailed by* the set of principles justifying the members of S. On that reading of 'flows from', A cannot have an independent justification in the way we imagined above. For the effect of (I) would now be to state, as a necessary condition on the justification of A, that A's justification be in or follow from a certain given set of justifications (namely, the justifications already underlying S).

Of course, we have not yet discussed what logical relation 'flows from' is supposed to capture. But already we have divided the possibilities into

[122] Natural law would, of course, take into account present traces of the past, including posited rules.

two classes. In the class of looser readings of 'flows from', we will say that A flows from S just in case A is not repugnant to or inconsistent with or precluded by S. The distinguishing feature of these looser readings is that A may be quite *new* in itself or in its justifications so far as the members of S are concerned. In the class of tighter readings of 'flows from', A will not be said to flow from S unless there is some relation like entailment between S (or its underlying principles) and A. In that sense, A cannot be entirely new. When Dworkin uses the phrase 'licensed or required by' as a gloss on 'flows from', it is clear that he is trying to keep his options open as between a looser and a tighter reading of coherence.

S, we know, is a set of political decisions reaching back in time. It is clear that at least some of the members of S must have had justifications that were formulated and found compelling on grounds other than integrity. Consider the earliest member of S. The justification for that decision could not have been that it flowed from S in the tighter sense of 'flowed from' that we have identified. The earliest decision must have been undertaken because it seemed desirable or just on some independent ground. Only when such an independent justification has been posited can a tight relation between S and its putative members arise. Of course, trivially, once the earliest decision is established as a member of S, then S entails that decision. Timelessly, that decision can be said to flow from the set of decisions of which it is the earliest member. But justification is a practical matter, and it is therefore time-sensitive. If (I) is read as a constraint on justification at the time a decision to perform or not to perform A is being contemplated, then it cannot have been read in the tighter sense with regard to all of the political acts of the community.

So much can be established *a priori*. In addition, we know that real live communities will take new political initiatives from time to time. Some of those initiatives will be thought of as new in the sense that the principles underlying them have never been appealed to before. For example, a community whose government has oriented itself in Lockian fashion to the preservation of life, liberty, and property may suddenly decide to develop programmes to foster the performing arts; or its government may decide to offer its services as a mediator or peace-keeper in international disputes. A principle of integrity would be quite unattractive, we think, if it operated to preclude all such political initiatives, or if it insisted that the government must always engage in the intellectual contortions necessary to establish *some line* between the new set of justifications and justifications that have been appealed to in the past.

This brings us to an extremely interesting point. In recent Anglo-American jurisprudence, most discussions of the nature of law have tended to focus on courts and on the reasoning processes followed by judges. Questions about right answers, discretion, fit, coherence, and precedent are all understood primarily in terms of how judges (particularly in appellate courts) should dispose of the legal issues that come before them. But in his account of the concept of law, Dworkin interprets (I) as a constraint on the justification of *all* governmental acts involving coercion, not merely the decisions of judges. That indicates that (I) is a constraint on legislators, too, and Dworkin recognizes that.

However, in his subsequent exposition, Dworkin suggests that (I) as it applies to legislators will differ somewhat from (I) as it applies to judges:

> It will be useful to divide the claims of integrity into two more practical principles. The first is the principle of integrity in legislation, which asks those who create law by legislation to keep that law coherent in principle. The second is the principle of integrity in adjudication: it asks those responsible for deciding what law is to see and enforce it as coherent in that way.[123]

One way of interpreting this distinction is to say that legislators are bound only by one of the looser understandings of coherence that we mentioned above, whereas the constraint of coherence that applies to judges is tighter. For a legislator, it is enough that his new bill does not disrupt whatever coherence there is among existing political decisions. A judge's decision, by contrast, is constrained by the requirement that it must, in some sense, follow from or be entailed by the set of existing decisions (made by earlier judges *and* by legislators). This interpretation is attractive since it provides room in a theory of law-as-integrity for new initiatives; however, these initiatives will come from the legislature, not the courts. The courts may occasionally say new and striking things, of course; but when they do, they must on this account go to some pains to show how their new principles follow from the set of principles they take to have been already accepted. Moreover, although this ability to accommodate new initiatives is an advantage, it does not justify the distinction between legislators and judges. The point about new initiatives provides an argument that at least *some* officials should be governed by a loose rather than a tight conception of coherence. But if so, why not apply the loose conception to *all* officials? So far there is no case for constraining some officials (such as judges) with a stricter conception of integrity than others.

Unfortunately, Dworkin never produces such an argument in *Law's Empire*. He says that judges are 'those responsible for deciding what the law is'.[124] But 'what the law is' is itself the phrase whose meaning is in question. A is part of 'what the law is' if A flows from set S of previous political decisions. Since there the issue between looser and tighter conceptions of 'flows from' is still outstanding, this particular description of the role of judges does not argue in favour of their being bound by a tighter rather than a

[123] Dworkin, *supra*, n. 1, at 167. [124] Ibid.

looser conception of integrity. Alternatively, even if Dworkin's account of judicial role does constrain judges with a stricter conception of coherence, he must still defend this account of the judicial role. Why say that the judge's role is to decide what the law is, in this sense? Why not say that the judge (as much as the legislator) has a duty to decide what the law is to be, bound only by the looser requirement of coherence with past decisions?

These questions are not self-answering. We must remember once again that the pragmatist is stalking Dworkin's theory every inch of the way. At every turn the pragmatist wants to ask: 'Why is the judge constrained from making the decision that best conduces to substantive justice?' The pragmatist thinks we should abandon integrity altogether (except to the extent that some of the requirements of integrity are generated by principles of justice). But he will also think that if we *must have* integrity as a *distinct* political virtue, we should have the weakest version of it possible. That way, at the margin, we enhance the chances of substantive justice actually being done. The challenge of the pragmatist is the pressure we respond to when we scour *Law's Empire* for defences of the particular conception of integrity that Dworkin favours.

The argument for integrity, as a distinct political virtue, is presented mainly in chapter 6 of the book. In setting the 'Agenda' for that chapter, Dworkin insists that it is integrity-for-legislators that he will be defending: 'Our main concern is with the adjudicative principle, but not yet . . . If the legislative principle of integrity is impressive . . . then the case for the adjudicative principle, and for the conception of law it supports, will already be well begun.'[125] That looks like a promise that, in the later chapters, he will produce an argument that takes us from the looser principle of integrity-for-legislators to a tighter principle of integrity-for-judges. But he never makes good on that promise. The claim about judges is restated several times but never defended.[126] In one passage, Dworkin does defend the view that judges are bound by integrity in some of the cases where legislators are not—cases where legislators are free to make decisions on grounds of policy as opposed to principle.[127] But he never defends the view that judges are bound by a duty of integrity that is tighter than the duty that binds legislators in those cases where legislators *are* bound by integrity.

In chapter 6 of *Law's Empire* Dworkin intimates a number of arguments in favour of integrity, including arguments for restraining legislators from passing bills that will introduce incoherence into the law, either in their own terms or in their coexistence with existing statutes and precedents. The arguments that he mentions are the following:

[125] Ibid., at 176. [126] See e.g. ibid., at 217, 225–6, 243.

[127] Ibid., at 244. That distinction remains terribly elusive in *Law's Empire*, and the defence of it in the passage we are referring to is not much more than an announcement that Hercules will think it matters.

(*a*) *The Community Argument*: '[A] political society that accepts integrity as a political virtue becomes a special form of community, special in a way that promotes its moral authority to assume and deploy a monopoly of coercive force.'[128]

(*b*) *The Anti-Corruption Argument*: 'Integrity provides protection against partiality or deceit or other forms of official corruption . . . There is more room for favoritism or vindictiveness in a system that permits manufacturers of automobiles and of washing machines to be governed by different and contradictory principles of liability.'[129]

(*c*) *The Organic Change Argument*: 'If people accept that they are governed not only by explicit rules laid down in past political decisions but by whatever other standards flow from the principles these decisions assume, then the set of recognized public standards can expand and contract organically, as people become more sophisticated in sensing and exploring what these principles require in new circumstances, without the need for detailed legislation or adjudication on each possible point of conflict.'[130]

(*d*) *The Self-Legislation Argument*: '[M]any of our political attitudes, collected in our instinct of group responsibility, assume that we are in some sense the authors of the political decisions made by our governors, or at least that we have reason to think of ourselves that way. Kant and Rousseau based their conceptions of freedom on this ideal of self-legislation. The ideal needs integrity, however, for a citizen cannot treat himself as the author of a collection of laws that are inconsistent in principle, nor can he see that collection as sponsored by any Rousseauian general will.'[131]

Of these arguments, (*a*) is the one that Dworkin develops most fully. Notice that (*a*) is not simply a reassertion of the *concept* of law that we discussed earlier: the principle that force must not be used by the government except in a way that coheres with past political decisions.[132] Argument (*a*) is a *defence* of that principle. The argument is that a requirement of coherence with past political decisions helps to forge us into a special sort of *community*. Such a community gives us a particular sense of *belonging*, and a particular sense of what Dworkin calls 'associative obligation'. He argues that the sense of obligation that flows from this communal belonging is the basis of our recognition that the community has moral authority over us. When the government exercises its power, then, we need not view it as brute force by an organization that just happens to dominate this territory. We connect the exercise of governmental power with our sense of belonging together, and this provides a better basis for the legitimation of that power than any of the traditional accounts of legitimacy and obligation that political theorists traditionally provide.

128 Ibid., at 188. 129 Ibid. 130 Ibid. 131 Ibid., at 189. 132 Ibid., at 93.

Community, then, is the crucial term in the argument. Dworkin is in effect undertaking to demonstrate that there is a sense of community that satisfies the two following conditions:

(i) its political decision-making is characterized by integrity; and

(ii) it generates a sense of belonging that provides a basis for political obligation and political legitimacy.

Of course, he will need to establish that (ii) is true in virtue of (i). Moreover, he will need to show that (i) is necessary for (ii). If there are forms of community that satisfy (ii) but not (i), this first argument of Dworkin's will have failed.

It will not be enough for him to show the converse, namely, that there is no form of community that satisfies (i) and not (ii). To show that is to show merely that integrity is sufficient for obligation and legitimacy. If it is sufficient but not necessary, then integrity will have been shown to be at most a good thing, but not something which is necessary or a duty. In particular, showing that integrity is merely a sufficient condition will not save Dworkin's argument if his opponent can show that a society that pursues only justice (and not integrity as a distinct virtue) can generate the requisite sense of belonging. And once again, the opponent we have in mind is the pragmatist.[133]

Let us examine, then, the steps in Dworkin's argument. In outline the argument goes like this:

(1) A political system is legitimate (in its use of coercive force) only if it is capable of generating political obligation.

(2) Traditional accounts of the features that a political system must have if it is to generate obligations do not work.

(3) The account that comes closest to working is the argument from fair play: if a person has [accepted?] received the benefits of some organization or scheme, he has an obligation to bear the burdens of it as well.

(4) But the argument from fair play works only if there is an associative background to the receipt of benefits and the requirement to bear the burdens. In other words, political obligation must be shown to be an instance of associative obligation.

(5) Associative obligations arising out of a given association must have (and be known by the members to have) each of the following four characteristics:

(i) they must be special (to those who are in the association) rather than applying to everyone whether he/she is a member of the association or not;

[133] Although Dworkin only says law as integrity is more legitimate than pragmatism, the above argument shows that his position requires that law as integrity is necessary for legitimacy.

(ii) they must be personal, that is, owed to the other members of the association as individuals rather than to the association itself;

(iii) each particular obligation must be thought of as flowing from an underlying and pervasive concern for the other members; and

(iv) they must be predicated not only on concern for the other members, but on equal and reciprocal concern.

(6) Now, a person's political obligations must include obligations laid down in explicit rules of law. But in order to satisfy condition (iii) above, the person's obligations cannot be thought of as exhausted by the explicit rules. People must think of themselves as having whatever obligations and rights can be shown to flow from the values of equal concern that underlie the explicit rules.

(7) People can infer such inexplicit obligations and rights from the values underlying the explicit rules only if the explicit rules are coherent.

(8) *Therefore*, tracing the line of necessary conditions all the way back through steps (7) to (1), a political system can have legitimacy only if its explicit rules are coherent.

As it stands, the argument from (1) to (8) is vulnerable at a number of points. Steps (3) and (4) assume that if the argument of fair play cannot be modified to explain political obligation, then nothing can explain political obligation. But there may be other arguments for political obligation that Dworkin has not considered. Or his arguments for step (2)—that is, his objections to the traditional defences of political obligation—may be unsound. He rather summarily rejects the duty to uphold just institutions and the traditional argument from fair play.

But we want to assume, for the sake of argument, that steps (1) through (5) are acceptable. What interests us is the argument from (5) to (8), that is, the argument to integrity from the conditions of associative obligation.

The condition that seems particularly germane to Dworkin's argument is condition (iii). We can undermine this argument by considering a form of community that exhibits condition (iii) but does not satisfy any requirement of coherence or integrity.

Suppose there is a community, some of whose laws are unjust. Several of the unjust laws are unjust for the same reason. For example, the statute governing employment in state agencies and the statute governing employment practices in large corporations both permit and encourage nepotism. A particular piece of legislation is passed repealing one (but only one) of these unjust laws: the law governing employment in public agencies is repealed to prohibit nepotism and allow equal opportunity. The new law is more just than the old one, but its promoters have been unable to secure sufficient political support to make consonant changes in the legislation governing private employment. Therefore, the effect of their action is what

Dworkin calls a 'checkerboard': nepotism is permitted and encouraged in private industry and prohibited and condemned in the public sector, and there is no distinction of principle between these contexts with respect to nepotism. As a result of this legislation, the integrity of the law relating to employment has been diminished.[134]

Has this diminished the ability of the citizens to regard themselves as belonging together in bonds of associative obligation? We shall assume that all the citizens understand the substantive arguments in favour of the new law, even though some of them are opposed to it.

Suppose now that several citizens in this society are debating with one another about some matter on which the explicit law is silent. There is an agency to distribute money to the arts, but the law does not lay down any criteria for such distribution, leaving it to the discretion of some official. The citizens are debating whether or not this official should be allowed to favour artists she knows as friends, or artists to whom she is related, in distributing the funds at her disposal.

By condition (iii), in step (5), it is important that these citizens be able to appeal to the deep principles that underlie the explicit laws of their community in resolving this issue. They must be able to say: 'We care for one another in a certain way in this community, and here is what that caring requires so far as the distribution of arts funding is concerned.' In order to do that, there must be some coherent conception of caring, underlying their law, to which they can appeal.

Under the old legislation they would be able to say: 'Our employment practices embody traditional values of nepotism. That is the sort of community we are. And that mode of equal concern generates the conclusion that the arts official ought to be allowed, nay, even encouraged, to distribute arts funds to her friends and family.' But they cannot say that now, because the employment legislation of their community is ambivalent on nepotism: some statues favour it, and some prohibit it. So they will be at a loss as to what to say. It looks as though the new law, leading as it does to a checkerboard situation, makes this sort of discussion among citizens more difficult. It makes it more difficult for them to infer implicit rights and obligations out of the principles and concerns underlying existing law. That is the move Dworkin wants us to make.

But it goes too quickly. Those who approve of the new legislation can say at least this: 'Though the new legislation only explicitly affects public-sector

[134] Readers who would deny that the integrity of the law relating to employment has been diminished because the government must act impartially, while private citizens need not, may change the example so that the new legislation creates equal opportunity only in the private sector, or choose their own example. If Dworkin claims that any change in the law can, by sufficiently imaginative reconstruction, be seen as coherent, then the constraint of coherence is empty.

employment (not private-sector employment and not public-sector grants), it is itself based on a new and improved conception of the concern we owe to each other in this community. We can use *that* conception to address our problem (about funding for the arts). Since our new law is based on a good conception of equal concern, and since that conception prohibits nepotism or anything like it, we can argue that the arts official should eschew any special favour for her family and friends.' That is a perfectly possible line for a supporter of the new legislation to take in arguing about the implicit obligations of the arts official.

So even though the new statute destroys the coherence (in terms of underlying principles) of existing employment law, it brings with itself a new set of coherent principles of equal concern that citizens can appeal to in debating their implicit rights and obligations. Condition (iii) is satisfied even though the requirement to maintain the integrity of existing law is not. Not only that, but there is no loss at all respecting condition (iii): we have not traded anything off here. Citizens can debate their implicit obligations as easily on the basis of the principles underlying the new law as they could debate them under the principles underlying the old, even though the conjunction of the former and the latter is radically incoherent.

These ideas demonstrate weakness in Dworkin's view of adjudication as well. Suppose a judge is deciding the arts funding question *before* the new legislation affecting public-sector employment has been passed. Suppose the judge believes (rightly) that nepotism is unjust. Then it seems to us that he should simply condemn the nepotism of the arts official, without any consideration of the gravitational force of the nepotistic principles underlying current employment legislation. Those principles, he will say, are repugnant to justice. The just thing to do is to require the arts official simply to eschew nepotism in her decision-making. The judge's decision to this effect is not capricious: it serves justice. Although that decision and its justification do not fit well with existing law, they do flow from the conception of justice to which the judge is appealing, and that conception will of course be internally coherent.

Someone may object that all this is a bit tough on those who disapproved of the new legislation. Are *they* required to use the conception of equal concern underlying laws they disapprove in order to infer their associated rights and responsibilities? Two answers are possible. They can appeal to the principles underlying the old legislation if they like when they debate with their fellow citizens about implicit rights and obligations; but they will meet with the response, 'that is not the conception of equal concern that we have around here any more'. The other answer concedes their difficulty but insists that *on any account* (Dworkin's as well as ours) of the nature of a pluralistic society, some people may find themselves out of sympathy with the current conception of equal concern taken to underlie the laws. That is inevitable and perhaps distressing, but it is not an objection to our account in particular.

The objection, however, may be used as a basis for reformulating Dworkin's argument. There is a phrase he uses in the elaboration of his case that suggests that we owe a deeper respect to those whose conception of justice is repudiated when new legislation is introduced. According to Dworkin, the idea of community 'commands that no one be left out, that we are all in politics together for better or worse, that no one may be sacrificed, like wounded left on the battlefield, to the crusade for justice overall'.[135] This suggests a different argument for integrity, one based on the respect that those who hold any given conception of justice (or equal concern) owe to those in the community who hold an opposing view. We have assumed that the new conception of justice is the better one, and that it has won the day, at least so far as public-sector employment is concerned. The defenders of nepotism have lost that particular battle. The question now is: how should the winners in this battle treat the losers? Should the losers be 'sacrificed, like wounded left on the battlefield, to the [winners'] crusade for justice'? Or should the winners pause in their crusade and pay their respects to those whose (wrong-headed) views they have defeated?

An argument for coherence, based on the respect that winners owe losers 'in the crusade for justice', might go as follows:

(9) There are different views about justice in any community. Some political decisions in the history of the community will have been made on the basis of one view; some will have been made on the basis of another.

(10) Any given political act will be based on a view of justice held by the faction who happen to have political power with respect to that decision at the time it is made. (Call these 'the winners'.) It will be opposed by a faction who lack the political power to defeat it. (Call these 'the losers'.)

(11) Though the losers have lost this particular battle, there are likely to be earlier decisions with respect to which *they* were the winners, earlier decisions in which *their* view of justice prevailed.

(12) If there are associative obligations in the community, they must (among other things) bind the winners and the losers together in ties of mutual respect.

(13) Mutual respect requires that the winners not treat the losers as though their views were of no consequence.

(14) If the winners appeal only to the conception of justice underlying their own political acts (for the purpose of inferring implicit obligations, and so forth), then they are treating the losers as though their views were of no consequence.

(15) Thus, for the purpose of inferring implicit obligations and so forth,

[135] Dworkin, *supra*, n. 1, at 213.

the winners must appeal to a conception of justice that pays attention to the views of the losers.

(16) But the conception of justice that is appealed to for this purpose must be a coherent conception, otherwise it cannot do the work specified in condition (iii) in step (5) of the argument.

(17) Therefore, the winners must take care not to make their decisions in a way that precludes the possibility of a coherent conception of justice that pays respect to the views of the losers.

(18) Therefore, the winners must make their decisions in a way that preserves an underlying coherence of principle between their acts and whatever political acts of the losers there are outstanding in the history of the community.

What shall we say about this argument? It seems to make a better case for integrity because it argues directly for the spirit of moderation and deference to precedents that integrity appears to involve.

However, a preliminary objection is that, as it stands, step (17) proves too much. One way to avoid checkerboard laws, the kinds of compromises which Dworkin believes violate the requirement of integrity,[136] is for the winners to repeal *all* losers' decisions at the time the winners gain power. Then all extant law will be supported by the winners' coherent conception of justice. But step (17) appears to preclude this. It suggests that even if the winners have it in their power to repeal all the bad old laws, they should keep some of them in force and modify their own legislation so that it coheres with it, purely out of respect for the losers. Indeed, if the losers have never managed to gain political power, though their views are current in certain sections of the community, step (17) seems to suggest that the winners must modify their legislation so that it is justified by a conception that *would have been* consonant with decisions taken by the losers had the losers ever and enough political clout to make a decision. But this is bizarre, and much more offensive to common sense (not to mention basic sanity) than checkerboarding.

A deeper objection focuses on step (14). Even if (13) is accepted—that is, even if we accept that the winners owe the losers some respect—why must the respect take *this* particular form? Why is it not enough that the losers' decisions stand (even though the losers are no longer in charge) unless and until they are explicitly repealed? From the winners' point of view, that is already a compromise—and, in their view, a compromise of justice at that. (These are not light matters that the winners and losers are disagreeing about.) The winners could treat all decisions taken by the losers as no longer having official effect. That they do not do so is a token of respect for their opponents. It adds insult to injury, however, to require the winners,

[136] Ibid., at 178–84.

not only to allow their opponents' legislation to stand (until repealed), but also to modify their own legislation so that its principles cohere with the principles underlying their opponents' legislation.

Another way of putting the point is this. Mutual respect among potential winners and potential losers is embodied already in the principle of political fairness. To embody it also in a distinct requirement of integrity takes mutual respect too far. The winners say to the losers that they are ready to submit to the losers' (unjust) views any time the losers can command a majority (or whatever is needed to gain political power). That is respectful. Why are they *also* required to moderate their own legislative initiatives just so that the conception of justice appealed to by the citizens can reflect their opponents' views as well as their own?

So step (14) seems unattractive. Maybe there are other arguments in favour of step (15) than those that take this route. Step (15), you will recall, is the following:

(15) Thus, for the purpose of inferring implicit obligations and so forth, the winners must appeal to a conception of justice that pays attention to the views of the losers.

There may be arguments for (15) that are based, not so much on mutual respect among winners and losers, but on doubts that the winners may have about the theory of justice they uphold. We have written as though the winners are sure that their views on justice are superior. But on complex matters they may not have this confidence that they are utterly right and their opponents utterly wrong. The truth, they may think, is likely to lie in between, and so they should tailor their legislation so that a coherent 'in between' conception of justice is possible.

But this is based on a quite naïve view about where truth is likely to be found in any political disagreement. (For example, many Democrats in the USA who have doubts about the justice of their own positions suspect that the truth of the matter lies, if anywhere, to the left of their position, not halfway to the right in a Republican direction.)

Another argument for (15) might be based on a Millian view of the marketplace of ideas, namely, that truth rarely can be grasped by a single mind and usually must emerge from a struggle between rival views. And so maybe it is best to go for the unsatisfactory tension of a compromise than the neat confidence of the views of a single faction.

The trouble with this as an interpretation of Dworkin is that it provides a positive argument *in favour of checkerboard law*. For what could be more tense and conflictual than that? The tensions and uneasinesses generated by checkerboard legislation will keep us all on our toes, and perhaps in time the truth will emerge.

Let us briefly summarize where the argument in this lengthy section has taken us. For purposes of this section we assumed, for the sake of argument, contrary to what we had demonstrated in earlier sections, that reconstructive methodology, the methodology of integrity, could produce determinate legal principles and their weights that were different from correct moral principles and their weights. We then examined Dworkin's arguments recommending integrity and found them wanting as a response to morally mistaken decisions. Past morally mistaken decisions should exert no force in present decision-making. Correct moral principles will take account of the past and its present traces in the morally appropriate way. Dworkin gives no sound arguments for abandoning correct moral views merely because those views were not followed in the past.

We have rejected Dworkin's argument for integrity as a response to moral disagreement manifested in official government actions, inconsistency that will ordinarily be among actions at differing times. We will now argue briefly but, we believe, powerfully that integrity is an inadequate response to the problem of political fairness: it cannot successfully resolve current disagreements among officials (or citizens).

What integrity demands is not compromise—Dworkin rules out explicit compromises like checkerboard statutes—but everyone's abandonment of her own moral principles. In other words, integrity demands a form of moral alienation, at least in the realm of governmental action.

First, if all the officials share the same moral principles, but a small segment of the community holds different ones, the officials must abandon their moral principles in favour of principles that neither they nor the minority hold. The officials have the power to do justice by their own lights, but integrity prevents them from doing so. They now must do what is unjust from everyone's perspective. Surely this is a perverse requirement.

If the officials themselves have different moral views, then conflicts will be inevitable under the natural law methodology we recommend. Different moral views held by different decision-makers will surely usher in a set of decisions that will not represent what anyone's moral theory would recommend.

The method of integrity will not change this. Recall that integrity has two axes, fit and moral acceptability. The latter axis will be interpreted differently by officials with different moral views. Put differently, if there is disagreement among officials' primary moral views, there will be disagreement among them regarding the principles integrity demands. What integrity results in, then, where officials disagree morally, is not the production of a coherent set of decisions, but rather the production of decisions that are both incoherent as a set and are individually morally repugnant to each official (since they represent no official's moral principles). With or without integrity, there will be disagreement 'all the way down'; but without integrity, at least some decisions will be correct by each official's own lights, and no official will be forced to alienate her own principles.

Surely, then, the correct way to respond to current moral disagreement is not to abandon principles one believes to be morally correct in favour of principles no one holds. Such alienation is the opposite of true integrity, as we argued above. And it is hard to see how it could provide a firmer basis for associative bonds and community dialogue than moral principles one regards as correct.[137]

V. LEGAL METHODOLOGY IN THE ABSENCE OF LEGAL PRINCIPLES

Legal methodology requires only two types of norms: correct *moral principles* and posited *legal rules.* It does not require *legal principles.* Moral principles themselves dictate the positing of legal rules—so that, for commonplace indirect consequentialist reasons, the moral principles themselves will be better realized over time—although the relation between moral principles and (even ideal) legal rules will be somewhat paradoxical (because of the potential gap in any particular case between what even ideal rules will dictate and what the moral principles will dictate).[138]

The existence of past morally incorrect decisions and morally incorrect legal rules that presently govern some legal domains does not alter this conclusion. Correct moral principles will always take account of the world in which they apply, a world that includes both past and present incorrect decisions and the rule of law, separation of powers, equality, and legitimacy considerations that affect how these incorrect decisions bear on what is now morally correct. The claim that the application of correct moral principles changes as the posited legal rules change—a claim that is true—is different from the false claim that correct moral principles should give way to different and perforce morally incorrect principles, that is, to legal principles.[139]

[137] Dworkin's integrity as a response to intra-temporal differences over moral principles bears a striking similarity to the view of liberalism as a set of political principles that can be accepted by those who disagree about comprehensive theories of the Good even though those theories dictate different political principles. In other words, Dworkin's integrity as a moral value that is somehow independent of and in some sense above the moral principles and theories it mediates functions like liberalism's principle of neutrality (among theories of the Good) and is subject to the same theoretical criticisms that have been levelled at the latter. See Larry Alexander, 'Liberalism, Religion, and the Unity of Epistemology', 30 *San Diego L. Rev.* 763 (1993).

[138] See, Larry Alexander, 'The Gap', *Harv. J. of Law & Pub. Pol'y* 695 (1991); id., *supra*, n. 47, at 39 n. 50, 53; id., *supra*, n. 23, at 432–4.

[139] See Alexander, *supra*, n. 47, at 39–41, 52; id., *supra*, n. 23, at 430–1; Alexander and Bayles, *supra*, n. 15, at 277.

In the end, the pragmatist or natural lawyer, who always follows correct moral principles, but who understands that those principles must be implemented through the conventionalist's posited rules and institutions, always occupies the normatively superior ground.[140] And legal principles, which offer neither the guidance virtues of rules nor the virtue of moral correctness, have no place in her legal methodology.

[140] See Alexander, *supra*, n. 23, at 432–3.

9

Legislators' Intentions and Unintentional Legislation

JEREMY WALDRON

I. AN ARGUMENT ABOUT AUTHORITY

In this paper, I shall discuss the latest attempt in analytic jurisprudence to revive the view that reference to legislators' intentions should play a role in the interpretation of statutes whose texts leave issues of meaning, purpose, or application unclear or controversial.

I use 'revive' advisedly: reference to legislative intention in one form or another is reasonably common among judges in the United States,[1] and the appeal to 'original intent' is common too in the politics of American constitutional law.[2] Philosophically, however, the idea of appealing beyond the statutory text to what legislators are thought to have intended has been subject to such powerful criticisms, most notably by Ronald Dworkin,[3] that one is surprised to find it appearing again in anything other than a trivial form in respectable academic jurisprudence.[4]

Earlier versions of this paper were presented in 1993 at a Conference on Law and Interpretation at Tel Aviv University and at a workshop at Brasenose College, Oxford, organized by the Oxford/USC Institute for Legal Philosophy. I am grateful to Andrei Marmor and to Martin Levine and Joseph Raz for invitations on those occasions, to Chaim Gans and Martin Levine for the responses that they prepared, and in general to Jules Coleman, John Finnis, Andrei Marmor, Michael Moore, Joseph Raz, Carol Sanger, and David Slawson for their helpful suggestions and criticisms.

[1] It is less common in England, though for a recent change of approach see the decision of the House of Lords in *Pepper* v. *Hart* 2 All E.R. [1993].

[2] See Edwin Meese III, 'Interpreting the Constitution', in Jack Rakove (ed.), *Interpreting the Constitution: The Debate Over Original Intent* (Boston: Northeastern University Press, 1990).

[3] Ronald Dworkin, *Law's Empire* (Cambridge, Mass.: Harvard University Press, 1986), 312–37.

[4] For a trivial version of intentionalism, see Stanley Fish, 'Play of Surfaces: Theory and Law', in Gregory Leyh (ed.), *Legal Hermeneutics: History, Theory and Practice* (Berkeley: University of California Press, 1992), 300–1: 'Intentionalism properly understood involves no methodology, no prescriptive direction . . . [T]here cannot be a distinction between interpreters who look to intention and interpreters who don't, only a distinction between the differing accounts of intention put forward by rival interpreters . . . [E]veryone who is an interpreter is in the intention business, and there is no methodological cash value to declaring yourself (or even thinking yourself) to be an intentionalist because you couldn't be anything else.'

Yet in a recently published book, entitled *Interpretation and Legal Theory*, Andrei Marmor makes an argument for the intentionalist thesis which is not only respectable, but novel and almost persuasive.[5] Its originality consists in eschewing any argument based on democratic considerations. Marmor advances no version of the claim that judges ought to defer to legislators' intentions because legislators are elected and judges are not.[6] His argument is based instead on a consideration of Joseph Raz's theory of the authority of law. The normal justification of X's having authority over Y, Raz says, is that Y is more likely to follow the reasons that apply objectively to his decisions if he follows the directives of X, than if he tries to work out the reasons himself.[7] If this is true of X's directives, Marmor reckons, it is likely to be true also of the intentions that lie behind those directives, even when such intentions are not fully disclosed in the directives themselves and have to be recovered by other means.

The application of this general argument to the case of legislation is obvious enough. A statute is conceived as the work of a lawmaker, X, and it is said to have authority just in case that X has some sort of technical or moral expertise in the field that the statute addresses. X is the expert and so ordinary citizens will do better by deferring to his directives than by trusting their own judgment on the matter. Now, this expertise is disclosed in the first instance in the explicit words of the statute that X has written. It is, however, unlikely to be exhausted by that. If his text turns out to be vague or infelicitous, his subjects may have recourse to his expertise in other ways, by gathering clues as to the thoughts and purposes that were in his mind at the time the original statute was passed. The law's authority, after all, is a matter of *X*'s authority, and that authority is defined dispositionally as the likelihood that others will do better by deferring to him. Thus, an argument for the authority of law based on the fact that the legislator is more enlightened than his audience may generate a case for appealing also to legislative intent as a further basis of enlightenment in determining what a citizen or official ought to do.

Now, an argument of this kind depends, at least for its initial attraction, on a rather primitive picture of legislation. It gains its greatest plausibility by stressing the features that statutes have in common with simple commands. If we understand legislation along Hobbesian lines—'where a man saith, *Doe this*, or *Doe not this*, without expecting other reason than the Will of

[5] Andrei Marmor, *Interpretation and Legal Theory* (Oxford: Clarendon Press, 1992), esp. ch. 8.

[6] Certainly, most appellate judges are not elected, i.e. most judges whose interpretations will be influential in the legal system. Moreover, those judges who are elected are seldom regarded by voters (and hardly ever regard themselves) as popular *representatives* in the way that legislators are.

[7] See Joseph Raz, *The Morality of Freedom* (Oxford: Clarendon Press, 1986), 53.

him that sayes it'[8]—we may indeed be inclined to turn to the lawmaker's intentions as a basis for interpreting the statutes that he has passed. For if there is something about his will that makes his original command authoritative, it seems natural to recur to that will—as far as one can ascertain it—if one is in need of further guidance in putting the command into effect.

It is not my aim here to rehearse the difficulties of this style of jurisprudence. They are familiar from H. L. A. Hart's criticisms of the 'Command Theory',[9] criticisms which go much deeper than the one that will be the focus of interest in this paper. For my purposes, what the account just sketched leaves out is that modern statutes are not the products of single expert authors. They are produced by the deliberations of large multi-member assemblies whose claim to authority in Raz's sense (if indeed they can make any such claim at all) consists in their ability to integrate a diversity of purposes, interests, and aims among their members into the text of a single legislative product. The modern situation, in other words, is not that of a *person's* having authority, but (at most) of a *group's* having authority, and of its having that authority only by virtue of the way in which it combines the interests and knowledge of its members in the act of legislating. In this situation, it is unwise to make any inference from the authority of legislation to the authority of anything said or any purpose expressed by members of the legislature that does not amount in itself to a legislative act. That, in outline, is the argument I shall make.

It is true, on the other hand, that sometimes the conditions under which a statute is passed may be such as to make single-author jurisprudence more appropriate. A particular law may have been conceived by just one legislator and his staff and passed 'on the nod', so to speak, by others in the chamber, in deference to his expertise in the area. So far as that particular piece of legislation is concerned, an argument for the authority of the statute may provide the basis for an argument for appealing to the author's intentions even when they are not disclosed in the text, along the lines that Marmor has intimated.[10]

All the same, we should remember that theories of legal authority (and any concomitant theories of interpretation) are usually purchased wholesale, not retail. The question is not about the authority or interpretation of this or that statute, but about the relation between authority and interpretation generally. We must ask, then, whether there is anything true in general about the way in which statutes are produced that makes appeal to

[8] Thomas Hobbes, *Leviathan*, ed. Richard Tuck (Cambridge: Cambridge University Press, 1988), ch. 25, p. 176.

[9] See H. L. A. Hart, *The Concept of Law* (Oxford: Clarendon Press, 1961).

[10] Chaim Gans insisted strongly on this point in the critical comments he made at the Tel Aviv Conference, and he was right to do so.

legislators' intentions a proper strategy of interpretation. How we answer that question will depend on what we take to be the most helpful general model of the legislative process, so far as theories of authority are concerned. My submission is going to be that, at that level, we will do better by eschewing any model that regards legislation as most commonly the intentional product of a single lawmaking author.

The argument that follows will proceed in three stages. After some preliminaries I will address the general issue of the intentionality of statutes. I will argue in Section 3 that, under the conditions of modern legislation, it is often implausible to describe legislative acts as intentional acts, even though they take place in an intentionally organized context. In Section 4 I will show how Raz's thesis about authority (or a plausible version of that thesis) might nevertheless apply to legislative acts, despite the fact that they are not conceived as intentional acts. Then, in Section 5, I will show that the best arguments for the authority of statutes produced under these conditions are arguments which actually preclude any appeal to the intentions of particular legislators as a general interpretive strategy. I will end the paper, in Section 6, with some further general comments on the significance of the considerations about legislation on which I have been basing my arguments.

2. SOME ASSUMPTIONS

First, I want to deal with some preliminary matters, to clear the ground, as it were. Like Marmor, I take the subject of this discussion to be statutory, not constitutional, interpretation.[11]

The hardest case for an opponent of the intentionalist strategy—and thus the case that I have to address—is a statute passed recently, in a deliberative session of which there is an undisputed public record, by legislators familiar with the conditions of the society to which it applies. If questions arise about the interpretation of a law enacted under these conditions, it is not implausible to suggest that they might be answered by looking to the public record of debates, committee deliberations, and so on to see what the legislators had in mind. Of course, such exercises are not always successful. Still, even if the judges get the legislators' intentions wrong, or if the legislators are for some other reason dissatisfied with the judges' answer, they can always enact another statute to impose the interpretation or the purpose that they prefer.[12]

None of this applies in constitutional adjudication. Despite its popularity among conservative politicians, the appeal to the intentions of the framers

[11] Marmor, *supra*, n. 5, 172–3. [12] Ibid. 173.

of the US Constitution is ludicrously implausible. Those who make the appeal disagree about who counts as a framer. Is it the drafters of the text, the members of the Philadelphia Convention, the ratifiers, or the people who elected the ratifiers? Not only that, but whoever the framers are taken to be, their actual intentions are largely a matter of conjecture, and at least as controversial as any less historical form of 'interpretation'. We know 'practically nothing', for example, about what went on in state legislatures during the ratification debates.[13] Moreover, even if we knew the framers' intentions, it would be unwise to rely on them. The framers lived two centuries ago and, despite their revolutionary virtue, they were utterly unacquainted with the conditions of modern politics and society in America. They lived in a loosely federated set of sparsely populated, post-colonial, white-supremacist states, whose economies were based on the exploitation of African slaves in agriculture, and whose politics were confined to those who owned slaves, women, or property. For the purposes of the Raz-Marmor argument, these men would not even have understood, let alone have had a better grasp than us of, the conditions for the subsistence of a continental superpower as a free and constitutional republic, under conditions of ethnic diversity, democratic equality, and post-industrial crisis. There may be a case for regarding the text of the Constitution as an stable and indispensable framework to house the volatility and vicissitudes of modern politics.[14] But that stabilizing function has more in common with co-ordinative authority—which Marmor acknowledges can generate no justification for an appeal to original intent[15]—than with the authority of moral expertise on which deference to framers' intentions is more usually based.

I take it, then, that we are to discuss the role of legislative intent in the interpretation of ordinary statutes under modern conditions.

I shall assume, in addition, that when we talk about legislation, we are envisaging the work of a congress, a parliament, or a state assembly: that is, a body comprising a number of members (usually in the hundreds) of various political persuasions, elected as representatives by the people of the state to whom the legislation is going to apply.

I shall assume, too, that the legislators are a diverse body of people, drawn from different groups in a heterogenous and multi-cultural society. I shall assume, in other words, that they are not necessarily transparent to one another, in the way that members of a tightly-knit *Gemeinschaft* or an 'old-boy's network' are often taken to be, and that there is very little in the

[13] Bernard Schwartz, *The Bill of Rights: A Documentary History*, ii (New York: Macmillan, 1971), 1171; I am obliged for this reference to Robert Post, 'Theories of Constitutional Interpretation', in Robert Post (ed.) *Law and the Order of Culture* (Berkeley: University of California Press, 1991), 22.

[14] See Hannah Arendt, *On Revolution* (Harmondsworth: Penguin Books, 1963), esp. ch. 4.

[15] Marmor, *supra*, n. 5, 179–80.

way of shared cultural and social understandings among them beyond the rather stiff and formal language that they address to one another in their legislative debates. If any one of them says to another, in the rather cozy way that people have who share tacit understandings, 'come on, you know what I mean', the answer is as likely as not to be: 'No, I don't know what you mean. You had better spell it out for me.'

I shall assume finally that the legislature possesses fastidiously defined procedures to determine how a piece of legislation is introduced, debated, and passed, what it comprises (that is, what its final authoritative text is), and when it takes effect. These procedures amount to the constitution of the legislature, and reference to them will form part of the rule of recognition for the legal system.

Though these assumptions are obvious enough in the modern world, they will turn out to be crucial for my argument against appeals to legislators' intentions; accordingly, I will spend some time examining their grounds in Section 6.

3. LEGISLATION WITHOUT INTENTION

It is often said, as though it were a truism, that anything we interpret must necessarily be conceived as a product of someone's intention.[16] The point is taken to be an elementary one about what counts as a linguistic artefact. Wave action on sand or the rustling of the wind might produce marks or noises that look or sound like a text. But one cannot treat them as a text—it is said—and set about discerning their meaning, unless one attributes their appearance to the intentions of some intelligent author. Stanley Fish puts the point this way:

> [I]n order to hear sense in arbitrarily produced sounds or marks we have to hear those sounds and marks within the assumption that they have been produced by some purposeful agent; that is, we have to hear them *as not arbitrarily produced*, even if to do so we must attribute purpose and intention to the waves or to the wind or to the great spirit that rolls through all things.[17]

The positing of intention, comes first on this account; the positing of meanings second.[18]

In exactly the same way, many legal theorists think it obvious that a statute must be conceived as something which has been produced intentionally;

[16] For the best-known recent argument to this effect, see Steven Knapp and Walter Benn Michaels, 'Against Theory', *Critical Inquiry*, 8 (1982), 723–42.

[17] Fish, *supra*, n. 4, 299.

[18] Stanley Fish, *Doing What Comes Naturally: Change, Rhetoric and the Practice of Theory in Literary and Legal Studies* (Durham: Duke University Press, 1989), 296.

and they infer from this that the only possible object of interpretation in the law is the meaning envisaged by those whose purposes constitute the intentionality of the provision under consideration.[19]

Thus, imagine that a piece of paper duly certified in accordance with proper parliamentary procedure appears in front of a judge with marks on it that look like the following:

Vehicles in the Park Act 1993. (1) With the exception of bicycles and ambulances, no vehicle shall be permitted to enter any state or municipal park. (2) Any person who brings a vehicle into a state or municipal park shall be liable to a fine of not more than $100.

According to Stanley Fish and the others who take the view that I am discussing in this section, if the judge views this as a statute, and begins the laborious business of working out, for example, whether its provisions apply to the proverbial jeep on a plinth,[20] then he must be treating the marks on the paper as the product of someone's intention.

Fish concedes that it is a further question whether we should search the legislative record in order to find intentionalist clues to the solution of the jeep-on-a-plinth problem. Acknowledging legislative intentionality, he says, is not the same as deferring to legislators' intentions, especially when the latter are not the intentions disclosed immediately in the text of the statute itself. We may end up answering our question about the jeep by reading the statute in a way that would have surprised its authors.[21] Still, the crucial point, according to Fish, 'is that one cannot read *or* reread independently of intention, independently, that is, of the assumption that one is dealing with marks or sounds produced by an intentional being, a being situated in some enterprise in relation to which he has a purpose or a point of view'.[22] The fact that 'intention' and 'meaning' are heavily theory-laden terms does not, according to Fish, undermine the point that interpreting a text is always a matter of determining what the intentional being who produced it meant. It is always, he says, a matter of discovering the meaning of which the statutory text was intended to be the expression.[23]

Though this position may seem uncontroversial with regard to novels and poems, it is confused—and significantly confused—with regard to modern legislation.

[19] See e.g. Steven Knapp and Walter Benn Michaels, 'Intention, Identity and the Constitution: A Response to David Hoy', in Leyh (ed.), *supra*, n. 4, 187.

[20] The case is from Lon Fuller, 'Positivism and Fidelity to Law: A Reply to Professor Hart', *Harvard Law Review*, 71 (1958), 633: 'What would Professor Hart say if some local patriots wanted to mount on a pedestal in the park a truck used in World War II, while other citizens, regarding the proposed memorial as an eyesore, support their stand by the "no vehicle" rule? Does this truck, in perfect working order, fall within the core or the penumbra?' The case is discussed by Marmor, *supra*, n. 5, 130.

[21] Hence the prescriptive triviality of Fish's intentionalism: see *supra*, n. 4.

[22] Fish, *supra*, n. 18, 99–100.

[23] Fish, *supra*, n. 4, 302.

Legislation, I have assumed, is the product of a multi-member assembly, comprising a number of persons of quite radically differing aims, interests, and backgrounds. Under these conditions, the specific provisions of a particular statute are often the result of compromise and line-item voting. It is perfectly possible, for example, that the our imagined Vehicles in the Park Act, considered as a whole, does not reflect the purposes or intentions of any of the legislators who together enacted it. Let me spell out this possibility. With regard to section (1) of the Act, the legislators might have been divided on the exception for bicycles (which I shall call B), on the exception for ambulances (A), and on the inclusion of state parks as well as municipal parks (S). Suppose the legislators divided into three equal factions on these issues:

Faction 1	*Faction 2*	*Faction 3*
B	B	~B
A	~A	A
~S	S	S

Successive majority voting on these various questions would produce our familiar statute—B, A, S—even though that combination corresponded to nobody's preference.

Someone might respond: surely, after the amendments are in, the legislators will vote on the bill as a whole, in its final form (B, A, S). Thus, even if they initially disagree, the enacted statute will at least reflect the intentions of a majority at that last stage, taking into account their awareness of what was politically possible, given their colleagues' views.

But this seems to me purely an artefact of our particular parliamentary procedures—that we have a third-reading debate and division, for example, after the amendment stage. One could imagine a legislature that proceeded quite differently. There might be a preliminary discussion during which all the issues likely to provoke a division were identified. General debate would ensue, at the conclusion of which members would feed their votes on the various issues into a machine which would produce the statute in its final form on the basis of the voting, and promulgate it automatically to judges, officials, and the population at large. The possibility of such a machine was considered by Richard Wollheim in his famous article 'A Paradox in the Theory of Democracy':

> I now want to go on and envisage Democracy in terms of a certain machine which operates according to [the following] method or rule. The machine—which we may for convenience call the democratic machine—operates in a discontinuous fashion. Into it are fed at fixed intervals the choices of the individual citizens. The machine then aggregates them according to the pre-established rule or method, and so comes up with what may be called a 'choice' of its own. Democratic rule is said to be

achieved if throughout the period when the machine is not working, the most recent choice of the machine is acted upon.[24]

Now, theorists of social choice are familiar with various tangles of cyclicity that such a machine might get into. Let's assume, however—as Wollheim did—that these are not a problem for the cases we are considering.[25] The point of this thought-experiment (which is not the same as Wollheim's use of it)[26] is that it enables us to envisage a piece of legislation that cannot be conceived as, in Fish's words, something produced 'by an intentional being . . . situated in some enterprise in relation to which he has a purpose or a point of view'.

Of course, this is just a model: in the real world, statutes are never produced exactly like that. But also, in the real world, statutes are never produced exactly as the product of one person's coherent intention. The interesting question is which picture is more helpful for our thinking about the intentionality of statutes under modern legislative conditions. Given the large part that is played by compromise, log-rolling, and last-minute amendments in contemporary legislation, my money is on the machine.

Fish might make another response. He might say: even if it is the product of Wollheim's machine, still the text of our statute is quite unlike the cases mentioned earlier of marks made by waves in the sand or noises in the wind.

He is right. There are three important differences. (1) The machine does what it does on the basis of the legislators' inputs, and those inputs are fully intentional. (2) The machine is programmed to produce the particular signs (words) that it does (under particular input conditions) because those signs are taken to have certain meanings by those who programme it. It is the programmers' intention, for example, that the English words 'with the exception of bicycles' be produced by the machine in the event that a majority of legislators press button 'B'. This is their expectation about how the

[24] Richard Wollheim, 'A Paradox in the Theory of Democracy', in Peter Laslett and W. G. Runciman, *Philosophy, Politics and Society*, second series (Oxford: Basil Blackwell, 1969), 75–6.

[25] Ibid. 75. I also want to evade a complaint that Ronald Dworkin might make, that the Wollheim machine might yield something like 'a checkerboard statute', that is, a statute that lacked internal coherence. (Dworkin, *supra*, n. 3, 178–84.) Even if Dworkin is right in thinking that there is something objectionable about a statute so compromised that it does not reflect any coherent set of principles or policies, he can hardly deny that it is a text and that a judge might make a good-faith effort to interpret it. Remember too that 'integrity', the value which Dworkin says is at stake here, is just one legal value among several, and must often be traded off against the others. In any case, the machine *need* not produce statutes that lack integrity. At most, a requirement of integrity would imply only that the machine's output *could* be interpreted as the product of someone's intention, not that it *must* be so interpreted.

[26] Briefly, Wollheim was interested in the question of why a person whose input into the machine was a firm and whole-hearted vote against policy A, should ever regard the machine's output as giving him a reason to act in favour of A.

machine's output—whatever it is—will be understood by those to whom it is sent: they will read it as a set of English sentences. And it is the expectation that the legislators share as they input their votes. (3) The whole system, the machine itself and the conventions surrounding its use, have been set up intentionally, pursuant to certain democratic procedural aspirations. The entire exercise, then, is an intentional one, and that is enough to distinguish it from waves in the sand.[27]

But it is not sufficient to establish Fish's conclusion that the text must be taken to embody *a particular intention*, for example, an intention to ensure that vehicles other than bicycles and ambulances do not enter state or municipal parks. For neither that intention nor anything like it figures among the intentional elements (1)–(3) that we have just identified. Accordingly, when the statute is read for the first time by an official or a citizen (or for that matter by a legislator interested to know what he and his colleagues 'decided'), Fish is not entitled to say that the aim of the reading must be to determine what somebody meant.

Max Radin once wrote that it is the job of a legislature to pass statutes, not form intentions.[28] A legislature is an artificial actor, and the passage of a statute is its action: indeed we refer to statutes as *acts* of congress or parliament or whatever. But though we use the language of agency in this way, we must not be misled by an obsessive analogy with the actions of natural persons into searching for a legislative equivalent for every event or state associated with action in the psychology of individual agents. Few would say, for example, that legislatures (as opposed to particular legislators) have motives as well as intentions associated with particular acts; or few would be willing to put the kind of weight on the motive–intention distinction that we apply in the individual case.[29] So why insist on a correlate for intention at all? Why not simply say that the act of a legislature is an artificial resultant of the acts of individual legislators, structured and related to one another through certain procedures, decision-functions, and perhaps machines? Why not say that while each of the latter acts—the

[27] Point (2) is sufficient to address the argument of Knapp and Michaels, 'Intention, Identity and the Constitution', *supra*, n. 19, 190–2, that the assignment of meaning to marks produced by chance involves an arbitrary choice among all actual and possible languages which might give semantic value to such marks. Knapp and Michaels say that 'the only plausible reason for restricting the text's meanings to the language in which the author wrote it is that one is interested in the author's intention; otherwise, the choice of this rule over an infinite number of others would be arbitrary' (192). But this argument is invalid, at least as it applies to our legislative example. Those who set up the Wollheim machine have determined intentionally that the marks it produces are to be understood as English words and sentences. But it does not follow from this that the particular marks that emerge from the machine should be taken to express the particular intentions of any user of the English language.

[28] Max Radin, 'Statutory Interpretation', *Harvard Law Rev.*, 43 (1930), 863; I am indebted for this reference to Michael Moore, 'A Natural Law Theory of Interpretation', *South. Calif. Law Rev.*, 58 (1985), 355.

[29] Cf. Marmor's discussion, *supra*, n. 5, 167.

individual acts—is of course the product of an intention, the resultant act—the act of the legislature itself—need not be?[30]

Part of the confusion tempting us to ascribe intentions to legislatures has to do with the concept of meaning. It may be thought that the very fact that legislation is a *speech*-act—the production of a meaningful utterance or text—means that it cannot be regarded as non-intentional.[31] What is it after all to say: 'No vehicle shall be permitted to enter any state or municipal park', but to utter a string of sounds with the intention to produce a certain effect or response in one's audience by virtue of its recognition of that very intention?[32] Even if one were to eschew the idea of a single utterer for cases like this and concentrate just on the meaning of the sentence, it remains the case that our most plausible accounts of sentence-meaning make that notion a function (albeit a complex one) of individual intention.

All the same, these considerations should not drive us towards any notion of legislative intentionality. I have noted already—item (2) above—that even a Wollheim machine would have to be programmed and operated on the basis of certain assumptions about the meanings of various signs and sounds. A legislator who votes for (or against) a provision like 'No vehicle shall be permitted to enter any state or municipal park' does so on the assumption that—to put it crudely—what the words mean to him is identical to what they will mean to those to whom they are addressed (in the event that the provision is passed). He can entertain that assumption only on condition that the words are meaningful elements in a language—that is, only on condition that there is a community in which it is well known that members of that community commonly use such words to produce a certain effect or response in their audience by virtue of the audience's recognition of that very intention.[33] That such assumptions pervade the legislative process shows how much law depends on language, on the shared conventions that constitute a language, and on the reciprocity of intentions that conventions comprise.[34] But though they indicate a place for referring to

[30] Then what becomes of the enquiries into legislative intention that are occasionally undertaken in constitutional law—for example, in querying whether a piece of legislation was intended unduly to burden some religious practice? What becomes of the familiar distinction between (a) neutral and non-neutral impacts and (b) neutral and non-neutral intentions? There is not space here to go fully into this issue. However, it has always seemed to me that the more useful distinction is between (a) consequential inquiry into neutrality of impacts, and (b*) justificatory inquiry as to whether there are neutral *reasons* favouring the legislation, whether or not those reasons surfaced in anyone's intentions at the time. If a court can discover a good neutral reason for a given law, the fact that it happens to have been enacted for a non-neutral purpose is surely not a justification for striking it down. We would be depriving ourselves of something useful purely in order to retaliate against the legislators' bad intentions.

[31] I am obliged to Joseph Raz for this point.

[32] See Paul Grice, *Studies in the Way of Words* (Cambridge, Mass.: Harvard University Press, 1989), 92.

[33] Ibid. 117–37.

[34] Legislation may also rely on certain quasi-linguistic conventions common to legislative draftsmen and the legal–judicial community. I am obliged to Joseph Raz for this point.

intentions—the intentions of language-users as such—in any comprehensive account of what is going on, they provide no warrant for the view that, simply because a particular piece of legislation has a linguistic meaning, it must embody a particular intention attributable to a language-user.

4. AUTHORITY WITHOUT INTENTION

It is one thing to play with the possibility of unintentional legislation, along the lines of my thought-experiment involving the Wollheim machine. But what becomes of the authority of a legislature if its statutes are not conceived as intentional acts? How can a legal provision be regarded as authoritative if the legislature employs a Wollheim machine to generate its laws? To address this question, we have to look again at the notion of authority.

The thesis about authority that Marmor invokes from Joseph Raz's book talks about 'the normal way to establish that *a person* has authority over another person'.[35] It is persons who have authority, on this account, not organizations or laws. In a subsequent chapter of the book, Raz asks whether anything changes when we move from a one-on-one situation to an issue involving the authority of the state. However, the change that seems to interest him there is the fact that 'political authorities govern groups of people' rather than particular individuals.[36] He does not appear to be interested in the ramifications for his thesis of the fact that political authorities, like legislatures, *are* groups of people.

The closest Raz comes to considering the issue is in the following passage that Marmor cites from an article published earlier than *The Morality of Law*: 'a directive can be authoritatively binding only if it is, or is at least presented as, someone's view of how its subjects ought to behave.'[37] Marmor glosses this as 'the idea that only an agent capable of communion with others can have authority over them'.[38] (He uses it to argue against Ronald Dworkin's view that the norms judges should take as authoritative are norms they themselves produce by a process of interpretive construction.)

The fallacy in Raz's thesis (or at least in Marmor's presentation of Raz's thesis) about the normal justification of authority lies in forging too tight a connection between *authority* and *authorship*. Authority cannot be systemic, on the Raz–Marmor account: it must be attributable to an author. Their claim seems to be that the reasons of ordinary citizens can be affected in the way that authority affects reasons only if there is some identifiable person (natural or artificial) who *has* the authority in question.

[35] Raz, *supra*, n. 7, 53 (my emphasis). [36] Ibid. 71.

[37] Joseph Raz, 'Authority, Law and Morality', *The Monist*, 68 (1985), 303, cited by Marmor, *supra*, n. 5, 114.

[38] Marmor, *supra*, n. 5, 115.

Thus Marmor assumes that a statute, S, can have authority only if the following is true about the person, X, who issued it: namely, that any person Y to whom the statute is addressed does better by following *X*'s view of the reasons that apply to Y's conduct than by attempting to work out those reasons for himself. For a statute to have authority, on this account, is for its author to have (or to have had) a view, and one which is superior in some regard to any view likely to be formed by the person to whom the statute is addressed.

I want to suggest, however, that the situation in which statutory authority is traceable back to personal authority is at most a special case. In other cases it should be possible to talk about the authority of the statute *tout court*, and develop a version of the normal justification thesis which refers only to the likelihood that a person subject to it will do better by following its provisions. What I have in mind is something along the following lines (which I shall label 'thesis [J]', because I will want to refer to it later):

> [J]: A statute (or any text) S has authority over a person Y only if person Y is likely better to comply with the reasons which apply to him by following the provisions of S, than if he tries to follow those reasons directly.

Now, [J] *may* be true on account of something about the views or the intentions of the person X who authored or voted for the statute. But that need not be the reason for its truth: S may satisfy [J] despite the fact that S has no author, or satisfy it in virtue of features that make no reference to any person's expertise.

Marmor of course does not consider [J]—for I have just invented it. However, in his discussion of Dworkin's arguments, he seems to suggest that whenever anything like [J] is true, we must either locate an individual X, whose view on the matter in question is taken to be superior to Y's, or we must *pretend* that there is some such individual. This insistence on producing or imagining an X is never defended (except by reference to Raz's formulations). I suspect, however, that it is due to an inability to conceive of how Y could do better by following the provisions of S than by following his own reason, unless S was an expression of someone else's view (someone who was smarter or more knowledgeable than he was). So let me explain how that might be possible.

First, a trivial example. I am very bad at keeping track of credit-card transactions. I use my card several times a week, but I do not keep the receipts or write down the amounts, so I am never sure how much has been charged to my account. Any attempt I made to work it out for myself would probably be inaccurate. Fortunately, the Bank of America provides an '800' number for me to call. I punch in my credit-card account number, and the last four digits of my Social Security number to verify my identity, and the disembodied 'voice' of a machine will say something like this:

Your current balance is FOUR hundred and *thirty* FIVE dollars and *sixty* cents. Your available credit is FIVE thousand FIVE hundred and *sixty* FOUR dollars and *forty* cents.

Now I am under no illusion that there is anyone at the bank who has worked all this out and is waiting to communicate it to me, any more than I think the 'voice' I hear is that of some individual at Bank of America headquarters, sitting patiently by the phone waiting for people like me to call. The deliverance I have just quoted is nothing but the product of a machine responding on the spot to my touch-tone input, to various inputs from retailers, and to its record of my credit limit. No one has worked out what my balance is: there are just the noises recorded above. Indeed, the machine may not even be storing a record of my balance; apart from the sending of my monthly account, it may be computed only as a response to my telephone call. Still, the machine's output is authoritative for me in terms of thesis [J]: I do better by relying on this text for information about the outstanding balance on my credit card than I would by relying on my own forgetful computations.

I know, of course, that someone has intentionally programmed the machine to produce outputs (in response to certain inputs) such that people who treat its sounds as English sentences will have reason to rely on the information such sentences conventionally convey. That is like the conditions (1)–(3) for the Wollheim machine that I mentioned in the previous section. But I can concede all that without saying (or pretending) that anyone is intentionally conveying to me the message that my outstanding balance is $435.60. That my reliance on the machine's output makes reference to someone's intentions (in programming the machine) does not make the machine, for me, an intentional system.[39]

In the case of the bank's computer, there are good reasons for me to respect the machine's output more than I respect the results of my own computations: the bank has an interest in keeping accurate records and no interest, as far as I can tell, in concealing the true state of my account from me. But legislatures are not banks. What reasons might there be for respecting the deliverances of a Wollheim machine?

I will consider three lines of argument: (A) the utilitarian argument, that a Wollheim machine might aggregate individual preferences in the way required by the applicable social welfare function; (B) the Condorcet theorem, that the view determined by a Wollheim machine to be that of the majority has a probability of being correct that is greater than the probability

[39] The philosopher Daniel Dennett is famous, among other things, for the claim that it is sometimes appropriate to treat machines as intentional systems. See Daniel Dennett, 'Intentional Systems'. But my claim falls far short of that here (even assuming Dennett's argument is accepted). It seems to me that an output S of a machine may sometimes be authoritative for a person in terms of thesis [J] whether that machine is (to be treated as) an intentional system or not.

that any given one of the views being counted is correct; and (C) the Aristotelian claim that a multitude of persons, by a process of deliberative synthesis, may forge a better view than even the wisest of them could up with on his own.

None of these arguments is watertight. But in common with Marmor and Raz, I do not want to make a watertight case for the authority of such legislation. The claim by Marmor that is under consideration is only that *if* (and *to the extent that*) there is reason to accord authority to a statute, there may also be reason to accord authority to the intentions of some or all of the members of the legislature which passed it, even when these intentions are not disclosed in the text of statute itself. My claim in Section 5 will be that this inference of Marmor's is invalid, at least to the extent that the authority of a statute is based on argument (A), argument (B), or argument (C).

Before moving to that, let me sketch out the three lines of argument in a little more detail.

(A) The Utilitarian Argument

Historically, the utilitarian case for democracy has been that a majoritarian decision-procedure at the level of public choice can sometimes model an aggregative social welfare function at the level of utilitarian morality. For both cases—that is, for both a majoritarian decision-procedure and a Benthamite social welfare function—the fact that a course of action promotes the satisfaction of some preference counts in its favour, and when it becomes apparent that not everyone's preferences can be satisfied, one adopts the course of action that satisfies as many of them as possible. Thus, as democrats, we follow the will of the majority; and as utilitarians, we try to promote the greatest aggregate happiness. The two may amount to roughly the same thing if individual votes are a reliable guide to the conditions of individual happiness.[40]

Now of course there are all sorts of difficulties with this equation. It presupposes that individuals are voting their own happiness; it assumes they are reliable judges of that; and it avoids altogether the question of the intensity of their preferences. Moreover, for the case of a representative legislature (as opposed to a directly democratic one), a number of epicycles have to be added to ensure that votes cast by each legislator accurately represent the proportion between various preferences of his constituents.

[40] This paragraph and the one that follows are adapted from my paper 'Rights and Majorities: Rousseau Revisited', in Jeremy Waldron, *Liberal Rights: Collected Papers 1981–91* (Cambridge: Cambridge University Press, 1993), 394–7. The paper was originally published in John Chapman and Alan Wertheimer (eds.), *Nomos XXXII: Majorities and Minorities* (New York University Press, 1990).

However, even if these difficulties cannot be perfectly overcome, it is easy to imagine that a Wollheim machine, registering and aggregating a large number of individuals' expressed preferences, might produce an output whose utilitarian credentials were much better than any rough-and-ready computation that could be made by an individual citizen. If an individual knows that his own computations of social utility are even less accurate than the machine's, and perhaps biased also by wishful thinking in his own favour, it might be wiser for him to forego self-reliance and rely instead on the somewhat less fallible outputs of the machine as his guide to what the general happiness demands. In these circumstances, anyone who believes that the truth about what ought to be done is utilitarian will have reason to regard the outputs of the machine as authoritative in the sense of thesis [J].

(B) Condorcet's Theorem

Under the previous heading we assumed that individual legislators were asking themselves different questions as they voted: each was asking 'What do I want?' (so that legislator W was asking 'What does W want?' and legislator X was asking 'What does X want?'). The same would be true if each legislator was asking himself, 'What are the preferences of my constituents?' We imagined that the Wollheim machine would take each person's preferences and aggregate them using a social welfare function to produce, for the first time in this process, a conclusion about the general good.

Often, however, legislators take themselves to be asking the *same* question: 'What is best for everyone, or for society at large, or what is most just?' Often, *each* takes himself to be expressing a view about the *general* welfare. When this is the basis of individual legislators' votes, is there any reason to believe that a Wollheim machine will produce an authoritative output, in the sense of thesis [J]?

There is; and the argument is a matter of simple arithmetic. Suppose that some voters are addressing a single question with two answers, one correct and one incorrect (for example, they are jurors deciding whether someone did or did not commit a robbery). Assume that the probability of each voter choosing the correct answer is greater than 0.5, that is, that each is more likely to get it right by thinking about the matter and then voting his best judgment than if he simply tosses a coin. Then provided the votes are cast independently of one another,[41] the probability that the answer chosen by a simple majority of them will be the correct answer is somewhat greater

[41] See also *supra*, n. 45.

than 0.5, and it rises toward the limit of certainty as the size of the group of people voting increases.[42]

This theorem, due to the Marquis de Condorcet, has its limits.[43] The same reasoning yields the conclusion that if the average competence of the individual voters dips below 0.5, then majority competence tends towards zero as group size increases. In other words, the theorem provides a ground for the authority of the outcome if individual voters are, on average, more likely than not to be correct in the alternative they choose; but it provides reason for doubting the authority of the outcome if on average the voters are more likely than not to choose incorrectly. Condorcet himself believed that, historically, average individual competence tended to decline as group size (for example, in a legislature) increased. But of course there is no reason to think that this truth (if it is a truth) of political sociology exactly cancels out the arithmetical effect we have been discussing.[44]

In any case, Condorcet's theorem indicates a reason for according authority to the output of a Wollheim machine in at least some circumstances. If a large number of legislators address themselves scrupulously to some objective issue, and if they each have a better-than-even chance of being right, then the ordinary citizen would be wise to trust the decision generated by a majoritarian machine out of their individual votes. Indeed, on Condorcet's reasoning *each individual legislator* will do much better by observing the

[42] Suppose there are three voters—V, W, and X—voting independently, each with a 0.6 chance of being right. When V casts his vote, there is a 0.6 chance he's right and a 0.4 chance he's wrong. When W casts his vote: there is a $0.6 \times 0.6 = 0.36$ chance that a majority comprising at least W and V will be right; a $0.6 \times 0.4 = 0.24$ chance that V will be right and W wrong; and a $0.4 \times 0.6 = 0.24$ chance that V will be wrong and W right. Now X casts his vote. If V got it right and W wrong, there is a $0.24 \times 0.6 = 0.144$ chance that a majority comprising only V and X will be right. And if V got it wrong and W right, there is the same chance (0.144) that a majority comprising only W and X will be right. The overall probability that a majority will be right then is

$$0.36 \text{ (VWX or VW)} + 0.144 \text{ (VX)} + 0.144 \text{ (WX)} = 0.648$$

which is higher than the 0.6 individual competence we began with.

For a sense of the difference that an increase in group size can make, consider that if we add to the group two additional voters of the same individual competence (0.6), we get a competence of 0.68256 for the five members deciding by a majority. To get a group competence of higher than 0.9, we need only add an additional 36 members with individual competences of 0.6. See Bernard Grofman and Scott Feld, 'Rousseau's General Will: A Condorcetian Perspective', *American Political Science Review*, 82 (1988), 571.

[43] Marquis de Condorcet, 'Essay on the Application of Mathematics to the Theory of Decision-making', in Keith Michael Baker (ed.), *Condorcet: Selected Writings* (Indianapolis: Bobbs-Merrill, 1976), 33–70.

[44] Ibid. 49: 'A very numerous assembly cannot be composed of very enlightened men. It is even probable that those comprising [*sic*] this assembly will on many matters combine great ignorance with many prejudices. Thus there will be a great number of questions on which the probability of the truth of each voter will be below. It follows that the more numerous the assembly, the more it will be exposed to the risk of making false decisions.' See the discussion in Jeremy Waldron, 'Democratic Theory and the Public Interest: Condorcet and Rousseau Revisited', *American Political Science Review*, 83 (1989), 1322–8.

authority of the machine-produced legislation than he would by trusting the reasoning that led to his own individual vote. This, as we shall see, is fatal to Marmor's case. But before we consider that, let us look at the third of our arguments for legislative authority.

(C) Aristotelian Synthesis

Condorcet's result is maddeningly mechanical. Forget truth, objectivity, and justice: the same arithmetical reasoning tells us about the prospects that a majority of balls pulled at random out of an urn will be black, given that more than half of the balls in the urn are black. Moreover, Condorcet's result takes no account of discussion, deliberation, and persuasion—the very processes that are likely to produce a legislative record to which Marmor's intention-seeking judge can appeal.[45]

The third line of argument I want to consider concentrates a little less on the Wollheim machine and the arithmetical blindness of its operations, and a little more on the real-world prospects that a multi-member legislature might come up with some result that satisfies condition [J]. Like the previous argument (and unlike the utilitarian theory), this one also assumes that legislators are addressing themselves in good faith—as they deliberate and vote—to a single question with an objective answer.

The argument this time is due to Aristotle. The question under discussion in the middle of Book III of his *Politics* is whether political power should be in the hands of the many or in the hands of the few men (or even the one man) of extraordinary wisdom and virtue. There is, says Aristotle, some truth in the view that political power should be in the hands of the multitude:

> For the many, of whom each individual is not a good man, when they meet together may be better than the few good, if regarded not individually but collectively, just as a feast to which many contribute is better than a dinner provided out of a single purse. For each individual among the many has a share of excellence and practical wisdom, and when they meet together, just as they become in a manner one man, who has many feet, and hands, and senses, so too with regard to their character and thought. Hence the many are better judges than a single man of music and poetry; for some understand one part, and some another, and among them they understand the whole.[46]

[45] See ibid., for a consideration of Grofman and Feld's view (*supra*, n. 42) that the applicability of Condorcet's theorem actually precludes deliberation among the citizens. That view is, of course, incorrect. It does not matter at all how the individual competences have been achieved, whether by discussion or by innate talent. What matters for the Condorcet result is that the individual competences be determined at the moment of voting, and that the votes be logically independent of one another.

[46] Aristotle, *The Politics*, ed. Stephen Everett (Cambridge: Cambridge University Press, 1988), III. xi. 1281^{b}1–10 (p. 66).

A little later he repeats the idea:

> Now any member of the assembly, taken separately, is certainly inferior to the wise man. But the state is made up of many individuals. And as a feast to which all the guests contribute is better than a banquet furnished by a single man, so a multitude is a better judge of many things than any individual.[47]

What lies behind this 'pot-luck' theory of politics is the idea that a number of individuals may bring a diversity of perspectives to bear on the complex issues under consideration, and that they are capable of pooling these perspectives to come up with better decisions than any of them could make on his own.

Suppose, for example, that the Athenian *ecclesia* is considering whether to mount an invasion of Sicily. One man might know the geography of the Sicilian coastline; another might know the character of the island's inhabitants; a third might have experience of amphibious expeditions to other regions; a fourth might be acquainted with the current state of the Athenian fleet; a fifth might be a bitter veteran of past military catastrophes; a sixth might know what is to be gained from the expedition; and so on. No one person might have all this information and experience himself. The most rational way to make the decision, then, is to pool the knowledge of the various individuals.[48]

That is why Aristotle takes it as the mark of man's political nature that he has been endowed with the faculty of *speech*.[49] Each can communicate to another experiences and insights that complement or qualify those that the other already possesses, and when this happens in dense interaction throughout a community it enables the group as a whole to attain a degree of wisdom and practical knowledge that surpasses even that of the most excellent individual member.

Now, there are two ways we can model what goes on in this pooling of knowledge and experience: (i) *individual synthesis* and (ii) *group synthesis*.

(i) Individual Synthesis

Each legislator listens carefully to the views of each of the others, and forms them into a synthesis which is then reflected in his voting. If he possesses a modicum of rationality and comprehension, the view that he ends up holding should count as authoritative, at least in comparison to the views of any persons who have not been exposed to a diversity of perspectives in this way. In addition, the view of a majority of such legislators would

[47] Ibid., III. xv. 1286^{a}27–31.

[48] This and the paragraphs that follow are adapted from my paper 'Religious Contributions in Public Deliberation', forthcoming in *Univ. of San Diego Law Rev.*, 30 (1993), 817–48.

[49] Aristotle, *supra*, n. 46, I. ii. 1253a.

have whatever authority stems from the fact that it appears to embody the most persuasive of the syntheses achieved in this way.

(ii) Group Synthesis

Alternatively, if the issue is a complex and subtle one, an authoritative synthesis may emerge at the level of group action without necessarily emerging at the level of individual understanding at all. This is the model of public deliberation—sometimes referred to as 'the market-place of ideas'—presented by John Stuart Mill:

> Truth, in the great practical concerns of life, is so much a question of the reconciling and combining of opposites that very few have minds sufficiently capacious and impartial to make the adjustment with an approach to correctness, and it has to be made by the rough process of a struggle between combatants fighting under hostile banners.[50]

Here the suggestion is that people simply fling their experiences and opinions into the public forum and, whether others understand them precisely or not, they will have their effect, and the truth will emerge by a sort of 'invisible hand' process, analogous to that by which Adam Smith thought efficiency would emerge from the operation of the market. The difference between this model and the first is that Mill does not presuppose that each person's contribution is being carefully taken on board by every other person and synthesized by him with his own view before he sends his modified opinion out to engage with the views of others in a similar way. According to Mill's model, quite incommensurable ideas may have a dialectical effect on one another, so that something better emerges in the discussion, even though the 'adjustment' between the various views has not been made by the deliberate synthetic activity of any 'single mind'.

If anything like this happens, then once again there is a reason to accord to the output of such a process the sort of authority intimated in thesis [J], even though there is no such reason for according authority to the particular views of any individual participant.

5. DISCOUNTING LEGISLATORS' INTENTION

I think it should be clear by now what my argument against Marmor's thesis is going to be. It is not simply that useful legislation can be conceived to emerge non-intentionally, through the impersonal or mechanical processes we have been discussing. I also want to argue that, in each of these cases, any reason we have for according authority to the resultant legislation is

[50] J. S. Mill, *On Liberty* (Indianapolis: Bobbs Merrill, 1955), ch. 2, para. 36 (p. 58).

also a reason for discounting the authority of the views or intentions of particular legislators considered on their own.

There is an intriguing point about the rule of law here. The model of authority used by Raz and Marmor presupposes that there is one person or group X, whose knowledge or situation is such that any ordinary citizen, Y, should trust the directives of X rather than his own reasoning. But it is an important part of our normative concept of legal authority that legislators themselves should be bound by the laws they enact.[51] On the Raz–Marmor approach, it is impossible that a law could have *authority vis-à-vis* a legislator, for it makes no sense to say that X has better reason to trust the directives of X than he has to trust his own reasoning on the matter that X is addressing. By contrast, the three arguments I have presented have the attractive ability not only to satisfy thesis [J] concerning the normal justification of authority, but also to make it clear why laws should have authority over those who vote for them.

Let me now go through the arguments in turn, to discuss their implications for the respect we should accord to the views, intentions, and other non-canonical opinions of the individual legislators.

(A) The Utilitarian Argument

On this account, each individual legislator is voting either in his own interest or the interests of his particular constituents. But the authority of the resultant legislation is based on its claim to represent the *general* interest. The reasons that led the legislator to vote as he did, then, are not the reasons that there are for respecting the result: the latter should be respected because it embodies a conclusion about *social* utility, whereas the former claims to be counted on the ground that it embodies individual or sectional utility. The ground of the law's authority, therefore, is not reflected in the views or purposes of any particular legislator.

Maybe in very simple cases we can say that the general interest just *is* the shared interest of a majority of voters. In a straightforward pork-barrel case, for example, the issue may be whether to benefit the East-Coasters with a new highway or to benefit the West-Coasters with a new dam (when we cannot do both). If the preponderance of individual preferences favours the latter, it might be thought that we *can* take the selfish purposes of the West-Coast voters as our best guide to the implementation of the socially favoured policy. The social decision is about who to benefit; once that has been decided, we might as well take the interests of the victors as our best guide to what the general utility requires.

[51] See F. A. Hayek, *The Constitution of Liberty* (London: Routledge & Kegan Paul, 1960), 155: 'The chief safeguard is that the rules must apply to those who lay them down and those who apply them—that is, to the government as well as the governed.'

But a case has to be staggeringly simple to have this feature. If the legislative choice is complex, if benefits and costs are indirect as well as immediate, or if the general interest dictates any form of compromise, then the pork-barrel authority of the individual voters in the majority (such as it is) simply evaporates.

(B) Condorcet's Theorem

Condorcet's theorem amounts precisely to the claim that one will do better by following the majority decision than by following the judgement of a given legislator. What is more, *ceteris paribus*, the wiser the legislators are on average the more reason there is to follow the majority decision than to follow the views of any legislator chosen at random.

Suppose, however, that one is not picking one's legislator out at random, but choosing a member of the majority. (This after all is Marmor's suggestion as to *which legislators* are the ones whose intentions we should defer to.)[52] Surely Marmor could argue that the fact that a given legislator, L, is a member of the successful majority, shows (by Condorcet's theorem) that one will do as well by following L's view as by following the view that emerged by majority voting.

This argument would be faulty, for two reasons. First, the Condorcet theorem concerns *ex ante* probabilities, and turns on the multiplicity of ways in which a majority can be constructed. Once a result has been arrived at by majority voting, the fact that L was a member of *the particular majority* that supported the result confers no additional authority on his judgment beyond the individual competence with which he began.

Secondly, the only way to determine whether L is a member of the majority—for the purposes of this argument—is by looking at whether his view matches the precise terms of the decision that has been arrived at by voting. It is only with regard to that issue that individual and majority competences have been established. To the extent that his view varies from this, nothing can be inferred as to its reliability. If it is even subtly different, then the numbers may differ—and the whole gist of the Condorcet result is that small differences may make a big difference, so to speak.

This difficulty, moreover, cannot be evaded by insisting that we consult L's intentions only when they correspond exactly to the issue that was voted on; for it is only to the extent that L's intentions are somewhat different from the *ipsissima verba* of the legislation that they can cast any light on

[52] There is an interesting and subtle discussion in Marmor, *supra*, n. 5, 159–65. Though he recognizes certain difficulties, Marmor's view seems to be that a legislator's intention is worth consulting when the legislator in question is a member of the majority who voted for the statute, and when the intention in question is also held by most (all?) other members of that majority.

interpretive problems that courts are facing over and above the light cast by the text itself.

Let me put this last point in a way that takes it slightly outside the mechanics of the Condorcet framework. All suggestions about consulting the intentions of legislators are suggestions about consulting views, purposes, and ideas that are not directly disclosed in the text of the legislation itself. (Or else what would be the point?) But it is only the text that has been voted on, and it is only relative to that text that we can talk about a majority view. Relative to any other understanding, the identification of a view as being held by the majority is always tendentious, and it is unlikely that it will ever be less controversial than the issue on which its alleged authority is supposed to cast light.

(C) Aristotelian Synthesis

Once again the immediate argument is obvious. Aristotle's doctrine of the wisdom of the multitude is precisely the view that a group decision is sometimes more to be trusted than the judgment of its most knowledgeable and distinguished member. The latter, then, should defer like a good citizen to the decision in which he participated; and if *he* should defer, then surely every member of the group should defer. The opinions and intentions, then, that he is subordinating to the text, can hardly be taken by us as a basis for supplementing it.

Substantively, the point here is that a particular legislator's intentions may reveal only a partial view of the synthesis embodied in the legislation. To interpret the legislation in the light of such intentions would be to distort an integrated whole by biasing it towards one of its parts.

Admittedly, this does not take account of the *ex post* situation. For after the deliberation and the pooling of knowledge and experience have taken place, it may be true that some (or perhaps even every one) of the legislators is better informed on the issue than he or anyone else would be coming to it cold, with the benefit of his own unaided judgment. That is the implication of model (i), of *individual* synthesis, which we considered towards the end of Section 4.

It may be thought, moreover, that such individual syntheses have to emerge at *some* stage or other in the process, otherwise voting by individual members would not ever reveal the wisdom of the multitude. John Stuart Mill's model (ii) might be all very well as a description of the informal emergence of veridical beliefs in a culture. But it is one of our basic assumptions about a legislature that its decisions are taken by *explicit* processes of voting. There are no invisible hands here; there are nothing but real, individual hands on the voting buttons.

All the same, an awareness of the second model helps us realize how narrowly circumscribed the first may be for the purposes of statutory interpretation. For if a judge appeals beyond the text of a statute to the intentions of particular legislators, he will be appealing to things said or done during the course of the bill's passage. At that stage the decisive synthesis may not have emerged or crystallized in individual minds, and we may be dealing with what can only be described *pro tem* as 'the reconciling and combining of opposites . . . by the rough process of a struggle between combatants fighting under hostile banners'.[53] At that stage, to take the inscriptions on any one banner as indicative of the ultimate synthesis underlying the statute may be most unreliable.

If, on the other hand, one waits for the final synthesis to emerge, one will be waiting in effect for the text of the final statute. So even if model (i) is the correct image of Aristotelian synthesis, it gives little comfort to anyone who wants to establish the authority of legislators' intentions expressed otherwise than in the chapter and verse of the text that embodies what the legislature ultimately decides.

6. LEGISLATORS VERSUS THE LEGISLATURE

I want to conclude with some remarks about the assumptions I have been making about the character of modern legislation. I assumed that any legislature worth discussing would be a large, multi-member assembly, comprising hundreds of persons with diverse views, affiliations, and allegiances. I assumed too that such a body would need formally specified procedures in order to determine what counted as its decisions. And I have assumed implicitly that any bills it considered and any statutes it enacted would be complex in their contents and accordingly complex in the process of their passage.

These assumptions, I submit, tend to undermine any talk about 'the intentions of the author' of a statute. To the extent that there is one author, it is the legislature, considered as a body and as distinct from the individual members (or any subset of the individual members) that it comprises. So far as that 'author' is concerned, all we have to go on are its formally specified acts; there is no question of our being able to discern or attribute to it any thoughts, intentions, motives, or beliefs beyond that. I argued in Section 3 that we do best to abandon all talk of such intentionality when we are considering such bodies. A slightly more conciliatory way of putting the same point is that we abandon all talk of legislative intentions apart from the intentionality that is part and parcel of the linguistic meaning (that is, the conventional or, in Gricean terms, 'sentence-meaning')[54] of the legislative

[53] Mill, *supra*, n. 50, 58. [54] Grice, *supra*, n. 32.

text itself. Beyond the meanings embodied conventionally in the text of the statute, there is no state or condition corresponding to 'the intention of the legislature' to which anything else—such as what particular individuals or groups of legislators said, wrote, or did—could possibly provide a clue.

The point, in other words is this. There is simply no fact of the matter concerning a legislature's intentions apart from the formal specification of the act it has performed. Certainly, the specification yielded by the decision-procedure (that is, by the legislature's constitution) will be of an action under a certain intentional description, for legislation is, as I said earlier, a speech-act. The intentional description will be that such-and-such words were used with their conventional English meaning. That, however, is *all there is to say* about the institution's intentions. In the case of a natural person, we can go beyond that. We can always ask: 'Well what did you have in mind, what were you thinking of, when you did (or said) X?' if the meaning of X is unclear. The person's answer, though not necessarily definitive of the contents of her intention at the time, at least provides us with a clue; for there is *some* link in the case of a natural person, though certainly not a direct link, between intention and occurrent thought. In the case of a legislature or a corporation, there is no such clue, for there is nothing amounting to *the institution's occurrent thoughts*.

What are we to say, then, about the particular thoughts and hopes of individual legislators? Do they bear no relation to the legislature's action or intentionality? The strict answer is 'no'. The intentional speech-acts of the legislature are constitutional functions of the intentional voting-acts of the individual members; but what matters here is simply the intentionality of 'yea' or 'nay' in relation to a given text, not any hopes, aspirations, or understandings that may have accompanied the vote. A legislature is impotent—incapable of action—unless there is a rule for aggregating or combining the votes of its members: the principle of majority-rules, for example. But it does not need, in addition, any rule for combining their thoughts, hopes, and understandings into something that would count as the thoughts or purposes of the institution. Its intentionality—such as it is—is quite secure apart from that.

Once again, the same point can also be stated in a more conciliatory form. Of course individual legislators have thoughts and intentions, and of course these can be loosely associated with the human authorship of the statute. The point is that there is no way of going beyond that sociological platitude to settle any interpretive dispute. People only appeal to legislators' intentions when there is a disagreement, for example, in a court, about what purpose (or whatever) to attribute to the statute. If the two competing views (or any pair like them) are represented among the non-canonical intentions of the legislators, then there is no way any *one* such view can be singled out as authoritative for the purpose of settling the dispute.

Marmor might make one last reply. Surely—he will say—it matters whether the view we have in mind corresponds to the intentions of the majority or the minority in the legislature. Surely the majority view is—by reason of the rules that allow it to prevail—the more canonical.

I think this is based on a deep misapprehension about the political authority of a legislature and about the principle of majority-rule. A statute passed in parliament is an *act of parliament*, not an act of the majority party. Certainly, it claims whatever authority it has in the community on the basis of that non-partisan characterization.[55] If we think, for example, that ordinary citizens supporting a minority party are bound to respect legislation sponsored by the majority, it is because they owe that respect to *the legislature*, and to the procedures and institutional forms that constitute it, not because they owe it to the majority as such.[56] Even if the legislative and elective procedures are majoritarian, the citizen's allegiance is to the principle of majority-rule not to the (members of the) majority.

Partly this is a matter of the complexity of modern legislation, of the multiplicity of views and considerations that must be brought to bear in debates and committee stages, and of the contribution that may be made by members of minority parties to the content of a bill through rhetoric, deal-making, or amendment. Our discussion of Aristotelian synthesis captures, I think, how important this can be, and how it undermines any simple appeal to the views of a few privileged members as providing us with a canonical legislative intention.

But above all it is a recognition that the elementary circumstance of modern politics is *plurality*[57] and that the form of legislation, as of all collective decision-making, is *e pluribus unum*. The authority of a law is its emergence, under specified procedures, as a '*unum*' out of a plurality of ideas, concerns, and proposals, in circumstances where we recognize a need for one decision made together, not many made by each of us alone. The '*unum*' does not abolish the plurality, nor is it insensitive to it. It is one *decision* we need, not necessarily one personality, and so it is not merely

[55] I have argued at greater length for this in Jeremy Waldron, *The Law* (London: Routledge, 1990), 8–28.

[56] Cf. Thomas Hobbes, *Leviathan* (Cambridge: Cambridge University Press, 1991), ch. xviii, p. 121: 'A Common-wealth is said to be instituted, when a Multitude of men do Agree, and Covenant, every one with every one, that to whatsoever Man, or Assembly of Men, shall be given by the major part, the Right to Present the Person of them all (that is to say, to be their Representative); every one, as well he that Voted for it, as he that Voted against it, shall Authorise all the Actions and Judgements, of that Man, or Assembly of men, in the same manner, as if they were his own, to the end, to live peaceably among themselves, and be protected against other men.'

[57] Cf. Hannah Arendt, *The Human Condition* (University of Chicago Press, 1958), 234: 'No man can be sovereign because not one man, but men, inhabit the earth.' I use 'circumstance of politics' in this sentence in roughly the same way that John Rawls describes scarcity and limited altruism as among the 'circumstances' of justice: see John Rawls, *A Theory of Justice* (Oxford: Oxford University Press, 1971), 126–30.

as a matter of logic that we should refrain from attributing mental states to the legislature. By the same token, however, there is no justification for privileging the mental states of any faction in the legislature as canonical with regard to the decision that has been made by the whole. The decision is made in the name, and for the sake, of the entire community, and one hopes it has been made in a way that encourages rather than precludes a plurality of contributions from a variety of directions. What the decision is—what *we* have done—is the text of the statute as determined by the institution's procedures. Those procedures make us *one* in action, and their identification of something as the text of a statute makes us *one* as the authors of a deed. Before that, however, and beyond that, we are many, and no further status as a part of the *unum* can be attributed to anything else that any one of us says or thinks.

The other side of this coin is that we should not underestimate the difficulties that stand in the way of a body of legislators understanding one another as they proceed through the stages of lawmaking. I said, in Section 2, that we must assume that we are not dealing with persons who are transparent to one another, or who share a comprehensive body of common understandings. Legislators will come to the chamber from different communities, with different ideologies and different perspectives on what counts as a good reason or a valid consideration in political argument. The only thing they have in common, in their diversity and in the welter of rhetoric and mutual misunderstanding that counts for modern political debate, is the given text of the measure currently under consideration. That is constituted by the conventions of the shared official language as the only landmark, the only point of reference or co-ordination, in a sea of possible misunderstanding—and even then it is fragile enough, and always liable to fly apart on account of the fragility of shared meanings. The point is that the text of the statute, carefully drafted, proposed, and amended in accordance with the most formalistic procedures, has a canonical status in legislation that is different in kind from any common view or shared sense of purpose that one might discern in the committee rooms or in the parliamentary corridors. The latter are always tendentious, always likely to be the exclusive province of a few like-minded legislators, whose cozy understandings tend to defeat the purpose of a solemn gathering of *all* the nation's representatives. By appealing to such views, the courts take the side of what was 'implicit' or 'understood', and that may be harmless enough in a small, homogenous legislature. But it strikes me that in a multi-cultural society, legislators are entitled to insist on the authoritativeness of the text and nothing but the text, as the only thing that one can be sure has been at the forefront of each member's legislative endeavours.

One final point—a little less pompous, I hope, in its tone. I hinted at the beginning of this paper that some American judges make a practice of appealing to certain statements on the legislative record (a formal committee report, for example, or the unchallenged statement of a bill's manager) which do not traditionally count as part of text of the statute they are considering. It seems to me that Ronald Dworkin has this exactly right when he says, in effect, that the judges are developing a practice of recognizing such statements as *acts of the legislature* and that legislators are responding to that recognition by producing statements that are intended to be taken in that way.[58]

Nothing I have said is incompatible with these practices: they represent, in effect, a gradual modification of the legal system's rule of recognition[59] from the judges' side, and, as far as the legislature is concerned, they represent a gradual modification of its constitutive procedures.

To the extent that these practices are well established, they may require us to modify our view (perhaps quite subtly) about what counts as *the text* of our statute. But they do not require us to deny that our best guide to what counts as that text are the reasons (related to the *e pluribus unum* considerations I mentioned a moment ago) for identifying certain things and not others as *acts* of the legislators in their *collective* capacity. Most importantly for the purposes of this paper, these practices lend no weight to Andrei Marmor's argument that the intentions of a legislator might have authority over and above their status as disclosed in whatever turns out to count in fact as the authoritative text of the legislation itself.

What I hope to have shown, then, in this paper is that the force of Marmor's argument is narrowly confined to those very rare cases where legislation is produced by an individual author, whose knowledge and expertise provide the same reason for respecting his intentions as for respecting the text he has produced. More positively, what I hope will follow from this is a greater recognition in jurisprudence of the conditions relating to plurality that are the very stuff and circumstance of politics.

[58] Dworkin, *supra*, n. 3, 342 ff.

[59] But I doubt that Dworkin would accept *this* part of my characterization. For his views on Hart's 'rule of recognition', see ibid., 34–5.

10

All or Nothing at All? The Intentions of Authorities and the Authority of Intentions

LARRY ALEXANDER

The scene is the town council meeting in Our Town. The proposal on the floor is—yes, you've heard this one before—an ordinance that reads: 'No vehicles are allowed in the park.' The members of the town council—Alice, Barbara, Charles, David, and Edith—are casting their votes.

Alice votes aye. She has been concerned about the safety of pedestrians, especially children, which she believes is jeopardized by the large number of cars, trucks, and motorcycles that now travel through the park.

Barbara votes aye. Her concerns are principally aesthetic. She finds the sight, sound, and smell of the vehicular traffic detract from the beauty and serenity that she would like the park to provide.

Charles votes aye. He himself, and many whom he represents, have become increasingly annoyed by the cut-up antics of skateboarders and rollerbladers. He cannot get others to join with him to ban skateboarders and rollerbladers specifically, a ban which he would prefer to the proposed ban on vehicles. But he prefers to ban all vehicles to banning none, if the ban includes skateboarders and rollerbladers, as he believes this ban does. (He has not, however, sought clarification regarding whether skateboarders and rollerbladers are included.)

David votes no. He represents such interests as skateboarders and rollerbladers as well as the many push-cart vendors who currently operate in the park. He believes the ordinance covers those whom he represents, though like Charles he has not obtained a definitive opinion on this issue from the rest of the council.

Edith also votes no. She is quite close to being an anarchist and generally opposes all regulations beyond the bare-bones criminal law and traffic laws. (She does not believe there is a safety problem in the park warranting further restrictions on traffic.)

The author would like to thank the following people for their very helpful comments on the ideas discussed herein: Paul Campos, Richard Kay, Brian Leiter, Stephen Perry, Steven Walt, and Christopher Wonnell.

The final vote is three to two in favour of the ordinance. Because the town council is legally empowered to pass regulations of this type by majority vote, the ordinance becomes law.

The scene now shifts to a short time after. The ordinance is on the books of Our Town. A veterans group wants to know if the ordinance forbids placing a military tank in the park to serve as a monument to Our Town's veterans. They are joined by skateboarders, rollerbladers, push-cart vendors, nannies pushing prams, and an advertising company that wishes to drop a car from a helicopter into the park to demonstrate the car's solidity and fine suspension. All of these groups are seeking to determine whether the ordinance applies to them.

The scene again shifts, this time to the much more distant future. The park is still there, and the ordinance is still on Our Town's books. Now, however, people travel around in bubble-like devices that ride on a cushion of air and are essentially invisible, emit no sounds or pollutants, and cause no injury or pain if they hit someone. The question has arisen whether these devices are allowed in the park in the absence of repeal of the ordinance.

These scenes are virtually all the props I need to explore the ever-vexing jurisprudential chestnut: what is the proper methodology for interpreting legal texts?

I. THE INTENTIONS OF AUTHORITIES

Much ink has been spilled on the question of how laws like the 'no vehicles are allowed in the park' ordinance should be interpreted.[1] With a few notable and rather recent exceptions, however, most of which involve contributors to this book, the debate over interpretive methodology has proceeded largely independently of the jurisprudential question, what is the nature of law? The two issues are intimately related, however. Knowing how to interpret laws requires knowing what laws *are*.

In what follows I shall attempt to illustrate how a theory about the nature of law carries with it the seeds of a theory of legal interpretation. I shall also attempt to demonstrate that many issues that are currently considered part of a theory of legal interpretation are actually part of a theory of authority instead. Debates over legal interpretation have been needlessly confused by lumping together questions of authority with questions of interpretive methodology.

[1] See e.g. Paul Brest, 'The Misconceived Quest for the Original Understanding', *Boston Univ. Law Rev.*, 60 (1980), 204–38, 209–13; Lon Fuller, 'Positivism and Fidelity to Law—A Reply to Professor Hart', *Harv. Law Rev.*, 71 (1958), 630–72; H. L. A. Hart, 'Positivism and the Separation of Law and Morals', *Harv. Law Rev.*, 71 (1958), 593–629.

A. The Task of Legal Authorities

The theory of law I find most persuasive is one most closely associated with Joseph Raz. According to this theory, law is the determinations of authorities of what ought to be done.[2] This theory is not a complete theory of law: as stated, it does not cover the status of the norms that designate who the authorities are and the scope of their authority, as well as certain other issues of authority that I shall mention in the second half of this paper. Are these norms, 'norms of authority', as I shall call them, legal norms, or are they moral norms? The theory in the simplified version I shall work with does not tell us.

Despite its neglect of issues of authority, this theory of law does have important implications. First, law is related to, but distinct from, morality. Morality concerns what ought to be done, and, on most meta-ethical accounts, its claims must be deemed to override all non-moral considerations. Law's task is to make moral principles determinate so that people can more easily ascertain what ought to be done than they can by direct recourse to abstract moral principles.[3] That means, however, that although law is handmaiden to morality in influencing people regarding what they ought to do, law can err. The determinations the authorities make regarding what morality requires can be mistaken. Law and morality can come apart. Thus, this theory of law is a positivistic theory. Law's enterprise is necessarily a moral enterprise, but its results are only contingently morally correct.[4]

The second implication of this theory of law is that law consists of a finite number of dateable determinations. (I leave aside the 'norms of authority'.) If law is what the authorities determine ought to be done, then it consists of those specific determinations which, being determinations, occurred at specific times and places. Again leaving aside 'norms of authority', there are no free-floating legal rules, rules not traceable to specific authorities at specific times and places.

(A corollary of this second implication is that there are no such things as legal 'principles' in Ronald Dworkin's sense, norms that are not identical to moral norms and that arise from, but are not reducible to, the determinations of the authorities.[5] On my account, the authorities either determine what ought to be done by enacting what in Dworkin's terminology are legal rules, or they enjoin people to act morally, a totally superfluous injunction given the already overriding nature of moral claims. If they 'enact' a legal 'principle'—say, the 'principle' of freedom of speech—either that 'principle'

[2] See Joseph Raz, 'Authority, Law and Morality', *The Monist*, 68 (1985), 295–324.

[3] Ibid. 304, 306.

[4] See Joseph Raz, *The Authority of Law* (Oxford: Clarendon Press, 1979), 233–49.

[5] See Ronald Dworkin, *Taking Rights Seriously* (Cambridge, Mass.: Harvard University Press, 1977), 105–23.

is a moral principle that they need not have enacted, or it is an incipient legal rule whose content has yet to be determined. It cannot be anything else.)[6]

A third implication of this theory of law follows from the fact that law's role is essentially epistemic. That is, law's role is to make what morality requires more determinate, which means more knowable, by those whom law governs. (Law's co-ordination and convention-establishing function is ultimately subsumable under the goal of making moral requirements more determinate.)[7] An implication of this role is that legal authorities fail in their task, not only when they merely restate moral norms, but also when the meaning of the rules they enact is as difficult to ascertain as the application of moral norms. Lon Fuller had a lot to say regarding this aspect of the lawmaking task.[8]

One issue within theories of law such as the one I am describing is whether law possesses practical authority or only theoretical authority. In other words, when the authorities determine what morality requires and enact their determinations as legal rules, are those governed by the rules to treat the rules as pre-empting their own independent moral assessments of what should be done (practical authority), or are they to treat the rules merely as sage advice but not practically pre-emptive?[9] Although the answer I favour is a mixed and paradoxical one—law has only (potential) theoretical authority but must claim practical authority[10]—this issue is one that I do not have to resolve for my present purposes. I think the methodology for interpreting authorities is independent of what kind of authority—practical or theoretical—the authorities possess.

To summarize, according to the theory of law that I favour, the role of law is to make moral requirements more determinate. That role entails the following: that law and morality are separate, and that law derives from social sources, namely, the acts of authorities (legal positivism); that law consists of a finite set of dateable rules; and that law fails in its task, not only when the authorities mis-gauge what morality requires, but also when their rules fail to guide better than unmediated moral norms.

B. Law, Texts, and Authorial Intentions

Law consists of the determinations of authorities of what ought to be done. Its function is to make what is morally required more determinate than

[6] See, in this volume, Larry Alexander and Kenneth Kress, 'Against Legal Principles', *supra*, Ch. 7.

[7] See Larry Alexander, 'Law and Exclusionary Reasons', *Philosophical Topics*, 18 (1990), 5–22, 16–19.

[8] Lon Fuller, *The Morality of Law*, rev. edn. (New Haven, Conn.: Yale University Press, 1969). See also Raz, *supra*, n. 4, at 163–79.

[9] See Heidi M. Hurd, 'Challenging Authority', *Yale LJ* 100 (1991), 1611–77.

[10] See Alexander, *supra*, n. 7, 19–20.

abstract moral norms. This means that the authorities' determinations must be communicated to the governed.

In modern societies the communication of authorities' determinations is usually achieved through written texts. Although a specific order might be communicated orally—in which case its statement consists of an oral text—most specific orders, as well as all constitutions, statues, and administrative rules, are embodied in written texts.

All texts are attempts by their authors to communicate, usually to other people, but occasionally to the authors themselves at some later time. Legal texts are attempts by authorities to communicate their determinations of what ought to be done to those they govern. Novels are attempts by novelists to communicate details of plot and character to readers. Scientific texts are attempts by scientists to communicate their scientific findings to their intended audience. And so on.

If texts are attempts by their authors to communicate, then *texts mean what their authors intend them to mean.* Take away the author's intentions, and you fail to have a text. If the proverbial thousand monkeys cavorting on typewriters produced *Moby-Dick*, it would be incoherent to ask, for example, what Ahab's quest for the white whale 'meant'. Indeed, we could not even ask what language *Moby-Dick* is written in, since our monkeys were not intending to communicate in any language. *Moby-Dick* the novel would not exist.[11] The same point holds true of legal texts. We assume the

[11] That the monkeys' marks resemble marks made by writers in English makes no difference. Is the flagpole outside my office the letter 'i'? And suppose there were a language, Shmenglish, that resembled English in every way, except that the nouns and verbs were switched around, so that 'dog' meant a domestic animal that meows, 'cat' meant a domestic animal that barks, 'whale' meant an ink-squirting mollusc, 'harpoon' meant a rapid-firing gun, 'walk' meant to move one's legs as quickly as possible, and so forth. Would we be able to interpret the monkeys' novel in such a case? Because they had no linguistic intentions, how can we decide in which of the infinite possible languages that could employ such marks their 'novel' was typed? In this connection, consider the following column by Dave Barry in the *San Diego Union*, 4 Dec. 1993: 'Meanwhile, out in Pinedale, Wyo., we have a situation involving: ARTISTS PAINTING ON COWS. You may have heard about this. Three artists got a $4,000 grant, some of which came from the federal government, to paint words from a pioneer woman's diary on the sides of live cows. I am not making this up. The idea was that the cows, with the words on their sides, would wander around and poop on symbolic representations of U.S. taxpayers.

No, seriously, the idea, as explained by one of the artists, was that the wandering cows would scramble the words so as to "create a new text." I think this is a terrific idea, and I believe that the government should seriously consider using wandering painted cows to generate the instructions for filling out federal tax forms. I bet cows would do a MUCH better job than whoever is doing this now (my guess is hamsters).'

For a good sampling of the literature in support of the general proposition that texts *qua* texts mean only what their authors intend them to mean, see Steven Knapp and Walter Benn Michaels, 'Intention, Identity, and the Constitution', in Gregory Leyh (ed.), *Legal Hermeneutics: History, Theory, and Practice* (Berkeley: University of California Press, 1992), 187–99, 190; Richard S. Kay, 'Original Intentions, Standard Meanings, and the Legal Character of the Constitution', *Const. Comm.*, 6 (1989), 39–50, 40–5; E. D. Hirsch, 'Counterfactuals in Interpretation', in Sanford Levinson and Steven Mailloux (eds.), *Interpreting Law and Literature* (Evanston, Ill.: Northwestern University Press, 1988), 55–68, 57; Steven Knapp and Walter Benn Michaels,

US Constitution is the attempt by the framers to communicate, in English, their determinations regarding how to structure and limit a national government. If we were to discover that the Constitution was the accidental product of spilled ink or the thousand monkeys, or that it was written in the framers' private code or in an exotic language that just superficially resembles English, our attitude toward it would completely change. If it were not a product of human design it would not be a text at all, and would have no meaning as one. If it were a communication, but one in a different language, then it would have meaning as a text, but its meaning would not be what we now think it is based on our assumption the framers were writing in English. The marks 'canard' mean different things in different languages and mean nothing if they are the result of wave action on a sandy beach.[12]

A text is an attempt by a particular author to communicate in a particular language or language-like code of some kind, and texts mean what their authors intend them to mean. That is not to say things that are not texts cannot be appropriated by authors and converted to texts. If someone had spilled ink in Philadelphia in 1787, and the resulting blots on paper looked just like letters that spelled out words in English, words that would express better than any others exactly what the framers had determined should be the fundamental law of the United States, the framers could adopt that ink-stained paper to represent their determinations and thereby convert it into a text. Similarly, Melville might have found the random peckings of the monkeys to have made just the markings he would have made to communicate his ideas of plot and character. Indeed, all authors appropriate marks and sounds that in themselves have no meaning and that could have been and are frequently produced with no intent to communicate, just as clouds can take the shapes of familiar objects without thereby becoming representational art.

Moreover, just as authors such as the framers or Melville can appropriate

'Against Theory 2: Hermeneutics and Deconstruction', *Critical Inquiry*, 14 (1987), 49–68, 54, 60; id., 'Against Theory', *Critical Inquiry*, 8 (1982), 723–42, 725–30; Walter Benn Michaels, 'The Fate of the Constitution', *Texas Law Rev.* 61 (1982), 765–76, 774. Even Stanley Fish, usually associated with the so-called 'reader response theory' of interpretation, which minimizes the role of the author and her intentions—see e.g. Robin West, 'The Aspirational Constitution', *Northwestern Univ. Law Rev.*, 88 (1993), 241–68, 257–8—has actually endorsed the centrality of authorial intention to interpretation. See Stanley Fish, 'Play of Surfaces: Theory and the Law', in Leyh (ed.), *Legal Hermeneutics*, 297–316, 299–300.

[12] Of course, I am speaking here of texts as communications. Texts can have plenty of meanings apart from their meaning as communications by their authors, just as can the marks made by waves in the sand. A text can be a sign of some event's occurrence in the sense that it is evidence of such an event. A statute may 'mean' that the legislature convened last year, or that the recorder of statutes was on the job, in this sense of 'mean', just as clouds can 'mean' rain or the marks on the beach can mean the high tide has occurred. See Heidi M. Hurd, 'Sovereignty in Silence', *Yale LJ* 99 (1990), 945–1028, 953–67 (discussing the Gricean analysis of communication).

non-texts for use as their texts, so too can some authors appropriate other authors' texts for use as their own.[13] If the framers meant something quite narrow by the phrase 'due process of law', such as legal regularity, but the Supreme Court ignores their intent and declares the phrase to encompass a broad array of substantive rights, then the Court has in effect re-authored the Constitution. It has taken the words of the Constitution and made them into a text more to its liking than the framers' text. The same point holds true for 'interpretations' of *Moby-Dick* that are not what Melville had in mind. (Note the relevance of this point to the question of whether the 'framers' of the Constitution for purposes of its interpretation are those who met in Philadelphia, the state legislatures that ratified the Philadelphia product, or others: each group could use the same words to communicate different determinations.)

In short, a text is always some author's text. It is whatever that author intended to communicate through the marks or sounds.[14] But one person's marks or sounds can be appropriated by other authors for use as *their* texts, just as one can cut the word 'canard' out of a French cookbook, where it refers to duck, for use in a note in English, where it refers to an untruth.

C. The Authorial Intentions of Legal Authorities

Law consists of the determinations of legal authorities of what ought to be done. Those determinations are communicated to their intended audience through legal texts. Legal texts, like all texts, are the symbolic vehicles for communicating what their authors intend to communicate, which in the case of law is the authorities' determinations of what ought to be done.

If we want to know what the law is, we must ascertain what the authorities have determined ought to be done. To ascertain that, we must look at their texts with an eye to discovering their authorial intentions. For *their* texts (as opposed to the texts that others could make out of the marks and sounds) are their vehicles for communicating to us what they have determined we should do, and mean only what they intended them to mean, which is the meaning we seek to discover if we seek to discover the law. This holds true no matter who the authorities are.

1. Speaker's Meaning and Dictionary Meaning

At this point, one will object that my analysis is much too simplistic. When I say that texts mean what their authors intend them to mean, have I not neglected such obvious distinctions as that between speaker's meaning on

[13] See the example in Paul Campos's 'Three Mistakes About Interpretation', *Mich. Law Rev.*, 92 (1993), 388–97, 389–90.

[14] See Jorge J. E. Garcia, 'Can There Be Texts Without Historical Authors?', *Amer. Phil. Q.*, 31 (1994), 245–53, 251–2; Paul Campos, 'Against Constitutional Theory', *Yale J. of Law & Hum.*, 4 (1992), 279–310, 301–2; id., *supra*, n. 13, 395–6. See also authorities cited *supra*, n. 11.

the one hand and dictionary and sentence meaning on the other? Although we must refer to an author's intention to ascertain that marks are a text and are written in a particular language, can we not dispense with the author's intentions at that point and ask what the text means in that language independently of what the author intended it to mean? In other words, can we not say that the author intended to use English when making the marks 'hippopotamus', and intended thereby to communicate the idea of an animal with a large trunk, but that 'hippopotamus' *means* something other than what the author intended it to mean?

The answer to this question is, as one might suspect, quite complicated. Let us say that the word 'hippopotamus' *means* a stocky African mammal that likes to wallow in mud and swim in rivers *in this sense*: the average reader of English who sees the word and assumes that it was intended by its author to be a word in the English language would assume it was intended to refer to such an animal (since such an animal is what most English speakers intend to refer to when they use the word). In other words, the word means what a standard dictionary would define it to mean. Let us call this type of meaning M_D for dictionary meaning, and let us distinguish it from speaker's meaning M_S, the ideas the speaker intends to communicate.

On the other hand, authors can use marks and sounds that have a particular M_D in a particular language to communicate ideas that are not part of M_D. Words can be used in non-standard and quite idiosyncratic ways. Of course, the authors who use words in such non-standard ways will frequently fail to communicate what they intend to, because the audience assumes the words are being used in a standard way. Ultimately, however, all meanings M_D depend on authors' intentions in the sense that audience understandings are attempts to decipher those intentions. Non-standard and idiosyncratic usages can become standard. M_D can change if speakers' meanings—M_S—change.[15]

At this point, then, we can distinguish among the following items: the author's intention to communicate certain ideas, such as, in the case of legal

[15] Of course, it is also true that successful communication of non-standard meanings usually depends on standard meanings or M_D. I cannot successfully communicate to you that I am using 'bad' to mean 'good', or that my touching my nose means 'bunt', unless I do so using some standard English meanings. If everything I said was non-standard, I would not be speaking in English but in a language of my own making. (Whether there can be truly private languages that are not constructed from public languages—or whether all languages are private in that no user's meaning can be perfectly translated by another—is an issue that I need not resolve.) See Anthony Dardis, 'How the Radically Interpreted Make Mistakes', *Dialogue*, 33 (1994), 415–35.

On the general relation between what I have called meaning$_D$ and meaning$_S$, see Donald Davidson, 'A Nice Derangement of Epitaphs', in Ernest LePore (ed.), *Truth and Interpretation: Perspectives on the Philosophy of Donald Davidson* (Oxford: Basil Blackwell, 1986), 433–46, 434, 439–40; Kay, *supra*, n. 11, 41. Both equate meaning$_D$ with the meaning usually intended.

authorities, what ought to be done (speaker's meaning M_S); the author's intention to convey those ideas through certain marks, sounds, or gestures (symbols); the author's intention to have those symbols be understood to be a particular language; and the meaning M_D that those symbols carry in the intended language. We have seen that M_S and M_D can come apart. The question then is whether communication can 'mean' M_D when M_D differs from M_S. Put differently, can communications mean something other than what their authors intend them to mean, even if meaning M_D in general at some level depends upon authorial intentions (M_S), and even if M_D in every case depends upon an authorial intent to communicate and to communicate in a particular language? Can we say that communications 'mean' what an author would intend them to mean if the author were speaking or writing in the correct standard version of the language that the author is intending to use?

I see no reason why we cannot speak about a communication's meaning in such a sense. On the other hand, in the context of legal texts the question is, why should we care what a communication's dictionary meaning M_D is (in the language intended by the authorities) if the authorities' meaning M_S is different? *Their* text is their attempt to communicate what they have determined ought to be done, and *that* text's meaning is M_S, not M_D, or so it would appear.[16] For if we disregard M_S in favor of M_D, why should we not as well disregard the language the authorities intended in favour of a language in which M_D is most to our liking? Put differently, why should the authorities be authorized to determine the symbols of legal texts and the language those symbols represent, but not be authorized to determine what the language shall mean when they use it?[17]

There is an obvious answer to this question, of course, one that relates to the rule of law and particularly the virtue of understandable legal commands. I shall address this answer and its effect on interpretation of legal texts in Part II. For the moment I wish to assume that a prima-facie case for making authorial intent the touchstone of legal interpretation has been established, and established on these grounds: (1) the role of legal authorities is to determine what ought to be done; (2) legal texts are communications from legal authorities to citizens and other legal authorities of those determinations of what ought to be done; (3) those texts mean what the authorities intend them to mean, M_S, namely, what they have determined

[16] Consider in this regard the Far Side cartoon by Gary Larson reprinted overleaf (courtesy of Richard Kay).

[17] See Campos, 'Against Constitutional Theory', *supra*, n. 14, at 283 n. 14. Query: can we ever say that the authorities determined the language of the symbols they chose if the language is given meaning different from what they intended? (See I.C.1. above.) In other words, how can we say they chose 'English' rather than 'Smenglish'? And does the same problem exist for the symbols they chose? What makes this 'a' the same symbol as this 'a'? See Knapp and Michaels, 'Intention, Identity, and the Constitution', *supra*, n. 11, 191–2.

"Wait! Wait! . . . Cancel that, I guess it says 'helf.' "

ought to be done. The intentions of the authorities are central because of the combination of what it means to be an authority and what it means to be a text.

2. *The Varieties of Speaker's Intentions*

Thus far I have treated speaker's meaning M_S as a univocal item, based on a univocal conception of the speaker's intention. At this point, however, it is useful to consider Gregory Bassham's distinctions among various types of speaker's intentions and beliefs and then to ask what hangs on such distinctions.[18]

[18] Gregory Bassham, *Original Intent and the Constitution* (Lanham, Md.: Rowman & Littlefield Publishers, 1992), 28–34.

Bassham distinguishes, on the one hand, between the legal authorities' beliefs about the legal effects of what they have authored and, on the other hand, other changes in the world that they expected or hoped would be accomplished by what they did intend to have legal effects.[19] (An example of the latter in our hypothetical case would be the town council's belief that park use will increase if the 'no vehicles' ordinance is enacted and enforced, or that the members of the town council will be re-elected. Neither of these beliefs, if mistaken, affects the legal effects of the ordinance.)[20]

Within the former category of authorities' beliefs about the legal effects of their enactment, Bassham distinguishes among (1) scope beliefs, (2) counter-factual scope beliefs, and (3) semantic intentions.[21] Scope beliefs are the actual occurrent beliefs the authorities hold at the time of enactment about the legal effects of that enactment.[22] Put differently, they are the actual beliefs of the authorities about what legal changes they have determined be implemented.

Counter-factual scope beliefs are the beliefs about such legal effects that the authorities would have held had they considered the particular application (of their text) in question.[23] Bassham gives as an example of a counter-factual scope belief the belief the framers of the US Constitution would have held regarding whether skyjacking is an 'infamous' crime within the meaning of the grand jury clause of the Fifth Amendment.[24] Obviously, the framers would not have had actual beliefs about skyjacking in 1791. None the less, Bassham considers it meaningful and sensible to ask what beliefs they would have held on the legal status of skyjacking under the Fifth Amendment had they considered skyjacking. Strict intentionalists are, for Bassham, all who would interpret legal texts solely according to scope and counter-factual scope beliefs, although the strictest of strict intentionalists look only to scope beliefs.

The authorities' semantic intentions are their intentions regarding the *meaning* of their legal texts.[25] Now this in itself is quite unhelpful because scope beliefs and counter-factual beliefs could be the exclusive determinants of the texts' *meaning*, in which case semantic intentions would merely be intentions to effectuate scope and counter-factual scope beliefs. Bassham points out, however, that a legislature that bans toxic substances may have in mind a particular concept of toxicity, or a particular definition or description of toxicity—semantic intentions—as well as some particular examples of toxic substances that they believed they were banning (scope beliefs).[26] It may turn out that the particular examples of toxic substances may not in fact be toxic according to the contemplated definition of toxicity. Or it may

[19] Ibid. 69–71.

[20] Bassham calls these latter intentions non-binding intentions and includes among them such things as the authorities' intentions regarding their own authority. Ibid.

[21] Ibid. 29. [22] Ibid. [23] Ibid. [24] Ibid. [25] Ibid. [26] Ibid. 32.

turn out that both the particular examples of toxic substances *and* the contemplated definition of toxicity are inconsistent with the best theory of the nature of toxicity as a concept.

Bassham labels as 'moderate intentionalists' those who would follow the authorities' semantic intentions when these conflict with the scope and counter-factual scope intentions.[27] With respect to which of the authorities' semantic intentions should dominate—their 'spare', realist intentions to use the terms consistently with the true nature of the terms' referents, or their 'rich', conventionalist intentions to use the terms according to the definitions or descriptions they have in mind—Bassham would apparently follow the authorities' own intentions on this question itself.[28] (If you discovered that your conception of toxicity was inconsistent with toxicity's true nature, which would you want to be controlling in terms of legal effect?)[29] Bassham himself believes that with regard to the US Constitution, the framers' semantic intentions were usually rich, not spare.[30] He concludes that the most defensible form of intentionalism in constitutional interpretation is moderate intentionalism in which the framers' rich semantic intentions trump their scope and counter-factual scope intentions.[31]

3. When the Authorities' Intentions Come Apart: Counter-factuality and Meaning

Although Bassham would deal with these various types of authorities' intentions—scope, counter-factual scope, and semantic, rich and spare—by choosing which one should be dispositive, I suggest that the question is not one of the interpreter's choice. The question is, what did the authorities intend to communicate that they had determined ought to be done? And prima facie that appears to be a datum about the world, not a matter of choice.

Choosing which one of Bassham's categories of intentions should be the basis of interpretation appears artificial for two reasons. First, whenever the various intentions conflict, there is no reason not to ask which intentions would the authorities wish to dominate in such a case. If semantic intentions conflict with scope intentions, there is no reason to choose semantic intentions as what the authorities 'intended' if the authorities would have chosen their scope intentions to dominate their semantic ones.

Secondly, I believe that Bassham's distinctions—and other analogous ones—ultimately collapse. I believe, for example, that within semantic intentions the distinction between sense and reference breaks down. Ultimately,

[27] Ibid. [28] Ibid. 32, 80–2. [29] Ibid. 32.

[30] Ibid. 79. They may not have always been rich, however. Bassham gives the example of a question that can arise under the 25th Amendment, namely, whether a president who has suffered cessation of brain activity but not respiration or circulation is 'dead'. Here, the framers arguably intended their realist intentions to trump their conventionalist intentions. Ibid. 82.

[31] Ibid. 51–6.

what a term refers to cannot be determined without a definition or description; but definitions and descriptions purport to be *of* something.[32] (We wouldn't know the thing that 'death' refers to without some description of it, though likewise we think that death can be mis-described.) Moreover, the distinction between semantic intentions and counter-factual scope intentions breaks down. Our definitions and descriptions can be fallible generalizations from particulars, and the particulars can be fallible inferences from generalizations.

In the end, I see no reason why a broad notion of counter-factual scope beliefs/intentions cannot subsume all of Bassham's categories of authorities' intentions. What we want to know—given some fact situation, the authorities' semantic understandings, the true nature of that to which their terms refer, and so on—is what they determined should be the legal effect of their action. Because the authorities' exemplars may be inconsistent with the definitions of the terms they employ, and the definitions may be inconsistent with the true nature of the terms' referents, the question is which did they intend to dominate in cases of such inconsistency.[33] In some cases, perhaps, referents will dominate definitions and exemplars.[34] In other cases, definitions or exemplars will dominate.[35]

What I have proposed, therefore, is to broaden Bassham's notion of counter-factual scope beliefs and intentions and to make it the touchstone of the authorities' meaning M_S. What the authorities mean by an enactment

[32] See generally Ralph Shain, 'Mill, Quine, and Natural Kinds', *Metaphilosophy*, 24 (1993), 275–92 (discussing problems with the concept of 'natural kinds'). See also Andrei Marmor, *Interpretation and Legal Theory* (Oxford: Clarendon Press, 1992), 144–5.

[33] Bear in mind that I believe that exemplars, definitions, and referents ultimately are interrelated and cannot be neatly opposed.

[34] Note that because the role of authorities is to determine what ought to be done—to make moral principles concrete enough to guide citizens and officials—when the authorities intend the true nature of the referents of the terms they employ to dominate their own inconsistent definitions and exemplars, they are in some sense defaulting on their role. In making legal effects turn on the true nature of moral terms, whatever that nature happens to be, the authorities have failed to give moral guidance; and in making legal effects turn on the true nature of natural kinds, they have left a good deal to the unknown (which is why I believe that reference cannot completely take leave of sense).

[35] The best discussion of why interpretation should not be tied to the true nature of the things to which the legal text's words refer is found in Stephen R. Munzer, 'Realistic Limits on Realist Interpretation', *South. Calif. Law Rev.*, 58 (1985), 459–75. Munzer, replying to Michael Moore's realist theory of legal interpretation, points out that many words do not name 'kinds' of any type (461–2), that words that name 'functional kinds' do not presuppose an underlying true nature of these kinds (466–8), that moral terms and natural-kind terms may not map on to reality in any neat way (462, 464), and finally, that for many legal texts, conventional understandings should dominate the true nature of terms' referents (468–70). In the latter category, Munzer places a statute limiting the harvest of 'fish' written at a time when whales were thought to be fish. Given certain purposes for the statute, it should be read to include whales (468–70). And see Dardis, *supra*, n. 15, 423–5 (discussing malapropisms, classic instances where semantic intentions come apart, not in terms of referent versus definition, but in terms of word chosen versus word meant).

is governed by how they would describe the enactment's legal effects in each possible circumstance. For example, if the enactment is, like our beginning hypothetical one, a prohibition of some behaviour, its meaning is what the authorities would say were their intended legal effects—prohibition or no prohibition—in the circumstances in question. If Alice, Barbara, and Charles all have in mind blue Chevrolets when they vote aye, but, if asked whether their ordinance would prohibit green Fords, would reply that it would, their counter-factual intention and thus the meaning of their enactment is that green Fords are prohibited.

We are at this juncture in the argument. Proper legal interpretation of legal texts must comport with the role of the authoring legal authorities. That role is to determine what ought to be done, which determination is what authorities intend to communicate to citizens and officials through legal texts. The meaning of such texts, therefore, just is what the authorities wish to communicate through them. And although the authorities might have various inconsistent beliefs and intentions embodied in their texts, when that is the case, the texts' meanings are still what legal effects authorities would declare the texts to have when confronted with such conflicts and inconsistencies.[36]

Two obstacles remain, however, before the case for adverting to the counter-factual scope beliefs and intentions of the authorities is secure, and both of them arise from the philosophically problematic nature of counterfactuals. The first obstacle is the problem of distinguishing between translations and corrections: we must leave room for the possibility that, in imagining the counter-factual dialogue with the authorities, we can envision their saying: 'We meant X but we now see that X was a mistake.' The second obstacle is whether the counter-factual inquiry is determinate: is there a fact of the matter regarding what the authorities would have believed and intended with respect to some situation not before them?

4. Counter-factual Scope Intentions: Leaving Room for the Possibility of Mistakes

Determining authorities' counter-factual scope intentions—which intentions, I have argued, are the key to interpreting legal texts—leads us to the following

[36] This approach to interpretation—frequently referred to as 'originalism'—has an impressive following. For example, William Eskridge, not himself an originalist, defines originalism almost identically to what I have called the meaning of the authorities' legal texts: 'This "intentionalist" [originalist] approach asks how the . . . [authorities] originally intended the interpretive question to be answered or would have intended the question to be answered had . . . [they] thought about the issue when . . . [they] passed the statute.' William N. Eskridge, Jr., 'Dynamic Statutory Interpretation', *Univ. Penn. Law Rev.*, 135 (1987), 1479–1555, 1479–80. See also Steven D. Smith, 'Law Without Mind', *Mich. Law Rev.*, 88 (1989), 104–19, 105–6; Earl Maltz, 'Some New Thoughts on An Old Problem—The Role of the Intent of the Framers in Constitutional Theory', *Boston Univ. Law Rev.*, 63 (1983), 811–51, 815–16 n. 14; Brest, *supra* n. 1, 222–3.

issue. Is it possible to distinguish between: (1) what the authorities *did determine* with respect to a factual situation that they were not adverting to at the time they authored their communication about what ought to be done; and (2) what the authorities *should have determined* with respect to such a situation? In other words, can we distinguish between counterfactual scope beliefs and intentions and (from our perspective) correct beliefs and intentions?

Consider one of the most carefully argued and persuasive recent attempts to describe proper interpretation in circumstances not envisioned by the authoring authorities. In 'Fidelity in Translation', Lawrence Lessig equates interpretation in such circumstances to translation.[37] Translation, says Lessig, requires two steps.[38] The first step is to read the text for the meaning it carries in its original context—how the authorities envisioned their determination would operate. The second step is to translate that meaning into the current context of application. Interpretation as translation requires that the meaning of a text be preserved as the contexts of application change. So long as the text's meaning in application is preserved through contextual change, the interpreters can be said to be carrying out what the authorities determined and communicated ought to be done rather than to be acting on their (the interpreters') own view of what ought to be done.

Lessig then goes on to describe translation of legal texts—how meaning in application is preserved through contextual changes.[39] The original context from which meaning is derived consists of the presuppositions of the authorities.[40] These, categorized broadly, consist of presuppositions about matters of fact, presuppositions about matters of law, and presuppositions about values. For example, the framers of the Fifth Amendment posited a privilege against self-incrimination in a factual setting in which there were no police forces and police interrogators like those we find today.[41] Therefore, even if the framers envisioned the clause's application to be restricted to interrogations at or before trial by magistrates or prosecutors, their meaning for the clause is preserved by applying it to the modern context of interrogation, namely, custodial interrogation of the defendant by the police. A difference in factual presuppositions between 1791 and today gets us from the Fifth Amendment to *Miranda* v. *Arizona*,[42] such that we can say that the *Miranda* decision is what the framers of the Fifth Amendment determined. In Lessig's terms, *Miranda* is a faithful translation of the Fifth Amendment's privilege against self-incrimination.

Lessig gives as an example of a change in legal presuppositions the case where a legal text is implicitly premissed on the existence of other legal doctrines, doctrines which in the interim between the promulgation of the

[37] *Texas Law Rev.* 71 (1993), 1165–1268. [38] Ibid. 1211. [39] Ibid. 1211 ff.
[40] Ibid. 1213–14. [41] Ibid. 1234–6. [42] 384 U.S. 436 (1966).

texts and the applications in question are judicially overruled or legislatively repealed.[43] As one example, Lessig points to the federal 'silver platter' doctrine—evidence is admissible in federal courts even if seized by state officials through a search and seizure that would have violated the Fourth Amendment were the states subject to that amendment, and even if the evidence would have been excluded from federal courts had federal officials been involved—and argues that the subsequently announced doctrine of incorporation should dictate a change in the doctrine's application to evidence seized by state officials.[44] As another example of a change in legal presuppositions that arguably requires a change in application, Lessig points to the expansion of federal power under modern judicial interpretations of the commerce clause, a change in legal presuppositions that arguably affects whether the Tenth Amendment, which might originally have been nothing but a legal truism, now has some affirmative legal bite in order to preserve a meaningful domain of state sovereignty.[45]

The problem with Lessig's approach, as Lessig himself recognizes, is that it threatens to efface the distinction between interpretation—fidelity in translating the authorities' determinations—and emendation, correcting those determinations that are, from the interpreter's point of view, mistakes.[46] In cases of interpretation, the authorities' role to determine what ought to be done is respected. In emendation, that role is usurped by the interpreter, who becomes the ultimate authority.

To see why this is so, imagine any case in which the interpreter has a view on what ought to be done, a view that superficially conflicts with what the authorities have determined. To take one of Lessig's examples,[47] consider that in 1864 Congress wrote a provision into the United States Code limiting the fee to 10 dollars that a veteran could pay an attorney for representation in a veterans' benefit suit. In 1864 10 dollars could purchase adequate legal services. Congress's intention was merely to limit what attorneys could charge veterans, not to exclude attorneys from veterans' benefits proceedings altogether. Today, however, because of over a century of inflation, the 10-dollar limitation would operate to exclude legal representation. The question then is, does fidelity in translation require us to read '10 dollars' to mean 'the cost of the amount of legal services that 10 dollars would have bought in 1864'?

Lessig is aware of the importance of this question, and he addresses it in the context of setting limits to his model of translation.[48] The important limit for my purposes is what Lessig calls 'structural humility'.[49] Humility in translation requires that the translator not improve the original text, that is, not correct mistakes that the text contains. The translator's job is to find equivalence in meaning between contexts, not to improve the meaning.

[43] Lessig, *supra*, n. 37, 1215–17. [44] Ibid. [45] Ibid. 1224–8.
[46] Ibid. 1251. [47] Ibid. 1176–7. [48] Ibid. 1251 ff. [49] Ibid. 1252–61.

Not all improvements are inappropriate, however, but only improvements that affect the task for which we hold the authors responsible.[50] Thus, it is okay for a translator of poetry to improve the poet's handwriting but not his poetry. We do not judge the poet by her handwriting. On the other hand, it is not okay to improve the handwriting in a child's paper if penmanship is part of the child's work to be evaluated. Lessig summarizes the point: 'What humility requires, then, is a claim about the background understanding of what it is the author is being held responsible for. Against this background, humility counsels the translator to stay clear of presuppositions that touch the author's responsibility.'[51]

Of what presuppositions of legal authorities must legal interpreters stay clear? Lessig answers that they must stay clear of 'political' or value presuppositions, but not factual or legal ones.[52] In other words, the interpreter, in faithfully translating a legal text, may correct for factual and legal presuppositions that turn out to be false, but not for value presuppositions with which the interpreter disagrees.

How does Lessig's analysis operate in the context of Congress's 10-dollar cap on attorneys' fees? Remember, the important questions for Lessig are whether there has been change in presuppositions (a change that would have resulted in a different text), and whether the changed presuppositions are factual or evaluative. The presupposition at issue that Lessig attributes to the 1864 Congress—that 10 dollars will purchase adequate legal representation—surely appears to be a factual one in Lessig's schema. Therefore, the faithful interpreter, who holds Congress responsible for its value choices but not its factual beliefs, would 'interpret' 10 dollars to mean whatever dollar amount is now necessary to purchase what 10 dollars would have purchased in attorneys' services in 1864. Moreover, one would suppose that similar results might be in order for the constitutional requirement that the president be 35 and serve four-year terms, that members of the House of Representatives serve two-year terms, and that senators serve six-year terms, or even that posted speed limits are to be taken literally.

Lessig does not justify his conclusion that we should hold authoring legal authorities responsible for their value presuppositions but not for their factual and legal presuppositions. Lessig realizes that correcting for all now-perceived-as-erroneous presuppositions of the authoring legal authorities in effect makes the interpreters, not the authoring legal authorities, responsible for governance.[53] Thus, he attempts to cabin such corrections by distinguishing between correcting erroneous value beliefs and correcting erroneous factual beliefs. Lessig's distinction, however, is unsatisfactory, both because the relation of fact and value is too messy, and because—as the attorneys' fees example suggests—we wish to make the authorities responsible for factual determinations.

[50] Ibid. 1253–4. [51] Ibid. [52] Ibid. 1254–5. [53] Ibid. 1253.

To take the latter point first, many disagreements interpreters have with the authorities whose laws they must interpret are disagreements about matters of fact. Does the 55 mile-per-hour speed limit save lives? Will Congressional term limits increase political accountability? Will ceilings on insurance rates actually work as forecast? And although Lessig's examples of fidelity in translation involve correcting factual and legal presuppositions that were correct when made but became incorrect over (a relatively long) time, there is no reason in principle that I can see why Lessig would not want interpreters to correct factual and legal presuppositions that were erroneous when made. Why should we not hold legal authorities responsible for failure accurately to predict the future and at the same time hold them responsible for failure accurately to assay the present?

In Lessig's scheme, it turns out to be impossible for the legal authorities to say that the law they enacted was premissed on a factual or legal error that should cause it to be repealed. For faithfully interpreted, the law's factual and legal presuppositions are all corrected. Repeals because of factual or legal error are never necessary. Because, however, we believe that such repeals are often necessary, there must be something amiss in Lessig's view of interpretation. Put differently, we think there is frequently a gap between what the authoring authorities *did determine* ought to be done and what, *in light of the facts*, they *should have determined*. Lessig's model of fidelity in translation, however, renders such a gap a conceptual impossibility.[54]

[54] Lessig could be read as endorsing a counter-factual test for determining the intentions of the authorities—for example, their intentions are what they would have enacted had they realized the conflict between their specific and their more general or abstract purposes. David Brink endorses just such a test, though he realizes that because authorities would always resolve such conflict between levels of generality of purpose in favour of the more abstract level, the approach threatens to make all laws into an injunction, 'do the right thing', which would not be an authoritative determination or in any way constrain interpreters. David O. Brink, 'Legal Theory, Legal Interpretation, and Judicial Review', *Phil. & Public Affs.*, 17 (1988), 105–48, 126–9. But see Marmor, *supra*, n. 32, 171–2 (advocating reliance on the highest level purposes of the authorities). (Marmor believes that giving precedence to how legislators intend their law to apply in given circumstances over what they intend to accomplish through such applications is incoherent. It seems to me, however, that I can intend to ban the bomb in order to promote peace and without any incoherence maintain that banning the bomb is what I intended even when confronted with arguments that peace is better maintained through nuclear arms.) See also Ronald Dworkin, *Life's Dominion* (New York: Alfred A. Knopf, 1993), 136–7; id., *supra*, n. 5, 134–6. The problem with such a counter-factual test is that it ultimately cannot distinguish two things that must be distinguished if authorities are to play their role: what the authorities *did* and what the authorities *would have done* (had they not made various mistakes). See Win-Chiat Lee, 'Statutory Interpretation and the Counterfactual Test for Legislative Intention', *Law & Phil.*, 8 (1989), 383–404, 397–401, 403–4.

With respect to factual and legal errors, Lessig's approach ultimately collapses the distinction between what is implied *in* a statute and what is implied *by* a statute. Many things about the world are implied by statutes but are not in them in the sense that they are legally operative. A law criminalizing prostitution may imply that the legislature holds a view of the world such that refusing to enforce contracts entered into by prostitutes would be desirable. None the less, it does not follow without more from this implication about the world that the law criminalizing prostitution itself renders prostitutes' contracts unenforceable. Or a law imposing a duty

Lessig's distinction between factual and legal presuppositions, which can be corrected by the interpreter, and value presuppositions, which cannot be corrected, is also problematic. It seriously underestimates the number of value disagreements that ultimately can be reduced to disagreements about facts or to mistakes in reasoning. For example, Lessig argues that something has gone amiss if we correct as erroneous the constitutional framers' presupposition that bicameralism is a 'better' form of government than unicameralism.[55] That presupposition was a value judgment for which the framers should be deemed responsible. It is hard to imagine, however, how that 'value' judgment is anything other than a judgment about facts—that is, about how efficient, liberty-protective, and responsive the two types of government will be. And the value presuppositions behind the preference for the superior form of government in terms of efficiency, liberty-protection, and responsiveness have arguably not changed a bit since the constitutional framing.

Lessig himself admits that the line between value and factual presuppositions will not be a clear or even a stable one.[56] Ultimately, the important question is, for what do we hold the authoring legal authorities responsible? Unfortunately for Lessig's analysis, he makes no case for the presupposition that we should hold authoring legal authorities responsible for their values but not their factual beliefs. Indeed, if the legal authorities' role is to make shared abstract moral notions much more determinate, the role of authorities in determining factual matters is in some sense more important than their role in determining values.

I began this section by asking whether it is possible to distinguish between what the authorities did determine and what the authorities should have determined with respect to factual situations to which they did not advert. Lessig fails to distinguish these things, namely, when what the authors determined changes with the context of application and when what they determined is shown to be mistaken by the context of application. Lessig's fidelity in translation effaces that distinction with respect to factual distinctions and assumes it with respect to value determinations. My question remains unanswered.

5. *The Ontological Status of Counter-factual Intentions*

The possibility of distinguishing what authorities did determine regarding applications to which they were not adverting from what they should have determined regarding those applications at bottom turns on whether there

regarding sex discrimination may imply that the legislature would view a private right of action to enforce that duty as a good idea were it to consider the question. In order to find such a private right of action to be implied *in* the law imposing the duty, however, it has to be such a good idea that we can infer that the legislature actually determined that it exist.

[55] Lessig, *supra*, n. 37, 1253. [56] Ibid. 1255.

is a fact of the matter about counter-factual beliefs and intentions. If we were to ask the legal authorities what they determined ought to be done with respect to an application not in mind at the time of legal enactment, is there some fact about the world at the time of enactment that makes the answers, 'we determined X' or 'we determined not-X', correct or incorrect? Or do all such answers reflect not merely reports of facts about the world, but also norms of interpretation, so that two authorities with exactly the same mental states could be said to have determined different things because the interpretive norms governing them are different?

To illustrate this issue, suppose that when Alice bans vehicles in the park she has in mind a blue Ford like one that had recently hit a pedestrian in the park. At the time the ordinance must be applied, however, the car in question is a green Chevrolet. Did Alice intend to ban it? Is there a fact of the matter about this?

Or suppose I give you my cheque-book and ask you to buy me curry powder for an Indian dinner I plan for tonight. You return with the curry powder and a $2,500 deduction from my cheque-book: there is a world shortage of curry powder, and the grocer wanted $2,500 for the last bottle in town. Or you come back, not with curry powder, but with alfalfa sprouts, explaining that since I wanted the curry powder because I enjoyed Indian food, what I really wanted was maximum gustatory pleasure, something that alfalfa sprouts will provide. Is there a fact of the matter whether I really did not intend to buy either $2,500 curry powder or possibly more pleasurable alfalfa sprouts?[57]

[57] See also Sanford Levinson, *Constitutional Faith* (Princeton, NJ: Princeton University Press, 1988), 82 ff. (posing a similar case). Consider in this regard Wittgenstein's famous example: 'Someone says to me: "Shew the children a game." I teach them gaming with dice, and the other says, "I didn't mean that sort of game." Must the exclusion of the game with dice have come before his mind when he gave me the order [to make this last statement true]?' Ludwig Wittgenstein, *Philosophical Investigations*, 3rd edn., G. E. M. Abscombe, trans. (New York: Macmillan, 1958), 33.

Consider also Jeremy Waldron's discussion of the determinacy of the command, 'Shut the door', given by Beth (the superior in the company) to Sam (the subordinate) as Sam enters Beth's office, an example given by Kent Greenawalt in *Law and Objectivity* (New York: Oxford University Press, 1992), 16–18, on which Waldron is commenting. 'As Sam goes to close the door he sees the company president approaching the entrance, evidently intending to enter. Should he interpret Beth's directive as instructing him to close the door in the president's face? Clearly not . . .'. Jeremy Waldron, 'Assurances of Objectivity', *Yale J. Law & Hum.*, 5 (1993), 553–68, 559. Waldron's answer—'clearly not'—suggests that he thinks there's a fact of the matter regarding the meaning of the command. He rightly rejects the language itself as the source of the answer. But he also rightly notes the problems one encounters if the meaning of a rule or command is located in the more general purposes and goals that underlie it. Although Waldron does not put it this way, the difficulty with the latter approach is that it collapses the rule into what the rule should have been (since every rule-issuer's highest-order goal is to do what is best). It does not create space for mistakes. Waldron does not himself answer the question of what makes Beth's command determinate in the sense that we know it does not require shutting out the company president. If there is a fact of the matter about what Beth intended for this application, even though she never adverted to it, then it is her intent that makes the answer, Beth is not commanding that Sam shut the door on the president, correct.

Or consider the Arkansas legislature that, in enacting a statute, voted for the fractured boiler-plate, 'all laws . . . are hereby repealed'.[58] Did the legislature intend to repeal the entire previously enacted code, as an opportunistic litigant contended? Is there some fact of the matter about this?[59] And compare this example to the situation in *United States* v. *Locke*,[60] in which the law in question required filing a claim 'before December 31'. Did Congress really intend to bar claimants who file on December 31? Is there a fact of the matter about this?

Pre-reflectively at least, there surely does seem to be a fact of the matter about such intentions. Alice would probably be quick to say that she intended to ban green Chevies. I am quite sure I did not intend to get alfalfa sprouts, even if I should have. And the Arkansas legislature would be quite adamant that it did not intend to repeal all prior laws.[61]

On the other hand, it is less clear to me that I did not intend, as opposed to should not have intended, to get $2,500 curry powder. Likewise, Congress might have trouble answering whether it intended erroneously to bar 31 December claimants or did not intend to bar them. And the town council of Our Town might be genuinely perplexed over whether it in fact prohibited the car dropped from the helicopter.[62]

This issue, I believe, lies at the core of the controversies about interpretation. The issue is not the shop-worn question of how transparent intentions are toward their objects (if I intend x, and x entails y, do I intend y?), an issue that seems to be one of how to use the term 'intention' and not one of what intentions are like in the world. The issue rather lies within the realm of transparency itself. If I say that in intending to outlaw vehicles, with a blue Ford as my exemplar, I intended to outlaw green Chevies, which I did not have in mind and may never have seen or imagined, am I reporting a fact about the world, or am I applying certain norms of interpretation to my own past act, norms that are derived from values?[63]

[58] See *Cernauskas* v. *Fletcher*, 21 Ark. 678, 201 S.W.2d 999 (1947).

[59] See also *In re Adams*, 619 F.2d 216, 222 (2d Cir. 1980), *cert. denied* 449 U.S. 843 (1980) (courts do not enforce obvious mistakes).

[60] 471 U.S. 84, 93–6 (1985).

[61] The case of the Arkansas 'repeal' illustrates the dual role that absurdity plays in interpretation. Sometimes absurdity plays the role of a normative constraint on the authority of the authorities' intentions. Thus, we might say that if a result is too absurd (or unjust), then it is beyond the scope of the authorities' authority, even if it is clear that they intended such a result. I discuss this and related points in Pt. II.

On the other hand, sometimes absurdity is used in an evidentiary way, namely, to establish what the authorities' intentions actually were (or were not). This use of absurdity seems to fit the Arkansas 'repeal' case better than the other use. See also Kay, *supra*, n. 11, 44.

[62] See also Brest, *supra*, n. 1, 210–11 (discussing such an example).

[63] This issue regarding the facticity of intentions has been noted by others. See e.g. Hirsch, *supra*, n. 11, 66–8 (asking whether, given that the world of the future, into which intentions project, will be different from the author's world, we can say that the author's intentions survive in that world). Some theorists are quite insistent that the content of intentions is a matter of fact. See e.g. Marmor, *supra*, n. 32, 156; Knapp and Michaels, 'Intention, Identity, and

I believe it is in part doubts about the facticity of intentions regarding non-contemplated applications that lead theorists to abandon authorial intentions as the key to interpretation.[64] Intention sceptics ultimately reject any distinction between 'What *did* you intend regarding unadverted situation S?' and 'What would you have intended regarding S had you adverted to it?' The latter question has no single answer, however, since what you would have determined regarding S had you adverted to it depends upon what you would have believed about S. And since you could have believed any number of things about S, anything from what we believe about S to very different beliefs, there is no fact of the matter about what you would have determined. And since what you did determine regarding S is what you would have determined, there is no fact of the matter about what you did determine.

To be a sceptic about the facticity of intentions regarding situations not adverted to, however, makes one a sceptic about the facticity of all intentions.[65] Intentions are future-directed, yet that future, no matter how accurately imagined at the time of intending, will frequently, if not almost always, at the time of consummation be somewhat different in relevant ways. More importantly, the set of intentions regarding situations not adverted to contains all intentions about which we think the authorities were mistaken (since mistakes always indicate a failure to advert at some level of analysis). Therefore, scepticism about the facticity of intentions regarding situations not adverted to leads to a denial that there is a fact of the matter about the authorities' intentions in any case in which those intentions could restrict us from doing what is right by our own lights. Such scepticism completely undermines the authorities' role.

Yet even the intention sceptics should be loath to see all intentions fall into the category of norm-governed interpretations about which there is no

the Constitution', *supra*, n. 11, 192–3. Others deny this. See Fish, *supra*, n. 11, 300; id., 'Wrong Again', in *Doing What Comes Naturally* (Durham, NC: Duke University Press, 1989), 99.

There is some relation between the issue of opacity–transparency of intent and the issue of whether there is a metaphysical fact of the matter about intentions. Those who deny the latter—intention sceptics—would claim that intentions are totally opaque to all unforeseen circumstances and thus cannot have any future applications—that is, any applications whatsoever. See generally Michael E. Bratman, *Intentions, Plans, and Practical Reason* (Cambridge, Mass.: Harvard University Press, 1987).

[64] Apart from doubts about the facticity of intentions, the other major impetus for abandoning authorial intentions is related to the paradoxical nature of authority: how is it possible to have good reasons for authorities' telling us that we must do *x*, and perhaps punishing us for not doing *x*, when we also have good reasons for not doing *x*? If in interpreting the authorities' prescriptions we can dispense with what they determined we should do in favour of what we now believe they should have determined, we can eliminate the paradox. Of course, in thus eliminating the paradox we effectively eliminate the authorities *qua* authorities, which by hypothesis we had good reason to have done.

[65] See Fish, 'Wrong Again', *supra*, n. 63, 99 (on our need to interpret even our own intentions).

fact of the matter. Not only must we say that, although the role of legal authorities is to determine what ought to be done in the future, there is never any fact of the matter about what they determine; we must also deny the legal authorities even the more limited roles that most theorists would grant them, such as determining the words to be interpreted, or the language of those words. If there is no fact of the matter about intentions regarding situations not adverted to, then there is no fact of the matter about, say, in what language the United States Constitution is written. For to say it is written in English normally means that that is the language its authors intended to use. And if English turns out to be in any relevant way different from what the authors contemplated, either with respect to sense or with respect to reference—as it almost always will[66]—so that there is no fact of the matter whether the authors intended *that* English, then there will be no fact of the matter about the language of the Constitution.[67]

We are left then in the following predicament. The facticity of intentions is problematic. There are surely cases where even the one whose intention is in question cannot answer confidently that he did or did not intend *that*.[68] And even when he is confident that he did or did not intend *that*, it is not at all clear on what such confidence is based. On the other hand, we are confident in most cases about what we intended, including cases where we believe we should have intended something different. And the price of denying the facticity of intentions is quite high. If the author's intention cannot extend beyond his world as he sees it at the moment of authoring, there is nothing but the norms and beliefs of the interpreter to determine what ought to be done at any later time, norms and beliefs which themselves cannot be projected authoritatively into the future.

[66] For related problems, see Shain, *supra*, n. 32 (discussing Problems in classifying objects as natural kinds); Dardis, *supra*, n. 15, 424, 428 (discussing malapropisms); Thomas S. Kuhn, 'Commensurability, Comparability, Communicability', *Phil. of Science Assoc.*, 2 (1982), 669–88 (discussing translation of languages with embedded mistakes about the world).

[67] Paul Campos has some useful things to say about this. See e.g. 'Against Constitutional Theory', *supra*, n. 14, 283–4. Michael Moore, in 'A Natural Law Theory of Interpretation', *South. Calif. Law Rev.*, 58 (1985), 277–398, gets caught in this predicament. Moore does not want to deny the facticity of intentions altogether. For example, he thinks there is a fact of the matter about whether legal authorities intend their marks or sounds to be a legal text and intend their text to be read in English. On the other hand, he denies that there is a fact of the matter about whether someone like Alice, who bans vehicles in the park while picturing a blue Ford, has a like intention regarding green Chevies (342–3). Moore, having used the authorities' intentions to establish that the text in question is indeed a legal text in English (see 355–7), dispenses with those intentions thereafter.

[68] To say that there must be some fact of the matter about counter-factual (that is, all) intentions is not to say that all possible applications must be covered by those intentions. With respect to some applications it is possible that the authorities lacked any intention, in which case nothing has been authoritatively determined regarding what ought to be done. But in some cases at least we must be able to say that *in fact* the authorities did determine what ought to be done, even if what they determined they now would believe to be mistaken.

6. *Summing Up: A Return to Our Town's Ordinance*

Let me tie the points of Part I together by returning to Our Town's ordinance prohibiting vehicles in the park. How will the ordinance apply to the military tank, skateboards, rollerblades, push-carts, prams, cars dropped from helicopters, and the quiet, clean, and safe vehicles of the future (bubble-mobiles)? If the ordinance is nothing more than the communication of what the authorities have intended to prohibit, then what are their intentions regarding these applications?

It is unlikely that either Alice's or Barbara's dominant intention is a semantic one, rich or spare. In other words, it is unlikely that they intended the conventional meaning of 'vehicle' or the true nature of vehicles as a functional kind[69] to dominate their scope and counter-factual scope intentions. Although each is probably aware that many 'non-vehicles' cause problems of safety or aesthetics and that some vehicles do not cause such problems, what they intend to prohibit, which they are attempting to describe through the word 'vehicle', may turn out to be different from the dictionary definition of 'vehicle' or the true nature of 'vehicle' as a functional kind.

Alice, whose concern is safety, may, for example, have a counter-factual scope intention that would include trains, trolleys, and electric golf carts even though she did not contemplate them at the time she cast her vote. On the other hand, she may have intended to ban the bubble-mobiles because they are sufficiently similar to what she had in mind by 'vehicles', even though they do not endanger anyone. And it may be uncertain, *even to her*, whether she intended to ban skateboards or rollerblades.

Barbara, whose concerns are aesthetic, may be certain that she did *not* intend to ban skateboards and rollerblades—they are sufficiently marginal as 'vehicles' and do not raise aesthetic concerns—though, like Alice, she probably did intend to prohibit the quiet, non-polluting bubble-mobiles because they are close to the core of what she means by 'vehicles'.

Charles clearly intends the ban on 'vehicles' to comprehend skateboards and rollerblades. His preference, it should be recalled, is to eliminate *only* skateboards and rollerblades, but he feels he has to join Alice and Barbara and prohibit vehicles to accomplish his goal. His understanding of 'vehicles' must be fairly broad to cover skateboards and rollerblades, and undoubtedly extends to many things that he regrets prohibiting (but none the less intends to prohibit).

We might then tally Alice's, Barbara's, and Charles's 'aye' votes as follows. None intends to prohibit the tank. At most one (Charles) intends to prohibit prams, push-carts, and the dropped automobile. At most two (Charles and

[69] See Michael S. Moore, 'Law as a Functional Kind', in Robert P. George (ed.), *Natural Law Theory* (Oxford: Clarendon Press, 1992), 188–242.

perhaps Alice) intend to prohibit skateboards and rollerblades. All three, however, intend to prohibit bubble-mobiles, though all three would regret having done so. (The bubble-mobiles are just unforeseen victims of an over-inclusive rule that must be amended to exempt them.)

Of course, the intention-sceptics would deny that there is any fact of the matter about what Alice, Barbara, and Charles determined regarding skateboards, rollerblades, push-carts, prams, and dropped automobiles, or indeed regarding the tank or the bubble-mobiles. Their intentions are a product of the norms of interpretation we impose on their actions; their intentions are not just there, independent of our values, like gravity, azaleas, and the Dog Star. But as I have said, the costs of intention-scepticism are very high. If authorities cannot intend for the unforeseen future, they cannot perform the role that legal theory posits for them. Past actions cannot determine present ones, and present ones cannot determine future ones. Nothing can be settled, and no guidance can be given.

What can we say about the status of skateboards, rollerblades, pushcarts, prams, and the dropped automobile? Of what significance is it that Charles would have voted no if skateboards and rollerblades were not prohibited, and that Alice and Barbara did not intend to prohibit them? And how, if at all, should we count the intentions of David and Edith, who voted no? When those who vote for a term in a law mean different things by that term, what are we to say that term has been determined to mean for purposes of the legal status of the conduct in question? And are the meanings attached to the term by those voting against the law material to what that term means? These are questions that the intentions of the authorities cannot answer because these questions concern the legal authority of the authorities' intentions themselves. And that is the topic of the next part.

II. THE AUTHORITY OF INTENTIONS

I have argued that the role of legal authorities is to determine what ought to be done in the sense that they are to translate abstract moral principles into more concrete and determinate norms. (Even if there were unanimous agreement on moral principles and universal willingness to follow them, there would still be such a role for legal authorities; for limits on knowledge about the world necessitate translating abstract moral principles into more knowable and determinate norms.) I have also argued that the texts that represent the legal authorities' communications of their determinations about what ought to be done mean only what the authorities intend them to mean. Any other meaning that is assigned to such texts represents an appropriation and re-authoring of the texts by others. In effect, those who re-author the texts by assigning them a meaning different from the authors' meaning have supplanted the authors and have become the legal authorities. Put more precisely, *they* (the re-authors) are the legal authorities for purposes of the text in issue if we recognize the legitimacy of their re-authoring, that is, their assigning of a meaning different from the meaning intended by the original authoring authorities.

A legal system in which one group of authorities had the role of choosing the words (the marks?) of legal norms but a second group then assigned *its* meaning to the words would be a decidedly weird system. In effect, the second group of authorities would actually be performing the role of determining what ought to be done, but it would be handicapped in its ability to communicate its determinations by the first group's choice of words (marks?).[70]

There *is* a case to be made, however, for a system that limits the authority of the determinations of the original authorities. Although it is the authorities' principal function to determine what ought to be done, the same 'preconstitutional norms' that establish who the authorities are might also constrain the authorities' determinations. Such constraints could take the form of constraints on the substance of the authorities' determinations. In addition, or alternatively, such constraints could take the form of restrictions on the form of the authorities' determinations. For simplicity, I shall label the former set of constraints substantive and the latter procedural.

Before I address substantive and procedural constraints on authorities' determinations, I should say a word about the status of the pre-constitutional norms that impose such constraints.[71] There is a large body of jurisprudential literature addressing such questions as whether a Hartian rule of recognition is itself a legal rule, a pre-legal convention, a moral rule, or some combination or relation of these possibilities; whether a rule of recognition is a single rule or instead a complex set of rules; and how rules of recognition relate to higher-order legal rules and practices, such as constitutions and institutions of judicial review.[72] I shall not enter these discussions here. All that I need to assume is that the norms that constrain the authorities' determinations, which determinations are paradigmatically 'law', are at the same jurisprudential level as the norms that establish who the ultimate legal authorities are. And the important point is that, although some legal authorities are designated as such by determinations of higher-level legal authorities, the highest-level legal authorities—for example, the constitutional 'framers'—are designated by norms that are not themselves determinations

[70] None the less, some theories of legal interpretation come close to recommending such a system.

[71] The concept of pre-constitutional norms is explicated in Richard S. Kay, 'Preconstitutional Rules', *Ohio State LJ* 42 (1981), 187–207.

[72] See e.g. Michael D. Bayles, *Hart's Legal Philosophy* (Dordrecht: Kluwer Academic Publishers, 1992), 69–85, 97–9, 168–72.

by (other) legal authorities. Because these pre-constitutional norms are not the determinations of legal authorities, they need not be 'interpreted' in the manner of texts.[73] They are conventions that are derived from our various views of what would be morally ideal, coupled with our recognition that our moral ideals can be best realized by establishing settled conventions with others who have different moral ideals or who share our ideals but not our views about how best to implement them. Because these conventional norms are convergences in practice and not authored texts, they do not fall within the purview of this discussion of interpreting authored texts, at least as texts to be interpreted. They enter the discussion of legal interpretation only in so far as they constrain authorities' determinations substantively and/or procedurally.

A. Substantive Constraints

Substantive constraints on authorities' determinations, although quite important practically, are relatively unproblematic jurisprudentially. We are quite used to the idea of substantive constitutional constraints on legislative, executive, and judicial acts. There is nothing fundamentally different about substantive pre-constitutional constraints on the authors of constitutions. For example, as a pre-constitutional matter, we could accept a norm that establishes as fundamental law the determinations of the 1787 constitutional framers, *except to the extent those that determinations are substantively absurd, unjust, and so on.*

Substantive constraints such as one denying the authority of any legal rule that is absurd or grossly unjust (by the interpreter's standards) are different from epistemological principles that help interpreters discover what the legal authorities intended ought to be done. That some result would be absurd or grossly unjust can be evidence—often strong evidence—that the authorities did not intend that result.[74] None the less, authorities can intend absurd or unjust results, even if not under those descriptions. That is, it is possible that: (1) authorities wish only to require what is just and not absurd; (2) authorities intend that X be done; and (3) X is unjust or absurd. Simply put, authorities can intend unjust or absurd results because they make mistakes.[75] And a norm that directs interpreters to disregard intended absurd or unjust results operates as a constraint on the authorities' power to determine what ought to be done rather than as an aid to understanding what the authorities did in fact determine.

Substantive constraints on the authorities' determinations can function as

[73] See Kay, *supra*, n. 71, 191–3.

[74] See the examples in Pt. I.C.5. showing how absurd results can be evidence that such results were not intended.

[75] See the discussion of Lessig, Pt. I.C.4.

absolute limits, much as do ordinary constitutional norms that limit the authority of governmental actors. Alternatively, they can function as do artificial evidentiary presumptions by directing interpreters to resolve uncertainties about the authorities' intentions in favour of certain outcomes. Thus, if the authorities' intentions are not clear, such substantive norms might direct interpreters to resolve the ambiguity in favour of the result that seems most just or wisest, rather than in favour of the result best supported by the evidence regarding the authorities' intentions, which evidence includes the fact that one result is more just or wise than the other.[76]

B. Procedural Constraints

The more interesting constraints on authorities' determinations are procedural constraints. Procedural constraints are norms that dictate the form that authorities' determinations must take and that handle cases where the authorities have apparently but not really determined what ought to be done. The norms that dictate form reflect the rule-of-law value of the accessibility of law. The norms that handle cases of failed law reflect both the rule-of-law value of accessibility and the more substantive value of consistent policy.

1. Norms of Form

We are quite familiar with certain formal constraints on authorities' determinations that must be satisfied before those determinations are deemed to have legal effect. For example, we have norms covering what counts as a 'vote', which 'vote' not only signifies that the voting authority's intention will be counted, but also marks the moment in time at which the relevant intention must exist. One who votes 'aye' when the roll is called is counted as in favour of the proposed bill for purposes of determining whether the bill has become law, even if she is subjectively opposed to the bill, and even if, moreover, she believes 'aye' means 'opposed'.

Notice that in the case of the authority who votes 'aye' thinking it means 'no', if the authority provides the necessary vote for passage, the law is deemed to have been passed even though a majority of the authorities intended that it not pass. In such a case, the law is not what the (majority of) the authorities determined ought to be done. When the law comes to be applied, what does it 'mean'?

We could have a norm that provided that in the case just described the

[76] Cass Sunstein's canons of statutory interpretation appear to function as substantively motivated, evidentiary presumptions rather than as either norms that define what legislation 'means' or norms that act as absolute limits on the authority of that meaning. Cass R. Sunstein, 'Interpreting Statutes in the Regulatory State', *Harv. Law Rev.*, 103 (1989), 405–508. For Sunstein urges following his canons *unless it is clear that the statute 'means' something at odds with the canons.* See e.g. ibid. 423, 434, 450, 456 (implying that statute could have a meaning distinct from the 'meaning' given by the canons).

law means what the authorities voting in favour thought it meant and intend it to mean in application, except that for the authority mistakenly voting 'aye', the law means merely what she thought it would mean if passed. She did not intend for it to mean anything in application because she did not intend for it to exist as law.

We need some such procedural norm because we have a gap to bridge: the gap between what the (majority of) authorities determined ought to be done—nothing—and what our norm regarding voting provides is the case, namely, that a law was passed. If we say that because of the mistaken and pivotal 'aye' vote a law was passed but it has no applications, we undermine the norm regarding what counts as 'aye' and 'no' votes. And without that norm, there will be continued uncertainty regarding what laws exist, an uncertainty that undermines the rule-of-law value of the knowability or accessibility of the law.

It is a short step from familiar procedural norms about voting to some similar but perhaps less obvious procedural norms. Consider the following procedural norms that might constrain the authorities' determinations. (1) All texts shall be interpreted as if they were written in the standard English of the date of enactment, both with respect to the meanings of the words used and also with respect to grammar and punctuation.[77] (2) All texts more than one hundred years old shall be deemed of no legal effect (or, more limitedly, of no legal effect if the standard English meanings of any of the text's words have changed in the hundred-year period).

Norm (1) reflects the rule-of-law value of legal accessibility. It bars authoring legal texts in the authorities' private code or in a different language from the populace. It thus prevents recondite law.

Norm (2) reflects the same value. Norm (2) reflects the fact that recovering authorities' intentions becomes more and more difficult as the moment of enactment recedes further and further into the past. With norm (1) in existence, norm (2) is perhaps less important but surely not unnecessary, especially if modified as indicated in parenthesis.

Norms (1) and (2) should be contrasted to proposals that might appear to be similar. For example, some have proposed that statutes be given the meaning their words would standardly carry if authored at the time of interpretation or application.[78] One impetus behind such a proposal is to make law's meaning even more accessible than it would be under norm (1), although there are also substantive concerns about policy obsolescence that underlie that proposal. This form of 'updating' of statutes, however, has a markedly different effect from norm (1) on the authorities' ability to carry

[77] See Kay, *supra*, n. 11, 48–50.

[78] See T. Alexander Aleinikoff, 'Updating Statutory Interpretation, *Mich. Law Rev.*, 87 (1988), 20–66. For replies to Aleinikoff, see Smith, *supra*, n. 36, 104–19; Larry Alexander, 'Of Two Minds About Law and Minds', *Mich. Law Rev.*, 88 (1990), 2443–9.

out their role. Norm (1) forces authorities to consult the dictionaries and grammars of their time in order to maximize their ability to effectuate their determination of what ought to be done. The 'updating' proposal, on the other hand, reduces their control to that of selecting the language (English) and the marks, but then leaves the translation of their determination to the fortuity of subsequent changes in the language.[79]

Calabresi has proposed that statutes be declared of no legal effect when they become 'obsolete'.[80] Unlike norm (2), Calabresi's proposal is not motivated primarily by rule-of-law concerns but rather is based on substantive policy considerations. Calabresi's test of statutory obsolescence is not one of mere age or even obscurity of meaning, but is rather one of substantive consistency with more modern statutes and judicial decisions.[81]

Norms (1) and (2) are purely procedural norms that attempt to reconcile the role of authorities—to determine what ought to be done—with the rule-of-law value of legal accessibility. Norm (2) effects the reconciliation by restricting the temporal scope of the authorities' authority. Norm (1) effects the reconciliation more or less well depending on the authorities' skill in drafting so as to communicate their determinations accurately according to the grammar and diction of the time. Where the reconciliation is imperfect—where the authorities fail to draft so that their determinations are conveyed in standard English—the law will not be what they determined ought to be done. Rather, the law will be a product of their determination regarding marks or sounds and the independent process of codifying standard English meanings and grammar. It will be to some degree 'mindless', in that the codification of meanings and grammar will not be a reflection of anyone's determination of what ought to be done in the world beyond dictionaries and grammar books. (Unlike Aleinikoff's proposal,[82] norm (1) does not deprive them of control over effectuating their determinations. It demands linguistic skills but not linguistic prescience.)

2. Norms for Failed Law

The procedural norms in this category are somewhat different from the norms of form in that, instead of addressing the problem of how to make the authorities' determinations more accessible, they address the problem of what to do when the authorities appear to have determined an issue but have not. Such cases of failed law, as I call them, are phenomena associated with multi-member legislative bodies. They occur when the legislating authorities individually intend different applications and thus mean different

[79] Query: do we have criteria for distinguishing when a language has undergone a change from when a new language has supplanted it? See Dardis, *supra*, n. 15, 420–1.

[80] Guido Calabresi, *A Common Law for the Age of Statutes* (Cambridge, Mass.: Harvard University Press, 1982), 2.

[81] Ibid. 2, 129–31.

[82] Aleinikoff, *supra*, n. 17.

things, despite having agreed on the language of their legislative text. In other words, norms for failed law deal with the problem of conflicting intentions within a multi-member legislative body.

When the general legislative norm is that authorities' determinations have the force of law only if a majority (or super-majority) of the authorities concur, and members of the (apparent) majority have made different and potentially conflicting determinations regarding what ought to be done despite having agreed on the words of a text, then it is possible that there is no majority determination having the force of law. Multi-member legislative bodies have no intentions regarding what ought to be done. Or, put differently, the only intentions such bodies have consistent with the role that legal authorities are supposed to play are some aggregation of the individual intentions of the members. Aggregation of individual intentions is not a problem if a majority have identical intentions. Where those intentions come apart, however, the passage of a law may be illusory in this sense: despite the appearance of legislative (majority) agreement that there be such a law, every possible application of that law would have been opposed by a majority of the legislative body. Put differently, no majority determined that any possible application ought to occur.

A norm of form such as one that irrebuttably assumes that all laws are intended to mean what they mean in the standard English of the date of enactment can save some laws from the failure to command a majority of consistent individual intentions. Such norms will not handle all cases, however, for even standard English will leave open the possibility of vagueness and ambiguity. The term 'vehicle' in Our Town's ordinance is vague beyond some core applications. The term 'canard' is ambiguous in that it means either 'lie' or 'duck', and has no single core of meaning. In either case, by application of Arrow's theorem, we face the possibility of majorities in favour of a law and its language but against all possible applications of that language.

Consider a case somewhat like our case involving vehicles. Legislators A, B, and C vote on term T. T is vague and can mean W, X, and Y or W, X, and Z. A votes aye, intending W, X, and Y. B votes aye, intending W, X, and Z. C votes no. A would have noted no had he been presented with B's definition as his only choice. B would have voted no had he been presented with A's definition as his only choice. Moreover, a truncated version of T, one that covered only W and X and neither Y nor Z, would likewise have been rejected. It is clear in this case that we have no majority of the authorities in favour of any possible meaning of T, even though we have a majority in favour of T itself.[83]

[83] See Kenneth A. Shepsle, 'Congress Is a "They", Not an "It": Legislative Intent as Oxymoron', *Int. Rev. of Law & Economics*, 12 (1992), 239–56.

Or consider a simple case of ambiguity, such as would occur if there were an ordinance forbidding 'canards in the park'. A voted for it to prohibit lying. B voted for it to prohibit ducks. C voted against it, as would have A or B had 'canard' clearly meant what the others intended by it.

One way to handle such cases of failed law is to bite the bullet and say that, despite appearances to the contrary, those legal texts are not laws. They are only apparent laws.

Alternatively, one might decide that having apparent laws on the books is undesirable for two related reasons. First, the existence of apparent laws confronts those subject to the laws with the spectre of uncertainty. In many or most cases, it will be difficult for the average subject of the laws to determine if a particular law is real and meaningful or only apparent. The uncertainty implicates the rule-of-law value of accessibility.

Secondly, the existence of apparent laws and the consequent uncertainty makes it difficult for legal authorities to carry out their function. For if they are uncertain about the content of the existing laws, they will be severely handicapped in deciding how best to legislate.

It might be desirable, therefore, to have pre-constitutional norms that direct official interpreters to breathe meaning into laws that are actually meaningless; in effect, to adopt the language of the existing laws but to 're-author' those laws so that the laws reflect the interpreters' determinations of what ought to be done (within the constraints of the norms of form). Such norms would make the official interpreters into the primary legal authorities, though constrained by the earlier authorities' choice of language.[84] Although many commentators propose such norms, they frequently make the mistake of conflating actions taken in pursuance of such norms with *interpretation* of the statutes or constitutional provisions that exhibit the failure of law. Those statutes and constitutional provisions are not being interpreted, however, for interpretation would conclude that they are meaningless marks. Rather, the statutes and constitutional provisions are being re-authored by a new set of legal authorities.

3. Levels of Generality of Authorities' Intentions

It is a common observation that the intentions of legal authorities can be described at various levels of generality. Thus, the authorities may intend a law to accomplish specific results R in order to further a more general purpose P, which purpose furthers a still more general purpose P_1, which purpose furthers Goodness and Justice. The authorities think those various intentions are consistent, which is why they passed the law in question. The intentions may turn out to be inconsistent in the view of those interpreting

[84] Note that the same problem of failed law would arise with respect to the interpreters' determinations if the interpreters were multi-member bodies, such as appellate courts.

the law, and inconsistent at any level. Thus, R may not in fact further P, P may not in fact further P_1, and P_1 may in fact be inconsistent with Goodness and Justice. If the interpreters are to give effect to what the authoring legal authorities intended, at what level of generality should that intention be described?[85]

I previously believed that this question could only be answered by reference to a pre-constitutional norm chosen because of its anticipated good results, and that the question could not be answered in the absence of such a norm.[86] I believed that when the intentions at the various levels of generality of description were inconsistent with each other, there was no fact of the matter about what the authorities intended. What they intended was rather the product of a norm that selected the appropriate level of generality at which to characterize their intention. My view on this issue was apparently widely shared.[87]

I now believe that view to be mistaken. A norm that directs interpreters to correct authorities' mistakes regarding how their specific intentions square

[85] An excellent case for illustrating how the possibility of describing the authorities' intentions at various levels of generality can affect judicial decision-making is the US Supreme Court's decision in *Home Building & Loan Association* v. *Blaisdell*, 290 U.S. 398 (1934). *Blaisdell* dealt with a Minnesota mortgage moratorium law that was challenged as violative of the clause in Art. I, § 10, forbidding the passage of any law 'impairing the obligation of contracts'. Justice Sutherland, dissenting from the Court's decision upholding the law's constitutionality, pointed out that not only was the law violative of the contract clause's literal command, but it was also exactly the type of law that the authors of the contract clause had in mind when the clause was drafted, i.e. a debtor-relief law enacted in a period of economic depression (448–50, 472). Chief Justice Hughes, on the other hand, writing for the majority, characterized the intent behind the contract clause at a higher level of generality. According to Hughes, the authors intended to proscribe debtor-relief laws that were unreasonable (427–43). Although they may have thought all such laws were unreasonable, even in depressions, their intention was only to proscribe unreasonable laws. See also Marmor, *supra*, n. 32, 171–72; Brink, *supra*, n. 54, 126.

For a different constitutional implication of the various levels of generality of the intentions of authorities, see Note, 'Legislative Purpose, Rationality, and Equal Protection', *Yale LJ*, 82 (1972), 123–54.

[86] See e.g. Larry Alexander, 'The Constitution as Law', *Constit. Comm.*, 6 (1989), 103–13, 111. See also id., *supra*, n. 78, 2447.

[87] Perhaps the foremost proponent of the view that what authorities intend is not a matter of fact but rather the product of a normative argument is Ronald Dworkin. See e.g. Ronald Dworkin, 'Bork's Jurisprudence', *Univ. of Chicago Law Rev.*, 57 (1990), 657–77, 663–4. This is also the official view of Cass Sunstein, though he equivocates at points. Cf. Sunstein, *supra*, n. 76, 411 ('Statutes do not have pre-interpretive meanings, and the process of interpretation requires courts to draw on background principles'), with ibid. 423, 434, 450, 456 (implying that statutes do have meanings that are independent of background principles). For a view similar to Sunstein's official view, see Note, 'Figuring the Law: Holism and Tropological Inference in Legal Interpretation', *Yale LJ*, 97 (1988), 823–43.

For a good statement of the opposing view, the one that I now endorse, see Campos, 'Against Constitutional Theory', *supra*, n. 14, 281–2 (arguing that interpretation is an empirical matter, not a theoretical one, since it seeks to uncover the 'fact' of the author's intention). See also id., 'That Obscure Object of Desire: Hermeneutics and the Autonomous Legal Text', *Minn. Law Rev.*, 77 (1993), 1065–95, 1092–3.

with their more general ones is one that threatens completely to undermine the authorities' role of determining what ought to be done. Because authorities always intend Goodness and Justice—or, if they are acting legitimately, can be presumed to intend Goodness and Justice—the interpreter can substitute his own views about what Goodness and Justice require for any specific intention of the authorities and still claim to be honouring their (more general) intent. For the interpreter would undoubtedly believe that had the authorities been disabused of all their mistakes of fact, mistakes of means/end reasoning, and mistakes in reasoning about values, they would have enacted what the interpreters would enact. In effect, a norm allowing the interpreter to disregard more specific intentions in favour of more general ones will convert the interpreter into the legal authority (and, of course, make the interpreter's determination subject to being corrected by a subsequent interpreter, and so on).[88] As I said earlier, in my discussion of Lessig's theory of interpretation,[89] if the authorities' mistakes are always to be corrected by interpreters, then there will be no authorities: if the interpreters are tantamount to the authorities, there can never be authorities for interpreters to interpret.

One might reply that while a norm directing interpreters to follow the authorities' most general intentions would undermine that authorities' role, a norm directing interpreters to follow the intentions characterized at some intermediate level of generality would not undermine that role. The interpreters could correct the authorities' most specific intention by reference to somewhat more general intentions, but not by reference to Goodness and Justice.

There are two problems with such a response, however. First, to speak of levels of generality of intention as if there were a discrete number of ways the authorities' intentions could be described is in some ways quite misleading. There is no one way to describe the levels of generality or to count them. Thus, it is impossible for a norm to specify the precise level of generality interpreters should look to in following the authorities' intentions.

Secondly, and more importantly, the choice to correct the authorities' specific intentions in light of their more general ones but not in light of their most general ones seems quite arbitrary. In some cases, for example, the authorities might specifically intend a result that is inconsistent with a more general intention they have, but which is in fact consistent with Goodness

[88] See Richard A. Epstein, 'A Common Lawyer Looks at Constitutional Interpretation', *Boston Univ. Law Rev.*, 72 (1992), 699–727, 703. 'The critical point is that theories of . . . interpretation are not theories of substantive transformation. No one should be able to win through interpretation what was lost in the initial drafting.'

[89] See Pt. I.C.4.

and Justice. In such a case they have done the right thing, although they have made two mistakes in reasoning from means to ends that happily cancel each other. The hypothesized norm directing interpreters to follow the authorities' intentions characterized at an intermediate level of generality would result in the interpreters acting contrary to Goodness and Justice when the enacting authorities, having made some lucky mistakes, would themselves have acted in a way consistent with Goodness and Justice.

None the less, if there were no fact of the matter regarding what the authorities intended in the sense of at what level of generality to characterize that intent, we would have no choice but to construct a norm that would prescribe the level of generality for interpreters to follow.[90] If there is a fact of the matter, as I believe there to be—so that, for example, there is a fact of the matter by virtue of which it is true that I did not intend you to bring me curry powder that cost $2,500 but I did intend you to bring me curry powder even if my total pleasure in life would be maximized by alfalfa sprouts—then the role of the authorities demands that that fact of matter be heeded.

This facticity about what the authorities determined ought to be done in the face of the various levels of generality at which their purposes could be described is what makes formal legal rules—rules that are opaque to their background purposes—possible. If there is a fact of the matter about what the authorities determined ought to be done, then that fact, as filtered through norms of form and norms for failed laws, should guide interpreters. Otherwise, interpreters are not interpreting and the role of the authorities does not exist.

D. Summary

There are two basic questions confronting interpreters that are easily and often conflated: (1) what did the authorities determine ought to be done?; and (2) what substantive and procedural norms constrain the authorities' determinations? The second question is as important as the first, but it is important to stress that, unlike the first, the second is not a question about interpretation in the sense of uncovering the text's meaning. The second question is really one about disregarding a text's meaning or creating a new text. Failure to distinguish the two questions can only lead to confusion, as Part III shall demonstrate.

[90] Of course, if there were no fact of the matter regarding the level of generality of the authorities' intentions, there might well not be a fact of the matter regarding the words or even the language through which they intended to communicate, which would leave interpreters with nothing to characterize at any level of generality.

III. CONFLATION AND AVOIDANCE: SOME RECENT ALTERNATIVE THEORIES OF INTERPRETATION

Recent scholarship on legal interpretation has tended to fall into one or the other of two categories. There is scholarship that focuses principally on what it means to interpret a text but avoids grappling with questions of the text's legal authority. I shall call this 'avoidance scholarship'. Then there is scholarship that is very much concerned with questions of texts' legal authority but that conflates such questions with questions of textual interpretation. I shall call this 'conflationist scholarship'. In this final part I shall give some brief examples from each category.

A. Avoidance Scholarship

The avoidance scholars are those with whom I feel the greatest kinship, for it is they who have stressed, as I have in Part I, the centrality of the intentions of the authorities in interpreting legal texts.

For example, Paul Campos has written a series of articles denying that a text *qua* text can mean anything other than what its author intended to mean by it.[91] Campos draws heavily on the works of Steven Knapp and Walter Benn Michaels,[92] who, as non-lawyers, are much more concerned with textual interpretation in general than with legal interpretation in particular.

What neither Campos nor Knapp and Michaels address in any sustained way is what authority the texts of legal authorities should possess. Should there be norms of form, substantive norms, and norms for failed law to circumscribe, supplant, or supplement the determinations of the authorities, and if so, what should those norms be? Campos has been preoccupied with debunking the idea, associated with the conflationists I address below, that legal texts can mean anything other than what their authors intended. That preoccupation, useful though it is, has left Campos with a position on textual interpretation but not one on textual authority.

Richard Kay, like Campos, has stressed the centrality of authorial intentions in legal interpretation.[93] Unlike Campos, however, he has at least adverted to some of the problems attendant on thoroughgoing intentionalism, at least in the context of constitutional interpretation. Kay argues that the most plausible theories for why the Constitution is authoritative would make authorial intent determinative of the Constitution's legal meaning.[94] Thus, he does relate his intentionalism to the role legal authorities occupy.

[91] See Campos, *supra*, n. 13, *supra*, n. 87, and 'Against Constitutional Theory', *supra*, n. 14.

[92] See Knapp and Michaels, articles cited *supra*, n. 11.

[93] See Kay, *supra*, n. 11; id., 'Adherence to the Original Intentions in Constitutional Adjudication: Three Objections and Responses', *Northwestern Univ. Law Rev.*, 82 (1988), 226–92.

[94] Kay, *supra*, n. 93, 231–4.

When Kay turns to the problem of group intentions and the spectre of a text the intended meaning of which no large enough group of authorities held in common, he recognizes the possibility that some portions of the constitutional text may be meaningless 'legal gibberish'—what I have termed 'failed law'.[95] He generally minimizes the possibility of failed law much more than I would, especially the possibility that the meaningful portion of a legal text—the domain of overlapping authorial intentions—might be sufficiently small that no one would have voted for it by itself (or so small in relation to the apparent meaning of the text as to make the text highly misleading).[96] Because Kay minimizes the possibility of failed law, he says virtually nothing about what authoritative interpreters should do when confronted with failed law.

None the less, although Kay's emphasis is on the intentions of (constitutional) authorities rather than on the authority of those intentions, he does not entirely neglect the latter. More than any other scholar, Kay has produced a theory of what legal texts *are* and what their authority should be, at least in the context of American constitutional law. His discussion of the authority of the constitutional text is sketchy and incomplete relative to his discussion of what the text is, but he does not totally avoid the former question.

B. Conflationist Scholarship

The conflationists are by far the more numerous group of those who offer theories of legal interpretation. While the details of the conflationists' theories differ, they all display one or the other of two general patterns. One pattern consists of 'combining' matters of authorial intentions with matters of the authority of such intentions. Because there is no way that matters of fact, such as what specific authors meant by a legal text, can be meaningfully combined with matters of value (the authority of the text), these theories are ultimately incoherent.

The other pattern of conflationist theories consists, not of conflation through combining matters of intention with matters of authority, but of conflation through reducing matters of intention to matters of authority. For these theorists, intentions do not matter at all, which means that texts and authorities do not matter. Ultimately, only what is morally right has authority. Practical authorities—human lawmakers—are oxymoronic.

To put matters slightly differently, one group of conflationists attempts to combine *will* (what the authorities determined) and *reason* (what they should have determined), while the other eliminates will altogether by reducing it to reason.[97] The latter group is perhaps less conflationist than eliminativist.

[95] Ibid. 249. [96] Ibid. 249–50.

[97] Cf. Alexander, *supra*, n. 78 (discussing the paradoxical relation of will and reason in law).

For them, legal interpretation is unnecessary because, in a very real sense, man-made law does not exist.

1. *Conflationists Who 'Combine' Fact and Value (Will and Reason)*

I have argued that legal texts represent the determinations of authorities regarding what ought to be done and that they mean what the authorities intend them to mean. I have argued that the intentions of the authorities are matters of fact, not matters of value-driven theory, and that if they were not matters of fact, the role of authorities would be impossible.

The first group of conflationists do not deny the facticity of authorities' intentions, but it believes those intentions must be 'combined' with certain values in interpreting legal texts. Although there are many conflationists of this type, perhaps the best example is Cass Sunstein in his article 'Interpreting Statutes in the Regulatory State'. Sunstein begins the article as if he is arguing for eliminativism, that is, making authorial intention into a matter of normative theory. Thus, Sunstein writes:

> The meaning of a statute inevitably depends on the precepts with which interpreters approach its text. Statutes do not have pre-interpretive meanings, and the process of interpretation requires courts to draw on background principles . . . drawn from the legal culture.[98]

Sunstein, however, backs away from the eliminativism this passage expresses. Instead, he endorses a position in which the meaning of a statute is a product of *both* the legislative intent and various substantive and procedural values, such as avoidance of constitutional invalidity, federalism, political accountability, the rule of law, antipathy to naked interest-group transfers, concern for property and contract rights, concern for welfare rights, deference to agencies, stare decisis, and so on.[99] Sunstein provides neither a lexical ordering of these values nor any other algorithm for how these various values should be combined. Nor is it all obvious how, for example, substantive values such as concern for property and contract rights can in any way be 'combined' with procedural values such as federalism.

Most importantly, however, Sunstein never explains how a statute's meaning can be in part what its authors intend it to mean but also in part what various values might suggest it ought to mean. In other words, Sunstein fails to explain how the *fact* of authorial intention can be meaningfully 'combined' with substantive and procedural *values*. Of course, this failure is not surprising; facts and values cannot be meaningfully 'combined'.

There are various indications that Sunstein is not really giving an account of statutory meaning but is offering instead a set of norms of authority that would constrain the authority of statutory meaning. In several places he

[98] *Supra*, n. 76, 411. [99] Ibid. 468–89.

makes statements to the effect that his canons should not be followed if they conflict with a statute's 'clear meaning'.[100] Such statements suggest that, notwithstanding the passage quoted above, Sunstein believes in a statutory meaning that *is* independent of value-based interpretive norms. If that is what Sunstein believes, then his canons do not determine what statutes mean. Rather, they are norms of authority that constrain the authority of that meaning by creating rebuttable presumptions that a statute's intended meaning is consistent with the various values Sunstein identifies. (The constraint is not absolute, in that statutes can contravene Sunstein's values if legislators make clear enough their intention to do so. If they fail to make their intentions sufficiently clear, their text will be read as if it had been authored by legislators with Sunstein's values.)

If this reading of Sunstein is correct, then his position is not incoherent, as it would be if he were actually advocating 'combining' authorial intentions and values. If he is merely proposing norms to constrain the authority of authorial intentions, then his is at least theoretically a tenable proposal. Unfortunately, the assessment of this reading of Sunstein's project is seriously impeded by the conflationist language in which it is wrapped.

If Sunstein can be read so that he escapes conflationism, there are many other theorists of interpretation who cannot. I have in mind principally those scholars who advocate the 'practical reason' approach to interpreting statutes. The practical reason approach suggests that in interpreting statutes, one should look to the words' meanings, the authors' purposes, norms regarding constitutional relationships, rule-of-law virtues, social norms, efficiency, and justice.[101] Moreover, in looking to this mixture of historical facts and different types of normative concerns, we should reject any algorithm or lexical ordering. Rather, we should combine these items non-mechanistically.[102]

The 'practical reason' approach to interpretation is pure conflationism. The questions of what the authorities intended by a statute and what authority that intent should possess are run together into one question of statutory interpretation that is supposed to give 'weight' to both factors. However, the two factors, one factual, the other normative, cannot be 'weighed' on the same scale.[103]

[100] See e.g. ibid. 423, 434, 450, 456.

[101] See e.g. Richard A. Posner, *The Problems of Jurisprudence* (Cambridge, Mass.: Harvard University Press, 1990), 130–2, 299–300; William N. Eskridge, Jr., 'Gadamer/Statutory Interpretation', *Columbia Law Rev.*, 90 (1990), 609–81, 633, 647–51; id. and Philip P. Frickey, 'Statutory Interpretation as Practical Reasoning', *Stanford Law Rev.*, 42 (1990), 321–84, 351–2; William N. Eskridge, Jr., *supra*, n. 36, 1479–555, 1483–4. See generally Larry Alexander, 'Practical Reason and Statutory Interpretation', *Law & Phil.*, 12 (1993), 319–28, 319–20.

[102] See Alexander, *supra*, n. 101, 326–8.

[103] Norms can designate the authorities whose determinations are in issue, norms can constrain those determinations, and norms can be weighed with each other, either algorithmically or non-algorithmically depending on the structure of the value theory from which the norms

2. *Conflationists Who Eliminate Authorial Intentions*

Several eminent theorists take positions on interpretation that purport to eliminate the intentions of authorities from any role in legal interpretation. For example, Jeremy Waldron believes that reference to legislative intentions should be restricted 'to those very rare cases where legislation is produced by an individual author whose knowledge and expertise provide the same reason for respecting his intentions as for respecting the text he has produced'.[104] In the standard case of legislation produced by large multimember bodies, the absence of shared intentions and/or the presence of conflicting ones makes the intentionalist theory of interpretation untenable.[105] Legislative texts must be interpreted without regard to any legislator's or legislative faction's intentions. More importantly, interpretation of this type is possible and even common. We do it daily, as, for example, when we 'interpret' the synthesized voice of the computer that tells us our bank balance.[106]

Waldron's principal focus is on what I have called failed law, cases where shared legislative intent is sufficient to cover the symbols to be enacted but not their meaning with respect to what legal subjects ought to do. In such cases, which Waldron may view as the rule rather than the exception, we need a norm of authority to tell us how to proceed, given that the authorities themselves have not determined what we ought to do. Waldron, however, would have such a norm of authority control even in cases where the authorities share intentions sufficiently so that we can say they *have* determined what we ought to do.

There are two quite distinct questions here that should not be conflated. One concerns the intentions of the authorities, that is, what have the authorities determined we ought to do. The other concerns norms of authority, that is, what ought we to do when the authorities have enacted symbols but have not determined what those symbols mean. We are not 'interpreting' the symbols when we follow some norm of authority that directs us to treat them as, say, symbols in English, perhaps with ambiguities resolved in

derive. But norms cannot be weighed with facts. As an ontological matter, therefore, legal texts cannot be what the proponents of the practical reason approach appear to believe. Legal texts can be the determinations of the authorities regarding what ought to be done, or they can be what the norms of authority dictate should be done in light of the authorities' determinations. They cannot be some combination of those things. Sometimes the practical reason approach to interpretation appears to be epistemological rather than ontological. That is, its proponents appear to be advocating a method for getting the meaning of legal texts right rather than giving an ontological account of what legal texts are. Without an ontological account, however, the epistemological proposal cannot be assessed. It is just a promissory note. (See generally ibid.)

[104] Jeremy Waldron, 'Legislators' Intentions and Unintentional Legislation', in this volume, *supra*, Ch. 9.

[105] Ibid. 331–2. [106] Ibid. 341–2.

favour of what the 'interpreter' believes is most just. That process is not interpretation of the text but appropriation of its symbols, as would be evident if the entire legislative body were actually speaking Esperanto.[107]

It is of course true that we can interpret mindless statements, such as those of the synthesized voice that tells us our bank account balance. We do so by implicit reference to the intentions of those who programme the bank's computer. If, for example, we were to learn that the programmers meant by 'one thousand' what we mean by 'one hundred', we might immediately cease writing cheques for fear that we might be overdrawn. If the computer were truly mindless—if it were programmed to give bank balances by reciting numbers randomly—we would 'interpret' what it says to us quite differently from the way we currently do.

It is also true that authorities can determine that what we ought to do should be decided by a mindless process, such as reading the entrails of an ox, flipping a coin, or what Waldron labels a 'Wollheim machine'.[108] At some point, the authorities in so determining cease to be authorities and abandon their role to that mindless process. None the less, specific and narrow delegations to mindless processes are quite compatible with the authorities' role.

Thus, it is conceivable that we could have a norm of authority that directed us to regard only the legislatively enacted symbols as authoritative, and to assign meaning to the symbols that they would carry if they had been authored by one intending to communicate in the standard English of the day. If the legislature enacts a prohibition on 'cats in restaurants', believing that cats are the animals that wag their tails and bark, what would be prohibited would be cats, not dogs.

Of course, even here reference to legislative intent is necessary to

[107] I realize that I am treading on hotly contested ground when I claim that assigning a meaning to symbols that one knows is not the meaning the author of the symbols intended by them is not 'interpreting' the symbols. In the end, because my concerns are with the nature of law and the role of authorities' determinations, and not with the true nature of the concept of 'interpretation', I could grant that assignment of unintended meanings to symbols in pursuance of some norm could count as interpretation, though of a quite different type from attempting to uncover what authors mean by the symbols they use. I prefer the narrower usage of interpretation, however, for two reasons. First, it seems closer to the colloquial meaning. Secondly, and more importantly, it allows me to avoid deciding what kinds of assignments of intended meanings are within the concept of interpretation and what kinds are without. Some would say that assigning symbols their dictionary meaning in a particular language counts as interpretation, even if it is clear that the meaning is not the intended one, but they would draw the line at that point. Others, however, would go beyond this and declare that making texts 'the best they can be' also counts as interpretation. See Ronald Dworkin, *Law's Empire* (Cambridge, Mass.: Harvard University Press, 1986), 313–54. Because I deny that assignments of meaning are interpretations even if they are justified, I can avoid this debate. For further remarks on this point, see the Appendix.

[108] Waldron, *supra*, Ch. 9, 336–8.

determine the symbols enacted. Beyond that minimum intention, however, the determination of what ought to be done is given over to the relatively mindless process through which words acquire standard dictionary meanings.

What is important here, and what Waldron neglects, is maintaining the distinction between interpreting the authorities' text and appropriating the authorities' symbols to make a different text. The norms of authority may direct us to do the latter, but the latter is not interpretation of the authorities' text. If we take the example of the prohibition of 'cats in restaurants' by a legislature that confused cats with dogs, and we follow a norm of authority that directs us to regard the text as having been authored by a competent English speaker even if we know it was not so authored, we must ban Puss but not Fido. If we do so it will not be because the authorities determined we should—they did not—but because they determined the symbols upon which an independent norm of authority operated. Moreover, if someone seeks to take a pet cheetah into a restaurant, it will be pointless to ask which of the possible meanings of cat is meant by the text. The legislature itself meant dog, and the norm of authority directs the interpreter to read the text as if it meant what it would mean in standard English, which norm leaves the status of cheetahs in restaurants unresolved. To resolve the status would require another such norm. When the norms of authority are exhausted, there is no sense asking what the text means on an unresolved point. Because it has been severed from authorial intentions, it means nothing.[109]

Several other theorists follow Waldron in abandoning what authorities intend in favour of norms of authority. Thus, in the context of interpreting the American Constitution, both Paul Brest and Gregory Bassham urge 'interpreters' to allow precedent and current values to trump what the Constitution's authors meant by it.[110] (Even Andrei Marmor, whose views on interpretation are otherwise very close to mine, distinguishes statutory interpretation, where he would ask what the authorities intended by their text, from constitutional interpretation, where he is reluctant to do so.)[111] There is nothing theoretically problematic with having pre-constitutional norms of

[109] Waldron gives three arguments for why his norm of authority—the legislature selects the symbols, which are to be read as if they were written by competent speakers of standard English—is superior to one that posits authority in the legislature to determine directly what ought to be done, even when there are sufficient shared intentions among the legislators. Those arguments are: a utilitarian one about aggregating the individual preferences of the legislators; one that relies on Condorcet's theorem about a majority's having a greater probability of being correct than a single individual; and one that relies on Aristotelian claims about forging views through deliberation. Ibid. 346–8. All of those arguments, however, appear to rest on some conception of the majority's view, which itself must rest on shared intentions. The mindless procedure of choosing symbols whose meaning is not transparent to the choosing legislature does not produce a view of any majority or any person.

[110] See Bassham, *supra*, n. 18, 98–102, 107; Brest, *supra*, n. 1, 228–9.

[111] Marmor, *supra*, n. 32, 172–3.

authority subordinate the authority of the Constitution to the Supreme Court's precedential rules, even if these themselves purport to be interpretations of the Constitution, or to certain substantive values. What *is* problematic is regarding the outcomes in such cases of subordination to be *interpretations* of the Constitution's text.[112] They are not. They are, rather, authoritative norms that, according to pre-constitutional norms, outrank the Constitution's text.

Finally, it should be noted that there will usually (but not always) be a convergence between what authorities mean by a text and what the norms of authority dictate the text shall mean authoritatively *so long as the norms of authority are of a certain type*. For example, a norm of authority that would have texts mean authoritatively what their symbols would mean in the standard English of the time of enactment would be a norm that a competent legislature could take account of in writing legislation. On the other hand, if the norm of authority transforms the text more mindlessly—as it would if it dictated that symbols be given their meanings in a language unfamiliar to the legislature, such as standard English *at the time of interpretation*, then convergence between what the authorities mean and the meaning that will be treated as authoritative will be unlikely.[113] In either case, we are *interpreting* the authorities' text only if we are seeking to determine what they meant by it. Otherwise, we are assigning meaning to it, even if the meaning we assign coincides with the meaning intended.

(Interestingly, those who would disregard the authorities' determinations fail to discuss how courts' decisions 'interpreting' statutes and constitutional provisions should themselves be interpreted. After all, courts are frequently multi-member bodies. And precedents can be quite ancient. Are future courts bound only by the precedent courts' symbols and not by what the precedent courts meant by them?)

Waldron, Bassham, and Brest conflate the questions of what the authorities' text means and what authority *that* text should have because they focus on the pathological case of failed law, where the authorities have not authored a meaningful text, or because they focus on concerns about stability (precedent) or dead-hand rule (obsolescence). Ronald Dworkin, however, would reduce the authorities' will to the sweet reason of moral correctness across the board. Dworkin is a conflationist who eliminates authoritative texts and the role of authority itself, leaving nothing for ordinary interpretation to interpret. He does so through two different techniques that ultimately lead to the same conclusion.

First, Dworkin argues for interpreting legal texts to embody moral concepts

[112] Again, recall that I am restricting the term interpretation to determining what was meant *by* a text and am not including the assignments of meaning *to* a text in pursuance of some norm.

[113] See Smith, *supra*, n. 36.

rather than the authors' specific conceptions of what those concepts require.[114] Because all authors of legal texts can be presumed to be attempting to achieve what is *really* just, fair, right, wise, and so on, we should 'interpret' their texts as directing us to achieve what is really just, fair, right, and wise. At this level of abstraction, a level at which the authoring authorities and their interpreters will always 'agree', the role of authority is eliminated. The interpreter will never encounter a situation where what the authorities determined ought to be done differs from what he believes ought to be done. Thus, authorities are redundant.

Dworkin's second technique is to argue for 'interpreting' legal texts to be 'the best they can be'.[115] But if texts are not anything prior to interpretation, then 'the best they can be' is to be an ideal text (in the eyes of the 'interpreter'). Texts are not matters of (another's) will but always reflect (the interpreter's) reason. If, on the other hand, texts *are* something prior to interpretation—if they have a facticity that cannot be 'interpreted' away—then they are what they are. Whether they are the best they can be will be a contingent matter. For that reason, Dworkin must be read as denying the facticity of legal texts, which means in effect eliminating them in favour of what is (in the eyes of the 'interpreter') what really ought to be done.[116]

Michael Moore's views on constitutional interpretation closely parallel Dworkin's views on interpretation generally and Waldron's views on statutory interpretation.[117] Moore believes that the authors of the Constitution are not authorities for us.[118] Because they are not authorities, what they intended to establish through the Constitution is not authoritative. Their text, however, is so.[119]

How can the constitutional framers' text—the Constitution—be authoritative if what they meant by it is not authoritative? For Moore, the authoritative Constitution is merely the symbols that the framers intended to produce.[120] Those symbols are the constitutional text, which is otherwise authorless.

And how can symbols be 'interpreted' without reference to the intentions

[114] See Dworkin, *supra*, n. 54, 136–7; *supra*, n. 5, 134–6.

[115] See Dworkin, *supra*, n. 107, 313–54.

[116] Consider Joseph Raz's criticism of Dworkin's theory of interpretation: 'If you regard the Constitution as an uninterpreted jumble of ink scratchings and regard legal theory (interpretation) as designed to give it meaning in accordance with the best moral theory there is, then there is no gap between ideal law and interpretation of existing law. Under these conditions one can interpret the Constitution to mean anything at all. It can be read to mean the same as Shakespeare's *Hamlet*.' Joseph Raz, 'Dworkin: A New Link in the Chain', *Calif. Law Rev.*, 74 (1986), 1103–19, 1103.

[117] See Michael S. Moore, 'Interpreting Interpretation', in this volume, *supra*, Ch. 1.

[118] Ibid. 14.

[119] Ibid. See also Michael S. Moore, 'Do We Have an Unwritten Constitution?', *South. Calif. Law Rev.*, 63 (1989), 107–39, 117–18. Moore's position has been criticized by Kay. See Kay, *supra*, n. 11, 43.

[120] Moore, *supra*, Ch. 1, 9–10, 17.

of their authors? Moore's answer is strikingly similar to Dworkin's: 'In the case of the American Constitution . . . the correct interpretation of the Constitution is the one that maximally furthers the peaceful resolution of fundamental political disputes . . . [so long as] the document . . . [does not make] too many moral mistakes.'[121] Although Moore acknowledges that sometimes—as in interpreting the request of a friend—'the values that justify us in treating certain phenomena as texts justify us in interpreting those phenomena by reference . . . to what their author meant',[122] in the case of interpreting the Constitution a valid interpretation is one that serves the value of peaceful resolution of political dispute (in a way generally consistent with justice and other moral values).[123]

Moore recognizes and worries about the problem that haunts Dworkin: if the constitutional text is always to be 'interpreted' to be the best it can be in resolving fundamental political disputes, why consult the text at all?[124] (Or, put differently, in what way does the text constrain its interpretation?) Moore's response is that,

> When we have reason to treat some phenomenon as a text, it is not just that we have reason to treat it as *any* kind of text. The legitimatization potential of the American Constitution, for example, not only gives us reason to consider that document as *some* kind of text; in addition, the kind of text it gives American citizens reason to interpret is one that respects the legitimizing potential of the document, *which means that the ordinary English meanings of the words the document employs must be respected.*[125]

Moore thus is arguing that the Constitution will serve its role if we deem the framers to have had authority to determine the symbols of our supreme law but not the meaning those symbols possess. The latter is supplied by, in my terms, a norm of authority that directs us to assign the meaning to those symbols that they would carry in standard English (of 1787? Today?).

Moore is not yet completely out of the woods that trap Dworkin, as he recognizes. For what if the standard English meanings of those symbols are inferior in terms of the guiding value or values, such as social peace, relative to some non-standard meaning? Will not the pressure of the guiding values overwhelm the constraints of, say, plain meaning and ultimately completely obliterate the text?[126]

Moore's answer to this worry is not entirely clear. On the one hand, he argues that this is a non-worry because interpreters must first treat the text

[121] Ibid. 17. [122] Ibid. 17–18. [123] Ibid. 17.
[124] Ibid. 18–20. [125] Ibid. 18–19 (final italics added).
[126] Ibid. 19–20. In some of Moore's earlier articles he appears to take the 'combining' conflationist's tack of putting authorial intentions and norms of authority into some weighing and balancing process. See e.g. Michael S. Moore, 'The Semantics of Judging', *South. Calif. Law Rev.*, 54 (1981), 151–293, 277–81; id., *supra*, n. 67, 277–398, 396–7.

as a text, not as anything they would like it to be.[127] Yet this argument does not work unless the text has a solidity to it that goes beyond its symbols and embraces what its authors intended to mean by it. After all, according to Moore, we assign the standard English meaning to the constitutional text, not because that is what its authors meant by it, but because that is what would be instrumentally useful. And if it proves not to be instrumentally useful to assign the standard English meaning to the symbols, what reason remains for doing so?

What I believe Moore intends here is that the Constitution can serve the goal of social peace—or any other such goal—only if its symbols are read as if they were authored by competent speakers of English, even if the instructions such a reading produces are inferior in terms of that goal than some other instructions would be. In other words, Moore is making the familiar rule-consequentialist move against an act-consequentialist reading of the Constitution: reading the Constitution as if it meant what its symbols would mean in standard English is a better long-term strategy for achieving social peace than trying to achieve social peace without the constraints that reading the Constitution as if it were in standard English produces.

I believe that Moore's reasoning for adopting his norm of authority—the constitutional symbols with their standard English meanings are authoritative—is the right kind of reasoning to employ in choosing norms of authority, namely, long-term consequentialist reasoning.[128] What should be noted, however, is that it is also the kind of reasoning that could support the position that Moore rejects, namely, that the constitutional framers are authorities. And the latter position would direct us to attend to *their* (the framers') *text*, not just their symbols. In other words, Moore's argument succeeds only if treating the framers as authorities and their text—what they determined ought to be done—as authoritative produces inferior consequences (in terms of our values) than treating them as authorities only for the limited purpose of determining symbols. And I do not see that Moore has given us any reason to believe that is the case.

IV. CONCLUSION

Legal authorities serve the role of making what is morally required more determinate. Their texts are their communications to us regarding their determinations of what ought to be done. If we are seeking to understand those determinations, then we must read the authorities' texts to mean what they intended to mean by them.

[127] Moore, *supra*, Ch. 1, 20.

[128] See Alexander, 'The Constitution as Law', *supra*, n. 86, 111.

On the other hand, we might wish to constrain the authority of legal authorities in various ways, both substantively and procedurally. Those constraints may direct us to ignore and supplant the *authorities'* texts for texts that are partially our own. When we observe these constraints, we are following our norms of authority, not the authorities' norms. Accounts of legal interpretation would be well served by maintaining the distinction between the authorities' texts and the constraints that limit those texts.

APPENDIX

Lest I be misunderstood with respect to monkeys on typewriters, marks made by waves on a beach, and so forth, let me briefly set forth a position that makes the monkeys' product, the wave marks, and other such items linguistically meaningful without reference to authorial intentions, which are obviously absent. (By qualifying 'meaningful' by the adverb 'linguistically', I mean to distinguish this position from the position that unintended marks and sounds can be meaningful as signs of events in the world, such as the curious and playful behaviour of monkeys, or the patterns that ocean waves take.) The position I here am considering goes something like this. Shapes and sounds that are not produced by an author intending to communicate something thereby may still be tokens of letters in an alphabet, and a string of such marks and sounds may be tokens of words in a particular language. That such shapes and sounds are words in a particular language is established by a public convention to that effect, not by authorial intent. Of course, the public convention itself is the product of past speakers' intentions, but once the convention takes hold, shapes and sounds and the words they produce have the meanings the public convention establishes independent of any author's or speaker's intention. In other words, what I have called dictionary meaning (meaning$_D$) can be attributed to objects with no authorial intent—such as wave marks on the beach, cloud formations, or monkeys' typing—or to words that were written or spoken with a speaker's meaning (meaning$_S$) different from meaning$_D$. Thus, a cloud formation that is shaped like the letters 'g' and 'o' means$_D$ 'go'. The monkeys' typing of 'whale' means$_D$ a large aquatic mammal. And when Mrs Malaprop refers to a 'nice derangement of epitaphs', 'derangement' and 'epitaphs' mean$_D$ what 'derangement' and 'epitaphs' mean in a standard English dictionary, even though Mrs Malaprop meant$_S$ something different by them. Moreover, the point remains true if it turns out that Mrs Malaprop is intending to speak Shmenglish, not English, Shmenglish being a language of Mrs Malaprop and a few of her friends that is identical to English except that 'derangement' in Shmenglish means 'arrangement' in English, and so forth.

Nothing I have said or will say is meant to deny this sense in which shapes, sounds, words, and arrangements of words can have meanings independent of the intentions of authors, meanings that arise from public conventions. (Much less do I deny the great utility of such public conventions—dictionaries, grammatical rules, and so forth—in successfully communicating to others what we intend to communicate.) Surely, when someone accidentally bumps into a typewriter with paper in it, and the 'i' key hits the paper, the mark on the paper *is* the letter 'i'. And if both the 'i' and 't' keys strike the page, those marks *are* the pronoun 'it'. This position is, however, of quite limited practical significance, and of absolutely no significance to questions of legal interpretation.

What does follow from the position is that we can use cloud formations, wave markings on the beach, monkeys' typings, and malapropisms to teach letter recognition, dictionary meanings, and misuses of language. If the waves make the marks of 'g' and 'o' next to each other, we can ask our children, who are learning English, what letters those marks form, and what words the letters form, even if both we and our children realize that no person with a communicative intent made those marks.

On the other hand, if our interests lie not in learning alphabets, dictionary meanings, or grammar, nor in learning ocean wave patterns or monkey behaviour, the absence of authorial intentions precludes any other inquiry into the meaning of such shapes and sounds. Whether our enterprise is literary criticism or legal interpretation, we need authors' intentions. If the shapes or sounds make a word with different meanings in different languages ('canard'), a word that could be a word with different meanings in different languages ('derangement' in English and Shmenglish), or a word with two or more different meanings in the same language ('bear' in English), it would make no sense in the absence of authors' intentions to ask which language those marks represent, or which of two meanings they have.

Therefore, what is important is that we be clear about what our practical enterprise is. What is less important—or perhaps completely insignificant—is whether meaning_S or meaning_D is more basic as a theoretical rather than practical matter. Legal interpretation is a practical endeavour, and my argument is that, given the practical role of legal authorities, and with the qualifications I have discussed, their authorial intentions and not dictionary meanings should be of primary importance.

11

Interpreting Authorities

HEIDI M. HURD

Despite its attempted exorcism, legal interpretation is haunted by intentionalism. This has puzzled those who have considered themselves successful in demonstrating the conceptual and normative indefensibility of intentionalist interpretation. In this chapter, I shall argue that the persistent spectre of intentionalism should come as no surprise to legal theorists whose battles with intentionalism have been fought in the shadow of traditional conceptions of the law's authority. For as long as the law is accorded the sort of authority that it has historically claimed, intentionalism will necessarily be accorded the sort of respect that it does not deserve.

In Part I I shall begin by demonstrating that the standard theories of legal authority locate the authority of law in the beliefs of lawmakers. They thus necessarily demand, at one point or another, that one seek the intentions of the legislature in interpreting democratically enacted laws. In Part II I shall very quickly canvass the multitude of reasons to think that intentionalist interpretation of legislation is either conceptually confused or empirically impossible. Collectively, these arguments support the conclusion advanced at the end of Part II that those who seek the content of legislation do best to eschew any inquiry into the authorial intentions of its drafters. In Part III I shall advance an alternative understanding of the law's authority—one that vests the authority of law in legal texts, not legal authors.[1] Such a theory, I shall argue, both relieves us of the need to interpret statutory texts in light of the intentions of those who drafted them and preserves the action-guiding function of law.

The argument structure, then, is this:

1. If one adopts any of the standard theories of the law's authority (influential authority, practical authority, or theoretical authority), then one is committed to locating the authority of law in the beliefs of lawmakers.

2. If one locates the authority of law in the beliefs of lawmakers, then one is committed to interpreting legal texts in light of the intentions of their authors.

[1] I developed in considerable detail the argument that legislation should not be thought of as a communicative enterprise in Heidi M. Hurd, 'Sovereignty in Silence', *Yale LJ*, 99 (1990), 945–1028. The same conclusion is advanced in this volume by Jeremy Waldron, *supra*, Ch. 9.

3. One cannot and should not seek to interpret legislative enactments in light of the intentions of their authors.

4. Therefore, one cannot and should not attribute to legislation any of the standard conceptions of legal authority.

5. If one adopts the non-standard theory of legal authority that I shall defend in Part IV, then one is committed to locating the authority of law in legal texts, and not in the beliefs of their authors.

6. If one locates the authority of law in legal texts, rather than legal authors, then one is not committed to interpreting those texts in light of any authorial intentions, but is free to use less-problematic interpretive techniques.

7. Either one must adopt one of the standard theories that locate legal authority in lawmakers, or one must adopt the non-standard theory that locates legal authority in legal texts.

8. Therefore, one should adopt the non-standard theory that locates legal authority in legal texts.[2]

I. STANDARD THEORIES OF AUTHORITY AND THE IMPLICATIONS FOR INTENTIONALIST INTERPRETATION

A number of contributors to this collection have converged upon the quite new claim that a theory of legal interpretation is necessarily related to, and indeed dependent upon, an antecedent theory about the nature of law's authority.[3] I think that this is true.[4] While it is not the case that each theory of authority logically entails a distinct and separate theory of interpretation, there are natural alliances between particular camps of authority theorists and particular camps of interpretation theorists. In what follows, I propose to trace the degree to which each of the traditional theories of legal authority is committed to an alliance with intentionalism. Specifically, I shall

[2] Throughout this paper, I shall make general references to legal authority and legal texts, instead of speaking always in terms of legislative authority and legislative texts. I do this because much of what I say is true of the authority claimed on behalf of all sources of law and all sorts of legal texts. However, I do make particular use of the interpretive problems generated by applying standard theories of legal authority to legislative enactments. I take these problems to discredit these theories of legal authority in all arenas of law, although I make no attempt to defend this assumption. When what I say is seemingly true only of (or particularly of) legislative enactments, I shall attempt to confine my thesis by speaking solely about the authority and interpretation of statutes.

[3] See e.g. Andrei Marmor, *Interpretation and Legal Theory* (Oxford: Clarendon Press, 1992), 155–84; Larry Alexander, 'All or Nothing At All? The Intentions of Authorities and the Authority of Intentions', in this volume, *supra*, Ch. 10; Waldron, *supra*, Ch. 9. See also Larry Simon, 'The Authority of the Framers of the Constitution: Can Originalist Interpretation be Justified?', *Calif. Law Rev.*, 73 (1985), 1482, 1486–9 (discussing the relationship between constitutional authority and constitutional interpretation).

[4] Indeed, I have so argued. See Hurd, 'Sovereignty in Silence', 1006–28.

demonstrate that intentionalism is necessarily implied, in one form or another, by all of the standard theories of legal authority.

A. Inspirational Authority

Let me begin with a kind of authority that has not, to my knowledge, been accorded to law (at least not to Anglo-American law), but upon which intentionalist interpretation most naturally leans. This is the sort of authority that many might attribute to God, but it is, I think, also the sort that is exercised by loved ones and friends, mentors and spiritual leaders. Joseph Raz has described this sort of authority as 'inspirational authority', and I shall employ his terminology.[5]

Consider a standard assertion of inspirational authority. It is common for my husband to find a new hike that he wants me to take. When he suggests that I take it, he wants me to do more than just traverse the nine miles he has described as four. He wants me to enjoy it! And the criteria of enjoyment are not up for grabs. He wants me to enjoy it for the specific reasons he enjoyed it; namely, because it is beautiful, challenging, and diverse. He wants me to say at the end of it: 'You were right. It's a great walk in all the ways you described!' His suggestion that I take the hike is thus designed to give me a complex reason for action: a reason to take and enjoy the hike for the reasons that he would take and enjoy the hike, namely, because it is beautiful, challenging, and diverse.

In so far as my husband can give me such complex reasons for action, he possesses, for me, inspirational authority. Put in precise terms:

> X has inspirational authority over Y if and only if when X says 'Do A', Y has a reason to do A for (and only for) the reasons that X values doing A.

The prescription of an inspirational authority thus gives one a second-order reason to do an action only for the first-order reasons that are valued by the authority.[6] If I say to my husband, 'Okay, I'll take the hike—but only because you want me to', he is bound to say that I am failing to act on his

[5] Joseph Raz, *The Morality of Freedom* (Oxford: Clarendon Press, 1986), 32.

[6] I may be departing here from Raz's conception of inspirational authority. Raz periodically says that an inspirational authority gives one a reason to do what is suggested for its own sake. Is doing something for its own sake different from doing it for the reasons that the inspirational authority would value? Raz himself appears ambivalent about the answer. As he says: 'One may, for example, come to enjoy Byrd's music because one's lover does and would be pleased if this taste were shared.' Ibid., at 32–3. This suggests my formulation of inspirational authority. But as he goes on to say: 'The point is that one comes to enjoy Byrd's music in itself.' One can imagine these formulations diverging. If an inspirational authority wants a loved one to do something for the sake of prestige, then on my formulation, the loved one acts on inspirational authority if she does it for prestige. But doing the act for prestige is not doing it for its own sake. Hence, if the Razian conception of inspirational authority requires action for its own sake, it is to be distinguished from the conception that I am here going to pursue under the name of 'inspirational authority'.

inspirational authority. As he would put it: 'Don't do it because I want you to. Do it because it is beautiful, challenging, and diverse.' If I then hike for any other reason save these (including for the reason that it will make him happy), I have failed to act on his (inspirational) authority.[7]

Consider a second example. Those who attribute inspirational authority to God's commands are inclined to insist that it is not enough simply to follow the letter of His law. It is not enough to give to the poor: one must do so for the reasons valued by God. If one gives to the poor to impress one's neighbours, or to garner a tax exemption, one fails to fulfill God's will. God's command is to be charitable, and charity amounts to sacrificing something one genuinely values for the good of another. One who gives what is not valued, or one who gives out of concern for one's own interests, fails to act on God's inspirational authority; and this is true even if one gives a fortune.

There plainly exists an intimate relationship between an inspirational theory of authority and an intentionalist theory of interpretation. The content of the reasons upon which one's actions must be based in order to act on the directives of an inspirational authority is given by the intentions of the authority. If the reasons behind an inspirational authority's directives are vague, a failure to interpret his reasons accurately will likely spell a violation of his authority. One cannot defend one's violation by simply saying: 'I did what you asked me to do.' For it is not enough to act in accordance with the plain meaning of an inspirational authority's words (it is not enough to give to the poor; it is not enough to hike the recommended miles). One must do so for the right reasons—for the reasons that motivated the authority to prescribe the action. And if those reasons are at all disguised, one is forced to engage in intentionalist interpretation. One is forced to ask: 'Why do you want me to do this?' Only then can one satisfy an inspirational authority, for only then can one act for the reasons that the authority desires one to act.

To attribute inspirational authority to the law would clearly commit one to an intentionalist theory of legal interpretation. One would act on the law's authority only when and to the extent that one did what the lawmaker required for the reasons that motivated the lawmaker to enact the law. If the point of prohibiting vehicles in the park was to reduce pollution, then a judge would accord the regulation inspirational authority only if she

[7] As Raz puts it: '[A]ffection for another often leads people to conceive desires and wishes, because the person toward whom they have the affection would be pleased if they had such wishes and tastes or acted on them . . . The desires I have in mind are to be strictly distinguished from desires to do certain things in order to please the other person.' (Ibid., at 32.) 'He may be pleased that I want to listen to Byrd to please him, but he does not want me to listen to Byrd for that reason . . . [H]e has another wish, namely that I should like Byrd. Here he wishes me to do it for a particular reason. Doing it for another reason would not be doing as he wishes.' Ibid., at 33.

allowed skateboards and banned automobiles *because* skateboards do not emit pollutants while automobiles do. If, on the other hand, the point of the regulation was to increase pedestrian safety, then the judge would accord the regulation inspirational authority only if she banned skateboards and allowed ambulances *because* by so doing she would increase pedestrian safety. In the event that the reasons for the regulation are opaque, the judge would have to seek the intentions of its drafters. For acting upon their motivations is the *sine qua non* of according the law inspirational authority.

While fulfilling the wants and desires of loved ones regarding the motivations with which we act is plausibly part of what it means to love them,[8] fulfilling the wants and desires of legislators regarding the motivations with which we obey their enactments is far less plausibly part of what it means to be law-abiding. That we genuinely imbue loved ones with inspirational authority thus serves as little precedent for according similar authority to lawmakers. It is not my object, however, to take issue with any of the theories of authority that I shall pair with intentionalism. My project is simply to determine the degree to which the various theories rely upon intentionalism. While there are good reasons to think that it would be a mistake to accord inspirational authority to the law, I shall say no more about them here.

B. Influential Authority

Let me now turn to a kind of authority that *is* predicated of law[9]—what I have elsewhere called 'influential authority'.[10] Like those of an inspirational authority, the directives of an influential authority have the power to give actors new reasons for action. But unlike those of an inspirational authority, the directives of an influential authority do not require that one act with any particular motivations. One merely has a new reason to act as the influential authority directs; one has no reason to do so for the reason that motivated the influential authority to issue the directive. Thus, imagine that a friend asks to borrow money. If one's friend functions as an influential authority, then her request, by itself, gives one a new reason (but not necessarily a sufficient reason) to give her money. It matters not what her reason for needing it is, and one need not give her the money for the reason that she wants it. One acts on her influential authority if one adds the fact that she has requested money to the antecedent reasons to lend her money—her

[8] As Raz maintains, 'The appearance of such desires is one necessary mark for affection to count as love.' Ibid., at 32.

[9] See Richard Flathman, *The Practice of Political Authority* (Chicago: University of Chicago Press, 1980); Frederick Schauer, *Playing by the Rules: A Philosophical Examination of Rule-Based Decisionmaking in Law and in Life* (Oxford: Clarendon Press, 1991); Michael S. Moore, 'Authority, Law and Razian Reasons', *South. Calif. Law Rev.*, 62 (1989), 829–96.

[10] Heidi M. Hurd, 'Challenging Authority', *Yale LJ*, 100 (1992), 1611–77, 1641–4.

obvious need for food and clothes, the fact that she has loaned one money in similar circumstances, the contribution that the loan would make to one's long-term friendship, and so on. One is then free to weigh all of these reasons against the antecedent reasons for not lending her money—the likelihood that she will spend the money on drugs and alcohol, the possibility that she will never repay the loan, the fact that others need the money more than she, and so on—and to act on the balance of the totality of reasons for action.

We can more formally define the concept of influential authority as follows:

> X has influential authority over Y if and only if when X says 'Do A', Y has a new reason to do A.

This concept of authority responds to the recognition that requests (and speech acts like them) are unique pieces of moral machinery. They serve to regulate charity and police intermeddling. While we have independent reasons to give to those in need, such persons may not appreciate our interference in their lives. The power to request (and to reject) thus equips them with a means of signalling when they are willing to have us act on their behalf. Their request adds the fact that they want to be aided to the antecedently existing reasons to aid them (if there are any). And those of us who give to homeless people who ask for donations, but not to ones who do not, well know the 'tipping power' of this added fact.

Like inspirational authority, influential authority is often premissed on the normative importance of a particular status or relationship. Not any and every request by any and every person gives one a new reason for action. Requests by homeless people do because there is something morally special about homelessness. Requests by friends and family do because there is something morally significant about friendships and familial relationships. To determine the moral importance of these special-status positions and personal relationships is to determine the conditions under which persons will have influential authority over us via their requests.

Those who attribute influential authority to democratically enacted laws conceive of those laws as analogues to requests. They give new reasons for action that are to be added to the balance of antecedently existing reasons for and against such action. Their reason-giving power derives from the same source as that of requests: respect for the autonomy of persons. Just as a request reflects an individual's interest in regulating her own affairs, so a democratic enactment reflects a majority's interest in regulating its own affairs. Those who accord influential authority to legislation must, of course, defend the claim that the sheer fact that a majority prefers something is a reason to do it. Just as one must give moral content to the significance of friendship or family ties in order to defend the attribution of influential authority to friends and family, so one must give moral content to the significance of a majority's will in order to defend the attribution of influential authority to a democratic legislature.[11]

If the attribution of influential authority to particular persons or groups is appropriate, how should one interpret their authoritative utterances? Specifically, must one detect their intentions in order to act on their authority? The answer is complex and calls for a distinction between two different sorts of intentions: semantic intentions and linguistic motivations.[12] Semantic intentions reflect what a speaker means by her utterance. They reflect her interpretation of her words given her theory of meaning. Linguistic motivations are those further intentions with which a speaker issues an utterance. They reflect the effects in the world that she seeks to achieve. When a friend asks to borrow a pin, one must necessarily detect her semantic intentions in order to discover which of the following her request gives one a new reason to lend her: a safety pin, a rolling pin, a hair pin, a hat pin, or a straight pin. But if she is just an influential authority, and not an inspirational authority, one need not necessarily detect her linguistic motivations. For why she needs the pin does not function as a reason that must motivate one to give it to her. Hence, one can act on her authority without acting on the linguistic motivations that prompted her request.

There are, of course, many instances in which one can detect semantic intentions only by detecting linguistic motivations. When I was growing up, my father would frequently say: 'Son, hand me a pin.' Now my father is from Missouri, with an accent and an attitude to show for it. What this request meant was: 'Heidi, hand me a ball-point pen.' His words reflected the semantic intention to have the utterance 'pin' mean 'ball-point pen' and the utterance 'son' mean 'daughter'. But of course, one could only know this if one appreciated his linguistic motivations: to procure a writing instrument from an off-spring of either sex. There was thus many a time that he puzzled over being handed a safety pin by my brother.

Those who attribute influential authority to persons or groups are thus committed to a theory of interpretation that *necessarily* requires a search for semantic intentions. Insofar as the reason to grant influential authority to persons or groups is a function of the moral importance of honouring their

[11] For an exploration and critique of the arguments advanced in defence of the influential authority of the law, see Hurd, 'Challenging Authority', 1644–66.

[12] Michael Moore first articulated this distinction in 1981 as a distinction between 'locutionary' and 'perlocutionary' intentions, and then re-described it in 1985 as one between 'semantic' and 'further' intentions. Michael S. Moore, 'The Semantics of Judging', *South. Calif. Law Rev.*, 54 (1981), 151; id., 'A Natural Law Theory of Interpretation', *South. Calif. Law Rev.*, 58 (1985), 277, 338–49. These distinctions were adopted and expanded by Gregory Bassham in his discussion of 'scope beliefs', 'counterfactual scope beliefs', and 'semantic intentions'. Gregory Bassham, *Original Intent and the Constitution* (Lanham, Md.: Rowman & Littlefield Publishers, 1992), 28–34. For a discussion of Bassham's rendition of these distinctions, see Alexander, *supra*, Ch. 10.

will, one must seemingly penetrate the plain meaning of their words in order to determine whether those words accurately capture their will. In the event that they have mis-spoken (uttering the word 'pin' when they mean 'pen'), or have used words in ways that are not conventionally identical to their semantic intentions (using the word 'son' when they mean 'daughter'), one must seemingly disregard the plain meaning of their words and act, instead, on their semantic intentions. For to give a friend what he asks for, as opposed to what he wants, is a cruel elevation of form over friendship (and it surely would have won me no points with my father).[13]

While the discovery of linguistic motivations may be helpful to detecting semantic intentions, a search for such motivations is not *necessitated* by the attribution of influential authority. It is this fact that makes the interpretation of an influential authority distinct from the interpretation of an inspirational authority. The interpretation of an inspirational authority *necessarily* requires a search for both semantic intentions and linguistic motivations. For complying with both sorts of intentions is what it *means* to act on inspirational authority. Such authority is vindicated only if one does what the authority semantically intends *and* does it for the reasons that linguistically motivate the authority.

Those who accord the law influential authority must thus necessarily seek the semantic intentions of lawmakers, but they need not necessarily seek the linguistic motivations with which the law was made. Inasmuch as the influential authority of legislation is premissed on the claim that the majority's 'requests' should function as reasons for action, it follows that one must detect the majority's semantic intentions in order to give adequate moral force to those 'requests'. If the views of the city council are genuinely representative of the views of the majority, and if the city council intended the word 'vehicles' to include skateboards, then a judge has a reason to prohibit skateboards in the park (whether or not the word 'vehicles' conventionally connotes skateboards). For only by so doing does the judge honour the will of the majority. But in so far as the city council's reasons for prohibiting skateboards in the park need not motivate the judge, the judge need not discover whether the prohibition was motivated by a concern for pedestrian safety or a concern for pollution unless such a discovery facilitates her understanding of the city council's semantic intentions.

In the end, then, those who attribute to law influential authority may be less rigorous intentionalists than those who attribute to it inspirational authority. But intentionalists they must be.

[13] As Oliver Wendell Holmes said, it would be puzzling to think that the separation of powers required a court to respond to a legislature's unclear or mis-stated enactments by saying: 'We see what you are driving at, but you have not said it, and therefore we shall go on as before.' Quoted in Learned Hand, *The Bill of Rights* (Cambridge, Mass.: Harvard University Press, 1958), 18.

C. Practical Authority

Those who think that laws function as commands rather than requests attribute to them what is known as 'practical authority'. A practical authority does not just give one a new reason for a particular action; it supplants all other reasons for and against that action.[14] One may not simply add the prohibition against vehicles in the park to the reasons for and against four-wheeling across the public lawn and disregard it in the event that the reasons for taking the ride outweigh the reasons against taking it (including the reason against taking it that is provided by its prohibition). Rather, one must take the prohibition as the answer to the question of whether one should drive one's jeep across the grass. One must substitute it for all of the antecedently existing reasons for and against the manœuvre, so that it alone informs one's choice.

We can more precisely define the concept of practical authority as follows:

> X has practical authority over Y if and only if when X says 'Do A', Y has a new reason to do A and a sufficient reason to disregard all other reasons for and against doing A.

Like the directives of an influential authority, the commands of a practical authority give one new reasons for action. Unlike those of an influential authority, however, these commands are pre-emptive. The reasons for action that they give take the place of all other reasons for and against action. The command of a practical authority thus leaves one with only one 'choice':

[14] Sophisticated practical authority theorists like Raz premiss the law's pre-emptive power on a finding that the law possesses *legitimate* practical authority and is within the *scope* of its jurisdiction. The legitimacy of a practical authority turns on the degree to which the authority comports with the 'dependence thesis'. The dependence thesis holds that 'all authoritative directives should be based on reasons which already independently apply to the subjects of the directives and are relevant to their action in the circumstances covered by the directive'. Raz, *The Morality of Freedom*, 47. The scope of a practical authority's jurisdiction extends to all those reasons for action that one will better act on if one follows the authority's directives instead of assessing them for oneself. Raz would thus qualify the claim that a law, if possessed of practical authority, supplants all other reasons for and against the required action. He would instead say that a law, if possessed of legitimate practical authority, supplants all other reasons for and against that action that are within the scope of its legitimate jurisdiction.

Both the requirement that the authority be legitimate and the requirement that it be acting within the scope of its jurisdiction are qualifications that are designed to make the exercise of practical authority morally palatable. I shall make no reference to these qualifications in the text because I am less concerned with spelling out the details of a morally defensible theory of practical authority than with deriving from the essential concept of practical authority a compatible theory of interpretation. Thus, my formulation of the concept of practical authority will represent a substantially simplified version of Raz's formulation. Those familiar with Raz's formulation may have grounds to complain that it is overly simplified. However, these complaints will matter for our purposes only if they would require modifications in the theory of interpretation that I derive from my simplified formulation of the concept of practical authority. For an analysis of Raz's theory of practical authority that is true to its details, see Hurd, 'Challenging Authority', 1620–44.

to do as one is told. Because a practical authority is not an inspirational authority, one need not do what is commanded for any of the reasons that motivated the practical authority to command it. Indeed, were one to add these motivating reasons to the reason for action provided by the command itself, one would fail to act on that reason for action alone. One would thus fail to act on practical authority, for one would be unable to say that the sole reason one acted was 'because I was told to'.

To make the exercise of practical authority morally intelligible, one must advance a theory about why individuals should sometimes surrender their judgment to others concerning what they ought to do. One strongly suspects that short of God, no one can plausibly claim that he deserves to be blindly obeyed solely because of who or what he is (that is, solely because of some status he occupies or some relationship he bears to those he commands). Parents often tell their children that they are owed blind obedience; religious figures often preach that blind faith in their word is the sole path to salvation; and some legal theorists have argued that legal authorities should tell similar tales to those they govern.[15] But it would be highly implausible for parents, preachers, and state officials to claim that they have a right to usurp persons' autonomy solely because they occupy the status of being a parent, a preacher, or a political leader. There are simply too many abusive parents, fanatical cultists, and corrupt politicians to enable us to believe that parents, preachers, and politicians are deserving of unquestioned authority. Like inspirational and influential authority, practical authority may be *accorded* to others on the basis of their status as legislators, parents, spiritual leaders, or friends. But unlike inspirational and influential authority, practical authority probably cannot be *justified* by an appeal to the moral significance of democracy, parenthood, religion, or friendship.

Recognizing that practical authority is implausibly premissed on a moral theory that accords special significance to particular relationships or status positions, Joseph Raz has defended the traditional attribution of practical authority to law on epistemic grounds. According to what he calls the 'normal justification thesis', persons or institutions have practical authority when and if their commands enable us to act on the balance of reasons for and against action more often than do our own judgments.[16] If abiding by another's directives enables one to do the right thing more often than one would if one took one's own counsel, then, argues Raz, the rational thing to do is to substitute those directives for the results of one's own judgment. For it follows that if one's own judgment is more fallible than that of the authority, one will do the right thing less often by second-guessing the directives of the authority than by following them 'blindly'. Upon establishing

[15] See e.g. Larry Alexander, 'The Gap', *Harv. Jo. Law and Public Policy* 14 (1991), 695–701; Alexander, *supra*, Ch. 10.

[16] Raz, *The Morality of Freedom*, 53.

another's practical authority, one will act most morally only if one acts 'because I was told to'.

Andrei Marmor has argued that those who advance an epistemic justification for the law's practical authority are likely to find a happy marriage with those who defend intentionalist interpretation.

> When one's reasons for acknowledging the authority of another are based on the assumption that the authority is more likely to have a better access to the right reasons bearing on the pertinent issue, it would typically be most sensible to take the authority's intentions into account when his directives require interpretation.[17]

Marmor's argument is compelling. If a legislature functions as a practical authority by virtue of being a better 'moral observer' than are individual citizens and officials, then citizens and officials would do well to abide by its enactments. And when those enactments are vague or ambiguous, citizens and officials should repair to the moral observations that motivated them. They should seek, that is, the mental states possessed by the individual legislators at the time of enactment, for the expertise that makes legislative enactments practically authoritative presumably resides in the beliefs and intentions that prompted individual legislators to act.[18]

Yet like any good marriage, this one is not without tension. Consider the case of *United States* v. *Kirby*,[19] in which a county sheriff was prosecuted under a federal statute that made it a crime 'to obstruct or retard the passage of the mail, or of any driver or carrier',[20] after he carried out a warrant to arrest an on-duty federal-mail carrier suspected of murder. By the plain meaning of the statute the sheriff committed a crime, for the carrier's arrest certainly delayed the delivery of the mail. But let us suppose, quite plausibly, that we have good evidence that (whatever else they intended) the legislators who enacted the statute did not intend for the mail to be delivered on time at any cost—including the cost of letting a murderer go free. Let us suppose that they did not intend for a sheriff to be arrested for obstructing the mail upon executing a lawful warrant against a murderous mail carrier. Rather, they intended for courts to recognize exceptions to the statute that would exculpate persons when they obstructed the passage of the mail for a higher purpose, for example, self-defence, defence of others, law enforcement, balance-of-evils necessity. Since the latter intention is

[17] Marmor, *Interpretation and Legal Theory*, 178.

[18] Marmor is quick to warn that legal directives may have practical authority because they solve co-ordination problems and dissolve prisoners' dilemmas. In so far as there are no right answers to co-ordination problems (there are merely salient solutions), those who have authored co-ordinating directives have little claim to any special moral expertise. There thus appears to be little reason to seek their intentions when their directives are ambiguous. One should simply seek less ambiguous, and hence, more salient, co-ordinating rules. Marmor, *Interpretation and Legal Theory*, 176–84.

[19] 74 U.S. (7 Wall. 482 (1868)).

[20] 74 U.S. at 483 (quoting 4 Stat. 104 (1825)).

presumably more authoritative than its imperfect expression in the federal mail obstruction statute, a court should ignore the language of the statute in favour of the legislative intent to exculpate those like Sheriff Kirby.

The problem with this solution is that it appears self-defeating, for it thwarts the purpose of ascribing practical authority to the law. While the exercise of practical authority may be justified on epistemic grounds, its role is to pre-empt individual judgment, to exclude moral enquiry, to usurp the role of private practical reasoning. Its point is to allow persons to act solely because they have been told to act. In so far as the directives of a practical authority bar one from second-guessing their wisdom, they seemingly cannot permit one to penetrate their plain meaning. Hence, when the commands of a practical authority possess a plain meaning, one is seemingly estopped from seeking their authorial intentions. For to do so implies that one is second-guessing their wisdom. And since they are not to be second-guessed precisely because in second-guessing them one will do worse than if one follows them blindly, the search for authorial intentions appears inconsistent with abiding by the commands of a practical authority when those commands possess a plain meaning.[21]

Only when the commands of a practical authority are vague, ambiguous, or open-textured do they invite intentionalist interpretation without apparent self-contradiction. In such cases, one cannot simply do as one has been told, because what one has been told to do admits of several possible interpretations. In order to identify correctly which of the various interpretations reflects the moral insight of the commander, one must seek the content of that insight. To do so, one must presumably employ an intentionalist theory of interpretation, for the beliefs that motivated the practical authority to issue the command are probably best reflected in the linguistic intentions (the semantic intentions and linguistic motivations) with which she spoke.[22]

[21] Marmor goes so far as to insist that what it *means* to follow a rule laid down by a practical authority (as opposed to set it aside) is to abide by its plain meaning. Were one to set the plain meaning of the rule aside in favour of purposive interpretation (or, presumably, an intentionalist interpretation) one would 'confuse[] the question of what *following a rule consists in* . . . with that of *whether a rule should be applied in the circumstances*'. Marmor, *Interpretation and Legal Theory*, 136 (emphasis in the original). Such a claim echoes the sentiments of Hart and Sacks when they wrote: '[Courts] cannot permit the legislative process, and all other processes which depend upon the integrity of language, to be subverted by the misuse of words . . . [T]hese policies of clear statement may on occasion operate to defeat the actual, consciously held intention of particular legislators, or of the members of the legislature generally . . . [T]hey constitute conditions of the effectual exercise of legislative power.' Henry Hart and Albert Sacks, *The Legal Process* (tentative edn., 1958), 1412–13. The analytic derivation of the plain meaning theory of interpretation from the concept of a practically authoritative rule is not altogether convincing. I find it more plausible to claim that the normative function of a practical authority is best preserved by interpreting its utterances according to their plain meaning.

[22] As I shall later make clear, what one cares about when disambiguating the statement of a moral expert are the moral beliefs that motivated the statement. Insofar as these beliefs may

Given the point of declaring lawmakers practical authorities, it would thus seem that intentionalism must play second fiddle to a plain-meaning theory of legal interpretation. Such a conclusion is puzzling, however, in just those cases in which the plain meaning of a legal text departs from the intentions of its authors. In such cases, the rule departs from its rationale. One should do as one is plainly told (for all other reasons for action are preempted), but the reason for doing as one is plainly told (the fact that the authority knows better what one should do) speaks in favour of refusing to do so.

It should be no surprise, however, that practical authority generates an interpretive paradox. For practical authority is itself inherently paradoxical.[23] Its point is to bar one from considering reasons for and against actions that determine the morality of those actions. Inasmuch as: (1) the morality of an action is determined by the balance of reasons for and against that action, all reasons considered; and (2) practical reason must therefore consist in weighing all of the available reasons for and against an action; and (3) practical authority bars one from considering all available reasons for and against an action save the fact that one has been told to do it, obeying a practical authority appears irrational. The most promising means of rescuing practical authority from the charge of incoherence is to insist, with Raz, that practical authority is properly possessed only by moral experts—by those whose commands reflect the balance of reasons for action more often than do one's own judgments. But to resolve the paradox of practical authority in this manner simply generates the paradox of interpretation described above. The epistemic defence of practical authority makes it rational to do as one is told by a practical authority; but what one is told to do may depart from what the authority intended. And since the expertise that justifies the exercise of practical authority resides in the authority's intentions, one fails to act rationally when one acts on the authority's words, rather than on the authority's intentions.

The interpretive paradox that is generated by a theory of practical authority says more about the problems with practical authority than it does about the problems with the particular theories of interpretation to which a theory of practical authority is hostage. Many may feel, however, that in so far as a theory of practical authority embodies a cardinal preference for abiding by the plain meaning of a text over its authorial intent, it catapults one out

best be gleaned by determining the linguistic intentions (the semantic intentions and linguistic motivations) with which the expert uttered the statement, one has a reason to engage in intentionalist interpretation. But the authority resides not in these linguistic intentions, but in the insights that motivated the formation of these intentions. See *infra*, text accompanying n. 26.

[23] For a lengthy discussion of what I call 'the paradox of practical authority', see Hurd, 'Challenging Authority', 1620–41.

of the frying-pan and into the fire. Any theory that allows a Sheriff Kirby to be convicted or that bars toddlers from riding Playskool three-wheelers in the park has problems that survive the vindication of its conceptual coherence.[24]

It is not the point of this part, however, to detail these problems. I have sought here merely to explore the theory of interpretation to which those who defend the law's practical authority are most plausibly committed. I have argued that Marmor is right in marrying an epistemically based theory of practical authority to a theory of intentionalist interpretation. But I have advanced reasons to think that this may be a fickle union. For the point of ascribing practical authority to a person or institution is best preserved by a plain-meaning theory of interpretation. One is permitted to appeal to the intentions of the authority only when its commands lack a plain meaning. Hence, intentionalist interpretation is implied only secondarily by an epistemic theory of practical authority.

D. Theoretical Authority

I have elsewhere argued that the law does not possess inspirational, influential, or practical authority.[25] At best, it serves as a theoretical authority about deontic propositions—a source of evidence about the antecedently existing moral maxims that alone obligate us. The law cannot give us reasons for action; only morality can do that. But it can give us reasons to believe that there are reasons for action, for it can function as a reliable guide to determining the content of morality. The law thus cannot command; but it can advise. It cannot pre-empt independent judgment, but it can serve as an efficient heuristic when independent judgment is difficult or impossible. In short, while the only real law is the moral law, the rules fashioned by human institutions can serve as rules of thumb that can and should be employed in practical reasoning as proxies for the rules of morality when those rules defy our clear understanding.

The question, for our purposes, is how the advice of theoretical authorities ought to be interpreted. In what follows, I shall outline why it is commonly thought that theoretical authorities demand intentionalist interpretation. I shall then, in Part II, turn my attention very briefly to the problems that plague intentionalism. In Part III I shall revisit the concept of theoretical

[24] These further problems were famously articulated by Lon Fuller in his critique of Hart's theory of interpretation. See Lon Fuller, *The Morality of Law*, rev. edn. (New Haven, Conn.: Yale University Press, 1969), 224–32; Lon Fuller, 'Positivism and Fidelity to Law: A Reply to Professor Hart', *Harvard Law Rev.*, 71 (1958), 630–72.

[25] Hurd, 'Sovereignty in Silence', 990–1028; 'Challenging Authority', 1611–66; 'Justifiably Punishing the Justified', *Michigan Law Rev.*, 90 (1992), 2222–4; 'Four Models of Authority', unpublished speech delivered at the University of Iowa Philosophy Department (available from author) (1991).

authority in order to demonstrate that it need not be linked to intentional communications by those possessing greater expertise. Hence, unlike the standard theories of legal authority, it need not be hostage to the fate of intentionalist interpretation.

It is initially plausible to think that just as those who defend the practical authority of law on epistemic grounds are committed to intentionalist interpretation, so those who defend the theoretical authority of law are committed to intentionalist interpretation. The argument for this is straightforward. It proceeds from what I shall call the 'standard conception' of a theoretical authority. On this standard conception, a theoretical authority is a secondary source of information. It 'sums up' other reasons for belief; it represents an evaluation of other, more primary evidence. Primary evidence signals the existence of a fact by virtue of being causally related to it. A theoretical authority signals the existence of a fact (be it moral or non-moral) by virtue of summing up the primary evidence for it. Thus, a thermometer is not a theoretical authority about the temperature. Its reading is, rather, evidence of the temperature, because, like the ice on the pond, the snow on the ground, the chill in the air, and the tingling in one's toes, it is caused by the temperature. The statement by the weatherperson that the temperature is below freezing is not, on the other hand, evidence of the temperature, for the temperature does not cause the utterance. Rather, if accurate, the utterance is theoretically authoritative: it summarizes the evidence of the temperature. Similarly, nausea, headaches, and muscular aches are not theoretical authorities about illness. They are, rather, evidence of illness, because they are presumably caused by it. The statement by a physician that one has a particular disease is not, on the other hand, evidence of that disease, for it is not a necessary result of it. Rather, if accurate, the utterance is theoretically authoritative; it sums up the evidence for the disease.

We can define the standard conception of theoretical authority about moral matters as follows:

> X has theoretical authority over Y if and only if when X says 'Do A', Y has a new reason to believe that there are reasons to do A.[26]

[26] This definition captures what might be called 'limited theoretical authority'. We might distinguish a notion of 'comprehensive theoretical authority' as follows: '*X has comprehensive theoretical authority over Y if and only if when X says "Do A", Y has a new reason to believe that the balance of reasons for action favours doing A.*' The difference between limited and comprehensive theoretical authority is one of degree, not kind. If another's advice accurately reflects some sorts of reasons for action, but not others, then we should say that it possesses limited theoretical authority. It does not give us an indication of what the balance of reasons requires, because it does not reflect all relevant reasons for action. It simply serves as a heuristic to a set of reasons which one must add to the balance of reasons when determining what to do. Thus, one might consult an economist for a cost–benefit analysis of a particular course of action, for in the absence of overriding obligations, the moral thing to do is typically the cost-efficient thing to do. But one should recognize that such an analysis may fail to reveal agent-relative obligations that bind one without regard to their costs and benefits. Hence, one would be wise to attribute limited theoretical authority to the conclusions of the economist.

Inasmuch as the standard exercise of theoretical authority involves summing evidence, and summing evidence is a rational endeavour, it would appear that only persons can exercise theoretical authority. Only persons can say 'do A' as a result of evaluating the reasons for and against doing A. When a theoretical authority issues advice, her words should presumably be treated as heuristics to the observations in which her theoretical authority resides. In the event that we distrust the heuristic value of her words (because they are vague, ambiguous, or apparent misstatements), we should seek directly the beliefs that motivated her advice. In so far as her linguistic intentions—that is, her semantic intentions and her linguistic motivations—are our best evidence of her beliefs, we should seek these intentions.

If the law functions as a theoretical authority about our moral obligations, then, on the standard conception, it must be by virtue of lawmakers reliably amassing and evaluating the relevant evidence concerning those obligations. In the event that we are in doubt about the moral lesson to be learned from the law, we should seek the beliefs of the lawmakers, for it is in these mental states—and not in their legal expression—that genuine theoretical authority resides. As a means of seeking the moral observations in which their theoretical authority resides, we would do well to seek their semantic intentions and linguistic motivations. For what they believed is probably best evidenced by what they meant by their utterances, and by what effects they meant to achieve in the world by those utterances. Hence, one who defends the theoretical authority of the law is committed, on the standard conception, to two theses: first, that the authority of the law resides in the moral expertise of lawmakers; and secondly, that the best means of 'tapping' that expertise is to discover the semantic intentions and linguistic motivations that best reveal the beliefs possessed by lawmakers.

In Part III I shall outline a 'non-standard conception' of the law's theoretical authority that rejects both of these theses. To motivate the claim that the authority of law is best captured by this non-standard conception, let me briefly make clear why the problems with intentionalism as a theory of legal interpretation render the standard theories of legal authority indefensible accounts of the law's authority.

If, in general, another's advice accurately reflects all (or most) of the relevant reasons for action, and accurately reflects the proper balance between them, then one should conceive of it as a source of comprehensive theoretical authority. While one is not estopped from judging for oneself the balance of reasons for action, one may be wise to defer to such a comprehensive theoretical authority when making one's own independent judgment would require a greater investment of time, energy, and resources than is merited by the issue at hand. By virtue of their intimate knowledge of our beliefs, desires, life plans, and circumstances, parents, spouses, and friends often claim comprehensive theoretical authority when they offer us advice. They purport to rest their advice on a summary of all considerations relevant to our decisions. And when we find ourselves unable to make our own judgments, many of us defer to such advice precisely because its comprehensive theoretical authority makes it rational to forgo further deliberation.

II. THE INDEFENSIBILITY OF INTENTIONALISM

If intentionalist interpretation is indefensible—because, for example, it is either empirically impossible to detect intentions or normatively undesirable to abide by them—then the theories of authority that necessitate it are indefensible. Few, however, would issue the blanket claim that intentionalism as a whole is indefensible. While the ability to read minds is a rare skill, most of us are fairly confident in our ability to detect the intentions of our family members, colleagues, friends, and enemies. Moreover, many of us plainly attribute either inspirational or influential authority to at least some of these persons (and some go so far as to accord them practical authority), implying thereby that we sometimes consider it morally appropriate to abide by their intentions. General scepticism about intentionalist interpretation thus appears unwarranted.

Scepticism about intentionalism in statutory interpretation stands in better stead. As one critic has put it: 'The folly of any attempt to conjure up a legislative intent has been asserted so often that many respectable scholars refuse to recognize the concept.'[27] But despite the brutal beatings it has received at the hands of critics, intentionalism in statutory interpretation will not die. The reason, I suspect, is that legal theorists implicitly attribute to the law one of the four sorts of authority outlined above—all of which entail a search for legislative intentions. They thus find themselves in a predicament: to borrow John Chipman Gray's words, their theory of legal authority requires them to search for a 'psychic transference of the thought of an artificial body [that] must stagger the most advanced of ghost hunters'.[28]

Legal theorists have performed some astonishing contortions to vindicate, conceptually and empirically, the search for legislative intentions. Some—call them 'pure realists'—have been so bold as to declare that groups can possess intentions in precisely the same manner as individuals.[29] Presumably these theorists would also argue that groups *qua* groups can experience moods, emotions, sensations, and memories that are not reducible to those of the individuals that comprise them. To make out these remarkable claims, however, pure realists would have to make out how groups can have minds distinct from those of their individual members. And they could

[27] Reed Dickerson, *The Interpretation and Application of Statutes* (Boston: Little, Brown 1975), 68. See e.g. Fuller, *The Morality of Law*, 86; Robert E. Keeton, *Venturing To Do Justice: Reforming Private Law* (Cambridge, Mass.: Harvard University Press, 1969), 81; J. A. Corry, 'Administrative Law and the Interpretation of Statutes', *Univ. of Toronto LJ*, 1 (1936), 286, 290; Moore, 'A Natural Law Theory of Interpretation', 345–52.

[28] John Chipman Gray, *The Nature and Sources of the Law*, 2nd edn. (Boston: Beacon Press, 1921), 170.

[29] These theorists have based their claims on the work of a small school of psychologists who maintain that masses do in fact manifest unique, non-reducible, psychological experiences. See Helen Silving, 'A Plea for a Law of Interpretation', *Univ. of Pennsylvania Law Rev.*, 98 (1950), 499, 510.

seemingly do this only if they could plausibly maintain that individuals in groups function in a manner analogous to neurons in a brain.

Those who are sceptical about the ontology of group minds have had to premiss their legislative intentionalism on the intentions of individual legislators. Their task has been to make sense of the notion of a singular 'legislative intent' in the face of their admission that the legislature, as such, lacks any such intent. Majoritarians have pursued this task by arguing that the legislative intent behind any particular statute is constituted by the intention shared by the majority of legislators at the time of enactment.[30] But the business of tabulating individual intentions is a messy one. First, whose intentions should count? Should one tally only the intentions of those who voted *for* the bill? Or should the intentions of those who voted *against* it be computed so as to determine the possible limits of the intent with which the statute was passed? What should be done in the face of multiple intentions, none of which commands a majority? And what of those legislators who had no intention one way or another concerning the enactment of a statute? Secondly, how should one count 'overlapping' intentions? Are the lesser included intentions of some legislators to be counted the same as, or different from, the more general intentions of other legislators within which they are included (as when one legislator intends to exclude white Jaguars from the park while another intends to exclude automobiles)? Thirdly, what should one do when legislators share the same linguistic motivations, but diverge from one another in their semantic intentions (as when all intend to prohibit vehicles in the park, but only some intend the word 'vehicle' to include skateboards)? And finally, what should one do when legislators share the same semantic intentions, but diverge from one another in their linguistic motivations (because, for example, they each possess a different ordering of the effects in the world that they seek to achieve)?[31]

In the face of the counting and combination problems that confront majoritarians, some theorists have sought to anthropomorphize the legislature so as to treat its enactments *as if* they were issued by a singular author.[32] They have argued that the diverse and sometimes conflicting intentions of legislators should be treated *as if* they were evidence of a coherent set

[30] Raz appears to have a majoritarian theory of legislative intent in mind when he urges that '[e]very attribution of an intention to the law is based on an attribution of a real intention to a real person in authority or exerting influence over authority'. Joseph Raz, 'Authority, Law and Morality', *Monist*, 68 (1985), 295, 318.

[31] For more extensive discussions of these sorts of counting and combination problems, see Ronald Dworkin, *A Matter of Principle* (Cambridge, Mass.: Harvard University Press, 1985), 38–55; Frank H. Easterbrook, 'Statutes' Domains', *Univ. of Chicago Law Rev.*, 50 (1983), 533, 547–8; Hurd, 'Sovereignty in Silence', 971–3; Moore, 'The Semantics of Judging', 266–70; Joseph Raz, 'Dworkin: A New Link in the Chain', (Book Review) *Calif. Law Rev.*, 74 (1986), 1103–19.

[32] See Scott Bice, 'Rationality Analysis in Constitutional Law', *Minnesota Law Rev.*, 65 (1980), 1, 26–33.

of intentions possessed by a single individual. One should reconstruct from such 'evidence' a unified account that represents what a rational person possessed of such intentions would intend. The problem, of course, is that one can hardly treat something as evidence when one knows that it does not evidence anything. Since there is literally nothing that the 'evidence' (the individual intentions of the legislators) evidences, the process of reconstruction is really just a process of creation. Anthropomorphic intentionalism thus stands to intentionalism as hypothetical consent stands to actual consent. Just as a rapist could hardly defend himself by claiming hypothetical consent on the part of his victim, so a judge could hardly claim an allegiance to legislative intent if she resolved conflicts between the particular intentions of legislators by assigning them new ones.

An alternative means of reducing, if not escaping, the counting and combination problems that plague majoritarian intentionalists is advanced by theorists who defend what has been dubbed a 'delegation model' of legislative intent.[33] According to this theory, the legislature's intent is constituted by the intentions shared by the small group of persons who actually drafted the statute. Other legislators are to be taken to have delegated to this small group the authority to speak (and intend) on their behalf. Yet two problems unite to befuddle the defence of such a theory. First, as a matter of psychology it would appear that few if any legislators have a second-order intention of the delegatory sort, namely, the intention that their intention should be taken to be whatever intention the drafters of the statutory language had in mind. Secondly, even if a majority of legislators had such delegatory intentions, the *legislature* itself would not have the requisite intentions. When a legislator delegates to draftspersons the power to intend something, without knowing or intending what it will be, the legislator is not intending what they intend—they are. When a legislator receives the bill from the draftspersons and transmits it by an affirmative vote without knowing what the draftspersons intended, the legislator is also not intending what they intended. By hypothesis, someone intends something (the draftspersons), but the delegation theory has no way of transforming that fact into the desired conclusion that the legislature *qua* legislature acts with a specific intention.

I have here canvassed only a smattering of the problems that confront those who attempt to defend intentionalism. The ones that I have mentioned can be characterized as counting and combination obstacles—that is, empirical problems that confront those who actually go in search of legislative intentions. I have elsewhere identified conceptual problems with the intentionalist's presupposition that legislative enactments are communications that

[33] See Gerald MacCallum, 'Legislative Intent', *Yale LJ*, 75 (1966), 754.

satisfy the complex conditions for communication famously articulated by Paul Grice.[34] Others have since advanced alternative arguments against conceiving of legislative enactments as intentional communications.[35] In light of the serious problems that confront any attempt to defend the conceptual coherence and empirical viability of appealing to legislative intent in the course of interpreting statutes, one has to wonder why theorists have been so reluctant to abandon the endeavour. The hypothesis that I advanced earlier is that they implicitly attribute to law an authority that demands intentionalist interpretation. Despite their nagging doubts about its conceptual and empirical viability, legal theorists feel persistent pressure to vindicate (or at least accommodate) intentionalism. Hence the contortions.

It would seem that the time has come to opt for the alternative solution: to abandon the theories of authority that commit theorists to the impossible task of vindicating intentionalism in statutory interpretation. The deduction that leads to this conclusion is simple. (1) If one assigns to statutory law inspirational authority, influential authority, practical authority, or the standard conception of theoretical authority, then one must adopt an intentionalist theory of statutory interpretation. (2) One cannot defend an intentionalist theory of statutory interpretation. (3) Therefore, one cannot assign to statutory law any of the four sorts of authority that commits one to intentionalist interpretation.

One has no reason, however, to buy the conclusion of this inference unless an alternative theory of authority is available that escapes intentionalism. For in the absence of a new alternative, one might as well keep trying to repair one of the old alternatives. In what follows, I propose to sketch a theory of the law's authority that both captures the unique role of law in guiding action and that invites interpretive strategies that avoid any appeal to authorial intentions.

III. ASSIGNING THEORETICAL AUTHORITY TO LAW, NOT LAWMAKERS

The standard conception of theoretical authority locates expertise primarily in the mental states of persons, and only derivatively in the statements that they use to express those mental states. It is no surprise, then, that when a theoretical authority's words fail to communicate her mental states, one should seek those mental states by means of other evidence. For according

[34] Hurd, 'Sovereignty in Silence', 947, 953–89. For defences of the intentionalist's assumption that statutes function as communications which employ a Gricean analysis of communication, see Geoffrey P. Miller, 'Pragmatics and the Maxims of Interpretation', [1990] *Wisconsin Law Rev.* (1990), 1179–227; M. B. W. Sinclair, 'Law and Language: The Role of Pragmatics in Statutory Interpretation', *Univ. of Pittsburgh Law Rev.*, 46 (1985), 373–420.

[35] The very creative arguments advanced in this volume by Jeremy Waldron are to this end. See *supra*, Ch. 9. See also *infra* text accompanying n. 46.

to the standard conception, one's reasons for belief are given by the observations that a theoretical authority makes and the conclusions that she derives thereby. One's interpretive strategies are thus to be judged in light of their ability to detect the beliefs and intentions that motivated the theoretical authority to speak.

I propose a modest Copernican revolution in the way we think about the theoretical authority of law. Instead of locating the theoretical authority of law primarily in the mental states of lawmakers, and only derivatively in the texts they produce, we should locate it primarily in the texts produced by lawmakers, and only derivatively (if at all) in the intentions with which they produced them. This, admittedly non-standard, conception invests the law—and not (necessarily) its authors—with theoretical authority. It treats legal texts as moral guides when complying with their language reliably assists us in satisfying our moral obligations. To the extent that detecting the intentions possessed by those who drafted the law would assist us in fixing the law with a determinate content, we have reason to look to their authorial intentions. But their intentions are, on this theory, mere heuristics to what is itself only a heuristic. For the intentions of lawmakers are, on this view, a heuristic guide to determining the content of the law, which is itself a heuristic guide to determining the content of morality. In the end, only morality obligates. All 'secondary principles' by which to determine the maxims of morality, and all interpretive techniques by which to fix the content of such secondary principles, should thus be judged by their ability to conform our conduct to the demands of morality. In the event that the law is ambiguous, we may do well to fix its content by reference to the intentions of its drafters. But in the event that these intentions are undiscoverable or unreliable,[36] they lose their heuristic value, and we would do well to fix the content of the law by other means, or to seek altogether an alternative guide to moral action.

This is the essence of my thesis. As a means of filling out its content, let me take up some concerns that would-be critics might have with it. First, the objection will be made that on the theory I have advanced, laws are just like seagull tracks in the sand. Without an understanding of their author's intentions, they are mere marks on paper. How can they be interpreted when one cannot even know, in the absence of authorial intentions, what language we should read them in? And why would one want to interpret them, given that we do not typically seek to interpret seagull tracks in the sand? Do we not have to assume that laws are communications in order to make sense of our attention to them?

[36] 'There is no more reason why a person who uses a word correctly should be able to tell what it means than there is why a planet which is moving correctly should know Kepler's laws.' Bertrand Russell, *My Philosophical Development* (New York: Simon & Schuster, 1959), 147 (quoting from id., *The Analysis of Mind*).

The answer to this challenge is straightforward. If the marks on paper laid down by lawmakers assist us in determining the content of morality when we invest them with meaning, then they should be thought theoretically authoritative. The same goes for seagull tracks in the sand and the oracular whistling of wind through rock walls. So long as the authorial intentions with which they were laid down do not give us reasons for action, we are not bound to determine the content of those intentions as a means of fulfilling our moral obligations. We are free, that is, to invest such marks with a meaning distinct from that contemplated by their authors if so doing better enables us to act on the balance of reasons for action. Of course, knowing what their authors intended might assist us in fixing the marks with a meaning that is maximally instructive. In the event that this is so, we have reason to seek such intentions. But if such intentions are non-existent (because the seagull lacked any to begin with) or unavailable (because we lack any readily available evidence of them) or conflicted (because we confront counting and combination problems that befuddle any attempt to detect them), we would do well to fix the meaning of the marks in other ways.

The next objection to my claim that the content of law should be thought distinct from the intentions of lawmakers follows close on the heels of this first objection. It goes like this: to interpret seagull tracks in the sand so as to achieve moral insight is not to *interpret* anything, and certainly not anything that can be called a 'text'. One who 'reads' and reasons from seagull tracks is simply engaged in the sort of moral reasoning that one engages in when short on seagull tracks. One's moral conclusions are phrased in the 'symbols' of the seagull, but they are not derived from those symbols. Similarly, to interpret marks on paper in the same manner as one interprets seagull tracks is not to *interpret* anything. One who reads and reasons from such marks is simply engaged in the sort of moral reasoning that one could engage in without such marks. One's conclusions might be expressed in terms of the marks on the paper, but their genesis lies elsewhere.[37]

Joseph Raz voiced this objection to the value-oriented interpretive theories defended by Ronald Dworkin and Michael Moore, and Larry Alexander revisits it in this volume when evaluating those theories.[38] Whatever be the responses available to Dworkin and Moore, mine is and must be epistemic.

[37] One could put this objection in the words of Bishop Hoadly: 'Whoever hath an *absolute authority* to *interpret* any . . . laws, it is *he* who is truly the Law-giver . . . and not the person who first wrote . . . them.' Quoted in Gray, *The Nature and Sources of the Law*, 172 (emphasis in original). If we are to avoid giving ourselves our own individual laws, we must interpret statutes as they were intended to be interpreted, for only by so doing do we preserve the role of the legislature as lawgiver.

[38] Raz, 'Dworkin: A New Link in the Chain', 1103–19; Alexander, *supra*, Ch. 10. See also Charles Fried, 'Sonnet LXV and the "Black Ink" of the Framers' Intention', *Harvard Law Rev.*, 100 (1987), 751–60.

We are constrained in our interpretation of seagull tracks by whatever seagull semantics maximize our moral insight. Suppose Jonathan Livingston Seagull smartly runs a pattern of the following shape: 'Duties of beneficence are not owed to all persons equally, but only to those near and dear.' In answer to the first objection, it matters not at all that Jonathan is an Italian seagull: we will do better to interpret these marks with English semantics. (This is, after all, pretty lousy Italian.) In answer to the second objection, we might better figure out to whom we owe duties of beneficence if we respect the normal English meaning of words like 'near' and 'dear' than if we try to reason our duties out *ab initio.*

Now why might this be true? The answer is that, for many people, moral insight is more easily achieved if they reason under the guise of interpreting an authoritative text than if they reason with Sartrean self-awareness that everything is up for grabs at once.[39] This I take to explain the staying-power of the world's popular religions. Despite their bizarre metaphysics, these religions give their believers authoritative moral texts the interpretation of which yields greater moral insight than believers are likely to achieve on their own.

Consider, as another example, how we should frame jury instructions when we wish a jury to make a moral determination. Let us suppose that the Royal Commission on Capital Punishment was right in advancing its 1954 recommendation: in criminal cases in which the insanity defence is raised, the jury should ultimately determine whether the defendant is so mentally diseased as to be irresponsible. One might none the less refuse to instruct a jury in these terms, because to do so would leave its members 'at sea'.[40] Instead, one might require it to focus on archaic questions like: 'Did he know the difference between right and wrong?'; or literally meaningless questions like: 'Was he irresistibly impelled to do what he did?'; or vague questions employing psycho-babble like: 'Did he lack a substantial capacity to conform his conduct to the requirements of law?' It may well be true that if jurors are asked to answer these curious questions, they will separate responsible from irresponsible defendants more accurately than if they are asked directly to determine defendants' responsibility.

The heuristic justification for paying attention to a text at all also gives us a reason to respect certain interpretive restraints, such as the ordinary semantics of English, when the text in question is a statute. The nature of these epistemically valuable restraints is a matter for extended discussion

[39] As Judge Posner has put it: 'When a court reads the Eighth Amendment, it is (or at least should be) looking for authoritative guidance, and it would get none if it felt free to give "cruel and unusual punishments" any meaning that the words wrenched free of their historical context might yield.' Richard A. Posner, *Law and Literature: A Misunderstood Relation* (Cambridge, Mass.: Harvard University Press, 1988), 227.

[40] This argument was made in Abraham Goldstein, *The Insanity Defense* (New Haven, Conn.: Yale University Press, 1967), 81–2.

elsewhere. One might think that the meaning of words in a statute should be given by their definitions, or by their paradigmatic exemplars, or by the nature of the things they denote, or by their conventional use amongst native speakers, or even by the intentions of their authors (if one could ever figure out how to overcome the counting and combination problems that prevent their detection[41]). One might be an eclectic about such semantic matters, employing different semantic constraints in different circumstances.[42] The point is that, like all heuristics, the only test of the value of interpretive restraints is their ability to generate insight. And nothing succeeds like success.

The next major source of criticism will probably originate with those who will argue that the reason why legal texts function as heuristic guides to moral action, while seagull tracks do not, is that the authors who draft them possess a certain moral expertise. They pick the marks they do because they know that we will invest them with conventional meaning, and if we do, we will be led to act on the balance of reasons for action.[43] We do well to look to law, as opposed to seagull tracks, the sounds of the whistling wind, works of fiction, the enactments of the local PTA, the advertisements at Woolworth's, or the pamphlets distributed door-to-door by missionaries, because lawmakers are better equipped to make moral judgments than are the authors of these works.[44] They possess extensive fact-finding powers, they enjoy unlimited time for debate and contemplation, they represent diverse points of view, and they have strong incentives to reach agreements that can be given a principled defence. Only the moral expertise of lawmakers can account for the comprehensive theoretical authority that the law enjoys[45]—a theoretical authority that, in contrast to every other theoretical authority, affects one's decisions about virtually every aspect of life. And if the law's comprehensive theoretical authority *is* a product of the moral expertise of lawmakers, then surely we should seek to discover the beliefs and intentions that motivated its enactment when its terms leave us in doubt about how to act.

[41] See Kent Greenawalt, 'The Enduring Significance of Neutral Principles', *Columbia Law Rev.*, 78 (1978), 982, 1014–16, arguing that there are several reasons (beyond counting and combination problems) why '[r]endering the theory [of original intent in constitutional interpretation] more plausible would virtually eliminate its utility'. Ibid., at 1016.

[42] For a defence of such an eclectic approach, see William N. Eskridge, 'Dynamic Statutory Interpretation', *Univ. of Pennsylvania Law Rev.*, 135 (1987), 1479, 1483.

[43] See Anthony D'Amato, 'Can Legislatures Constrain Judicial Interpretation of Statutes?', *Virginia Law Rev.*, 75 (1989), 561–603 (arguing that a legislature can manipulate the interpretation of its enactments by employing its audience's theory of interpretation to give meaning to its statutory terms).

[44] So I have argued in my past work. For an extended defence of the claim that legislators possess both the motivations and capacities of good moral observers (in large part because of the institutional constraints of their setting that procedurally check their self-interested motives and afford them extensive fact-finding opportunities), see Hurd, 'Sovereignty in Silence', 1010–15.

[45] See *supra*, n. 26.

Those persuaded by this rejoinder would do well at this point to read Jeremy Waldron's contribution to this volume. Waldron quite cleverly argues that democratic decision procedures yield results that are morally superior to those generated by the individual judgments of legislators. He advances three reasons for this claim. First, it is likely that democratic decision procedures aggregate individual preferences in the manner required by the applicable social-welfare function. Secondly, democratic decision procedures plausibly yield results that comport with the Condorcet Theorem—namely, the probability that they are correct is greater than the probability that any one of the views tabulated is correct. Finally, democratic decision procedures are likely to forge a 'deliberative synthesis' that is superior in content to any view that even the wisest of individuals could come to hold on her own.[46] As Waldron concludes, these arguments do not just give us reasons to think that theoretically authoritative results could be generated by a 'democracy machine' of the sort that Richard Wollheim famously hypothesized[47]—a machine that generates results which 'cannot be conceived as . . . something produced "by an intentional being . . . situated in some enterprise in relation to which he has a purpose or point of view" '.[48] More radically, in so far as these arguments give us a reason to accord theoretical authority to democratic enactments, they also give us 'a reason for discounting the authority of the views or intentions of particular legislators considered on their own'.[49] That is, they give us a reason to think that while democratic legislation may itself possess a certain moral expertise, individual legislators do not. If Waldron is right, one need not, and should not, concede that the only reason to think legislation theoretically authoritative is that legislators possess moral beliefs superior to those of citizens or officials. One can rather maintain that legislation is theoretically authoritative just in case its terms (interpreted without recourse to any legislators' intentions) enable one to act morally more often than one otherwise would.

Let me now turn to two objections to my thesis that take their leave from particular meta-ethical theories. The first derives from a defence of non-natural realism. Non-natural realists maintain that while moral facts exist, they are not natural facts. In order to know them one must possess a 'sixth sense'—a special faculty of perception that G. E. Moore called 'moral intuition'.[50] Only persons can possess moral intuition, and hence, only persons can possess theoretical authority about moral matters. To say that the law—

[46] Waldron, *supra*, Ch. 9.

[47] Richard Wollheim, 'A Paradox in the Theory of Democracy', in Peter Laslett and W. G. Runciman, *Philosophy, Politics and Society* 2nd series (Oxford: Basil Blackwell, 1969), 75–6.

[48] Waldron, *supra*, Ch. 9 (quoting Stanley Fish, *Doing What Comes Naturally: Change, Rhetoric and the Practice of Theory in Literary and Legal Studies* (Durham: Duke University Press, 1989), 99–100.).

[49] Ibid., at 336–8.

[50] G. E. Moore, *Principia Ethica* (Cambridge: Cambridge University Press, 1903), 1–36.

as distinct from its authors—can be theoretically authoritative about morality is thus absurd.

Even if non-natural realism were defensible,[51] this argument would fail. For while moral insight might require the exercise of moral intuition, one might find that one can assist one's moral intuition by experiencing phenomena that do not themselves originate from moral intuition. When particular phenomena reliably induce useful moral insights, they can be taken to give reasons to believe that one has reasons for action. That is, they can rightly be thought to possess theoretical authority. Thus, while legal texts may not reflect, or be interpreted in light of, moral intuitions possessed by lawmakers, they may serve to trigger useful moral insights on the part of readers who possess moral intuition.

The second meta-ethically based challenge to my claim that the law's theoretical authority should not be thought to reside in its authors derives from the claims of conventionalism. Conventionalists maintain that moral truths are natural facts, but they equate them with sociological facts about the beliefs of the community. Such a view gives rise to the claim that beliefs of persons are the only source of evidence about what one should do. While the beliefs of individuals might depart from the beliefs of the community as a whole, they offer the only source of theoretical authority concerning the content of conventional morality. Hence, only persons can possess theoretical authority.

This argument invites the same response as did the last one. Even if conventionalism were defensible,[52] it would not give us a reason to think that only persons possessed of the beliefs that constitute the content of morality could serve as theoretical authorities about those beliefs. On the contrary, for precisely the sorts of reasons that Waldron outlines, a democracy machine might better capture the beliefs of the majority.[53] Alternatively, examining what most people *do*, as opposed to what most people *say*, might better guide one's judgment about what most people believe. And if most people follow the letter of the law, and not its intent (assuming there is such a thing), then the letter of the law, and not the intent behind it, will better serve to capture the beliefs of the majority.

A final challenge may be made by those who fear that, in advancing the thesis that law should be thought distinct from the intentions of lawmakers, I have unwittingly fallen in with the rebel forces who champion a post-structuralist revolution in jurisprudence. As Judge Posner has noted, '[t]he thread that connects the various schools of poststructuralism is their

[51] I have elsewhere argued that it is not. See Hurd, 'Sovereignty in Silence', 1000–6.

[52] I have argued extensively that it is not. See Heidi M. Hurd, 'Relativistic Jurisprudence: Skepticism Founded on Confusion', *South. Calif. Law Rev.*, 61 (1988), 1459–1506.

[53] For just such an argument, see Robert W. Bennett, 'Mere Rationality in Constitutional Law: Judicial Review and Democratic Theory', *Calif. Law Rev.*, 67 (1979), 1049, 1095–7.

determination to reverse the traditional primacy of author over reader in the interpretation of texts'.[54] By rejecting intentionalist interpretation and denying legal texts anything more than theoretical authority, have I not really made the reader the sole and only source of meaning and moral authority? Have I not joined the ranks of those who wave the banners of 'deconstructionism', 'postmodernism', and 'critical legal studies', in protest against any and all who would defend the objectivity of law? And are not my conclusions therefore subject to the same criticisms that have been directed against the claims of the Academic Left?

I have addressed above a number of criticisms that echo those directed at post-structuralist theories of law. In the course of so doing, I have sought to make clear that law can be accorded an authority distinct from that possessed by either its authors or its readers. Such a thesis is not motivated by, nor does it threaten, the meta-ethical subjectivism that makes one an apostle of post-structuralism. Legal post-structuralists use arguments against the authority of law and the relevance of lawmakers' intentions as means of undermining claims about the objectivity of the rules by which we are governed. Most radically, they claim that the meaning of legal texts rests not in their authors but in their readers. When judges claim to derive meaning from legal texts they disguise what they are really doing: imposing their own (economically, racially, and sexually privileged) biases on those who lack their power. On this theory, there are no objective moral maxims that bind us. And there are no institutionally created laws or principles that genuinely operate to constrain us. We are hostage only to the exercise of power at the hands of the powerful. And in many cases we ought to recognize that we are operating as the captors, and not the hostages.

On my theory, there are objective moral maxims that bind us. We cannot invest legal texts with any meaning whatsoever without running the risk that they will mislead us about our moral obligations. If legal texts are to assist us in acquiring subjective moral beliefs that better cohere with objective moral maxims, we cannot interpret legal texts so that they simply mirror our own subjective moral beliefs. We must, instead, employ semantic restraints that generate a proverbial market-place of ideas. We must adopt interpretive techniques that yield moral conclusions distinct from our own moral beliefs. Only by so doing are we able to test our own beliefs in contrast. Institutionally created laws and principles should thus be thought to have an autonomy all their own. And when they provide reliable insights into the content of the moral maxims that bind us they indeed constrain us. They give us reasons for belief that as practical reasoners we are epistemically bound to consider. One cannot derive from my theory, as one can from the

[54] Richard A. Posner, *Law and Interpretation: A Misunderstood Relation*, 216. See e.g. Jonathan Culler, *On Deconstruction: Theory and Criticism after Structuralism* (Ithaca, NY: Cornell University Press, 1982), ch. 3.

claims of post-structuralism, the conclusion that law is only a ruse for power and politics. It is, rather, a source of education about antecedently existing moral obligations, which, like any good educator, derives its authority from its ability to inspire insight into genuine truths.[55]

There undoubtedly remain many concerns about a theory that makes law significant if and only if our interpretation of it assists us in doing what we already have reason to do. Many of these concerns will involve the claim that law cannot do the action-guiding tasks it is called upon to do (for example, solve co-ordination problems and defuse prisoners' dilemmas) if it is thought to possess only theoretical authority.[56] If legitimate, these concerns would be enough to motivate a return to one of the standard theories of legal authority with its concomitant commitment to intentionalist interpretation. I have argued elsewhere, however, that we need make no such retreat.[57] And so long as a theory that accords law theoretical authority can preserve the action-guiding functions of law, we have reason to prefer such a theory to one that would require us to engage in intentionalist interpretation.

CONCLUSION

I have argued that the authority we assign to law determines, in large part, the method by which we must interpret legal texts. The standard theories of legal authority that dominate contemporary jurisprudence all require, in one way or another, an appeal to the intentions of lawmakers. This is why intentionalism continues to haunt the jurisprudence of those who reject it.

The time has come to fish or cut bait. Either legal theorists should confess their commitment to intentionalism and reconcile themselves to its conceptual and empirical obstinacy, or they should abandon the standard theories of legal authority that commit them to it. I have argued here that only the latter alternative is genuinely available to them. Legal theorists should cease to locate the authority of law in lawmakers. Instead, they should recognize that the law itself, as distinct from its authors, has a claim to authority. While it cannot claim inspirational, influential, or practical authority, it can claim theoretical authority when and if our interpretation of it (by non-intentionalist means) assists us in abiding by our antecedently existing moral obligations.

[55] My thesis thus subscribes far more to what Judge Posner has described as 'New Criticism', than to the post-structuralist challenge that he calls 'reader response criticism'. As he describes them, 'Intentionalism assigns primacy in the creation of the meaning of the work . . . to the author, reader-response criticism to the critic or other reader, New Criticism to the work itself'. Ibid., at 221.

[56] As one critic has maintained, 'The legislature cannot adequately discharge its responsibility of shaping the future unless the integrity of the accepted communication process is maintained'. Dickerson, *The Interpretation and Application of Statutes*, 11.

[57] Hurd, 'Sovereignty in Silence', 1015–22.

12
Interpreting Official Speech

MEIR DAN-COHEN

My starting-point is a narrow but persisting problem: the role, if any, of legislative intent in statutory interpretation. But though this is my starting-point, it is not my main target. My aim is instead to identify and characterize a wider category of speech—I call it *official speech*—of which legislation forms just one part. Placing the interpretation of statutes in such a broader context puts the ongoing debate in a new light. The contribution is, however, not in the form of added ammunition to one of the contending parties. Rather, my analysis will take us outside that debate, revealing a layer of normative considerations not usually addressed in the current discussion. They concern the ways in which different strands in our interpretive practices help construct various social roles—specifically the role of 'official'—and the selves that occupy those roles.[1]

THE STANDARD SEQUENCE AND ITS BREACHES

The question of the interpretive relevance of legislative intent arises against the background of the ordinary relationship between intention and speech.[2] We ordinarily view a speaker's intentions as highly relevant to the meaning of her utterances. Why? A simple answer can be given in terms of what I shall call *the standard sequence.* On this picture, a speech act consists in a speaker having or forming an intention which she proceeds to express or convey by an utterance. This can be schematically represented as S → I → U, where S is the speaker, I the intention, and U the utterance. The standard sequence embodies what has become one of the central elements in the

I would like to thank my friends and colleagues Bruce Ackerman, Chaim Gans, Ruth Gavison, Sanford Kadish, Andrei Marmor, Robert Post, Eric Rakowski, Jan Vetter, Jeremy Waldron, and Frank Zimring for their helpful comments.

[1] Much of the literature on legislative intent is concerned with the difficulties that result from the fact that the legislature is a collective body. I don't address these issues in this article; I focus instead on the speech and intentions of single legislators whether or not they are part of a collective legislature, and more generally on single officials.

[2] Throughout this essay I use 'intention' broadly and interchangeably with 'mental state' to include such things as beliefs, emotions, and desires.

analysis of speech acts: the condition of sincerity. Both the meaning and significance of this condition are most famously highlighted by John Searle (1969: 60–5; 1979: 4–5). As he points out, saying, for example, 'Thank you, but I'm not really grateful', does not involve a logical contradiction, yet is linguistically odd. The oddity results from the implicit background assumption, labelled the *condition of sincerity*, that saying 'thank you' is ordinarily designed to express the speaker's gratitude.

The condition of sincerity describes the standard speech situation from which there are many deviations, and speech-act theory spends considerable effort analysing and documenting them. Insincere speech is thus widely recognized, commonly diagnosed as a lack of correspondence between intention and utterance: as in saying 'thank you' without being grateful, or as in dissembling more generally. Such cases of insincere speech can be seen as disruptions of the normal connection between intention and utterance. In terms of our notation they can be accordingly rendered as S → I –/→ U, where the broken arrow signifies the lack of correspondence between the speaker's state of mind and what she says. However, as the notation clearly suggests, there is a second, though I think a less well recognized, way in which the standard sequence can be disrupted, one in which the breach in the sequence occurs, as it were, between the speaker and the intention: S –/→ I → U in our notation. I will label a speech act that fits this description *detached speech*. Detached speech, I argue, provides the key to understanding official speech and the role of speakers' intentions in interpreting it. But what kinds of speech acts fit this description? And what exactly is meant by a separation between the speaker and the intention? To answer these questions we need to consider some examples.

THE AT&T OPERATOR AND DETACHED SPEECH

As an occasional user of the services of AT&T, the reader may have observed that the operator invariably concludes each exchange with the refrain: 'Thank you for using AT&T.' Now notice that in this case we find an opposite oddity to the one involved in denying one's gratitude subsequent to saying 'thank you'. It would be equally out of place for an over-zealous operator to add the words 'I'm really grateful'. Such an explicit affirmation of the state of mind supposedly expressed by the 'thank you' expression is as incongruous in this case as its denial would be in the ordinary instance. Why?

Now it should be first noted that this is not a case of insincerity that involves deception of any kind. The operator does not pretend to be grateful while failing to possess that state of mind. Indeed, the explicit affirmation of gratitude would be just as inappropriate even if while speaking to the customer the operator did in fact experience a surge of gratitude. It seems, in other words, that the operator is not in violation of the condition of sincerity, but rather that this condition does not at all apply to him. What accounts for its suspension?

It might be suggested, in response, that the condition of sincerity is not really suspended here at all, but that it is merely displaced. According to this suggestion, the operator does not speak on his own behalf but rather on behalf of someone else. He engages in what I will call *representative speech*. Given his representative capacity he is simply the wrong person in whom to search for the intentions that animate the speech in question. Now, as a general proposition, this suggestion is quite plausible. Take a simple example: R reads to A a thank-you note she received from S. If R were to interrupt the reading and add the words 'and I'm really grateful', referring to herself, we would think her deeply confused. But it would be altogether appropriate for her to interject the phrase 'and he is really grateful', referring to S, on the evidence, let us suppose, of the large bouquet that accompanied the note. Some speech situations, in other words, may present a question as to who is the real speaker whose intentions ought to control the interpretation of a given utterance. But they are not exempt from the condition of sincerity. Once the real speaker is identified, the standard sequence would be restored and the condition satisfied.

Plausible as the suggestion is in the simple case, it does not seem to apply to our main example. If we try to track down the origin of the operator's speech, we are most likely to be led to an AT&T public-relations office or to an advertising firm. Someone in some such outfit must have come up with the idea that a standardized display of politeness on the operator's part would enhance AT&T's public image. The idea quite likely needed and received the approval of someone in the corporation's management, whereupon the appropriate instruction was inserted into the operators' manual. The most important aspect of this hypothetical scenario is that at no point does it involve anyone's actual gratitude that the operator's utterance would purport to express. It may seem, though, that this search for the real speaker, on whose behalf the operator utters the 'thank you' refrain, overlooked the most obvious candidate, namely the AT&T corporation itself. Doesn't the operator simply speak for the corporation? However, ascribing the speech to the corporation does not restore the standard sequence in this case. No matter how sanguine one may be about the agency of collective entities, one would be hard put to impute to the corporation an actual intentional state of gratitude of which the operator's speech is the sincere expression.[3] Whatever the basis and the meaning of ascribing speech

[3] I don't mean to suggest here that gratitude is a pre- or extra-linguistic sensation. Gratitude may well be constituted by the relevant social and linguistic practices and is in this sense inseparable from the conventions for expressing it. However, once these practices are in place

to corporations, such ascription must involve the recognition that it may proceed without anyone possessing the intentions that the speech is ostensibly designed to convey. The suggestion that the operator is merely a shadow-speaker, thanking on behalf of someone else, does not accordingly remove the difficulty presented by the seeming exemption of his speech from the condition of sincerity. The anomaly of his speech situation requires a different diagnosis, one that acknowledges the breach in the standard sequence that I have mentioned and tries to account for it. To improve the chances of diagnostic success, we need first acquaint ourselves with more symptoms of the problem. The following example should help us do so.

THE JUROR AND CAPACITY DISCLAIMERS

Consider the utterance 'guilty as charged' made by F, the forewoman of a jury stating the jury's verdict to the judge. Suppose that F had been heard earlier to argue to the jury in favour of acquitting the defendant, a view she has not changed. Would this fact vitiate her declaration of the defendant's guilt or at least impugn her sincerity? The answer to both questions is clearly negative. For F's utterance to count as a valid verdict it must be only true that a majority of the jurors voted for conviction;[4] and the only relevant beliefs implicit in F's utterance concern such facts about the jury's vote.

However, this should not be understood as suggesting that F uses the phrase 'guilty as charged' in a new sense, namely as meaning 'a sufficient majority of the jury voted to convict the defendant'. We must draw here a crucial distinction between the evidentiary grounds for a proposition and its truth conditions. The fact that the jury voted the way it did counts as sufficient grounds for F's declaration of the defendant's guilt. Still, the meaning of the phrase 'guilty as charged' is not affected by this fact; the phrase retains its ordinary meaning, namely that the defendant is guilty as charged.[5] How are we then to explain the fact that F is pronouncing the defendant's guilt while believing in his innocence? Is she dissembling?

they do permit us to entertain, identify, and label a mental state of gratitude, and to interpret utterances conveying gratitude as expressing, in the standard case, that state of mind. My point is that such an interpretation would make no sense in the case of the corporation.

[4] For the sake of this example I simply stipulate a majority rule for the jury's decision rather than a requirement of unanimity. Nothing substantive in my argument depends on this stipulation.

[5] I don't think that the performative aspect of the forewoman's utterance bears on this analysis, but in any event we can stipulate that aspect away. We can hypothesize that it is only the judge who proceeds to perform the institutional act of convicting the defendant, based upon the forewoman's statement. This would make it clearer that the performative aspect is separate from and depends upon the propositional content of the forewoman's utterance.

The puzzle arises out of a seeming conflict between what F says and what we have taken to be her actual view as expressed during the jury's deliberations. Let us now probe the latter. Imagine that during a recess in the jury's deliberations F had been heard to divulge to her friend her belief in the defendant's guilt. Would this discovery impugn her sincerity in arguing to her fellow jurors in favour of acquittal? Not necessarily. When speaking to the jurors, F is bound by legal rules and standards, both evidentiary and substantive, and her position may reflect her conviction regarding the right decision given these legal guide-lines. Her acting as a conscientious juror, however, is compatible with her holding the view, expressed during the break, that the defendant is guilty. But even as we acknowledge the compatibility we must also recognize that we have replicated the earlier puzzle, this time arising out of the flat contradiction between F's exculpatory attitude conveyed to her peers and her condemnatory beliefs revealed by the statement to her friend. As before, the puzzle reflects a conflict between what F says (to the jury) and what we *now* take to be her true point of view.

The story need not stop here. F, it turns out, is a newcomer to California, speaking to her Californian friend. The criminal charges in question concern smoking in a public place. F had just moved from another state, say New York, where public smoking, let us assume, is common and generally approved. Finally, F had been earlier heard talking to an old New York friend about those 'poor innocents persecuted by the Californians for their smoking habits'. Does this additional information render F's statement to her Californian friend fallacious and insincere?

I think there is some doubt here, which further facts would perhaps help remove. But whichever way we lean at this point, this much seems clear. F could easily escape such charges of falsehood or insincerity by appending to her statement of the defendant's guilt addressed to her Californian friend the explanation: 'I'm saying this in my capacity as a Californian.' A similar qualification—call it a *capacity disclaimer*—would be in order, and is indeed implicit, in the other situations we've imagined: 'I'm saying this in my capacity as a juror', or 'in my capacity as forewoman'. The capacity disclaimer, I suggest, highlights the presence in these situations of the second kind of breach in the standard sequence that I have distinguished, where the speaker is separated from the intention conveyed by her speech. To see how this can be we need to look at an analogical case concerning fictional speech. We must go to the theatre.

FICTIONAL ROLES

A, an actor in a play, rages against her 'husband', played by B, exclaiming 'I hate you!' Now suppose that in order to add conviction to her acting, A can bring herself to a high level of emotional involvement in the play, so that at the relevant point in the plot she is in fact provoked into intense rage. Clearly, her exclamation expresses this emotion. At the same time, it would be ludicrous to conclude that A does in fact hate B, even momentarily. A and B are the best of friends, and their friendship is forged rather than suspended during their common performances. The situation seems clearly to illustrate the kind of disruption in the standard sequence that issues in detached speech: the utterance expresses an intention, but in an important sense the intention does not belong to the speaker. It is also easy to see what accounts in this case for the separation between the speaker and the intention: it is the role which A performs and the fact that she utters her lines in her fictional capacity as B's wife in the play. But though this account seems clearly on the right track, it is not very informative. How exactly does the fact that A performs the role of a wife affect her relationship to the emotion she expresses? What precisely does it mean to say that her speech is detached?

One source of difficulty arises from the fact that A's exclamation of hatred on the stage is accompanied by a surge of rage no different in intensity from what A might feel and express at home. The difference between the theatrical performance and its domestic counterpart is not simply phenomenological. Nor should we say that A is merely performing the *role* of a wife in the theatre. The concept of role extends beyond the theatre and reaches into the household. There too, to be a wife—or a husband—is to perform a role. The distinction then must be made in terms of some characteristic other than that of occupying a role: perhaps by pointing out that one role is 'fictional' while the other one is 'real'. But describing the two situations respectively in such terms simply restates the puzzle rather than solving it: we want to know precisely what makes one role-performance 'real' and another 'fictional'.

Some easy answers should be dismissed right away. For example, it would be a mistake to emphasize the limited duration of the actors' enactment of their roles as husband and wife. In a long-running play their engagement on stage can outlast in the aggregate some real marriages. Nor is the intermittent nature of the theatrical role of great significance. The real marriage is no different in this regard, and the fact that we think only of the latter as continuous, that is, as persisting even when the parties are off enacting other marriages on stage, is part of the puzzle rather than part of the solution. Next, I want to discard summarily the possible suggestion that the crucial difference between the two kinds of marriage lies in the fact that the theatrical role is scripted and directed by others, whereas the domestic one is not. We can imagine in response an improvised play in which the actors enjoy no less textual and behavioural freedom than that allowed a couple who live, let us say, under the constantly vigilant scrutiny of parents and in-laws. Finally, it cannot be said that the real spousal role differs from the theatrical in the former's greater importance to its occupant. The opposite may well be the case. An actor may value his on-stage role as Desdemona's husband, and Desdemona her role as Othello's wife, much more than they value their relationships with their respective partners at home.

SPEECH AND SELF

The distinction we seek is not simple, and is likely to involve different kinds of factors. But one way of drawing the line that looks to me promising is in terms of a particular conception of the self. I cannot provide in this space a detailed description of this conception or deploy the arguments that support it. However, the picture of the self on which I rely is familiar and a rough sketch is all I need. The self, on this view, is at least in part constituted by social roles and mental states.[6] But a self is not merely a concatenation of roles and intentions. To form a single self, a bunch of roles and intentions must be unified in some fashion. A self, we might say, is an integrated set of social roles and mental states.[7] What does the integration consist in? The answer I suggest is metaphorical. The different roles and intentions must form a dovetailing, interrelated, and interacting arrangement that we can imagine as possessing a certain 'density' or as forming a 'core'. Such a spatial depiction of the self makes immediate room for the possibility that a person—by which I mean a human individual as ordinarily understood—may occupy roles and entertain mental states that are too tenuously connected to the elements forming that core to count as parts of the self. Such a possibility, as well as the underlying spatial imagery, are implicit in Erving Goffman's notion of *role distance*: it describes the possibility of enacting a social role without fully integrating it into the self.[8] Analogously, Harry Frankfurt (1977, 1987) drew attention to the distinction between 'internal' and 'external' mental states. In both cases a spatial metaphor is used to demarcate a certain boundary line around the self and to separate out some elements that ordinarily would likely be ascribed to the same individual.

The sketch of the self I have drawn so far is static, but in order for it to meet our present needs I must add to it a dynamic component. Let me call

[6] I don't mean to maintain a sharp distinction between roles and mental states. On the present view the appropriate state of mind under given circumstances is indicated by a role (or by the role's 'script') as much as the expected behaviour.

[7] The primary modern text on the social origins of the self is Mead (1934). For a more recent statement see Berger and Luckmann (1966: 173–80). The dramaturgical imagery I employ is closest to Erving Goffman's. The most comprehensive statement of his approach is in Goffman (1974).

[8] See Goffman (1961*a* and *b*). Although I borrow the notion of role distance from Goffman, I modify it for my present purposes and employ it in ways that depart from his own use.

the process by which a new role or mental state gets attached to the pre-existing constituents of the self—*identification.* A person identifies with a particular element (a role or a mental state) in so far as this element is allowed to sprout enough connections with existing constituents of the self. The proclivity for identification with any new role or intention can be understood in terms of the dynamic properties of the person's existing roles and intentions: how prone they are to hook up or interact with the new addition. Identification describes, accordingly, an inner or subjective process by which the self is shaped and modified. But the self has also a public, interpersonal existence. The contours and properties of this objective entity are a product of what we may call the process of *interpretation* by others. Just as identification is constitutive of the subjective self, so is interpretation of the objective one. One of the important aspects of interpretation is the interpreter's willingness and ability to connect various roles and intentions, and his decision, in light of his overall interpretive scheme, as to which roles or intentions sufficiently interrelate to form an integral whole and which are distant or external.

Although identification and interpretation are thus clearly distinguishable, they are also obviously related. First, each person has available to her the outside perspective on herself, either by learning how others interpret her or by taking a direct interpretive glimpse at herself from the outside, as it were. Such interpretive input is likely to play a role in the process of her identification. Conversely, one of the interpretive resources likely to have a significant import on interpreting one's public self is the subject's own self-understanding. A third reason for the tendency of identification and interpretation to converge is perhaps even more important than the first two. Roles and mental states are shaped by a social and cultural context shared by both the subject and her external interpreters. The tendency of such roles and intentions to interrelate or to separate in various contexts and combinations is accordingly a generally known piece of social or cultural data. This tendency is, in other words, part of the shared vocabulary of the self, a shared vocabulary that underlies and to a considerable degree unifies identification and interpretation.

In light of these observations it is easy to see why the interpretation I have described can be labelled *constitutive* interpretation. First, such interpretation is the process by which the public self is constructed. Secondly, this construction is refracted in the subject's own self-understanding both through her interpretive perspective and as a result of the way in which the properties of the roles and intentions that compose her self and determine its identifications are themselves the products of society's interpretive practices.

Although rough, this sketch of the self can help us now clarify the contrast between the marriages on stage and at home. This contrast is a matter of the different degrees of integration between the respective roles and their associated states of mind on the one hand and the subject's self on the other. Unlike the domestic role, the theatrical one is distant: it is relatively removed or disconnected from the actor's other roles. Similarly, the rage she experiences and conveys on stage is external: it is seen neither by A nor by others as continuous and intertwined with A's other mental states. Evidence for these characterizations can be found in our respective approaches to construing the theatrical and the domestic episodes. In the former case, our explorations would be strictly confined to the theatrical role, implying a sharp separation between this segment of A's life and the rest of it. In trying to understand fully A's on-stage verbal assault, we would not deem relevant information such as A's relationship and attitudes to other people or even to B himself. By contrast, all such information would be highly relevant to our understanding of a corresponding domestic feud. We would naturally view the emotional outburst as of a piece with other roles A may occupy, such as a mother or a sister, and as related in important and potentially revealing ways to her other mental states, such as her attitudes toward other people, her aspirations, frustrations, and the like.

Moreover, these contrasting interpretive practices do not only testify to the difference between the two episodes, but they also help constitute it. Our refusal to transgress the boundary of the theatrical role in our interpretation of A's on-stage utterance helps constitute that role as distant, just as by not exploring A's mental life on that occasion we help constitute the on-state rage as an external intention, cut off from A's genuine mental self. Finally, these two aspects of our interpretive practice help constitute A's on-state utterances as detached speech. In short, to call an utterance, an intention, or a role fictional is, among other things, to activate with respect to it a set of interpretive practices that help constitute it as separate from the subject.

This conclusion raises the following question: Why do we create and enact such disparate interpretive practices? More specifically, what is the point in separating certain utterances, intentions, and roles from their subjects and in treating them as self-enclosed and detached? The question is, of course, much too broad and involved to be adequately treated in this space, but our theatrical example suggests some preliminary points. As the prevalence of gossip columns and voyeurism testifies, people find pleasure in observing others' private lives. The interpretive practice we call 'fiction' or 'theatre' gives us the benefit of a public display of scenes from a private life while controlling most of the potential damage inherent in publicly enacting such scenes.[9] The potential benefits of such an arrangement can

[9] I don't mean to suggest that these benefits provide the main reasons or explanations for the theatre, but only that they can be usefully extrapolated from the theatre example in order to illuminate the nature of official roles.

be subsumed under three headings. The first concerns reduced *responsibility*. In our example, A will not be perceived as the offending party when she utters offensive words, and correspondingly she will not be made to bear the personal consequences that might be otherwise attached to her behaviour. The second implication of the theatrical role is to reduce *vulnerability*: the distant role B enacts provides him with a kind of immunity; the insults are hurled at his role, not at himself. Consequently, A and B can remain good friends with no hurt feelings despite the daily display of mutual hostility beheld by a large crowd of observers. Finally, the actors' distant role increases their *versatility*: they can assume and shed roles at will without deep repercussions and corresponding adjustments in any other parts of the self. By reducing responsibility and vulnerability, and by increasing versatility, the distant nature of the theatrical role can accordingly be said to augment freedom of speech and action: it allows A to do (say) things that might be otherwise inappropriate; it allows B to have things done or said to him that would otherwise be injurious; and it permits both actors to engage in a larger variety of activities than would be otherwise feasible.

CONSTRUCTING OFFICIALS

Every analogy is imperfect—otherwise it would be an identity—and the one between my examples of the theatre and the jury is no exception. None the less, our foray to the theatre can shed some light, I believe, on the issues raised by our jury example.[10] There we observed that a 'capacity disclaimer' can reconcile apparently conflicting statements regarding a defendant's guilt made by the same person F on different occasions. How does this capacity disclaimer work? Let us consider the first instance in which F, speaking in her capacity as forewoman, pronounces the verdict. In analogy to our theatre example, the distinguishing mark of the forewoman role, I suggest, is that it is a distant role. Consequently, although F utters U ('guilty as charged') with the requisite intention—to convey the belief that the defendant is guilty as charged—that intention is an external one, meaning that the belief in question is not continuous or integrated with F's other beliefs and intentions. These features of the role and the intention define F's utterance as detached speech, similar in this regard to the actor's exclamation on stage.

Drawing further on our discussion of the theatre, our interpretive approach toward F's speech can be characterized as a constitutive interpretation. Our refusal to explore the relationship between the belief in the defendant's guilt implicit in F's statement and her other beliefs and intentions is a

[10] On the use by sociologists of the theatre analogy to explore the nature of social roles, cf. Burns (1972).

constitutive move in constructing the role of foreperson as a distant one. The point of such an interpretive practice has also been suggested, at least in outline, by the theatrical analogy. For example, the distant nature of F's role and the correlatively detached character of her speech help mitigate F's personal responsibility for the defendant's fate.

The foreperson case can be now generalized. It highlights a set of interpretive practices that treat official speech as detached by locating its underlying intentions outside the configuration of the speaker's mental states, thereby helping to constitute the role of official as distant. In this way such interpretive practices participate in constructing the familiarly impersonal nature of officialdom. Such construction of the official role diminishes officials' personal responsibility as well as their vulnerability. Things can be done and said by officials and to them without engaging them personally and thus without the costs that such engagement might sometimes carry. The impersonal nature of an official role also increases versatility by reducing the personal costs of being assigned to different tasks and positions or of moving out of the official career into other pursuits.

The forewoman example presents a clear case of detached speech produced in one's capacity as a holder of a distant role. But this clarity is in a way deceptive. It suggests a sharp line between detached and non-detached speech and a correspondingly clear divide between distant roles and roles that are integral to the self, as well as between external and internal intentions. In other words, the example implies a rigid and well-defined boundary of the self by reference to which these binary distinctions can be sharply and confidently drawn. The subsequent stages in our story of F were designed to dispel this impression.

As you may recall, F's profession of the defendant's innocence was made in her capacity as juror. Here we are presumptively inclined to ascribe the speech to her as non-detached and to view the underlying intentions as internal. But as the example suggests, this presumption can be easily rebutted by a reminder that being a juror is an official role of sorts, which F can enact at a distance, forming *ad hoc* intentions appropriate to the role but disconnected from her other views and beliefs.

We would be, however, less receptive toward a similar use of the capacity disclaimer in the next stage of the story, when F points out that her condemnatory statement to her friend is only made in her capacity as a Californian. We would likely view such a disclaimer as intelligible but jarring. Both components of this mixed reaction are noteworthy. We can imagine treating one's newly acquired California residency as a quasi-official role, mouthing without conviction politically correct opinions and exhibiting upon cue the expected attitudes without integrating them with one's erstwhile New York self. It is, of course, possible that one is simply dissembling. But this would mark one's speech as insincere in the first, straightforward sense that I've distinguished early on. The scenario I have in mind is a different one. F has an image of what is expected of a Californian, and she sets out in good faith to meet the expectations. But this entire package—role, attitudes, and speech—is somewhat alien to her. There is a split or a disjunction between her role as Californian and the other roles and intentions that have so far formed her identity. We can even imagine an extreme case in which over time aspects of F associated with her role as Californian may have grown in bulk and importance and her former New York identify shrivelled to the point where at least over a certain range of issues and attitudes the question who is the real F has no clear answer.

These considerations make F's use of the capacity disclaimer intelligible and under some circumstances credible even in the case of her Californian role. But the circumstances are rare and the invocation of the disclaimer in this kind of case artificial and jarring. The reason is clear. The role of Californian is ordinarily enacted in a non-distant fashion; views and beliefs one holds in this capacity are treated as integral to the self; and one's speech accordingly is construed as non-detached.

These problematic uses of the capacity disclaimer should serve to correct the impression created by the foreperson example and the theatrical analogy that the distinctions I have drawn between kinds of roles, intentions, and utterances are binary and that the self to which they apply is clearly and rigidly bounded. Taken together, these examples reveal a more complicated picture. Roles—and their related intentions and utterances—can be arranged on a spectrum defined by a variable role distance. At one end we will find, among other things, strictly official roles whose bearers are expected to keep them at a distance. The other end is defined by personal roles that are uniformly expected to be an integral part of the self. In-between these two poles matters are more flexible and negotiable. The negotiation concerns the proper relation of a given role with its attendant intentions and utterances to the self, and correlatively the proper way of drawing a given segment in the boundary of the self. The negotiation can arise in different contexts and take many forms, but one of them will be that of a dispute over the interpretive practice appropriate to a given type of utterances, and more specifically over the role of a speaker's intentions in interpreting her speech.[11]

LEGISLATIVE INTENT

Earlier I distinguished three ways in which speech can seem to fail the condition of sincerity: by being deceptive, representative, or detached. All

[11] A similarly scalar conception of self is argued for by Parfit (1984: pt. III).

three categories can potentially apply to legislators and influence the way their speech is interpreted. Politicians are notorious practitioners of the noble and not-so-noble lie, and as such their discourse is sometimes deceptive. Legislators also act in a representative capacity, and at least on some conceptions of political representation, approximated perhaps in certain settings, it makes sense to think of the legislators merely as mouthpieces or conduits for someone else. I will not dwell, however, on these possibilities and on their implications for the role of legislators' intentions in interpreting statutes. My main purpose has been to identify and describe the third category—detached speech—as potentially applicable to the case of legislators. What bearing does it have on the role of intentions in statutory interpretation?

Our analysis of detached speech suggests two sets of considerations: reactive and constructive. By reactive considerations I mean the inquiry as to whether the legislative role is generally understood and enacted in a distant or a non-distant manner. Here we are trying to fit the interpretive approach to the social facts.[12] Clearly, if the legislative role is distant and the speech in which it issues detached, then it would make little sense to mine a legislator's mental life that lies outside the boundary of her legislative role for added insight into the meaning of her official utterances. The point can be amplified by contrasting it with a seemingly unexceptionable comment made by Professor Gerald MacCallum in his well-known essay on legislative intent. In arguing for the possibility of imputing intentions to other people, including legislators, MacCullum maintains that doing so 'may require a fair degree of intimacy with the person whose intentions are being considered' (1966: 773). On the present view, this statement applies to non-distant roles only. 'Intimacy' involves close familiarity with someone across a wide range of non-distant roles. Because of the interconnections among such roles, one's speech and behaviour in any one of them can be better understood in light of the interpreter's acquaintance with that person's enactment of the other roles. We can more easily and confidently impute an intention to a mother if we know her also in her capacities as, say, wife, sister, and friend. But such intimacy is irrelevant to the construal of detached speech. Since *ex hypothesi* the intention we impute is unrelated to the states of mind that belong in the core of the speaker's self, intimate familiarity with that core and the roles that compose it is quite unnecessary, and can only mislead.

How are we to assess the distance of the legislative role so as to choose the appropriate interpretive approach? We can think of many kinds of

[12] Describing the investigation as factual should not of course hide the normative component in it. The way a role is enacted—as distant or non-distant—is itself a normative matter. However, in this part of the investigation we are concerned to find out what norms of distance in fact apply to a given role in a given society, seeking to adjust our interpretive practices to these normative understandings.

relevant evidence, but let me just give one example. Consider the public-figure exemption that present-day libel law creates for expressions that would be otherwise defamatory.[13] Here we have a legal doctrine that legitimates the exposure of politicians' private lives to public scrutiny. Such a doctrine both reflects and foments the effacement of the boundary between the politician's self and her role, thereby signalling a reduction in the acceptable role-distance in this case.[14] An increased willingness to consult legislative intentions in our practices of statutory interpretation would accordingly seem consistent with this piece of evidence.

The constructive considerations that our analysis implies relate to the constitutive aspect of interpretive practices. How widely we cast our net in search of legislative intentions deemed pertinent to the interpretation of official utterances is a constitutive move in determining the relationship of the legislative role to the self. Consequently, in contemplating the adequacy of an interpretive practice we must also examine the normative question: where *should* the boundary of a politician's self be drawn? What is the desirable relationship between a legislator and his role?

Again, the question is too multi-faceted to be adequately considered here. But we can attempt a first stab at it by recalling the kinds of general considerations that we have earlier identified as relevant to the creation of distant roles: decreasing responsibility and vulnerability and increasing versatility. Are such effects desirable in this case? Consider responsibility first. The limitation of responsibility implicit in role distance means that as long as the legislator acts within the confines of the role, he is given personal immunity from the adverse consequences of his official actions and decisions. These consequences can affect him only in his official capacity, and at most will cost him his job, but they will not have direct personal ramifications on him beyond that. Is such a system of limited liability advantageous? The answer depends on many considerations that we cannot canvass here, but we can briefly mention some obvious ones. Should legislators be encouraged to be risk-takers or risk-averse? How adequately can sanctions that are limited to the legislators' role police their conduct? Specifically, is the risk of losing the role altogether—by being removed from office or by failure to get re-elected—sufficient to deter official misconduct? Finally, how important is such a limitation of responsibility for recruiting worthwhile candidates to such political roles?

It should be noted that the issue here goes beyond legal liability. Politicians are often faced with the 'dirty hands' moral dilemma: they are called upon, sometimes by duty and public interest, to perform morally repugnant

[13] See e.g. *New York Times Co.* v. *Sullivan*, 376 U.S. 254 (1964).

[14] Cf. the increased First Amendment protection given to abusive language directed to police officers as reflecting and encouraging an increased role-distance in their case. See *Lewis* v. *New Orleans*, 408 U.S. 913 (1972).

actions. If relatively good people are to be attracted to such tasks, some devices may be necessary to alleviate somewhat the moral burden beyond the removal of whatever material or physical sanctions might be otherwise attached to such behaviour. Role-distance can be such a device. Instituting a visible distance between the role and the self can be a way to exempt the politician from some of the moral responsibility for discharging his official duties.[15]

Limiting politicians' responsibility by expanding their role-distance can have an additional advantage. Politicians do and say many nasty things to each other as well as to people outside their circle. Role-distance and the implicit invocation of the capacity disclaimer may somewhat soften these blows. In the relationship among the politicians themselves these devices can help instil a measure of civility—legislators can go out together for a drink even after the most acrimonious exchanges. In the relationship with the citizenry, legislators' role-distance is linked to the ethos of law's impersonal nature and to the ideal of being ruled by laws rather than by other people. For reasons that we cannot even start to explore here, it is sometimes preferable—less injurious to one's self-esteem—to sustain the same insults or aggravations when these are not perceived as directly inflicted by another human being but are instead mediated or authored by an impersonally held social role.

Role-distance, we saw, also reduces the role-holder's vulnerability. A distant role helps legislators be thick-skinned about the insults and aggravations to which they are subjected by both their constituents and their peers. A complicated judgment is, of course, required to determine whether it is desirable on balance to fit politicians with such a shield. The kinds of considerations that bear on this question are quite obvious though, and they resemble those that arise under the heading of responsibility. Vulnerability to insult and aggravation may help keep politicians in line, so the trade-off would seem to be between policing legislators' conduct and providing incentives for good and sensitive people to run for office.

Finally, role-distance increases politicians' versatility. It encourages people to make relatively short stints as legislators by reducing the damage to the self that might be otherwise involved in giving up one's office or losing it. The resulting revolving-door politics has its obvious attractions, but also some potential disadvantages, such as reduced commitment and expertise.

Taken together, the three groups of considerations that I have listed should help us to select an adequate interpretive practice regarding statutes and other legislative pronouncements. On the present analysis, taking full account

[15] This point can be seen as complementary to Bernard Williams' suggestion that we are better off with politicians who are sensitive to the immorality their task sometimes requires. See Williams (1978). On the 'dirty hands' dilemma' in politics, cf. also Nagel (1978) and Walzer (1974).

of legislative intentions represents a choice, with constitutive ramifications, in favour of effacing the boundary between self and legislative role and integrating the latter into the former. Limiting resort to legislative intentions has the reverse implication, representing a vote for role-distance in this case. By a careful examination and weighing of the conflicting considerations we can accordingly hope to resolve the prevailing uncertainty regarding the interpretive relevance of legislative intent, and thus help constitute the desirable relationship between legislators' selves and their roles.

But such a stark choice between identification and distance in the legislative role is not, in fact, forced upon us. I want to mention briefly in closing another possibility. The prevailing indecision and ambiguity in statutory interpretation need not represent uncertainty on the question of role-distance, but may rather provide the right answer to this question. To recognize this possibility, recall the scaler aspect of the role-distance imagery. Some roles, we said, occupy a middle ground between those that are detached from the self and those that are bound up with it. One's identification with such roles is typically qualified or selective rather than wholehearted or wholesale. In light of the conflicting considerations I have listed, such intermediate and variable role distance is perhaps the best we can hope for in this case, and a wavering, fluctuating interpretive practice the best way to achieve it. We started this essay by noting the problem marked by the mixed views and practices concerning legislative intent in statutory interpretation. Recognizing the crucial difference between an unresolved problem and one solved by a compromise, we can now see that what we initially took to be the problem may in the end turn out to be part of the solution.

REFERENCES

Berger, P. L. and Luckmann, T. (1966), *The Social Construction of Reality* (New York: Doubleday).

Burns, E. (1972), *Theatricality: A Study of Convention in Theater and in Social Life* (New York: Harper & Row).

Frankfurt, H. (1977) 'Identification and Externality', in *The Importance of What We Care About* (Cambridge: Cambridge University Press, 1988), 50–68.

—— (1987), 'Identification and Wholeheartedness', in *The Importance of What We Care About* (Cambridge: Cambridge University Press), 159–76.

Goffman, E. (1961*a*), 'Role Distance', in *Encounters: Two Studies in the Sociology of Interaction* (Indianapolis: Bobbs-Merrill Co.).

—— (1961*b*), 'The Underlife of a Public Institution: A Study of Ways of Making Out in a Mental Hospital', in *Asylums: Essays on the Social Situation of Mental Patients and Other Inmates* (New York: Anchor Books).

—— (1974), *Frame Analysis* (New York: Harper & Row).

MacCallum, Jr. G. C. 'Legislative Intent' (1966), 75 *Yale LJ* 745.

Mead, G. H. (1934), *Mind, Self, and Society* (Chicago: Chicago University Press).

Nagel, T. (1978), 'Ruthlessness in Public Life', in *Mortal Questions* (Cambridge: Cambridge University Press, 1979), 75–90.

Parfit, D. (1984), *Reasons and Persons* (Oxford: Clarendon Press).

Searle, J. (1969), *Speech Acts* (Cambridge: Cambridge University Press).

—— (1979), *Expression and Meaning* (Cambridge: Cambridge University Press).

Walzer, M. (1974), 'Political Action: The Problem of Dirty Hands', in M. Cohen, T. Nagel, and T. Scanlon (eds.), *War and Moral Responsibility* (Princeton, NJ: Princeton University Press).

Williams, B. (1978), 'Politics and Moral Character', in *Moral Luck* (Cambridge: Cambridge University Press, 1981), 54–70.

Index

THE FAR SIDE By GARY LARSON

The manufacturer's authorised representative in the EU for product safety is Oxford University Press España S.A. of el Parque Empresarial San Fernando de Henares, Avenida de Castilla, 2 – 28830 Madrid (www.oup.es/en or product.safety@oup.com). OUP España S.A. also acts as importer into Spain of products made by the manufacturer.

www.ingramcontent.com/pod-product-compliance
Ingram Content Group UK Ltd.
Pitfield, Milton Keynes, MK11 3LW, UK
UKHW022025150926
475595UK00013B/289
9780198264873